Darwin's
Laboratory

Evolutionary
Theory
and Natural History
in the
Pacific

Darwin's Laboratory

Edited by
Roy MacLeod
and
Philip F. Rehbock

University
of Hawai'i
Press
Honolulu

99 98 97 96 95 94
5 4 3 2 1

**Library of Congress
Cataloging-in-Publication Data**
Darwin's laboratory :
  evolutionary theory and natural history
  in the Pacific /
  edited by Roy MacLeod
  and Philip F. Rehbock.
      p.   cm.
  Outgrowth of a symposium
  held in Hamburg in 1989.
  Includes bibliographical references
  and index.
  ISBN 0–8248–1613–7 (acid-free paper)
  1. Natural history—Pacific Area—
History—Congresses.
2. Evolution (Biology)—History—
Congresses. 3. Anthropology—
Pacific Area—History—Congresses.
4. Social Darwinism—Pacific Area—
History—Congresses.
I. MacLeod, Roy M. II. Rehbock, Philip
F., 1942– .
QH198.A1D37   1994   94-20341
508.9—dc20   CIP

Book design by Cameron Poulter

Contents

Part Three: Natives, Colonials, and Anthropologists

Part Four: Social Darwinisms

Figures

Preface

In 1836 HMS *Beagle,* with Darwin its ship's naturalist, memorably sailed through the Strait of Magellan and entered the Pacific. From that time onward, from the Andes and the Galapagos to Australia, the Pacific played a central role in shaping Darwin's experience of Nature and the nature of modern science. Before Darwin's time the Pacific was for Europeans a source of inspiration, discovery, and exploration. After him it became a vast resource of evidence upon which geological and biological theories could draw and a seemingly limitless natural laboratory in which propositions about organic evolution could be tested.

As the Pacific shaped Darwin, so Darwin shaped the Pacific. And if in the region we can locate the biographical Darwin and empirical Darwinism, so also in the Pacific can we see the earliest, tentative applications of Social Darwinsim. To explore this conceptual and regional conjuncture, we offer the following essays. This book had its origins in a symposium devoted to Western Science in the Pacific, held as part of the International Congress for the History of Science at Hamburg in 1989. In a wider sense, its origins bespoke a conscious attempt to look away from the specifically cultural and political character of European scientific debates. In fact, however, the Pacific was, no less in science than in naval strategy and commerce, quintessentially part of European debate and in many ways essential to that debate. In the Pacific lay opportunities for phenomena to be observed and theories to be tested. What applied to botany and geology applied equally to native peoples—as it would to oceanography, meteorology, marine biology, and eventually nuclear weapons.

Expeditions, observations, collections, debates, exchanges, and demonstrations—these were to become the hallmarks of the Darwinian Pacific. From European, then North American "centers of calculation" came the concept of the Pacific as an intellectual space to be commanded and controlled. The conquest of the Pacific was vital to the success of the Darwinian program; the Pacific supplied both evidence for Darwinism and field training for its missionaries. That their "mission" may have despoiled the peoples of the region and the environment in which they lived was not yet counted part of the cost.

These essays canvass recent American, British, and Australasian scholarship.There is undoubtedly much more that will be added in coming years from French, Russian, and Japanese sources. If their focus is unapologetically regional—whether speaking of islands or "rim"—the conclusions they draw are global. If, as is now widely argued, we believe that locality has helped shape the context of discovery it is time to see how the Pacific shaped some of the most influential and debatable propositions about the nature of life.

As with our earlier book, *Nature in Its Greatest Extent,* we are again indebted to colleagues and librarians on three continents. We wish in particular to thank the University of Hawai'i Press for its continuing commitment to this project. While the Asia-Pacific region has long been a research site for Europeans, it has at last become a field of intense interest for historians of science who line the "rim" and whose task it is to follow the complex traffic in ideas, between metropolis and periphery, between traditional and Western beliefs, and across racial and cultural frontiers.

Roy MacLeod	Philip F. Rehbock
Sydney	Honolulu

ROY MACLEOD

AND PHILIP F. REHBOCK
Introduction

June 10th [1834]—In the morning we made
the best of our way into the open Pacific.
—CHARLES DARWIN

With this spare journal entry Darwin noted his arrival and that of
HMS *Beagle* in the Pacific hemisphere.[1] Within the next two years, the
Pacific would determine the directions of his later research. In the
southern winter of 1834, Darwin had not yet confronted the phenomena whose interpretation he would make famous—the uplift of the
Andes, the biota of the Galapagos, and the coral atolls of Polynesia
and the eastern Indian Ocean. But by the end of the 1830s, his knowledge from the Pacific had begun to shape modern understanding in
geology, biology, and anthropology, and to redefine the European
concept of "the Pacific" itself.

The Pacific was not, however, the *Beagle*'s destination. Its captain,
Robert FitzRoy (1805–1865), had orders to survey the coast of South
America, a task in which he had previously participated, and to carry
out a chain of longitudinal measurements around the globe, returning
to England (it was expected) in two years or so. The voyage also gave
the scientifically enthusiastic FitzRoy opportunities to use the new
Beaufort scale to reckon wind forces around the world. The focus of
his expedition, however, was South America—Argentina, Chile, and
Tierra del Fuego. British capital had begun to flow into the region,
and the importance of safe, efficient, competitive coastal navigation
was recognized by private investors as well as by government. The
dedicated FitzRoy responded to this challenge by producing no fewer
than eighty-two coastal charts and eighty harbor plans.[2]

Only twenty-six years of age in 1831, Captain FitzRoy was concerned about the effects of isolation. Accordingly, he requested a gentleman companion of a scientific inclination. Darwin thus sailed, not

as the *Beagle's* official surgeon-naturalist (by then a well-established billet in the Royal Navy), but as an unpaid, supernumerary naturalist. Suffering regularly from seasickness, Darwin spent as much time ashore as possible. While the *Beagle's* crew endured two-and-a-half years charting the Brazilian and Argentinian coasts, Darwin reveled in the diversity of the tropical rain forests and rode with gauchos in Patagonia. The geology of the continent intrigued him, especially when a severe earthquake on the Chilean coast caused a permanent elevation of the land above sea level in areas he was able to observe. The Galapagos Islands, now central to Darwinian legend, were not reached until September of 1835, nearly four years into the voyage and barely a year before returning to England. But with subsequent landfalls at Tahiti, New Zealand, Australia, Tasmania, Keeling Island, Mauritius, the Cape of Good Hope, and—yet again—the coast of Brazil, it was a busy year indeed. At these outposts of discovery, the origin of coral atolls and the future of native races were in Darwin's thoughts far more than the fabled "mystery of mysteries"—the origin of species. But Pacific observations, collections, recollections, and correspondents would play a central part in Darwin's thinking for the rest of his life.

Darwin could not have known a great deal about the natural history of the Pacific in 1834. Few naturalists had explored the Pacific since Cook's voyages sixty years earlier, and most of those had not published in English. Neither Alexander von Humboldt nor Charles Lyell, Darwin's heros, had been to the Pacific. So when he returned to England in 1836, at the age of just twenty-seven, he could with justification regard himself an authority on Pacific matters. "People's ideas of the Pacific are most false," he wrote to Charles Lyell from his London lodgings in December 1837.[3] He was referring to the common misconception that the Pacific, especially the South Pacific, was so crowded with islands that a sailor was rarely out of sight of land. To the contrary, Darwin went on to say, "In the thick archipelagoes—in a long day's sail, you will often only see one or two islands."[4] The experience of the *Bounty*—of "breadfruit Bligh" and his eighteen loyal sailors who crossed three thousand five hundred miles of ocean from Tonga to Timor without sight of land—had either been forgotten or was never grasped.

The young Darwin—well connected by birth, education, and religious inclination—would probably never have strayed from the traditional conception of Nature's Order had it not been for his exposure, during the *Beagle* voyage, to conditions entirely at variance with his previous experience. These new conditions were both natural—from the superabundant verdure of the Brazilian rain forest to the stark geology of the Galapagos—and social—from the vicious warfare of the gaucho army of General de Rosas to the marginal existence of the natives of Tierra del Fuego. How could his sense of the order of nature and of society—and the theology that rationalized that order—not be seriously disturbed, even overturned, by such experiences? From these encounters with the unaccustomed, from this "shock of the new," to borrow Robert Hughes' phrase, came heterodox theories and values. Such experiences must explain, at least in part, why Darwin—and Wallace—came to understand nature so differently from their cohorts, the amateur, weekend or armchair, naturalists of Britain; so differently too from the leading natural history theorists of the preceding decades, the French triumvirate of Cuvier, Lamarck, and Geoffroy Saint-Hilaire.

What has not been sufficiently grasped in our own time is the impact of the Pacific upon the thought of Darwin and those who followed him. For nineteenth-century Europeans, the Pacific hemisphere was still largely an imagined world: a world of the exotic, the contradictory, the "other"—much as the Near East and the Orient had been constructed by Europeans in the eighteenth century. Scientifically, such a world could be ignored by those who had never visited it. Distance alone could protect conventional thinking from confrontation by uncomfortable facts or unorthodox notions. It could also be argued that experience in that opposite, contradictory half of the world gave one the license to entertain unorthodox beliefs within a society otherwise wedded to Creationist orthodoxy. Through his encounters with the "other," Darwin could see himself, and be seen, as no longer tied to conventional society.[5] But to appreciate the Pacific as Darwin saw it, we must retrace the course that earlier Europeans had followed, the course that had defined "the Pacific" in the Atlantic mind.

Darwin and the Invention of the Pacific

The Pacific occupies an enduring place in the Atlantic memory. European encounters with the Pacific helped define the region in European eyes. As Arif Dirlik has suggested, the Pacific was "invented" as it was conceptualized in a global vision, binding the region and its people to the economic and political interests of Europe.[6] Similarly, the interests of European science—what we will call "Atlantic science"—helped "invent" the Pacific as a conceptual space whose dimensions were to embrace both theory and observational experiment. The Pacific, read through Atlantic eyes, became a comprehensive, vast, but incomplete text, a text translated into European languages, according to rules and methods derived from Atlantic preoccupations. Nowhere was this more relevant than in the "discovery"—and "invention"—of the Pacific by European naturalists.

What was "the Pacific" to the Atlantic naturalist? It was, at one level, a vast collecting ground, at first a *terra incognita,* or an *oceanus incognita.* From the days of Joseph Banks onward, it was a venue for the acquisition of knowledge, plants, and animals for Atlantic collections. A legion of collectors, from Sir Stamford Raffles to the brothers Allan and Andrew Cunningham, scoured the Pacific for patrons' cabinets, museums, gardens, and herbaria.[7]

But the Pacific was more than a collecting field for trophy hunters; it was also a "laboratory"—invented as a site for testing "Atlantic" theories. Nowhere was this more evident than in the sciences of the natural and human environment, where European scholars sought data to confirm or refute hypotheses central to the Darwinian program. David Lowenthal has described the conditions under which geographic spaces can be reinvented as conceptual spaces.[8] In the Pacific, European science transformed a physical area into a conceptual laboratory. That space was essential to complete Europe's catalogue of the world; that space Europeans came to occupy, often at the cost of local systems of knowledge and belief. In this process, haphazardly and by design, European naturalists fueled the invention of a region and a particular social construction of material and human artifacts that served European interests in conquest, settlement, and trade.

The cognitive space Europeans produced was, in effect, a "Pacific science" drawing upon the historical laboratory of the "outdoors." "Atlantic science" was epitomized by the experimental, "indoor" laboratory, a space devoted to the exact sciences and to the testing of testable hypotheses, reproducible under controllable conditions.[9] "Pacific science" occupied a different space, observational, outdoors, and difficult to reduce to exact measurement. Perhaps because it conveys connotations of traditional, amateur, or anecdotal collections of beliefs, rather than universal application, this space has been neglected by historians of science. However, because localities reflect global biodiversities, and frames of reference are key to the taxonomic sciences, we see the history of Pacific science as equal in importance to the history of modern physics and molecular biology.[10]

Few, at least, would deny the importance of the Pacific to modern oceanography, geology, anthropology, and biology. Travel and exploration to the largely uninhabited, dotted landfalls surrounded by vast tracts of sea altered perceptions of what Europeans thought to be knowable. Dramatic contrasts—in plants, rain forests to lichens; in animals, iguanas to birds of paradise; in geological formations, high islands to coral atolls—were formative to Atlantic theories of nature. Eighteenth-century voyagers to the Pacific sought not only to determine where the boundaries of land and sea lay, but to confirm or disprove Alexander Dalrymple's theory of a "balancing" southern continent. And in the nineteenth century, it was the Pacific laboratory that yielded answers to such questions as the origin of coral atolls, the extent of continental elevation and ocean-floor subsidence, the causes of biogeographic discontinuities, and the migratory histories of New World peoples.

However, the text had to be read *in situ*. Not least for that reason, the Pacific, or at least much of it, was viewed as an essential library and museum for imperial interests of Britain, France, and Germany. Once hydrographic surveys were complete, natural histories of Pacific lands and seas became means of sustaining an imperial presence.[11] The forebears of "Big Science"—including atomic testing—were the research teams that sailed with Cook and La Pérouse, Wilkes and the *Challenger*.[12] As imperial interests invested the region, so they helped create a venue for discovery within spheres of political influence.

In its encounter with the Pacific, "Atlantic" science met a multiplicity of beliefs and understandings of nature, indigenous to the islands, many of which were soon displaced. Ironically, such beliefs now play an increasing role in understanding the Pacific, even as defined in Atlantic terms.[13] During the nineteenth century, however, the Pacific became a region of intellectual colonization by Darwinians, as evolutionary theory was called upon to explain the survival through adaptation of certain organisms and races and the disappearance of others. The regime afforded by Darwinism provided both method and morality. Both involved the active interaction of observation and theory in particular localities. From the "coral episode" to the "species question," the Darwin encounter lent testimony to the belief that knowledge of nature, including human nature, is particular and local, and that local knowledge, by becoming cosmopolitan, fosters a global synthesis. Only with his reading of Lyell's *Principles of Geology* did Darwin begin to appreciate the value of theories "by which to work" and to conclude that "no one could be a good observer unless he was an active theorizer."[14] But Darwin treated theories as frameworks for arranging and interpreting observations, rather than as tentative explanations to be confirmed or refuted. By the late nineteenth century, there were "Darwinian theories" in abundance—theories whose confirmation rested on geological and biological data acquired primarily in the Pacific. The region, invented first as an emporium, then as a mission, became reinvented as a laboratory for the investigation of theories essential to science, trade, settlement, and control.

Darwin Studies and the Pacific

Given the impact of Darwin on the Pacific, it is not untimely to seek the Darwinian dimensions of "Pacific science." Regrettably, the literature on Darwin and Darwinism in the Pacific is in a very early state.[15] Of course, the history of exploration, manifest most clearly in the "Cook industry,"[16] has always lured scholars to Pacific themes. During the 1980s, however, when the Pacific began to engage historians of science, the literature broadened significantly.[17] The activities of anthropologists, the relationship of colonial scientists to metropolitan centers, the origins of scientific institutions in the Pacific, and the clash of cultures, reflecting what Alan Moorehead called the "fatal impact," began to win fresh attention.[18] And while discovery and exploration remained central, they required new approaches, often revealing complex interplays among political, economic, commercial, and scientific activity.

None of the recent scholarship on Darwin will lead the reader easily into Pacific waters. The word "Pacific" is rarely a category to be found in indices. Even in the 38-page index to David Kohn's *Darwinian Heritage,* there are no geographical or conceptual references for "Pacific," "Polynesia," "Melanesia," "Micronesia," "Australia," or "New Zealand." The "Galapagos" carries six references, but the only entry for the "tropics" refers to Darwin's reactions to the Brazilian forest. A "chart" for the Darwin scholar navigating the Pacific must therefore begin with the few scholars who have looked toward the Pacific dimensions of Darwinian themes. Frank Sulloway has substantially revised our understanding of the role of the Galapagos finches in Darwin's thinking,[19] David Stoddart has devoted much thought to Darwin's work on coral reefs and his influence in geography,[20] and Sandra Herbert has recently made a fresh examination of his *Beagle* geologizing.[21] Nichols and Nichols have plotted Darwin's travels in Australia, and James Pusey has followed the course of Darwinian ideas in late nineteenth- and early twentieth-century China.[22] More recently, Eugene Cittadino has described the export of Darwinian ideas to the German empire by plant ecologists.[23] And George Stocking's studies of Victorian anthropology have touched the Pacific at many points.[24]

Biographies and autobiographies provide more material. As the

Pacific won prestige for nations, it showered fame on individuals. To go where few have gone before has always been a shortcut to immortality, and many naturalists became famous after expeditions to the Pacific. Joseph Banks would have reached the pinnacle of Georgian science without Cook's first voyage, but less well-born men like John Gould and Samuel Stutchbury[25] (not to mention Joseph Hooker, Thomas Huxley, or James Dana) found their fortunes enhanced if not entirely transformed by a few years in the Pacific. For many others, it offered a refuge, a way of dealing with a world known to Somerset Maugham, awaiting more prosperous times, when opportunities for a paying career in the metropolis again might open. William Swainson and, to a lesser extent, even Alfred Russel Wallace saw the Pacific in these terms.[26] The Pacific was thus both a first opportunity and a last resort, and in both respects it commanded the presence of talented naturalists.

The Pacific Landscape

Our intention in this volume is to restore the Pacific to a more central place in the Darwinian literature—to bring the "periphery" closer to the center—by presenting a number of cases that demonstrate the variety and richness of science in the Pacific. We hope to show how the Pacific created a laboratory for natural history and the theory of evolution; and to show how Darwinian ideas helped invent and refine a particular conception of the Pacific. From that intention we trust will emerge an extensive program, of which the following essays will form just a beginning.

This Pacific project begins with the recognition that the Darwinian program was driven by the need to collect, comprehend, and explain by imparting structure to nature. In many ways, this helped establish the Pacific as a realm of political subordination and intellectual occupation. Dirlik's insistence that "Euro-Americans invented the Pacific region because they created a structure out of the area that had not been there earlier"[27] applies to Darwinian naturalists as well as to colonial governors and clipper capitalists. A principal feature of the Darwinian program was the way in which it threw "a girdle round the earth" through communication networks of exchange in plants, animals, and ideas. Networks were part of the business of botany long before Darwin, and acclimatization societies owed little to his work. But the flood of new evidences of nature flowing to Europe through these networks fueled both theoretical debate and practical application.

None of these debates was more vigorous than that surrounding

the nature and diversity of human races. Darwin's most vivid Pacific
memories were of the native peoples he encountered. Subsequently—
for European missionaries, anthropologists, and colonial administrators—conceptions of race, behavior, and progress became part of the
agenda of settlement and rule. They acquired an important position in
the Atlantic interpretation of the Pacific when, during the 1890s, the
reading of Darwinism as Social Darwinism became a dominant theme
in Atlantic political theory. Whether Darwin was himself a Social
Darwinian continues to be debated. But it is clear that Darwinism
was deployed as a naturalistic justification for an array of rival political preferences.

With such issues in mind, the following essays selectively traverse
four chapters in the history of Darwinism in the period between Darwin's own *Beagle* experiences of the 1830s and the *fin de siècle,* when
biologists faced what Peter Bowler has called the "eclipse" of natural
selection.[28] The struggle for existence would be rewritten in the language of neo-Lamarckians, Mendelians, environmental determinists,
and Social Darwinists interpreting Darwin as social theory. The
"Modern Synthesis" in evolutionary biology lies outside our pages;
we limit ourselves to applications of evolutionary principles that for
more than a century justified the European presence in the Pacific and
as such retain a central role in the history of "Atlantic science."

Darwin found his earliest scientific success as a geologist. Hence,
we begin in part 1 with David Stoddart's analysis of the friendly relations, parallel development, but often divergent views of Darwin and
the American geologist James Dwight Dana. Educated formally at
Yale but trained practically in the Pacific as a member of the U.S.
Exploring Expedition, Dana agreed with Darwin's reading of coral
atoll formation in all but details. The persistence of their disagreement over evolutionary theory Stoddart attributes to differences in
personalities and priorities.

Pacific islands, like coral atolls, were microcosms where evolutionary phenomena occurred on a more visible, manageable scale—laboratories more convenient for observing the effects of migration,
dispersal, barriers, and isolation, as Alison Kay shows in her survey of
Pacific biogeography in the wake of the *Origin.* Explorer-naturalists
as early as J.R. Forster in the 1770s had begun to invent a Pacific biogeography, but Darwinians were especially quick to notice and eager
to explain the curious features of island biotas: the paucity of species
compared to equal continental areas, the high rates of endemism, and
the isolation of species to limited areas.

From the central Pacific we pass to the Indo-Pacific frontier, with

Jane Camerini's study of Wallace's line. One of the most striking and unexpected faunal boundaries to be mapped in the nineteenth century—the line through the East Indies separating the Asian and Australian faunas—was hinted at by Darwin but constructed fully only by Wallace in the late 1850s. Camerini posits that Wallace's visualization of the line was not only coincident with, but integral to, the development of his evolutionary views. Maps, "mental and actual," were crucial to naturalists in creating order out of the chaos of Indo-Pacific data. She notes that the inventing of the region developed precisely in parallel with the mapping of social and economic variables and rise of statistical thinking among the leading imperial nations of the era.

Ronald Amundson continues the biogeographic theme in his study of the Hawaii-born naturalist-missionary, John Thomas Gulick. From his intimate knowledge of the natural history of the islands Darwin had longed to visit, Gulick became an early advocate of the importance of isolation in the formation of new species and a critic of deterministic adaptationism. The latter belief led inevitably to fatalism, anathema both to Gulick's religious views and to his socialist political leanings. To counter both adaptationism and fatalism, Gulick developed the notion of the "active organism," whose spontaneous behavioral changes could alter its environmental relations and thus the direction of its evolution. In leading us through the complexities of Gulick's thought, Amundson also shows how Gulick, the son of a Calvinist missionary family and a missionary himself, found meaning for his Christian beliefs within his evolutionary biology.

To conclude part 1 we turn from the anomalies of biogeography to the anomalies of evolutionary embryology. Roy MacLeod charts the careers of the early Balfour Students, demonstrating how Cambridge scholars came to see and use the Asia-Pacific hemisphere as a laboratory for the confirmation of Darwinism. Inspired by the foresight of Michael Foster, the example of Frank Balfour, the supervision of Adam Sedgwick, and the opportunities of British dominion, Balfour Students were able to travel the globe as few before them, making important contributions to mammalian taxonomy, endocrinology, invertebrate morphology, and the study of variation.

In part 2, we turn to communication between peripheries and "centers of calculation,"[29] examining the development of networks for the exchange of correspondence, specimens, and plant material. Janet Garber opens with a cataloguing of Darwin's Pacific correspondents. A host of Pacific "lab assistants" provided Darwin with data relating to all his principal theories. Garber classifies these contacts and accomplices across the full range of Darwin's interests—from geology, biogeography, and variation to domestication, human origins, and earthworms—yielding a new sense of the extent and depth of his continuing presence in the Pacific after the *Beagle* voyage.

By the closing decades of the nineteenth century, Darwinian theory was influencing the work of naturalists well outside Darwin's network. In his study of Seattle's Young Naturalists' Society, Keith Benson assesses the prevalence of Darwinian presuppositions among the budding collectors of the Pacific Northwest. Like collectors elsewhere, the Young Naturalists rarely concerned themselves with higher theoretical matters. But integral to the advance of evolutionary theory was the investigation of species variation with respect to geography. Little-explored regions like the Pacific Northwest had much to offer the student of variation, and the naturalists exemplified by P. Brooks Randolph traded on their locale to the benefit of professional naturalists in the eastern United States, as well as for their own curiosity. While not a direct motivation, Darwinian theory gave coherent meaning to the collecting and ordering of Nature by such amateur devotees.

Moving to the opposite extremity of the Pacific, and from pure to applied natural history, Pauline Payne explores the life of Richard Schomburgk to demonstrate the cultural significance of entrepreneurial botany at the periphery of empire. As director of Adelaide's botanical garden from 1865 to 1891, Schomburgk established and exploited a botanical exchange network, connecting Australia with Europe, Africa, India, and the Americas—an enterprise especially important in a country with no prior agricultural tradition and few cultivable species. While Darwin was at home exploring the power of movement in plants, Schomburgk and other government botanists, responding to the more utilitarian needs of colonial existence, were transporting plants and exchanging experimental experience across the world.

In part 3, the focus shifts to the natural history of mankind, one of Darwin's dominant interests post-*Origin* and a field that, as the science of anthropology, intensified during the closing decades of the century. Janet Browne opens a new perspective on the *Beagle* voyage itself, demonstrating the intensity of Darwin's anthropological interests—even at that early stage in his career—and their accord with the views of his otherwise argumentative captain, Robert FitzRoy. Revisiting the traditional view of Darwin and FitzRoy as philosophical adversaries from divergent backgrounds, Browne finds clear convergences in their opinions on the unity of the human race, the "civilized potential" of aboriginal peoples, the merits of missionary activity, and the possibility of progress—convergences arising directly from their shared experiences in the southern hemisphere.

Pacific missionaries were themselves active contributors to natural history and ethnography throughout the nineteenth century, as Niel Gunson amply demonstrates. Gunson finds few of the "genesis versus geology" antagonisms here; on the contrary, Pacific missionaries— Evangelicals as well as nonconformists—were widely sympathetic to science, Dissenting counterparts of the traditional Anglican parson-naturalist. Ideally positioned to assist other naturalists, both visitors and correspondents, missionaries also collected and published their own accounts, in scientific as well as religious journals. For the most part, missionaries believed that Pacific Islanders had little hope of competing with European races, but wished to recognize indigenous cultures as having qualities worthy of preservation and study. It could be argued, as Gunson does here, that the "truth" of human history was to lie somewhere between evolutionary theory and a "nonliteral understanding of the Bible."

The missionary connection in anthropological research, introduced by Gunson, is examined in detail by Sara Sohmer in her study of the missionaries to Melanesia in the 1860s and 1870s. Missionaries were much more anthropologically enlightened and much more likely to contribute to the research programs of anthropologists than our traditional stereotype of them has allowed. Sohmer finds a particularly strong intellectual symbiosis operating between the Melanesian mission of the Church of England, beginning under the leadership of Bishop John Coleridge Patteson and the Reverend Robert Codrington, and Victorian academic anthropologists such as Friedrich Max Müller, Edward Tylor, and Henry Maine. This symbiosis was grounded in their common Oxbridge experience, subsequently enhanced, at least indirectly, by Darwinian theory. With this common spirit, missionaries were useful collectors of anthropological data, and essential in the study of the languages of aboriginal peoples. But, as the case of Codrington demonstrates, missionaries could become substantial theorists as well.

By the close of the century, evolutionary theory had become part of the anthropologist's discourse, though it was Lamarckian theory rather than Darwinian, as Henrika Kuklick shows in her study of the Torres Strait expedition. Led by A. C. Haddon, who would later become Cambridge's first full-time anthropologist, the Torres Strait team applied an evolutionary outlook to a psychological problem. The problem was to specify the origins, biological or cultural, of differences in perception—when is "the color blue" identified as blue, and why? Their method was to abandon the laboratory for the field, to examine the behavior of traditional peoples in their native environment. The result for psychology was the abandonment of widely held Lamarckian notions that long-established habits could induce changes in physical endowment, and a greatly increased appreciation of the role of social conditioning. This would influence both theory and therapy well beyond World War I. For anthropological method, the expedition had far-reaching effects as well, convincing the next generation of workers of the necessity of field work. The hope of the missionary had become the expectation of the anthropologist.

In the final section, we turn to Social Darwinism, or rather Social Darwinisms, for our authors demonstrate that the social ideologies associated with Darwin's name took a variety of forms. Barry Butcher offers a reassessment of the relations of Darwinism, Social Darwinism, and anthropology in nineteenth-century Australia. Observing the sea change in the recent historiography of Social Darwinism—shifting responsibility for the ideology away from Herbert Spencer and toward the larger, pre-*Origin,* Victorian context—Butcher follows the implications of this revisionism for understanding colonial attitudes toward the Aborigines. He then shows how this seamless biosocial ideology helped construct the data that Australian observers Alfred Howitt and Walter Baldwin Spencer contributed to evolutionary anthropology. Thus, ironically, Social Darwinism helped create biological Darwinism; the latter reciprocated by adding its authority to the comfortable, racist conclusions of Victorian anthropology.

Across the Tasman, Darwinian biology was invoked by leading New Zealand *pakeha* (white) leaders to justify their domination of the Maori and of the white underclass as well, yielding what John Stenhouse calls the "dark and dubious side" of the Darwinian enlightenment. Stenhouse explains that early plans to create a "new and better Britain" by careful screening of immigrants fell short of the ideal, while expectations of easy appropriation of Maori lands were diminished after 1840 by the Treaty of Waitangi. But despite the outcry from Christian missionaries that Maori rights be upheld, *pakeha* politicians insisted that the sovereignty of Her Majesty's government was supreme and invoked the law of nature—that superior species and races supplant inferior ones—to defend their position. The Maori were judged unfit—physically, morally, and culturally—to occupy their own lands. Darwin's *Origin,* appearing just before the New Zealand Wars, provided ammunition for commentators throughout the remainder of the century to argue that colonial ascendancy and

Maori decline were legitimized by nature itself. Darwin's own writings on the future of indigenous peoples, though more neutral in tone, acquiesced to the reality of racial extinction.

A quite different tack was taken by the Sydney-educated geographer Griffith Taylor. Nancy Christie describes Taylor—founder of the geography departments at the Universities of Sydney and Toronto—as an eclectic, but strongly Lamarckian, evolutionary geographer in the decades between the decline of natural selection at the end of the nineteenth century and its rebirth as the "Modern Synthesis" in the 1940s. Taylor's effort to explain the origins and distribution of the races of humankind was driven by a strict environmental-climatic determinism. He then expanded this theory to encompass the phenomena of a range of disciplines, from philology to urban planning. Christie traces the diverse Australian, European, and American roots of this holistic evolutionary philosophy and shows how Taylor moved against contemporary currents of eugenics and racism to advocate racial migration and intermarriage.

In the closing contribution, John Laurent uncovers in Australia, Japan, and Hawaii, a "spectrum" of Social Darwinisms, extending in both directions from the standard, Spencerian, laissez-faire version. To the political right, he finds evidence of a genocidal model of Social Darwinism, foreshadowing fascism. To the left, he finds several variations: a model of embryological differentiation, according to which society proceeds from "incoherent homogeneity" to "coherent heterogeneity;" a collectivist model that notes the tendency of many species to congregate for survival; and an internationalist model that points to the tendency for wars to exterminate the most fit, and the need to eliminate war so that natural selection can be allowed to operate normally.

Just as the Pacific has, in geological time, served as a grand laboratory for biological divergence, so in recent times the Pacific has provided niches for many divergent "species" of scholarship. These themes add a fresh dimension to Darwinian studies. Taken as a whole, they are suggestive of the possibilities for research in the history of Darwinism and its place in the laboratory of the Pacific.

Notes

1   Charles Darwin, *Voyage of the "Beagle,"* edited with an introduction by Janet Browne and Michael Neve (London: Penguin, 1989), 204.

2   The political, economic, and hydrographic circumstances of the *Beagle* voyage are set forth in George Basalla, "The Voyage of the *Beagle* without Darwin," *Mariner's Mirror* 49 (1963): 42–48.

3   *The Correspondence of Charles Darwin,* ed. Frederick Burkhardt and
     Sydney Smith, 10 vols. (Cambridge: Cambridge University Press,
     1985–1994), 2:65.

4   Ibid.

5   Such arguments apparently gave Darwin little comfort from the anxi-
     eties he suffered from his heresy, however, as documented in the
     recent biography by Adrian Desmond and James Moore, *Darwin*
     (London: Michael Joseph, 1991).

6   Arif Dirlik, "The Asia-Pacific Idea: Reality and Representation in
     the Invention of a Regional Structure," *Journal of World History* 3
     (1992): 55–78.

7   Philip F. Rehbock, "The Banksian Legacy in the Pacific: British
     Botanists from Brown to Moseley," paper presented at the Visions of
     Empire Conference, Los Angeles, 17–19 January 1991.

8   David Lowenthal, "Geography, Experience and Imagination:
     Towards a Geographical Epistemology," *Annals of the Association of
     American Geographers* 51 (3) (September 1961): 241–260.

9   David Gooding, Trevor Pinch, and Simon Schaffer, eds., *The Uses of
     Experiment: Studies in the Natural Sciences* (Cambridge: Cambridge
     University Press, 1989); H. E. Le Grand, ed., *Experimental Inquiries:
     Historical, Philosophical, and Social Studies of Experimentation in
     Science* (Dordrecht: Kluwer, 1990).

10   Scott Atran, *The Cognitive Foundations of Natural History: Towards
     an Anthropology of Science* (Cambridge: Cambridge University Press;
     Paris: Editions de la Maison des Sciences de l'Homme, 1990).

11   James A. Secord, "King of Siluria: Roderick Murchison and the Impe-
     rial Theme in Nineteenth-Century British Geology," *Victorian Studies*
     25 (1982): 413–442; Robert A. Stafford, *Scientist of the Empire: Sir
     Roderick Murchison, Scientific Exploration and Victorian Imperial-
     ism* (Cambridge: Cambridge University Press, 1989).

12   See, especially, Herman J. Viola, and Carolyn Margolis, eds.,
     Magnificent Voyagers: The U.S. Exploring Expedition, 1838–1842
     (Washington, DC: Smithsonian Institution, 1985); and Harold L.
     Burstyn, "Pioneering in Large-scale Scientific Organisation: The
     Challenger Expedition and Its Report. I. Launching the Expedition,"
     Proceedings of the Royal Society of Edinburgh (B) 72 (1971–1972):
     47–61.

13   Conference Report, Science of Pacific Island Peoples Conference,
     Suva, Fiji, 6–10 July 1992.

14   *The Autobiography of Charles Darwin and Selected Letters,* ed. Fran-
     cis Darwin (New York: Dover, 1958), 43, 101. Elsewhere, of course,
     Darwin disclaimed his dependence on theories, insisting that he
     "worked on true Baconian principles" (ibid., 42); but as Michael

Ghiselin has argued in *The Triumph of the Darwinian Method* (Berkeley and Los Angeles: University of California Press, 1969), this was far from the case.

15   The literature generated by the Darwin industry is, of course, vast. As a benchmark, one might simply observe the output of books during the single year 1990: volume 6 of the *Correspondence* (1856–1857); the 700-page *A Concordance to Charles Darwin's Notebooks, 1836–1844,* edited by Donald J. Weinshank, Stephan J. Ozminski, Paul Ruhlen, and Wilma M. Barrett (Ithaca, NY: Cornell University Press); the first volume of *Charles Darwin's Marginalia,* edited by Mario A. Di Gregorio (New York: Garland); and two biographies: John Bowlby, *Charles Darwin, A Biography* (New York: Norton) and Peter J. Bowler, *Charles Darwin: The Man and His Influence* (Oxford: Blackwell). Also appearing in 1990 were the following monographs on Darwin's influence in various realms: Eugene Cittadino, *Nature as the Laboratory: Darwinian Plant Ecology in the German Empire, 1880–1900* (Cambridge: Cambridge University Press); Lucille B. Ritvo, *Darwin's Influence on Freud: A Tale of Two Sciences* (New Haven: Yale University Press); and James Rachels, *Created from Animals: The Moral Implications of Darwinism* (Oxford: Oxford University Press). Finally, James R. Moore edited the festschrift *History, Humanity, and Evolution: Essays for John C. Greene* (Cambridge: Cambridge University Press, 1990); and reprints of Alvar Ellegård, *Darwin and the General Reader: The Reception of Darwin's Theory of Evolution in the British Periodical Press, 1859–1872,* and of the most influential work of Darwin's early life, Charles Lyell, *Principles of Geology,* 3 vols., were published, both by University of Chicago Press.

The list for 1990 may be expanded by essays and journal articles, some of the most notable being: M. J. S. Hodge, "Darwin Studies at Work: A Re-examination of Three Decisive Years (1835–1837)," in *Nature, Experiment and the Sciences: Essays on Galileo and the History of Science in Honour of Stillman Drake,* ed. Trevor H. Levere and William R. Shea (Dordrecht: Kluwer Academic), 249–274; Joel S. Schwartz, "Darwin, Wallace, and Huxley, and *Vestiges of the Natural History of Creation,*" *Journal of the History of Biology* 23 (1990): 127–153; John Angus Campbell, "Scientific Discovery and Rhetorical Invention: The Path to Darwin's *Origin,*" in *The Rhetorical Turn: Invention and Persuasion in the Conduct of Inquiry,* ed. Herbert W. Simons (Chicago: University of Chicago Press), 58–90; Linda S. Bergmann, "Reshaping the Roles of Man, God, and Nature: Darwin's Rhetoric in *On the Origin of Species,*" in *Beyond the Two Cultures: Essays on Science, Technology and Literature,* ed. Joseph W. Slade and Judith Yaross Yee (Ames: Iowa State University Press), 79–98; Frederick R. Prete, "The Conundrum of the Honey Bees: One Impediment to the Publication of Darwin's Theory," *Journal of the History of Biology* 23 (1990): 271–290; Fabienne Smith, "Charles Darwin's Ill Health," *Journal of the History of Biology* 23 (1990): 443–459; Gordon Russell Chancellor, ed., "Charles Darwin's St. Helena Model Notebook," *Bulletin of the British Museum (Natural History),* History Series, 18 (1990): 203–228; and several of the essays in the collection edited by Andrew Cunningham and Nicholas Jardine, *Romanticism and the Sciences* (Cambridge: Cambridge University Press).

This ever-expanding literature has been made more readily accessible through the periodic publication of excellent review articles: Bert James Loewenberg, "Darwin and Darwin Studies, 1959–63," *History of Science* 9 (1965): 15–54; Ernst Mayr, "Open Problems of Darwin Research" (essay review of Charles Darwin, *The Life and Letters of Charles Darwin,* Johnson Reprint), *Studies in History and Philosophy of Science* 2 (1971): 273–280; Michael Ruse, "The Darwin Industry: A Critical Evaluation," *History of Science* 12 (1974): 43–58; John C. Greene, "Reflections on the Progress of Darwin Studies," *Journal of the History of Biology* 8 (1975): 243–273; David R. Oldroyd, "How Did Darwin Arrive at His Theory? The Secondary Literature to 1982," *History of Science* 22 (1984): 325–374; Antonello La Vergata, "Images of Darwin: A Historiographic Overview," in *The Darwinian Heritage,* ed. David Kohn (Princeton: Princeton University Press, 1985), 901–972; and Ralph Colp, Jr., "Charles Darwin's Past and Future Biographies," *History of Science* 27 (1989): 167–197.

The 77-page bibliography contained in Kohn's massive *The Darwinian Heritage* displayed the extent of the frontier of Darwin studies by the 1980s. The appearance of path-breaking works since 1990 demonstrates that the Darwin industry continues to thrive. Among them are an issue of the *British Journal for the History of Science* devoted to "Darwin and Geology" (vol. 24, pt. 2 [1991]); and the widely acclaimed biography *Darwin,* by Adrian Desmond and James Moore (London: Michael Joseph, 1991; New York: Warner Books, 1992).

16   E.g., Robin Fisher and Hugh Johnston, eds., *Captain James Cook and His Times* (Vancouver: Douglas and McIntyre, 1979), papers from the Cook Bicentennial Conference, Simon Fraser University, Burnaby, British Columbia, 26–29 April 1978.

17   The work of several scholars, including Lewis Pyenson and Roy MacLeod, has directed attention to Pacific science in the past decade. For a survey suggesting the breadth of previously unexplored topics, see Roy MacLeod and Philip F. Rehbock, eds., *Nature in Its Greatest Extent: Western Science in the Pacific* (Honolulu: University of Hawaii Press, 1988).

18   Alan Moorehead, *The Fatal Impact: An Account of the Invasion of*

the South Pacific, 1767–1840 (London: H. Hamilton; New York: Harper and Row, 1966). This theme was pioneered in A. Grenfell Price, *The Western Invasions of the Pacific and Its Continents: A Study of Moving Frontiers and Changing Landscapes, 1513–1958* (Oxford: Clarendon Press, 1963). The biological ramifications of impact have been explored in Alfred W. Crosby, *Ecological Imperialism: The Biological Expansion of Europe, 900–1900* (Cambridge and New York: Cambridge University Press, 1986).

19   Frank J. Sulloway, "Darwin and His Finches: The Evolution of a Legend," *Journal of the History of Biology* 15 (1982): 1–53; idem, "The *Beagle* Collections of Darwin's Finches (Geospizinae)," *Bulletin of the British Museum (Natural History), Zoology* series, 43, no. 2 (1982); idem, "The *Beagle* Voyage and Its Aftermath," *Journal of the History of Biology* 15 (1982): 325–396.

20   David R. Stoddart, "Darwin, Lyell, and the Geological Significance of Coral Reefs," *British Journal for the History of Science* 11 (1976): 199–218; idem, "Darwin's Impact on Geography," in *The Conceptual Revolution in Geography*, ed. Wayne K. D. Davies (Totowa, New Jersey: Rowman and Littlefield, 1972), 52–76; and idem, *On Geography and Its History* (New York: Basil Blackwell, 1986).

21   Sandra Herbert, "Charles Darwin as a Prospective Geological Author," *British Journal for the History of Science* 24 (1991): 159–192.

22   F. W. Nichols and J. M. Nichols, *Charles Darwin in Australia* (Cambridge: Cambridge University Press, 1989); James Reeve Pusey, *China and Charles Darwin* (Cambridge: Harvard University Press, 1985).

23   See n. 15.

24   George W. Stocking, Jr., *Victorian Anthropology* (New York: Free Press; London: Macmillan, 1987).

25   Gordon C. Sauer, *John Gould, the Bird Man: A Chronology and Bibliography* (Melbourne: Landsdowne Editions; London: Henry Southern, 1982); David F. Branagan, "Samuel Stutchbury: A Natural History Voyage to the Pacific, 1825–27, and Its Consequences," *Archives of Natural History* 20: 69–91.

26   Paul Lawrence Farber, "Aspiring Naturalists and Their Frustrations: The Case of William Swainson (1789–1855)," in *From Linnaeus to Darwin: Commentaries on the History of Biology and Geology*, ed. Alwyne Wheeler and James H. Price (London: Society for the History of Natural History, 1985), 51–59.

27   Dirlik, "The Asia-Pacific Idea," 65.

28   Peter Bowler, *The Eclipse of Darwinism: Anti-Darwinian Evolution Theories in the Decades around 1900* (Baltimore: Johns Hopkins University Press, 1983).

29   Bruno Latour, *Science in Action: How to Follow Scientists and Engineers through Society* (Milton Keynes: Open University Press, 1987); David P. Miller, "Joseph Banks, Empire, and 'Centres of Calculation' in Late Hanoverian London," in *Visions of Empire,* ed. Peter Reill (Cambridge: Cambridge University Press, forthcoming).

PART ONE

Nature's Diversity and the Research Site of the Pacific

DAVID R. STODDART

1 "This Coral Episode"
Darwin, Dana, and the Coral Reefs of the Pacific

Charles Darwin disembarked from HMS *Beagle* at Falmouth on 2 October 1836, after four years and nine months circumnavigating the globe. James Dwight Dana, exactly four years Darwin's junior—both were born on February 12—sailed under Lieutenant Charles Wilkes from Norfolk, Virginia, with the U.S. Exploring Expedition almost two years later, for three years and nine months at sea, the greater part of it in the Pacific.

Perhaps no significant personal relationship in nineteenth century natural science is so problematic and so unexamined, or indeed so systematically forgotten, as that between Darwin and Dana in the field of their earliest specialty.[1] The similarities in their research interests and their careers have often been remarked,[2] but in a remarkably unproblematic manner.[3] With the exception of Sanford's paper on Dana's reaction to Darwinism,[4] no attention has been given to the intellectual tensions between the two. Their earliest and almost contemporary work on coral reefs led to a constantly uneasy association between them that continued until Darwin's death in 1882. This relationship reflected not only the scientific issues at stake, particularly over the development of coral reefs, but demonstrates also the importance of personal and social issues, as well as international rivalries, in the development of nineteenth-century science.

Darwin's Originality

Darwin's remarkable insight into the development of coral reefs during the voyage of the *Beagle* is well known.[5] He was initially impressed both by his experience of earthquake-induced uplift on the coast of Chile and by his discovery of recent marine faunas at high altitudes in the Andes. This led him to the speculations that even high mountain ranges could have been formed by the cumulative effects of individually minor elevations and also that such continental uplift must be balanced by equivalent subsidence in the ocean basins. It was his genius to apply this idea, and to calibrate it, by interpreting the various forms of coral reefs—fringing reefs, barrier reefs, and atolls—as stages in an evolutionary sequence defined by the slow subsidence of the foundations on which the reefs had grown.[6] In its elegant simplicity, Darwin's explanation both incorporated the recent realization that corals can grow only in shallow surface waters and also avoided the manifest improbabilities of previous explanations of reef form.[7]

It was Darwin's first major contribution to science, and it established his reputation. When he returned to England he soon made contact with Charles Lyell, who in his *Principles of Geology* had produced the improbable if superficially plausible suggestion that atolls were simply coral reefs growing on the rims of slightly submerged volcanic craters. When Darwin told Lyell of his new interpretation Lyell fell into a state of "wild excitement and sustained enthusiasm"[8] in which he actually "danced about and threw himself into the wildest contortions, as was his manner when excessively pleased."[9] Darwin read a paper at the Geological Society of London on his theory in 1837,[10] published an outline as chapter 20 of his *Journal and Remarks* in 1839,[11] and produced his treatise on *The Structure and Distribution of Coral Reefs* in 1842.[12] Lyell briefly noted the new explanation in his *Elements of Geology* in 1838[13] and treated it at length in the sixth edition of *Principles of Geology* in 1840.[14]

Paradoxically, given the range of his theoretical views, Darwin's actual field experience of coral reefs was very limited. He first saw atolls in the Tuamotus, from shipboard, on 9 November 1835, and was initially unimpressed.[15] Later that month he both observed the reefs of Tahiti and saw from that island the barrier reef encircling the island of Moorea. His main field observations of reefs were at Cocos-Keeling Atoll in the eastern Indian Ocean, where he outlined his theory in his *Diary* entry for 12 April 1836:

If the opinion that the rock-making Polypi continue to build upwards, as the foundation of the Isd from volcanic agency, after intervals gradually subsides, is granted to be true; then probably the Coral limestone must be of great thickness. We see certain Isds in the Pacifick, such as Tahiti & Eimeo [Moorea], . . . which are encircled by a Coral reef separated from the shore by channels & basins of still water. Various causes tend to check the growth of the most efficient kinds of Corals in these situations. Hence if we imagine such an Island, after long successive intervals to subside a few feet, in a manner similar, but with a movement opposite to the continent of S. America; the coral would be continued upwards, rising from the foundation of the encircling reef. In time the central land would sink beneath the level of the sea & disappear, but the coral would have completed its circular wall. Should we not then have a Lagoon Island [atoll]?—Under this view, we must look at a Lagoon Isd as a monument raised by myriads of tiny architects, to mark the spot where a former land lies buried in the depths of the ocean.[16]

He had previously written out a fuller statement while on board the *Beagle* between Tahiti and New Zealand, in December 1835.[17]

Both the intellectual power and the general acclaim for his theory gave Darwin great satisfaction. Toward the end of his life, in the *Autobiography* he wrote in 1876, he recalled:

No other work of mine was begun in so deductive a spirit as this; for the whole theory was thought out on the west coast of S. America before I had seen a true coral reef. I had therefore only to verify and extend my views by a careful examination of living reefs. But it should be observed that I had during the two previous years been incessantly attending to the effects on the shores of S. America of the intermittent elevation of the land, together with the denudation and the deposition of sediment. This necessarily led me to reflect much on the effects of subsidence, and it was easy to replace in imagination the continued deposition of sediment by the upward growth of coral. To do this was to form my theory of the formation of barrier-reefs and atolls.[18]

The Wilkes Expedition

The U.S. Exploring Expedition of 1838–1842 was the first coordinated investigation of the Pacific organized by the government of the United States. Its achievements in hydrographic surveying and in science are rightly celebrated.[19] But anyone who has ever been on a scientific expedition at sea will recognize it as the ultimate nightmare. It began with years of controversy, was executed through four years of malice, ineptitude, and frustration, and ended with decades of animosity and recrimination. Many if not all of its difficulties must be attributed to its commander, Charles Wilkes, a man of shallow intellect, meager understanding, and emotional instability. Even before the expedition began he was seen as "exceedingly vain and conceited."[20] At times during the expedition his very sanity seemed in doubt; he was, as Stanton comments, a leader of a seagoing expedition who was neither leader nor seaman. At his subsequent court-martial he was variously described as violent, overbearing, and insulting; incoherent and rude; and offensive in the highest degree.[21] In the annals of exploration there can have been few leaders more crass, foolish, and inept than Wilkes. The commander of the *Beagle*, by comparison, who was far from the easiest of men, appears positively benign by comparison.

In the earliest planning stages of the expedition, the problem of coral reefs was recognized to be important. A memorandum from the American Philosophical Society to the secretary of the navy in October 1836 makes the point:

> We would enjoin a close study of all the geological phenomena connected with causes now in action, as well the volcanic where such occur, as those arising from the operation of the ocean upon the land. The circular figure and deep water of the Coral Islands having given rise to the conjecture that these fabrics of the Zoophytes are based upon the craters of submarine volcanoes, the collection of any facts calculated to throw light upon this subject will form one of the interesting duties of the Geologists.[22]

Wilkes thought it all nonsense. In his *Narrative* he said that he "was unable to believe that these great formations are or can possibly be the work of zoophytes. . . . It seems almost absurd to suppose that these immense reefs should have been raised by the exertions of a minute animal"; he suggested instead that the reefs were formed by "the lightning of tropical regions, and the electric fluid engendered by submarine and other volcanoes which abound in the South Seas."[23]

The two "scientifics" with particular responsibility for reef science were Joseph P. Couthouy, serving as conchologist, and James Dwight Dana, as geologist. They had unparalleled opportunities for reef studies. The tracks of the Exploring Expedition (figure 1.1) constituted the most comprehensive exploration of the Pacific since the time of Cook, though of course in very different circumstances. The expedition entered the reef seas in the eastern Tuamotus at Reao and made many running surveys of atolls all the way to Tahiti. After a month in Samoa the expedition proceeded to New Zealand and Australia. Wilkes then made a separate and contentious excursion to Antarctica before the squadron again left Sydney for New Zealand and then Tonga, Fiji, and Hawaii. One vessel continued exploring the Line Islands and the Tuamotus, others the Phoenix Islands, the Tokelaus, Samoa, the Gilberts (Kiribati), and the southern Marshall Islands. It was (and remains) the single most comprehensive survey of Pacific atolls and reef-encircled volcanic islands ever carried out.

Couthouy collected corals and other marine invertebrates as well as molluscs, and the smell of their decay on board ship (Couthouy was assigned to the flagship *Vincennes*) soon aroused Wilkes' ire. One small specimen of each was the limit, and everything on deck, was his ruling. When Couthouy suggested that previous expeditions had

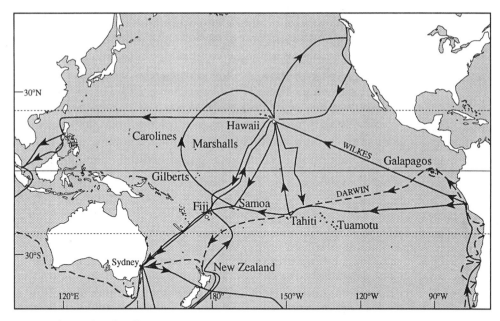

1.1 Pacific tracks of Wilkes expedition (Dana) and H.M.S. *Beagle* (Darwin).

made decent collections of similar material Wilkes told him that he "did not give a damn" what any previous expedition had done. At least in the early days in the Tuamotus the scientifics took second place to the prime purpose of the expedition (as seen by Wilkes) of hydrographic surveying, and at some atolls they were even prevented from going ashore at all. Couthouy complained that whereas fifty thousand specimens had been sent home from already well-collected Rio de Janeiro, the first five atolls visited in the Tuamotus yielded less than a cigar box of specimens. In Samoa, Wilkes publicly accused Couthouy of "fomenting discord." When Wilkes demanded his notebooks and records, Couthouy refused to hand them over, on the grounds that understanding of his collections required constant reference to previous notes and drawings. To the arrogant Wilkes this was tantamount to mutiny. Finally Couthouy gave up: he was ill in Sydney and did no further work. Wilkes dismissed him from the expedition and all its works and thus lost a fine field naturalist.[24]

Thus it happened that Dana's duties were expanded from geology alone to include responsibility for the "zoophytes" or coelenterates and other marine invertebrates. It meant too that he alone had experience of the vast reef tracts of Fiji and Tonga, which the expedition worked through after leaving New South Wales. This is of particular significance, since Dana always held that he heard of Darwin's theory on arriving at Sydney at the end of November 1839:[25]

> Soon after reaching Sydney, Australia, in 1839, a brief statement was found in the papers of Mr Darwin's theory with respect to the origin of the atoll and barrier forms of reefs. The paragraph threw a flood of light over the subject, and called forth feelings of peculiar satisfaction, and of gratefulness to Mr Darwin, which still come up afresh [more than thirty years later] whenever the subject of coral islands is mentioned.[26]

This statement by Dana is referred to by all who have subsequently commented on his reef work, though it is curious that there appears to be no reference to Darwin's theory in any Sydney newspaper, either while Dana himself was in Australia or for the twelve months preceding his arrival.[27] Dana had in fact two alternative means of learning of Darwin's ideas, both of which are highly probable. Lyell included a single sentence about the theory in his new *Elements of Geology*, published in 1838, citing the account in Darwin's *Journal of Researches*, which did not appear until the following year.[28] Dana took a copy of the *Elements* with him on the expedition, and it is scarcely conceivable that he did not read what Lyell had to say on reefs. Unfortunately, this copy was lost when the *Peacock* was wrecked in July 1841, and so we cannot know if any annotation revealed Dana's recognition of the importance of the passage.[29]

But Dana also spent much time in Sydney with the Reverend W. B. Clarke, a student of Adam Sedgwick in Cambridge who had emigrated from England on 27 January 1839 and who became the colony's principal geologist. Whether Clarke actually met Darwin in the fifteen months after the latter's return to England is not known, but six weeks before Clarke left England Sedgwick wrote to him, asking if he knew of the new coral reef theory and urging him to call on Darwin before he left.[30] Again, it is scarcely conceivable that Clarke and Dana did not discuss Darwin and coral reefs during the three-and-a-half months they spent together in New South Wales, though Dana nowhere makes reference to any such exchange.

In his later published works on reefs, Dana came close to suggesting that Darwin's explanation had occurred to him quite independently during the course of the expedition.[31] Indeed, many years later, Dana commented that Darwin's "work on Coral Reefs appeared in 1842, when my Report on the subject was already in manuscript,"[32] as if to suggest that their discoveries were contemporary. Darwin, however, after first publishing his theory in May 1837, began his book in October 1838 and sent the manuscript to the printer in January 1840;[33] Dana on the other hand was saying in February 1845 that his book would be completed in eight months, and his manuscript was not actually received until December 1847.[34]

Whatever happened in Sydney, however, Dana's knowledge of Darwin's theory had profound significance for his interpretations as the expedition sailed back into the reef seas. After speaking of his gratitude for Darwin's insight, Dana continued:

> The Gambier Islands, in the Paumotus, which gave him the key to the theory, I had not seen;[35] but on reaching the Feejees, six months later, in 1840, I found there similar facts on a still grander scale and of more diversified character, so that I was afterward enabled to speak of this theory as established with more positiveness than he himself, in his philosophic caution, had been ready to adopt.[36]

Dana's Coral Reef Achievements

Dana's have been called "the most fundamental and enduring contributions of the U.S. Exploring Expedition,"[37] and certainly with cause. Twenty-five years old when the expedition sailed, he had already published a paper on volcanic activity on Vesuvius, based on observations during previous naval service, and a textbook, *System of Mineralogy,* that in various formats was to survive for over a century. The breadth and virtuosity of Dana's technical contributions to the expedition's reports are astonishing. Among the massive quarto volumes of results, unbelievably produced in minute editions by order of the Congress and unavailable therefore even to their authors,[38] Dana was responsible for the treatment of the "zoophytes" (volume 7), the Crustacea (volumes 13 and 14), and the geology (volume 10).

The volumes on the corals and their relatives extended to 740 pages.[39] Dana himself privately saw it, with good cause, as potentially "the most complete work on the subject ever published."[40] In the report itself he made large and justified claims: "a large amount of new information was obtained"; he found "numerous errors in the received systems" of classification; and he had "suggested changes of fundamental importance."[41] Of the 483 species of corals he described, 229 were new to science. The work remains a fundamental taxonomic reference in what is a notoriously difficult group, more especially because Dana ignored Wilkes' orders to confine himself to describing specimens and instead reviewed and revised the whole field of knowledge. His text was accompanied by a folio atlas of 64 plates, including 1,008 figures, of which 54 were from Dana's own illustrations.[42]

The report on the Crustacea totaled more than 1,600 pages and included some 650 new species.[43] It too was accompanied by a folio atlas of 96 plates based on Dana's own drawings.[44] The text included substantial essays on the classification of the Crustacea and on their geographical distribution. These were later issued separately, together with a substantial memoir on sea surface temperature.[45]

In the present context, however, the most significant and generally accessible report was that on the geology.[46] This was a text of 756 quarto pages, with a separate folio atlas of 21 plates. A partial version of the text was published serially in the *American Journal of Science* in 1851–1852[47] and as Dana's first reef book, *On Coral Reefs and Islands,* in 1853.[48] This subsequently evolved into *Corals and Coral Islands,* published in 1872, with further editions in 1874 and 1890.[49] The reception and content of these books will be discussed below. The three reports taken together represented more than a decade of intensive effort and must have greatly taxed their author. There is no question that, in terms of magnitude of output, Dana's results from the Wilkes Expedition greatly exceeded the formal publications on Darwin's own collections, even if the latter had greater ultimate significance.[50]

Two Expeditionaries

Thus we have two remarkable expeditions to the tropical Pacific, closely spaced in time, with two remarkable field naturalists, each of them working on the nature, origin, and distribution of coral reefs. Of the two men, Darwin had clear priority in the development of the theory to which his name has always subsequently been attached. Darwin's insight established his reputation: Lyell's reaction has already been described, and Darwin had the satisfaction of seeing his views accepted in the sixth edition of *Principles of Geology* in 1840.[51] Darwin's book *The Structure and Distribution of Coral Reefs* in 1842 was a model of conciseness and clarity, has gone through countless editions, and remains in print a century and a half after it first appeared.[52] Darwin's reef work is still constantly discussed, both in its historical context and in its modern interpretations.[53] In spite of his reputation during his lifetime, Dana's writings on reefs excite no contemporary interest, and his *Corals and Coral Islands* appears to have merely antiquarian value.[54]

This apparent paradox can be in large degree explained by the way in which the personalities of the two men governed their scientific interactions, as well as by the way these interactions can be set in cultural context. The cautious Darwin knew the value and originality of his insight well enough: still in his early thirties, he was able to share in the exuberance of Lyell's response. But he was equally aware of the paucity of his own field experience. He had seen atolls from the deck of the *Beagle* in the Tuamotus as the ship sailed through; he saw the fringing reefs of Tahiti and the reef-encircled island of Moorea from a distance; he passed by the almost-atoll of Aitutaki in the southern Cooks; and finally in 1836 he landed for eleven days on Cocos-Keeling Atoll in the eastern Indian Ocean. The data he assembled in his book came mainly from published nautical charts and the surveyors who made them possible: J. S. Henslow, for example, was instrumental in obtaining information from Moresby, which Darwin used freely. He handled the information beautifully, but much of it was library science nevertheless, and Darwin must have been aware of it. Yet he remained calmly confident in the correctness of his views and never showed the slightest doubts or hesitation.

Dana, by contrast, was a highly strung person, desperately hard working, who had not only endured the physical hardships and dangers and the mental stresses of the expedition but who then spent more than a decade of his life committed to the minute study of his collections and the compilation of his reports. He "had undergone a strenuous and emotionally debilitating bout of religious conversion shortly before the squadron sailed"[55] and was the kind of person—he has been called "prissy"[56]—who was deeply shocked by the licentiousness and drunkenness of the Tahitians and indeed of the ships' companies themselves. It is hard to resist the view that he must have been a somewhat tedious shipboard companion, though doubtless he was heartened by the chaplain's issue of testaments to all on board.[57] Wilkes' diary entry praising Dana, in contrast to his manifest contempt for and dislike of the other scientifics, must surely raise a question about Dana's personality.[58] And indeed that question was put as soon as the squadron returned to the United States: Dana blundered almost at once.

The Couthouy Affair

Wilkes had dismissed Couthouy from the expedition in Hawaii, but that was far from the end of him. He made his way back to the United States and was present in Boston in the second half of October 1841 when Charles Lyell gave the Lowell Lectures to audiences of more than three thousand.[59] Couthouy came to know of Darwin's theory through one such lecture. Less than two months later, on 15 December 1841, Couthouy read a long paper on reefs, based on his observations during the first part of the Wilkes Expedition, to the

Boston Society of Natural History. This was published as "Remarks upon Coral Formations in the Pacific" in 1842.[60]

The paper was written entirely from memory, since Wilkes had impounded both Couthouy's specimens and field notes, but it contains detailed descriptions of many reef features fully as precise as those of Darwin; indeed, Couthouy was critical of Lyell's own inadequate grasp of what reefs are really like. Couthouy refers specifically to Lyell's outline of Darwin's theory, commenting that

> having personally examined a large number of these islands, and also residing eight months among the volcanic class, I may be permitted to state that my own observations have impressed a conviction of the theory here advanced by Mr Darwin. Indeed without being aware at the time that such views were entertained by anyone else . . . I was led, more than two years ago . . . to similar conclusions as to their origin, with those recently published by that gentleman; though not to entertain his opinions respecting limited and definite areas of subsidence and elevation.[61]

He then specified evidence for recent uplift following earlier subsidence.[62]

Taken as a whole Couthouy's paper is remarkable—for its discussion of the geometry of subsidence, of beachrock and reefrock, of the depth of lagoons and the factors controlling it, and of the dissection of high volcanic islands, all in advance of the availability of Darwin's book. All were topics Dana was later to address. When Dana arrived back on the East Coast later in 1842, the discovery that he had once again been anticipated caused him both chagrin and dismay.

Couthouy had begun his paper with an observation on the way in which the depth at which corals could grow was limited by temperature; he ended it with an extended discussion of the way in which low temperatures caused by oceanic circulation patterns excluded corals and coral reefs from the eastern parts of the tropical oceans. At a meeting of the American Association of Geologists and Naturalists, 29 April 1843, Dana accused Couthouy of plagiarism, saying that he had shown him his own manuscripts on these very subjects at Hawaii in 1840. Dana's criticism was published for all to see in the *American Journal of Science*.[63] He followed this with a second paper, on subsidence in the Pacific, which while admitting that Darwin's theory "has been fully confirmed by the investigations of the Exploring Expedition," nevertheless proposed that Darwin's "regions of subsidence and elevation, and the conclusion that these changes are now in progress, appear to have been deduced without sufficient examination." He even went so far as to receive Darwin's eyewitness observations of Andean uplift "with some hesitation."[64] Here is Dana nervous and dismayed, doubly outflanked and anticipated after years of effort, fighting to stake his claims.

Couthouy replied at length on 28 August in "astonishment, indignation and sorrow" to Dana's accusation.[65] The details of this voluminous rebuttal are not relevant here, except for Couthouy's assertion that he had sent a written statement of his views to friends at home from Sydney in December 1839: unfortunately he could not find the statement, and his own field notebooks had been impounded and had apparently been mislaid. Dana would not let the matter lie. He responded somewhat sanctimoniously in astonishment that the Sydney manuscript could not be found. More, he revealed that Couthouy's field books had been found in the expedition's archives, that he had had the seals broken, and that upon inspection he found nothing in them relevant to the content of Couthouy's paper.[66] Couthouy countered this in a letter, which the editor of the *American Journal of Science* printed as a separate appendix ("which subscribers can at their option retain or reject"), in which he announced the discovery of the missing documents: they did indeed show that Couthouy had the substance of his material together when in Australia in 1839.[67] Dana was obliged publicly to withdraw and apologize;[68] Couthouy was suitably magnanimous, while repeating his arguments.[69] This bizarre and distasteful episode reflected both Dana's own temperament and doubtless his exhaustion at the end of the expedition.

Dana's *Geology* and Its Impact

Dana's *Geology* finally appeared in 1849: he at once sent a copy of the unofficial issue to Darwin. *On Coral Reefs and Islands*, part of the main report, was commercially published in 1853; it is Dana's equivalent to Darwin's *Structure and Distribution of Coral Reefs*. The book is a masterpiece of organization, bringing a remarkable range of observations from all over the Pacific to bear on the subject. In texture of organization and wealth of detail, based as it largely was on his own observations, Dana's *Coral Reefs* undoubtedly surpasses Darwin's.[70]

In this book Dana had a very difficult path to pursue: he could scarcely challenge Darwin's priority over a theory he himself supported, but at the same time he could not simply abandon his own claims to independence and originality. His solution was ingenious: he mentions Darwin only nine times, four of them in footnotes, and with one exception all of these references are to matters of detail rather than substance. He makes Darwin's contribution explicit in but one short paragraph:

> A study and comparison of the reefs of different kinds,—fringing, barrier, and atoll,—throughout the oceans, is the only philosophical mode of arriving at any conclusions on this subject. This course Mr Darwin has happily and successfully pursued, and has arrived, as we have reason to believe, at the true theory of Coral Islands. It is satisfactory, because it is a simple generalization of facts. The explorations of the Expedition afford striking illustrations of his views, and elucidate some points which were still deemed obscure, establishing the theory on a firm basis of evidence, and exhibiting its complete correspondence with observation.[71]

But in the final and crucial chapter in the book—"On Changes of Level in the Pacific Ocean"—Darwin's name does not appear. It was a less than generous acknowledgment.

The detailed points of difference that Dana raised between Darwin's views and his own are not of present significance. They concerned rates of coral growth, the influence of temperature on coral distribution (a topic to which Dana returned in 1853,[72] reviving memories of the Couthouy affair), and the existence of widespread recent elevation in areas of prior subsidence including a rather labored attempt to delineate areas of elevation and subsidence in the Pacific on a basis somewhat different from Darwin's.

Dana did, however, add two important points to Darwin's synthesis. One was his recognition that Pacific volcanoes are frequently distributed in linear and even parallel array and that within individual chains there is a regular age distribution from end to end. Thus in the Hawaiian Islands the oldest volcano, Kauai, is in the northwest, and the youngest, Hawaii, in the southeast. The same is true of the Societies and other groups.[73] Appleman[74] has pointed out that Dana mistook the mechanism for this apparent progression, while Couthouy apparently got it right, but the distribution of age itself made it possible to calibrate the stages of Darwin's temporal succession of reef stages. The second point was Dana's recognition that the valleys of tropical volcanic mountains were carved by fluvial erosion, and that if they were submerged the flooding of their lower reaches by the sea would yield a deeply embayed shoreline. This independent proof of subsidence has been named Dana's Principle by W. M. Davis,[75] and it is often said that Dana recognized it during his ascent of Mt. Aorai in Tahiti in 1839.[76] If so his recognition of volcanic subsidence would have been independent of Darwin's. Dana himself, however, made no such claim. In his *Geology* he made the connection,[77] but it seems likely that the significance of embayments came to him after 1839.

Darwin's initial response to Dana's work was generous enough: on 8 October 1849 he wrote to Dana saying, "You cannot imagine how much gratified I have been that you, to a certain extent agreed with my coral reef notion."[78] Then Dana's *Geology* arrived. Darwin's first reaction, written in a letter to Lyell, 4 December 1849, was ecstatic: "I am astonished at my own accuracy!! if I were to rewrite now my coral book, there is hardly a sentence I shd. have to alter." But then he went on: "When I say all this, I ought to add, that the *consequences* of the theory in areas of subsidence are treated in a separate chapter to which I have not come."[79] He wrote in similar vein to Dana the following day: "I have not yet come to the chapter on subsidence. . . . I consider that now the subsidence theory is established."[80]

It was a different matter when Darwin did read that chapter over the next couple of days. He wrote at once to Lyell:

> I utterly disbelieve his statements that most of the atolls over the whole have been lately raised a foot or two; he does not condescend to notice my explanation for such appearances. He misrepresents me, also, when he states that I deduce without restriction elevation from *all* fringing reefs & even from isld. without any reefs!! . . . Dana puts me in a passion several times by disputing my conclusions, without condescending to allude to my reasons. . . . He strikes me as a very clever fellow; I wish he was not quite so great a generaliser.[81]

But he did not apparently say anything directly to Dana.

The specific points of contention on which Darwin and Dana initially disagreed, and continued to do so for the rest of their lives, were less to do with the origin of atolls through the subsidence of their foundations than on the reality of recent slight uplift of reefs and islands, on sea temperature as a controlling factor in coral distribution, and on the effects of submarine volcanic activity on coral growth. While it is clear that Darwin was broadly correct in his main theoretical insight, there is little doubt that Dana, with his wider field experience, made telling criticisms, which Darwin could not satisfactorily answer and which have subsequently been sustained.[82]

The Barnacle Interlude

There is much else of interest in the correspondence just quoted between Darwin and Dana, for each had decided views also on volcanic structure and erosion on which they disagreed. But these points of difference were muted, except in Darwin's correspondence within his own private circle. A major factor in this abatement of discord was undoubtedly the emergence of a collaboration between the two men that in a sense established neutral ground.

Darwin had become interested in barnacles in South America, and he began to work on their structure and taxonomy in earnest in 1846. At the suggestion of Augustus Gould, who had replaced Couthouy as author of the expedition's report on the Mollusca, Darwin wrote to Dana in mid-1849 about his interest in the Cirripedia. The letter does not survive, but it initiated a remarkably good-natured exchange of information between the two, which extended over many years. Both were in agreement that barnacles are crustaceans rather than molluscs, and they were able to exchange many taxonomic and anatomical details. Dana could not, however, loan Darwin any of the expedition's material, which was considered the property of the U.S. government.

Darwin's own volumes on the living Cirripedia appeared in 1851 and 1854 and on the fossil forms in the same years; Dana identified the corals for Darwin in the former.[83] Dana's two volumes on the expedition Crustacea appeared in 1852 and 1853. Darwin saw Sir John Lubbock's copy and wrote handsomely if slightly condescendingly about it to Dana on 27 September 1853: "Forgive me presuming to estimate your labours, but when I think that this work has followed your Corals & your Geology, I am really lost in astonishment at what you have done in mere labour. And then, besides the labour, so much originality in all three works."[84] The collaboration rather than competition in the treatment of barnacles thus helped smooth the rougher edges of the coral reef controversy. And both men now had solid achievement behind them; both were in middle age (Darwin forty-one in 1850 and Dana thirty-seven); and Dana had perhaps lost some of the intemperance of the immediate post-expedition days.

The Impasse of Evolution

But simultaneously a more serious problem was looming between them. Darwin had opened his first notebooks on the transmutation of species in 1837. He read Malthus in 1838, wrote the abstract of his species theory in 1842, and his fuller sketch in 1844. After the Cirripedia he devoted himself to working on his big book, until prompted by Wallace's intervention to publish *On the Origin of Species* in 1859. In spite of his intensive, systematic work on the corals and the Crustacea and on the difficulties of demarcating taxa, and in spite too of his uniformitarian geology, Dana's zoology remained resolutely creationist and catastrophist.[85] Dana's conversion to Christianity in 1837 has already been noted; even as Darwin was writing the *Origin*, Dana was debating issues of "Science and the Bible" in *Bibliotheca Sacra*.[86] Almost symbolically, in 1859 he suffered a complete nervous collapse from which he never fully recovered.

Darwin had warned Dana on 29 September 1856 that "I am becoming, indeed I shd. say have become, sceptical on the permanent immutability of species" and forecast that Dana would be "rather indignant" at this news.[87] He sent Dana a copy of the *Origin* two weeks before publication, noting that it would "horrify" him, but in the "hope that you will read my book straight through" and "would spare time to read it with care."[88] He wrote again to Dana on 30 July 1860 that "whenever you are strong enough to read it I know you will be dead against me, but I know equally well your opposition will be liberal and philosophical."[89] But Dana did not—could not? would not? or did he?—read the book. "Many long months, and now even years, have passed by, and still your book, *The Origin* remains unopened," wrote Dana on 4 December 1862.[90] Again on 5 February 1863: "I have still to report your book unread; for my head has all it can now do in my college duties."[91]

Darwin must have seen this for what it was: sanctimonious evasion rather than simply illness. Given that Dana was well enough and had the time to publish his *Manual of Geology* (812 pages) in 1862 and a dozen papers on zoological systematics and geology in 1863, his protestations cannot be taken seriously. Moreover, even though he had not (as he said) read Darwin's *Origin*, he nevertheless specified his objections to evolutionary ideas in the *Manual*.[92] These he repeated in the letter to Darwin of 5 February 1863 quoted above.[93] Darwin replied rather stiffly that "perhaps it would have been better if, when you condemned all such views [in the *Manual*], you had stated that you had not been able to read it [the *Origin*]. But pray do not suppose that I think for one instant that, with your strong and slow acquired convictions and immense knowledge, you could have been converted. The utmost that I could have hoped would have been that you might possibly have been here or there staggered."[94] You old humbug, we hear Darwin say.

The rest of Dana's life is seen by William Stanton as "a progressive surrender to Darwinism,"[95] although William Sanford attempts to see the gradual shifting in Dana's position in a more positive light.[96] The first admission of Dana's conversion came in the second edition of the *Manual* in 1874;[97] it was complete by 1883,[98] but by then Darwin was dead.

The Coral Reef Controversy Revived

Meanwhile the coral reef controversy of the 1840s lingered on: neither of the contestants would give it up. Dana published his *Corals and Coral Islands* in 1872. It was a more attractive book than its predecessor of 1853, but its content, with some updating and additional material on corals as animals, was essentially the same. He sent his son to present a copy personally to Darwin in England.[99] A second edition appeared in 1890.

Darwin likewise published a second edition of *The Structure and Distribution of Coral Reefs* in 1874, appropriately enough immediately before the voyage of HMS *Challenger* led to a concerted attack on his views and initiated a new phase in reef studies. In the preface Darwin sets out once more his dissatisfaction with Dana's arguments on the influence of temperature on corals, on the negative effect of volcanic activity on reefs, and on evidence for elevation as well as subsidence in the Pacific: it had a very familiar ring.[100] Dana reviewed the book at once in the *American Journal of Science,* but similarly simply repeated his arguments of thirty years before.[101]

There was a brief resurgence too of controversy over the geology of volcanic islands, which forms a separate issue. Darwin's *Volcanic Islands* of 1844 was issued as a second edition (in fact an unaltered reprint) in 1876. Dana's *Characteristics of Volcanoes,* picking up themes from his *Geology* of 1849, appeared in 1890.[102]

Darwin died on 18 April 1882. Dana was thus allowed the last word in the forty years of debate between the two on the coral reef results of their two expeditions. Ostensibly in response to a presidential address by Archibald Geikie (who never saw a coral reef), given to the Royal Physical Society of Edinburgh in 1883, Dana set out to summarize the arguments made so long before by Darwin and himself, together with the objections raised by a variety of reef workers over the previous decades.[103] And for the first time he gave Darwin his unequivocal support:

> The subsidence which the Darwinian theory requires has not been opposed by the mention of any fact at variance with it, nor by setting aside Darwin's arguments in its favor; . . . Darwin's theory therefore remains as the theory that accounts for the origin of coral reefs and islands.[104]

It was in a sense too late, for new issues were by then being debated in coral reef studies.[105] Dana joined Darwin in death on 14 April 1895. Their particular "coral episode" was over.

Conclusion

Ever since their Pacific explorations, Darwin and Dana were in fundamental agreement on coral reef theory. It was indeed Darwin's theory, but each of the points Dana added, though Darwin was unconvinced by them, were in fact sound. Together they left the theory in a much stronger position than when it was first announced.

It follows that the controversy between the two was to some degree artificial. Partly this was a result of temperament, partly of circumstance. Darwin was keen to defend his first major achievement in science from the claims of others. The excitable and highly strung Dana was equally determined that his own hard-won results should not go unacknowledged. In consequence, he dramatized a series of relatively minor differences of fact and opinion to make them appear of more fundamental importance and indeed in his published work gave Darwin less forthright acknowledgment than was his due. Darwin's own interests soon moved on to wider fields, and Dana mellowed over the years. Their interest in barnacles gave them common and uncontentious ground, though the question of evolution soon proved to be a greater issue for Dana than the origin of coral reefs.

There were other considerations, too, dating back to the voyages themselves. Both men were in naval vessels subject to the rigid naval discipline of the time; both expeditions had as their primary function nautical surveying. The captain of the *Beagle*, Robert FitzRoy, was an aristocrat, and Darwin a gentleman; indeed, except at times of tension, Darwin messed with the captain. Neither Wilkes nor Dana could be described as an aristocrat, and Wilkes from his behavior was certainly no gentleman. Dana came from a modest background and was obliged to earn his own living all his life; Darwin lived in comfort at his house in the country and devoted himself to his own research. Naval officers could bring themselves to tolerate scientific gentlemen; hired hands were another matter, even if they were scientifics. Darwin's was one of the last expeditions of the kind pioneered by Sir Joseph Banks; Dana's was perhaps the first of those staffed by professionals. Darwin was his own man so far as his scientific work was concerned; Dana had his instructions and moreover was one of a team, each member with prescribed duties that often overlapped. Darwin's niche was secure from the outset, Dana had to carve his out.

Like Thomas Henry Huxley, Dana had, after the expedition's work was done, to create a paid career for himself in both teaching and research as the nineteenth-century idea of the university developed.

Dana wrote textbooks; it would have been unthinkable, if only socially, for Darwin to do so, and indeed he had no need to.

Above all, Darwin was—and Dana knew it well—at the hub of the greatest metropolitan center of science in the world. He knew everyone who mattered and had first the approbation and then the friendship of world leaders, especially Lyell, in what were then the most exciting of the field sciences. Given his talents, achievements, and connections, it was almost inevitable that he became a world leader himself. For Dana, even Yale University was on the far periphery; organizations such as the National Academy of Sciences and what became the American Association for the Advancement of Science were but pale imitations of the Royal Society and the British Association. Dana had to seize recognition in that wider world, since science in America still had far to go before it could match that in Europe.[106]

Darwin's recognition came rather readily: he was elected Fellow of the Royal Society in 1839, awarded its Royal Medal for his reef and barnacle work in 1853, and its highest distinction, the Copley Medal, in 1864. Darwin, Lyell, and Huxley discussed the election of Dana as a Foreign Member of the Society in 1855, but the proposal came to nothing. Dana was indeed awarded the Copley in 1877 but had to wait until 1884 for his Foreign Membership, two years after Darwin's death: no one interested in his work on coral reefs forty years earlier signed his certificate of election.[107]

Between them also were the scientific issues themselves. Gruber has called attention to the striking formal resemblance between Darwin's theory of coral reefs and his theory of evolution,[108] a theme strongly echoed by Michael Ghiselin.[109] Both involve ideas of sequential and irreversible change of form through time, of population growth and struggle against the elements and other organisms, and of the keys to process afforded by spatial distribution. Perhaps the comparison was not lost on Dana as 1859 approached.

Finally, however, the issue was one of two very different naturalists themselves in competition. They were not unique in that, of course. Indeed, it would be instructive to reflect on the role of the Harvard botanist Asa Gray, who though not a member of the Wilkes Expedition authored one of its reports, and the very different relationship to that of Dana which he developed with Darwin over the same period of time.[110]

Yet in spite of the often unnecessary convolutions of this coral reef episode, it must in the end be acknowledged that no one since Dana has made so great a contribution to knowledge of both the zoology and geology of coral reefs as he did, just as no one since Darwin has given us greater insight on the fundamental processes of reef development.

Notes

I acknowledge the enormous value in writing this essay of previous studies of the Wilkes Expedition cited in notes 2, 3, and 19. My work in the Mitchell Library, Sydney, was made possible by Dr. David H. Montgomery of the Western Society of Naturalists. I am grateful to a reviewer for drawing my attention to oversights and making useful suggestions.

1   Thus Dana is unmentioned in such major works of interpretation as G. Himmelfarb, *Darwin and the Darwinian Revolution* (London: Chatto and Windus, 1959); M. T. Ghiselin, *The Triumph of the Darwinian Method* (Berkeley: University of California Press, 1969); M. Ruse, *The Darwinian Revolution* (Chicago: University of Chicago Press, 1979); P. J. Bowler, *Charles Darwin: The Man and His Influence* (London: Blackwell, 1990); and P. J. Bowler, *Evolution: The History of an Idea* (Berkeley: University of California Press, revised edition, 1989). There is only the most trivial reference to him in J. R. Moore, *The Post-Darwinian Controversies: A Study of the Protestant Struggle to Come to Terms with Darwin in Great Britain and America 1870–1900* (Cambridge: Cambridge University Press, 1979). In recent biographies of Darwin, Dana's name does not appear in P. Brent, *Charles Darwin: "A Man of Enlarged Curiosity"* (London: Heinemann, 1981); is mentioned once in J. Bowlby, *Charles Darwin: A New Life* (London: Hutchinson, 1990); and briefly but twice in A. Desmond and J. R. Moore, *Darwin* (London: Michael Joseph, 1991). Astonishingly Dana's name is absent from both D. Kohn, ed., *The Darwinian Heritage* (Princeton: Princeton University Press, 1985), and R. C. Olby, G. N. Cantor, J. R. R. Christie, and M. J. S. Hodge, *Companion to the History of Modern Science* (London: Routledge, 1990).

2   D. E. Appleman, "James Dwight Dana and Pacific Geology," in *Magnificent Voyagers: The U.S. Exploring Expedition, 1838–1842*, ed. H. J. Viola and C. Margolis (Washington: Smithsonian Institution Press, 1985), 89–117.

3   See, for example, H. H. Bartlett, "The Reports of the Wilkes Expedition, and the Work of the Specialists in Science," *Proceedings of the American Philosophical Society* 82 (1940): 601–705; J. E. Hoffmeister, "James Dwight Dana's Studies of Volcanoes and of Coral Islands," *Proceedings of the American Philosophical Society* 82 (1940): 721–732.

4   W. F. Sanford, Jr., "Dana and Darwinism," *Journal of the History of Ideas* 26 (1965): 531–546.

5   C. M. Yonge, "Darwin and Coral Reefs," in *A Century of Darwin*, ed.
        S. M. Barnett (London: Heinemann, 1958): 245–266.

6   C. R. Darwin, "Coral Islands," with introduction, map, and remarks
        by D. R. Stoddart, *Atoll Research Bulletin* 88 (1962): i–iv, 1–20.
        Darwin's assertion decades later in his *Autobiography* that "the
        whole theory was thought out on the west coast of S. America before
        I had seen a true coral reef" (*The Autobiography of Charles Darwin,
        1809–1882*, ed. N. Barlow [London: Collins, 1958], 100) has been
        confirmed by F. W. Burkhardt's analysis of letters and field books,
        demonstrating that Darwin perceived a connection between continen-
        tal uplift and oceanic subsidence as early as April 1835, when still in
        Valparaiso: F. W. Burkhardt, "Darwin's Early Notes on Coral Reef
        Formation," in *The Correspondence of Charles Darwin*, ed. F. W.
        Burkhardt and S. Smith, 10 vols. (Cambridge: Cambridge University
        Press, 1985–1994), 1:567–571. Nevertheless, Sandra Herbert has
        shown from his manuscript geological notes that Darwin continued
        to speculate on alternative atoll origins while in the Galapagos dur-
        ing September and October 1835: S. Herbert, "Charles Darwin as a
        Prospective Geological Author," *British Journal for the History of
        Science* 24 (1991): 159–192; see 188–189.

7   See the analysis by D. R. Stoddart, "Darwin, Lyell, and the Geological
        Significance of Coral Reefs," *British Journal for the History of Sci-
        ence* 9 (1976): 199–218.

8   J. W. Judd, "Darwin and Geology," in *Darwin and Modern Science*,
        ed. A. C. Seward (Cambridge: Cambridge University Press, 1909),
        337–384; reference on 358.

9   J. W. Judd, "Critical Introduction," in C. R. Darwin, *On the Structure
        and Distribution of Coral Reefs, also Geological Observations on
        the Volcanic Islands and Parts of South America visited during the
        Voyage of H.M.S. "Beagle"* (London: Ward, Lock, 1909), 3–10;
        reference on 5.

10   C. R. Darwin, "On Certain Areas of Elevation and Subsidence in the
        Pacific and Indian Oceans, as Deduced from the Study of Coral For-
        mations," *Proceedings of the Geological Society of London* 2 (1838):
        552–554.

11   C. R. Darwin, *Journal and Remarks, 1832–1836* [also subsequently as
        *Journal of Researches into the Geology and Natural History of the
        Various Countries Visited by H.M.S. "Beagle"*] (London: Henry Col-
        burn, 1839), 539–569.

12   C. R. Darwin, *The Structure and Distribution of Coral Reefs* (Lon-
        don: Smith, Elder, 1842).

13   C. Lyell, *Elements of Geology* (London: John Murray, 1838), 36.

14   C. Lyell, *Principles of Geology*, 6th ed. (London: John Murray, 1840);
        see vol. 3, chap. 18 ("Formation of Coral Reefs"), 366–406.

15 They "have a very uninteresting appearance; a long brilliantly white beach is capped by a low bright line of green vegetation. This stripe on both hands rapidly appears to narrow in the distance & sinks beneath the horizon.—the width of dry land is very trifling: from the Mast-head it was possible to see at Noon Island across the smooth lagoon to the opposite side.—This great lake of water was about 10 miles wide": *Charles Darwin's "Beagle" Diary*, ed. R. D. Keynes (Cambridge: Cambridge University Press, 1988), 365.

16 Ibid., 418.

17 Darwin, "Coral Islands." For further commentary see Herbert, "Charles Darwin," 186–189.

18 *Autobiography*, ed. Barlow, 98.

19 For narratives of the expedition, see D. B. Tyler, *The Wilkes Expedition: The First U.S. Exploring Expedition (1838–1842)* (Philadelphia: American Philosophical Society, 1968); and W. Stanton, *The Great U.S. Exploring Expedition of 1838–1842* (Berkeley: University of California Press, 1975). For descriptions of results, see D. C. Haskell, *The United States Exploring Expedition, 1838–1842 and Its Publications 1844–1874* (New York: New York Public Library, 1942); Bartlett, "Reports of the Wilkes Expedition"; and Viola and Margolis, eds., *Magnificent Voyagers.*

20 Stanton, *Great U.S. Exploring Expedition*, 20.

21 Ibid., 139–140. Wilkes is denounced and documented as "a false and malignant villain" in Lieutenant Reynolds' letters: *Voyage to the Southern Ocean: The letters of Lieutenant William Reynolds from the U.S. Exploring Expedition, 1838–1842*, ed. A. H. Cleaver and E. J. Stann (Annapolis: United States Naval Institute, 1988), 115–120; at the outset Reynolds had been one of Wilkes' most fervent supporters.

22 E. G. Conklin, "Connection of the American Philosophical Society with our First National Exploring Expedition," *Proceedings of the American Philosophical Society* 82 (1940): 519–541; reference on 541 (memorandum by Henry D. Rogers to Mahlon Dickerson). Similar though more specific instructions for surveying and scientific work on atolls were issued by the hydrographer, Captain Beaufort, to FitzRoy shortly before the *Beagle* sailed. See R. FitzRoy, *Narrative of the Surveying Voyages of His Majesty's Ships "Adventure" and "Beagle,"* vol. 2, *Proceedings of the Second Expedition, 1831–1836* (London: Henry Colburn, 1839), 38.

23 C. Wilkes, *Narrative of the United States Exploring Expedition during the years 1838, 1839, 1840, 1841, 1842*, 4 vols. (Philadelphia: C. Sherman, 1844), 4:270. Darwin evidently met Wilkes in November 1836 when the latter was in London to buy instruments for the expedition (Darwin to Wilkes, 7 November 1836, *Correspondence*, 1:517–518), but if he did there appears to be no record of their meeting (I am

grateful to a reviewer for drawing this letter to my attention). Wilkes himself mentions no one he met in London during that visit. W. J. Morgan, D. B. Tyler, J. L. Leonhart, and M. F. Loughlin, eds., *Autobiography of Rear Admiral Charles Wilkes, U.S. Navy, 1798–1877* (Washington, DC: Naval History Division, Department of the Navy, 1978), 323–324. See D. E. Borthwick, "Outfitting the United States Exploring Expedition: Lieutenant Charles Wilkes' European Assignment, August–November, 1836," *Proceedings of the American Philosophical Society* 109 (1965): 159–172. Darwin was unimpressed a decade later when J. D. Hooker loaned him Wilkes' *Narrative:* "what a feeble book in matter & style, & how splendidly got up." Darwin to Hooker, 10 February 1845, *Correspondence,* 3:140.

24   Stanton, *Great U.S. Exploring Expedition,* 121, 219.

25   Dana arrived in Australia on 30 November 1839 and stayed until 19 March 1840.

26   J. D. Dana, *Corals and Coral Islands* (London: Sampson Low, Marston, Low and Searle, 1875); reference on xi.

27   The collections of Australian newspapers for the period January 1839 to March 1840 in the Mitchell Library, Sydney, contain only a single reference to Darwin's work on the *Beagle* voyage (to petrified trees in Chile). Dana may of course have seen English newspapers of the previous two years.

28   Lyell, *Elements,* 96.

29   M. L. Prendergast, *James Dwight Dana: The Life and Thought of an American Scientist* (Ann Arbor: University Microfilms International, 1978).

30   D. R. Stoddart, "Joseph Beete Jukes, the 'Cambridge Connection,' and the Theory of Reef Development in Australia in the Nineteenth Century," *Earth Sciences History* 7 (1988): 99–110; reference on 101.

31   J. D. Dana, "Origin of Coral Reefs and Islands," *American Journal of Science,* 3d ser., 30 (1885): 89–105, 169–191; see 92, where Dana states that he realized the reality of "great subsidence" in the Society and Marquesas Islands in September 1839, i. e., more than two months before he arrived in Sydney. But he did not claim to have made the connection between subsidence and reef upgrowth, as Tyler suggests (*Wilkes Expedition,* 101).

32   Dana, *Corals and Coral Islands;* reference on xi.

33   F. Darwin, ed., *The Life and Letters of Charles Darwin, including an Autobiographical Chapter,* 3 vols. (London: John Murray, 1887); see 1:291 and 302.

34   Bartlett, "Reports of the Wilkes Expedition."

35   Darwin never saw the Gambiers; Dana's reference should be to the Society Islands and in particular Moorea. Dana's mistake is repeated in W. Stanton's entry on Dana in *Dictionary of Scientific Biography,*

18 vols. (New York: Charles Scribner's Sons, 1970–1990), 3:549–554; see 550–551.

36 Dana, *Corals and Coral Islands;* reference on xi.

37 Appleman, "Dana and Pacific Geology," 88.

38 The story is told that Dana finally received a copy of the official edition of his *Geology* when an American found the set of the reports that had been presented to the emperor of China for sale in a market stall in Canton and bought the book for its author (only 100 copies had been printed and of these 30 were destroyed by fire). Stanton, *Great U.S. Exploring Expedition,* 351–352.

39 J. D. Dana, *Report of the United States Exploring Expedition . . . ,* vol. 7, *Zoophytes* (Philadelphia: C. Sherman, 1846).

40 Haskell, *The United States Exploring Expedition,* 50.

41 Dana, *Exploring Expedition,* 7:i–iii.

42 Ibid., *Atlas. Zoophytes* (Philadelphia: C. Sherman, 1849).

43 Ibid., vols. 13–14, *Crustacea* (Philadelphia: C. Sherman, 1852–1853).

44 Ibid., *Atlas. Crustacea* (Philadelphia: C. Sherman, 1855).

45 J. D. Dana, *On the Classification and Geographical Distribution of Crustacea: From the Report on Crustacea of the United States Exploring Expedition . . .* (Philadelphia: C. Sherman, 1853); idem, "On an Isothermal Chart, illustrating the Geographical Distribution of Marine Animals," *American Journal of Science,* 2d ser., 16 (1853): 153–167, 314–327.

46 Dana, *Exploring Expedition . . . ,* vol. 10, *Geology* (Philadelphia: C. Sherman, 1849).

47 Dana, "On Coral Reefs and Islands [some title variation]," *American Journal of Science,* 2d ser., 11 (1851): 357–372; 12 (1851): 25–51, 165–186; 13 (1852): 34–41, 185–195, 338–350; 14 (1852): 76–84.

48 J. D. Dana, *On Coral Reefs and Islands* (New York: Putnam, 1853).

49 J. D. Dana, *Corals and Coral Islands* (New York: Putnam, 1872; 2d ed., 1874; 3d ed., 1890; for the London edition see n. 26).

50 For assessment see W. M. Davis, *The Coral Reef Problem* (New York: American Geographical Society, 1928).

51 Lyell, *Principles,* 3:366–406.

52 C. R. Darwin, *The Structure and Distribution of Coral Reefs* (Berkeley: University of California Press, 1962; Brussels: Editions Culture et Civilisation, 1969 [facsimile of the first edition]; New York: Abrahams Magazine Service, 1972 [facsimile of the third American edition]; Tucson: University of Arizona Press, 1984). The book has also been translated into French, German, Italian, Russian, and Japanese. R. B. Freeman, *The Works of Charles Darwin: An Annotated Bibliographical Handlist,* 2d ed. (London: Archon Books, 1977).

53 B. R. Rosen, "Darwin, Coral Reefs, and Global Geology," *BioScience*

32 (1982): 519–525; T. P. Scoffin and J. E. Dixon, "The Distribution and Structure of Coral Reefs: One Hundred Years since Darwin," *Biological Journal of the Linnean Society* 20 (1983): 11–38.

54   There is, however, a great deal of factual material on reefs and islands many of which have been little studied since.

55   Stanton, *Great U.S. Exploring Expedition,* 129.

56   Stanton, *Scientific Biography,* 3:550.

57   Stanton, *Great U.S. Exploring Expedition.*

58   Morgan et al., *Wilkes,* 480.

59   C. Lyell, *Travels in North America in the Years 1841–2,* 2 vols. (New York: Wiley and Putnam, 1845); see 1:86.

60   J. P. Couthouy, "Remarks upon Coral Formations in the Pacific; with Suggestions as to the Causes of Their Absence in the Same Parallels of Latitude on the Coast of South America," *Boston Journal of Natural History* 4 (1842): 66–105, 137–162.

61   Ibid., 77. Lyell gave Darwin a reprint of Couthouy's paper (it is in the Cambridge University Library collection of Darwin pamphlets), and Darwin was able to refer to it in *The Structure and Distribution of Coral Reefs* (81) by adding a note while the book was still in proof.

62   Couthouy, "Remarks," 140.

63   J. D. Dana, "On the Temperature Limiting the Distribution of Corals," *American Journal of Science* 45 (1843): 130–131.

64   J. D. Dana, "On the Areas of Subsidence in the Pacific, as Indicated by the Distribution of Coral Islands," *American Journal of Science* 45 (1843): 131–135; see 131–132.

65   J. P. Couthouy, "Reply of J. P. Couthouy, to the Accusations of J. D. Dana, Geologist to the Exploring Expedition, Contained on pp. 130 and 145 of this Volume," *American Journal of Science* 45 (1843): 378–389.

66   J. D. Dana, "Reply to Mr. Couthouy's Vindication against the Charge of Plagiarism," *American Journal of Science* 46 (1844): 129–136.

67   J. P. Couthouy, "Review of and Strictures on Mr. Dana's Reply to Mr. Couthouy's Vindication against His Charge of Plagiarism," *American Journal of Science* 46 (1844): appendix, 1–11.

68   J. D. Dana and J. P. Couthouy, "Acknowledgments Relative to a Charge of Plagiarism," *American Journal of Science* 47 (1844): 122–123.

69   J. P. Couthouy, "Some Remarks Explanatory of the Extent of His Views Relating to the Influence of Temperature on the Development of Corals, as Compared with Those Entertained by Jas. D. Dana, Esq.," *American Journal of Science* 47 (1844): 123–126.

70   Dana, *On Coral Reefs and Islands.*

71 Ibid., 88–89.

72 Dana, *Classification and Geographical Distribution of Crustacea;* idem, "Isothermal Chart."

73 Dana, *Exploring Expedition,* 10:12.

74 Appleman, "Dana and Pacific Geology"; idem, "James Dwight Dana and Post-Darwinian Evolution of Pacific Geology," *Abstracts* (Hamburg: International Congress for the History of Science, 1989), 4, 13.

75 W. M. Davis, "Dana's Confirmation of Darwin's Theory of Coral Reefs," *American Journal of Science,* 4th ser., 35 (1913): 173–188; and idem, *Coral Reef Problem,* 43–50.

76 Hoffmeister, "Dana's Studies," 725.

77 Dana, *Exploring Expedition,* 10:379–393; idem, *On Coral Reefs and Islands,* 118–119.

78 *Correspondence,* 4:266.

79 Ibid., 284–285.

80 Ibid., 286–288.

81 Ibid., 288–290.

82 On the question of recent emergence of Pacific atolls, either by uplift or sea-level fall, there is little question that Dana was right and Darwin was wrong. There is, however, much local variability, even between adjacent reefs, and Darwin's discussion of the controls of coral growth was remarkable for its insight. See Dana's catalogue of evidence for higher sea levels in J. D. Dana, "Notes on the New Edition of Mr. Darwin's Work on the Structure and Distribution of Coral Reefs (1874)," *American Journal of Science,* 3d ser., 8 (1874): 312–319; (1875): 284–298, following Darwin's own discussion in *The Structure and Distribution of Coral Reefs,* 2d ed. (London: Smith, Elder, 1874), 168–193. Curiously, in the first edition of the book (1842) Darwin himself had described emersed ledges of coral conglomerate at Cocos-Keeling Atoll of precisely the kind that supplied Dana's Pacific evidence, but without realizing what they meant; he noted too that such ledges appeared to occur in the Maldives, Chagos Archipelago, and Marshall Islands, but seems to have been misled by Captain Beechey's accounts into thinking they were absent in the Tuamotus (ibid., 25–26). For modern evidence of recent emergence, especially in the Tuamotus, where Dana derived many of his data, see L. F. Montaggioni and P. A. Pirazzoli, "The Significance of Exposed Coral Conglomerates from French Polynesia (Pacific Ocean) as Indicators of Recent Relative Sea-Level Change," *Coral Reefs* 3 (1984): 29–42; and P. A. Pirazzoli and L. F. Montaggioni, "Holocene Sea-Level Changes in French Polynesia," *Palaeogeography, Palaeoclimatology, Palaeoecology* 68 (1988): 153–175. Recently the reality of both Pleistocene subsidence and of Holocene emergence has been demonstrated at Cocos-Keeling Atoll itself by C. D. Woodroffe, H. H. Veeh, A. C.

Falkland, R. F. McLean, and E. Wallensky, "Last Interglacial Reef and Subsidence of the Cocos (Keeling) Islands, Indian Ocean," *Marine Geology* 96 (1991): 137–143; and C. D. Woodroffe, R. F. McLean, H. A. Polach, and E. Wallensky, "Sea Level and Coral Atolls: Late Holocene Emergence in the Indian Ocean," *Geology* 18 (1990): 62–66.

Dana was also undoubtedly right in emphasizing the importance of sea temperature in "accounting for the non-distribution of central-Pacific species of corals to the Panama coast, and the paucity of species there" ("Isothermal Chart," 314). But neither Darwin nor Dana could appreciate the relative importance of present dispersal processes and plate tectonics in the development of biogeographic distribution patterns. See E. D. McCoy and K. L. Heck, Jr., "Biogeography of Corals, Seagrasses, and Mangroves: An Alternative to the Center of Origin Concept," *Systematic Zoology* 25 (1976): 201–210; and K. L. Heck, Jr., and E. D. McCoy, "Long-distance Dispersal and the Reef-building Corals of the Eastern Pacific," *Marine Biology* 48 (1978): 349–356.

Finally, Darwin and Dana argued inconclusively on the consequences of submarine volcanic activity for coral growth, on which neither had direct observations. Corals can in fact rapidly colonize submarine lava flows; see R. W. Grigg and J. E. Maragos, "Recolonization of Hermatypic Corals on Submerged Lava Flows in Hawaii," *Ecology* 55 (1974): 387–395.

83   *Correspondence*, 5:79–81, esp. Darwin to Dana, 15 February 1852, n. 9.

84   Ibid., 157.

85   Sanford, "Dana and Darwinism."

86   J. D. Dana, "Science and the Bible," *Bibliotheca Sacra* 13 (1856–1857): 80–129, 631–656; 14 (1857): 388–413, 461–524.

87   *Correspondence*, 6:235–237.

88   *Correspondence*, 7:367–368; this is also quoted by Sanford, "Dana and Darwinism," 535.

89   *More Letters of Charles Darwin*, ed. F. Darwin and A. C. Seward, 2 vols. (London: John Murray, 1903), 1:159.

90   D. C. Gilman, *The Life of James Dwight Dana: Scientific Explorer, Mineralogist, Geologist, Zoologist, Professor in Yale University* (New York: Harper and Brothers, 1899), 311.

91   Ibid., 313.

92   J. D. Dana, *Manual of Geology* (Philadelphia: T. Bliss, 1863), 602.

93   Gilman, *Life of James Dwight Dana.*

94   Ibid., 315.

95   Stanton, *Scientific Biography,* 3:553.

96   Sanford, *"Dana and Darwinism."*

97   J. D. Dana, *Manual of Geology,* 2d ed. (Philadelphia: T. Bliss, 1874), 603–604.

98   J. D. Dana, *New Text-book of Geology,* 4th ed. (New York: American Book, 1883).

99   J. D. Dana to C. R. Darwin, 23 May 1872, in Gilman, *Life of James Dwight Dana,* 315.

100   C. R. Darwin, *Structure and Distribution of Coral Reefs,* 2d ed., v–ix.

101   Dana, "Notes on the New Edition"; Dana did, however, express "the fullest satisfaction in his [Darwin's] theory for the origin of atoll and barrier forms of reefs," in spite of his disagreement on specific points (319).

102   C. R. Darwin, *Geological Observations on the Volcanic Islands Visited during the Voyage of H.M.S. "Beagle"* (London: Smith, Elder, 1844; 2d ed., 1876); J. D. Dana, *Characteristics of Volcanoes with Contributions of Facts and Principles from the Hawaiian Islands* (New York: Dodd, Mead, 1890).

103   A. Geikie, "Address," *Proceedings of the Royal Physical Society of Edinburgh* 8 (1883–1885): 1–31; also in *Nature* 29 (1883): 107–110, 124–128.

104   Dana, "Origin of Coral Reefs and Islands," 190.

105   See Roy MacLeod: "Imperial Reflections in the Southern Seas: The Funafuti Expedition, 1896–1904," in *Nature in Its Greatest Extent: Western Science in the Pacific,* ed. R. MacLeod and P. F. Rehbock (Honolulu: University of Hawaii Press, 1988), 68–82.

106   N. Reingold, ed., *The Sciences in the American Context: New Perspectives* (Washington, DC: Smithsonian Institution Press, 1979); idem, *Science in America: A Documentary History, 1903–1939* (Chicago: University of Chicago Press, 1981).

107   While the Copley Medal frequently went to foreigners, it was unusual for it to go to one not already a foreign member of the society; see E. C. Smith: "The Copley Medal and Its Founder," *Nature* 174 (1954): 1034–1037. The president of the Royal Society at the time of Dana's award was J. D. Hooker. Dana was unable to receive the medal in person (*Proceedings of the Royal Society* 26 [1877]: 446–447; and Dana to Hooker, 23 March 1878, Royal Society Archives). Darwin himself had proposed Dana for foreign membership as early as June 1855, stating that "his Volcanic Geology is admirable, and he has done much good work on coral reefs" (Darwin to T. H. Huxley, 10 June 1855 [*Correspondence,* 5:351–352]), and Lyell concurred (C. Lyell to Darwin, 23 April 1855 [*Correspondence,* 5:318–319]). But Dana failed to be elected. He was finally successfully proposed nearly thirty years later by Joseph Prestwich (Prestwich to T. H. Huxley, 17 June 1884, Royal Society Archives). There is an obituary of

Dana, based largely on his own writings, in *Proceedings of the Royal Society* 58 (1895): lvii–lx, by "L. F." This was Sir Lazarus Fletcher, then keeper of minerals in the British Museum (Natural History). I am indebted to D. J. H. Griffin of the Royal Society for much of the information in this note.

108   H. E. Gruber and V. Gruber, "The Eye of Reason: Darwin's Development during the *Beagle* Voyage," *Isis* 53 (1962): 186–200; H. E. Gruber, *Darwin on Man: A Psychological Study of Scientific Creativity* (London: Wildwood House, 1974), 101–102.

109   Ghiselin, *Triumph of the Darwinian Method*, 21–27.

110   Cf. A. Hunter Dupree, *Asa Gray, 1810–1888* (Cambridge, MA: Belknap Press, 1959).

E. ALISON KAY

2   Darwin's Biogeography and the Oceanic Islands of the Central Pacific, 1859–1909

"... that grand subject, that almost keystone of the laws of creation, Geographical Distribution."
—CHARLES DARWIN (1845)

It is now a commonplace that biologists have gained much of their insight into evolutionary processes by studying the biology of islands. Darwin himself began to recognize the importance of islands in recounting the unique features of the biota of the Galapagos,[1] and his theory of biogeography ultimately rested on "the inhabitants of islands."[2] Although they are cited in only two instances,[3] the animals and plants of the oceanic islands of the tropical Pacific played a major role in the development of Darwin's theory of biogeography, and the Pacific island biotas comprised a significant element in subsequent theory following the publication of the *Origin of Species*.

Geographical distribution was both the starting point of Charles Darwin's ideas on the origin of species and a test of their validity.[4] In seeing the connection among patterns of distribution, dispersal mechanisms, and barriers, Darwin established both theory and method in biogeography and discovered the definitive evidence for evolution.[5] The substance of his biogeographic argument is summarized in a mere two chapters (12 and 13)[6] which stand as a theory within the theory of the *Origin of Species*.

The crux of Darwin's theory of biogeography lies in "three great facts" cited in the first three pages of chapter 12 and elaborated on thereafter: (1) "neither the similarity nor the dissimilarity of the inhabitants of various regions can be wholly accounted for by climatal and other physical conditions;" (2) "barriers of any kind, or obstacles to free migration, are related ... to the differences between the productions of various regions;" and (3) there is affinity among "the productions of the same continent or of the same sea, though species themselves are distinct at different points and stations."[7] These "facts" are simply explained in the *Origin:* dissimilarities arise from variation and natural selection, degrees of dissimilarity are controlled by migration, and the bond of affinity is inheritance.

The earliest indication of Darwin's influence in the Pacific appears in an essay by John T. Gulick, son of a missionary in the Hawaiian Islands, who, on reading the *Journal of Researches* in 1853,[8] recognized that the principles of distribution were "nowhere . . . more beautifully and strikingly displayed than in the natural history of isolated groups . . . and these Hawaiian Islands." Ten years later, another naturalist in Hawaii, William Harper Pease, discussing the distribution of animals and plants on Pacific islands, was clearly influenced by the Darwinian notions of speciation on islands separated from each other by great distances and of the colonization of these islands by migration. In an unpublished manuscript read at the Newcastle meetings of the British Association for the Advancement of Science in 1863, Pease wrote, "The material so far furnished from the Pacific province, . . . is very defective . . . [and] the chief cause, arises from the great number of separate localities, isolated in position, with a common Fauna, abounding subsequently in specific variation." Pease also emphasized that the species of land snails found on low coral atolls did not furnish "the slightest evidence of recent creation of species, for we suppose them to have been transported by natives, on cocoa husks or some plant, from distant Islands."[9]

The Inhabitants of Oceanic Islands

If there is the slightest foundation for these remarks, the Zoology of Archipelagoes—will be well worth examining.
—CHARLES DARWIN (1835)

The principles of distribution that Gulick saw illustrated in the Hawaiian Islands were summarized by Darwin in a list of the characteristics of the biotas of oceanic islands in the *Origin.* The list illustrates Darwin's "first great fact," that neither climate nor physical conditions fully accounts for the characteristics of the biotas of oceanic islands—that is, fewer species exist on islands than on equal areas of continents; terrestrial mammals, amphibians, and reptiles are absent; and there is a high proportion of endemic species.[10] Examples are cited from Madeira, St. Helena, Bermuda, the Galapagos, and New Zealand, yet most of the features mentioned had been described by the explorer-naturalists who sailed the Pacific from the time of Cook. Notebooks, letters, and early drafts of the *Origin* show that Darwin was familiar with sources of these observations,[11] although they were not specifically credited in the *Origin*.

The paucity of species, particularly the want of insects[12] and sighting of only two commonly found mammals, "the vampyre and the common rat," were remarked on by Johann Reinhold Forster, naturalist on Cook's second voyage. That there were no reptiles or amphibians on Pacific islands was noted by Quoy and Gaimard, who sailed with Freycinet on the *Uranie,* and Adolphe Lesson with d'Urville on the *Astrolabe* fifty years later, while Richard Brinsley Hinds, surgeon on the *Sulphur,* wrote that in the ocean, "large and important groups" of countless mollusks "are entirely absent." J. F. W. Meyen, botanist on the Prussian ship *Prinzess Louise* visiting Hawaii in 1831, noticed that the absentees were replaced by other animals: in Brazil, "seldom does one touch the branch of a tree or the leaf of a plant without coming upon various sorts of insects. . . . Here on the Sandwich Islands nature has placed countless land snails instead of insects on the leaves of trees."[13]

Struck by the high percentage of peculiar species of animals on the Galapagos Islands, Darwin also observed that although the peculiar species belonged to the same genera as those found on the South American mainland, each species was limited to its own island.[14] Joseph Hooker found this "unequal dispersion" of the plants Darwin had collected in the Galapagos "the most singular feature" of the Galapagos, and Asa Gray termed the phenomenon "Hooker's rule."[15] Gray, using U.S. Exploring Expedition collections, found his own example in the central Pacific: in the Hawaiian silverswords, species of *Argyroxiphium* are found on Maui and Hawaii, and *Wilkesia* on Kauai. The Hawaiian land shells were described by Gulick in like manner: "*Achatinella,* a genus of land shells found on these islands and nowhere else, . . . each island and each valley has its own peculiar species."[16]

These observations of the explorer-naturalists were but fragmentary hints of the intriguing nature of the animals and plants of the island Pacific. Darwin had summarized their major features, but he recognized the deficiencies as he indicated in an 1859 letter to J. D. Hooker: "How I wish you would work out the Pacific floras . . . but of all places in the world I should like to see a good flora of the Sandwich Islands."[17] P. L. Sclater echoed Darwin eleven years later, suggesting that the British station for observation of the 1874 transit of Venus on Oahu in the Hawaiian Islands would afford a

favorable opportunity for "a thorough examination of the whole
fauna and flora of the Hawaiian Archipelago;" and Thomas Blackburn, who had spent six years looking at Hawaiian insects during his
tenure as chaplain to the Episcopal bishop of Honolulu, wrote of
"luring fresh explorers to the islands."[18] Darwin's emphasis on insular
biotas in the *Origin of Species* singled them out for special attention.
As the British entomologist Peter Cameron observed in 1887,

> The investigation of the natural history of oceanic islands is now rightly
> regarded as a subject of great interest and importance. Not only do their
> faunas and floras throw much light on the manner in which species have
> been distributed over the globe, but many of the species themselves are,
> from the peculiarities of their structure, of extreme value in throwing light
> on the origin of species.[19]

A few naturalists managed to travel into the Pacific in the waning
years of the nineteenth century. Scott B. Wilson was sent to collect
birds in the Hawaiian Islands in 1887 by the ornithologist Alfred
Newton; Philip Palmer was sponsored by Lord Rothschild on a
similar collecting trip in 1890.[20] Newton argued before the British
Association Committee meetings in 1890 for more field work in the
Hawaiian Islands, an argument that succeeded in 1890 when the
Sandwich Islands Committee was established to organize such an
investigation, which would be partly funded by a government grant
from the Royal Society, and R. C. L. Perkins, who had studied entomology at Oxford, was sent to the islands as a collector in 1892.[21]

Three years of rigorous collecting and nearly thirteen years of compilation resulted in the publication of the *Fauna Hawaiiensis,* an
exquisitely detailed study of an oceanic island fauna. The characteristics of biotas so succinctly listed by Darwin were confirmed, and
many of their implications were elaborated. One could walk for
miles through a forest and see not a single conspicuous insect, but
there were in fact thousands of species of minute, inconspicuous
insects; insects and other animals were limited to a small variety of
types, but they were often rich in species which "fill up vacancies
caused by the absence of many forms of life almost ubiquitous elsewhere." "There is a tendency of island creatures to limit their range
and to specialize their habits;" "whole families of birds . . . far better
adapted to cross wide extents of ocean are quite unrepresented in the
Hawaiian Islands;" and "the distribution of genera within the islands
is very unequal with distinct species and genera on different
islands."[22]

Barriers and Isolation

These *Achatinellinae* never came from Noah's Ark.
—J. T. GULICK (1853)

Darwin's "second great fact" of geographical distribution was that "barriers ... are related ... to the differences between the productions of various regions." The French botanist Charles Gaudichaud had earlier suggested a role for barriers: "The littoral plants, so abundant in the Moloques [Moluccas] and Mariannes [Mariannas], begin to desert the shores of the Sandwich Islands. Shall we search for the cause in the isolation of this archipelago?" Darwin hinted at the same idea in an 1837 notebook jotting: "We find/species few in proportion to the difficulty of transport."[23]

But Darwin also saw barriers as separating different biotas, for example between "the New and the Old Worlds." Indeed, in the unpublished *Natural Selection* he wrote that "barriers were the most important element in distribution."[24] He reasoned that because different animals and plants do not always have coextensive ranges, barriers must not be the same in all cases: what is a barrier to a land snail may not matter to a bird. This diversity of opportunity becomes significant in terms of what actually colonizes oceanic islands.

A third role for barriers, the consequent isolation of a biota, was recognized early in his thinking when Darwin noted, "animals, on separate islands, ought to become different if kept long enough—apart, with slightly different circumstances" and "animals [of the same class] differ in different countries in exact proportion to [the] time they have been separated." In the essay of 1844 he regarded geographic isolation as the main means of formation of new species; in the unpublished *Natural Selection* he was less emphatic, writing "It must not be supposed that isolation is at all necessary for the production of new forms." Yet in the *Origin,* isolation becomes merely "an important element in the modification of species through natural selection." When Moritz Wagner proposed in 1868 that isolation was a necessary element for the formation of new species, Darwin was adamant: "I can by no means agree."[25]

As Darwin had worked from observation and question in the *Journal of Researches* to theory in the *Origin* over a period of twenty years, so had J. T. Gulick's studies of the Hawaiian land shells, *Achatinella,* led him from observation of distribution in 1853 to questions and theory in 1872–1873. On 18 July 1872, Gulick's paper

"The Variation of Species as Related to their Geographical Distribution" was published in *Nature*. In this he provided "some ... remarkable facts" on the *Achatinellinae*: each of four provinces into which the Hawaiian Islands could be divided has a separate set of species and one genus or more peculiar to it; Kauai, separated from the other islands by the widest channel, has forms that differ most from those of the other islands; on Oahu each valley has "its own species; the degree of difference between several species of the same group is in proportion to their separation in space; the average length of the area occupied by different species is perhaps five miles." The facts raised questions: "How can we account for the species being restricted in their distribution to such narrow limits? Why do not the species of North-eastern Oahu pass over their narrow bounds and become mingled throughout the whole extent of that short mountain range?"[26]

On 6 August, Gulick visited Darwin at Down. In a letter of thanks, Gulick wrote, "In the *Origin of Species* ... you say, 'I am convinced that Natural Selection has been the most important but not the exclusive means of modification.' I have attempted to suggest some of the other conditions that have influence." With the letter, Gulick enclosed an outline of another manuscript, "On Diversity of Evolution under One Set of External Conditions." Gulick asked Darwin to recommend the paper to the secretaries of the Linnean Society: "I have not heard from the secretaries. ... A paper that deals so largely with theories is very liable to be thrown out unless it is ... recommended, by one who appreciates its bearing upon theories that have already awakened the greatest interest." Darwin's reply was noncommittal: "I do not think I can do anything about your paper. The Secretaries act somewhat like judges and might properly demur to any suggestion being made to them."[27]

"On Diversity of Evolution" was, however, published the following year. Outlining the same group of facts on the achatinelline land snails that he had emphasized in *Nature*, Gulick observed that

> I think the evolution of these different forms cannot be attributed to difference in their external conditions: ... in different valleys on the same side of the mountain where food, climate and enemies are the same, there is still a difference in species; ... if we suppose separation without a difference of external circumstances is a condition sufficient to ensure variation, it renders intelligible the fact that in nearly allied forms on the same island, the degree of divergence in type is in proportion to the distance in space by which they are separated.[28]

Gulick had identified isolation as a factor in the formation of species, and he elaborated on the idea in 1888 in a paper now considered a major turning point in what had become a lively debate on the issue.[29]

For the next thirty years, Gulick tenaciously advocated the role of isolation in speciation.[30] His ideas were confirmed by studies of another Pacific land snail, *Partula,* in Tahiti. Alfred G. Mayer concluded, "It is probable that geographical isolation plays a most important part. . . . If two valleys be adjacent, their snails are closely related. . . . The wider the separation between any two valleys, the more distant the relationship between their snails."[31]

Gulick's advocacy of a role for isolation in evolutionary theory was joined almost simultaneously by David Starr Jordan, ichthyologist and first president of Stanford University, when Gulick published his most ambitious work, *Evolution, Racial and Habitudinal* (1905). Jordan took up Gulick's cause with a lead article in *Science,* "The Origin of Species through Isolation," in which he highlighted as examples the land shells studied by Gulick, Hawaiian passerine birds, and his own work on Pacific fishes.[32] Like Gulick, Jordan reached his position on isolation from studies (among others) of geographical distribution on islands in the Pacific. A series of visits to the Hawaiian Islands, the Philippines, Japan, and Samoa between 1899 and 1905 resulted in descriptions of new species and genera and conclusions about the distribution and origin of the fish fauna of Pacific islands. In a paper on the fishes of Samoa, Jordan cited what is now known as Jordan's Law: for any given species the one nearest related will be found in neighboring waters, but not in the same waters. However, he concluded, "the Samoa species of small [gobies] . . . form an exception. . . . Here closely related species live in the same region. . . . [T]he isolation of different coral masses is sufficient to prevent the migration of individuals, . . . thus producing distinct species in regions not far separated."[33]

The Theory of Migration

[A]ll the grand leading facts of geographical distribution are
explicable on the theory of migration.
—CHARLES DARWIN (1859)

In chapter 13 of the *Origin,* Darwin turned to the question of the "third great fact," migration. Affinity presents the greatest amount of difficulty with respect to distribution, "on the view that not only all the individuals of the same species have migrated from

some one area, but that allied species, although now inhabiting the
most distant points, have proceeded from a single area."[34]

Dispersal was not a new idea. Cook, after a visit to Palmer-
ston Island on the third voyage, described "the plants that may have
Vegetated from Cocoanuts, roots and seed b[r]ought there by the
wind, birds, or thrown up by the sea." Forty years later, Adelbert von
Chamisso on the *Rurick* wrote that "the sea brings . . . the seeds and
fruits of many trees, most of which have not yet grown there . . .
[to Ratak and others of the Marshall Islands,] many of them appearing . . . to have not yet lost the capability of growing." In the
Hawaiian Islands, Gaudichaud observed that it was "more natural
to attribute the plant life . . . to the air or marine currents, to the
birds, . . . than to search for the germs of all living things of these
islands, within the center of the earth." Hinds a decade later wrote
of the few "peculiar species" in the Pacific "being chiefly fed by
migration from other seas," and James Dwight Dana and Charles
Pickering, both of whom sailed through the Pacific with the U.S.
Exploring Expedition (1838–1841), cited the role of dispersal in the
distribution of plants and animals. Dana visualized "the migration of
species [of Crustacea] from island to island through the tropical
Pacific." Pickering suggested that "every species of animal and plant
had an original home, a point from which its generations are continually pressing outwards, migrating as far as the means of support and
the constitutional relation to climate permit, unless checked by some
direct barrier."[35]

But where was "home" in the Pacific? The obvious similarity of the
endemic animals and plants in the Galapagos to those on the South
American mainland led Darwin to conclude that "the most striking
and important fact . . . is the affinity of the species which inhabit
islands to those of the nearest mainland."[36] From which of the two
continents bordering the Pacific were the animals and plants of Pacific
islands derived?

Forster had said that "the plants which grow on south-sea isles
partly resemble those of America and partly those of Asia, with the
resemblance to India becoming more apparent the further west."
Later explorer-naturalists echoed Forster: Chamisso commented that
the flora "seems to have become more scanty . . . from the west
towards the east;" Hinds noticed that westward from the Marquesas
"additional Indian species appear at every group, and the conchology
becomes gradually more rich and abundant."[37] An explanation for
these observations was provided by P. A. Latreille in 1821 in an essay
on the distribution of insects in the

archipelagoes of the great southern ocean, . . . [where] these islands . . . form a chain which unites them to those of the west, and from which they have been able to receive their productions. But on the American side, there are no groups of coral islands to afford such a mode of communication. Hence it happens that many of these islands are American by geographical position, but Asiatic in regard to the animal and vegetable productions of their soil.[38]

Darwin's explanation of the westerly similarities was essentially that of Latreille. There is a tentative reach for the explanation in a notebook jotting: "birds & bats have certainly travelled from East Indies, . . . Wide space of sea, to west of America, would account for this." But he clearly states it in the *Origin*: "Westward of the shores of America, a wide space of open ocean extends, with not an island as a halting-place for emigrants; here we have a barrier of another kind, and as soon as this is passed we meet in the eastern islands of the Pacific with another and totally distinct fauna."[39]

Given virtually unanimous agreement that Pacific islands were colonized by migration, it is not surprising that the dispersalist tradition in the Pacific should continue after the publication of the *Origin*. Alexander Agassiz attributed migration in currents as the "principal cause of the extensive range of so many species" of echinoderms. William Hillebrand declared that Hawaiian plants owed their origin to the "current that deposits drift on the shores." Botting Hemsley reported on the botany of the *Challenger* expedition that "all the data coming under my notice bearing on the dispersal of plants . . . sufficiently accounts for the vegetation of low coral atolls."[40] Other dimensions to the dispersalist thesis emerged at the end of the century when the Australian malacologist Charles Hedley focused on the distribution of marine organisms and H. B. Guppy, the English botanist who traveled widely in the Pacific, studied seed dispersal.

Drawing attention to the distribution of marine organisms on the islands of the central Pacific, Hedley adopted Darwin's distinction between continental and oceanic islands and elegantly described the biotas of the two kinds of islands.

The first received its population by normal methods of migration, while it was part of . . . the mainland; the second received only such animals and plants as might cross actively by flight or swimming, or be borne passively. . . . Since such transmission would be easy for a few, difficult for many and impossible for most, the fauna and flora of an Oceanic Island will bear to an appreciative eye the distinctive stamp of its selective origin.[41]

The critical observation was "the absence of certain forms [rather] than the presence of others" on oceanic islands: various species of *Melo, Voluta,* and *Nautilus* were abundant and conspicuous throughout the continental islands nearest Funafuti, but

> the line which I draw between the oceanic and continental islands, is, however, an insuperable barrier to these, though it is none to such genera as *Mitra, Conus* or *Cypraea.* The reason suggested is that the former lay eggs of great size, the young have no trochosphere stage and are already bulky when hatched. They are not therefore capable of crossing spaces of open sea like the others. . . . I should suppose indeed that the bulk of the molluscan fauna reached Funafuti in the larval swimming stage.[42]

Guppy focused on another aspect of dispersal, seed buoyancy, as the common thread of a series of investigations undertaken among the islands of the Pacific during the last years of the century. Hundreds of observations led him to the conclusion that long-distance dispersal is fortuitous: "The great variety of structures concerned with buoyancy are regarded in the main . . . as not arising from adaptation. . . . Buoyancy is connected with structures that now serve a purpose for which they were not originally developed. It cannot have been provided for by previous adaptation, . . . it is . . . selective and in that sense accidental."[43] Guppy also found, as had Darwin, that seawater dispersal of plants accounts for relatively few island plants. Curiously, although there are references to Darwin's observations and experiments with seeds, there is no mention of either the *Origin* or of natural selection in Guppy's work.

A second source area for the Pacific biota was further developed in the years immediately following the *Origin.* J. D. Hooker found a remarkable difference between floras of the New Hebrides and New Caledonia and those of Fiji and the islands to the east. In the former, there were New Zealand and Australian types, in the latter almost exclusively Indian forms.[44] Hedley followed that scheme for land shells, "populating the Central Pacific islands by drift from Melanesia," and suggested a route via New Guinea to Fiji and then into Samoa. W. H. Pease assigned a different origin for the marine mollusks, however: they are, he wrote, "generically & to a great extent specifically the same as those of the Philippines & apparently from the variation which can be traced in many species, passing from one group of Islands to another eastwardly, originated there." The same theme was adopted forty years later by David Starr Jordan, who traced a path for marine fishes from the center of dispersion in the East Indies through a series of islands to the central Pacific.[45]

Dispersal

Why not extend a continent to every island in the Pacific?
—CHARLES DARWIN (1856)

Dispersal was Darwin's most persuasive argument in explaining the distribution of the biotas of oceanic islands: "Although terrestrial mammals do not occur on oceanic islands, aerial mammals do occur on almost every island.... The Viti [Fiji] Archipelago, the Bonin Islands, the Caroline and Marianne Archipelagoes, ... all possess their peculiar bats. Why... has the supposed creative force produced bats and no other mammals on remote islands?" His answer was that the limited number of species, endemism, and the absence of whole classes of animals such as amphibians and terrestrial mammals could be explained "better with the belief in the efficiency of occasional means of transport, carried out during a long course of time, than with the belief in the former connection of oceanic islands."[46]

Darwin's question was posed again in 1900 by Henry A. Pilsbry, malacologist at the Academy of Natural Sciences in Philadelphia. Why had families of land snails dominant elsewhere failed to take advantage of the means of dispersal used by the dispersalists to account for oceanic island biotas?[47] But Pilsbry's answer was a grand mid-Pacific continent, possibly two-thirds as large as Australia, extending from the Cook Islands to the Marquesas to accommodate the Pacific land snails. His reasoning was that many genera of land snails reach back to the Oligocene unchanged save in specific characters, and the Pacific islands were tenanted almost entirely by the most primitive and oldest groups of land snails. Therefore "zoogeographic 'provinces' based upon the distribution of land snails or earthworms ... recall older arrangements of sea and land than those based upon the distribution of terrestrial vertebrates."[48]

Darwin had argued time and again that continental extensions were not the answer to the problem of distribution, both on geological grounds and because "they do not accord for all the phenomena of distribution on islands."[49] His arguments did not dissuade all bridge builders, however, and even his friends and allies slipped continents into the Pacific Ocean. Hooker proposed that the similarities among the floras of New Zealand, Tasmania, and temperate South America were due to their being remnants of a flora that "had once spread over a larger and more continuous tract of land than now exists in that ocean." Huxley, explaining "a great difference between the Fauna of the Polynesian Islands and that of the west coast of

America," proposed that "a gradual shifting of the deep sea, which at present bars migration, between the easternmost of these islands and America took place to the westward" and also postulated a continent in the Pacific. The English conchologist and Darwin correspondent S. P. Woodward also proposed an early Pacific continent, on which Darwin remarked, "Woodward . . . does not seem to doubt that every island in the Pacific and Atlantic are the remains of continents." Although Hooker's continent did not include the islands of the South Seas, later bridge builders, including Captain Frederick W. Hutton, a geologist in New Zealand, and Hermann von Jhering, a German naturalist, suggested extensions of a southern continent to include some, if not all, of the islands of the tropical Pacific.[50]

There were earlier Pacific "continents." A. A. Gould, writing of the land snails collected on Pacific islands during the U.S. Exploring Expedition, suggested that the "mountain peaks evident now indicate or constitute, the islands with which it [the Pacific] is now studded. . . . We think there are strong indications that some groups of islands have an intimate relation to each other, and belonged, at least, to the peaks of the same mountain ranges, before they were submerged."[51]

Three Pacific continents had been proposed prior to the publication of the *Origin of Species;* in the fifty years after publication at least ten were proposed to accommodate various elements of the Pacific biota, including not only Pilsbry's land snails but monotremes, birds, lizards, eels, insects, and the coral *Pocillopora.*[52] Most of these continents accounted for apparently related species on widely separated islands and could be countered with additional distributional data or phylogenetic interpretation.

Pilsbry's continent, however, provided a new dimension to the biogeography of Pacific islands, for his idea was that "far from being a dependency of the Australian or Oriental regions, Polynesia has every appearance of being a region which started with a fauna long antedating the present Australian and Oriental faunas."[53] Polynesia had been recognized as a botanic subdivision by Schouw as early as 1853, and Swainson appended it to the Australian province because the islands were then but "obscurely known." Sclater and Wallace recognized the "Pacific Islands" as a subregion and also appended them to the "Australian Region," although Wallace indicated that the biota of the Hawaiian Islands was very peculiar and indicative of "the relics of a more extensive land." What Pilsbry contended was that there was a Polynesian fauna that had developed "along its own lines, retaining old types because they did not come into competition with the higher groups developed on the greater and less isolated continents,"[54] and hence a fauna that had originated in the Pacific.

Conclusion

The *Origin of Species* was both an immediate success and a center of controversy. Bowler suggests that field naturalists found the *Origin* less controversial than did the Darwinians who did not work in the field.[55] In the Pacific, the field naturalists had made the observations that Darwin's theory explained, and the success of the *Origin* was particularly evident in their virtually unquestioned acceptance of Darwin's dispersalist thesis.

Field collecting in the Pacific in the years immediately following the publication of the *Origin* not only provided confirmation of earlier observations but permitted their elaboration. Darwin's intuition that the Hawaiian Islands would provide a rich resource of plants was borne out by Hillebrand, while the land shells studied by Gulick and the passerine birds described by Wilson, Henshaw, and Perkins were cited as classic examples of insular evolution in early twentieth-century texts on biogeography and evolution.[56] Isolation was separated from selection as a factor theoretically distinct in great part through the work of a Pacific naturalist (J. T. Gulick) and indeed, as Bowler has pointed out,[57] David Starr Jordan could conclude his essay of 1905 on isolation and the origin of the species by saying that there were scarcely any field naturalists at that point who did not accept isolation.

The widely held assumption that concepts of organic change first put forward by Darwin and Wallace mark the beginning of modern biogeography is disputed by Janet Browne, who suggests that "from Noah's Ark to the advent of evolutionary theory, the study of animal and plant geography displayed a rich and complex history."[58] The evolution of idiosyncracies in the distribution of animals and plants is surely a part of that long history. The explorer-naturalists who plied the Pacific in the late eighteenth and early nineteenth centuries distinguished the pieces of the puzzle; naturalists later resident in the islands provided insight and hypothesis. What Darwin did was to construct a framework into which the pieces fit. Restricting himself in the *Origin* to establishing general principles to account for the facts of distribution as part of his larger argument, he was nevertheless fully cognizant of the peculiarities of Pacific island biotas and incorporated them in his argument. Much of the confirmation of the three great facts that were the crux of Darwin's theory of biogeography lies in those observations.

Notes

1   Charles Darwin, *Journal of Researches into the Natural History and Geology of the Countries Visited during the Voyage Round the World of H.M.S. "Beagle" under Command of Captain FitzRoy, R. N.*, 2d ed. (London: John Murray, 1902).

2   Charles Darwin, *On the Origin of Species*, 6th ed. (London: John Murray, 1872; reprint New York: P. F. Collier & Son, 1909). The sixth edition, the most widely accessible edition of the *Origin*, is used throughout this study.

3   Darwin, *Origin*, 351, 353. Bats of Viti (Fiji), the Carolines, and the Marianas, and the endemic land shells reported by Gould are mentioned.

4   William Thiselton-Dyer, "Geographical Distribution of Plants," in *Darwin and Modern Science*, ed. A. C. Seward (Cambridge: Cambridge University Press, 1910), 299; Philip J. Darlington, Jr., "Darwin and Zoogeography," *Proceedings of the American Philosophical Society* 103 (1959): 307, 315; Michael T. Ghiselin, *The Triumph of the Darwinian Method*, 2d ed. (Chicago: University of Chicago Press, 1984), 38, 43.

5   Ghiselin, *Triumph*, 38.

6   Darwin, *Origin*, 353.

7   Ibid., 316–318.

8   John T. Gulick, MS journal, Hawaiian Mission Children's Society Library; John T. Gulick, "The Distribution of Plants and Animals, Read before the Punahou Debating Society, April 7, 1853," Gulick MS, Bancroft Library, University of California, Berkeley, and abstracted in Addison Gulick, *Evolutionist and Missionary John Thomas Gulick* (Chicago: University of Chicago Press, 1932), 114–116; quote on 115. (See also chapter 4 herein.)

9   William Harper Pease, MS, not paginated, Bernice P. Bishop Museum Library. The last page of the manuscript bears the notation "W. Harper Pease Honolulu, Sandwich Islands, January, 1863" in Pease's hand and another note written by Philip Pearsall Carpenter who acted as Pease's agent in England, "Returned at your request. I read a part at the Newcastle meeting. I put a short note in the Transactions. P." The "short note" is an abstract, "On the Principal Divisions of the Pacific Fauna," *Report of the British Association for the Advancement of Science* (1864), 101–102. Pease mentions Darwin in a September 1860 letter to the naturalist Andrew Garrett, then in Tahiti: "Darwin's ideas on the origin of species, appears to be absorbing all the attention. . . . Agassiz . . . comes down strong on Darwin. In fact so near as I can learn, Darwin has but few backers" (original in Pease-Garrett correspondence, Bernice P. Bishop Museum Library). See also E. Alison Kay and William J. Clench, "A Biobibliography of

William Harper Pease, Malacologist of Polynesia," *Nemouria* 16
(1975): 1–50.

10   Darwin, *Origin,* 431–435.

11   Reading lists and notes in *Charles Darwin's Notebooks, 1836–1844,*
ed. Paul H. Barrett, Peter J. Gautry, Sandra Herbert, David Kohn, and
Sydney Smith (Cambridge: The Press Syndicate of the University of
Cambridge, 1987); *The Correspondence of Charles Darwin,* ed. Fred-
erick Burkhardt and Sydney Smith, 10 vols. (Cambridge: Cambridge
University Press, 1985–1994), vol. 1, appendix 6, "Books on the *Beagle*"; *Life and Letters of Charles Darwin,* ed. Francis Darwin (New
York: Appleton, 1896); and Nora Barlow, *Charles Darwin and the
Voyage of the "Beagle"* (London: Pilot Press, 1945). These works indi-
cate Darwin had read most of the voyages such as those of Cook,
Beechey, and Kotzebue. An early synthesis of observations of Pacific
island biotas from the Cook voyages is that of James Cowles Prichard,
ed., *Researches on the Physical History of Mankind* (London: John
and Arthur Arch, 1826), whom Darwin cites in notebook B (*Darwin's
Notebooks,* ed. Barrett et al.) and who was cited extensively in
Charles Lyell, *Principles of Geology* (London: John Murray, 1832),
vol. 2. Prichard has been given his due by anthropologists (see George
W. Stocking, Jr., "From Chronology to Ethnology: James Cowles Prichard and British Anthropology 1800–1850," in *Researches,* ed. Prichard (1826; reprint Chicago: University of Chicago Press, 1973),
ix–cx, but is little recognized for his contributions to biogeography.

12   J. R. Forster, *Observations Made during a Voyage round the World,
on Physical Geography, Natural History, and Ethic Philosophy...*
(London: G. R. Robinson, 1778) 186–187. See Darwin, n. 54, notebook C, *Notebooks,* ed. Barrett et al. The scarcity of insects on Pacific
islands was noted by several of the explorer-naturalists. Thomas
Blackburn and David Sharp, "Memoirs on the Coleoptera of the
Hawaiian Islands," *Scientific Transactions of the Royal Dublin Society,* 2d ser., 3, (1885):119–208, summarized what was known about
the scarcity of insects in the Pacific: "One of the most remarkable factors in Hawaiian entomology is the extreme rarity of specimens, in
comparison of the number of species, . . . my experiences in this matter agrees with that of previous explorers in the islands of the Pacific
Ocean, many of whom allude to the extreme paucity of insect life
there." J. R. C. Quoy and P. S. Gaimard, "Zoologie," in Louis C. C. De
Freycinet, *Voyage autour du Monde... sur les corvettes "l'Uranie"
et de "la Physicienne"... 1817, 1819, 1820* (Paris: Chez Phillet aine,
1824), xx. R. P. Lesson, *Voyage autour du Monde... sur la corvette
"La Coquille,"* 2 vols. (Paris: P. Pourrat Freres, 1838), in Darwin,
notebook C, no. 27e, *Notebooks,* ed. Barrett et al. R. B. Hinds, "The
Mollusca," in E. Belcher, *Narrative of a Voyage round the World...
1836–42* (London: Smith, Elder, 1844), 3.

13   J. F. W. Meyen, in *A Botanist's Visit to Oahu in 1831*, ed. M. A. Pultz,
      an excerpt from the original publication, *Reise um die Erde . . . Preus-
      sischen Seehandlunge-schiffe, "Prinzess Louise"* (Honolulu: Press
      Pacifica, 1981), 44–45.

14   Darwin, *Journal*, 401.

15   Joseph Dalton Hooker, "On the Vegetation of the Galapagos Archi-
      pelago, as Compared with that of Some Other Tropical Islands and of
      the Continent of America," *Transactions of the Linnean Society Lon-
      don (Botany)* 20 (1851): 235–262; Asa Gray, "On Some Plants of
      Order Compositae from the Sandwich Islands," *American Associa-
      tion for the Advancement of Science Proceedings*, 2 (1849): 397–398.
      A later expression of "Hooker's Rule" is "Jordan's Law"; see n. 33.

16   Gulick, "Distribution of Plants and Animals," 118.

17   Charles Darwin to J. D. Hooker, 1850, cited in *More Letters of
      Charles Darwin: A Record of His Work in a Series of Hitherto
      Unpublished Letters*, ed. Francis Darwin and A. C. Seward, 2 vols.
      (London: John Murray, 1903), 1:459.

18   P. L. Sclater, "The Transits of Venus in 1874 and 1882," *Nature* 1
      (1870): 527; and see idem, "Remarks on the Avifauna of the Sand-
      wich Islands," *Ibis* 1, ser. 3 (1871): 356–362; Blackburn and Sharp,
      "Memoirs on the Coleoptera," 119–208.

19   Thomas Blackburn and Peter Cameron, "On the Hymenoptera of the
      Hawaiian Islands," *Manchester Literary and Philosophical Society
      Memoir* 10 (1887): 194–244.

20   Alfred Newton, "Ornithology of the Sandwich Islands," *Nature* 45
      (1892): 465–469; Lionel W. Rothschild, *The Avifauna of Laysan and
      the Neighbouring Islands; with a Complete History to Date of the
      Birds of the Hawaiian Possessions* (London: R. H. Porter, 1893–1900).

21   Newton, "Ornithology"; and see Anita Manning, "The Sandwich
      Island Committee, Bishop Museum, and R. C. L. Perkins: Cooperative
      Zoological Exploration and Publication," *Bishop Museum Occa-
      sional Papers* 26 (1986): 1–46, for an excellent summary of the intri-
      cacies involved in the formation of the Sandwich Islands Committee
      and its successful conclusion.

22   David Sharp, ed., *Fauna Hawaiiensis; or, the Zoology of the Sand-
      wich (Hawaiian) Isles Being Results of the Explorations Instituted by
      the Joint Committee Appointed by the Royal Society of London for
      Promoting Natural Knowledge and the British Association for the
      Advancement of Science, and Carried on with the Assistance of Those
      Bodies and of the Trustees of the Bernice Pauahi Bishop Museum at
      Honolulu*, 3 vols. (Cambridge: Cambridge University Press, 1890–
      1913); Perkins, "Introduction," *Fauna*.

23   Darwin, *Origin*, 396; Charles Gaudichaud, "The Vegetation of the
      Sandwich Islands as Seen by Charles Gaudichaud in 1819: A Transla-

tion, with Notes, of Gaudichaud's *Iles Sandwich,* Harold St. John and Margaret Titcomb, eds., *Occasional Papers of B. P. Bishop Museum* 25 (9) (1983): 1–16; Darwin, notebook B, no. 158, in *Notebooks,* ed. Barrett et al.

24 Darwin, *Origin,* 396; *Charles Darwin's Natural Selection Being the Second Part of His Big Species Book Written from 1856 to 1858,* ed. R. C. Stauffer (Cambridge: Cambridge University Press, 1975), 584.

25 Darwin, notebook B, no. 7, in *Notebooks,* ed. Barrett et al.; Darwin, notebook D, no. 23, in ibid.; Charles Darwin, in *The Foundations of the Origin of Species: Two Essays Written in 1842 and 1844,* ed. Francis Darwin (Cambridge: Cambridge University Press, 1909); Darwin, *Origin,* 116, 416; Charles Darwin's *Natural Selection,* 254.

26 John Thomas Gulick, "The Variation of Species as Related to their Geographical Distribution, Illustrated by the Achatinellinae," *Nature* 6 (1872): 222–224.

27 Gulick to Darwin, 8 August 1872, original in the Cambridge University Library, copy in Linnean Society of London, cited in Gulick, *J. T. Gulick,* 234–235; Darwin to Gulick, 8 August 1872, copies in the Linnean Society of London and Bancroft Library, University of California at Berkeley; original in the American Philosophical Society, Philadelphia.

28 John Thomas Gulick, "On Diversity of Evolution under One Set of External Conditions," *Linnean Society Journal of Zoology* 11 (1872): 496–505.

29 Ernst Mayr, "Darwin, Wallace, and the Origin of Isolating Mechanisms," in *Evolution and the Diversity of Life* (Cambridge: Belknap Press, 1976), 129–134, has pointed out that in these early papers on isolation, and in those of others such as Wagner and Romanes, the term "isolation" was applied in two ways, in one sense meaning geographic isolation or (in modern terms) the division of a gene pool into two independent pools by strictly extrinsic factors, and in the second, reproductive isolation, which refers to the prevention of interbreeding of populations by intrinsic mechanisms now called isolating mechanisms. The distinction was not recognized until about 1940 when Theodosius G. Dobzhansky in *Genetics and the Origin of Species* (New York: Columbia University Press, 1937) drew attention to it. See also John E. Lesch, "The Role of Isolation in Evolution: George J. Romanes and John T. Gulick, *Isis* 66 (1975): 483–503; and Hampton L. Carson, "The Process Whereby Species Originate," *Bioscience* 37 (1987): 715–720. Frank J. Sulloway, "Geographic Isolation in Darwin's Thinking: The Vicissitudes of a Crucial Idea," *Studies in History of Biology* 3 (1979): 23–65, also distinguishes two meanings of "isolation" in Darwin's writings.

30   Gulick published sixteen papers on the subject 1872 to 1914 in the
      *Journal of the Linnean Society, American Journal of Science, Ameri-
      can Naturalist,* and *Nature,* culminating with John T. Gulick, *Evolu-
      tion Racial and Habitudinal* (Washington, D.C.: Carnegie Institution,
      1905).

31   Alfred Goldsborough Mayer, "Some Species of *Partula* from Tahiti,"
      Memoirs of the Museum of Comparative Zoology at Harvard College
      26 (1902): 117–135.

32   David Starr Jordan, "The Origin of Species through Isolation," *Sci-
      ence* 22 (1905): 545–562. Jordan cites W. B. Henshaw, Hans Gadow,
      and Scott B. Wilson as his authorities on speciation in Hawaiian
      birds. Jordan was also author of Gulick's obituary. David Starr Jor-
      dan, "John Thomas Gulick, Missionary and Darwinian," *Science* 43
      (1923): 509. George John Romanes, another staunch advocate, wrote
      of Gulick, "To his essays on the subject I attribute a higher value than
      to any other work in the field of Darwinian thought since the date of
      Darwin's death." Gulick's portrait forms the frontispiece of George J.
      Romanes, *Darwin and after Darwin* (Chicago: Open Court, 1906).

33   David Starr Jordan and Alvin Seale, "The Fishes of Samoa," *Bulletin
      United States Fish Commission* 25 (1905): 175–445. David Starr
      Jordan and Vernon Kellogg, *Evolution and Animal Life* (New York:
      Appleton, 1908), stated that "given any species, in any region, the
      nearest related species is not to be found in the same region nor in a
      remote region, but in a neighboring district separated from the first by
      a barrier of some sort or at least by a belt of country, the breadth of
      which gives the effect of a barrier" (120). J. A. Allen, "Mutations and
      the Geographic Distribution of Nearly Related Species in Plants and
      Animals," *American Naturalist* 41 (1908): 653–655, called the gener-
      alization "Jordan's Law." See also David Starr Jordan, "The Law of
      Geminate Species," *American Naturalist* 42 (1908): 73–80. Jordan's
      generalization would appear to be a later statement of what Asa Gray
      had called "Hooker's Rule" (n. 15).

34   Darwin, *Origin,* 431.

35   James Cook, in *The Journals of Captain James Cook: The "Reso-
      lution" and "Discovery," 1776–1780,* pt. 1, ed. J. C. Beaglehole
      (Cambridge: Cambridge University Press, 1967), 95. Adelbert von
      Chamisso, "Remarks and Opinions of the Naturalist of the Expe-
      dition," in O. Kotzebue, *A Voyage of Discovery into the South
      Seas . . . in the Years 1815–1818,* 3 vols. (1821; reprint, New York:
      Da Capo Press, 1967), 155; Gaudichaud, "Vegetation of Sandwich
      Islands," 11; Hinds, "Regions of Vegetation," 11; James Dwight
      Dana, "On the Geographical Distribution of Crustacea," *American
      Journal of Science,* 2d ser., 20 (1855): 349–361; Charles Pickering,
      Botany, vol. 15, pt. 2 of *Report of the United States Exploring Expe-
      dition* (Philadelphia: C. Sherman, 1854), 5.

36 Darwin, *Origin,* 439.

37 Forster, *Observations,* 174; Chamisso, "Remarks and Opinions," 365; Hinds, "The Mollusca," 4.

38 P. A. Latreille, "On the Geographical Distribution of Insects," *Edinburgh New Philosophical Journal* 6 (1822): 51–62; Darwin, notebook C, no. 21, *Notebooks,* ed. Barrett et al.: "Consult Latreille, Geographie des insectes."

39 Darwin, notebook B, no. 7, in *Notebooks,* Barrett et al., ed. Barrett; Darwin, *Origin,* 397.

40 Alexander Agassiz, "Revision of the Echini, Parts I and II," *Illustrated Catalogue of the Museum of Comparative Zoology at Harvard College* (Cambridge: Harvard University Press, 1872), 208; William Hillebrand, *Flora of the Hawaiian Islands* (New York: B. Westermann, 1888), xv; W. B. Hemsley, "Report on Present State of Knowledge of Various Insular Floras, being an Introduction to the First Three Parts of the Botany of the *Challenger* Expedition," *Report of the Voyage of H.M.S. "Challenger," (Botany)* (1), (1885), 1–75.

41 Charles Hedley, "A Zoogeographic Scheme for the Mid Pacific," *Proceedings of the Linnean Society of New South Wales* 24 (1899): 391–423. Ernst Mayr, "The Origin and History of the Polynesian Bird Fauna," in *The Evolution of Diversity,* ed. Ernst Mayr (Cambridge: Belknap Press, 1940), 601–617, defines "oceanic island" as a "term created by zoogeographers and with no geological significance."

42 Hedley, "Zoogeographic Scheme."

43 H. B. Guppy, *Observations of a Naturalist in the Pacific between 1896 and 1899* (London: Macmillan, 1906). Sherwin Carlquist, *Island Biology* (New York: Columbia University Press, 1974), 53, notes that Guppy's work provides "most of the information we have on the dispersal of Pacific plants."

44 Joseph D. Hooker, "On the Origination and Distribution of Species: Introductory Essay to the Flora of Tasmania," *American Journal of Science and Arts,* 2d ser., 29 (1860): 1–25.

45 Hedley, "Zoogeographic Scheme," 405; Pease, MS; Jordan and Seale, "Fishes of Samoa," 180.

46 Darwin, *Origin,* 437.

47 Henry A. Pilsbry, "The Genesis of Mid-Pacific Faunas," *Proceedings of the Academy of Natural Sciences Philadelphia* (1900): 568–575.

48 Ibid., 569. The American climatologist W. D. Matthews responded to Pilsbry in a letter in *Science* 43 (1900): 686: "Dr. Pilsbry may have overlooked the fact that the older a given group, the longer time for chance overseas dispersal, hence greater probability of reaching the islands."

49   Darwin to Lyell, in Thistleton-Dyer, "Geographical Distribution,"
        303.

50   Joseph Dalton Hooker, *The Botany of the Antarctic Voyage of H.M.
        Discovery Ships "Erebus" and "Terror" in the Years 1839–43*, vol. 2,
        Flora Novae-Zelandiae, pt. 1, *Flowering Plants* (London: Lovell
        Reeve, 1853), xxi. Hooker's continent has in fact stood the test of
        time, although Hooker abandoned the idea of "continental exten-
        sions" in 1867. T. H. Huxley, "Anniversary Address Delivered before
        the Geological Society," *Nature* 1 (1870): 437–443; Darwin to Lyell,
        25 June 1856, in *Life and Letters,* 2:74; W. Hutton, "Theoretical
        Explanation of the Distribution of Southern Faunas," *Proceedings of
        the Linnean Society of New South Wales* 21 (1876): 36–47; H. von
        Ihering, "On Ancient Relations between New Zealand and South
        America," *Transactions of the New Zealand Institute* 24 (1893):
        431–445.

51   A. A. Gould, "Mollusca and Shells," *Report of the United States
        Exploring Expedition during the Years 1839–1842 under the Com-
        mand of Charles Wilkes, U.S.N.* (Philadelphia: Sherman, 1859–
        1861), 12:xiv.

52   Pilsbry, "Genesis"; and, for example, G. Baur, "New Observations on
        the Origin of the Galapagos Islands, with Remarks on the Geological
        Age of the Pacific Ocean," *American Naturalist* 31 (1897): 864–896;
        Lord Walsingham, "Microlepidoptera," in *Fauna Hawaiiensis*, ed.
        Sharp, 1:469–759; E. Meyrick, "Macrolepidoptera," in ibid., 1:123–
        275; Andrew Murray, "On the Geographical Relations of the Chief
        Coleopterous Faunae," *Journal of the Linnean Society of London* 11
        (1873): 1–89; G. Budde-Lund, *A Revision of "Crustacea Isopoda Ter-
        restria,"* with additions and illustrations (Copenhagen: H. Hagenup,
        1904), 2:40.

53   Pilsbry, "Genesis," 573. It is somewhat ironic, in light of Darwin's
        opposition to continents in explaining distribution of insular biotas,
        that a continent should emerge as a heuristic device, but Pilsbry's con-
        tinent did serve as the stimulus for the recognition of a Pacific biota.

54   J. F. Schouw, *Grundzüge einer allegemeinen Pflanzen-geographie*
        (Berlin: G. Reimer, 1823); William Swainson, *A Treatise on the
        Geography and Classification of Animals* (London: Longman, Green,
        1835); P. L. Sclater, "On the Geographical Distribution of the Mem-
        bers of the Class Aves," *Journal of the Linnean Society of London
        (Zoology)* 2 (1858): 130–145; A. R. Wallace, *The Geographical
        Distribution of Animals*, 2 vols. (London: Macmillan, 1876), 1:442;
        Pilsbry, "Genesis," 573.

55   See Carson, "The Process Whereby Species Originate"; Peter J.
        Bowler, *Evolution: The History of an Idea* (Berkeley: University of
        California Press, 1989), 236.

56   See, for example, Edward D. Cope, *The Primary Factors in Evolution* (Chicago: Open Court Publishing, 1904); Vernon Kellogg, *Darwinism Today* (New York: Henry Holt, 1908).

57   Bowler, *Evolution,* 236.

58   Janet Browne, *The Secular Ark: Studies in the History of Biogeography* (New Haven: Yale University Press, 1983), 221.

JANE R. CAMERINI

3 Evolution, Biogeography, and Maps

An Early History of Wallace's Line

A year after his return from eight years of traveling and collecting animal specimens in the East Indian Archipelago, Alfred Russel Wallace presented a paper on the physical geography of the region to the Royal Geographical Society of London.[1] The map accompanying the article (figure 3.1) depicted the boundary between the Asian and Australian biotas by a single line, known shortly thereafter as "Wallace's line."[2] In that although Wallace's line is one of the most disputed topics in biogeography and his evolutionary theorizing has been the focus of intensive scrutiny, the close connection between the formulation of the line and his evolutionary hypotheses has been overlooked by historians of science.[3]

The relationship between Wallace's line and evolutionary theory is explored here. Contemporary descriptions of faunal regions referred vaguely to the area then known as the East Indian Archipelago as the place where the Asian and Australian biotas met. Wallace and Charles Darwin each struggled with the precise location of the boundary between these two faunal regions at a critical stage in the development of his evolutionary theory. Mapping the boundary between the Asian and Australian faunas served multiple functions: it was a method for organizing and communicating faunistic data, a potential device for predicting range limits of other species, a modern method of argumentation and representation that was familiar to their peers, and, most important, a method of analysis that tested positively with evolutionary hypotheses. In more general terms, maps of faunal regions served as instruments both of thought and of persuasion.

While I shall not ignore the relationship of Wallace's and Darwin's maps to those of other naturalists, or the role of maps as a means of biogeographic argumentation, my emphasis here is on maps as instruments of thought, as visual and flexible components of their concep-

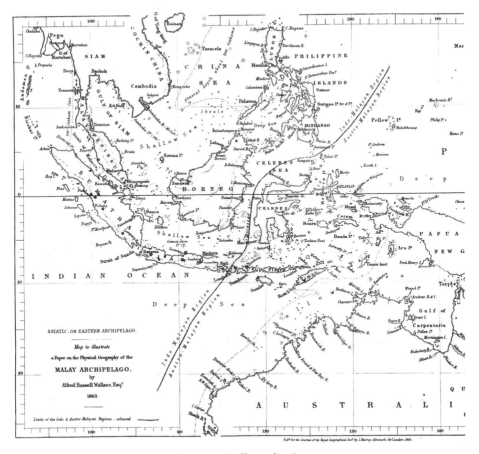

3.I A portion of the first map showing "Wallace's line"
(published in the *Proceedings of the Royal Geographical Society,* in 1863).

tual framework. From this vantage point one can examine how
Darwin and Wallace used both actual and mental maps in an effort to
find order in a mass of complex biogeographical data. I emphasize
actual *and mental* maps to encompass not only the maps each made
or used, but the map-based images that became elements of their
thought.[4]

Map-based observations of, for example, discontinuous distributions or altitudinal zonations were frequently expressed in words as
well as pictures. By studying different or sequential versions of such
map-based conceptual frameworks, one can readily identify changes
in map meaning. Maps of faunal regions in the pre-Darwinian period
generally portrayed the static distribution of plants and animals in

terms of "nations" with stable boundaries. Darwin's and Wallace's mental and actual maps showed the same stable regions, but theirs outlined the result of historical and evolutionary transmutation of the organisms themselves, not only the result of past movements of organisms. If it is fair to say that Wallace's line came to represent not only geographical boundaries of existing species but their history as well, then we must articulate how the map came to have this meaning. In other words, if both evolutionary and nonevolutionary faunal regions can be portrayed by the same (or similar) maps, then how can we speak about what the maps mean?

Two issues about visual geographical representations are raised here. The first is the capacity of a map to look the same but change in meaning over time, from one map-maker to another, or from one map-user to the next. The second issue, a corollary of the first, is the notion that the meaning of a map resides not only in the map, but in relation to the written text of which it is a part and the larger historical context in which it appears. Both of these issues—the potential for historical change in meaning and the relation of the map to the text—are largely unexplored in the burgeoning body of literature devoted to visual representation in the history of science.[5]

In the introduction to his classic "The Emergence of a Visual Language for Geological Science," Martin Rudwick laments the neglect of illustration by historians, attributing it to "the lack of any strong intellectual tradition in which visual modes of communication are accepted as *essential for the historical analysis and understanding of scientific knowledge.*"[6] In the last twenty-five years or so, numerous historians have established the central, constitutive (as opposed to "merely illustrative") role of mapping in the emergence and practice of geology.[7]

Rudwick identified the striking discrepancy between the pervasive use of diverse visual tools in geological practice and their meager use in historical work. Not only is the use of maps in modern geology commonplace, but it is considered natural and unproblematical. This discrepancy is even more true in biology as a whole, and evolutionary biology in particular, with the exception of illustrations of plant and animal specimens.[8] Mapping in biology never became as conscious or explicit a goal as it did in geology, and biogeography never stabilized into a highly integrated or self-contained discipline. Thus, the nature of mapping in biology remains far more tacit than it does in geology, with the consequence that both the evidence for, and arguments about, "bio-cartography" are subtler. This does not render maps of biological themes any less essential to historical understanding than geological maps or visual representations in other physical sciences, but it partly explains why it has taken longer to establish connections between the history of pictorial representation and the history of evolutionary thought.

Recent work in cartography and geography demonstrates a new-found concern with manifold levels of map meaning, the rhetorical power of maps, and mapping as a mode of knowing.[9] Although this literature informs the present work, the former is not concerned with how levels of map meaning participate in the development of particular sciences.

In reconstructing the story of Wallace's line, it is my purpose to examine part of a larger issue, the complex role of visual representation in the history of evolutionary biology. The legacy of the line, its numerous map progeny and their role in shaping twentieth century biogeographical thought, is another, yet unwritten chapter in the history of evolutionary biogeography. Here I will simply try to demonstrate the integral relationship between mapping and Darwin's and Wallace's evolutionary understanding of the biogeography of the East Indian Archipelago. Because Darwin's work on the Asian/Australian boundary is difficult to date with precision, it cannot be implicated as clearly in specific theoretical formulations as can Wallace's work. Wallace's articles of 1855 and 1858 on evolutionary theory, his formulation of the faunal line, and his 1863 paper on the physical geography of the Malay Archipelago are fundamentally interrelated, conceptually and temporally. The mapping of biological distributions was not merely coincident with the formulation of these men's theories, nor did it play a simple causal role; it was a pictorial embodiment of evolutionary processes, part and parcel of the conceptual framework that produced the theory of evolution. Wallace's line used available cartographic techniques to forge evolutionary meaning onto the familiar geographical map; pictures of faunal ranges became traces or "outcrops" of faunal histories.

In order to place Darwin's and Wallace's use of faunal maps in perspective, I will briefly discuss the salient features of early nineteenth-century biological mapping and ideas about biological regions, both botanical and zoological. In the sections on Darwin and Wallace, only their work on zoological regions is analyzed.[10]

Regions and Maps

Natural historians in the late eighteenth and early nineteenth centuries increasingly focused on the description and explanation of plant and animal distribution.[11] Based on the groundwork laid by

Carolus Linnaeus and Georges de Buffon, geographical distribution became a new object of study, and diverse approaches developed to make sense out of a plethora of new information. One of these approaches, the regionalization of plant and animal distribution, became a compelling goal for a growing number of naturalists.

Biological regions formed the framework for Charles Lyell's discussion of geographical distribution in *The Principles of Geology*. His introductory comments to the first of three chapters devoted to geographical distribution are quoted below for their clear articulation of the importance of biogeography. The single most important element in his statements is the notion of regionalization. By this time, the 1830s, maps had become shared cultural images, and Lyell was able to refer to zoological and botanical regions without actually presenting a map:

> Next to determining the question of whether species have a real existence, the consideration of the laws which regulate their geographical distribution is a subject of primary importance to the geologist. . . .
>
> But the extent of this parceling out of the globe amongst different nations, as they have been termed, of plants and animals,—the universality of a phenomenon so extraordinary and unexpected, may be considered as one of the most interesting facts clearly established by the advance of modern science.[12]

Regionalization was considered a remarkable fact forming a paradigmatic basis for the study of geographical distribution. That different regions of the globe are inhabited by different organisms is partly explained by the environmental requirements of organisms. These factors, such as climate, moisture, and soil, define the station of a species (what we could call habitat). The problem that Lyell stressed is that the known facts of distribution could not be accounted for by a study of stations alone; he cited Alexander von Humboldt as among the first to perceive that similar climates do not have identical productions. In order to explain the distribution of species, what was then called "habitation"—that is, the areas or regions (rather than the kinds of environments) over which they are distributed—Lyell discussed a different set of factors, i.e., the history of dispersal and migration of organisms in changing environments.[13]

Although Lyell did not advance a single scheme of regions, he thought that Augustin de Candolle's system of twenty great botanical provinces provided a trustworthy prose description of the "lines of demarcation" of native areas and was not likely to be substantially altered by new evidence.[14] Implicit in his discussion of plant provinces was that the "lines of demarcation," the boundaries between the provinces, represented a barrier to migration and dispersal over time.

Faunal provinces came under a separate discussion; there was no mention of the possibility that plant and animal regions might be the same. Lyell's demarcations of zoological provinces were based on the distribution of mammals and were loosely extended to other groups of animals. He mentioned some ten different provinces, referred to in approximated geographical terms: for example, "The whole arctic region has become one of the provinces of the animal kingdom" or "New Holland is well known to contain a most singular and characteristic assemblage of mammiferous animals."[15] Lyell discussed birds, fish, reptiles, and marine organisms, all of which were known to differ from region to region, but he did not enumerate provinces.

Questions of species origin and species distribution were inextricably linked. Neither environmental requirements, nor present-day geographical habitation (range) alone could explain the distribution or the origin of species. One had to consider the co-development, as it were, of the earth and its productions. The notion of "nations" of plants or animals was paradigmatic in that it prescribed a set of questions regarding species origins and distribution, carrying with it the assumption that geographical boundaries between regions of existing organisms were also critical barriers to migration over time.

Following the masterful lead of Humboldt, many other naturalists discussed regional plant and animal geography at length. In Britain, for example, we might select James Cowles Prichard, known chiefly for his espousal of a quasi-evolutionary theory of human races; William Swainson, whose zoological works were widely read but only partly trusted; and Robert Chambers, whose *Vestiges of the Natural History of Creation* was scorned by scientists but was nonetheless a best seller.[16] Chambers' twelve-page essay on geographical distribution is among the earliest discussions of the importance of isolation for the maintenance of botanical and zoological provinces.[17] Prichard's treatment of the subject is similar in broad outline to that of Lyell, both authors borrowing generously from one another in the successive editions of their books. Prichard accepted de Candolle's twenty floristic provinces and described his own division of the earth into seven zoological provinces, based on the aggregation of endemic species.[18] Among these, he named Australia, the Indian Archipelago, and Polynesia (with its center in New Guinea) each a separate province, but he did not precisely describe the boundaries between them.

The work of these authors reflects both the prevalence of a regional approach to geographical distribution and the substantial range of theoretical orientation within this approach from about 1805 to 1850. Regions were essential to creationist and evolutionist alike. When Darwin and Wallace read these overviews of biological regions, the two became well informed of the basic problem: physically similar distant areas have different characteristic species; therefore, the history of species and the history of the earth must be studied together in order to explain observed patterns of distribution. Lyell's emphasis led the way for Darwin's and Wallace's research, but his description of biological regions, with its emphasis on impassable barriers separating the major provinces, did not prepare them for the peculiar distribution of the mammals and birds of the East Indian Archipelago, where two widely different faunas are found in extreme proximity.

But this account of the regional approach to problems of geographical distribution does not present a complete picture of pre-Darwinian biogeography. The surge in mapping activities is one of the characteristic features of early nineteenth-century natural history.[19] With mapping, the notion of biological distribution became concrete. The cartographic representation of the range of a plant, animal, plant assemblage, or faunal region employs distinct variables—color, shape, and area—that everyone can see. Sophisticated graphic representations of comparative social, economic, and political characteristics of states coincided with new methods in the study of the natural environment.[20] There was a remarkable expansion of science into the public domain—with museums, displays of experiments and inventions, and "coffee table" narratives of scientific exploration in exotic countries all playing a part in the popularization and visualization of scientific knowledge. The use of maps in popular as well as scientific documents was a pervasive and ubiquitous vehicle for communicating scientific values in this "age of science."[21] Distribution maps displaying spatial variations of an extensive range of objects, from star clusters and comets to minerals and forests, from occurrences of cholera to the correlation of drunkenness to income, formed a characteristic feature of the visual culture.[22]

The iconography of this period is replete with cartographic "firsts" from virtually all fields of study, noteworthy among which was Eberhardt von Zimmermann's 1777 map of the distribution of mammals.[23] Zimmermann indicated major regions by outlining them in color; the map also portrayed range limits of numerous species. While naturalists in Germany, England, and France followed up the theme of animal and plant regions, few maps of zoological regions were made after Zimmermann's until the mid-nineteenth century. But other approaches to botanical distribution resulted in different kinds of maps, such as the map of botanical regions of France by de Candolle, Humboldt's map of the distribution of plant assemblages according to altitude, and the twelve maps of plant distribution by the Danish botanist J. F. Schouw, whose work became known through summaries published in English journals.[24] The legacy of these authors is their diverse approaches to mapping and the novel terminology they developed to describe biogeographical concepts. Thus, not only did regions become part of the discourse of natural history, but new terms, such as *isotherms, life zones, plant community, vegetation assemblage,* and *species range,* gave additional evidence of the increasing role of map-based concepts in the study of geographical distribution.

The new role for cartographic representation in the study of plant and animal distributions was consolidated in the second quarter of the nineteenth century. New cartographic symbols continued to co-evolve with novel concepts; mapping was now a recognized tool in the visual technology of natural history. A new genre of atlas, the physical atlas, contained only distribution maps, excluding political or "geographical" maps. Alexander K. Johnston's *Atlas of Physical Phenomena* was the most popular of these in England and was well known to both Darwin and Wallace.[25] It appeared in various editions from 1846 to 1856; a typical edition included twenty-four distribution maps, seven of which portrayed various themes of botanical and zoological geography.

The zoogeography of the East Indian Archipelago found its way onto a map in the first German physical atlas, Heinrich Berghaus' *Physikalisher Atlas* (figure 3.2). The map was made by Berghaus in his effort to summarize and display the findings of the Dutch naturalist Saloman Müller. Berghaus called the map, along with another on mammals of Austria, "Mammalian Monographs."[26] Darwin, who saw some of the sheets of the Berghaus atlas as they were published, may well have seen the map; it is unlikely that Wallace was aware of it.

In sum, by the time Darwin and Wallace began to study geographical distribution, various schemes for plant and animal regions had been described verbally but few had been mapped, the exceptions being the maps of Zimmermann for mammalian regions and Schouw for botanical regions. Detailed information about animal distributions was accumulating rapidly. Why did Darwin and Wallace synthesize this knowledge by mapping zoological regions? Maps were clearly a necessary practical tool for traveling naturalists; what was their value as tools of biogeographical thought?

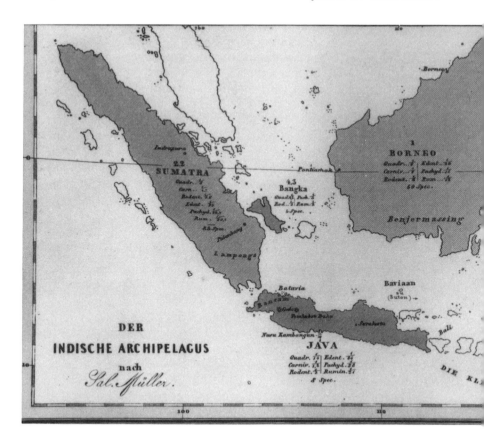

Darwin and the East Indian Archipelago

In the course of his extensive writing and research in the decade following the voyage of the *Beagle* (1831–1836), Darwin confronted the complex distribution patterns of East Indian mammals. His published and unpublished writings reveal that the boundary between the Asian and Australian faunal regions was a focal point in his struggle to account for the regionality of organisms according to his developing theory of common descent. He attempted to delineate the location of this faunal boundary using tables, nautical charts, and maps as well as verbal descriptions of species locations. From an evolutionary point of view, a naturalist would not expect an archipelago of physically similar islands to be populated with strikingly different animals on its western and eastern ends. Darwin would find the solution to this problem in the realization that deep water (rather than a

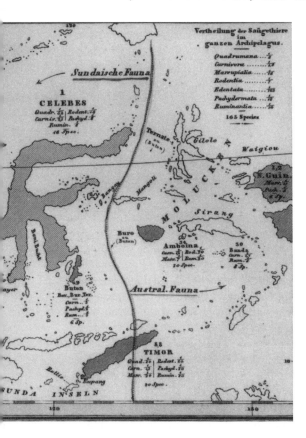

3.2 Heinrich Berghaus'
"Mammalian Mono-
graphs" of the East Indian
Archipelago, 1845 (from
the *Physikalischer Atlas*,
Section 6, Animal
Geography Plate No. 6).

large expanse) between certain islands could account for the observed differences in the fauna of the East Indian Archipelago.

Darwin employed the idea of regions as a conceptual scaffolding for a complex combination of geological, biological, and geographical phenomena. He explicitly and repeatedly tried to account for the regionalization of animals, from the early entries in his first transmutation notebook ("I think a very strong case might be made out of world before zoological regions"), to notes for *Natural Selection,* and through the chapters on geographical distribution in the *Origin of Species.*[27] In his approach to biogeography, regional, map-based thinking appears as an instrument of thought rather than an end in itself: Darwin's goal was to account for the accepted "fact" of zoological regions in accordance with his evolutionary theory, not to define faunal boundaries. But there was an important fact missing—the location of the boundary between the Asian and Australian faunas in an area where there was no single obvious barrier to migration. Darwin eventually found the relationships that made sense of the phenomena—elevation and subsidence, formation of new species, the importance of barriers to mammalian distribution, and depth of water—that recur in conjunction with his efforts to locate this regional dividing line.

In spite of the many changes and refinements during the long gestation of his theory of evolution by natural selection, there is a stability in Darwin's maplike frame of reference for the study of patterns of animal geography. This backdrop, the geographical base map of his biogeography, grew out of his extensive experiences with maps on the journey of the *Beagle,* including the numerous geological profiles and maps he made himself. Most important, he carefully compiled a detailed world map of the distribution of coral reefs, which played a central role in *The Structure and Distribution of Coral Reefs.*[28] His manuscripts and published work provide substantial evidence that he also relied on published exploration and distribution maps, as well as on his own mental maps, during many phases in the development of his theories.[29]

Darwin's enduring interest in geographical distribution can be categorized into three loosely defined stages: the notebooks and unbound notes of the late 1830s, his unpublished essays on species from the 1840s, and the manuscripts and books of the 1850s, including *On the Origin of Species.*[30] During the post-*Beagle* decade, Darwin became extremely well versed in contemporary thought on geographical distribution through his voracious reading of natural history journals and books, travel reports, and exploration surveys, and his voluminous correspondence and professional relationships with leading naturalists of the day. Darwin's collection of information and ideas about the occurrence and ranges of animals in the East Indian Archipelago is well documented in these notebooks and loose notes.[31] He was concerned with the areal extent of species ranges, with ascribing animals to the Asian or Australian fauna, and with the pattern of species variation among the islands, drawing analogies to the pattern he saw in the Galapagos. Darwin sought information about animal distribution in the East Indian Archipelago from a wealth of sources, most notably James Horsburgh's *India Directory,* René Lesson and Prosper Garnot's *Zoologie* from the voyage of the *Coquille,* Jean-René Quoy and Paul Gaimard's *Zoologie* from the voyage of the *Astrolabe,* Jacques de Labillardière's account of the voyage of *La Pérouse,* Coenraad Temminck's contribution to the *Fauna Japonica* by Phillip von Sie-

bold, and Sir George Windsor Earl's book *The Eastern Seas*.[32] Many
of these works were consulted in conjunction with his research on
coral reefs, which occupied much of his time from late 1838 until
early 1842.[33]

At an early stage in his evolutionary theory, Darwin imagined that
isolation, brought about by subsidence of once-continuous land, was
critical in differentiating the three forms of rhinoceros (Indian, Jav-
anese, and Sumatran). He claimed that if Sumatra and Java were to be
reunited by continued elevation of the islands, the two species would
remain distinct. His research on the Malay region combined one of
his major geological preoccupations, island elevation and subsidence,
with his interest in the distribution of mammals. Because mammals
have more difficulty in crossing presumably permanent oceanic barriers than do birds or insects, their island distribution took on greater
importance. The mammal-rich East Indian Archipelago, in contrast
with the mammal-poor Galapagos Islands, provided a unique setting
for mammalian evolution.[34] An example of the confluence of Darwin's interest in species distribution and in elevation and subsidence is
found in Notebook B, the first of his transmutation notebooks, begun
in the second half of 1837. Although somewhat cryptic, the following
quotations show Darwin speculating about speciation as a result of
repeated elevation and subsidence of islands in the East Indian Archipelago:

> The motion of the earth must be excessive up & down.—Elephants in
> Ceylon—East Indian archipelago.
>
> . . . Species formed by subsidence. Java & Sumatra. Rhinoceros. Elevate &
> join keep distinct. two species made. elevation and subsidence continually
> forming species.—
>
> . . . When breaking up (the primeval.) continent. Indian Rhinoceros. Java
> & Sumatra ones all different.—Join Sumatra & Java together, by eleva-
> tions now in Progress, & you will have two.[35]

An interesting example of Darwin's notes on these matters is a table
he drew comparing the mammalian fauna of Borneo, Sumatra, Java,
Malacca, and other small isles (figure 3.3; see figure 3.4 to locate
these places). The table is an undated entry among Darwin's portfolio
"scraps"; it was almost certainly made in conjunction with his reading of Temminck's *Coup-d'oeil sur la faune des Iles de la Sonde et
l'empire du Japon* in 1839,[36] and illustrates his strong interest in variations among closely related island species. He noted whether a species was unique (endemic) to an island, and whether or not it had a

Borneo	Sumatra	Java	Malacca	Small isles near these great ones
p.6 { Orang Outang Semnopithecus nasique Gibbon NS Felis macrocelis Tupaia 2 spe. NS Semnopithecus 2 spec Ursus malaianus Felis 2 spec NS Hypsiprimnus ursinus	Orang Outang p.6	—0—		Cervus Kuhlii proper to smaller isles of Bassian near Java, but never found on Java. p.11
	Ursus	— 0	Ursus malaianus	Muka Kambing (p.12) has a Pteromys 1/3 larger than P. nitratus so common in Java. – it is found on some other isd's but never in Java.
	Elephant Tapir	0 0	Elephant 0	
	Rhinoceros bicorna p. 8	1 spec Rhinoceros unicorna p. 8	Rhinoceros unicor. 2 Spe p8	
	Bos arni	Bos banting	Bos sylhetanus – D'???ii Coch??i ?????	
	Cervus russa p. 80 — hippelaphus 90	Cervus nipa 0		
	Sus – 3' spec. ? –	Sus verrucosus – vittatus	Sus verrucosus	
	0 ——— 0 ——— 0 ——— 0 ——— yet there are many species of these 2 genera p 9	Hylobates leuciscus Semnopth: mitratus (p. 9 mauris auratus or pyrrhus		
	Galeopth: marmoratus	— 0 —		
	— 0 —	Galeopithecus variegatum	— — —	Found in all these isd's even to Amboina or Timor
	Hylogales or Claddeus			

3.3 A transcription of Darwin's table of mammals of the Malay Archipelago (from DAR 205.3.211).

close relative on another island. On the same sheet Darwin made some notes of a more speculative nature, pointing to the ever-present theoretical problem of common descent. In searching for a solution to the relation of mammalian species in the archipelago, he looked to the depth of water between islands and the possibility of former land connections between them, penciling in the phrase "relation of character of quadrupeds to soundings."[37]

Darwin struggled with the role of elevation and subsidence in the formation of new species, at times finding subsidence or elevation, or both, the critical factor in favoring speciation. In the course of his research for *The Structure and Distribution of Coral Reefs,* Darwin found evidence of recent elevation in the East Indian Archipelago and came to the conclusion that changes in land elevation over time were the key factor in speciation.[38] His interest in elevation and subsidence led Darwin to focus on the depth of water between adjacent islands in the region. He was concerned with soundings because he inferred (correctly) that shallow depths between islands meant that they had been united in the not-too-distant past. Shallow water indicated a recent land connection and close biological affinities, deep water a far more ancient barrier to migration and more distant biological relationships.

Elevation and subsidence were of fundamental importance in explaining the diversity of species because Darwin's theory at this time still required new physical conditions to stimulate variations within a species; he did not yet see the tendency to vary as an inherent (genetic) trait in wild species. Elevation and subsidence were also important in favoring or impeding migration: subsidence would isolate individuals, elevation would allow them to vary as they expanded their ranges into newly emerged land, and repeated oscillations would favor the creation of a great number of new species. His theory at this stage was based on his highly visual geological view of the world; it was largely dependent upon isolation for the production of new species.[39]

As part of his research on elevation, Darwin studied a Dutch chart of the region around Java that listed measurements of soundings between the islands of the archipelago.[40] On this list, made as early as 1839, he noted deep water in several places, including on the west coast of Celebes (between Celebes and Borneo), and between Gilolo and Celebes, Bali and Lombock, Ceram and New Guinea, and Gilolo and the Philippine Islands. Remarkably, three of these locations are on the line Wallace later drew dividing the Asian and Australian biotic regions. Darwin's conclusions from these charts, tables, and musings on the relation of water depth to mammalian distribution were roughly drawn together in his two essays on species.

All of the above-mentioned threads woven into Darwin's theoretical framework appear in these essays (known as the pencil sketch of 1842 and the essay of 1844). Again we find the major faunal regions, depth of water, and elevation and subsidence as central themes.[41] Here the story of three closely related oriental species of rhinoceros, descendants of their more distant African ancestor, provided one of his strongest arguments in the summary of his theory of common descent. In this discussion he sarcastically refuted Chambers' evolutionary hypothesis, which was based on inorganic origins of species. Darwin wrote: "Shall we then allow that the three distinct species of Rhinoceros which separately inhabit Java and Sumatra and the neigh-

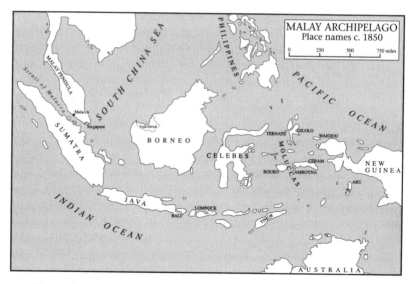

3.4 The Malay Archipelago, ca. 1850.

boring mainland of Malacca were created, male and female, out of the inorganic materials of these countries?"[42]

The regionalization of mammalian distribution provided a conceptual and at the same time visual framework for Darwin's first attempts at presenting his theory. In both of these essays Darwin began his discussion of geographical distribution with the concept of mammalian regions. He suggested initially that there were three or four main regions, with the East Indian Archipelago forming a single region along with North America, Europe, and Asia. In the essay of 1844, Darwin discusses two-, three-, and four-fold divisions of the globe before settling on a scheme of five regions: Australia and New Guinea, South America, North America and Eurasia, Madagascar, and Africa.[43]

In the essay of 1844, Darwin revealed one of his cognitive schemes by "placing" his five regions on a base map. "Inspection of a map of the world at once shows that the five divisions, separated according to the greatest amount of difference in the mammifers inhabiting them, are likewise those most widely separated from each other by barriers which mammifers cannot pass."[44] With either an actual or a mental map of the world before him, he overlaid an image of the regional distributions of mammals and then saw the congruence of the boundaries of the regions and major barriers to migration of mammals. As his theory began to take shape, he tested the zoological regions according to his ideas of dispersal from a single point of origin and common descent. Darwin synthesized all of the geological and biological patterns and processes he believed were involved, and then saw that the regions were in fact following an expected pattern.

Although Darwin's notes display some uncertainty as to the exact location of the line between the Eurasian and Australian regions, he had, by 1844, settled on the idea of deep water as forming the critical boundary. He concluded that "New Guinea and its adjoining islets are cut off from the other East Indian islands by deep water."[45]

In the 1844 essay Darwin pointed to deep water separating the Australian region from the other East Indian islands. He did not, however, specifically mention Celebes. The placement of Celebes in one or the other region would concern Darwin for some time, and several of his loose notes from the 1840s and 1850s dealt with affinities of the Celebes fauna and with the connection of Celebes with New Guinea and nearby smaller islands.[46] In the following year he read Earl's article "On the Physical Structure and Arrangement of the Islands in the Indian Archipelago" and began to rely on Earl and other authorities for their placement of Celebes.[47]

Earl grouped most of the islands separated by shallow depths into either the Great Asiatic or the Great Australian Bank. Those islands separated by deeper channels he took to be younger and of volcanic origin. The map accompanying the article, which was noted by Darwin, shows the banks as stippled areas (figure 3.5). Earl found these geographic results significant in that "all the countries lying upon these banks partake of the character of the continents to which they are attached"; he offered evidence from plant, animal, and mineral distributions.[48]

Some years later, in a letter to Wallace, Darwin referred to soundings in the archipelago, indicating how important Earl's remarks had been to him. "Are you aware that Mr. W. Earl published years ago the view of distribution of animals in the Malay Archipelago in relation to the depth of the sea between the islands? I was much struck with this, and have been in the habit of noting down all facts on distribution in the Archipelago and elsewhere in this relation."[49] It seems that Earl's article, rather than his own research, became a firm reference point for this correlation, and Darwin would later point to "the relation between soundings and distribution," invoking Earl's name.

Darwin's lasting insight into mammalian distribution in the East Indian Archipelago was his (and Earl's) idea of relating depth of water to degree of biological affinity. The record of soundings was a shorthand for a history of repeated elevation, subsidence, and changes of sea level. "The distribution of mammals with relation to soundings" is a phrase found repeatedly in Darwin's drafts from the mid 1850s

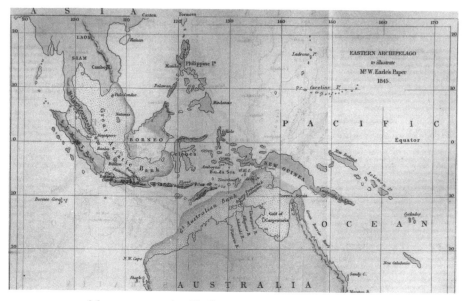

3.5 Map accompanying Sir George
Windsor Earl(e)'s article, "On the Structure and
Arrangement of the Islands in the Indian
Archipelago" (published in the *Journal of the
Royal Geographical Society* in 1845).

for his longer book on evolution, *Natural Selection*.[50] By this time, the
phrase seems to have solidified in his mind, its significance being that
water depth, rather than visible barriers to migration, could in fact
account for the known patterns of mammalian distribution; his theory of common descent from a single pair of ancestors was thereby
sustainable.

By the time Darwin wrote the *Natural Selection* manuscript and the
Origin of Species itself, zoological regions were not of importance as
areas per se; it was the barriers between them that were critical to his
argument on geographical distribution. He noted for the first time in
print that the region comprising Australia, New Guinea, and its
adjoining islets was separated from the islands of the East Indian
Archipelago and the rest of the Eurasian region by deep water. He
referred to the deep ocean near Celebes as the boundary between
these major faunal regions:

> . . . there is also a relation, to a certain extent independent of distance,
> between the depth of the sea separating an island from the neighbouring

mainland, and the presence in both of the same mammiferous species or of allied species in a more or less modified condition. Mr. Windsor Earl has made some striking observations on this head in regard to the great Malay Archipelago, which is traversed near Celebes by a space of deep ocean; and this space separates two widely distinct mammalian faunas. On either side the islands are situated on moderately deep submarine banks and they are inhabited by closely allied or identical quadrupeds.[51]

Zoological regions were a necessary step in the development of Darwin's theory. Although he used the concept and a map image of mammalian regions in the early formulation of his argument for common descent and continued to be interested in regional schemes, the regions themselves faded from his writing after the 1850s.[52] He became more interested in the process of natural selection, in the origin of adaptations, and in explaining the evolutionary significance of certain distributional patterns, such as disjunct alpine distributions, than in the overall geographic regional patterns that resulted.

Wallace Draws the Line

Even before he set on his journey in the Amazon (1848–1852), Wallace wrote to his friend Henry Walter Bates that his principal interest was in resolving the problem of the origin of species through detailed study of his favorite subject, "the variations, arrangements, distribution, etc., of species."[53] Knowledge of animal distribution was a major goal of his Amazonian research, and his publications from this journey clearly demonstrate his emphatic concern with detailed and accurate geographical information.[54] In 1854, when he began his extensive travels in the East Indian Archipelago, Wallace was equipped with an awareness of contemporary views on geographical distribution, as well as with firsthand knowledge of the practical difficulties of field work. In the course of the eight years he spent in the Malay Archipelago (1854–1862), he published some thirty-eight papers and letters in British natural history journals, including the historic sketch of his theory of evolution by natural selection that induced Darwin to get his own theory into print quickly.[55]

Small and large fragments representing Wallace's extraordinary intellectual activity in the course of his Malay travels are extant in two field notebooks, four journals, and two species registers.[56] Wallace traveled about 14,000 miles within the archipelago, collected well over 100,000 specimens, and persevered in his speculations and theories in spite of being criticized for doing so instead of just collecting facts.[57] His correspondence with Bates (his companion in South

America), his English friend George Silk, his agent Samuel Stevens, Charles Darwin, and others, along with his publications in British natural history journals, makes this a scientifically well-documented period of his life.

For Wallace, the significance of the geographical patterns that he observed, both local and global, was in their relation to his views on the origin of species. In this retelling of the genesis of Wallace's line from 1855 to 1863, two methodological themes are paramount. The first is his combination of features of physical geography with species change, a continuation of the kind of reconstruction of species origins and earth history he sought in his Amazonian research. The use of maps constitutes the second facet of his approach. Maps served Wallace as a conceptual framework, a metaphor, and a tool for synthesizing and communicating his results—they were the mental and actual space on which the processes of biological, geological, and geographical change formed a comprehensible pattern.[58]

The first public announcement of Wallace's evolutionary hypothesis was the so-called Sarawak paper, published in 1855: "On the Law Which Has Regulated the Introduction of New Species."[59] The article, also known as the "law" paper, has been carefully analyzed in relation to Wallace's zoological observations by several historians;[60] only a few points relevant to his understanding of faunal regions need be made here. Wallace recognized the underlying importance of geographical and geological proximity of closely allied species for the problem of species origins. The propositions of his argument, listed as ten main facts of organic geography and geology, were generalizations of known patterns of biological distribution. Wallace's argument about distributions in geographical space and geological time begins with large groups (as in the first excerpt below) and ends with species (the last excerpt below). The numbers Wallace assigned to the propositions are included:

> 1. Large groups, such as classes and orders, are generally spread over the whole earth, while smaller ones, such as families and genera, are frequently confined to one portion, often to a very limited district. . . .

> 3. When a group is confined to one district, and is rich in species, it is almost invariably the case that the most closely allied species are found in the same locality or in closely adjoining localities, and that therefore the natural sequence of the species by affinity is also geographical. . . .

> 6. Most of the larger and some small groups extend through several geological periods. . . .

9. As generally in geography no species or genus occurs in two very distant localities without being also found in intermediate places, so in geology the life of a species or genus has not been interrupted. In other words, no group or species has come into existence twice.[61]

The statements lead logically to his tenth and last proposition: "The following law may be deduced from these facts:—*Every species has come into existence coincident both in space and time with a pre-existing closely allied species.*"[62] As can be seen in these excerpts, Wallace carefully avoided a direct confrontation of creation and transmutation theories, although the article is rife with implications of evolutionary relationships. The thread that holds Wallace's law together is proximity: close phylogenetic affinity (Wallace's pre-existing closely allied species) corresponds to proximity in geographical space and in geological time.

In the same paper, Wallace conjectured that the Galapagos Islands, an ancient volcanic group, had originally been populated by South American forms that had arrived there by winds and currents. The original species became extinct, being replaced by newly modified forms; Wallace's words—"differently modified prototypes were created"—left undefined the mechanism of creation.[63] But the high degree of endemism in the Galapagos and the faunal and floral alliances with South America were explained by the great antiquity of the islands and the "descent" of their inhabitants from those of the nearest continent.[64] Wallace compared these phenomena to patterns of faunal distribution he observed in the East Indian Archipelago. Among these islands, he hypothesized, a once-continuous fauna became disconnected by the isolating effects of volcanic activity, which separated formerly continuous land masses into islands. The effects of isolation were partial, with some species identical on neighboring islands and some closely allied but not identical. The numerous closely allied representative species on different islands reflected the substantial time that had elapsed since their separation. Wallace's explanation of the fauna of the western portion of the Malay Archipelago (Malacca, Java, Sumatra, and Borneo) took account of biological affinity, geographical proximity, and geological history.

The organic results we see in the very considerable number of species of animals common to some or all of these countries, while at the same time a number of closely allied representative species exist peculiar to each, showing that a considerable period has elapsed since their separation. The facts of geographical distribution and of geology may thus mutually explain each other in doubtful cases, should the principles here advocated be clearly established.[65]

In spite of Wallace's circumspect style of addressing the issue of common descent, his intended meaning is clearly implied by a passage in the final paragraph: his law "claims a superiority over previous hypotheses, on the ground that it not merely explains, but necessitates what exists."[66] What would be the necessity (or importance) of the "law" if species were the product of special creation? If Wallace did not believe that species evolved from one another, his law would be trivial. He later wrote that his law paper suggested the "when" and the "where" of evolution—that it could only occur through natural generation—but that the "how" remained unknown.[67]

In Wallace's notebook from this period we find an analogy that secures the notion that his understanding of the origins and distributions of organisms through space and time was in fact conceived of in map imagery: "System of Nature, compared to fragments of a dissected map—a picture or a mosaic—approximation of fragments shew that all gaps have been filled up."[68] What is interesting here is that the map, as a pictorial metaphor, served as a unifying framework for disparate bits of information about insect, bird, and mammalian forms at their respective locations. The conceptual gap (between affinities of closely related forms on different islands and the lack of affinity in species of geographically proximate islands) was closed by putting the pieces of the puzzle together as a map. Given that by this time Wallace believed in common descent, the map metaphor served as a means of combining evolutionary origins and distribution patterns in a single representation.

In the following year, 1856, Wallace visited Bali, Lombock, and Celebes, thus completing his first survey of the western islands of the archipelago. In traversing the narrow strait between Bali and Lombock (see fig. 3.4), he was impressed by dramatic changes in the distribution of birds; he wrote to Samuel Stevens, his agent in London, of the sharp discontinuity in the fauna of the archipelago:

> The Islands of Baly and Lombock, for instance, though of nearly the same size, of the same soil, aspect, elevation and climate, and within sight of each other, yet differ considerably in their productions, and, in fact, belong to two quite distinct zoological provinces.[69]

Immediately, this crucial portion of what would become Wallace's line (identified by Darwin in unpublished notes) caught Wallace's attention and remained a location of fundamental importance. In numerous subsequent descriptions of the boundary between the Malay and Australian faunal regions, Wallace expressed the significance of this faunal change by referring to a map. His frame of reference was a map that not only showed the proximity of Bali and Lombock, but the physical similarities of these islands as well.[70] He was also struck shortly thereafter by the absence in Celebes of entire genera and families characteristic of the major islands of the western portion of the archipelago, promptly reporting his findings, along with a disappointing assortment of birds, shells, and insects, to Stevens.[71]

The significance of these findings—that is, the absence of certain groups in Celebes and the distinctiveness of the avifaunas of Bali and Lombock—is best understood when viewed in relation to the assertions of Wallace's 1855 paper. All other things being equal, one would have expected the faunas of Bali and Lombock to have been similar (see above proposition 3). How can we understand his statement that these islands belonged to two distinct zoological provinces? We must assume that Wallace *saw* that the strait between these two islands had prevented the natural geographical sequence of closely related forms from developing.

He soon observed another piece of the Malayan faunal puzzle, on his extensive visit to the Aru Islands in 1857. Wallace reported on his observations of the natural history of the Aru Islands in a paper written during and after his six-month residence in the area.[72] He found what he considered to be an unusual degree of identity between the families, genera, and some species of birds and mammals of Aru and those of New Guinea, and similarities (but not identity) with those of Australia. Citing evidence from other regions, he argued that biological affinities between other similarly placed islands and continents (such as Ceylon in relation to India, or Sardinia in relation to Italy) were not as faunistically strong as those between Aru and New Guinea and Australia. Several species of marsupial mammals on the Aru Islands gave further evidence of a former connection with Australia.

At the same time, none of the families of birds and mammals characteristic of the western Malay Archipelago were found on Aru. In seeking the "full development of such interesting details," Wallace boldly contradicted previous hypotheses about zoogeographical relationships, specifically confronting what he saw as a fundamental contradiction in Lyell.[73] He claimed that Lyell's description of the extinction of entire faunas in response to large-scale changes in the earth's environment (e.g. volcanism and mountain building), followed by the resettlement of an entirely different set of species suited to the new physical environment, simply did not fit the observed pattern in the Malay Archipelago. On the basis of water depths, physical geography, and, most important, animal distributions, he postulated that the islands had once been part of New Guinea, which itself had been connected to Australia. Some of the information Wallace used to formulate his reconstruction was collected by other naturalists; he almost certainly had Earl's paper on the physical structure of the archipelago.[74] Wallace's resolution of the contradiction between Lyell's prediction and the observed faunas was to apply his own "law": if every new creation was closely allied to some species already existing in the same region, and if gradual extinction and introduction of new species were taken into consideration, then the faunal alliances between the Aru Islands and New Guinea and Australia would follow an expected pattern.

This extensive theorizing in what could have been a purely descriptive natural history of the Aru specimens sent to England demonstrates Wallace's need to seek explanations.[75] His hypotheses were built on the accrual of detailed studies of species distributions and the belief in the modification of species from pre-existing ones. Geographical relationships provided the crucial link between biological processes (the production of new species from existing ones) and geological processes (the separation of New Guinea from Australia and a more recent separation of the Aru Islands from New Guinea). In the case of the Aru fauna, as in his other initial researches, he tried to comprehend the system driving his "law." By combining the physical history of the islands with the history of their faunas, he perceived their regional alliances.

Wallace saw another part of the boundary line separating the two major faunal regions by January 1858, nearly halfway through his stay in the region. After traveling to Bali, Lombock, and Celebes, he wrote of the boundary; his clear description read as if he had seen a line on a map. This lucid account of "Wallace's line" occurs in a letter to his friend Bates from the island of Amboina, dated 4 January 1858.[76] Several phrases are identical with those in his paper on the Aru Islands and with others in his notebook, demonstrating unquestionably the gradual synthesis of his findings.

> In this archipelago there are two distinct faunas rigidly circumscribed, which differ as much as do those of Africa and South America, and more than those of Europe and North America; yet there is nothing on the map or on the face of the islands to mark their limits. The boundary line passes between islands closer together than others belonging to the same group. I believe the western part to be a separated portion of continental Asia, while the eastern is a fragmentary prolongation of a former west Pacific continent. In mammalia and birds the distinction is marked by genera,

families, and even orders confined to one region; in insects by a number of genera, and little groups of peculiar species, the families of insects having generally a very wide or universal distribution.[77]

What is most remarkable about this passage is its context. In the same letter, Wallace wrote that he was gratified by Darwin's agreement with his 1855 law paper, and he described both his own and Darwin's plans for a fuller explication of the theory. Immediately before the passage quoted above, in regard to the boundary line between the two faunas, Wallace wrote:

> Your collections and my own will furnish . . . material to illustrate and
> prove the universal applicability of the hypothesis. The connection between
> the succession of affinities and the geographical distribution of a
> group . . . has never yet been shown as we shall be able to show it.[78]

It is not a coincidence that less than two months after this, Wallace pieced together his famous feverish account of natural selection. Here is a clear connection between the faunal boundary line, Wallace's ideas about evolution (the succession of affinities), and his pivotal theoretical paper of 1858. Apparently, when Wallace wrote in January 1858 "the connection between the succession of affinities and the geographical distribution of a group," he was referring to his evolutionary insight into the phylogenetic relationship of closely allied Asian forms whose ancestry was distinctly different from that of the Australian forms in the eastern portion of the archipelago. Wallace's "law," his line, and his theory of evolution by natural selection were all pieces of the same puzzle and were essentially in place by February 1858.

After writing his natural selection paper, a more confident Wallace turned his attention to extending his biogeographical findings in an evolutionary framework. In a letter written in March 1859 to the journal *Ibis,* he described his views on patterns of distribution in response to the publication of Philip Sclater's paper on zoological provinces of the globe.[79] Sclater described verbally and diagrammatically six regions determined by bird distributions but did not delineate boundaries between the regions on a map. Sclater could not define precisely the boundary between the Indian and Australian faunas, naming only a few islands that could be allied to one or the other region with some certainty. Wallace's letter corrected and delimited Sclater's regional scheme and extended it to include the whole of the plant and animal kingdoms. He also gave a clear description of his line in presenting the limits of the Asian (i.e., Indian) faunal region:

"Its south-eastern limits I draw between the islands of Bali and Lombock, and between Celebes and Borneo, and the Moluccas and the
Philippines."[80]

He remarked that the boundary between the Indian and Australian
regions was most extraordinary and seemingly inexplicable, dividing
as it did an apparently homogeneous region into two provinces having less in common than any other two upon the earth. The key to
this "inexplicable" problem was to understand that the ancestry of
Asian forms was largely separate from that of Australian forms—
which, however, Wallace did not openly aver—and then to look at a
map and consider the number of groups in common for each pair of
islands; former land connections would then become clear.

With a solution to the problem of the boundary basically in hand,
Wallace elaborated on these ideas in an 1860 paper entitled "On the
Zoological Geography of the Malay Archipelago," considering in
greater detail the characteristics of the Australian and Asian faunal
regions.[81] Although he again agreed with Sclater's general scheme, he
sought to refine the boundaries of the two regions "and to call attention to some inferences of great general importance as regards the
study of the laws of organic distribution."[82] These inferences dealt
with vast changes in the surface of the earth and the hypothesis of
evolution. Wallace based his analysis on the presence or absence of a
variety of species, including insects, birds, and mammals. He compared the Indian and Australian faunal elements of the eastern and
western portions of the archipelago and defined a boundary line only
where the two regions are closest: "the Strait of Lombock (only 15
miles wide) marks the limits and abruptly separates two of the great
Zoological regions of the globe."[83]

In his efforts to extend the boundary line in a precise manner, Wallace found that the Philippine Islands and Celebes posed difficulties.
Later, in 1863, he placed the Philippines in the Indian region despite
the lack of some characteristic features, such as mammals. He
resolved this problem by assuming a more ancient separation from
the Asian continent for the Philippines than for the other eastern
Malayan islands. The situation was further confused in 1868, when
T. H. Huxley referred to "Wallace's Line" but drew a line passing to
the west of the Philippines.[84]

Celebes was far more difficult to interpret, because of its peculiar
mix of Asian and Australian animals and the presence of genera having little or no affinity with those of adjacent islands. This fact suggested that this island was more ancient than the others, but its
marked affinities with Africa made it particularly anomalous. Wallace

hypothesized that the Celebes group represented the eastern fragment of a former Indian Ocean continent, but he did not commit himself in 1860 as to which faunal region it belonged to, although he had done so in 1859 in the letter to *Ibis*, and would do so again in 1863, only to reverse his opinion much later.[85] The faunistic evidence from Celebes led him to conclude in later work that "it will perhaps ever remain a mere matter of opinion" whether it should be considered part of the Asian or Australian region, remarking that "there is no other example on the globe of an island so closely surrounded by other islands on every side, yet preserving such a marked individuality in its forms of life; while, as regards the special features which characterize its insects, it is, so far as yet known, absolutely unique."[86]

For Wallace, zoological regions reflected patterns of faunal similarity and dissimilarity because of the "fact" of evolution. Given common descent, the proximity of closely allied species could be of great utility in making inferences about geological history. Although his results were inextricably tied to his evolutionary perspective, Wallace did not mention natural selection, evolution, or his own or Darwin's theory in the 1860 article. He stated simply that those who viewed island productions as inexplicable or anomalous were wrong.

> We really require no speculative hypothesis, no new theory, to explain these phenomena; they are the logical results of well-known laws of nature. The regular and unceasing extinction of species, and their replacement by allied forms, is now no hypothesis, but an established fact, and it necessarily produces such peculiar fauna and flora in all but recently formed or newly disrupted islands, subject of course to more or less modification according to the facilities for the transmission of fresh species from adjacent continents.[87]

Shortly after his return to England in 1862, Wallace drew the map delineating his division of the Australian and Indian faunas. He presented the map (see figure 3.1) when he read his paper "On the Physical Geography of the Malay Archipelago" to the Royal Geographical Society in June 1863. After describing and delimiting the area, he considered the major geographic features of the archipelago—volcanism, vegetation, climate, bathymetry (water depths), and geological and zoological relations to Asia and Australia. Wallace drew together several lines of evidence in reconstructing the most likely evolutionary history of the region and its inhabitants. As in previous accounts, he called attention to the unusual fact that the striking disparity in the organisms of the two regions did not correspond to their physical or climatic features.

Following Lyell in citing contradictions to the old doctrine that animals and plants are directly dependent on the physical conditions of their environment, Wallace argued strongly that both biological and geological history are necessary to account for observed patterns in the geographical distribution of plants and animals. Just as geological and physical features provide clues to biological evolution, the evolutionary relationships and geographical distribution of animals provide essential clues to former land connections. On this point, however, we find in 1863 a shift from the reliance on major continental movements to a belief in the permanence of the major continental land masses.[88] This shift did not appreciably alter Wallace's reconstruction of past changes in the gradual fragmenting of land from Asia and Australia to form the islands of the East Indian Archipelago. The pro-permanence view provided solid ground for his subsequent treatises on geographical distribution and earned him the full support of Lyell and Darwin. According to Darwin, Wallace's 1863 paper epitomized "the whole theory of geographical distribution."[89]

Conclusion

Although the idea of faunal regions existed well before Darwin and Wallace came on the scene, it was Wallace's placement of his line *on a map* that forged evolutionary meaning onto the notion of regions. This meaning does not inhere solely in the line—the map has to be seen in the context of the text in which it appears. The same is true of Darwin's mental maps of faunal regions—they are part of a larger text. I have argued that Darwin and Wallace engaged in a strikingly similar process of evolutionary theorizing about the origins of East Indian fauna, leading to the delineation of a boundary line. Wallace's map served as a conceptual framework, as well as a means of argumentation and, when published, of persuasion.

The tenacious and controversial legacy of Wallace's line becomes clearer when its development is viewed in its close relation to the development of Darwin's and Wallace's evolutionary theories. The East Indian Archipelago is of interest both as a case study in the formulation of Darwin's theory and as an emblem of his sensitivity to the faunal complexities of a region that later became famous in Wallace's and subsequent zoogeographic analyses. Darwin described an approximate boundary between the two major faunal regions in the Malay Archipelago, anticipating one of the critical portions of Wallace's line between Bali and Lombock. The passages relating to the region in the *Origin of Species* make more sense when viewed against the background of his more extensive and earlier notes.

Wallace is less well known for his lifelong insistence on the necessity for precise species distribution maps than he is for his much-disputed line. Detailed knowledge of species distribution was the basis for Wallace's efforts to formulate a general scheme of faunal regions. In one image, Wallace's map redefined and unified the various notions of biological regions current in the first half of the nineteenth century, embodied the evolutionary history of the diverse biota of the East Indian Archipelago, and participated in a genre of visual representation extending into the contemporary culture.

Darwin's and Wallace's mental and actual maps were the table on which the evolutionary scheme was played out, comparable in importance to the geological time scale. The enduring program of drawing boundary lines is a concrete manifestation of the extent to which cartographic constructs provided a framework for the development of the two men's theories and for the subsequent development of evolutionary biogeography.

Notes

This chapter is reprinted with minor changes from *Isis* 84 (December 1993): 700–727. It is reproduced by permission of the University of Chicago Press (© 1993 by the History of Science Society, Inc.).

The research for this chapter was supported by a post-doctoral fellowship and a grant-in-aid from the American Council of Learned Societies. I thank David Kohn for pointing out the references to the East Indian Archipelago in Darwin's Notebooks, and Hal Cook, Faye Getz, Roy MacLeod, Lynn Nyhart, Fritz Rehbock, as well as the referees, for their generous comments on various drafts. I am grateful to Peter Gautrey, Underlibrarian at the University Library, for his help in correcting my transcriptions of Darwin's notes. The Syndics of Cambridge University Library have kindly granted permission to reproduce tables and excerpts from the Darwin manuscripts.

1   Alfred R. Wallace, "On the Physical Geography of the Malay Archipelago," *Journal of the Royal Geographical Society* 33 (1863): 217–234.

2   To my knowledge, Thomas Huxley coined the term "Wallace's Line" in his paper on gallinaceous birds, "On the Classification and Distribution of the Alectoromorphae and Heteromorphae," *Proceedings of the Zoological Society of London,* 1868: 294–319.

3   References to articles on Wallace's line can be found in Wilma George, "Wallace and His Line," in *Wallace's Line and Plate Tectonics,* ed. T. C. Whitmore (Oxford: Oxford University Clarendon Press, 1981), 3–8; Ernst Mayr, "Wallace's Line in the Light of Recent Zoogeographic Studies," *Quarterly Review of Biology* 19 (1944): 1–14; and George G. Simpson, "Too Many Lines: The Limits of the Oriental

and Australian Zoogeographic Regions," *Proceedings of the American Philosophical Society* 121 (1977): 107–120.

4   Major references to theories of mind or of cognition that describe the role of visual imagery are discussed in Jane Camerini, "Darwin, Wallace, and Maps" (PhD. dissertation, University of Wisconsin, 1987), 4–6. In recent years, interest in cognitive aspects of scientific practice has grown immensely; for references to this literature see David Gooding, *Experiment and the Making of Meaning* (Dordrecht: Kluwer, 1990) and Nancy J. Nersessian, "The Cognitive Sciences and the History of Science," Conference on Critical Problems and Research Frontiers, 30 Oct.–3 Nov. 1991, Madison, WI, pp. 92–115.

5   Peter Taylor and Ann Blum note, in their article "Pictorial Representation in Biology" (*Biology and Philosophy*, 6 [1991]: 125–134), that these two issues are insufficiently addressed. Other recent work relevant to visual representation in biology is found in Barbara Maria Stafford, *Voyage into Substance: Art, Science, Nature, and the Illustrated Travel Account, 1760–1840* (Cambridge: MIT Press, 1984); Bruno Latour and Steve Woolgar, *Laboratory Life: The Construction of Scientific Facts,* 2d ed. (Princeton: Princeton University Press, 1986); Londa Schiebinger, "Skeletons in the Closet: The First Illustrations of the Female Skeleton in Eighteenth-Century Anatomy," *Representations* 14 (1986): 42–82; Michael Lynch and Steve Woolgar, eds., *Representation and Scientific Practice* (Cambridge: MIT Press, 1990); and Greg Myers, *Writing Biology: Texts in the Social Construction of Scientific Knowledge* (Madison: University of Wisconsin Press, 1990). Work on visual representations in physics includes Samuel Y. Edgerton, Jr., "The Renaissance Development of the Scientific Illustration," in *Science and the Arts in the Renaissance,* ed. John W. Shirley and F. David Hoeniger (Cranbury, NJ: Associated University Presses, 1985), 168–197; Arthur I. Miller, *Imagery in Scientific Thought* (Cambridge: MIT Press, 1986); Gooding, *Experiment and the Making of Meaning;* William Ashworth, Jr., "The Scientific Revolution: The Problem of Visual Authority," Conference on Critical Problems and Research Frontiers, 30 Oct.–3 Nov. 1991, Madison, WI, pp. 326–348; Mary G. Winkler and Albert Van Helden, "Representing the Heavens: Galileo and Visual Astronomy," *Isis* 83 (1992):195–217. Visual representation in art history and critical theory is the subject of W. T. J. Mitchell, ed., *The Language of Images* (Chicago: University of Chicago Press, 1980); idem, *Iconology: Image, Text, Ideology* (Chicago: University of Chicago Press, 1986); *Picturing Power: Visual Depiction and Social Relations,* ed. Gordon Fyfe and John Law (London and New York: Routledge, 1988). Other recent works are cited in Jan Golinski, "The Theory of Practice and the Practice of Theory: Sociological Approaches in the History of Science," *Isis* 81 (1990): 492–505, on p. 498; and *Science as Practice and Culture,* ed. Andrew Pickering (Chicago: University of Chicago Press, 1992).

6   Martin J. S. Rudwick, "The Emergence of a Visual Language for Geo-
         logical Science 1760–1840," *History of Science* 14 (1976): 149–195,
         p. 149 (emphasis added).

7   See Rhoda Rappaport, "The Geological Atlas of Guettard, Lavoisier,
         and Monnet: Conflicting Views of the Nature of Geology," in *Toward
         a History of Geology,* ed. Cecil J. Schneer (Cambridge: MIT Press,
         1969), 272–287; Marcia Pointon, "Geology and Landscape Painting
         in Nineteenth-Century England," *British Society for the History of
         Science* 1 (1979): 84–108; Martin Rudwick, "Visual Language";
         idem, *The Great Devonian Controversy: The Shaping of Scientific
         Knowledge among Gentlemanly Specialists* (Chicago: University of
         Chicago Press, 1985); idem, *Scenes From Deep Time: Early Pictorial
         Representations of the Prehistoric World* (Chicago: University of
         Chicago Press, 1992); Gordon L. Herries Davies, *Sheets of Many
         Colours: The Mapping of Ireland's Rocks 1750–1890* (Dublin: Royal
         Dublin Society, 1983); James A. Secord, *Controversy in Victorian
         Geology: The Cambrian-Silurian Dispute* (Princeton: Princeton
         University Press, 1986); Homer E. Le Grand, "Is a Picture Worth
         a Thousand Experiments?" in *Experimental Inquiries: Historical,
         Philosophical and Social Studies of Experimentation in Science,* ed.
         H. E. Le Grand (Dordrecht: Kluwer, 1990), 241–271; Mark Hineline,
         "Beyond Mere Description: William Morris Davis, Block Diagrams,
         and Genetic Description," paper presented at the History of Science
         Society Annual Meeting, 30 Oct.–3 Nov. 1991, Madison, WI.

8   The most comprehensive references in this regard are Gavin D. R.
         Bridson and James J. White, *Plant, Animal and Anatomical Illustra-
         tion in Art and Science: A Bibliographical Guide from the 16th Cen-
         tury to the Present Day* (Winchester: St. Paul's Bibliographies, 1990)
         and Brian Ford, *Images of Science: A History of Scientific Illustration*
         (London and New York: The British Library and Oxford University
         Press, 1992). Also see the several volumes in I. B. Cohen's series
         Albums of Science (New York: Scribner); F. David Hoeniger, "How
         Plants and Animals Were Studied in the Mid-Sixteenth Century," and
         Philip Ritterbush, "The Organism as Symbol: An Innovation in Art,"
         in *Science and the Arts,* ed. Shirley and Hoeniger, 130–148, 149–167;
         Evelyn Hutchinson, "Zoological Iconography in the West after A.D.
         1200," *American Scientist* 66 (1978): 675–684; David Knight, *Zoo-
         logical Illustration: An Essay towards a History of Printed Zoological
         Pictures* (Kent, England, and Connecticut: Dawson and Archon
         Books, 1977); Knight's chapter on "Discourse in Pictures" in his book
         The Age of Science (Oxford and New York: Basil Blackwell, 1986),
         109–127; and most recently Ann S. Blum, *Picturing Nature: Ameri-
         can Nineteenth-Century Zoological Illustration* (Princeton: Princeton
         University Press, 1993).

9   Arthur H. Robinson and Barbara B. Petchenik, *The Nature of Maps*
         (Chicago: University of Chicago Press, 1976); Stafford, *Voyage into*

Substance; Dennis Wood and J. Fels, "Designs on Signs: Myth and Meaning in Maps," *Cartographica* 23 (1986): 54–103; J. Brian Harley and David Woodward, *The History of Cartography* (Chicago: University of Chicago Press, 1987), vol. 1, chap. 1; David Turnbull, *Maps Are Territories: Science as an Atlas* (Victoria, Australia: Deakin University Press, 1989); Harley, "Deconstructing the Map," *Cartographica* 26 (1989): 1–20, and "Cartography, Ethics and Social Theory," *Cartographica* 27 (1990): 1–23. Of interest, although not bearing directly on the present study, is Wilma George, *Animals and Maps* (Berkeley: University of California Press, 1969), which deals with the meaning of animal drawings on maps before 1800.

10   Darwin's interest in botanical geography is discussed in Janet Browne, *The Secular Ark: Studies in the History of Biogeography* (New Haven: Yale University Press, 1983). Wallace's work on the geography of human races is discussed by Martin Fichman, *Alfred Russel Wallace* (Boston: Twayne, 1981); references to and some excepts from Wallace's publications on human geography are found in Charles H. Smith, ed., *Alfred Russel Wallace: An Anthology of His Shorter Writings* (Oxford: Oxford University Press, 1991).

11   The long tradition of identifying plants and animals with particular places is discussed in Janet Browne, "C. R. Darwin and J. D. Hooker: Episodes in the History of Plant Geography, 1840–1860" (Ph.D. diss., University of London, 1978), chap. 3. Other works focusing on the history of biogeography include Browne, *Secular Ark;* Philip F. Rehbock, *The Philosophical Naturalists: Themes in Early Nineteenth Century British Biology* (Madison: University of Wisconsin Press, 1983); James Larson, "Not without a Plan: Geography and Natural History in the Late Eighteenth Century," *Journal of the History of Biology* 19 (1986): 447–488; and Gareth Nelson, "From Candolle to Croizat: Comments on the History of Biogeography," *Journal of the History of Biology,* 11 (1978): 269–305.

12   Charles Lyell, *The Principles of Geology,* 3 vols. (London: John Murray, 1830–33), 2: 66.

13   Lyell's discussion of the distinction between stations and habitations is explicitly based on his reading of the "luminous" essay of 1820 by the renowned botanist Augustin de Candolle. In explaining the distinction between stations (the locality where each species grows in reference to climate, soil, etc.) and habitations (the geographical range of species), Lyell complained that two terms have often been confused, and that it was important to realize that they express two distinct ideas. Ibid., 69.

14   Ibid., 71.

15   Ibid., 88.

16   Robert Chambers, *Vestiges of the Natural History of Creation* (Lon-

don: Churchill, 1844); J. C. Pritchard, *Researches into the Physical History of Mankind*, 3rd ed. (London: Sherwood, Gilbert and Piper, 1836); William Swainson, *A Treatise on the Geography and Classification of Animals* (Lardner's Cabinet Cyclopedia, vol. 2) (London: Longman Rees, 1835).

17   Chambers, *Vestiges*, 251–262.

18   Prichard, *Researches*, 32–33, 68–71.

19   The sharp increase in mapping activities in the early nineteenth century was considered a central characteristic of "Humboldtian science" by Susan F. Cannon in *Science in Culture: The Early Victorian Period* (New York: Dawson, 1978).

20   The quantification of biogeographical phenomena, such as the development of botanical arithmetic, is not independent of the development of statistical thinking and of political and moral statistics. Several recent books treat the history of statistics in the nineteenth century, including Theodore M. Porter, *The Rise of Statistical Thinking 1820–1900* (Princeton: Princeton University Press, 1986). The development of new methods in the presentation of statistical information is described in Arthur H. Robinson, *Early Thematic Mapping in the History of Cartography* (Chicago: University of Chicago Press, 1982); and in Edward R. Tufte, *The Visual Display of Quantitative Information* (Connecticut: Graphics Press, 1983).

21   The quotation marks acknowledge the title of David Knight's book on the scientific worldview in the nineteenth century, *The Age of Science*.

22   The term "visual culture" is attributed to Michael Baxandall in Svetlana Alpers, *The Art of Describing: Dutch Art in the Seventeenth Century* (Chicago: University of Chicago Press, 1983), xxv.

23   The map first appeared in Eberhardt A. W. von Zimmermann, *Specimen zoologiae geographicae, quadrupedum domocilia et migrationes sistens* (Leiden Batavorum, Theodorum Haak, 1777), and in a slightly altered form in Zimmermann, *Geographische Geschichte des Menschen und der Allgemein Verbreiteten Vierfüssigen Thiere* (Leipzig: Weygandschen, 1778–1783). An explanation of the map in German was published separately: Zimmermann, *Tabula Mundi Geographico-zoologicae Explicatio Brevis* (Leipzig: n.p., 1783). The burgeoning of thematic cartography during this period is described by Robinson in *Thematic Mapping*.

24   Augustin de Candolle and Jean B. A. P. M. de Lamarck, *Flore Française...*, 3rd ed. (Paris: Desray, 1805); Alexander von Humboldt and Aimé Bonpland, *Essai sur la Géographie des Plants* (Paris: Levrault, Schoell, 1805); Joachim F. Schouw, *Pflanzengeographischer Atlas zur Erläuterung von Schouws Grundzügen einer allgemeinen Pflanzengeographie* (Berlin: Reimer, 1823). Humboldt's maps are discussed in Thomas R. Detwyler, "Humboldt's *Essay on Plant Geogra-*

phy: Its Relevance Today," *Michigan Academician* 1 (nos. 3 and 4)
(1969):113–122; Camerini, "Maps," chap. 2; and Malcolm Nicolson,
"Alexander von Humboldt and the Geography of Vegetation," in
Romanticism and the Sciences, ed. Andrew Cunningham and Nicholas Jardine (Cambridge: Cambridge University Press, 1990), 169–185.

25   Darwin had already made use of the singly issued plates of the origi-
     nal German version of the atlas, Heinrich Berghaus, *Physikalisher
     Atlas* (Gotha: Justus Perthes, 1836–1848), in research for *The Struc-
     ture and Distribution of Coral Reefs. Being the First Part of the Geol-
     ogy of the Voyage of the "Beagle," under the Command of Capt.
     Fitzroy, R. N. during the Years 1832 to 1836* (London: Smith Elder,
     1842; reprinted Tucson: University of Arizona Press, 1984). Darwin
     made extensive notes on and references to several different editions of
     Alexander K. Johnston, *The Physical Atlas of Natural Phenomena*
     (Edinburgh and London, William Blackwood, 1848, 1850, 1856) in
     Darwin Archive (hereafter DAR), Manuscript Room, Cambridge Uni-
     versity Library, Cambridge, 72: 32–56; DAR 205.2.89; and *Charles
     Darwin's Natural Selection,* ed. Robert C. Stauffer (Cambridge: Cam-
     bridge University Press, 1975, paper, 1987), 55n1, 535, 539n3. The
     1850 edition of Johnston's *Physical Atlas* was in Wallace's personal
     library (now at the Linnean Society Library, London).

26   Berghaus, *Atlas,* 2: text p. 21 cited his source as the classic overview
     of the fauna of the East Indian Archipelago by Salomon Müller in the
     Annalen der Erdkunde, 1842, pt. 1 (March): 251–266; pt. 2 (April):
     289–333). A similar overview by Müller appeared the year after the
     map was printed: "Ueber den Charakter der Thierwelt auf den Inseln
     des Indisches Archipels," *Archiv für Naturgeschichte* 12 (1846): 109–
     128. The Berghaus Atlas and the plant and animal maps therein
     are discussed in Jane R. Camerini, "The Physical Atlas of Heinrich
     Berghaus: Distribution Maps as Scientific Knowledge," in *Non-
     Verbal Communication in the History of Science,* ed. R. Mazzolini
     (Florence: Olschki, 1993). Another Dutch student of the East Indian
     fauna was H. Zollinger, "Over het begtip enden omvang eener Flora
     Malesiana," *Natuurkundig Tidschrift voor Nederlandisch-Indie,* 13
     (1857): 293–322. There is no evidence that Lyell, Darwin, or Wallace
     was aware of either of these authors before 1863; Wallace cited
     Zollinger in Alfred R. Wallace, *The Malay Archipelago: The Land
     of the Orang-Utan and the Bird of Paradise* (1869; 6th ed., London:
     Macmillan, 1877), 202.

27   *Charles Darwin's Notebooks, 1836–1844,* ed. Paul. H. Barrett, Peter
     J. Gautrey, Sandra Herbert, David Kohn, and Sydney Smith (Ithaca:
     Cornell University Press and the British Museum [Natural History],
     1987), B.95; Darwin, *Natural Selection,* 584–585; DAR 205.2.89
     verso; and Charles Darwin, *On the Origin of Species by Means of
     Natural Selection* (London: John Murray, 1859; Penguin, 1968), 393
     (summary of chaps. 11 and 12).

28   Darwin made two compilation maps of his coral reef map, which
          hang in Down House; these are reproduced and discussed in Cam-
          erini, "Maps," 95–98. *The Structure and Distribution of Coral Reefs*
          is the first of Darwin's three volumes on his geological research from
          the *Beagle* voyage; the other volumes are *Geological Observations on
          the Volcanic Islands Visited during the Voyage of H.M.S. "Beagle,"
          Together with Some Brief Notices of the Geology of Australia and the
          Cape of Good Hope. Being the Second Part of the Geology of the
          Voyage of the "Beagle," under the Command of Capt. Fitzroy, R. N.
          during the years 1832 to 1836* (London: Smith Elder, 1844); and
          *Geological Observations on South America. Being the Third Part of
          the Geology of the Voyage of the "Beagle," under the Command of
          Capt. Fitzroy, R. N. during the Years 1832 to 1836* (London: Smith
          Elder, 1846). Darwin's numerous articles on his geological research
          are reproduced in *The Collected Papers of Charles Darwin,* ed. Paul
          H. Barrett (Chicago: University of Chicago Press, 1977).

29   Darwin refers to scores of maps in *The Structure and Distribution of
          Coral Reefs;* in addition to the profiles and maps published in the vol-
          umes on geology, two unpublished geological maps and numerous
          profiles are among his manuscripts in DAR 34.1, DAR 34.2, DAR
          39.2, DAR 41, and DAR 44. These maps are discussed in Camerini,
          "Maps," 72–90; and in each of the three contributions by James Sec-
          ord, Sandra Herbert, and Frank H. T. Rhodes to a special issue of *The
          British Journal for the History of Science,* 24 (1991), devoted to
          "Darwin and Geology." Notable exceptions to the traditional neglect
          of visual representation in Darwin's thought are Michael T. Ghiselin,
          The Triumph of the Darwinian Method (Berkeley: University of Cali-
          fornia Press, 1969), 13–24; and Howard E. Gruber, "Darwin's 'Tree
          of Nature' and Other Images of Wide Scope," in *On Aesthetics in Sci-
          ence,* ed. J. Wechsler (Cambridge: MIT Press, 1978), 121–140.

30   The present analysis is based primarily on Darwin's writings as found
          in *Darwin's Notebooks;* his essays of 1842 and 1844 in *Charles Dar-
          win and Alfred Russel Wallace: Evolution and Natural Selection,* ed.
          Sir Gavin De Beer (Cambridge: Cambridge University Press, 1958);
          his big book on species, *Natural Selection;* and three volumes of Dar-
          win's portfolio notes on geographic distribution bound in archival
          volumes DAR 205.2, 205.3, and 205.4. Darwin's interest in geo-
          graphical distribution is analyzed by Philip J. Darlington, Jr., "Dar-
          win and Zoogeography," *Proceedings of the American Philosophical
          Society* 103, no. 2 (1959): 307–319; Ghiselin, *Triumph of the Dar-
          winian Method,* 32–45; Alan R. Richardson, "Biogeography and the
          Genesis of Darwin's Ideas on Transmutation," *Journal of the History
          of Biology* 14 (1981):1–41; and Browne, *Secular Ark.*

31   Appendix I of Camerini, "Maps," has some forty references to the
          East Indian Archipelago in Darwin's notebooks and loose notes from
          before 1840.

32   James Horsburgh, *India Directory,* 4th ed., 2 vols. in one (London, 1836); René P. Lesson and Prosper Garnot, *Zoologie,* in Louis I. Duperrey, *Voyage autour du monde . . . sur la corvette de sa 'Majesté,' 'La Coquille' pendant les années 1822, 1823, 1824 et 1825,* 6 vols. (Paris, 1825–1830); Jean-René C. Quoy and Paul J. Gaimard, *Zoologie,* in J. S. C. Dumont d'Urville, *Voyage de la corvette 'l'Astrolabe' . . . pendant les années 1826–1827–1828–1829,* 14 vols. and atlas (Paris, 1830–1835); Jacques J. H. de Labillardière, *Relation du voyage à la recherche de 'La Pérouse' . . . pendant les années 1791, 1792, et pendant la 1ère et la 2ème année de la Republique française,* 2 vols. and atlas (Paris, 1800); Coenraad J. Temminck, *Discours preliminaire. Coup-d'oeil sur la faune des îles de la Sonde et de l'empire du Japon,* in Phillip F. von Siebold, *Fauna Japonica; . . . conjunctis studiis C. J. Temminck et H. Schlegel pro vertebratis, atque W. de Haan pro invertebratis elaborata,* 6 vols. in four (Leiden and Batavia, 1833–1850); and George W. Earl, *The Eastern Seas, or Voyages and Adventures in the Indian Archipelago, in 1832-33-34 . . .* (London: W. H. Allen, 1837).

33   Darwin had begun to theorize about coral reef formation while on the *Beagle.* See David R. Stoddart, "Coral Islands by Charles Darwin, with Introduction, Map and Remarks," *Atoll Research Bulletin* 88 (1962): 1–20; idem, "Darwin, Lyell, and the Geological Significance of Coral Reefs," *British Journal for the History of Science* 9 (1976): 199–218; and Frederick Burkhardt, "Darwin's Early Notes on Coral Reef Formation," *Earth Sciences History* 3 (1984): 160–163.

34   The Galapagos have one genus of indigenous rodents and one bat species.

35   See *Darwin's Notebooks,* B: 80, 82, and 241, for Darwin's additions and deletions to these entries.

36   DAR 205.3.211. The table is dated on the basis of an entry in Notebook E.170 which includes a note with a page reference to Temminck, *Discours preliminaire.* Darwin's table is drawn on the same large sheet of paper on which notes from Temminck were made. In the second column there is a page reference written alongside the small circles. Darwin's note here reads: "yet there are many species of these 2 genera p 9."

37   This portion of Darwin's notes reads: "Relation of character of quadrupeds to soundings is explicable when same species occurs on the opposite sides, as Britain & Sicily etc—but what relation a creationist.—but these obviously differing in this troubled region of the world studded with craters, in correction on my theory for they might formerly have been connected and the same parent species" DAR 205.3.209.

38   Proofs of recent elevation in the East Indian Archipelago are summarized in Darwin, *Coral Reefs,* 134–135.

39   Frank Sulloway, "Geographic Isolation in Darwin's Thinking: The
      Vicissitudes of a Crucial Idea," *Studies in the History of Biology* 3
      (1979): 23–65, treats the changing role of isolation in Darwin's think-
      ing, from the Notebooks of the late 1830s through later editions of
      the *Origin*.

40   DAR 205.3.59; watermark on paper is 1839. The chart he took notes
      from is very likely one he referred to in *Coral Reefs* (1842, 1984
      p.175): "In a Dutch MS. chart on a large scale of Java, which was
      brought from that island by Dr. Horsfield, who had the kindness to
      show it me at the India-House."

41   Dov Ospovot, *The Development of Darwin's Theory* (Cambridge:
      Cambridge University Press, 1981), treats in detail the development of
      Darwin's theories and emphasizes the geological basis of the essay of
      1844.

42   De Beer, *Darwin and Wallace*, 83, 249.

43   Ibid., 65, 169, 170.

44   Ibid., 171.

45   Ibid.

46   Notes on alliances of Celebes forms to other species are found in *Dar-
      win's Notebooks* C.13,14; DAR 205.2.112; DAR 205.3.179. Refer-
      ences to former land connections with Celebes are found in DAR
      205.2.112 (Celebes and Philippines); DAR 205.2.129 ("Crawford
      tells me . . . Earl has written on connection of the Bank of Borneo
      with Celebes," dated May 5); DAR 205.3.113 (Celebes and New
      Guinea, dated Aug. 1844); and DAR 205.3.182 (Celebes and New
      Guinea, dated Aug. 1856). When Darwin consulted *Johnston's Atlas*
      he noted that "Celebes is outlier (as far as soundings concerned) in
      map—Ceram and Timor being boundary to west,—& belongs to Aus-
      tralia" (in DAR 72.35; phrase in parentheses inserted by Darwin).
      Darwin's and Wallace's sensitivity to the significance of deep water as
      a barrier to migration and their attention to the difficulties of placing
      Celebes in one region or another are all the more interesting in light of
      recent findings of plate tectonics. See M. G. Audley-Charles, "Geolog-
      ical History of the Region of Wallace's Line"; and T. C. Whitmore,
      "Introduction," in *Plate Tectonics,* ed. Whitmore, 1–2; 24–36.

47   George Windsor Earl, *Eastern Seas;* and idem, "On the Physical
      Structure and Arrangement of the Islands in the Indian Archipelago,"
      Journal of the Royal Geographical Society 15 (1845):358–365. The
      spelling of Earl(e)'s names varies in his publications, and in Darwin's
      references to him. Darwin notes Earl's 1837 book in Notebook E.18
      and E.182; he refers to the 1845 article in DAR 205.2.50; DAR
      205.2.129; and DAR 205.3.153 (entry dated 1845). On Earl's map
      Celebes falls (almost) in the Asian bank, but is colored green, as are
      Borneo and New Guinea, to indicate volcanic land.

48   Earl, "Physical Structure," p. 359. According to Wallace, "On the

Physical Geography of the Malay Archipelago," *J. Royal Geog. Soc.*
33 (1863):217–234 (p. 10 of reprint), Earl believed that there had
been a former connection between Asia and Australia.

49   Letter, Darwin to Wallace, 9 August 1859, in James Marchant, ed.,
      Alfred Russel Wallace: Letters and Reminiscences (New York and
      London: Harper and Brothers, 1916), 114; and DAR 205.2.89.

50   The phrase is found in DAR 205.2.89; DAR 205.2.91 (in two places,
      see "On Barriers" in Stauffer, *Natural Selection,* 1987, p. 585 and
      585n); and DAR 205.3.171.

51   Darwin, *Origin* (Penguin, 1968 ed.), 383.

52   His ongoing interest is evidenced by an annotated clipping of an arti-
      cle from *Nature,* 30 March 1871, on a suggested new division on the
      earth into zoological regions (DAR 205.3.17).

53   Alfred R. Wallace, *My Life: A Record of Events and Opinions,* 2 vols.
      (London: Chapman and Hall, 1905), 1:257. The standard references
      on Wallace's life and work are: Marchant, *Alfred Russel Wallace;*
      Wilma George, *Biologist Philosopher: A Study of the Life and Writ-
      ings of Alfred Russel Wallace* (London: Abelard-Schuman, 1964);
      H. Lewis McKinney, *Wallace and Natural Selection* (New Haven: Yale
      University Press, 1972); Arnold C. Brackman, *A Delicate Arrange-
      ment* (New York: Times Books, 1980); Fichman, *Alfred Russel Wal-
      lace,* John L. Brooks, *Just Before the Origin: Alfred Russel Wallace's
      Theory of Evolution* (New York: Columbia University Press, 1984);
      and Charles H. Smith, *Alfred Russel Wallace: An Anthology of His
      Shorter Writings* (Oxford: Oxford University Press, 1991).

54   Alfred Russel Wallace, "On the Monkeys of the Amazon," *Proceed-
      ings of the Zoological Society of London,* pt. 20 (1852): 107–110;
      idem, "On the Habits of the Butterflies of the Amazon Valley," *Trans-
      actions of the Entomological Society of London,* 2d ser., 2 (1854):
      253–264; idem, *Palm Trees of the Amazon* (London: Van Voorst,
      1853). Wallace's emphasis on geographical distribution is discussed
      by McKinney, *Wallace,* 13–26; Brooks, *Just Before,* 32–55.

55   Charles Darwin and Alfred R. Wallace, "On the Tendency of Species
      to Form Varieties; and on the Perpetuation of Variation and Species
      by Natural Means of Selection," *Journal of the Proceedings of the
      Linnean Society of London (Zoology)* 3 (1858): 53–162. Wallace's
      sketch was mailed to Darwin from Ternate in March 1858. The story
      of Wallace's sketch and its joint publication with Darwin's extracts
      is well-thrashed history: see George, *Biologist Philosopher;* Barbara
      Beddall, "Darwin and Divergence: The Wallace Connection," *Journal
      of the History of Biology 21 (*1988): 1–68; McKinney, *Wallace;*
      Brackman, *Arrangement;* Fichman, *Wallace;* Brooks, *Just Before;* and
      M. J. Kottler, "Charles Darwin and Alfred Russel Wallace: Two
      Decades of Debate over Natural Selection," in *The Darwinian Heri-*

tage, ed. David Kohn (Princeton: Princeton University Press, 1985), 367–432.

56   The notebooks and journals are housed in the Linnean Society Library; the first notebook is referred to as the Wallace 1854 notebook, the second as the Wallace species notebook (begun in 1855). The four journals are referred to by their consecutive dates. The species registers are notebooks containing primarily lists of species Wallace collected in the Malay, 1855–1860, and are at the British Museum (Natural History); letters to Samuel Stevens, Wallace's agent in London, are reproduced in Brooks, *Just Before,* 22–26, 138–139, 140–143, 144–147, 174.

57   In his autobiography Wallace records that soon after his 1855 "Law" paper appeared, his agent wrote to him that he had heard several naturalists express regret that he was "theorizing" instead of collecting more facts (*My Life,* 1:355). It does not seem to have discouraged Wallace from doing so; however, it probably added to his circumspect style in writing about common descent. Wallace's collecting activities are described in Wilma George, "Alfred Wallace, the Gentle Trader," *Journal of the Society for the Bibliography of Natural History* 9 (1980): 503–514.

58   Wallace's lifelong concern with maps and his use of other graphical forms of representation are discussed in Camerini, "Maps," 136–188.

59   Alfred R. Wallace, "On the Law Which Has Regulated the Introduction of New Species," *Annals and Magazine of Natural History,* 2d ser., 16 (1855): 184–196.

60   Barbara Beddall, "Wallace, Darwin, and the Theory of Natural Selection," *Journal of the History of Biology* 1 (1968): 273–280; McKinney, *Wallace,* 44–53; Fichman, *Wallace,* 34–45; Browne, *Ark,* 171–174; Brooks, *Just Before,* chap. 5.

61   Wallace, "Law," 185–186.

62   Ibid., 186.

63   Ibid., 188.

64   Wallace had read Darwin's *Journal of Researches,* probably both the first and second editions (Wallace, *My Life,* 1:256). Wallace's notes about island speciation, with specific reference to the Galapagos, are found in his species notebook, and many passages from it are reproduced in McKinney, *Wallace.*

65   Wallace, "Law," 189.

66   Ibid., 196; Chambers made essentially the same point in 1846: "That plan necessitates the facts of distribution, which the other hypothesis does not" (Chambers, *Vestiges,* 289).

67   Wallace, *My Life,* 1:355.

68   Wallace, species notebook, 53r ('r' refers to the pages numbered 1–

179 in the Notebook, 'v' refers to pages numbered 1–70 in the opposite direction of the same notebook). The entry is located after one dated 27 June 1855 and just before one dated March 1856; the probable date of the "System of Nature" entry is January or February, 1856. This entry ends a twenty-five page section that includes a discussion of—more precisely an argument with—Lyell's ideas on species change; this section of the notebook is discussed by McKinney in *Wallace*, 32–43; and Brooks, *Just Before*, 68–69.

69   Letter, Wallace to Samuel Stevens, 21 August 1856, from Lombock; in Brooks, *Just Before*, 138–139.

70   Wallace repeatedly refers to a nonspecific map of the region that I refer to as a mental map. For example, the following quotation indicates Wallace's (map) frame of reference: "If we look at a map of the Archipelago, nothing seems more unlikely than that the closely connected chain of islands from Java to Timor should differ materially in their natural productions. . . . The remarkable change in natural productions which occurs at the Straits of Lombock, separating the island of that name from Bali; and which is at once so large in amount and of so fundamental a character, as to form an important feature in the zoological geography of our globe." Wallace, *Malay Archipelago* (1877), 202. Also the quotation on pages 92–93 describing the location of Wallace's line makes a similar reference to this nonspecific map of the region.

71   Letter, Wallace to Stevens, 1 December 1856, in Brooks, *Just Before*, 140.

72   Alfred R. Wallace, "On the Natural History of the Aru Islands," *Annals & Magazine of Natural History*, 2d ser., suppl. to 20 (1857): 473–485.

73   Ibid., 479.

74   Earl, "Physical Structure and Arrangement."

75   See note 57.

76   Letter, Wallace to Bates, 4 January 1858, in Wallace, *My Life*, 1:358–359.

77   Ibid., 358–359.

78   Ibid., 358.

79   Alfred R. Wallace, "Letter on the Geographical Distribution of Birds," *Ibis*, 1 (1859): 449–454; Philip L. Sclater, "On the General Geographical Distribution of the Class Aves," *Journal of the Proceedings of the Linnean Society (Zoology)* 2 (1858): 130–145.

80   Wallace, "Distribution of Birds," 450.

81   Alfred R. Wallace, "On the Zoological Geography of the Malay Archipelago," *Journal of the Proceedings of the Linnean Society*

(Zoology) 4 (1860): 172–184 (communicated to the society by Charles Darwin, 3 November 1859).

82 Ibid., 172.

83 Ibid., 173–174.

84 George, "Wallace and His Line," 4.

85 Ibid., 4–5; see also note 46 above, on Darwin and Celebes.

86 Alfred R. Wallace, *Island Life* (London: Macmillan, 1880), 432, 434.

87 Wallace, "Zoological Geography of the Malay Archipelago," 182.

88 Martin Fichman describes changes in Wallace's views about the permanence of continents in "Wallace: Zoogeography and the Problem of Land Bridges," *Journal of the History of Biology* 10 (1977): 45–63.

89 Letter, Darwin to Wallace, 29 January 1865, in Marchant, *Alfred Russel Wallace,* 132.

RON AMUNDSON

4 John T. Gulick and the Active
Organism
Adaptation, Isolation, and the Politics of Evolution

The Hawaiian Islands are the most geographically isolated island archipelago in the world. They had been inhabited for more than a thousand years by people of Polynesian ancestry before the first European contact occurred in 1778. American Protestant missionaries began arriving from New England in 1820. The Reverend Peter Johnson Gulick was in the third wave, arriving in 1827. In 1832, on Kauai, his wife bore the third of seven children, John Thomas Gulick. Gulick's biographer refers to him as "evolutionist and missionary." This description gives only a hint of the uniqueness of Gulick's life and work. He became not merely an evolutionist, but, according to one recent assessment, "one of the most influential evolutionists in the world at the turn of the century."[1] Gulick's role in the history of evolutionary theory comes from his very early advocacy of the importance of isolation in the formation of new species. According to current thinking, isolation is a crucial element in speciation, but in the 1880s this was a minority position. But there was much more to Gulick's story than isolation. This study will focus on aspects of Gulick's thought that provide a context for his views on isolation: the antiadaptationist aspects of his theory, his view of organisms as active participators in the evolutionary history of their lineage, and the commitment he expressed late in life to socialist political ideas.

John Gulick lived in Hawaii until 1853, when he traveled to the United States for his education at Williams College and Union Theological Seminary. He began his missionary career on an unofficial basis in Yokohama, Japan, in 1862, and was given an official assignment in north China in 1864. Reassigned to Japan because of poor health in 1875, he worked at Kobe and Osaka until his retirement in 1899. He then lived and wrote for five years in Oberlin, Ohio, returning to Honolulu in 1905. He died in 1923. During his thirty-seven years as a missionary, his only travels outside of Asia were two-year furloughs in 1871–1872 and 1888–1889. On each trip he visited with British and American evolutionists.

After a long period of neglect, Gulick has recently begun to receive the attention of historians of science. Their studies discuss the nine-teenth-century debates on the importance of isolation and Gulick's contributions to the development of modern views of speciation. As Lesch has argued, "The principal source of this new recognition [of the importance of isolation in evolution], at least among English and American biologists, must be sought in the debates surrounding the work of Romanes and Gulick in the two decades after 1886."[2]

The three topics of adaptationism, the active organism, and politics intertwine to varying degrees with Gulick's isolationist views on speci-ation. The challenge to adaptationism is tied in quite closely, and recent commentators (especially Provine) have given it attention. But although the concept of the active organism is at least as important in Gulick's mature thought on matters of biology and politics and to some extent on religion, there is little recognition of this aspect of his thought in the modern literature. The most striking passages in this vein by Gulick are in refutation of what he called "fatalism." Stephen Jay Gould in 1969 made half-joking reference to Gulick's refutation of fatalism, but there has been little other discussion.[3]

I hope to show that Gulick's rejection of fatalism was more deeply rooted in biological theory than in religious doctrine, notwithstanding the moral and political uses to which he put his biological argumenta-tion. An ironic outcome of these observations will be that certain bio-logical and political ideas developed by Gould himself and others in recent years show far closer affinities to J. T. Gulick than Gould could have expected in 1969.

Adaptationism and Its Critics

How do we explain why organisms have the traits they do? One dominant theme in the history of thought on this subject is the notion that structure follows function. Explaining the presence and structure of a trait involves identifying what purpose or function that trait serves for the organism in the environment it occupies. It is pre-sumed that, by some means or other, the trait has been shaped so that it will perform the function it can be seen to have. This sort of "func-tional" approach contrasts with the view that organic structure occurs by random accident or that it arises out of structural or mechanical causes insensitive to functional needs. These nonfunc-tional alternatives would imply that the uses and functions served by organic traits are merely opportunistic byproducts of the traits' structures: the functions were not involved in the creation of the structures. The functional approach is intuitively pleasing, and dates to antiquity. It was prominent in British natural theology, and (following Darwin) it remains today a central part of evolutionary biology. The modern version of the approach has recently been labeled "adaptationism" by certain critics, and that term will be used in the present work. Even though adaptationism was labeled in order to be more conveniently criticized, modern evolutionists seem unoffended by the term. For our purposes, as a first approximation, a biologist is an adaptationist who considers biological form or structure to be explained by biological function.

It is important to recognize that adaptationism is an environmentalist approach to the study of biological form. This is so even for preevolutionary versions of adaptationism, such as British natural theology. The relevant difference between natural theologians and neo-Darwinians is not in whether biological traits serve biological purposes, but rather in the mechanism by which the adjustment of the trait to its purpose is achieved. Darwinians favor natural selection, natural theologians supernatural design. Whatever the cause of the adaptation, the trait serves its purpose in virtue of its adaptedness to the environment in which the organism lives. The dependence of structure on function is recognized by adaptationists whether the cause of the adaptedness is believed to be a history of natural selection or a creative act of God.

Any particular version of adaptationism involves both a strategy for research and explanation and a central factual belief. The research strategy may or may not be coupled with high standards for explanatory acceptance. Natural theologians had a rather lax set of explanatory standards. They sometimes seemed satisfied when they had merely dreamed up a conceivable function a trait might serve. Modern adaptationist evolutionists may begin a study with a similar imaginative speculation about possible functions, but their scientific program includes a broad system of constraints arising from genetics, accepted mechanisms of natural selection, and ecology.

Besides the research-guiding aspect of adaptationism, it carries with it a central factual belief, namely that the world is rich in adaptations. Adaptationists do not merely look about for adaptations in the hopes of finding them. Rather, they expect to find adaptations almost everywhere they look. In classical times this expectation was expressed by the slogan that Nature does nothing in vain. The slogan, with a suitably depersonalized "Nature," is not inconsistent with much of modern evolutionary theorizing.

Almost as ubiquitous as adaptationists have been their critics. A common complaint is that adaptationists are too facile with their explanations—purposes are just too easy to invent. Voltaire's Doctor Pangloss, who proposed that human noses exist as a platform for spectacles, was a parody on this aspect of Leibniz's cosmic adaptationism. The more focused and important criticisms of adaptationism offer alternative explanations of organic form. Two broad groups of alternatives are proposed. The first sort argues that the adaptive force (natural selection, in modern biology) is too weak to restrain nonadaptive, free variation in organic form, such as genetic drift. The second argues that the adaptive force is too weak to overcome nonadaptive conservative constraints on organic form. The modern version of the second approach emphasizes "developmental constraints."[4]

Adaptationist debates predated Darwinian evolution theory. One example pitted the adaptationist Cuvier against the morphologist Geoffroy St. Hilaire. Cuvier claimed that the demands of the environment, what he called "conditions of existence," dictated biological form. Geoffroy argued that related organisms show affinities in character that cannot be explained by environmental demand; these traits were to be explained by the nonadaptive principle of "unity of type." The morphological approaches of Geoffroy and other French biologists were carried to Britain and used in opposition to the adaptationist arguments of William Paley and other advocates of the theological Argument from Design. The followers of Paley were well aware of the challenge from the morphologists, as can be seen in the pious, adaptationist Bridgewater Treatises.[5]

Adaptationism and Politics

Humans are biological entities. While any scientific endeavor carries social and moral implications, the social implications of the biological sciences are more immediate than most. Recurring themes during the past two centuries have been the alignment of biological adaptationism with social and political conservatism and attacks on adaptationism originating from scientists who support progressive or radical political causes. This alignment held in the Geoffroy versus Cuvier debates and in early nineteenth-century Britain. The most recent rebirth of this alliance occurred in the late 1970s as politically radical (and/or progressive) biologists began a vigorous attack on sociobiology. It was argued by Richard Lewontin, Stephen Jay Gould, and others that sociobiology was an "adaptationist program" (this was in fact the origin of the term "adaptationism") and that the conservative political implications of sociobiology were tainted by the conceptual flaws of adaptationism itself.[6]

It would, of course, be a mistake to suggest a one-to-one correlation of politics to science. It is possible to interpret particular scientific theories in ways that make them seem to support any number of different political views.[7] Scientific disputes on topics like adaptationism can be conducted in contexts remote from politics. As far as I can tell, most adaptationist disputes in the history of biology were not overtly related to social or political issues. The importance of political aspects of adaptationism also varies greatly from author to author. Lewontin, for example, became interested in a critique of adaptationism because of what he saw as the political implications of sociobiology; his interest in the topic continues to be informed by his political views. Gould's approach, while influenced by political concerns, was also informed by his work in at least two other biological areas, paleontology and embryology. These studies took place after his 1969 proadaptationist criticism of Gulick and before the debates on sociobiology. Much of the current discussion of adaptationism shows little overt connection with the politically volatile rebirth of interest in the topic.[8]

Nonetheless, the historical correlation of adaptationism with conservative politics is more than an accident. Let us consider an explanation of the adaptationist/conservative correlation.

Teleological or adaptationist explanations of phenomena are usually constructed in the absence of direct knowledge of the causal origins of those phenomena. William Paley, Charles Darwin, and modern evolutionists alike must examine a biological trait, observe the effects the trait has upon the life of the trait holder, and designate one (or more) of the effects of the trait as the purpose or function of the trait. This function is seen to benefit the organism in some way.

Recall the two aspects of adaptationism addressed above. The adaptationist has a strategy of explanation for traits that are determined to be adaptations and also believes that adaptations are rife in the biological world. But there is a problem concerning the criteria by which a trait is identified as an adaptation. Functions can be dreamed up for any trait one happens to pick out; Candide's Dr. Pangloss and Kipling's "Just So Stories" exploit this fact. An adaptationist can defend against the charge of dreamed-up functions only by showing that the identification of the functions of observed traits is subject to other criteria than mere imaginableness. The adaptationist Bridgewater Treatises were in part a demonstration of the ingenuity of creationist adaptationists, an ingenuity the authors share with modern Darwinian adaptationists. But the treatises equally demonstrate the extreme lack of constraints natural theologians placed on the identification of functions and purposes. This lack has been largely remedied by modern evolutionary theory—subject, of course, to the modern critiques of adaptationism.

Why does adaptationism have a politically conservative flavor? Because, by its own principles of explanation, the first explanatory move is to treat currently observable traits as having currently identifiable functions and as having been historically produced by an adaptive force (whether natural or supernatural). Observed traits, treated *ceteris paribus* as "adaptations," are explained not by a mere cause, but by a sort of reason or rationale. The rationale lists beneficial results of possession of the trait and says it exists because of those benefits. This explanation carries a strong hint that if it were possible to modify or abandon the trait, some loss of benefit would follow. Moreover, it depicts the trait as "natural" in the commendatory sense of the term—not just one of the features of nature, but one of the fruits of nature.

It must immediately be acknowledged that this approbation of the status quo is only provisional and only the initial step in a conscientious adaptationist endeavor. Conscientious modern adaptationists subject their hypotheses to a wide range of tests. Nor need an adaptationist see all of an adaptation's consequences as desirable. An adaptive trait may have maladaptive by-products, and an originally valuable trait might have since become undesirable under changed conditions.[9] An adaptationist need not endorse the status quo in all of its details; but because the first step in an adaptationist explanation provides an initial endorsement, the adaptationist argument can easily be made to serve conservative ends. Social traits (like biological ones) that are seen as flowing naturally from the adaptive trends of nature will also be seen as resistant to the attempts of reformers. We can't fool Mother Nature.

The pre-Darwinian French and British debates on adaptationism mentioned above fit this pattern. Cuvier's adaptationism was associated with social conservatism, Geoffroy's morphological approach with social change. Many of the early British antiadaptationist "transcendental anatomists" were political radicals. Meanwhile, the wealthy and privileged biological followers of Paley made it quite clear that their adaptationism provided a scientifically sanctioned defense against social upheaval, revolution, and moral chaos.[10] In these cases at least, adaptationist endorsement of the biological status quo went hand in hand with endorsement of the social status quo. I will interpret the Gulick critiques of adaptationism and fatalism in such a context.

J. T. Gulick: Early Years

The theological climate in the Gulick family was an ascetic and other-worldly Calvinism, far more bleak than the British Anglicanism that underwrote Paleyan natural theology. J. T. Gulick had been fascinated by nature all of his life, but he had seen no special connection between nature and religion. John's oldest brother Halsey, born in 1828, had been sent at the age of twelve to the United States for his education. Halsey returned in 1852 as an ordained missionary with an M.D. and a collection of books on natural history and natural theology. He introduced John to both topics. John's journal shows the personal importance of natural theology. The vision of nature as an expression of God's will was a great intellectual and religious liberation. "A vast field of thought and study has within a few days been rapidly opening to my view. It is the study of God's character, as displayed in his stupendous works and in the history of man." Within a short period, perhaps no more than a year, his new theology came to embrace evolution itself, although he was at the time uncertain of how many species had evolved from common ancestors. In 1853 he gathered a mammoth collection of Hawaiian land snails, mostly *Achatinella*. He later recalled that one of his earliest evolutionary insights was "all these *Achatinellae* never came from Noah's Ark."[11]

Gulick's evolutionary leanings could not have arisen from the pure empirics of his collected shells. By 1853 he had read works on the consistency of religion with science, but until 1857 he read nothing that openly advocated evolution. From the lists of readings in his journals (most of the books borrowed from Halsey) the probable pre-1853 sources of his evolutionary ideas are geologist Hugh Miller's *Footprints of the Creator* and Charles Darwin's *Voyage of the "Beagle."* Miller's book was intended to refute evolutionary theories, in particular the one expressed in *Vestiges of Creation,* but it may have planted a seed in Gulick's mind. Nothing in *Footprints,* however, would have convinced Gulick of the scientific importance of systematic shell collecting. Darwin's *Voyage of the "Beagle"* was certainly the source of that interest.[12]

The second edition of the *Voyage of the "Beagle"* (the edition Gulick read), published fourteen years before the 1859 publication of the *Origin of Species,* reported on the natural history of the places visited but did not openly discuss biological evolution. The *Voyage* is now famous for its description of Darwin's visit to the Galapagos Islands; contrariwise, the Galapagos are now famous because of Darwin. This assessment is hindsight, of course. The Galapagos discussion is chapter 17 of twenty-one chapters. It does contain the famous passage about the finches in which Darwin observes that "one might really fancy that from an original paucity of birds in the archipelago, one species had been taken and modified for different ends." But even including this pregnant phrase, it is not obvious that chapter 17 would have seemed especially striking to a contemporary (nonevolutionist) reader. To J. T. Gulick, however, it was by far the most striking chapter. The Galapagos are, like Hawaii, a geographically isolated island archipelago. In April 1853 Gulick gave a speech to a debating society at Punahou School, the school set up in 1841 to educate the children of the missionaries. Citing Darwin's *Voyage*, Gulick urged his classmates to take up the study of natural history. "Nowhere is the operation of these [biogeographic] principles more beautifully and strikingly displayed than in the natural history of isolated groups such as the Cape Verd [sic] Islands, the Galapagos Group, and these the Hawaiian Islands."[13] Darwin had discussed Cape Verde and the Galapagos. The young Gulick boldly added Hawaii.

The probable significance of Darwin's *Voyage* for Gulick has been underestimated by his commentators. The *Voyage*, for Gulick, was not just natural history, nor even island-oriented natural history, nor yet evolution-flavored island natural history. It offered a unique opportunity for Gulick at a crucial point in his life. His religious tradition had not only made the study of nature seem secular; it had burdened him with guilt about his own ambitions. A month before the visit from brother Halsey he had sorrowfully confessed in his journal that "it has always been my ambition to be a great man and that even my desires after holiness were in a measure a love of distinction."[14] Ascetic Calvinism made him ashamed of this pride. The discovery of natural theology showed how to accommodate his interest in natural history to religion. Darwin's *Voyage* was to offer a specific and important task in natural history suitable to his ambition as well as to his newly revised religious faith.

Modern mythology places Darwin's experiences with the Galapagos tortoises and finches at the very crux of his scientific thought. The facts are different. Frank Sulloway has shown how poorly Darwin originally understood his Galapagos collection and how distorted is the modern myth. Darwin's *Voyage* discussion of the tortoises and finches was not itself dishonest. The myth was a later, heroic, creation. Darwin's report was extremely suggestive, but admittedly inconclusive. In chapter 17 he virtually admits having botched the job of Galapagos biogeography. The huge land tortoises were reported to differ in form from island to island. This had not been a personal observation. Darwin attributed it to Mr. Lawson, the Galapagos vice-governor. Darwin had himself collected several species of finches, but he failed to record the islands on which he found most of them. After he returned to England he reconstructed the locations by comparing his collections to the better-annotated collections of other members of the expedition (including his own servant) and reported in the *Voyages* that the different species seemed to live on different islands. Darwin then charmingly confessed his frustration at having realized only after leaving the Galapagos that a careful record correlating form to location on this remote archipelago would have been useful. Several important points are revealed in that passage.

> I never dreamed that islands, about 50 or 60 miles apart, and most of them in sight of each other, formed of precisely the same rocks, placed under a quite similar climate, rising to a nearly equal height, would have been differently tenanted; but we shall soon see that this is the case. It is the fate of most voyagers, no sooner to discover what is most interesting in any locality, than they are hurried from it; but I ought, perhaps, to be thankful that I obtained sufficient materials to establish this most remarkable fact in the distribution of organic beings.

It is clear that Darwin's regret applied to the inadequacy of the collections of both finches and tortoises. Later in the chapter he emphasized again the environmental similarity of all the islands. The first sentence of the above passage, reporting similarity of environment together with difference of organic form, was quoted verbatim by Gulick in his 1853 Punahou speech.[15]

Darwin's *Voyage* not only provided Gulick with a hint of evolutionism and encouragement about the value of island biology. It also described an important scientific task that had not yet been accomplished, the task of studying and cataloging the variations in form of closely related but geographically isolated organisms, and especially those found on remote islands. Gulick, unlike Darwin, was eminently able to collect and record such organisms. Within a year of reading the *Voyage* he had done so. Darwin had described an important biological phenomenon, variation of form associated with isolation in identical environments. He had then confessed that that important phenomenon had been inadequately studied. This presented the newly non-Calvinist Gulick a task suited both to his ambition and to his religion.

With the help of a network of native collectors, Gulick spent much of 1853 gathering shells on Oahu and carefully logging their locations. He left Oahu for college in the United States on 21 November of that year. On the day-long horseback ride from the family home in Waialua to the Honolulu docks, Gulick stopped twice to purchase more shells from his native collectors. He carried his entire collection with him to the United States.[16]

Darwin's amazement in the *Voyage* at the richness of varieties in an environmentally homogeneous region had deep repercussions for Gulick. Less so for Darwin. He had mentioned in the 1845 *Voyage* and repeated in the 1859 *Origin* the close affinities among many Galapagos species, their close gradations of form, and their clear relations to continental American groups. But he referred not at all to the now-famous Galapagos tortoises and finches in the *Origin*—an interesting and somewhat puzzling elision. The passage quoted above from the *Voyage* carries a strong implication that adaptation to environment might not have been the cause of the differences among the species of finches and tortoises. But by 1859 Darwin had come to doubt the importance of isolation as a condition for natural selection to operate; he was in this way a stronger adaptationist than he had been in 1845. He avoided the isolationist implication by explaining that the Galapagos Islands must have differed from one another in the plant and animal life they contained even though they were climatically and geologically similar. If different species had originally tenanted the various Galapagos islands, then members of the original immigrant finch species that landed on different islands would live under different biological environments. This situation would account for the evolution of different forms on climatically similar islands. And thus was removed what would otherwise have been an adaptationist's anomaly: differences of form caused by something other than differences of environment. Also eliminated was any need to discuss the Galapagos tortoises and finches or the poverty of Darwin's knowledge about their precise geographical distribution.[17]

The young Gulick must have felt betrayed by Darwin's retraction in the *Origin* of the *Voyage*'s account of the importance of Galapagos isolation, but he waited thirty years to complain. In a paper read to the Linnean Society in 1889 he remarked that the *Origin*'s explanation of Galapagos diversity would imply "that if every species that gained access to any island had at the same time gained access to the other islands of the archipelago, there would then have been no occasion or opportunity for the divergences we now find."[18] Gulick found this absurd.

By the time Gulick read the *Origin* the die had been cast. Darwin might thenceforth doubt the reality of nonenvironmentally controlled speciation, but Gulick wouldn't. His *Voyage*-inspired *Achatinella* collection had already convinced him of the reality of the phenomenon Darwin had marveled at in 1845; closely related Hawaiian land snails *did* show both variation and speciation independently of any differences in environment. Gulick's description and interpretation of the *Achatinella* collection to the scientific community would be delayed another thirteen years until 1872, but it would have significant impact on evolutionary debate in the years to come.

College, China, and Britain

Gulick spent the period from 1853 to 1861 in the eastern United States, much of the time at Williams College and Union Theological Seminary. His biological reading continued; he read the pro-*Vestiges* book *The Bible of Science* in 1857 and Darwin's *Origin* shortly after its 1859 publication. He gave minor talks on the Hawaiian shells and talks in religious contexts containing somewhat obscure allusions to evolution, with titles like "Nature's Law of Change" and "Death and the Struggle for Existence."[19] In 1861 Louis Agassiz saw and was impressed by the *Achatinella* collection and hired Gulick to collect for him in South America. Gulick traveled as far as Panama before political chaos in the region stymied Agassiz's plan. Gulick abandoned the project and began a migration back across the Pacific. His shell collection had been left in New York.

Gulick's missionary career began unofficially in Japan in 1862. The American Board of Commissioners for Foreign Missions (ABCFM) gave him an official assignment to north China the next year. The demanding work and climate was a strain on his always frail health, and he was granted a medical leave in 1871. He was reunited with his collection in New York, and he carried a large part of it to England, in hopes of selling it to the British Museum. Most of 1872 was spent in England. This was Gulick's first opportunity for full-time science among fellow scientists. The British Museum turned down his shells but offered him research facilities. He met with Darwin, contacted Wallace, and presented papers to the British Association and the Linnean Society. Four papers were published from this period, two systematic and two theoretical.

The first theoretical publication, a letter to *Nature* in 1872, began by recalling Darwin's observations on the Galapagos preparatory to discussing the distribution of *Achatinella*. The 1873 *Linnean Society Journal* paper introduced Gulick's observations on the inadequacy of natural selection to explain the geographical variations observed. The main reason was the one Darwin had proposed in the *Voyage:* biological variations overshot environmental differences. Gulick first described the finely graded variations among *Achatinella* across the ridges and valleys of Oahu. He concluded: "The conditions under which [the species] are found are so completely similar, that it does not appear what ground there can be for difference in the characters best fitting the possessors for survival in the different valleys in which they are found." "If . . . we suppose that a difference in the external conditions is necessary to the evolution of distinct forms, these and other similar facts remain unexplained." His data were far more detailed than Darwin's had been, and he was able to support more detailed critiques of adaptationism. For example, the rainfall difference between the windward and leeward sides of a ridge was the only significant environmental difference he could find. But "we find no greater difference in the species when we pass from the more rainy to the drier side, than when we compare the forms from valleys on the same side of the mountain, separated by equal distances."[20]

In the papers from the 1870s, Gulick argues for the inadequacy of natural selection to explain speciation but offers relatively little in its place. There are references to the importance of an "inherent tendency to variation," but little else. Nor is there much reference to the importance of behavior, a topic that would later become central. Habits are usually mentioned only as species traits that reveal evolutionary relationships. He makes one brief behavioral reference to nongeographical segregation of the sort that George John Romanes came to endorse and that in the 1880s drew Gulick and Romanes together. This passage describes the caste system of India as an example of nongeographical segregation of breeding.[21] If the same passage had been written in 1890, Gulick would surely have argued that the Indians themselves adopted the caste system, thereby affecting future evolutionary influences; external nature did not impose castes on the Indian people.

Japan and Biological Thought

By 1873 Gulick was back in the north China mission. In 1875 he transferred to Kobe, Japan, an assignment that offered a climate gentler to his failing health. It also offered greater opportunity and stimulus for scientific thought, though this was presumably far from the minds of the commissioners of the ABCFM. Japan had changed greatly since Gulick's 1862 visit. The shogun had been overthrown and the emperor restored, and the Doshisha School, a Christian school that grew into Doshisha University, was being set up in Kyoto. Japan in the Meiji era (1867–1912) was exploring ways to come to terms with modern Western culture, especially Western science. The Doshisha School had been sponsored by the conservative wing of the Congregationalist mission, but even the conservatives realized that access to Western scientific thought was important to their Japanese students. Gulick was invited in 1878 and 1879 to give a series of lectures on biological evolution. The synopsis of these lectures shows that Gulick was beginning to consider the ethical and political implications of the various versions of evolutionary theory.[22] This line of thought led him to an interest in the evolutionary importance of the active organism and to his refutation of "fatalism"; it may also have been a stimulus for the increasingly detailed critiques of adaptationism that marked his publications of the 1890s.

When a professional missionary introduces evolution to a religious clientele, one must expect that theology would be involved. The extent of the involvement will be discussed below. But another context provides more specific insight into Gulick's thought. The recent political changes in Japan had made political theory a prime topic of intellectual debate. Like everywhere else in the world, the developments in evolutionary biology were seen to have deep social significance. The main influence of Western biology in Japan during the Meiji era was the impact of so-called Social Darwinism. This unfortunately named ideology invoked the scientific images of the "struggle for existence" and "survival of the fittest" in the context of social policy, either to support laissez-faire capitalism as a struggle between individuals or (as the occasion arose) to support aggression or oppression between races, nations, or classes. The external environment was supposed to ensure human progress by rewarding the victorious participants in this "struggle."[23]

In its Japanese incarnation, as elsewhere, Social Darwinism was opposed to ideals of equality and liberal democracy on the grounds that they were "unnatural." Hiroyuki Kato, president of Tokyo University from 1881, expressed the political implications of evolutionary biology as follows:

> According to this theory [evolution], the gradations of inferior and superior exists [sic] in plants and animals and is a result of the double process of heredity and mutation. Consequently, to accomplish the purpose of the maintenance and growth of life, mutual competition is generated in which the superior always conquers and the inferior is defeated. Only in this way is life carried on. . . . [T]he survival of the fittest is easily proven by the his-

torical evidence of societies from ancient times to the present and, perforce, wipes out any specious proof of the existence of natural rights to liberty, independence, and equality. . . . The division of mankind into inferiors and superiors leads to a continual struggle for the survival of the fittest. . . . The proponents of wild fancies, not being able to know this indisputable and clear principle of truth, have eagerly advocated natural rights. These people do not know that such rights as we do have are those which have been taken by force from others.[24]

This passage was written in 1882. In Kato's view, the disparities that exist between various classes of people are a natural result of the environment favoring the superior in the struggle for existence. According to his reading of evolutionary theory, "only in this way is life carried on." In 1893 Kato published a book entitled *The Struggle for the Right of the More Powerful.* He was never one to mince words.

Gulick took the opportunity in his Doshisha lectures to develop an interpretation of evolutionary theory opposed to Social Darwinism. His first published critique of "fatalism" was in an 1883 paper containing passages noticeably similar to the notes of his 1878–1879 lectures. After urging that Darwin underestimated the contribution of internal spontaneous causes of variation to evolutionary change, Gulick continued:

It may appear to some a matter of small importance whether the course of evolution is attributed to conditions found in the species, or to conditions external to it. When, however, we come to human evolution we shall find that the latter theory lands us in fatalism. If for each species there is but one kind of nature and instinct that can be developed under one set of conditions, and if there is but one set of actions that can possibly result from that predetermined nature acting under predetermined circumstances, then the course of all evolution is predetermined by mechanical laws, and no effort on the part of individuals or nations can in any way effect [sic] the result; for we cannot change our circumstances without acting, and our acting is already determined by our circumstances. The knot may be cut by assuming that man's rational nature sets him free from the law that controls the rest of animated nature; but a truer science finds in nature a very different law, a law of spontaneous variation and of discriminating endeavour, in accordance with which faculties are evolved, and external conditions subdued and appropriated for ever widening uses; in a word, a law of advancing conquest by which the Material is conformed to the Ideal.[25]

Note that Gulick declines the special appeal to human rationality, which would exempt only humans from fatalism. The "truer science" rejects fatalism in a manner equally applicable to humans and land snails. Admittedly the rejection is on somewhat obscure—and pontifical—grounds: "discriminating endeavor" and "Material . . . conformed to the Ideal." But the argument was soon to improve.

In the first of two 1885 papers Gulick began with an especially elegant synopsis of the reasoning behind evolutionary biology. He went on to identify the fatalist culprit more directly: Herbert Spencer, the natural father of Social Darwinism, with some contributions from Darwin himself. Gulick first asked the question "Can change in the character of the Natural Selection be initiated and continued through change in the organism, without any change in the environment, except what is produced by the action of the organism?" Spencer was quoted as answering in the negative: "That there may be continuous changes in the organism there must be continuous changes in the incident forces." Spencer again: "Vital actions remain constant so long as the external actions to which they correspond remain constant. There must be maintained a tolerably uniform species so long as there continues a tolerably uniform set of conditions in which it may exist." In sum, "Herbert Spencer rests his denial of the freedom of the human will on the biological assumption that all vital activities are predetermined by activities in the environment." Gulick described Darwin's views as more ambiguous, giving some of the credit for the effects of selection to the nature of the organism itself. But Gulick highlights one passage in the *Origin* as truly environmental and adaptationist. It is the passage at the end of chapter 6: "The law of Conditions of Existence is the higher law; as it includes, through the inheritance of former adaptations, that of Unity of Type."[26]

Gulick's critique of this view was subtle and far-reaching. In response to the fatalist's claim that external conditions control changes in the organism, he argued that the term "external conditions" is ambiguously used.

> Are not its external conditions changed when a variety takes up a new habit of feeding? If they are, external conditions and external nature are certainly not identical. The external conditions are not external nature, but *the relations in which the organism stands to external nature*. . . . [C]an anything be surer than that through the activities of the organism changes in its relations to the environment [are] often produced; and that through these changes the character of its success is changed, and so the character of its Natural Selection.[27]

So selection involves not a force on the organism from the preexisting, independent environment. It is rather an interactive result created in part by the activities of the organism itself. Selection occurs not through the actions of "external nature" alone but through the activities of the organism that place it into specific relations with "external nature."

This relational concept of selection was important to Gulick's later thought. It came up not only in later discussions of the fatalism issue[28] but also in more purely biological discussions. His most influential scientific work was surely the 1888 paper, "Divergent Evolution through Cumulative Segregation," which allied him with George John Romanes and against Alfred Russel Wallace on the issue of adaptation versus isolation as the primary cause for speciation. In this paper "the environment" was carefully classified as "nature lying outside of the Intergenerant." (The Intergenerent is the breeding population.) Gulick pointed out that changes in the organism's relations to the environment can be caused by "change in the environment," by "entering a new environment," or by "change in the organism." A basic category of segregation (breeding isolation) is "Environal segregation," or isolation of breeding populations caused by "the relations in which the organism stands to the environment." "The environment" is not an autonomous, shaping force. It is rather one of the relata in that organism/environment relationship the character of which constitutes natural selection.[29]

Wallace roundly criticized the 1888 paper both on its obscurity and complexity and on theoretical grounds. Gulick's supposedly nonselective causes of speciation were argued to be selective after all. In a response, Gulick showed convincingly that Wallace had again equivocated on exactly what "the environment" comprised. Examples are whether the actions of species members on one another were or were not a part of the "environment" and whether geographical isolation was a feature of the "environment" or of the species itself.[30]

First introduced in the fatalism refutation, the relational concept of selection made its way into all of Gulick's later biological work. The original concept had referred only to the activities of the organism as changing its relations to "external nature." Gulick soon saw that any spontaneous change in the organism—behavioral or physical—could change its relations to the environment; this is evident in the above passages from 1888. Gulick never neglected the behavioral application of his views. But as his work became important and controversial in biology, the physical rather than behavioral applications of his approach received more attention.

Fatalism?

What exactly was this "fatalism" Gulick is arguing against? It is clearly opposed to human freedom and allied with "predetermination." But it does not quite fit into the standard metaphysical problem of freedom of the will. In metaphysics, the position that causal determinism prohibits freedom of the will is called "necessitarianism." Is fatalism necessitarianism? Gulick argued that the spontaneous activities of different organisms may place them into different relations with the external environment and that these relations determine how natural selection will act on the organisms. But if Gulick is arguing as a pure metaphysician, he has left his flank open. He failed to refute the claim that the organism's "spontaneous" activities themselves were causally determined, either by the environment or by causes internal to the organism itself. In modern terms, he never addressed himself to the ontogeny (so to speak) of an organism's behavior, but only to the phylogeny of the species' "nature and instinct." He showed that a species' current "nature and instinct" have been shaped not directly by the external environment (as Spencer had claimed) but by the relations with the environment that arose out of the activities of ancestral organisms themselves. Organisms contribute to the evolution of their own species; external causes cannot alone control that evolution.

Notice how irrelevant this approach would seem to a necessitarian, who believes that the individual actions of individual organisms are causally determined and (therefore) unfree. Gulick sometimes even seemed to help the necessitarian refute him. He offered a nice analogy in comparing the flow of water down a hill to the paths two horses took down the same hill; water will always take the same path, but the two horses could choose different paths. So far, so good. But then he says, "[O]ne horse being thirsty took the path that leads to the spring, another being hungry chose the shortest road to the clover-field."[31] Aha! shouts the metaphysician. So the paths taken by the horses were causally determined after all, by their internal states of thirst and hunger. Either Gulick was a clumsy metaphysician, or he was not really arguing against necessitarianism at all.

The best interpretation of this apparent failure is that Gulick's "fatalist" opponent was not really the necessitarian. It was the Social Darwinist. Many have argued, before and since Gulick's time, that the causes operating on an organism within its own lifetime so rigorously control its behavior as to prohibit freedom of the will.[32] But neither Darwinism nor Social Darwinism requires such a premise. As seen in the Kato quote above, Social Darwinism depicts the status quo, including class distinctions, oppression, and aggression, as an inevitable outcome of the evolutionary process. The argument carries the same force whether or not the actions of individual organisms are causally determined. Indeed, Darwinism presupposes spontaneous variation in heritable traits. It doesn't matter to Darwinism (or Social Darwinism) whether the source of variation is genuinely random or causally determined by factors insensitive to the environmental needs of the organism. Darwin himself did not believe heritable variation to be truly random, but only random with respect to adaptation. His theory addresses itself to a phylogenetic level of explanation. As long as the source of variation is nondirected ("random" in a broad sense) with respect to adaptation, causal determinism is an irrelevant issue.

But if both Gulick and the Social Darwinists (as well as other Darwinian adaptationists) agree on the spontaneity of variation, how can the Social Darwinists endorse the "fatalism" Gulick so deplores? The answer has to do with the nature of the variation and how it relates to the external environment. The notion of a spontaneously active (or spontaneously varying) organism was regarded as vitalistic and antiscientific through much of the nineteenth century. The attitude attributed by Gulick to Spencer was dominant: the organism would be expected to be inert unless goaded into action by its environment. Challenges to this view came from Darwin's natural selection, along with the discovery of the spontaneous activity of the nervous system[33] and assisted by the growth of other probablistic disciplines such as thermodynamics.

The sort of fatalistic adaptationism condemned by Gulick—the acceptance of the status quo as inevitable and natural—can nevertheless be salvaged from the spontaneity of variation in which Darwinism is rooted. All that is needed is for the spontaneous variation to be small, ever present, and closely supervised by environmental pressures. If these conditions are met, the probablistic basis of Darwinian evolution approximates ever so closely a direct molding of the malleable organism by the all-powerful environment. This is why Gulick and other antiadaptationists often challenge the existence of hypothetical supersensitive selective pressures (Gulick calls them "occult influences")[34] and why they emphasize the ways in which small variations can create large changes in the selective regime. It is why Gulick argued that activity affects an organism's relation to its environment. And it is why Gulick didn't bother to argue for the metaphysical nondeterminedness of organismic behavior; he argues instead that admittedly spontaneous behavior makes a difference in the evolutionary history of the organism's lineage.

Religion

All but a few of Gulick's comments on the relations between religion and evolutionary biology sound remarkably modern and naturalistic. This is especially curious given that they were published in journals with religious affiliations, three of which had missionary and presumably conservative connections. The fourth, *Bibliotheca Sacra,* was published by liberal Oberlin College, where Gulick eventually spent five years after retiring from his mission work.[35]

Many of Gulick's observations on religion and biology were standard conciliation arguments; the relation between man and God remains unchanged, for example, "whether his creation was carried through many successive stages of long duration, or was completed in one brief moment." Gulick's early Biblical training revealed itself in many quaint-sounding allusions to scripture: "Everywhere we find creatures called upon to work out their own salvation; for it is God that worketh in them, that they may attain complete fitness to the environment in which they have been placed." The first two clauses paraphrase a Biblical verse from Saint Paul, a verse Gulick repeated in a later paper. Paul had been speaking only of humans, of course, and had not mentioned "fitness to the environment." From the context it is clear that "working out one's own salvation" is (for Gulick) a reference to the activity of organisms, whose choices partly determine the evolution (salvation?!) of their species.[36]

In an especially interesting passage, Gulick discussed "the need that a rational animal has for the support of religion." He assumed that both rational and nonrational animals might be called upon to struggle both for their own existence and for that of their family or species (their "aggregate"). He then pointed out that rational animals, unlike nonrational animals, can foresee the consequences of individual loss and sacrifice. "When [a man] sacrifices himself for the good of his family, or nation, or race, he knows that he is making sacrifice. He cannot, like the beast and bird, sacrifice himself without any thought of the consequences." This horrible awareness of the consequences of self-sacrifice is ameliorated by religion. Religion offers a higher context into which the rational animal can place its actions. "The law of nature seems to provide for the success of the race, without regard to the fate of the individual. But religion offers the highest blessedness to the individual while devoting himself to the service of the race, through love of God." In other words, a self-sacrificing rational animal could not evolve without resolving the conflict between self-sacrifice and knowledge of its consequences. Religion resolves that conflict.[37]

This explanation of the evolutionary function of religion makes no reference to the truth of religious doctrine. It is purely naturalistic. The two papers Gulick published in 1885 had been read as one to the Protestant Missionary Conference in Osaka in 1883. Addison Gulick has speculated on how his father was able to express his progressive notions in such a conservative religious climate. Part of the answer is that his opinions didn't touch the day-to-day evangelical concerns of the missionaries; another may be that the isolation of the Asian missions kept them from close American supervision. One suspects a third possibility—that Gulick's creative scriptural allusions obscured rather than illuminated his evolutionary message, and his religious audience simply didn't follow the niceties of his biological thought.[38]

Evidence for this interpretation comes from later commentary by the comparatively liberal *Bibliotheca Sacra*. In prefaces to Gulick's works the editor showed pride in Gulick's importance in science and twice quoted paragraphs of Romanes' effusive praise of Gulick the scientist. One of these papers was a reprint of a letter from Gulick to Romanes explaining Gulick's views on Christianity. (Jesus is described as a "new type" in rational evolution, analogous to new biological types in organic evolution.) The editor of the journal rather boastfully claimed that Gulick's letter was "among the prominent influences which led to Mr. Romanes' substantial return to the Christian faith." (Romanes had converted to Christianity shortly before his death in 1894.) Gulick and his son emphatically rejected this claim, the latter pointing out that his father had always considered science and religion to be based on identical forms of reason, while Romanes claimed that only intuition, not reason, could support a belief in God. Gulick: "The unity and harmony of truth is a fundamental axiom which cannot be set aside. If fatalism is true for the naturalist, it is also true for the rest of mankind."[39]

Another blunder can be seen in the editor's attempt to comment on Gulick's biology. Short passages from his scientific articles were quoted, describing how the radius of distribution of a species depends directly on its powers of migration and inversely on its heritable plasticity and variability. The editor says that these conclusions "rule chance out of the problem [of organic origins], and reveal a law whose source is invisible but all-powerful."[40] Darwinian references to chance had been a perfectly dreadful feature of Darwinian evolution to many religious people, and especially to Calvinists. Gulick did not share the Calvinists' love of deterministic law. Always arguing in opposition to the "fatalistic" environmental determinism of adaptationism, he attributed evolutionary change to spontaneous change in the organism. The "laws" of distribution cited by the editor were, to Gulick, simply a by-product of different organisms' modes of spontaneous variation. They were not imposed from above by an all-powerful Deity. It is almost comical to see Gulick, the lifelong champion of the spontaneously active organism and the foe of fatalism, described by a coreligionist as having imposed the rule of divine "law" over "chance." This editor did not understand Gulick's biological thought.

Influences, Large and Small

Gulick kept his journal only until he was married in 1863, so it is more difficult to trace the development of his thought as an adult than as a youth. The evolutionary work from the 1880s onward shows increasing biological sophistication. His 1870s papers were important for the data on the snails and had some remarkable insights (e.g., the recognition that a small isolated population is more likely to vary from the species mean than is a large isolated population). But they referred primarily to the "power of variation" as the alternative to simple natural selection. Recognition of the importance of breeding isolation came in the 1880s, and reference to variation as a "power" declined. From this point on he replaced variational "power" with detailed discussions of the ways in which isolation interacted with spontaneous phenotypic and behavioral variation to influence evolution. I suspect that this development was influenced both by his 1870s contacts with biologists (the papers of that decade had been written before he had visited England) and his early 1880s struggles with Social Darwinism.

Gulick's monumental and baroque "Divergent Evolution through Cumulative Segregation" appeared in 1888, his first publication in a scientific journal since 1873 and his most important theoretical paper. It put him in touch with George John Romanes, himself in the midst of a debate with Wallace over the importance of segregation for speciation. Romanes found an important ally in Gulick. The 1888 paper was long, complex, and somewhat self-indulgent with neologisms; according to Wallace it contained names for thirty-eight distinct forms of segregation. Gulick confessed his isolation from colleagues and libraries. A more elegant paper might have been written from a less isolated scientific environment. Nevertheless, the paper was influential.[41]

The debate with Wallace and the alliance with Romanes brought Gulick, his views on isolation, and his *Achatinella* work to the attention of evolutionists everywhere. There is a fairly direct link to the "Modern Synthesis" of evolutionary theory. Gulick's work was described sympathetically in *Darwinism To-day,* an important 1908 work by Vernon Kellogg (who also advised Addison Gulick on the writing of his father's biography). Provine has learned that Sewall Wright, one of the founders of the Modern Synthesis in the 1930s, had been strongly influenced by Kellogg's report. "Seventy five years after he read this account of Gulick's data and conclusions Wright had a keen recollection of how deeply impressed he had been with it." So at least one line of influence on modern views regarding the importance of isolation can be traced to Gulick. His views on the importance of spontaneous behavior, derived from his critique of "fatalism," didn't benefit from the same publicity; they weren't at the center of a similar debate. The closest Kellogg came to mentioning Gulick's views on behavior is the possibility that "a change of instinct determining migration to another area, or occupation of a different habitat in the same area" would create isolation.[42]

There was one line of thought in which Gulick's ideas of spontaneity might have found a better home. This was the notion of "organic selection" or the so-called Baldwin Effect, an evolutionary mechanism independently proposed by James Mark Baldwin, Conwy Lloyd Morgan, and Henry Fairfield Osborn in the 1890s. Of this group, Baldwin, at least, was motivated by an opposition to Spencerian Social Darwinism, and the other two had some sympathies with Lamarckism, possibly for similar reasons. The Baldwin Effect showed how Lamarckian-appearing evolutionary results could occur even without the inheritance of acquired characters. Organisms make individual adaptive changes during their lifetimes, adaptively modifying their physical traits (e.g., gaining strength) or developing skills or otherwise modifying their behavior. These ontogenetic adaptations are not inherited directly. Suppose that a species takes to tree climbing and that therefore certain ontogenetic adaptations need to be reacquired each generation (e.g., the strengthening of tree-climbing muscles). Individuals that inherit a tendency for their tree-climbing muscles to respond rapidly to exercise will have a selective advantage over those whose muscles grow slowly. In a case like this, descendent generations would have strong muscles at younger ages than ancestor generations, and it would appear that they had responded in a Lamarckian way to the acquired strength of their ancestors' tree-climbing muscles. In fact there is no Lamarckian inheritance of tree-climbing muscles but rather a Darwinian selection for the (heritable) ability rapidly to acquire strong muscles. What was originally an ontogenetic adaptation gradually becomes selected for in a Darwinian manner. The theory stresses the plasticity of the phenotype, and especially the plasticity of behavior. In this way ontogenetic plasticity becomes a part of the explanation of new phylogenetic adaptations, but it does so without invoking Lamarckian inheritance.[43]

Baldwin himself acknowledged Gulick's work, and it is hard to

believe that Lloyd Morgan (protégé of Romanes just as Romanes had
been protégé of Darwin) was unaware of it. Baldwin's huge *Dictionary of Philosophy and Psychology* cites Gulick under several head-
ings, including the following from the "Organic Selection" entry:

> Or again, two or more different accommodations may subserve the same
> utility, and thus conserve different lines of variation. To escape floods, for
> example, some individuals of a species may learn to climb trees while oth-
> ers learn to swim. This has been recognized in Gulick's *Change of Habits*
> as a cause of segregation and thus of divergent evolution.[44]

So both Kellogg and Baldwin present Gulick's "change of habits" as
important only because habits can produce isolation and segregation,
which can in turn lead to divergent evolution. This is not a false
account of Gulick's ideas about behavior, but it is impoverished. It
implies no more than had been offered in Gulick's 1873 example of
the Indian caste system. In his later thought, behavior played a much
more active role in evolution than merely one more cause of segregation. The antifatalist writings of the 1880s had begun to describe
behavior as productive of new evolutionary adaptations, just as
would the Baldwin Effect. At least ten years before the Baldwin Effect
was proposed, Gulick had pointed out that when an organism
behaves in a new way, it places itself in new relations to the external
environment and thereby changes the selective forces that influence
the evolution of its lineage. To this insight, the Baldwin Effect added
only a new emphasis on ontogenetic adaptive changes.

In the 1940s the geneticist C. H. Waddington described a complex
phenomenon he called "genetic assimilation." At the time he hadn't
known of the Baldwin Effect (which never reached the evolutionary
mainstream), but he later realized the similarities between the effect
and genetic assimilation. He praised the early writers on the effect for
understanding, better than "the conventional Neo-Darwinist theories
of Haldane and Fisher (and to a lesser extent Sewall Wright) . . . the
importance of behavior in influencing the nature of selective forces."[45]
Had he known of it, Waddington might have cited John Thomas
Gulick's priority on that insight.

Science in Its Political Context

The personal journals that give us so much insight into the
thoughts of the young J. T. Gulick ended in 1863. The early journals
pointed us to Darwin's *Voyage* as an influence on Gulick's biological
development. We have no similar hints for the development of his
political thought. The above suggestion of Japanese Social Darwinism

as a motivating influence is based on circumstantial evidence. We do know that Gulick had read the journal *Dawn,* an organ of the Christian Socialists, in 1892. He was a confirmed socialist by 1905 and participated in forming a branch of the Socialist Party of America in Honolulu in 1907. Addison Gulick dates his socialism (almost apologetically) to 1905, but the tenor of the writings of the 1880s hints at an earlier acquaintance with socialist ideas.[46]

Gulick's most openly political publication appeared in the *International Socialist Review* in 1907. It discusses the "habitudinal" (social and behavioral) analogs to the biological evolutionary processes he had worked out in his 1905 book. He argued that capitalism produces "increasing divergence [of traditions and interests] between the capitalist class and the laboring class" by segregating the interests of the two classes. "Community of interest is blotted out. Moreover, [the workers] observe that with their class the struggle is for the necessities of life, while with those who are pre-eminently the capitalists there is an ever increasing competition in extravagance of display."[47] The dig at the capitalist class' "competition in extravagance of display" is a clear allusion to the evolutionary mechanism of sexual selection, a mode of competition universally acknowledged not to increase organisms' adaptation to the external environment.

One modern dismissal of Gulick's relational view of selection is especially tempting. He had shown that not all of "external nature" exerts selective force on an organism, but only the part with which the organism interacts. An easy response to this is that Gulick simply lacked the concept of the *evolutionary niche.* Now that we know that organisms occupy niches, we can see that it is the selective forces associated with the niche (and not all of the features of the external environment) that shape the organism. We have no further need for Gulick's odd-sounding distinction between "external conditions" and "external nature" or his peculiar notion that organisms themselves somehow control the forces that exert selection on them.

Perhaps this solution is correct, and Gulick's active organism is unnecessary for the understanding of evolution. If so, it is not because of the concept of the niche. The evolutionary niche is subject to precisely the same critique Gulick had brought to bear against the "fatalist" in 1885. After the initial heat of the sociobiological debate in the 1970s, Richard Lewontin began constructing a deeper and openly ideological examination of neo-Darwinian adaptationism. Some of it appeared in *The Dialectical Biologist,* coauthored with Richard Levins. "Indeed it is a sign of the Marxist dialectic with which we align ourselves that scientific and political questions are inextricably

interconnected—dialectically related." In this book Lewontin criti-
cizes the standard concept of the environmental niche for giving the
false appearance that

> the external world poses certain well-defined "problems" for organisms;
> those that best survive and reproduce are those whose morphological,
> physiological, and behavioral traits represent the best solutions to the
> problems. . . . The word "adaptation" reflects this point of view, implying
> that the organism is molded and shaped to fit into a preexistent niche,
> given by the autonomous forces of the environment, just as a key is cut and
> filed to fit into a lock.

This view is said to be mistaken, first because "organisms determine
what is relevant," that is, what is and what is not within the niche,
and second because "the organism-environment relationship defines
the 'traits' selected."[48] But recall Gulick: "can anything be surer than
that through the activities of the organism changes in its relations to
the environment [are] often produced . . . and so the character of its
Natural Selection." Like Gulick, Lewontin cites both physical and
behavioral traits of organisms as placing the organisms into new relations with the external environment. Clearly Lewontin's criticism of
niche determinism makes precisely the same point as Gulick's critique
of a broader form of environmental determinism ("fatalism"). If
Gulick was mistaken about the nature of natural selection, it was not
because of his ignorance of evolutionary niches.

The adaptationism debates continue despite the gathering of
massive amounts of empirical evidence about natural species. The
politically inspired critiques of strongly environmentalist versions
of Darwinism have likewise survived a hundred years of fine tuning
of evolutionary theory. I take the similarities between Gulick and
Lewontin as circumstantial evidence that Gulick's attack on fatalism
may have been influenced by specific socialist sources, even though
I am unable to identify the precise influence.[49] But even if Gulick
were motivated by more general liberal opposition to Social Darwinism, he represents yet another alignment between conservative
politics and adaptationism, progressive politics and critiques of
adaptationism.

Notes

This paper has benefited from information, discussion, and commentary from
Alison Kay, Hampton Carson, Will Keim, David Purcell, and Don Hemmes
and from insightful editorial advice from Philip Rehbock. I am indebted to
Stephen Jay Gould and Richard Lewontin for discussions of biology and its

political context. I also wish to thank my research assistant Lisa Martin and the heroic librarians of the Edwin Mookini Library.

1   Addison Gulick, *John Thomas Gulick: Evolutionist and Missionary* (Chicago: University of Chicago Press, 1932); William B. Provine, *Sewall Wright and Evolutionary Biology* (Chicago: University of Chicago Press, 1986), 217.

2   Provine, *Sewall Wright;* John E. Lesch, "The Role of Isolation in Evolution: George J. Romanes and John T. Gulick," *Isis* 66 (1975): 483–503; Malcolm Jay Kottler, "Isolation and Speciation" (Ph.D. dissertation, Yale University, 1976); W.-E. Reif, "The Work of John Th. Gulick (1832–1923): Hawaiian Snails and a Concept of Population Genetics," *Zeitschrift für zoologische Systematik und Evolutionsforschung* 23 (1985): 161–171. See also Hampton Carson, "The Processes Whereby Species Originate," *Bioscience* 37: (1987) 715–720. Quote is from Lesch, 503.

3   Kottler (perhaps unfairly) reads Gould as attributing the refutation of fatalism, and even Gulick's antiadaptationism, to Gulick's religious preconceptions. Here are the relevant passages: "This missionary-scientist even read cosmic significance into his claim [about speciation], using it to defend human free will against an encroaching scientific determinism." Stephen Jay Gould, "Character Variation in Two Land Snails from the Dutch Leeward Islands: Geography, Environment, and Evolution," *Systematic Zoology* 18 (1969): 186. "We are removed nearly a century from the time when land snails first played devil's advocate to Darwinism. The advocate: *Achatinella.* Mephisto: none other than the Reverend Gulick." Idem, "Environmental Control of Form in Land Snails: A Case of Unusual Precision," *Nautilus* 84 (1971): 86. Gould recently expressed a new and higher opinion of Gulick in "Unenchanted Evening," *Natural History* 100 (10) (September 1991): 6–7.

4   J. Maynard Smith, R. Burian, S. Kauffman, P. Alberch, J. Campbell, B. Goodwin, R. Lande, D. Raup, and L. Wolpert, "Developmental Constraints and Evolution," *Quarterly Review of Biology* 60 (1985): 265–287.

5   Toby Appel, *The Cuvier-Geoffroy Debate: French Biology in the Decades before Darwin* (New York: Oxford University Press, 1987); Philip F. Rehbock, *The Philosophical Naturalists* (Madison: University of Wisconsin Press, 1983); Adrian Desmond, *The Politics of Evolution* (Chicago: University of Chicago Press, 1989).

6   On the nineteenth-century debates, see Appel, *Cuvier-Geoffroy Debate;* Eveleen Richards, "The 'Moral Anatomy' of Robert Knox: The Interplay Between Biological and Social Thought in Victorian Scientific Naturalism," *Journal of the History of Biology* 22 (1989): 373–436; Desmond, *Politics of Evolution;* Philip F. Rehbock, "Transcendental Anatomy," in *Romanticism and the Sciences,* ed. Andrew

Cunningham and Nicholas Jardine (Cambridge: Cambridge University Press, 1990). On the current debates, Sociobiology Study Group of Science for the People, "Sociobiology—Another Biological Determinism," *Bioscience* 26 (1976): 182–186; Richard C. Lewontin, "Sociobiology as an Adaptationist Program," *Behavioral Science* 24 (1979): 5–14; Stephen Jay Gould and Richard C. Lewontin, "The Spandrels of San Marco and the Panglossian Paradigm: A Critique of the Adaptationist Programme," *Proceedings of the Royal Society of London,* B, 205 (1979): 581–598. For a response to the 1976 paper, Edward O. Wilson, "Academic Vigilantism and the Political Significance of Sociobiology," *Bioscience* 26 (1976): 183–190.

7   See Peter J. Bowler, *Evolution: The History of an Idea* (Berkeley: University of California Press, 1984), chap. 10 on the wide range of social views Lamarckism has been used to support.

8   Stephen Jay Gould, *Ontogeny and Phylogeny* (Cambridge: Harvard University Press, 1977); Niles Eldridge and Stephen Jay Gould, "Punctuated Equilibrium: An Alternative to Phyletic Gradualism," in *Models in Paleobiology,* ed. J. M. Schopf (San Francisco: Freeman Cooper, 1972). Information on Gould's and Lewontin's motivations from personal discussion during spring 1986. For nonpolitical discussions see, e.g., the papers in John Dupre, *The Latest on the Best: Essays on Evolution and Optimality* (Cambridge: MIT Press, 1987).

9   Malthus surely regretted the fact that poverty was an inevitable consequence of the beneficial and God-given laws of population growth; the sociobiologist E. O. Wilson fears that the marvelously adapted human intelligence might lead to world annihilation since intelligence wasn't selected for in a high-technology world environment.

10   Desmond, *Politics of Evolution.*

11   A. Gulick, *John Thomas Gulick,* 55, 113.

12   Hampton Carson and Alison Kay remind me that Gulick had been an avid collector and lover of nature since he was a child and that not only Gulick but all of his classmates at Punahou School had been stricken with "shell fever." Darwin and natural theology were certainly not the cause of Gulick's love of nature, but (I suggest) they probably were the cause of his dedication beginning in 1853 to the systematic study of nature.

13   Charles Darwin, *Voyage of the "Beagle,"* 2d ed. (New York: P. F. Collier and Son, 1845), 384; A. Gulick, *John Thomas Gulick,* 115. The biogeographic principles mentioned included the "center of origin" from which each species radiated, the distinctness of the biota in different geographic locations irrespective of common climate, and the relatedness of many island biota to forms on neighboring continents.

14   A. Gulick, *John Thomas Gulick,* 53.

15   Frank J. Sulloway, "Darwin and His Finches: The Evolution of a Leg-
      end," *Journal of the History of Biology* 15 (1982): 1–53; "Darwin
      and the Galapagos," *Biological Journal of the Linnean Society* 21
      (1984): 29–59; Darwin, *Voyage,* 398 (quote); A. Gulick, *John
      Thomas Gulick,* 116.

16   A. Gulick, *John Thomas Gulick,* 133.

17   See Dov Ospovat, *The Development of Darwin's Theory* (Cambridge:
      Cambridge University Press, 1981), 193ff., on Darwin's gradual rejec-
      tion of the importance of isolation between 1845 and 1859.

18   John T. Gulick, *Evolution, Racial and Habitudinal* (Washington,
      D.C.: Carnegie Institute of Washington, 1905), 216.

19   A. Gulick, *John Thomas Gulick,* chap. 6.

20   John T. Gulick, "On the Variation of Species as Related to their Geo-
      graphical Distribution, Illustrated by the *Achatinellinae*," *Nature* 6
      (1872), 224; idem, "On Diversity of Evolution under One Set of
      External Conditions," *Zoological Journal of the Linnean Society* 11
      (1873), 505, 498.

21   J. T. Gulick, "Diversity of Evolution," 499.

22   A. Gulick, *John Thomas Gulick,* 391.

23   Masaaki Kosaka, ed., *Japanese Thought in the Meiji Era,* vol. 9 of
      Japanese Culture in the Meiji Era, David Abosch, trans. (Tokyo: Pan-
      Pacific Press, 1958); Masao Watanabe, "John Thomas Gulick: Ameri-
      can Evolutionist and Missionary in Japan," *Japanese Studies in the
      History of Science* 5 (1966): 140–149, on Social Darwinism in Japan.
      Peter J. Bowler, *The Non-Darwinian Revolution* (Baltimore: Johns
      Hopkins Press, 1988), chap. 7, on the non-Darwinian nature of
      "Social Darwinism."

24   Masaaki, *Japanese Thought,* 155–156.

25   John T. Gulick, "Darwin's Theory of Evolution Applied to Sandwich
      Island Mollusks," *Chrysanthemum* 3 (1883): 6–11 (11).

26   John T. Gulick, "Evolution in the Organic World," *Chinese Recorder*
      16 (1885), 246; idem, *Evolution, Racial and Habitudinal,* 215; idem,
      "False Biology and Fatalism," *The Friend* (Honolulu), June 1907: 12–
      14; August: 10–11; Charles Darwin, *On the Origin of Species* (Lon-
      don: John Murray, 1859), 206. "False Biology and Fatalism" was
      reprinted in *Bibliotheca Sacra* 65 (1908): 358–367.

27   J. T. Gulick, "Organic World," 247, emphasis added.

28   A short passage in *Evolution, Racial and Habitudinal* and again in
      "False Biology and Fatalism."

29   John T. Gulick, "Divergent Evolution through Cumulative Segre-
      gation," *Zoological Journal of the Linnean Society* 20 (1888), 201,
      222.

30   John T. Gulick, "The Inconsistencies of Utilitarianism as the Exclusive

Theory of Organic Evolution," *American Journal of Science* 40 (1890): 5ff. See also *Evolution, Racial and Habitudinal*, 197.

31   J. T. Gulick, "Sandwich Island Molluscs," 8.

32   E.g., B. F. Skinner, *Beyond Freedom and Dignity* (New York: Knopf, 1971).

33   Robert Boakes, *From Darwin to Behaviorism* (Cambridge: Cambridge University Press, 1984), 101.

34   J. T. Gulick, "Inconsistencies of Utilitarianism," 7.

35   *Chrysanthemum, The Chinese Recorder, The Friend,* and *Bibliotheca Sacra.*

36   John T. Gulick, "The Theory of Evolution in Some of Its Relations to Christian Theology," *Chinese Recorder* 16 (1885b): 296; "False Biology and Fatalism," 11. The scriptural allusion is to Philippians 2:12–13.

37   J. T. Gulick, "Christian Theology," 297. "Race" should be read as "species." The Gulick family was ardently antiracist.

38   A. Gulick, *John Thomas Gulick,* 265ff. On the other hand, Ronald Numbers has pointed out to me that there were Christian Darwinists among the Calvinist conservatives, including George Frederick Wright, Gulick's editor at *Bibliotheca Sacra.* Numbers, "George Frederick Wright," *Isis* 79 (1988): 624–645.

39   John T. Gulick, "Christianity and the Evolution of Rational Life," *Bibliotheca Sacra* 53 (1896), 74; A. Gulick, *John Thomas Gulick,* 294; J. T. Gulick, "Christian Theology," 295.

40   J. T. Gulick, "Rational Life," 69.

41   The details of this debate are well covered by Lesch, Kottler, and Provine. J. T. Gulick, "Inconsistencies of Utilitarianism," 13; idem, "Divergent Evolution," 105.

42   Provine, *Sewall Wright,* 228–229; Vernon L. Kellogg, *Darwinism To-Day* (New York: Henry Holt, 1908), 250.

43   See James Mark Baldwin, *Development and Evolution* (New York: Macmillan, 1902), for a full account of the debate; Boakes, *Darwin to Behaviorism,* 44, on social motives. The emphasis on behavior by these men made sense. Lloyd Morgan and Baldwin, following Romanes, were in the process of inventing comparative psychology. It is ironic that the role of behavior in the process of speciation had first been recognized not by the proto-psychologist Romanes, but by the more purely biological Gulick.

44   James Mark Baldwin, ed., *Dictionary of Philosophy and Psychology,* New edition, with corrections, 3 vols. (New York: Macmillan, 1925), 2:215.

45   C. H. Waddington, *The Evolution of an Evolutionist* (Ithaca, NY: Cornell University Press, 1975), 280. Note that Sewall Wright, the

"Neo-Darwinist" most influenced by Gulick, was seen by Waddington to be more sensitive to the role of behavior than were the other
founders of the Modern Synthesis.

46   A. Gulick, *John Thomas Gulick*, 309, 334, 355–356.

47   John T. Gulick, "The General Laws of Evolution as Seen in Social
      Evolution," *International Socialist Review* 7 (1907): 490.

48   Richard Levins and Richard Lewontin, *The Dialectical Biologist*
      (Cambridge: Harvard University Press, 1985): viii; 97–102.

49   The similarities between Lewontin and Gulick are striking, but I
      confirmed with Lewontin that he had read none of Gulick's writing
      before 1985. Lewontin now sees Gulick's "Fatalism and False Biol-
      ogy" as primarily a commentary on the third of Karl Marx's "Theses
      on Feuerbach." Personal communication, 20 December 1987.

ROY MACLEOD

5 Embryology and Empire
The Balfour Students and the Quest for Intermediate Forms in the Laboratory of the Pacific

"Monotremes oviparous, ovum meroblastic." This short message from W. H. Caldwell, relayed on 29 August 1884 by Professor Archibald Liversidge in Sydney to Professor H. N. Moseley, veteran of the *Challenger* and chairman of the Biology Section of the Congress of the British Association for the Advancement of Science (BAAS) then meeting at Montreal, forms a turning point in the history of imperial science in the Pacific.[1] "No more important telegram in a scientific sense had ever passed through the submarine cables," Moseley told his audience.[2] And as the tendrils of imperial communication told the world at large that the platypus and echidna laid eggs with thin shells, so they reminded the world of science of the familiar paradox by which colonial discoveries would become internationally known and rewarded only when recognized by the metropolis. Caldwell's announcement effectively asserted intellectual property rights for Britain over a central fact and artifact of Australia's "bright and savage land."[3] Even so, within two years, his discovery would propel widely separated "transplanted Britons" to form an Australasian Association for the Advancement of Science, with an announced interest in studying the Pacific from tropic to pole.[4] The elusive platypus, long a scientific puzzle, had proved a political catalyst as well.

A century later, Caldwell's discovery—of facts presumably well known to the Aboriginal trackers who guided him—cannot be divorced from the circumstances that brought the young Englishman to Australia's shores. These form a chapter in the history of British science in which the advancement of research proceeded in harmony with the expansion of political and commercial interests. In this case, the Asia-Pacific region, like other regions under British influence, was confirmed as a key site for field research, a "privileged space for doing science," as essential to science as the museum, lecture room, and laboratory.[5] As such, it becomes an important locus for historical inquiry.[6]

140

In the Pacific, scientific interests and political opportunism combined to make the history of science relevant to European imperialism. Conversely, for more than two hundred years, the Pacific offered Europe a supremely diversified testing ground, a garden, a zoo, and a quarry for the discovery, demonstration, and refutation of established theories. Nor did Pacific experience leave untouched those Europeans who ventured into the region.[7] European science in the Pacific—or, more usefully, the Asia-Pacific region—divides easily into periods of exploration and discovery, of contact and survey, and of modern systematic research. Each stage left residues which have influenced the culture of science in the region. The significance of these becomes more tangible when individuals and their discoveries are retrieved from the iconographic literature, and placed within the social and geographical contexts that gave them rise. In Darwinian biology, circumstances shaped cases, as British naturalists drew upon opportunities made possible by the expansion of British interests, and on sites made accessible by the presence of a friendly flag.

The Imperial Impulse

In the history of Western exploration and discovery—in the Americas, then in Africa—Asia and the Pacific provided both motive and means.[8] By the age of Banks and Cook, British men of science deployed tactics structured by metropolitan institutions and mandated by "interlocking directorates" of scientific, commercial, moral, and political interests. In tracing linkages among the factors underlying science and empire, we may canvass widely for cause and effect, argument and justification.[9] It is tempting to place such developments within range of debates about agency and contingency in the history of ideas. Scientific theories are commonly influenced by their cognitive environments, while their applications have frequently acquired political influence, shaped by ideological preferences.[10] There seems, however, little need to debate claims for "strong forces," mandating causal links between external influences and "internal" scientific developments, so long as there is such abundant evidence of contingent relationships between the pursuit of natural knowledge, political investment, and commercial enterprise. Such relationships were to culminate in policies for development in the colonial and post-colonial world. But in the nineteenth century, these interests were not the only, or even the most dominant, influences at issue in the Pacific, where intellectual rivalries and international prestige were also at stake.

Trade, it is said, follows the flag, but in the Pacific, curiosity accompanied both. From Magellan to Cook, Europeans entered the Pacific impelled not only by visions of conquest but also by a metropolitan thirst for illustrations of nature—for the unusual, the exotic, and the bizarre. The region's rich diversity, its unique flora and fauna exposed exceptions and errors in received wisdom. Intermittent forays of discovery gave way to intensive surveys, linked with political and naval display. European naturalists, geographers, and astronomers visited the Pacific to record the movements of the ocean, the history of its inhabitants, the patterns of its skies, the distribution of its species, and the natural history of its islands, atolls, and shores. For the Netherlands, France, and later Germany, such engagements generated explosive quantities of information for museums, laboratories, and galleries of art. In England, such returns were audited in the botanical house of Kew, in the ethnography cabinets of the British Museum, and in the collections of a dozen museums and galleries, both public and private.[11]

An imperial presence conveyed an unequivocal (if debated) sense of place and ownership. The naming of parts—geographical, geological, botanical, and zoological—established a broader claim—notably put, as James Secord has written, by Roderick Murchison—that the natural history of regions belonging to or protected by the British Crown belonged also to British science.[12] In the Pacific, Britain was easily the dominant naval power. By a series of maneuvers completed by the early 1900s, the Union Jack was raised over Fiji, Tonga, Papua, the Solomons, the Gilbert and Ellice Islands (now Kiribati and Tuvalu), and (with France) over the New Hebrides (now Vanuatu).[13] In ways that mirrored the "scramble for Africa," the European powers partitioned the Pacific, claiming its islands and cataloging its peoples and resources. Now, more than ever, there was opportunity for British scholars to capitalize upon regions of the map that European geographers conveniently colored red.

This development was relevant to the interests of British science in at least two ways. The interests of "imperial science" were present in the Pacific since the voyages of Cook. But by the late 1840s, as Lord John Russell's administration laid the foundations of the "second" British Empire, the scientific institutions of Britain acquired a representative interest in its colonies outside North America—many of which Britain acquired, borrowing the famous phrase, in a "fit of absence of mind." From the 1870s, when Lord Kimberley began forward moves in West Africa, Malaya, and Fiji, through the 1880s, when explorers and governments assumed the civilizing mission of Froude and Seeley, Disraeli and his successors committed Britain to a colonial empire beyond India.[14] Within the political economy of this new imperialism came a special role for science, as for technology. The steamship, the telegraph, the railroad, and tropical medicine were obvious "tools of empire," underwriting British rule from Calcutta to the Cape, and from Vancouver to Hobart.[15] But by the 1880s, what Lord Milner called the "essential principles of organic imperial unity"[16] were complemented by the unifying rhetoric supplied by new discoveries in geology, biology, and natural history.

The "imperial idea" of the 1880s coincided with a new phase in scientific exploration. The age of discovery that opened with Cook, climaxed in the great surveys of the *Challenger*. Thereafter, voyages of survey were overtaken by expeditions having as their object the testing of particular hypotheses in the laboratory of the Pacific. Students of anthropology, zoology, and botany traversed the islands, archipelagos, and rim, consolidating the pioneering geographical and navigational discoveries of the 1830s and 1840s. Some expeditions were assisted by the Admiralty and the learned societies. Others were led independently. But by the 1890s, most would be found working within an intellectual domain shaped by the writings of Darwin and Wallace. For these investigators, species new or unfamiliar to European science offered fresh evidence of geological and biological change. Little-known or ill-understood peoples, many "protected" by the British crown, seemed to test Darwinian theories of variation. Perhaps it could be demonstrated that "primitive" societies recapitulated earlier stages of civilization; certainly, the observation of transitional species could "naturalize idealistic morphology,"[17] improve knowledge of phylogenetic relationships, and suggest possible evolutionary mechanisms. Ultimately, to seize such opportunities was to open a new chapter in the history of British biological imperialism and in the history of the Darwinian program.

Cambridge and Comparative Morphology

Perhaps nowhere in England were the imperial mission and Darwinian program so completely and artlessly combined than among the young naturalists who came to prominence in the "reformed" Cambridge of the 1880s. At a time when Sir John Seeley's lectures on the "Expansion of Europe" were charting Britain's historical future beyond India, Africa, the Caribbean, and the Orient, many scholars embraced an imperial destiny defined by overseas field-work. Foremost among them was the physiologist Michael (later Sir Michael) Foster, who migrated from University College London to Trinity College in 1870, recommended by T. H. Huxley as the man most fitted to launch a program of research in experimental biology.[18] Emerging from three decades of reform in its statutes and practices, Cambridge was stirring from its dogmatic slumbers.[19] While James Clerk Maxwell introduced laboratory physics to the newly established Cavendish, Foster took under his tutelage some of the most talented undergraduates then reading for the Natural Sciences Tripos,[20] and inspired them to take up research. Like Huxley, Foster saw science as a unifying agency of empire, and was an evangelist for an "imperial vision" in British science.[21] He moved resolutely into domains of physiology and anatomy hitherto dominated by Europeans, and by the 1890s, Cambridge had bred a generation of scholars —including Sydney Vines, F. O. Bower, and later, A. E. Shipley, S. F. Harmer, Hans Gadow, and Walter Gaskell—who were to "imperialize" large domains of research in the plant and animal kingdoms.

Among Foster's men, working within the new Darwinian synthesis, comparative morphology was to prove as exciting as physiology. The theoretical othodoxy that had dominated the field derived from the 1830s, and the work of Georges Cuvier and Geoffroy Saint-Hilaire.[22] By 1880, it had become identified in England with Professor Richard Owen, symbolically commanding the impregnable heights of the Royal College of Surgeons and the British Museum.[23] Owen spoke for a tradition that gave prominence to fossil evidence as demonstrating serial development, but transgressing neither the *scala naturae* nor the temporality of individual forms. His influence within and upon Australasia was profound.[24] With Darwin, however, had come a more dynamic view of morphology, one that called, *inter alia,* for the discovery and description of *living* organisms to supply—as Carl Gegenbaur put it—"evidence of the doctrine of development in anatomical enquiry."[25] In the search for living evidences of evolution, the race would pass to the swift and soon favored those who enjoyed an imperial view of the world.

Within the Darwinian framework, comparative morphologists gave a special place to the doctrine of recapitulation.[26] This body of theory, derived in its pre-Darwinian form from the transcendental arguments of *Naturphilosophie,* argued that ancestral adult stages have been, and are, repeated in the ontogeny of individual animals and are observable in the embryonic stages of their descendants. That this theory eventually became encumbered by its own vocabulary is a commonplace,[27] and, as early as 1850, anatomists were wrestling with its contrasting, conflated, and confused positions.[28] In particular, authoritative opinion was divided between those who accepted what E. S. Russell has called the "Meckel-Serres law," which argued that stages of ontogeny run in parallel with the sequence of adults of different species, arranged in a linear chain of being,[29] and those who preferred to follow Karl Ernst von Baer, who argued that development did not require recapitulation.[30] Embryos, wrote von Baer, are undifferentiated general forms, not previous adult ancestors. Distinguishing features were, he argued, added later, as development proceeds from the general to the specific (or, in the phrase later popularized by Herbert Spencer, as homogeneity precedes heterogeneity).[31]

For Darwinians, there were problems with the theory of recapitulation that logic alone could not solve. It was unclear how natural selection could be applied to the process of "condensation" between different stages, which must occur if phylogenetic changes are to mimic an animal's ontogenetic passage through its ancestral stages.[32] Yet some Darwinians were confident that a solution was possible, and many followed the example of Ernst Haeckel, who had given the doctrine the force of "law" as the "biogenetical principle"—encapsulated in the famous phrase, "ontogeny recapitulates phylogeny."[33]

In morphological circles, controversy turned largely on logical predictions of what might or ought to occur; far less was known about what actually occurred in nature.[34] If physical comparisons revealed homologous structures in the embryological development of two forms, one could hypothesize that those structures shared a recent phylogenetic relationship. But this required a descriptive embryology, sufficiently unequivocal to permit the inference of evolutionary relationships. This in turn presupposed a series of careful observations, under laboratory conditions, of different reproductive systems and fetal stages, and the composition of life histories, if possible, of intermediate, and possibly transitional species. Of such rare specimens, little was known.

As Ernst Mayr reminds us, Darwin had looked to embryology to supply evidence for evolution and common descent, arguing that variations, appearing at a "very early period" in an organism's life, must offer "by far the strongest single class of facts in favour" of evolution.[35] He based his explanation of development on the origin of variation. But post-Darwinian debate continued to revolve around pre-Darwinian premises, as scholars from Maine to Munich offered different explanations to account for successive embryonic comparisons and their implications for evolutionary theory. Not surprisingly, the challenge of working in this, the "most productive of the morphogenetical specialised spheres," as Nordenskiöld put it, eventually attracted "the most eminent biologists of the time."[36]

At first, however, few in England rose to the challenge. E. Ray Lankester, in his preface to the first English translation of Gegenbaur's *Elements of Comparative Anatomy* in 1876, deplored England's lack of interpretative morphological research. Discounting the largely fossil-based reputations of Owen and even T. H. Huxley's popular manuals, there was, he said, "no modern work on comparative anatomy" to illustrate that "throughout and without reserve the Doctrine of Evolution appears as the living, moving investment of the dry bones of anatomical fact."[37] In effect, British comparative anatomy was late to take up the "morphological explanation of the phenomena of form met with in the organisation of the animal body." This in turn required a perspective of global diversity, as well as an orientation toward function, which combined the lessons of physiology and embryology, of tissues and organs as well as fossils.[38]

Among Englishmen, this new Darwinian morphological and embryological program, begun in Europe, and soon applied—as Keith Benson has shown—in the United States,[39] had its most influential advocates in Cambridge. There, the challenge was picked up by Francis Maitland (Frank) Balfour (1851–1882), the tall, energetic, good-looking, almost mythic aristocrat. Educated at Harrow and Trinity, younger brother of the former philosopher and future prime minister, and an excellent sportsman (figure 5.1), Balfour parted company with traditional classificatory biology soon after taking a First in the Natural Sciences Tripos in 1873. His teacher, Michael Foster, who indefatigably encouraged undergraduates showing any scientific inclination, "either suggested to him or acquiesced in his own suggestion that he should . . . set to work on some distinct research" and set him to dissecting layers of chick blastoderm. In December 1873, Foster sent Balfour to the Naples Zoological Station where he was to study the embryology of elasmobranch fishes (including sharks and rays), about which "little was known, . . . but which . . . could not help proving of interest and importance."[40] There he soon revealed the relationship between sharks and other vertebrates—in Foster's words, making "them tell the tale of evolution."[41] Some authors had suggested that blood relationships were the best guiding principles; others, homologies of structure, shown in embryonic change.[42] Accepting that the principal aim of comparative embryology was the clarification of phylogenetic relationships, Balfour set about collecting evidence that would throw light on evolutionary development.

In 1874, Balfour was elected a Fellow of Trinity College, and, in 1876, College Lecturer in animal morphology. There he assisted Foster in completing a small book on embryology, and began publishing

5.1 A portrait of F. M. Balfour (1851–1882). From *The Works of Francis Maitland Balfour,* ed. Michael Foster and Adam Sedgwick (London: Macmillan, 1885). Courtesy of the Royal Society of London.

on the elasmobranchs. Espousing what Mayr might call a "mild version" of recapitulation, Balfour seems to have avoided a general theory of development; his methods were those of a practical embryologist, who believed his work could be best use to evolutionary theory by remaining detached from ideological positions. In consequence, it is possible to read him in different ways. The man who, in Stephen Gould's words, became "England's staunchest recapitulationist"[43] is, to Peter Bowler, an example of token lip-service paid to Haeckel and a conscious advocate of the opposing position of von Baer.[44] Above all, however, Balfour refused to let theory stand in the way of research. His account of the elasmobranchs, which appeared in 1878 with a sensitive dedication to Darwin, was soon enhanced by his work on the ancestry of all vertebrates, reflecting a new tradition of university research, replacing heady popular clamor for "missing links" with a scholarly, dispassionate quest for evidence of relationships among the earliest metazoans.

Undergraduates attending Balfour's lectures heard him state Darwin's view that "embryos of the most distinct species belonging to the same class are closely similar."[45] To this message, Balfour added his own Darwinian conviction. "The embryological record," he wrote, "is almost always abbreviated in accordance with the tendency of nature (to be explained on the principle of the survival of the fittest) to attain her ends by the easiest means."[46] To unravel these "embryological abbreviations" became the object, and field "detective" work, the means:

> When the life history of a form is fully known, the most difficult part of the task is still before the scientific embryologist. Like the scholar with his manuscript, the embryologist has by a process of careful and critical examination to determine where the gaps are present, to detect the later insertions, and to place in order what has been misplaced.[47]

In 1880, Balfour took his message to the British Association;[48] and the same year, he began a series of studies, published as "from the Morphological Laboratory," in affectionate tribute to Foster's pioneering *Studies from the Physiological Laboratory* in the 1870s.[49] In 1880 also appeared the first of two volumes devoted to his *Treatise on Comparative Embryology,* a work of "unrivalled importance at the time" and what Nordenskiöld has called a powerful defense of Darwinian biology in its classical form.[50] Indeed, Darwin, on receiving a copy, pronounced that its young author "will someday be the chief of the English Biologists."[51] In less than five years, Balfour had set a course for others to follow. He was exalted by the Royal Society (F.R.S., 1878; Royal Medal, 1881), honored by Glasgow (LL.D, 1881), and courted by Oxford and Edinburgh, until at Foster's insistence, Cambridge in 1882 created for him a personal chair for life, the first in animal morphology in England.[52]

That year, alas, was to be, in Huxley's famous words, "a dark year for English science."[53] That year, Darwin died peacefully at Down House. So also died his young acolyte, Frank Balfour, in a tragic Alpine accident. Balfour was only thirty-one. "Probably few lives of this generation were so full of promise as the one thus cut short," Foster mourned.[54] Immediately, friends, students, colleagues from around the world contributed to a research fund in his memory. By the end of the year, there was £8,446, enough to establish the "Balfour Studentship"—the instrument by which his memory was to reach beyond Cambridge and encompass the world for Darwinian biology.[55]

Balfour's Progeny

By its terms of foundation, the Balfour Studentship was to promote "original research in Biology, especially Animal Morphology; and to further by occasional grants original research in the subject."[56] It was specified that, unlike college fellowships, typically awarded on the basis of Tripos examination results and restricted to members of the university, these would be open, and awarded on the basis of promise alone.

As it was construed, that promise soon reflected well on Cambridge biology. Since 1883, there have been more than thirty Balfour Students. Fourteen of these were appointed before World War I; but in certain respects the years of the first nine constitute the Studentship's "heroic age".[57] At a time when few Oxbridge College fellowships were filled by natural scientists, and when, outside the Exhibition of 1851 awards, there were no government scholarships for research, the Balfour awards were highly unusual in England.[58] Led by the shining example of Johns Hopkins, some North American universities had already begun to award graduate fellowships. But few British universities had such adornments; and at Cambridge, the princely stipend of £200 a year for three years promised to produce a new generation of research scholars—in fact, if not in name, equivalent to the first "post-doctorals" at any British university.

Of the first nine Students, three distinguished themselves in the Pacific, three in the Indian Ocean. Of the Pacific trinity, Caldwell is perhaps the most widely remembered. His scholarly life was well advanced before he left Cambridge. Taking a First in the Natural Sciences Tripos in 1881 and a Fellowship at Caius in 1883, he became the university's first Demonstrator in Comparative Anatomy and a protégé of Balfour. Highly skilled, Caldwell invented the first automatic microtome to be used at Cambridge for cutting thin sections, and inspired its later manufacture by the Cambridge Scientific Instrument Company.[59]

In the autumn of 1881, Balfour followed Foster's example, and sent Caldwell to the table reserved for Cambridge at the Zoological Station at Naples, directed by Haeckel's student, Anton Dohrn.[60] At Capri, Caldwell fell ill with typhoid; he was rescued by his teacher, who succumbed to the disease himself.[61] Under Balfour and Dohrn, Caldwell entered the first stage of the embryologist's rite of passage—in his case, some years of laboratory work on eggs and embryos, notably of the *Peripatus,* a genus of tropical terrestrial invertebrates thought to lie between the annelids and the arthropods.[62] But to pursue the *Peripatus* involved further travel overseas—a proposition not anticipated by the Balfour Trustees and at first opposed by the university on administrative grounds. Eventually, however, the point was conceded. Caldwell and his successors were destined to work overseas.

The immediate stimulus for Caldwell's famous mission to Australia followed upon a suggestion—also originating with Balfour—that he find and study living examples of *Ceratodus,* the Queensland lungfish,[63] which had been discovered in 1871 and proclaimed to be a "living fossil." Specimens of the lungfish, revealing fresh evidence of evolutionary anatomy, had reached Cambridge (thanks to Archibald Liversidge) in 1879; its study *in situ* might, it was thought, throw light on the evolution of amphibians from ancestral fish.[64] While in Australia, Caldwell was also given a second task. He was to learn what he could about two persisting and controversial questions in European biology—the reproductive system of the marsupials and monotremes and the correct classificatory relationship of the monotremes (including the echidna and the platypus). The first dried platypus had arrived in Europe in 1797. For generations, its proper place in the animal kingdom had been disputed.[65] European taxonomists held that all milk-giving animals gave birth to live young; and classified all warm-blooded, egg-laying animals as birds, and all egg-laying quadrupeds as reptiles. Having characteristics of all three groups and appearing to be neither exclusively reptile nor bird, amphibian nor mammal, monotremes were symbol and substance of the "land of contrarieties"—a place of creatures that, in Darwin's words, "might cause an unbeliever in anything beyond his reason" to believe that "two distinct Creators must have been at work."[66]

The central questions were: do these animals give milk, and do they lay eggs? Reports from Australia in the early 1800s confirmed that monotremes laid eggs, but the discovery in 1824 that they also gave milk provoked vigorous debate. Georges Cuvier and Richard Owen argued that they were true ovoviviparous mammals—that is, hatched their young from eggs within their bodies, giving milk and producing live young. In contrast, Geoffroy Saint-Hilaire, who was prepared to accept evidence for an anomalous, possibly transitional creature, claimed that they laid eggs and did not give milk. Both schools of thought worked from preserved specimens; both tried to fit the known evidence—that is, evidence reaching Europe—within preconceived categories.[67] In Sydney, George Bennett, a leading colonial "physician-naturalist" and first secretary of the Australian Museum, who had found evidences of milk for which Owen had received published credit, had spent years looking for specimens to confirm Owen's theory.[68] That theory was disputed by Johann Louis Gerhard Krefft, the volatile and ultimately defrocked Darwinian curator of the Australia Museum. But, in the absence of living evidence, or of testimony from Aborigines, who must surely have known the truth, the official London view—associated indelibly with Owen—prevailed.[69]

Not for the first time in British history, comparative anatomy dissolved easily into politics,[70] and it was no accident that a student of Foster, himself a student of Huxley, was given the task of resolving the question. It was a departure equally important for the standing of

Cambridge biology, for the new field of experimental embryology, and for the reputation of British comparative morphology. Caldwell sailed in 1883 for Sydney, where he was given the use of a laboratory by Archibald Liversidge, another former pupil of Foster, and a staunch empire man, who since 1874 had held the chair of chemistry at the University of Sydney. With Liversidge's help, Caldwell spent several months analyzing specimens and preparing for what would prove an eventful expedition to outback Queensland.

Caldwell's subsequent exploits on the Burnett River are well known.[71] Thanks to knowledgeable Aboriginal trackers, whose contribution he scarcely credited, Caldwell was given a supply of echidna eggs and eventually a platypus which, sadly, he shot.[72] That unfortunate creature and its eggs achieved instant immortality. The eggs confirmed the belief that monotremes were oviparous (that is, laid eggs then hatched them) like birds and reptiles and furthermore demonstrated that the eggs were thin shelled, like those of reptiles.[73] The news was flashed to Liversidge in Sydney, thence to Montreal. A nearly simultaneous announcement by a colonial scientist in South Australia was overlooked,[74] and the imperial announcement was formally communicated to the Royal Society in London by Foster.[75] With this imprimatur, Caldwell's "discovery" overturned the orthodoxy of Owen. When assimilated by naturalists in Europe, it forced revisions in the classification of Mammalia that were to remain unchallenged for the next eighty years.[76]

Caldwell's three-year studentship was renewed in 1886. His academic future seemed secure. His work in the Pacific had underlined the growing importance of Cambridge to the forward movement of British biology and its willingness to send men overseas for empirical field work. In the end, however, he did no further work of importance. Caldwell returned a hero, but, for reasons which remain unclear, became a hostage to oblivion. Little more was heard of the "platypus man," who left science to become a paper maker in Scotland.[77]

A kinder fate awaited both his department and his successor. William Bateson (1861–1926), son of the master of St. John's, next won the Studentship, on his second application in 1887.[78] Peter Bowler has suggested that once Balfour was gone, his students soon began to lose interest in evolutionary speculation. This is only partly true and has the ring of hindsight, for Bateson had come to embryology through Balfour and spent his early research demonstrating what were thought to be evolutionary affinities between vertebrates and the wormlike *Balanoglossus*. As a Balfour Student, Bateson worked closely with Adam Sedgwick, Balfour's pupil and successor as Reader in Morphology, who had recently translated Gegenbaur's *Textbook of Zoology*.[79] Indeed, from the late 1880s, Cambridge zoology—nominally chaired by its professor, Alfred Newton, the ornithologist—was largely directed by Sedgwick, aided and abetted by Foster in physiology. Advanced biology courses in the Tripos were placed in the hands of Balfour's "second generation" of students, Harmer and Shipley, who taught invertebrate biology, and Hans Gadow, who taught vertebrate biology. With their senior demonstrator, John Stanley Gardiner, they led Cambridge into the mainstream of modern biology.[80]

As he consolidated his position in Cambridge, Sedgwick used the Balfour Studentship to run his department's writ into research sites throughout Asia and the Pacific. For a decade, this effort mirrored Cambridge's confidence in the embryological program and in the likely outcome of searches for empirical confirmations of evolutionary theory. In 1891, Alfred Marshall, speaking to the British Association, devoted his presidential address to the biogenetic law, which, he said, "forms the basis of the science of Embryology, and which alone justifies the extraordinary attention this science has received."[81] Within a decade, however, the program had come under attack, not least from Sedgwick. By 1894, Sedgwick had come to believe that neither Haeckel's nor von Baer's theories could be reliably demonstrated.[82] Early stages of growth in fact did not reveal ancestral relationships, outside the developmental stages of larvae—which retained for this reason a fascination for morphologists.[83] Otherwise, evidence was inconclusive. Sedgwick did no more in this area, and for a time the baton passed again to Germany, where Wilhelm Roux was startling traditional morphologists from their preoccupation with what Garland Allen has called the "evolutionary kaleidoscope." Roux had shown the importance of the experimental study of causes of differentiation, using laboratory techniques for the modification of embryos. His work was to mark an early stage in the *fin de siècle* "revolt from morphology" and the beginnings of "mechanistic embryology."[84] A second aspect of the "revolt" came at Cambridge, when Sedgwick's pupil, Bateson, seeking other mechanisms to explain the theory of natural selection, turned away from the Balfour tradition altogether, and took up the study of heredity instead.[85]

Like Caldwell, Bateson traveled to the Asia-Pacific—in his case, across the steppes of Russia, where he studied the relationship between environmental variation and variability among animal populations. In early work on the Chordates, published before he was awarded a studentship, he had remarked that the morphological search for genealogical trees had become the "subject for some ridicule, perhaps deserved."[86] Like Balfour, however, Bateson subjected theory to the "touchstone of fact."[87] The first results of his field work in Asia were made known in his *Materials for the Study of Variation,* published in 1894. The systematic study of many organisms led Bateson to conclude that variations are discontinuous and as such are determined by heredity. His book produced a much publicized uproar among those who favored continuous variation and from the biometricians led by Karl Pearson and Francis Galton;[88] but he proceeded with animal breeding experiments and in some respects anticipated Mendel's discoveries some years before their "rediscovery" in 1900. At the end of his studentship, Bateson returned to Cambridge and, ultimately, to the foundation chair at the John Innes Institution.[89]

However much he broke with the Balfour tradition, Bateson was not to be the last of the Balfour line. The third Balfour Student was Walter Heape (1855–1929), who came to Cambridge from Owen's College, Manchester, via the superintendency of the Marine Biological Laboratory at Plymouth. Like Caldwell, Heape was an inventor and a protégé of the Balfour program. Like him, he collected specimens of *Peripatus*—this time, at the Cape. He spent his three studentship years (1890–1893) in India, studying the reproductive system of monkeys, a study that formed the basis of pioneering work on sex hormones. He held no further academic appointments, but he did produce well-known guides to fertility, one of which, usefully entitled *Preparation for Marriage,* appeared in 1914.[90]

His successor, the fourth Balfour Student, Arthur Willey (1867–1942), came from University College London and retraced Caldwell's steps to Sydney and the Pacific. There he spent months searching New Guinea, New Caledonia, and the Loyalty Islands for the elusive pearly nautilus, in hopes of establishing its relationship to the squid and cuttlefish. In the end, the creature's reproduction eluded him, but Willey succeeded in bringing back ample quantities of specimens to furnish Sedgwick's laboratory shelves. His studentship, awarded in 1893, was renewed in 1897 and 1898; his impressive *Zoological Results* was published by Cambridge University Press between 1898 and 1902. Building on Bateson's work, Willey established the evolutionary status of the well-known protochordate, *Amphioxus.* In 1902, he decided to remain in the East, where he became director of the Colonial Museum in Ceylon. There he remained for eight years, before becoming head of the department of zoology at McGill University in Montreal, thus virtually circumnavigating the empire.

In some respects, the fifth Balfour Student, John Stanley Gardiner (1872–1946), owed his selection in 1899 to his earlier experience of the Pacific. Sent by Cambridge to work in Naples, he returned to England to take part as a volunteer naturalist on the first Coral Reef Expedition led by Professor W. J. Sollas, subsequently of Oxford, to the atoll of Funafuti. Gardiner's reports of the expedition, which failed to confirm Darwin's theory of subsidence, pitted him against Darwinians, who led a subsequent, Australian-based expedition, directed by T. W. (later Sir) Edgeworth David.[91] But Gardiner's experience brought him preferment. With his Balfour Studentship, he again went overseas, this time to the Laccadive and Maldive Islands, where again he studied the morphology of corals. The least "embryological" of the early Balfour Students, Gardiner was the earliest to reach high academic position. Elected to the Royal Society in 1908, he became professor of zoology at Cambridge in 1909.[92]

Following Gardiner, the sixth Student, John Budgett (1872–1904), died at the age of only thirty-two, before he could make a name from his studies in Africa.[93] But the seventh, Reginald Punnett (1875–1967), a Fellow of Caius who joined Sedgwick's department in 1902, held the studentship during four years from 1904 before returning to the demonstratorship left vacant by Gardiner's rapid promotion. By the time of Punnett's appointment, however, the zoology department had begun to shift its emphasis, and his career mirrored that change. When Mendel's work came to light, Cambridge zoology moved rapidly from the study of transitional species to the eggs of individual species, away from the biogenetical principle, toward the study of heredity. In both cases, this led away from the field, into the farm and the laboratory. Like Bateson and other famous Mendelians who had begun their careers as recapitulationists in the tradition of speculative phylogeny, Punnett left morphology and systematic zoology; in 1905 he produced a volume on *Mendelism,* a book so timely and popular that it became a best seller. The studentship gave him time to develop the next stage of his career, when he joined with Bateson (whose papers he later edited) in launching the *Journal of Genetics* in 1911. Ironically, given his origins in Frank Balfour's image, he ended his long professional life in 1940 as the first Arthur Balfour Professor of Genetics at the University of Cambridge.

The last two prewar Students, Clifford Dobell (1886–1949) and John Fortescue Fryer (1886–1948), marked the full transition of Cambridge zoology from comparative morphology, in the Balfourian idiom, to genetics and applied biology in the post-Mendelian sense. Their tenure also coincided with the last days of Adam Sedgwick and the end of the direct Balfour intellectual line. Dobell was already a Fellow of Trinity when he was elected a Balfour Student; he spent his studentship in Ceylon with Punnett, where both visited Willey, who by then had become director of the Colombo Museum. All enjoyed close associations and together strengthened Cambridge's links with colonial research, often at official levels. Dobell's early work in proto-zoology and parasitology culminated in a career lasting thirty years with the National Institute for Medical Research.[94] Fryer, the son of a Cambridgeshire farmer, chased butterflies in Ceylon on his student-ship, returning in 1913 to pioneer the use of genetics in entomology and agriculture. He became secretary of the Agricultural Research Council in 1944 and was knighted in 1946.[95]

By 1914, no one doubted that the program in evolutionary embry-ology sustained by Balfour had run its course. Bateson was later to recall the logical objection that embryological evidence could only help "tell the story" of evolution when it established as a general prin-ciple that embryological stages did indeed reveal lines along which a given species has developed. The proof of this proposition depended on inferred resemblances; but general principles were inferences from special cases that could not themselves lay claim to general truth.[96] Jane Maienschein has persuasively argued that descriptive embryol-ogy failed because it left unanswered, or, more strictly, unasked, the problem of causation. If the causes of differentiation lay in factors of heredity or in the environment of the cell, morphology as then con-ceived was unable to address either domain.[97]

Stephen Gould has argued that Mendelianism ultimately disproved the "laws" of evolution that recapitulation required.[98] The effect of this discovery was to displace careers and unsettle long-standing con-victions. For some, the adjustment was painful. Toward the end of his life, according to his biographer, Arthur Willey could not come fully to terms with the lack of progress in demonstrating ancestral relations by the discovery of anatomical resemblances between different animal types. "Conclusions which had come to be regarded as almost sacred ... had with the increase of knowledge become suspect [and] not [been] altogether worthy of the absolute faith which had been accorded to them."[99] In any event, given the complexity of organisms, the prospect of tracing ancestral lines was doomed to disappoint-ment.[100] The process of evolution, Willey argued, must be viewed as a total process; and as this view gained currency, comparative embryol-ogy eventually discarded its Victorian predilection for hypothetical ancestral forms.

Conclusion

In the Asia-Pacific region, discoveries made possible by the convenience of imperial possesssion and biological diversity were shaped by Darwinian strategies that both assumed and sought for evidences of evolution. The laboratory of the Pacific gave unique opportunities, ably seized by Cambridge and British scholars elsewhere, that sustained a metropolitan research program for almost a generation. By the close of the century, the intellectual dominion of Haeckel's biogenetic law had been eclipsed, leaving behind much confusion as to the way (or whether) ontogeny is, or is not, related to phylogeny. While some organisms appear to recapitulate the adult stages of their ancestors, other adult stages resemble the juvenile stages of their ancestors. Simple metazoans that seem alike are not necessarily related. The consequences of their study for Darwinism remained unresolved. For those who later viewed evolution as a holistic process, meeting the requirements of what Donald Anderson has called "functional gradualism," Darwinian theory did not exclude the possibility of parallel or convergent evolution.[101] In such directions, however, comparative morphology offered few prospects for closing theoretical debate.

But this is to look ahead. In the last analysis, the early Balfour program and its Students provided a highly visible, practical application of a coherent, open theoretical discourse, significant for the development of British biology and its presence overseas. Under Sedgwick's leadership, the Balfour Studentships made Cambridge a focal point in the new biology that followed this discourse. As fashion shifted, so did Balfour's successors, moving away from morphology and macrozoology, toward the applications of genetics to agriculture. After World War I, Cambridge saw proposals to explore evolutionary linkages through chemical embryology, a subject that interested Joseph Needham in the 1930s.[102] These were ultimately overtaken by the rise of molecular biology. But although the research interests of Balfour Students changed, their reputation endured, and the studentship became a significant rite of passage for those highflyers destined to take up leading positions in British biology. Drawn from men of proven ability, the first generation of Students predictably reached the top of their profession. Seven of the first nine became Fellows of the Royal Society. One died too young to achieve greatness. Only Caldwell, with whom it all began, failed to reach high scientific honors; he is today remembered only by his microtome, in a displayed case outside the Cambridge zoology department, suitably named after Balfour.

Caldwell and his early successors traversed the progression of biological expeditions in the Pacific, from the pre-Darwinian voyages of survey and collection, symbolized by the *Beagle* and the *Rattlesnake*, to the modern era of systematic exploration, begun by the *Challenger* and continuing with government and privately financed expeditions of international significance. In his generation, the imperial network sustained British biology, drawing upon colonial observers as participants, even where isolation made participation difficult. When, by the second quarter of our century, the Pacific became less a place in which to look for transitional organisms than a place to study global variation, the contribution of the early Balfour Students had become an established part of Cambridge scientific memory. Its Darwinian tradition, and its Asia-Pacific encounters, gave this aspect of Cambridge science an epistemological and thematic unity.

Ironically, Australia, which supplied so much evidence for the Darwinian debate, witnessed both the beginning of the Balfour program and its end. In 1914, on the eve of the European war, William Bateson, perhaps the equinoctial Balfour Student—bred in the Balfour tradition, and yet its severest critic—was invited to Australia as the president of the British Association for the Advancement of Science on the occasion of the B.A.'s first (and only) visit to the southern continent. The congress was widely welcomed as an imperial event, rekindling old arguments about imperial federation, but also giving Australians an unparalleled opportunity to meet their British mentors.[103] In greeting biologists at the periphery, Bateson chose as his subject the history and future not of Darwinism, but of Mendelian theory. His message was not irrelevant to the future of empire itself. If biological analogies could be applied to social systems, Britain's dominion, Bateson predicted, would endure through a process of discontinuous, creative individualism, and not through a policy of social imperialism.[104] "The teaching of biology," he told his Sydney audience, "is perfectly clear. We are what we are by virtue of our differentiation."[105] Science itself had progressed "not by imperceptible mass-improvement, but by the sporadic birth of penetrative genius."[106] His message appealed to a country destined to recapitulate British ideologies and institutions, but seeking different evolutionary directions. That prospect held high promise, and not least for the independent representatives of Australian biology, already at work forming their own research traditions in the laboratory of the Pacific.

Notes

For their advice and assistance in the preparation of this essay, I wish to thank Professor Donald Anderson, F.R.S., and Professor Charles Birch, F.A.A., University of Sydney; Dr. A. V. Grimstone, Pembroke College, Cambridge; Professor Fritz Rehbock, University of Hawaii; and Dr. Elisabeth Leedham-Green, University Archivist, Cambridge University.

1   Roy MacLeod, "On Visiting the Moving Metropolis: Reflections on
         the Architecture of Imperial Science," *Historical Records of Austra-
         lian Science* 5 (3) (1982): 1–16, reprinted in *Scientific Colonialism:
         A Cross-Cultural Comparison,* ed. Nathan Reingold and Marc
         Rothenberg (Washington, DC: Smithsonian Institution Press, 1987),
         217–250.

2   H. N. Moseley, "On the Ova of Monotremes," *Report of the British
         Association for the Advancement of Science* (Montreal), 54 (1884):
         777.

3   To borrow the fine title of Ann Moyal, *A Bright and Savage Land:
         Science in Colonial Australia* (Sydney: Cassell, 1986).

4   Cf. Roy MacLeod, ed., *The Commonwealth of Science: ANZAAS
         and the Scientific Enterprise in Australasia, 1888–1988* (Melbourne:
         Oxford University Press, 1988).

5   The uses of the "laboratory" in the field sciences, with their special
         connotations, awaits the careful treatment now being accorded the
         so-called experimental sciences. See David Gooding et al., eds., *The
         Uses of Experiment: Studies in the Natural Sciences* (Cambridge:
         Cambridge University Press, 1988).

6   Jeffrey L. Sturchio, Editorial, "Artifact and Experiment," *Isis* 79
         (1988): 369.

7   See Roy MacLeod and P. F. Rehbock, eds., *"Nature in Its Greatest
         Extent": Western Science in the Pacific* (Honolulu: University of
         Hawaii Press, 1988).

8   See Morris Berman, *Social Change and Scientific Organisation: The
         Royal Institution, 1799–1844* (London: Heinemann, 1977); Reingold
         and Rothenberg, eds., *Scientific Colonialism.*

9   See the alternatives posed in R. W. Home, ed., *Australian Science in
         the Making* (Sydney: Cambridge University Press, 1988); and in Lewis
         Pyenson, "Science and Imperialism," in *Companion to the History
         of Modern Science,* ed. R. C. Olby et al. (London: Routledge, 1989),
         920–933, idem, "Pure Learning and Political Economy: Science and
         European Expansion in the Age of Imperialism," in *New Trends in
         the History of Science,* ed. R. P. W. Visser et al., (Amsterdam: Rodopi,
         1989), 209–278.

10   Three forms of influence are commonly cited. One infers evidence
         of religious or economic belief or analogy on the pursuit of natural
         knowledge, as in the relationship between puritanism and the scien-
         tific revolution in England or Darwin's use of Malthus; a second
         records the influence of a given ideology upon research, as in the
         bearing of Lysenkoism on genetics; and a third develops the influence
         of philosophical theory upon political theory, as in the relations
         between Spencerian Darwinism and politics, ethics, and education

and between Bergsonian organicism and the conception of the state. See Ingemar Bohlin, "Robert M. Young and Darwin Historiography," *Social Studies of Science* 21 (4) (1991): 597–648.

11   See, for example, Lucile Brockway, *Science and Colonial Expansion: The Role of the British Royal Botanic Gardens* (New York: Academic Press, 1979); William T. Stearn, *The Natural History Museum at South Kensington* (London: Heinemann, 1981); Lynn Barber, *The Heyday of Natural History 1820–1870* (Garden City, NY: Doubleday, 1980).

12   James Secord, "King of Siluria: Roderick Murchison and the Imperial Theme in Nineteenth-Century British Geology," *Victorian Studies* 25 (4) (1982): 413–442.

13   For the political history of Britain in the Pacific, see W. P. Morrell, *Britain in the Pacific Islands* (Oxford: Clarendon Press, 1960); W. Ross Johnston, *Sovereignty and Protection: A Study of British Jurisdictional Imperialism in the Late Nineteenth Century* (Durham, NC: Duke University Press, 1973); W. David McIntyre, *The Imperial Frontier in the Tropics* (London: Macmillan, 1967); the many works by Deryck Scarr, including *Fragments of Empire: A History of the Western Pacific High Commission, 1877–1914* (Canberra: Australian National University Press, 1967); and more specialized works such as Barrie Macdonald, *Cinderellas of the Empire: Towards a History of Kiribati and Tuvalu* (Canberra: Australian National University Press, 1982). For Australia's role, see Roger C. Thompson, *Australian Imperialism in the Pacific: The Expansionist Era, 1820–1920* (Melbourne: Melbourne University Press, 1980).

14   Eric Hobsbawm, *The Age of Empire, 1875–1914* (London: Weidenfeld and Nicolson, 1987); C. E. Carrington, *The British Overseas: Exploits of a Nation of Shopkeepers* (Cambridge: Cambridge University Press, 1950), 803–805.

15   Daniel Headrick, *Tools of Empire: Technology and European Imperialism in the Nineteenth Century* (New York: Oxford University Press, 1981).

16   For contemporary use of the "organic analogy" applied to imperial affairs, see Charles Sydney Goldman, *The Empire and the Century: A Series of Essays on Imperial Problems and Possibilities by Various Writers* (London: John Murray, 1905). See also Bernard Semmel, *Imperialism and Social Reform: English Social-Imperial Thought, 1895–1914* (London: Allen and Unwin, 1955); A. P. Thornton, *The Imperial Idea and Its Enemies: A Study in British Power* (London: Macmillan, 1959).

17   M. A. Di Gregorio, "A Wolf in Sheep's Clothing: Gegenbauer, Haeckel, the Triumph of Homology, and the Survival of Richard

Owen in Evolutionary Morphology," paper given to the Richard Owen Centenary Conference of the Society for the History of Natural History, London, 29 April 1992.

18   Gerald Geison, *Michael Foster and the Cambridge School of Physiology: The Scientific Enterprise in Late Victorian Society* (Princeton: Princeton University Press, 1978).

19   D. J. Winstanley, *Later Victorian Cambridge* (Cambridge: Cambridge University Press, 1947, 1977); Sheldon Rothblatt, *The Revolution of the Dons: Cambridge and Society in Victorian England* (London: Faber, 1981).

20   Roy MacLeod and Russell Moseley, "Breaking the Circle of the Sciences: The Natural Sciences Tripos and the Examination Revolution," in *Days of Judgement: Science, Examinations, and the Codification of Knowledge in Victorian Britain,* ed. Roy MacLeod (Driffield: Nafferton, 1982), 189–212; Roy MacLeod and Russell Moseley, "The Naturals and Victorian Cambridge: Reflections on the Anatomy of an Elite, 1851–1914," *Oxford Review of Education* 6 (2) (1980): 177–195.

21   For Foster's extensive imperial sympathies, evidenced during his long tenure as biological secretary of the Royal Society, president of the BAAS (1899), chairman of the International Commission on Scientific Periodicals, member of the British Science Guild, and member of Parliament, see Roy MacLeod, *Imperial Science under the Southern Cross: Archibald Liversidge and the Culture of Anglo-Australian Science* (Melbourne: Melbourne University Press, forthcoming), chap. 7; for his influence upon imperial ethnology and in the training of several eminent anthropologists, including A. C. Hadden, see Henrika Kuklick, *The Savage Within: The Social Context of British Anthropological Thought, 1885–1945* (New York: Cambridge University Press, 1991), chaps. 2 and 4.

22   See Toby Appel, *The Cuvier-Geoffroy Debate: French Biology in the Decades before Darwin* (Oxford: Oxford University Press, 1987); P. L. Farber, "The Type-Concept in Zoology during the First Half of the Nineteenth Century," *Journal of the History of Biology* 9 (1976): 93–119.

23   For an indicative account of Owen's position in London, see Adrian Desmond, *Archetypes and Ancestors: Paleontology in Victorian London, 1850–1875* (London: Blond and Briggs, 1982) and Nicolaas Rupke, "Richard Owen's Vertebrate Archetype," *Isis* 84 (1993): 231–251. Owen's life and influence will be extensively treated in Rupke, *Richard Owen* (New Haven: Yale University Press, forthcoming).

24   See Ann Mozley Moyal, "Sir Richard Owen and his Influence on Australian Zoological and Palaeontological Science," *Records of the Australian Academy of Science* 3 (1976): 41–56.

25 Carl Gegenbaur, *Elements of Comparative Anatomy,* trans. F. Jeffrey Bell (London: Macmillan, 1876), Foreword.

26 Michael Bartholomew, "Huxley's Defence of Darwin," *Annals of Science* 32 (1975): 525–535.

27 Pere Alberch et al., "Size and Shape in Ontogeny and Phylogeny," *Paleobiology* 5 (3) (1979): 296–217.

28 The convoluted routes taken by this debate have been well mapped by E. S. Russell, *Form and Function: A Contribution to the History of Animal Morphology* (London: John Murray, 1916), 246–60, and more recently by Stephen Gould, *Ontogeny and Phylogeny* (Cambridge: Harvard University Press, 1977), and Ernst Mayr, *The Growth of Biological Thought: Diversity, Evolution, and Inheritance* (Cambridge: Harvard University Press, 1982).

29 After J. F. Meckel and Étienne Serres. Cf. Russell, *Form and Function,* 91–93, 101.

30 Ibid., 120–123, 304.

31 Mayr, *Growth of Biological Thought,* 472–473.

32 Gould, *Ontogeny,* 100–101.

33 Ernst Haeckel, *The Evolution of Man: A Popular Exposition of the Principal Points of Human Ontogeny and Phylogeny,* 2 vols. (London: Beccles, 1879).

34 Balfour Zoological Library (Cambridge), Biog. D 4/A, "William Bateson, 1861–1926," 1.

35 Quoted in Mayr, *Biological Thought,* 470.

36 Eric Nordenskiöld, *The History of Biology* (New York: Tudor Publishing, 1928), 528.

37 Gegenbaur, *Elements,* Preface.

38 For background, see Mark Ridley, "Embryology and Classical Zoology in Britain," in *A History of Embryology,* ed. T. J. Horder, J. A. Witkowsky, and C. C. Wylie (Cambridge: Cambridge University Press, 1986), 35–67.

39 Keith Benson, "Problems of Individual Development: Descriptive Embryological Morphology in America at the Turn of the Century," *Journal of the History of Biology* 14 (1) (1981): 115–128.

40 Michael Foster, "Introduction," in *The Works of F. M. Balfour,* ed. Michael Foster and Adam Sedgwick (London: Macmillan, 1885), 7, 9.

41 M[ichael] F[oster], "Francis Maitland Balfour, 1851–1882," *Dictionary of National Biography,* 22 vols., 1:971.

42 Mayr, *Biological Thought,* 475.

43 Gould, *Ontogeny,* 176.

44 Peter Bowler, "Development and Adaptation: Evolutionary Concepts

in British Morphology, 1870–1914," *British Journal for the History of Science* 22 (3) (1989): 290.

45   Charles Darwin, *On the Origin of Species,* 6th ed. (London: John Murray, 1872), 387.

46   F. M. Balfour, *A Treatise on Comparative Embryology* (London: Macmillan, 1880–1881) 1:3–4.

47   Ibid., 4.

48   F. M. Balfour, "Address to the Department of Anatomy and Physiology of the British Association for the Advancement of Science, " in *Works,* ed. Foster and Sedgwick, 698–713.

49   F. M. Balfour, ed., *Studies from the Morphological Laboratory in the University of Cambridge* (London: William and Norgate, 1880), vol. 1.

50   Nordenskiöld, *History of Biology,* 531.

51   Foster, "Introduction," in *Works,* ed. Foster and Sedgwick, 23.

52   Cambridge University Archives, CUR 39. 36. See J. Willis Clark, *Old Friends at Cambridge and Elsewhere* (London: Macmillan, 1900), 282–291.

53   Leonard Huxley, *The Life and Letters of T. H. Huxley,* 2 vols. (London: Macmillan, 1900), 2:37.

54   F[oster], "Balfour," 972.

55   Foster, "Introduction," in *Works,* ed. Foster and Sedgwick, Preface. The studentship papers are to be found in the Cambridge University Archives, Zoo 10/1 "Balfour Memorial"; in ZOO 10/2, Balfour Managers; and in Cambridge Corrrespondence, vol. 100:100–101.

56   J. R. Tanner, ed., *The Historical Register of the University of Cambridge* (Cambridge: Cambridge University Press, 1910), 275.

57   See *The Historical Register of the University of Cambridge* (Cambridge: Cambridge University Press, 1966–1970), Supplement.

58   See Roy MacLeod, "The Support of Victorian Science: The Endowment of Science Movement in Great Britain, 1868–1900," *Minerva* 9 (1971): 197–230; "The Resources of Science in Victorian England," in *Science and Society,* ed. Peter Mathias (Cambridge: Cambridge University Press, 1972), 111–166.

59   Sir Richard Threlfall, "The Origin of the Automatic Microtome," *Biological Reviews* 5 (1930): 357–361. The Cambridge Instrument Company was founded by Darwin's son, Horace.

60   See Charles Atwood Kofoid, *The Biological Stations of Europe,* U.S. Bureau of Education Bulletin 440 (Washington, DC: Government Printing Office, 1910), 7–8.

61   Foster, "Introduction," in *Works,* ed. Foster and Sedgwick, 19.

62   John Graham Kerr, "Arthur Willey, 1867–1942," *Obituary Notices of Fellows of the Royal Society* 4 (November 1943): 403.

63   For details, see Ronald Strahan, *Rare and Curious Specimens: An*

Illustrated History of the Australian Museum, 1827–1979 (Sydney: Australian Museum, 1979), 29 et passim.

64   See MacLeod, *Imperial Science,* chap. 5.

65   For the prevailing range of such questions, see M. A. Di Gregorio, "In Search of the Natural System: Problems of Zoological Classification in Victorian Britain," *History and Philosophy of the Life Sciences* 4 (1982): 225–254.

66   Quoted in Gavin de Beer, *Charles Darwin* (London: Nelson, 1963), 107, and in Ann Mozley Moyal, *Scientists in Nineteenth-Century Australia: A Documentary History* (Sydney: Cassell, 1976), 60.

67   For an intepretation of the central theoretical issues and their relationship to colonial scientific relations, see Kathleen G. Dugan, "The Zoological Exploration of the Australian Region and Its Impact on Biological Theory," in *Scientific Colonialism,* ed. Reingold and Rothenberg, 79–100, esp. 86–89.

68   See George Bennett, "Notes on the Natural History and Habits of the *Ornithorhynchus paradoxus* Blum," *Transactions of the Zoological Society of London* 1 (1835): 240; Richard Owen, "On the Marsupial Pouches, Mammary Glands, and Mammary Foetus in the *Echidna hystrix,*" *Philosophical Transactions of the Royal Society* 159 (1865): 684. For Bennett, see A. H. Chisholm, "George Bennett (1804–1893)," *Australian Dictionary of Biography* (1966), 1:85–86.

69   Strahan, *Rare and Curious Specimens.*

70   The prevailing *leitmotif* of political intrigue in scientific matters in England is delicately handled by Adrian Desmond, *The Politics of Evolution: Morphology, Medicine, and Reform in Radical London* (Chicago: University of Chicago Press, 1989); see also Evelleen Richards, "A Question of Property Rights: Richard Owen's Evolutionism Reassessed," *British Journal for the History of Science* 20 (1987): 129–171.

71   For the Australian side of the story, see Moyal, *Scientists,* 73–75.

72   For local accounts, see W. H. Caldwell, "On the Development of the Monotremes and Ceratodus," *Journal and Proceedings of the Royal Society of New South Wales* 18 (1884): 117–122; idem, "The Royal Society of New South Wales: Mr. Caldwell's Australian Researches," *The Southern Science Record,* n.s., 1 (1) (January 1885): 16–20.

73   Owen Archives (Royal College of Surgeons, London), George Bennett to Owen, 10 September 1884, cited in Moyal, *Scientists,* 83.

74   Wilhelm Haacke, "Meine Entdeckung des Eierlegens der *Echidna hystrix,*" *Zoologischer Anzeiger,* 7 (1884): 647–653, cited in Dugan, "Zoological Exploration," 100.

75   W. H. Caldwell, "The Embryology of Monotremata and Marsupialia, Part I," *Philosophical Transactions of the Royal Society* 178B (1887): 463–486.

76   The monotremes are now included in a subclass of Mammalia. Harry
        Burrell, *The Platypus, Its Discovery, Zoological Position, Form and
        Characteristics, Habits, Life History, etc.* (Sydney: Angus and Robert-
        son, 1927).

77   "William Hay Caldwell," in *Alumni Cantabrigienses*, ed. John Venn
        (Cambridge: Cambridge University Press, 1922); *Biographical His-
        tory of Gonville and Caius College* (Cambridge: Cambridge Univer-
        sity Press, 1948), 5:160.; G. P. Bidder, "Mr. W. H. Caldwell," *Nature*
        148 (8 November 1941): 557–559.

78   Beatrice Bateson, *William Bateson, F.R.S., Naturalist, His Essays and
        Addresses, together with a Short Account of His Life* (Cambridge:
        Cambridge University Press, 1928), 17–19.

79   C. C. Gegenbaur, *Textbook of Zoology*, 4th ed., trans. Adam Sedg-
        wick (London: Swan Sonnenschein, 1892).

80   F. A. E. Crew, "Reginald Crundall Punnett, 1875–1967," *Biographical
        Memoirs of Fellows of the Royal Society* 13 (November 1967): 313.

81   Alfred Marshall, "Presidential Address," *Report of the British Associa-
        tion for the Advancement of Science, 1890* (Leeds, 1891) 60: 826–852.

82   Adam Sedgwick, "On the Law of Development Commonly Known
        as Von Baer's Law; and on the Significance of Ancestral Rudiments
        in Embryonic Development," *Quarterly Journal of Microscopical
        Science*, n.s., 36 (1894): 35–52, reprinted in Adam Sedgwick, ed.,
        *Studies from the Morphological Laboratory in the University of
        Cambridge* 6 (1894): 75–92.

83   Adam Sedgwick, "The Influence of Darwin on the Study of Embryol-
        ogy," in *Darwin and Modern Science*, ed. A. C. Seward (Cambridge:
        Cambridge University Press, 1909), 171–184.

84   Garland Allen, *Life Science in the Twentieth Century* (New York:
        John Wiley, 1975), 25, 33–39.

85   See ibid., 50–52. See also the biographical memoir in Beatrice Bate-
        son, *Bateson*.

86   Wiliam Bateson, "The Ancestry of the Chordata (1886)," reprinted in
        The Scientific Papers of William Bateson, ed. R. C. Punnett, 2 vols.
        (Cambridge: Cambridge University Press, 1928), 1:1–31.

87   William Bateson, *Materials for the Study of Variation* (London:
        Macmillan, 1894), chap. 25; J. B. F., "William Bateson, 1861–1926,"
        Proceedings of the Royal Society B101 (1927): ii.

88   See Robert Olby, "The Dimensions of Scientific Controversy: The
        Biometric–Mendelian Debate," *British Journal for the History of Sci-
        ence* 22 (3) (1988): 299–320; Donald MacKenzie, *Statistics in Britain,
        1865–1930: The Social Shaping of Scientific Knowledge* (Edinburgh:
        Edinburgh University Press, 1981).

89   Robert Olby, "Scientists and Bureaucrats in the Establishment of the

John Innes Horticultural Institution under William Bateson," *Annals of Science* 46 (1989): 497–510.

90 F. H. A. M, "Walter Heape, 1855–1929," *Proceedings of the Royal Society* B106 (1930): xv–xviii.

91 Roy MacLeod, "Imperial Reflections in the Southern Seas: The Funafuti Expeditions, 1898–1904," in *Nature in Its Greatest Extent*, ed. MacLeod and Rehbock, 159–194.

92 C. Forster-Cooper, "John Stanley Gardiner, 1872–1946," *Obituary Notices of Fellows of the Royal Society* 5 (1947): 541–553.

93 John Venn, "John Samuel Budgett (1872–1904)," *Alumni Cantabrigienses* (Cambridge: Cambridge University Press, 1922).

94 Cecil A. Hoare and Doris L. Mackinnon, "Clifford Dobell, 1886–1949," *Obituary Notices of Fellows of the Royal Society* 7 (1950): 35–61.

95 H. McD. Edelstein, "John Claud Fortescue Fryer, 1886–1948," *Obituary Notices of Fellows of the Royal Society* 7 (1950–1951): 95–106.

96 So argued Bateson. See Beatrice Bateson, *Bateson*, 32.

97 See Jane Maienschein, "Shifting Assumptions in American Biology," *Journal of the History of Biology* 14 (1) (1981): 89–113.

98 Gould, *Ontogeny*, 202.

99 Kerr, "Willey," 405.

100 Ibid., 404.

101 D. T. Anderson, "Origins and Relationships among the Animal Phyla," *Proceedings of the Linnean Society of New South Wales* 106 (2) (1981): 151–166. I am indebted to Professor Anderson for this reference.

102 Cf. Joseph Needham, *History of Embryology* (Cambridge: Cambridge University Press, 1934; 2d ed. New York: Abelard Schuman, 1959); *Chemical Embryology*, 2 vols. (New York: Hafner, 1963). With the war came Needham's interest in the history of Chinese science; but that Pacific connection is another story.

103 Peter Robertson, "Coming of Age: The British Association for the Advancement of Science in Australia, 1914," *Australian Physicist* 17 (1980): 23–27.

104 Michael Worboys, "The British Association and Empire: Science and Social Imperialism, 1880–1940," in *The Parliament of Science: Essays in Honour of the British Association*, ed. Roy MacLeod and Peter Collins (London: Science Reviews, 1981), 170–187.

105 William Bateson, "Presidential Address," *Report of the British Association for the Advancement of Science 1914* (Melbourne, 1914) 84:37.

106 Ibid., 21.

PART TWO

Exchange Networks
and the Organization of Research

JANET GARBER

6 Darwin's Correspondents in the Pacific

Through the Looking Glass to the Antipodes

How funny it'll seem to come out among the people that walk
with their heads downwards! The Antipathies, I think—
—LEWIS CARROLL, 1865

Darwin was in the Pacific less than two years, from 10 June 1834
when he sailed "for the last time" from Tierra del Fuego to 14 March
1836 when the *Beagle* stood out of King George's sound. Yet his brief
landfalls on the Galapagos and Australia were central to the development of his theory of natural selection, while the Andes and the Keeling Islands provided laboratories to test his geological theories.[1] And
it was a peculiar barnacle from the Pacific coast of Chile that stimulated him to undertake his investigation into the whole subclass of cirripedia in 1846.[2]

Subsequently, however, it fell to Darwin's correspondents to com-
pensate for his own relative lack of direct contact with the Pacific by
providing the supporting evidence he needed: geological measurements of the Andes and of coral islands, and observational and experimental data for his studies of distribution, variation, and inheritance.
Darwin used his Pacific contacts to bolster all his major hypotheses,
incorporating what he learned into his books and papers.[3] These
hypotheses include not only his geological theories and his theory of
natural selection, but also his concept of diversity; his beliefs in the
common origin of domestic breeds, in the monogenesis of man, and
in the interrelatedness of all nature; and his theory of pangenesis: the
influence of the environment on the "reproductive elements" as a
cause of variation.

Darwin in turn had a profound influence on science in the Pacific.
He knew before he left England that the Pacific was not merely the
back side of the globe, a mirror of the English side. The Pacific was

through the looking glass to the converse of any kind of rational expectations in natural history, expectations that were difficult enough to fulfill in the Atlantic realm.[4] Those who attempted to classify the plants and animals brought back from the Pacific revealed the intransigence of the data to the imposition of order. To give just one example, John Edward Gray of the British Museum, on trying to identify the fishes brought back by Phillip P. King (appendix 1) from the waters off Western Australia (1818–1822) wrote that "so little is known of the genera and species of this department of Natural History, that I am not inclined to describe them as new, for fear of increasing the confusion at present existing."[5] Even Joseph Hooker, more than twenty years later, when working on Darwin's Galapagos plants, found all his "preconceived notions" of species migration overturned by the "extraordinary difference between the plants of the separate islands."[6] It was not until Darwin explained that extraordinary difference to be caused by selective survival of variants—that is, provided a "theory to work by"—that light was cast on the mysteries of classification and distribution in the Pacific. Much of Darwin's correspondence is not well known,[7] and more awaits both identification[8] and analysis. This paper summarizes what is known about Darwin's correspondents who lived in the Pacific or visited long enough to contribute to its natural history. Sources of information include the *Calendar of the Correspondence of Charles Darwin*, the eight volumes of the *Correspondence of Charles Darwin* thus far published, Darwin's published works, national biographical dictionaries, and *Isis* cumulative bibliographies.

The Correspondents

According to extant letters and accounts, Darwin's correspondents in the Pacific number (so far) fifty-five persons (see appendix 1). Most (30) lived in Australia; a few (10) in New Zealand.[9] Others lived on the west coast of North or South America, Hawaii, China, Borneo, or Malaya. The letters date from 1830, a year before the *Beagle* sailed, to 1881, the year before Darwin died. For most of Darwin's Pacific correspondents, the *Calendar* lists only one or two letters; for several others there are none listed—only statements in other letters or in Darwin's books.[10] Some exchanges, however, continued for as many as sixteen years. Most were begun after 1859, and only two or three of Darwin's Pacific area correspondents wrote to him both before and after the watershed year of 1859–1860.[11] These patterns are consistent with Darwin's correspondence on scientific matters as a whole.[12] Before 1870, supporters of natural selection in England and

Europe as well as in the Pacific included museum directors and amateur naturalists, but not university professors, contrary to earlier beliefs that this situation was true only of colonial science.[13] Even well after 1870, for some in "establishment" posts in the new—as well as in the old—metropolitan centers, science still consisted of collecting and naming.[14]

In two other ways, however, Darwin's post-1859 Pacific correspondents differed from those in Great Britain and Europe. The correspondents at "home" were younger, and those in the Pacific were more amenable to accepting his theory than their cohorts who had stayed in Europe. Persons who had personal contact with living nature were more likely to find evolution understandable and acceptable than were those who confined their studies to the dried and pressed specimens in herbaria or to animals preserved in spirits.

Second, in contrast to Europeans, most of whom wrote to Darwin first,[15] Darwin generally took the initiative with his Pacific correspondents, because he wanted answers to specific questions. Most of his questions concerned the expression of the emotions, but other queries concerned glacial drift, cross-fertilization of flowers, coral reefs, movements of plants, and the origin of domestic breeds of birds. That Darwin sought out information from Pacific residents underscores the importance he attached to data from the Pacific.

Among Darwin's correspondents were travelers to the Pacific—ships' officers, naturalists on exploring expeditions, private collectors, or geologists—who influenced Darwin's conception of the Pacific and/or aided him in his research. Many of these travelers resided in the Pacific for years—some of them so long that they are difficult to categorize as visitors—but their correspondence with Darwin dates from their return to England or to Europe or the United States (see appendix 2).[16] In China, Japan, the Philippines, Malaysia, and the widely scattered islands of the Pacific, in contrast to New Zealand and Australia and to some extent Hawaii, Europeans collected specimens as visitors, not as colonists developing an indigenous science.

Darwin's Influence on Natural History in the Pacific

Darwin realized the significance of many of his observations and collections only after returning to England and after having his specimens examined. And only after he had been home for ten years did Darwin find time to work on the unusual cirripede from the coast of Chile,[17] work that led to his "botanical arithmetic" and ultimately resulted in his concept of diversity.[18] These revelations necessitated correspondence with those on the scene or recently returned when he began writing his *Journal of Researches* (in later editions titled the *Voyage of the "Beagle"*), the three parts of the *Geology of the Voyage of the "Beagle,"*[19] and his monographs on cirripedes. Both his letters and his books were stimuli to science.

Beginning with the publication of his *Journal of Researches,* Darwin provided research programs for those interested in the new biology—the study of life. Darwin's own science was largely experimental, and in his writings he provided techniques of observation and experiment to follow.[20] As his books circled the globe, each offered new inspirations for the investigation of nature. For instance, one of Darwin's most influential books, *The Various Contrivances by Which Orchids Are Fertilized by Insects,* included an "Explanation of Terms," a complete description of the anatomy of orchids, of "how this complex mechanism acts," and of how the experimenter with only a pencil as a tool could repeat his experiments, the whole copiously illustrated.[21] That experimentation was an ideal of scientists and that Darwin's experiments could be carried out by scientists who did not accept evolution explain much of the popularity of his book on orchids.

But his explanation of how evolution might have occurred profoundly stimulated natural historians. In the *Origin of Species* (1859) Darwin succeeded in encompassing all nature under the theory of evolution by natural selection, ending the vain search for order and symmetry[22] with a mirror held up to nature itself for a weapon. It may be argued that, as natural history became modern biology only after Darwin, the practice of natural history rapidly matured into the new biology in proportion to the extent to which it was Darwinian.[23]

Darwin supervised the conduct of experiments by correspondence as well as through his books. Most of his correspondence was directed to particular persons, but Darwin also used questionnaires, which he distributed as widely as he could.[24] He sent his "Queries on Expression" to a number of his Pacific correspondents for his book on the expression of the emotions, asking the correspondents in turn to find responsible persons in contact with people who had had little previous acquaintance with Europeans. In addition, nearly every one of Darwin's scientist correspondents was subjected to a barrage of questions that ranged widely, often beyond the recipient's field of expertise. As early as his *Coral Reefs* (1842), Darwin's geology was subsumed under the problem of distribution of living species, until his geology and biology were one, but that was not true of many of his correspondents. Thus while Darwin did succeed in broadening the outlook of a number of naturalists, he did not always get what he asked for. Few flatly denied his requests, but judging by extant letters, several apparently did not reply.

Darwin's Pacific area correspondents contributed to his work in roughly six areas: geology, classification and distribution (including his work on cirripedes), theories of variation (including cross-fertilization and environmental influences), the origins of domestic breeds, of the human species, and finally of all plants and animals. I shall consider each in turn.

Geology

Darwin's geological investigations and related correspondence began with his studies of the Andes and continued across the Pacific and Indian oceans to coral islands and the great southern continent.

For his work on the elevation of the Andes, Darwin used information obtained from five English residents of Valparaiso whom he met there in 1834: Robert Alison, Richard Corfield, Charles Douglas, Mr. Gill, and Mr. Lambert; and he used information obtained from Alexander Usborne and William Kent, master's assistant and assistant surgeon on the *Beagle,* for papers read before the Geological Society of London in 1838,[25] to show that "the earth's crust floats . . . on a sea of molten rock,"[26] and for his *Journal of Researches,* where he concluded that "Nothing is so unstable as the level of the crust of this earth."[27] Darwin made use of the data again when, in *Coral Reefs,* he maintained that there were areas of elevation of the earth's crust to balance the subsidence of large areas of the Pacific and "that nearly the whole line of the west coast of South America . . . has undergone an upward movement during the late geologic period."[28] By the mid-1850s, when Darwin began the draft for his "big book,"[29] the principle had become an essential underpinning for his biogeography. He was pleased years later to see a succession of young travelers to the west coast of South America confirm his observations.[30]

Most of those who contributed to Darwin's data on coral reefs were travelers rather than residents.[31] The only Pacific resident was the *Beagle* artist Conrad Martens (1801–1878), whom Darwin visited while in Australia. Martens informed Darwin of a terrace—possibly marine—a hundred feet above the sea on the Cook Islands.[32] One of the earliest of Darwin's informants was also one of the earliest of experimenters in the Pacific, Dr. J. Allan, who spent the years 1830–1832 on Madagascar transplanting corals to study their growth. After returning to Edinburgh, Dr. Allan sent Darwin his testimony on the elevation of the Seychelles.[33]

A long-term resident of the Pacific who made significant contributions to *Coral Reefs* was the naturalist Hugh Cuming (1791–1865). Cuming returned to England in 1839 after an absence of twenty years, bringing with him extensive collections of living and fossil shells and of plants from the Pacific. He provided Darwin with considerable data on the coral reefs about the Philippine Islands, the geology of the islands, and the distribution of marine species, including cirripedes, throughout the Pacific.[34]

During his brief visit to Australia, Darwin discussed Australian geology with Sir Thomas Mitchell (1792–1855), surveyor-general of New South Wales and one of the great explorers of Australia. Mitchell shared the results of his geological investigations in the Blue Mountains with Darwin both in Australia and later on a visit to England.[35] Darwin found the information gleaned from Mitchell useful for explaining the distribution of plants and animals in the Pacific.

Classification and Distribution of Species

After returning to London, Darwin began to realize that his specimens from the antipodes supplied important clues to the origin of species, a realization aided by specialists in London such as those who wrote the volumes on Vertebrates for the *Zoology of the "Beagle"* and naturalists such as Hugh Cuming. Darwin met Hugh Cuming shortly after the latter's return from his long sojourn in the Pacific in 1839. From Cuming, Darwin learned that half of the Galapagos shells he had collected were endemic to the archipelago, "a wonderful fact, considering how widely distributed sea-shells generally are."[36] Of the remaining shells, some were common to the west coast of America and some to the central Pacific; only in the Galapagos were both found together.[37] Both of these "wonderful facts" reinforced the uniqueness of the Galapagos as a natural laboratory of evolution.

Four years later, Cuming was one of the many from whom Darwin borrowed cirripede specimens.[38] It was in a cirripede Cuming collected in the Philippines that Darwin discovered, parasitic on the female, several "complemental males"; he named it *Ibla cumingii.*[39] Another early stimulant to Darwin's study of cirripedes was a paper on barnacles and mollusks collected off the west coast of Australia by Phillip Parker King (1793–1856), who had commanded the *Adventure,* a companion ship to the *Beagle* on its first surveying voyage, 1826–1830. Darwin met King in England in 1831 and again at King's home near Sydney in 1836.[40] Darwin did not refer to King's paper in his volumes on cirripedes, but in his notebook he suggested that the North-South ranges of shells (cirripedes and mollusks) might be worked out, using his own, Cuming's, and King's collections.[41]

When Darwin began his study of Cirripedia, he developed an extensive network of correspondents, including Hugh Cuming, Samuel Stutchbury,[42] and James Dwight Dana,[43] who had collected in the Pacific. Syms Covington, Darwin's servant on the *Beagle*, was the only Pacific resident who sent him specimens.[44] In 1854, nearing the end of his eight-year study of cirripedes, Darwin wrote to Philip Gidley King, who had been a mate on the *Beagle* and settled in Australia, to ask for a duplicate specimen of *Scalpellum papillosum* collected by his father, Phillip Parker King, from Patagonia, but it apparently was not sent to him.[45]

In 1854, having packed up the last of the barnacles, Darwin was ready to start the "big book" in which he meant to expound his theory of natural selection. Of his many projects, three involved the Pacific: to gather information on the means of distribution of plants and animals across geographical barriers; to learn the cause or causes of variability; and to reveal the common origins of domestic breeds of animals and plants in order to demonstrate the power of artificial selection.

After reading Alfred Russel Wallace's paper, "On the Law Which Has Regulated the Introduction of New Species" (1855),[46] Darwin wrote to him in Malaya on 1 May 1857: "One of the subjects on which I have been experimenting, and which cost me much trouble, is the means of distribution of all organic beings found on oceanic islands; and any facts on this subject would be most gratefully received."[47] Wallace had been studying just that, and it was the subject of much of his correspondence with Darwin over the next twenty-five years.[48] Distribution in both space and time—over the surface of the earth and in geological strata—had indeed long interested Darwin. He began the experiments that cost him "much trouble" after conversations with John Gould and Joseph Hooker in 1844 on wide-ranging genera and species.[49] The large number of Pacific correspondents on distribution, most of them long-time residents of the Pacific, is a measure of its importance to him throughout his career.

Darwin needed to explain the presence of identical species on Australia and New Zealand; to explain the dispersal of northern hemisphere plants to the southern hemisphere, particularly to Australia; and to gather evidence for the passage of vast amounts of time since the formation of the earth necessary for both the dispersal of plants and for evolution of new species. Information he obtained from Sir Thomas Mitchell in 1836 convinced Darwin that New Zealand and Australia had never been united,[50] implying that identical species had to have been transported across the ocean from one to the other; he

Pacific Correspondents on Distribution

On distribution of Cirripedes *(1846–1854)*
Syms Covington
Hugh Cuming
Samuel Stutchbury
James Dwight Dana

Plants and animals other than Cirripedes

1830s	1840s
John Gould	Joseph Hooker
Hugh Cuming	Richard Brinsley Hinds
William Sharp Macleay	Charles Pickering
Sir Thomas Mitchell	

1850s	1860–1880
James Dwight Dana	William B. Clarke
Walter Mantell	Robert Swinhoe
Alfred R. Wallace	Julius von Haast
Charles Moore	Berthold C. Seeman
Ferdinand Mueller	William Swale
William Sharp Macleay	Thomas Belt
	James Hector

remained convinced until years later, when Hooker's biogeographical data and the views of an Australian geologist, the Reverend William B. Clarke, shook that conviction, allowing for the possibility of land dispersal.

One-way dispersal of northern plants to the southern hemisphere required some other explanation. On the basis of data supplied by Cuming and others,[51] including the American botanist Charles Pickering,[52] Darwin postulated a worldwide cool period at the time of the last glacial era in the northern hemisphere.[53] In 1854, seeking further confirmation of this hypothesis, Darwin wrote to Walter Mantell[54] in New Zealand, requesting information on erratic boulders and marks of glaciers on that island.[55] Mantell sent sketches of fragments of quartz that he judged to be "erratic boulders," moved from their original locations by glaciers.[56]

After publication of the *Origin of Species,* Darwin obtained additional evidence of glaciers in Australia from Clarke and in New Zealand from Julius von Haast and James Hector and of a cool period in Central America from Berthold Seeman[57] and Thomas Belt.[58] Clarke (1798–1878) had been a prominent scientist in London before emigrating to Australia in 1839. Darwin knew him from Geological Society meetings.[59] For thirty years Clarke served Church and Science in Australia, long being the only field geologist in the colonies.[60] His field work prepared Clarke for acceptance of Darwin's theory: geological evidence at the Australian coal seams revealed a vast amount of time separating the fossils above and below the coal. In 1861, Clarke wrote to congratulate Darwin on the *Origin,* adding his confirmation of the existence of Australian glaciers.[61] Clarke also sent evidence that New Zealand had once been an appurtenance of Australia, countering Mitchell's earlier findings[62] and adding to Darwin's store of data on subsidence in the Pacific.

In 1862, Hooker alerted Darwin to the work of Johann Franz Julius von Haast (1824–1887), government geologist at Canterbury, on glacial drift in New Zealand.[63] Darwin wrote to Haast, who had explored much of the Southern Alps since his arrival from Germany in 1858[64] and had become an authority on glaciation.[65] During his explorations, Haast discovered bones of gigantic extinct birds;[66] he was one of the first to document his discoveries with photographs and sent some to Darwin.[67] Haast later founded both the Canterbury Museum and the Canterbury Collegiate Union (later the University of Canterbury), where he was a professor of geology. In thirteen letters to Darwin, Haast revealed himself to be one of Darwin's avid supporters;[68] he published a favorable review of the *Origin,* provided valuable data on everything from glaciers to gold and from paleontology to pangenesis, and circulated Darwin's queries on expression. Darwin encouraged Haast's own research and sponsored him for election to the Royal Society. Like Clarke and like most of Darwin's supporters, Haast faced nature directly and saw with his own eyes evidences for the evolution of species and for an ancient earth, "the geological age of which is incalculable."[69]

Darwin attempted to get geologists Mantell, Clarke, and Haast to look at distribution of life over the globe as a biological as well as a geological problem. In 1856 he asked Mantell, and six years later he asked Haast, to try to procure specimens of the native rat and frog.[70] "A frog and rat together would," he wrote, "to my mind, prove former connection of New Zealand to some continent,"[71] but apparently both men were unsuccessful.[72] Darwin had more luck in 1863, when he asked Haast for facts on the spread of European plants[73] and both Haast and Clarke to observe introduced animals.[74] In the early 1860s Darwin was collecting data on biological distribution for a planned sequel to *The Variation of Animals and Plants under Domestication,* on variation and selection in nature. He never did complete the sequel, and the biological information he gleaned after 1860 from Mantell, Haast, Clarke, and others, as opposed to their geological contributions, has never been published.

Darwin postulated that if the entire world were cold during the last glacial age in the northern hemisphere, subarctic plants would be more successful in crossing the equator and establishing themselves in the southern hemisphere than would subtropical or temperate region plants. Moreover, when the climate began to warm, retreat would be impossible for the subarctic plants. In 1856 he began to wonder how those plants were surviving in warm-temperate regions such as South Africa and Australia.[75] A year later, in a letter to Hooker, Darwin wrote, "I have to beg one other favour; viz name of any intelligent Curator (& permission to use your or Sir William's name as introduction) of any Botanic Garden in hot or hottish & dryish country, as Sydney or Cape of G. Hope, that I may inquire about temperate plants withstanding dryish heat, for my Glacial Chapter."[76] Hooker suggested writing to Ferdinand Mueller and Charles Moore in Australia.[77] Darwin took his friend's advice.

From Moore (1820–1905), director of Sydney's Botanic Garden,[78] Darwin received a list of British perennials that seeded in New South Wales, noting those that were so successful they had become weeds.[79] For ten years, Moore had paid particular attention to plants that had become pests in New South Wales, so could provide Darwin with a reasonably complete list.[80] It added to Darwin's growing evidence against the old assumption of the balance of nature—that all species maintain constant populations—as well as giving evidence for natural selection. Moore's letter arrived after Darwin had begun the manuscript of the Origin, and the data he sent was never published.

Ferdinand von Mueller (1825–1896),[81] first government botanist of Victoria, was in 1857 the recently appointed director of the Melbourne botanical garden, where he built the "first great botanical collection in the Southern Hemisphere."[82] Darwin asked Mueller whether British or Northern European plants could withstand the climate of South Australia, "my point being whether they could withstand the heat,"[83] and what he gained was evidence against one theory of variation and for distribution of species. He found Mueller's reply very useful; in the chapter on geographical distribution in Natural Selection there is a remarkable passage in which Darwin demonstrated his ability to make creative use of observational data. In it Darwin discussed the relevance of distribution to evolution and the evidences for a worldwide cold period and for long-distance migration of plants:

Long since Robert Brown showed that there were several northern [hemi-sphere] plants in Australia, which could not be considered as naturalized by man's aid. Recently, Dr. F. Muller has found on the Australian Alps sev-eral European plants . . . found no where else in the southern hemisphere.

I should suppose that these plants had migrated into Australia during the cold period . . . by the islands of the Malay archipelago: perhaps through New Guinea;...Between New Guinea & Java, where northern forms are found, the sea in parts is deep, but it is studded with an extraor-dinary number of islands, so that by strides of 50 miles the interspace can be crossed on dry land; & there is some evidence in parts of subsidence.[84]

Just as Darwin had earlier woven his own observations on the living and fossil animals he collected in South America into a story recount-ing the natural history of the extinct animals in his *Journal of Researches*,[85] so now he incorporated the "fact" presented to him by a correspondent into a coherent adventure story of plants with eight-league boots in corroboration of his hypothesis of plant migration. Darwin was thus able to argue that the plants under discussion—and by extension every species of plant and animal—had only one "center of creation."[86] It was also evidence that phenotypic variation is not inevitable, or driven by internal clocks in every organism—the hypothesis later called "orthogenesis."

A few years later, in 1861, Mueller was "too busy to help" Darwin with experiments on the mechanism of fertilization of flowers;[87] but in 1867, when Darwin sent him a copy of his questionnaire on expression, Mueller distributed it to various acquaintances in Austra-lia.[88] It has been claimed that Mueller refused to experiment for Dar-win because he did not wish to help sustain a theory "dangerous to our Christian faith,"[89] but his conviction does not seem to have deterred him five years later from collecting evidence that human beings had evolved from lower animals. A number of Darwin's friends[90] and correspondents both at home and abroad[91] were capable of divorcing empirical science from theory both at meetings of scien-tific societies[92] and in letters to Darwin. Perhaps this was true of Mueller as well by 1867. Nor did Mueller's opposition to Darwin's theory prevent him from asking Darwin for data. Thus in 1874, Mueller requested input from Darwin for his work on timber trees and other plants of value to industry.[93]

In 1858 Darwin requested information on the replacement of the native Australian bee by the introduced hive bee from English natural-ist William Sharp Macleay (1792–1865), who had emigrated to Aus-tralia in 1839.[94] Darwin used the information for later editions of the

Origin, in which he included a statement about the hive bee driving out the stingless native bee of Australia.[95] Macleay, author of the "Quinarian System" of classification, had supported publication of the *Zoology of the "Beagle,"* "because it keeps together a series of observations made respecting animals inhabiting the same part of the world."[96]

Darwin continued to collect intriguing bits of data on distribution for his never-published sequel to *Variation.* New Zealand fruit growers were pleasantly surprised in 1856 at the arrival of small birds that had flown to New Zealand from Tasmania, twelve hundred miles away, and rid them of an aphid called the "American Blight." In 1870 Swale, a nurseryman with whom Darwin had corresponded previously on cross-fertilization, sent Darwin his notes on the habits of the bird, which had come to be called the "American Blight bird."[97]

The Causes of Variation

The second of Darwin's projects about which he wrote to Pacific correspondents beginning in 1854 for his "big book" was to try to learn the cause or causes of variability in plants and animals. Contrary to the opinion of many, it was Darwin's belief that the tendency to vary, and perhaps each variation, had a cause.[98] The enormous diversity of cirripedes strengthened Darwin's resolve to determine the causes of diversity and ultimately speciation. As with diversity, the large number of Darwin's correspondents on the causes of variability underscores its importance to him. He entertained three different hypotheses about the cause of variation but discussed only two with Pacific correspondents. The third hypothesis was that there was some sort of impetus leading to a constantly increasing rate of variation.

Hypothesis 1: Cross-fertilization

Since at least 1841, when he read Sprengel's *Nature's Secret Revealed,*[99] Darwin had looked for some purpose to bees' attendance on flowers and for evidence of cross-fertilization.[100] The advantage of sexual reproduction to both plants and animals must, he reasoned, be sufficient to overcome the enormous expenditure of energy in wasted pollen or sperm. Darwin read all he could find on the matter, wrote to everyone he could think of, put queries in the *Gardeners' Chronicle,*[101] and experimented to try to learn the frequency of cross-fertilization of flowers and its effects on the health of the offspring. He was particularly interested in the flowers of the pea family (Papilionaceae or Leguminoseae), which were widely assumed to be self-fertilizing, even though they were commonly visited by bees.

He read "in an old number of the 'Gardeners' Chronicle' ... an extract ... from a New Zealand newspaper, in which much surprise is expressed that the introduced clover never seeded freely until the hive-bee was introduced." Darwin experimented and discovered that common clover in England left uncovered and "seen daily visited by my bees ... produced just ten times as much seed as the covered."[102] Excited that the statement supported his hypothesis about Papilionaceous flowers, Darwin checked his current issue of the *Gardeners' Chronicle* for someone in New Zealand of whom he could inquire further. He later reported that he "wrote to Mr. Swale in Christchurch in New Zealand, and asked him whether Leguminous plants seeded there freely before the hive-bee was introduced; and he, in the most obliging manner, has sent me a list of twenty-four plants of this order which seeded abundantly before bees were introduced."[103] Those plants, Mr. Swale suggested, were natives, which were probably fertilized by other insects, and gave some examples, supporting Darwin's contention that pea flowers are not self-fertilized.[104] Mr. Swale, a Norfolk gardener who emigrated to Christchurch in 1857, confirmed that the results of Darwin's clover experiments held true in New Zealand with both introduced clover and garden lupines.

There were irregular flowers other than peas, including orchids and bell-shaped flowers such as the Goodeniaceae.[105] They had curved pathways to their nectar and thus were commonly believed to be self-fertilizing. Darwin believed that all irregular flowers had structures that made it impossible for birds or insects to reach the nectary without picking up or depositing pollen, but insects adapted to the peculiar shapes of flowers transplanted from abroad were often absent from England. *Leschenaultia formosa,* an Australian flower in the family Goodeniaceae, was one of these. He needed someone to observe the flower in its native habitat and appealed to Hooker, "Remember that the *Goodeniaceae* have weighed like an incubus for years on my soul."[106]

At Hooker's suggestion, he applied to James Drummond, *Leschenaultia's* original collector, government naturalist, and superintendent of government gardens in Western Australia.[107] Drummond confirmed that *Leschenaultia* was indeed cross-fertilized by insects— and Darwin triumphantly sent off a notice to the *Gardeners' Chronicle.*[108] Then he attempted—unsuccessfully—to get Mueller and Clarke to confirm Drummond's results in eastern Australia.[109] In the same year (1860), Darwin observed that the peculiar shapes of orchids supported his thesis that most plants are adapted for cross-fertilization. He began a new series of experiments, culminating in *Orchids* (1862), the first of his post-*Origin* books. Such was the inpouring of new information from botanists and amateur gardeners around the world following its publication that Darwin published a supplement in 1869[110] and a second edition in 1877. Among correspondents who contributed to the second edition of *Orchids* were Henry Fletcher Hance in China, Thomas Frederick Cheeseman (1846–1923) in New Zealand, and Robert Fitzgerald in Australia. Hance, a civil servant who collected plants in China, wrote merely to correct a statement in the first edition of *Orchids*,[111] but Cheeseman and Fitzgerald sent copies of papers or books to Darwin, reporting experiments on the fertilization of orchids performed according to the example set by Darwin in his book. The article sent in 1873 by Cheeseman, curator of the Auckland Museum, started a six-year exchange of letters with Darwin on the fertilization of New Zealand orchids.[112] In *Orchids* Darwin reported Cheeseman's discoveries that insect aid was essential to the fertilization of many New Zealand orchids.[113]

Robert D. Fitzgerald (1830–1892), enthusiastic amateur ornithologist and plant collector, was deputy surveyor to the Department of Lands, chief mining surveyor, and controller of Church and School lands in New South Wales in 1875 when he sent volume 1 of his *Australian Orchids* to Darwin. Darwin promptly suggested further observations,[114] and Fitzgerald's second volume arrived at Darwin's door just as the second edition of *Orchids* was about to go to press.[115] Darwin noted that Fitzgerald had collected sixty-two species of orchids within one mile of Sydney[116] and had proved the necessity of insect fertilization for most of them.[117] More of the Australian orchids were self-fertilizing than Darwin would accept without further investigation, however.[118] Fitzgerald investigated further and sent five more volumes of observations on orchids to Darwin by 1881. A few of the orchids were intransigent; further experiments revealed their constancy in self-fertilizing.

In the 1870s Darwin published two more books on the cross-fertilization of plants, demonstrating that most flowering plants do cross-fertilize and that cross-fertilization results in physiological advantages to the plants. Extending his principle to many foreign trees was difficult, but J. Gerhard von Krefft (1830–1881), curator of the Australian Museum from 1864 to 1874, sent him proof of the dichogamous nature of eucalyptus trees (which ensured their cross-fertilization). Krefft assured Darwin that many insects visited the trees and asked a colleague to collect their flowers and the insects that visited them for Darwin.[119]

Cheeseman, Fitzgerald, and Krefft initiated correspondences with

Darwin, a pattern typical of Darwin's post-*Origin* experience around the world. All three made important contributions to natural science employing evolutionary theory. All three had opportunities for direct contact with living nature, an almost universal characteristic of Darwin's supporters. Their reputations as scientists benefited from their contacts with Darwin, but while Cheeseman in New Zealand remained as curator of the Auckland Museum until his death in 1923 and Fitzgerald's career was unaffected, Krefft lost his job in 1874. While the *Origin* and *The Descent of Man*, which interested Krefft, were controversial, *Orchids* was very popular worldwide, stimulating experiment among creationists as well as among evolutionists.[120] Most of his readers did not realize that with *Orchids,* Darwin was making a "flank movement" around his opposition.[121]

Hypothesis 2: The Environment as Inducer of Variability

For fifty years, Darwin toyed with the idea that somehow changes in the environment (the "conditions of life") induce variations. In the 1850s he started several experiments,[122] but as he realized the long-term nature of such trials, he attempted to recruit younger men to carry them out.[123] The results were generally inconclusive, and pervasive belief in the inheritance of acquired characteristics fortified Darwin's own bias in that direction. Carl Semper (1832–1893), a German zoologist who lived in the Philippines from 1858 to about 1865, studying the ethnography and zoology of the islands, began corresponding with Darwin after joining the faculty of zoology at Würzburg. Semper wrote frequently to Darwin on what he interpreted as the effects of the environment on species modification in marine animals he observed in Philippine waters.[124]

In 1881, Darwin wrote to Semper that he was "staggered" by reports of experiments which decisively countered the hypothesis of the direct effect of the environment on variation.[125] In that same year, Darwin received confirmation from an Australian sheep raiser, Peter Beveridge (1829–1885), that factors in the environment do not necessarily lead to variations. Beveridge wrote to Darwin in October 1881, after reading Darwin's article in *Nature* about 'Black Sheep;'[126] Darwin had postulated that the black sheep exhibited reversion to the ancestral color. Beveridge disagreed, commenting on the lack of black sheep at his father's sheep station. Beveridge also noted that neither repeated brandings of sheep nor a woman's withered leg were inherited.[127] Beveridge confirmed what Darwin had observed over twenty years earlier: that most ordinary breeders knew far more than most naturalists of the "laws of inheritance."[128]

The Origins of Domestic Breeds

Darwin's third project for his "big book" that involved Pacific correspondents was to trace the pedigrees of domestic animals in order to demonstrate the power of selection. He inquired around the world for skins and skeletons, including the Pacific, and collected the most diverse breeding stocks of small animals he could obtain for his experiments. The results finally appeared in *The Variation of Animals and Plants under Domestication* in 1868.

One of Darwin's most generous early suppliers seems to have been the rajah of Borneo, the British adventurer James Brooke (1803–1868). Brooke sent Darwin "some of his pigeons and fowls and *cats'* skins from the interior of Borneo and Singapore,"[129] skins of ducks from Bali, pigeons from the South Natunas Islands,[130] and notes on inherited characteristics of orangutans.[131] Others from whom Darwin requested skins and skeletons were Sir George Grey,[132] Walter Mantell,[133] and A. R. Wallace. In 1860 Darwin resumed the task of tracing the lineage of domestic animals he had put aside in 1858 to write the *Origin of Species*. Beginning in 1862, Robert Swinhoe (1836–1877), English consul on Taiwan, regularly sent Darwin specimens of domestic pigeons[134] and guinea pigs of China and bits of information as evidences for evolution by natural selection,[135] distribution, and expression of the emotions.[136] When in England on leave Swinhoe visited Darwin at Down, and Darwin proposed him for election to the Royal Society.[137] Henry Fletcher Hance, who had commented on *Orchids,* sent Darwin an article on early Chinese domestication of goldfish.[138]

Darwin on Men and Worms

After completing *The Variation of Animals and Plants under Domestication,* Darwin decided not to publish the remaining two volumes of his trilogy and turned to more limited works, several of which were intended to demonstrate the common origins of all human beings, then of all plants and animals including *Homo sapiens*.[139]

The Descent of Man

Darwin's Pacific correspondents who contributed to *The Descent of Man and Selection in Relation to Sex* included a number of his acquaintances who had spent considerable time in the Pacific, such as A. R. Wallace, T. H. Huxley, John Gould, Cuthbert Collingwood, David Forbes, and Thomas Belt. Darwin took most of the information he credits to them from their published works reporting on their stays in Asia, Australia, Peru, or Nicaragua, although he also carried on written correspondences and personal conversations with them. Letters containing data for *Descent* came from a diverse group: an English actor in California, Henry Edwards; a young American in Japan, Edward S. Morse; and Darwin's faithful informant in China, Robert Swinhoe. All of it was used by Darwin for his discussions of sex ratios and sexual selection in various animals, including humans.[140]

Several other contributors to the *Descent* were new correspondents, who furnished information for Darwin's discussion of the decline of native populations in the Pacific, a problem of which he became aware during his visit in 1835.

In 1835 Darwin believed the Maoris to be an exception to the observed decreases in human populations,[141] but he learned from Ernst Dieffenbach (1811–1855) in 1843 that they, too, were diminishing in numbers. Dieffenbach, who had spent the years 1839–1843 exploring and collecting in New Zealand,[142] wrote that the Maoris' mode of living provided sufficient cause to account for many of their diseases.[143] Darwin took that into account, but he believed that the spread of disease was insufficient to account for the population decreases and that somehow, changes in the conditions of life (environment, food, behavior) could bring about a decline in fertility leading to eventual extinction. Darwin also dismissed the hypothesis of inbreeding. He wrote, "It is known that the present inhabitants of Norfolk Island are nearly all cousins or near relations, . . . and yet they seem not to have suffered in fertility."[144] He cited a book by Sir William Denison, *Varieties of Vice-Regal Life,* to which he was referred by Lady Denison.[145] During Denison's tour as governor of New South Wales (1854–1861), the Pitcairn Islanders—descendants of mutineers of the *Bounty*—were removed to Norfolk Island, and Denison had visited them twice to investigate their well-being.

Darwin suggested other possible causes of population decline: "increased mortality, particularly of the children," probably from infanticide of girls, judging by the preponderance of male children,[146] or "lessened fertility," possibly due to "the profligacy of the women" or more probably to "changed habits of life," which could upset the "reproductive elements," leading either to variability or to lessened fertility or both. Information he received from zoological gardens and animal breeders, botanists, and nurserymen seemed to him to support this conclusion.[147] He wrote: "One of my informants, Mr. Coan, who was born on the islands, remarks that the natives have undergone a greater change in their habits of life in the course of fifty years than Englishmen during a thousand years."[148] Mr. Coan was Titus Munson

Coan, M.D. (1836–1921), the son of a New England missionary to Hawaii, Titus M. Coan (1801–1882). From his home in New York, Dr. Coan passed on his father's answer to Darwin's query about Hawaiian infanticide[149] and sent statistics on the declining population of the Hawaiian islands[150] and articles on the phenomenon gleaned from the press.[151]

Another of Darwin's informants was Thomas N. Staley (1823–1898), Anglican Bishop of Honolulu. Darwin had read an article by Staley in the *Journal of the Royal Geographic Society* on volcanic activity of the Sandwich Islands. Never hesitating to ask questions outside his correspondents' own interests, Darwin wrote to Staley to ask for information on the decline in population and on infanticide in the islands.[152] Darwin considered the changes in the diet of Hawaiians noted by Staley—the introduction of new fruits—to be a significant alteration of their conditions of life.[153] Darwin trusted both his hypothesis and his informers on the general influence of the conditions of life on fertility, but felt himself on less sure ground on the possibility of infanticide. He wrote, "I cannot decide whether what I have found is trustworthy" and concluded, "I now see that the problem is so intricate that it is safer to leave its solution for the future."[154] Why did he discuss it at all? Darwin never shied from including incomplete information in his books. As part of his strategy to stimulate further research, he always expressed hope that others would take up the problems he left unsolved.

Expression of the Emotions

More than a third of Darwin's correspondents who lived in the Pacific contributed to his second book on the origins of humans, *The Expression of the Emotions in Man and Animals* (1872). Of the thirty-six replies to Darwin's queries on expression, twenty-one were from his Pacific correspondents (see table 2), thirteen from Australia alone.[155] Six were missionaries.[156] Mining engineers, a police magistrate—"whose observations, as I am assured, are highly trustworthy"[157]—a pastoralist (sheep rancher), two German naturalists, and the Rajah of Borneo were some of the others who contributed notes replying to Darwin's questions on the expressions of persons "in a state of nature"—or as close to that as was possible.[158] Of course, in order to be observed, the Aborigines had to encounter "civilized" persons. Half of those who contributed to his project did so through intermediates, who forwarded their replies to Darwin. Very little is known about many of these persons today, although some of their letters are extant.[159]

Because Darwin's informants were transplanted Britons or Europe-

Contributors to *Expression of the Emotions*

Acted as intermediate	Wrote through intermediate
Alfred R. Wallace	Fred Geach, Malay
Julius von Haast	James Stack, New Zealand
Ferdinand Mueller	Mrs. Green, Australia
Ferdinand Mueller	Sir Samuel Wilson, Australia
Ferdinand Mueller	Charles Walter, Australia
Ferdinand Mueller	Friedrich Hagenauer, Australia
Robert Smyth	H. B. Lane, Australia
Robert Smyth	Archibald Lang, Australia
Robert Smyth	J. Bulmer, Australia
Robert Smyth	Templeton Bunnett, Australia
Edward Wilson	Dyson Lacy, Australia

Wrote directly to Darwin:
George Taplin, Australia
Philip Gidley King, Australia
Rajah Charles Brooke, Borneo
Robert Swinhoe, China
Adolph Meyer, Philippines
David Forbes, South American Indians
George Gibbs, North American Indians

Wrote to Darwin after publication of Expression:
Alfred Howitt, Australia
James Dawson, Australia
Henry Nottidge Moseley

ans, it was impossible for him to screen out their biases. His theory of evolution demanded the conclusion that expressions of emotions are similar in all human beings everywhere, and thus that all humans are siblings, or at least cousins. Including the Australians and New Zealanders in the human race was, however, one more way to turn the whole world "right side up." The antipodes were no longer the "antipathies." *Expression of the Emotions* was, like all of Darwin's books, a stimulant to hopeful correspondents, but there was no second edition or supplemental report, so Darwin made no use of Howitt's, Dawson's, or Moseley's observations.[160]

Movements in Plants

After his son Francis joined him as his research assistant in 1874, Darwin took up an investigation of the movements of germinating plants. He had published a preliminary study of climbing plants in 1865 and had become convinced that all plants when very young exhibit the same types of motions as climbers, motions brought about by the same mechanisms as in animals. Darwin collected seeds from as many parts of the world as possible. Two donors were from the Pacific region. Volney Rattan (1840–1915), a botanist and school-teacher in San Francisco, sent seeds of a climbing plant in the gourd family (Curcurbitaceae), *Megarrhiza californica* Torr. (California Man-root), and sketches of its germination via Asa Gray at Harvard, a long-time correspondent of Darwin's.[161] John Murray, a plant collec-tor in Queensland, sent Darwin a specimen of an Australian insectivo-rous plant (*Drosera* sp.); Darwin thanked Murray for sending the specimen, but it was too late for citation in any of his publications.[162]

The Formation of Vegetable Mold

Two of Darwin's Pacific correspondents helped him with his last biogeological project, a demonstration that the generally despised earthworms exist worldwide, that they act everywhere to turn the soil and to increase its fertility, and that, like human beings, worms are able to learn. Haast, who had so helpfully provided data on glacial drift and plants introduced into New Zealand, sent him information on the burial of ancient tools by worms.[163] Krefft sent a package of New South Wales worm castings and assured Darwin of their abun-dance.[164] With the help of his correspondents, Darwin showed that worms, which like coral animals are small, seemingly unimportant creatures, also like coral animals can accomplish great works, altering the surface of the earth.

"Normal Science"

The number of evolutionists who wrote to Darwin about their own research after publication of the *Origin* increased each year until about 1872, then held steady until his death. Many were amateurs, as were his earlier correspondents Fitzgerald, Beveridge, Rajah Brooke, Swinhoe, and Clarke. Darwin's campaign to convert scientists every-where to evolution was strengthened by encouraging his correspon-dents to publish.

Natural Selection

John Thomas Gulick (1832–1923), missionary and member of a Hawaiian missionary family, was, as were Cheeseman, Fitzgerald, and Alfred Howitt, inspired by reading Darwin to embark on his own Darwinian research program. For Gulick it was the *Journal of Researches*, where Darwin mentioned he had collected land shells (snails) on the Galapagos Islands peculiar to the archipelago.[165] In 1851–1852, the young Gulick began collecting the colorful Hawaiian tree snails (Achatinellidae). On a visit to England in 1872, he received a coveted audience with Darwin, who encouraged him in his work.[166]

Henry Edwards (1830–1891), an English actor who traveled with a theatrical company in Australia, Peru, Panama, California, and Mexico, collected insects, plants, and shells wherever he went. He was elected a member of the California Academy of Sciences in 1867.[167] Inspired by the *Origin* and *Insectivorous Plants,* Edwards wrote to Darwin in 1873 about the honey-making Mexican ant, *Myrmecocystus mexicanus*[168] and in 1874 about an insectivorous pitcher plant *(Darlingtonia californica)* and dimorphism in butterflies.[169]

Samuel Butler (1835–1902), grandson of the headmaster of the Shrewsbury school that Darwin attended as a boy, went to New Zealand in 1859 to escape going into the Church. After publication of the *Origin of Species,* Butler took up what he considered to be the tyranny of natural selection in a succession of articles and books, most published after his return to England in 1865. Both his writings and his correspondence with Darwin centered on the theoretical aspects of evolution and its philosophical implications for human life.[170]

Voices from the Challenger

The voyage of HMS *Challenger* (1872–1876) was the last of Britain's great nineteenth-century voyages of exploration. Darwin corresponded with two of the expedition's "scientifics," Henry Nottidge Moseley (1844–1891) and Charles Wyville Thomson (1830–1882), director of the scientific staff. Moseley dedicated his book, *Notes by a Naturalist on the "Challenger"* (1879), to Darwin.[171] Thomson offered Darwin the opportunity to examine the cirripedes from the *Challenger* collections and obtained his advice on the selection of a scientist to undertake their description.[172]

Emigrants Abroad

Wallis Nash, one of Darwin's neighbors, had corresponded with him on inheritance of traits in dogs. Nash visited Oregon and wrote a book on his adventure, then emigrated there in 1879 and wrote to Darwin about life there.[173] Some writers wanted information, others to correct statements in Darwin's books. Thomas Stanley in New South Wales wrote to Darwin to ask for a reference to the work of von Haast and Hector on New Zealand glaciers.[174] Frank Simmons wanted to correct a statement in the *Descent of Man* on the Maoris.[175] Many letters were frivolous, such as those from James Sinclair in

Aukland, who wanted Darwin's opinion on his theories of "organic disturbance" and of "organic combination,"[176] and Johann Riedel, who wrote from the Celebes about skin pigmentation and moveable tail bones on natives.[177]

In the last years of his life, Darwin received numerous honors. One of them came from the antipodes. Thomas Moreland Hocken (1836–1910), lecturer in surgery at and president of Otago University, New Zealand, in 1880 sent Darwin a copy of an address commemorating the twenty-first anniversary of the *Origin*. Darwin in his reply to Dr. Hocken said that he had "read every one of the volumes of the New Zealand Institute from the first" and congratulated the country on the great progress in science made in such a short time.[178]

In the last year of Darwin's life, William Nation (1826–1907), a Kew-trained botanist who became a professor at Guadeloupe College in Peru, was prompted by Darwin's accounts of the European cuckoo in the *Origin*[179] to send him a note on the behavior of the Peruvian cowbird, *Molothrus,* which lays eggs in other birds' nests. Darwin could not have been more pleased, as his contention that the habits of the cuckoo were developed by natural selection was controversial. He sent Nation's letter to *Nature,*[180] one of his final salvos for natural selection.

Conclusion

Darwin's extensive experiences in observation and experiment enabled him to see clearly through the looking glass to the other side of the world to discover explicable patterns in nature and to gain the authority to direct others' experiments and observations. Darwin knew before he had been home for three years what he wanted from correspondents residing in or returned from the Pacific and effectively extended his brief sojourn for forty-five years. Subsequently, guided by the principle of diversity and the theory of natural selection, scientists the world around took up Darwin's research programs on their own.[181]

As Darwin had predicted, those who endorsed his theory came largely from a younger generation. Many of his Pacific correspondents, however, were exceptions to the rule. James Drummond and W. B. Clarke, both born in the previous century, willingly aided Darwin. Titus B. Coan, American missionary to Hawaii, born in the first decade of the nineteenth century, wrote to Darwin for the first time in the last decade of his—and Darwin's—life.[182] Hawaiian missionaries were apparently, like Clarke, who was an Anglican minister, "quite relaxed about evolution."[183] The Australians James Dawson and

Edward Wilson, the New Zealanders James Stack (another missionary)[184] and William Swale, and the American George Gibbs are other examples of "older" men who accepted evolution.[185] All lived in the Pacific for years and could have been those of whom Frederick Burkhardt observed, "many of the strongest early Darwinists were those who studied species and varieties as they occurred in nature."[186] In Australia, New Zealand, and the Pacific islands, naturalists observed for themselves the extraordinary wonderland of animals and plants, both living and extinct. The data of geographical distribution and geological succession were consistently more explicable from the Darwinian than from the creationist standpoint. William Sharp Macleay, while not ready to accept Darwin's theory, in 1860 referred to Darwin as "an old friend of mine" and said that he hoped Darwin's book would "make people attend to such matters, and to be no longer prevented by the first chapter of Genesis from asking for themselves what the Book of Nature says on the subject of Creation."[187]

London was the metropolitan center for Darwin from 1838 to the end of his life—near Lyell and Huxley; the Athenaeum; the Geological, Zoological, and Linnean societies; the British Museum; and Kew Gardens. But science for Darwin also required Alpine meadows and breeders' pastures, oceans and tropical forests. Accordingly, he did not distinguish between science carried out in Ireland or the United States, in Germany or Brazil, in the mid-Pacific or at Kew. All were equally peripheral and equally "colonial." Thus the cirripede study, though requiring specimens from all over the world, was not "colonial science" in any meaningful sense. Except for Australian barnacles sent to him from Covington, all Pacific cirripede specimens came from travelers (Cuming, Stutchbury, Dana) and from the collections in the British Museum. Darwin's chief Pacific sources for skins, skeletons, and living specimens for his experiments on domestic animals were the amateurs, Rajah Brooke and Robert Swinhoe, neither of whom could be called a colonist.

If one attempts to define "colonial science," one must identify the "colonial scientists." Émigrés to Australia, New Zealand, India, or South Africa; government servants in China, Japan, or South America were all British citizens, free to return home at the end of an assignment or if new opportunities beckoned at home. Missionaries from the United States or from Britain to the Pacific often stayed for half a lifetime but returned "home" to retire. W. B. Clarke always referred to England as "home," and after more than thirty years in Australia he did go home, where he was honored for his contributions to geology, in 1870. Hugh Cuming stayed in the Pacific for twenty years, but he was not a colonist; he was a British scientist doing a bit of work half a world away from home.

Scientists who made their careers in Australia or New Zealand occasionally felt the sting of being treated like "colonials": Clarke and Macleay, both recognized scientists before going out to Australia, complained of such treatment by Richard Owen in the identification and description of fossil animals. Mueller was not granted the opportunity to travel to England to "work up" his own plant collections: Bentham, who like Owen had never traveled to the Pacific, thought he could do it better.[188] Krefft on the other hand saw his innovations hampered by trustees and the scientific elite at home in Sydney as much as by Owen in England.[189] Haast in New Zealand could be termed a colonial, as he made his life as well as his career in the Pacific. Yet he was a respected scientist both there and in England. Haast was never treated like a "colonial," whose function was to supply data and specimens to the experts at home, but like the accomplished scientist he was.

One facet of Darwin's Pacific science could be labeled "colonial." A problem with any science that is particularly acute with natural history is that of obtaining trustworthy observations of phenomena. Experiments can be reproduced, but observations in nature are often of fleeting phenomena; the conditions under which they are made rarely remain stable. Moreover, the kind of observations Darwin wanted for *The Descent of Man* and *The Expression of the Emotions,* to which a number of his contacts in the Pacific region contributed, required subjective interpretation. Like Gilbert White of the previous century, Darwin trusted men of the cloth—ministers and missionaries—college professors, and government officials in responsible positions, as well as personal acquaintances. Many of his correspondents for *The Expression of the Emotions* numbered among such trustworthy observers. That was colonial science, and it was Baconian science as it was understood by Victorians—science that was not limited to professionals, but that made use of the abilities of many persons in many walks of life.

Darwin asked for considered judgment on the part of his informers regarding the success of introduced plants or animals, the decline of local populations, the conduct and results of experiments, or the meaning of facial expressions. He made his correspondents aware of their participation in a vast enterprise; his citations of their work contributed to their careers as well as to his cause. Many of the letters he received in the last decade of his life—and most papers and books published in the life sciences since then—reveal that his work was, as he intended it to be, a springboard for future research, research to strengthen the hold of his theory on the imaginations of us all.

Appendix 1: Darwin's Correspondents in the Pacific[190]

Name	Years of correspondence	Number of letters	Country of residence	Vocation if known
Alison, Robert	1834–1835	2	Chile	writer
Beveridge, Peter	1881	1	Australia	pastoralist
Brooke, Rajah Jas.	(1850s)	(?)	Borneo	ruler
Brooke, Rajah C.	1870	1	Borneo	ruler
Bulmer, J.	1867 or 1868	(1)	Australia	missionary
Bunnett, Templeton	1868	(1)	Australia	missionary
Cheeseman, Thomas F.	1873–1879	5	New Zealand	botanist
Clarke, William B.	1861–1862	6	Australia	minister
Coan, Titus M.	1874–1879	4	Hawaii	missionary
Corfield, Richard H.	1835	2	Chile	
Covington, Syms	1843–1859	10	Australia	postmaster
Dawson, James	1881	2	Australia	farmer
Denison, Caroline	1872	2	Australia	lady
Douglas, Charles	1835–1836	2	Chile	surveyor
Drummond, James	1860	5	Australia	botanist
Edwards, Henry	1873–1875	4	Australia; United States (Calif.)	actor
Fitzgerald, Robert D.	1875–1881	7	Australia	engineer
Geach, Fred F.	1867–1868	2	Malaya	engineer
Green, Mrs.	1867 or 1868	(1)	Australia	
Grey, Sir George	1846–1855	4	Australia; New Zealand	governor
Gulick, John Thomas	1872	4	Hawaii	missionary
Haast, J. F. J. von	1862–1879	22	New Zealand	geologist
Hagenauer, Friedrich	1867–1868	2	Australia	missionary
Hance, Henry F.	1863–1868	2	China	civil servant
Hector, Sir James	1872	1	New Zealand	geologist
Hocken, Thomas M.	1881	1	New Zealand	surgeon
Howitt, Alfred	1874	2	Australia	anthropologist
King, Philip G.	1854–1869	6	Australia	manager
King, Phillip P.	1836	1	Australia	admiral
Krefft, J. G. von	1872–1876	16	Australia	zoologist
Lacy, Dyson	1867 or 1868	(1)	Australia	

continued

Lambert, Mr.	1835	1	[Chile]	
Lane, H. B.	1867 or 1868	(1)	Australia	policeman
Lang, Archibald	1867 or 1868	(1)	Australia	missionary
Macleay, William S.	1839	1	Australia	entomologist
Mantell, Walter B.	1854–1869	5	New Zealand	geologist
Martens, Conrad	1862	1	Australia	artist
Mitchell, Sir Thomas	1838–1839	2	Australia	surveyor
Moore, Charles	1858	1	Australia	botanist
Mueller, Ferdinand	1858–1874	6	Australia	botanist
Murray, John	1880	1	Australia	plant collector
Nation, William	1881	1	Peru	botanist
Rattan, Volney	1880	2	United States (Calif.)	teacher
Simmons, Frank C.	1871	1	New Zealand	teacher
Sinclair, James L.	1869	2	New Zealand	journalist
Smith, Chas. H., Jr.	1872	1	Australia	army officer
Smyth, Robert B.	1868	1	Australia	mining engineer
Stack, James West	1867	1	New Zealand	missionary
Staley, Thomas N.	1874	4	Hawaii	bishop
Stanley, Thomas	1872	1	Australia	
Swale, William	1858–1870	2	New Zealand	nurseryman
Swinhoe, Robert	1862–1874	18	Taiwan (China)	diplomat
Taplin, George	1867 or 1868	1	Australia	missionary
Walter, Charles	1867	1	Australia	naturalist
Wilson, Sir Samuel	1867	1	Australia	pastoralist

Appendix 2: Darwin's Correspondents Who Worked in the Pacific but Lived Elsewhere[191]

Name	Years of correspondence	Number of letters	Country of residence (work)	Vocation if known
Agassiz, Alexander	1869–1881	12	United States (Pacific)	engineer
Allan, Dr. J.	1832–1845	(?)	Scotland (Madagascar)	medicine
Belt, Thomas	1867–1877	15	England (Central America)	engineer

Butler, Samuel	1865–1880	13	England (Australia)	writer
Coan, Titus, MD	1874–1879	4	United States (Hawaii)	physician
Collingwood, Cuthbert	1861–1868	4	England (China)	naturalist
Cuming, Hugh	1845–1849	3	England (Pacific)	naturalist
Dana, James D.	1849–1874	30	United States (Pacific)	geologist
Dieffenbach, Ernst	1843–1847	12	Germany (New Zealand)	naturalist
Forbes, David	1860–1872	12	England (Chile)	chemist
Gibbs, George	1867	1	United States	ethnologist
Gould, John	1838–1866	4	England (Australia)	ornithologist
Hinds, Richard	1843	2	England (Pacific)	naturalist
Hooker, Joseph	1843–1882	1394	England (Pacific)	botanist
Huxley, Thomas	1851–1882	285	England (Australia)	anatomist
Jukes, Joseph B.	1838–1864	8	England (Australia)	geologist
Meyer, Adolf B.	1868–1872	4	Germany (Philippines)	writer
Morse, Edward S.	1871–1880	8	United States (Japan)	zoologist
Moseley, Henry	1876–1882	21	England (Pacific)	naturalist
Nash, Wallis	1871–1880	5	England (Oregon)	lawyer
Orton, James	1869–1870	6	United States (Ecuador, Peru)	zoologist
Pickering, Charles	1850	1	United States (Pacific)	botanist
Ridley, Henry N.	1877–1878	4	England (Malay)	botanist
Riedel, Johan G.	1875–1877	2	Netherlands (East Indies)	writer
Seeman, Berthold	1862	1	Germany (United States)	botanist

continued

Semper, Carl G.	1874–1881	17	Germany (Philippines)	zoologist
Stokes, John Lort	1846	4	England (Beagle)	naval officer
Stutchbury, Samuel	1846–1854	(?)	England (Australia)	naturalist
Thomson, Charles W.	1870–1878	6	England	naturalist
Usborne, Alexander	1835	1	England (Beagle)	master's assistant
Wallace, Alfred R.	1857–1881	186	England (Malay)	naturalist
Wilson, Edward	1867–1869	8	England (Australia)	politician

Notes

The following abbreviations are used for volumes of Darwin's correspondence and publications.

APS   *An Annotated Calendar of the Letters of Charles Darwin in the Possession of the American Philosophical Society,* ed. P. Thomas Carroll (Wilmington: Library Publication, 1976).

Calendar   *Calendar of the Correspondence of Charles Darwin,* ed. Frederick Burkhardt and Sydney Smith (New York and London: Garland, 1982).

Coral Reefs   *The Structure and Distribution of Coral Reefs. Being the First Part of the Geology of the Voyage of the "Beagle"* (London: Smith, Elder, 1842).

Correspondence   *The Correspondence of Charles Darwin, 1821–1860,* ed. Frederick Burkhardt and Sydney Smith, 10 vols. (Cambridge: Cambridge University Press, 1985–1994).

CP   *The Collected Papers of Charles Darwin,* ed. Paul H. Barrett et al., 2 vols. (Chicago: University of Chicago Press, 1977).

Descent   *The Descent of Man and Selection in Relation to Sex* (London: John Murray, 1871).

Geology   *Geological Observations on the Volcanic Islands and Parts of South America, Visited during the Voyage of H.M.S. "Beagle." Being the Second and Third Parts of the Geology of the Voyage of the "Beagle"* (London: Smith, Elder, 1844, 1846; 2d ed., 1876, text unchanged).

LL   *Life and Letters of Charles Darwin,* ed. Francis Darwin, 2 vols. (New York: Basic Books, 1959); the original edition (London: John Murray, 1887), in three volumes, is used by current editors of Darwin's *Correspondence;* it contains some letters omitted from the two-volume edition.

ML   *More Letters of Charles Darwin,* ed. Francis Darwin and A. C. Seward, 2 vols. (London: John Murray, 1903).

Natural Selection   *Charles Darwin's Natural Selection: Being the Second Part of his Big Species Book Written from 1856 to 1858,* ed. R. C. Stauffer (Cambridge: Cambridge University Press, 1975).

Origin   *On the Origin of Species* (London: John Murray, 1859; facsimile, Harvard University Press, 1964; 6th ed., 2 vols., Chicago and New York: Rand McNally, 1872).

Variation   *The Variation of Animals and Plants under Domestication* (London: John Murray, 1868; 2d ed., 1872; reprint, 1900).

Voyage   *The Voyage of the "Beagle"* (New York: Doubleday, Natural History Library edition, 1962, reprint of 3rd ed., 1860).

1   The Keeling Islands are in the Indian Ocean but were important to Darwin's theory of coral reefs. Darwin learned that the Indian Ocean is biologically a part of the Pacific (*Origin*, 348).

2   *Origin,* 6th ed., 1:437; Charles Darwin, *A Monograph on the Subclass Cirripedia: The Balanidae* (London: Ray Society, 1854), 564.

3   For example, *CP,* 1:41 contains information supplied by Alison and Douglas, two of Darwin's correspondents in Chile, while *CP,* 2:19 contains data sent by Mr. Swale in New Zealand, *CP,* 2:36, 42, and 162 report experiments by James Drummond in Australia, and *CP,* 2:235–236, is based on information from William Nation, a correspondent in Peru.

4   A discussion of the problems of ordering "the chaotic diversity of nature" in the first half of the nineteenth century is presented in Neal C. Gillespie, "Preparing for Darwin: Conchology and Natural Theology in Anglo-American Natural History," *Studies in the History of Biology* 7 (1984): 93–145; quotation from 116.

5   Gray, "Pisces," in Captain P. P. King, *Narrative of a Survey of the Intertropical and Western Coasts of Australia, 1818–1822,* 2 vols. (London: John Murray, 1827), 2:436.

6   Letter from Hooker to Darwin, December 1843, in *Life and Letters of Sir Joseph Dalton Hooker,* ed. Leonard Huxley, 2 vols. (London: John Murray, 1918), 1:436; also in *Correspondence,* 2:421.

7   Papers have been published on some of Darwin's correspondents in New Zealand, Australia, and Hawaii: Garry J. Tee, "Charles Darwin's Correspondents in New Zealand," *Proceedings of the Australasian Association for the History, Philosophy, and Social Studies of Science* 12 (2) (1980–1981): 367–379; Barry W. Butcher, "Darwin's Australian Correspondents: Deference and Collaboration in Colonial Science," in *Nature in Its Greatest Extent: Western Science in the Pacific,* ed. Roy MacLeod and Philip F. Rehbock (Honolulu: University of Hawaii Press, 1988), 139–158; Frank W. Nicholas and Jan M. Nicholas, *Charles Darwin in Australia* (Cambridge: Cambridge University Press, 1989); and John H. R. Plews, "Charles Darwin and Hawaiian Sex Ratios, or Genius Is the Capacity for Making Com-

pensating Errors," *Hawaiian Journal of History* 14 (1980): 26–49.

8   Letters are still being discovered; for instance, two of Darwin's letters to Philip Gidley King, published in Nicholas and Nicholas, *Darwin in Australia,* were not found in time for one dated 1854 to be included in *Correspondence,* vol. 5. But see *Correspondence,* 7:489 (Supplement, 1821–1857).

9   Garry J. Tee in "Darwin's Correspondents in New Zealand," 369–378, mentions several other of Darwin's contacts not listed here: James Busby, William Williams, William Colenso, Frederick Wollaston Hutton, Thomas Jeffery Parker, Dr. Andrew Sinclair, and William Thomas Travers. Either there are no extant letters between Darwin and those persons, or there were no statements by Darwin that there had been letters, or the persons had emigrated after corresponding with Darwin. Hutton (1836–1905) is of importance as a geologist and Darwinist in New Zealand. He obtained many skeletons of the extinct moa, *Dinornis;* he was the author of *Darwinism and Lamarckism Old and New,* 1899, and *The Lesson of Evolution,* 1902 and 1907; see the *Dictionary of New Zealand Biography.*

10 For instance, no letters from the following are listed in the *Calendar,* but Bulmer, Bunnett, Green, Lacy, Lane, Lang, and Taplin are listed as correspondents in *The Expression of the Emotions in Man and Animals* (New York and London: D. Appleton, 1872; reprint Chicago: University of Chicago Press, 1965), 19–20; Bulmer, Bunnett, Hagenauer, Lane, and Lang are mentioned in a letter from Robert Smythe to Darwin, 13 August 1868 (*Calendar,* no. 6314); Dr. J. Allan in *Voyage,* 14, 463; and Rajah Brooke in *Natural Selection,* 112, and in *Variation,* 1:191, 289, and in letters from Darwin to Wallace (*Correspondence,* 6:387, May 1857), Fox (*Correspondence,* 6:135–136), and Teqetmeier (*Correspondence,* 6:295–296, 344–345,393–394, and 397).

11 Mueller, Swale, and possibly Mantell; see appendix 1. Letter no. 6520 to Walter Mantell may have been erroneously dated [1869?], as it appears to be a sequel to no. 1663 of [1855].

12 James R. Moore, "Essay Review: *A Calendar of the Correspondence of Charles Darwin, 1828–1882,*" *Isis* 76 (1985): 570–580, esp. 573; Janet Bell Garber, "Charles Darwin as a Laboratory Director" (Ph.D. dissertation, UCLA, 1989), 161–167, 381, 470–471, 512–516, 663.

13 Butcher, "Darwin's Australian Correspondents," 144–147; the United States was an exception: Asa Gray and Jeffries Wyman at Harvard were among early supporters of natural selection.

14 Bailey, "Concise History of Australian Botany," in his Presidential Address to the Royal Society of Queensland, July 1891, in *Proceedings of the Royal Society of Queensland* 8 (1891): xvii–xli, xlv–xlvii;

Ann Mozley, *A Guide to the Manuscript Records of Australian Science* (Canberra: Australian Academy of Science in association with Australian National University Press, 1966), xii.

15   William Montgomery, "Editing the Darwin Correspondence: A Quantitative Perspective," *British Journal of the History of Science* 20 (1987): 13–28; see 17.

16   Persons who corresponded with Darwin only before their emigration or while traveling to the Pacific or whose letters to Darwin do not concern the Pacific realm are omitted from this study.

17   *Correspondence*, 4: "Introduction," xvii–xx, and appendix 2, "Darwin's Study of the Cirripedia," 388–409.

18   See Janet Browne, *The Secular Ark: Studies in the History of Biogeography* (New Haven: Yale University Press, 1983) 196–214, and Dov Ospovat, *The Development of Darwin's Theory: Natural History, Natural Theology, and Natural Selection, 1838–1859* (Cambridge: Cambridge University Press, 1981), 170–194. On the Galapagos birds, see Frank J. Sulloway, "Darwin and His Finches: The Evolution of a Legend," *Journal of the History of Biology* 15 (1982): 1–53.

19   *Coral Reefs* and *Geology*.

20   Others have noted Darwin's ability to use correspondence as a means to conducting research on a wide scale: Barry G. Gale, *Evolution without Evidence: Charles Darwin and the Origin of Species* (Albuquerque: University of New Mexico Press, 1982); and Frank N. Egerton, "Darwin's Method or Methods?" essay review of Michael T. Ghiselin, *The Triumph of the Darwinian Method,* in *Studies in the History and Philosophy of Science* 2 (1971): 281–286.

21   *On the Various Contrivances by Which British and Foreign Orchids Are Fertilised by Insects . . .* (London: John Murray, 1862; 2d ed., 1877), 1–15. (1877). See especially Fig. 2, p. 12.

22   Mary P. Winsor, *Starfish, Jellyfish, and the Order of Life: Issues in Nineteenth-Century Science* (New Haven: Yale University Press, 1976), 175; for a discussion of the search for "laws of the living realm" among nineteenth-century British and European naturalists, see Philip R. Rehbock, *The Philosophical Naturalists: Themes in Early Nineteenth-Century British Biology* (Madison: University of Wisconsin Press, 1983), esp. 4–11, 32–114, 192–193.

23   This was in spite of appointments of "creationists" to university posts; see Butcher, "Darwin's Australian Correspondents," 140–141, 147, 153.

24   For instance, his "Questions about the Breeding of Animals." R. B. Freeman and P. J. Gautrey, *Journal of the Society for the Bibliography of Natural History* 5 (1969): 220–225; also see *Correspondence,* 3:404–405 for another set of queries on the same subject.

25   *CP*, 1:41–43, 53–86; see also *Correspondence*, 1:390, 450–457, 464–
      465, 475–481, and 550–551.

26   1:81–82.

27   *Voyage*, 256 (entry of 23 July), 278 (entry of 16 November 1834),
      321–323.

28   *Coral Reefs* (1851), 141–2. Darwin made similar remarks in *Geology*
      (1876), 237–239, 244–245, 272, 295, 298, 397, 541, 573.

29   *Natural Selection*, 545, 561.

30   David Forbes, "On the Geology of Bolivia and Southern Peru," *Quar-
      terly Journal of the Geological Society* 17 (1861):184; *Origin*, 6th ed.,
      2:97; *Calendar*, no. 6751, letter from Darwin to Lyell, 20 May 1869,
      in *ML* 2:144 and n. 2; letters from Darwin to James Orton: *Calendar*,
      nos. 6570 and 7117, 23 January [1869] and 24 February [1870];
      *Letters and Recollections of Alexander Agassiz with a Sketch of His
      Life and Work*, ed. G. R. Agassiz (New York: Houghton Mifflin,
      1913), 140.

31   Travelers who contributed to *Coral Reefs* were John Lort Stokes,
      Richard Brinsley Hinds, James Dwight Dana, Joseph Beete Jukes, and
      Charles H. Smith. For *Beagle* Mate Stokes see Darwin, *Coral Reefs*,
      86. For Hinds, see *Correspondence*, 2: 357, 375. For Dana, see *Cor-
      respondence*, 4: 266, 284–286, 289; *Calendar*, nos. 8349, 9240,
      9556; James Dwight Dana, "On the Areas of Subsidence in the
      Pacific, as Indicated by the Distribution of Coral Islands," *Edinburgh
      New Philosophical Journal* 35 (1843): 341–345; and idem, *Corals
      and Coral Islands* (New York: Dodd and Mead, 1872). For Jukes see
      Correspondence, 4:87. For Smith, see *Calendar*, no. 8131. (Smith's
      father, Col. Charles H. Smith [1776–1859], was one of the experts at
      home whom Darwin consulted on subsidence of islands in the Pacific;
      see *Correspondence*, 1: 178, 3:126, 129, 131, and *CP*, 1: 227–249,
      esp. 246).

32   Darwin, *Coral Reefs*, 132. Martens (1801–1878), artist aboard the
      Beagle for part of the voyage, sailed ahead to Australia and settled
      there.

33   *Voyage*, 14, 77–78, 463; *Coral Reefs*, 14, 55, 77, 122n, 136, 185–
      188; *Geology*, 141.

34   *Coral Reefs*, 58, 135, 179–180.

35   *Voyage*, 437 (entry of 18 January 1836); *Correspondence*, 2: 68
      [1838], 195 [1839]; *Geology*, (1844), 38 and fig. 4.

36   *Voyage*, 390–391.

37   *CP*, 1:204.

38   *Correspondence*, 4: 264, letter from Darwin to Cuming, [October?]
      1849 (in *APS*, no. 82).

39   *Correspondence*, 4:128, 129 n. 7, 249, 250 n. 3.

40   Nicholas and Nicholas, *Darwin in Australia*, 63; *Correspondence*, 1:148, 149, 481, 483, 561.

41   Darwin's "Zoology Edinburgh Notebook" (1837–1839), 13, in *Charles Darwin's Notebooks*, ed. Paul H. Barrett, Peter J. Gautrey, Sandra Herbert, David Kohn, and Sydney Smith (Cambridge: Cambridge University Press, 1987).

42   Matthews L. Harrison, "Samuel Stutchbury and Darwin's Cirripedes," *Notes and Records of the Royal Society of London* 36 (1982): 261–266; no letters between Darwin and Stutchbury are listed in the *Calendar*, but Darwin acknowledged his aid in *Living Cirripedia: Lepadidae*, vi; and see letter to Mrs. Stutchbury, 22 August [1854], *Correspondence*, 7:492.

43   See Herman J. Viola and Carolyn Margolis, eds., *Magnificent Voyagers: The United States Exploring Expedition, 1838–1842* (Washington, DC: Smithsonian Institution Press, 1985), esp. 90–91; and Daniel C. Gilman, *The Life of James Dwight Dana* (New York: Harper and Bros., 1899), 304–306 (letters also published in *Correspondence*, 4:247, 265, 286; the last is also published in *ML*, 2:227).

44   *Correspondence*, 4: 230, 369.

45   See letter from Darwin to P. G. King, 21 February 1854, published in Nicholas and Nicholas, *Darwin in Australia*, 133, and in *Correspondence*, 7:489.

46   *Annals and Magazine of Natural History*, 2d ser., 16 (1855): 184–196; *Alfred Russel Wallace: Letters and Reminiscences*, ed. James Marchant, 2 vols. (London: Cassell, 1916; reprinted 1975), 1:29–34, 107.

47   *Correspondence*, 6: 387; also in *LL*, 2:95, and in *Alfred Russel Wallace*, ed. Marchant, 1:107–109.

48   Wallace was in the Pacific for the first five of those years; Wallace's discovery that a deep ocean trench near the Celebes was significant for distribution particularly interested Darwin (*Origin*, 6th ed., 2:113).

49   See Darwin-Hooker letters of 11 January and 23 February 1844 (*Correspondence*, 3:1–3, 11); *Origin*, 1st ed. 404; and Darwin's "Questions and Experiments" notebook (1839–1844), 17 (questions to ask Hooker), in *Darwin's Notebooks*, ed. Barrett et al.

50   *Natural Selection*, 563–564, 580.

51   Others were Hooker, Dana, Lyell, and Louis Agassiz; for Cuming's contribution, see *Correspondence*, 3:90–94, 232–235, and *LL* 1:339. Richard B. Hinds, naturalist on HMS *Sulphur*, wrote to Darwin but contributed nothing useful (*Correspondence*, 2: 357, 375).

52   Letter to Darwin, 9 January 1850, *Correspondence*, 4: 299.

53   *Natural Selection*, 529; *Origin*, 1st ed. 365–382.

54   *Correspondence,* 2: 192, 529; 4:313. Mantell, son of London geolo-
      gist Gideon Algernon Mantell, emigrated to New Zealand in 1840.

55   *Correspondence,* 5: 238, 17 November 1854. Darwin had attempted
      unsuccessfully to obtain the same information seven years earlier
      from Sir George Grey (1812–1898), then governor of New Zealand,
      who had offered to help with his researches; see *Correspondence,*
      3:263, 362–365; 4:95–96; and Tee, "Darwin's Correspondents in
      New Zealand," 372 and n. 11.

56   Mantell's reply is missing from the *Correspondence* but is reported in
      Natural Selection, 546.

57   Berthold C. Seeman (1825–1871), was a naturalist aboard the HMS
      Herald, 1847–1851. See *Natural Selection,* 550 n. 1; *ML,* 1:473; and
      Origin, 6th ed., 2:100.

58   Thomas Belt (1832–1878), *Naturalist in Nicaragua* (London: John
      Murray, 1874), 248–272.

59   *Correspondence,* 2: 251, 22 January 1840, to the Geological Society;
      ibid., 3:79, from a letter to Hooker, 10 November 1844. See also *CP,*
      1:200 n. 8.

60   Ann Mozley Moyal, *Scientists in Nineteenth-Century Australia: A
      Documentary History* (Sydney: Cassell, 1976), 131–132. On the dis-
      covery of fossil bones in Australia, see W. B. Clarke, *Sydney Morning
      Herald,* 30 November 1847, p. 2; 6 December 1847, p. 2.

61   Moyal, *Scientists in Nineteenth-Century Australia,* 187; *Calendar,* no.
      3222.

62   *Origin,* 6th ed., 2: 97, 111.

63   *Calendar,* no. 3374.

64   Darwin cited Haast in *Origin,* 6th ed. 2: 97. The passage also credits
      Sir James Hector with supplying similar information, although their
      extant letters do not include the subject.

65   Rewa Glenn, *The Botanical Explorers of New Zealand* (Wellington:
      A. H. and A. W. Reed, 1950), 111–127; see 123.

66   Haast's discoveries included a moa (*Dinornis,* an extinct flightless
      bird resembling an ostrich) and an eagle.

67   Haast sent photos to Darwin of skeletons of *Dinornis; Calendar,* no.
      10722, 16 December 1876.

68   Thirteen is the minimum number of letters from Haast; some may
      have been lost (*Calendar,* nos. 3851, 4026, 4160, 4249, 4264, 4285,
      4518, 4900, 5158, 5207, 5534, 5705, 10722); Darwin wrote at least
      nine letters to Haast (nos. 3935, 4245, 4356, 4956, 5079, 5423,
      5808, 10756, 12284); in addition, eleven letters between Darwin and
      Hooker concerned communications from Haast (nos. 3374, 3391,
      3731, 3735, 4133, 4216, 4324, 4325, 4339, 4341, 4954).

69   *Calendar,* no. 4249, letter from Haast to Darwin, 21 July 1863.

70   *Correspondence,* 6:130, Darwin to Mantell, 5 June [1856]. *Calendar,*
      no. 3851, Haast to Darwin, 9 December 1862; no. 3935, Darwin to
      Haast, 22 January 1863, *LL* 2:190.

71   Darwin explained his desire for information on a New Zealand rat
      and frog to Hooker in 1862; *Calendar,* no. 3735, *ML* 2:154. Neither
      the rat nor the frog can survive long immersion in salt water (*Origin,*
      6th ed., 2:112), and neither is found on oceanic islands (ibid., 2:52).

72   No New Zealand frog or rat is mentioned in later letters or any of
      Darwin's books. There was a native frog (an early arrival), but not a
      rat (see *Correspondence,* 6:130 nn. 3–4).

73   *Calendar,* no. 4324, Darwin to Hooker [30 October 1863], and no.
      4325, Hooker to Darwin after 30 October 1863.

74   *Calendar,* no. 3298, Darwin to Clarke, 25 October 1861; no. 3392,
      Clarke to Darwin, 16 January 1862; no. 4339, Hooker to Darwin 11
      November 1863, and no. 4341, Darwin to Hooker [13 November
      1863], both on a report by Haast regarding introduced animals; no.
      4356, Darwin to Haast 12 December 1863, thanks for report on nat-
      uralization of animals in New Zealand.

75   *Correspondence,* 6: 271–274, letters between Darwin and Hooker,
      15–18 November [1856].

76   *Correspondence,* 6: 498, letter from Darwin to Hooker, 4 December
      [1857]

77   *Correspondence,* 6: 498, letter to Darwin from Hooker, 6 December
      [1857].

78   Lionel Gilbert, *The Royal Botanic Gardens, Sydney: A History, 1816–
      1985* (Melbourne: Oxford University Press, 1986), 72–113.

79   *Correspondence,* 7: 151, 11 August [1858].

80   Gilbert, *Royal Botanic Gardens,* 94.

81   Mueller anglicized his name after settling in Australia; Sophie C.
      Ducker, "Australian Phycology: The German Influence," in *People
      and Plants in Australia,* ed. D. J. Carr and S. G. M. Carr (New York:
      Academic Press, 1981), 116–138, esp. 123.

82   Moyal, *Scientists in Nineteenth-Century Australia,* 172–174; Carr
      and Carr, eds., *People and Plants in Australia,* xii.

83   *Correspondence,* 6: 501 [8 December 1857]; it was thought that
      all correspondence between Mueller and Darwin was lost (Butcher,
      "Darwin's Australian Correspondents," 155 n. 7), but preparation
      of the *Calendar* has resulted in locating six letters.

84   *Natural Selection,* 553–554; a briefer statement of Mueller's contribu-
      tion is to be found in the *Origin,* 375. Also see *Correspondence,* 7:
      236–237, 242–243, letters from Darwin to Hooker, 20 and 28 Janu-
      ary [1859].

85   Stan P. Rachootin, "Owen and Darwin Reading a Fossil," in *The*

Darwinian Heritage, ed. David Kohn (Princeton: Princeton University Press, 1985), 155–184, esp. 167–168.

86   Only a year or two earlier Hooker was still arguing with Darwin that the existence of European plants on the Australian alps was only explicable by double creations; letters from Hooker to Darwin, 6–9 June 1855 (*Correspondence,* 5: 345–346) and 10 July 1856 (*Correspondence,* 6:175).

87   Letter from Darwin to William B. Clarke, 25 October [1861], *Calendar,* no. 3298, published in Moyal, *Scientists in Nineteenth-Century Australia,* 193–195 (*Correspondence,* 6:175).

88   *Calendar,* nos. 5424, 5620, 5626, 5677; Darwin, *Expression of the Emotions,* 19–20.

89   Ann Mozley, "Evolution and the Climate of Opinion in Australia, 1840–1876," *Victorian Studies* 10 (4) (June 1967): 412–430; quote from 422; also see Moyal, *Scientists in Nineteenth-Century Australia,* 181.

90   Examples are Darwin's geology professor at Cambridge, Adam Sedgwick, and the geologist Hugh Falconer, who remained Darwin's friends in spite of their adverse opinions of Darwin's theory of natural selection. See letter from Sedgwick to Darwin, 24 November 1859, *LL,* 2: 247–250 (*Correspondence,* 7:5396), and letter from Falconer to Darwin in 1862, *ML* 1:205.

91   Examples are James West Stack, a missionary in New Zealand (see Tee, "Darwin's Correspondents in New Zealand," 376) and James Dana (see Garber, "Darwin as a Laboratory Director," 253–262).

92   Frederick Burkhardt, "England and Scotland: The Learned Societies," in *The Comparative Reception of Darwinism,* ed. Thomas F. Glick (Austin: University of Texas Press, 1974), 32–74 (reprint, Chicago: University of Chicago Press, 1988).

93   *Calendar,* no. 9494; Baron Ferdinand von Mueller, *Select Extra-Tropical Plants Readily Eligible for Industrial Culture or Naturalisation* (Sydney: Thomas Richards, 1881).

94   J. J. Fletcher, "The Society's Heritage from the Macleays: Part 1," *Proceedings of the Linnean Society of New South Wales* 45 (1920): 568, 623–624. Darwin made the request through his neighbor, John Lubbock.

95   *Origin,* 6th ed., 1:57. Lubbock reported to Darwin on the effects of the introduction of bumble bees into Australia in 1867 (*Calendar* no. 5716, letter from Lubbock to Darwin).

96   *Correspondence,* 2:15, letter from Darwin to Leonard Jenyns, 10 April 1837. The only extant letter between Darwin and Macleay is a request from Darwin in 1839 asking Macleay in Sydney to help Syms Covington find employment. *Correspondence,* 2: 194, 29 May 1839.

97   *Calendar,* no. 7109; the aphid is *Schizoneura lanigera;* the bird is a
     White-eye, *Zosterops lateralis;* Walter L. Buller, *Manual of the Birds
     of New Zealand* (Wellington: Colonial Museum and Geological Sur-
     vey Dept., James Hector, Director, 1882), 13; Bruce Campbell and
     Elizabeth Lack, *A Dictionary of Birds* (Vermillion: University of
     South Dakota Press, 1985). (Darwin subscribed to Buller's serial pub-
     lication of *History of the Birds of New Zealand* [vol. 1, 1873] and
     sponsored Buller as F.R.S. [see Tee, "Darwin's Correspondents in New
     Zealand," 378], but no letters between them are known.)

98   *Origin,* 197–198; Darwin's theory of pangenesis, at least in part, was
     a hypothesis of a cause for variations; see *LL,* 2:157–158, 3:72; *ML,*
     1:197–198; and *Variation* (1900), 2:238–239; *Correspondence,* 6:
     281–282. Letter from Darwin to Hooker [23 November 1856].

99   *The Autobiography of Charles Darwin,* ed. Nora Barlow (New York
     and London: W. W. Norton, 1958), 127.

100 *CP,* 1: 142–145.

101 *CP,* 1:263, 264, 273, 275, 277, all 1855–1857.

102 Letter to Hooker, 12 January [1858], *ML,* 2: 255–256; *Correspon-
     dence,* 7:5. Bees were introduced into New Zealand in 1839; the
     native bees, which are solitary, not social insects, still exist (*Ency-
     clopedia of New Zealand* 1:187). Clover is a member of the pea
     family.

103 *CP,* 2: 20–21, reprinted from *Annals and Magazine of Natural
     History,* 3d ser., 2 (1858): 459–465 (also *Gardeners' Chronicle,* 13
     November 1858, 828–829). For William Swale (1816–1875), see Tee,
     "Darwin's Correspondents in New Zealand," 373 and n. 17; William
     Swale, "Garden Memoranda: Mr. Wilson's Nursery," *Gardeners'
     Chronicle,* 20 February 1858, 131–132.

104 *Correspondence,* 7:134 (*Calendar,* no. 2308), 13 July 1858. Darwin
     quoted part of Swale's letter in *CP,* 2:21, and in *The Effects of Cross-
     and Self-Fertilisation in the Vegetable Kingdom* (London: John Mur-
     ray, 1876), 150; another extract of the letter was published in the
     Gardeners' Chronicle, 13 November 1858, 829.

105 Goodeniaceae are in the order *Campanulales* (bellflowers). Darwin's
     correspondence with Hooker on them is in *Correspondence,* 8:111,
     162–174, 181, 191–192, 205–211; it took place between February
     and May 1860.

106 Letter of 7 June 1860, in *Correspondence,* 8:245–246, and *ML,*
     2:257–258.; *ML,* 2: 259; see Francis Darwin's notes on *Leschenaultia,*
     ML, 2:257–258.

107 *Correspondence,* 8:213–214; see Butcher, "Darwin's Australian Cor-
     respondents," 142–144, for more about Drummond's correspondence
     with Darwin. Drummond sent plants to John Lindley and to William
     Hooker and wrote accounts of Australian flora for Hooker's *Journal*

of Botany and for *Gardeners' Magazine.* His plant collections are to be found in twenty-five herbaria in Britain, Europe, the United States, and Australia. Mea Allan, *The Hookers of Kew, 1785–1911* (London: Joseph, 1967), 99; E. Charles Nelson, "James and Thomas Drummond: Their Scottish Origins and Curatorships in Irish Botanic Gardens," *Archives of Natural History* 17 (1) (1990): 49–65; L. Diels, "Extra-tropical Western Australia," in *People and Plants in Australia,* ed. Carr and Carr, 47–78; esp. 56; Carr and Carr, "James Drummond and the Royal Cork Institution," 280–287, ibid.

108   *Calendar,* no. 3162, *CP,* 2:42.

109   *Calendar,* no. 3298, 25 October [1861]; no. 3392, 16 January 1862; Moyal, *Scientists in Nineteenth-Century Australia,* 193–195.

110   *CP,* 2:138–150.

111   *Calendar,* no. 4152; *Orchids* (1862), 236–238; *Orchids* (1877), 197n; Darwin gave evidence of which Hance was unaware, that two orchids formerly placed in different genera were the male and female of the same species.

112   *Calendar,* nos. 8955, 9048, 11204, 11277, written from Cheeseman to Darwin in the years 1873–1879.

113   *Orchids* (1877), 88, 90, 280; also *Cross- and Self-Fertilization,* 392; Glenn, *Botanical Explorers of New Zealand,* 160–171.

114   *Calendar,* no. 10069, 17 July 1875; Butcher, "Darwin's Australian Correspondents," 150–153.

115   *Calendar,* no. 10579, Darwin to Fitzgerald, 18 August [1876].

116   *Orchids* (1877), 279–281.

117   Ibid., 89–91.

118   Fitzgerald found that *Spiranthes australis* and two species of *Thelmitra* regularly self-fertilize; ibid., 114–115, 127, 279–281, 290–291.

119   *Calendar,* no. 9124, Krefft to Darwin, 1 November 1873. Dichogamous flowers contain both male and female organs, but they mature at different times, so cannot ordinarily self-fertilize. Krefft's information was too late for the sixth (and last) edition of the *Origin* but Darwin mentioned Australian trees as a problem (1:76). Krefft is not cited in Darwin's *Cross- and Self-Fertilisation,* but Darwin discussed eucalyptus trees, under their family name, Myrtaceae; Darwin wrote that although they do not have separate sexes, as do most trees, "I have been assured that the flowers of the prevailing Australian trees, namely, the Myrtaceae, swarm with insects" (414ff.).

120   For instance, the *Botanische Zeitung* ignored the *Origin;* but after publication of *Orchids,* Darwin's botanical works received a great deal of attention: 21 (1863): 1–7, 9–16, 188–190, 241–243, 309–314, 321–328, 329–333; contrast with 20 (1862) and previous volumes.

121   Darwin to Asa Gray (American botanist), 23 July [1862], *Calendar,* no. 3662, *ML,* 1:202.

122   *Correspondence,* 5:359, 364, 373, 490; 6:142, 465, 467, from 27 June 1855 to 18 October 1857 (also in Nora Barlow, *Darwin and Henslow, the Growth of an Idea* [London: John Murray, 1967], letters 81, 82, 84, 91, 97, 101, 102); *Natural Selection,* 127–128 (written between 1 December 1856 and 31 January 1857).

123   For example, *Correspondence,* 7:15, letter from Darwin to George Henry Thwaites, 7 February [1858]; *Origin,* 139–143.

124   *Calendar,* nos. 9255, 10942, 11050, 11760, 11767, 11776, 11777, 12245 (*LL,* 3:182), and 13040, written between January 1874 and February 1881; see also Robert M. Stecher, "The Darwin-Bates Letters: Part II," *Annals of Science* 25 (1969): 115.

125   *Calendar,* no. 13251, Darwin to Semper, 19 July 1881, published in Herbert G. Baker, "Charles Darwin and the Perennial Flax—A Controversy and Its Implications," *Huntia* 2 (1965): 161, and in *LL,* 3:344. The experiments were done by Hermann Hoffmann (1819–1891) in Europe.

126   *CP,* 2:224.

127   *Calendar,* no. 13369, 3 October 1881.

128   *Origin,* 29.

129   Letter from Darwin to Wallace, 1 May 1857, *Correspondence,* 6: 387 (*LL,* 2:95, and *Alfred Russel Wallace,* ed. Marchant, 107); see *Variation,* 1:242.

130   *Variation,* 1:191, 289.

131   *Natural Selection,* 112.

132   *Variation,* 1:321.

133   *Correspondence,* 6:70, Darwin to Mantell, 3 April [1856].

134   *Variation,* 1:152, 192, 212.

135   *Calendar,* nos. 3803, 3892, 4094, 4257, 4268: all Swinhoe to Darwin, dated 12 November 1862 to 14 August 1863; see *Variation,* 1:59, 300.

136   *Calendar,* nos. 4449, 4727, 5041, 5598, 6303, from Taiwan and from China, April 1864–August 1868. *Calendar,* no. 4970 to Sclater, no. 5202 to Swinhoe, no. 5702 to Hardwicke's *Science Gossip* (*CP,* 2:137), no. 7580 (14 March 1871), no. 8824 (26 March 1873). See *Expression of the Emotions,* 21, 206, 246, 316.

137   *Calendar,* no. 6940 (16 October 1869); nos. 7080, 7450, Darwin to A. Gunther (16 January [1870] and 21 January [1871?]); no. 7095, Swinhoe to Darwin (2 February 1870); nos. 9242, 9277, 9291 (from Gunther), 9295, 9330 (Darwin to Tristram), 9329 (Darwin to the secretary of the Royal Society), all January–March 1874.

138   *Calendar*, no. 6348, Hance to Darwin, 3 September 1868; *Variation*, 1:306, 307 n. 53 (a reference to "an old Chinese work" on the culture of goldfish).

139   *The Descent of Man* (1871), *The Expression of the Emotions* (1872), *Insectivorous Plants* (1875), *The Power of Movement in Plants* (1880), and *The Formation of Vegetable Mould, through the Action of Worms* (1881), all London: John Murray.

140   Darwin listed all of these people in the index to *Descent of Man* and cited their works in footnotes. For more on Edwards, see following section, "Normal Science."

141   *Voyage*, 433–434.

142   Glenn, *Botanical Explorers of New Zealand*, 69–74. Dieffenbach translated Darwin's *Journal of Researches* into German and supplied him with tidbits on genetic curiosities; see *Variation*, 1:24, 47, 447; *Correspondence*, 5: 428, 429 n. 4.

143   *Correspondence*, 2: 423, Darwin to Dieffenbach, 16 December 1843; Dieffenbach, *Travels in New Zealand*, 2 vols., translated from the German (London: Braunschweig, 1844), 2:19–20.

144   *The Descent of Man*, 2d. ed. (New York: Hurst, 1874), 205.

145   *Calendar*, no. 9241, 14 January 1874; no. 9246, 17 January [1874].

146   *Descent*, 273–278, 615; Plews, "Hawaiian Sex Ratios," 28–36 (Plews used a Modern Library edition of *The Descent of Man*; 273–278 in the edition to which I referred are 606–612 in his copy).

147   *Variation*, 2:126–138; *Descent*, 46–47.

148   *Descent*, 202–204. The passage from which this is taken is too long to quote here, but the interested reader is urged to read it in its entirety.

149   *Calendar*, no. 9506, Coan to Darwin, 22 June 1874.

150   *Calendar*, no. 9290, Coan to Darwin, 14 February 1874; *Descent*, 186–188 and n. 42; 203 and 204. On 204 n. 43, Darwin states: "I owe the census of the several years to the kindness of Mr. Coan, at the request of Dr. Youmans, of New York." Edward Livingston Youmans (1821–1887) was an American writer, editor, promoter of science education, and founder of *Popular Science Monthly* (1872); he wrote to Darwin in 1870; *Calendar*, nos. 7324, 7325.

151   *Calendar*, no. 9949, Coan to Darwin, 24 April 1875; no. 12171, Coan to Darwin, 25 July 1879.

152   *Calendar*, no. 9239, Darwin to [Staley], 13 January [1874], Plews, "Hawaiian Sex Ratios," 26–49.

153   *Calendar*, no. 9286, Staley to Darwin, 12 February 1874; no. 9307, Staley to Darwin, 20 February 1874; no. 9314, Staley to Darwin, 25 February [1874].

154   *Descent*, 274, 278.

155   *Expression of the Emotions,* 16, 19.

156   The missionaries were J. Bulmer, Templeton Bunnett, Friedrich
       Hagenauer, Archibald Lang, and George Taplin, all of Australia, and
       James West Stack of New Zealand.

157   *Expression of the Emotions,* 20.

158   Robert Smyth was a mining engineer (and honorary secretary to the
       Board for the Protection of the Aborigines); H. B. Lane was a police
       magistrate, whose reply was sent via Smyth; Sir Samuel Wilson was
       an Irishman who emigrated to Victoria and became a wealthy pasto-
       ralist (*Calendar,* no. 5677); Edward Wilson was a neighbor of Dar-
       win's who lived in Melbourne from 1842 to 1864; Charles Walter was
       a German naturalist who collected plants in Victoria and sent his
       replies through Mueller (*Calendar,* no. 5626); Walter is not cited in
       Expression of the Emotions; Adolph Meyer was another German nat-
       uralist, who had made a major study of the Philippines; the second
       rajah of Borneo was Charles Anthony Johnson (1829–1917), who
       succeeded his uncle, the first rajah of Borneo, James Brooke, in 1863.

159   For Geach, see *Alfred Russel Wallace,* ed. Marchant, 148–149;
       Expression of the Emotions, 20. For Haast, see *Calendar,* nos. 5534
       and 5705, 12 May 1867 and 4 December 1867. For Smyth, see *Cal-
       endar,* no. 6314, 13 August 1868. For Edward Wilson, see *Calendar,*
       nos. 5672, 5896, 5916, and 6419 (enclosing the reply from Dyson
       Lacy, no. 6374). For Brooke, see *Calendar,* no. 7386, 30 November
       1870, written from Sarawak. For Meyer, see *Calendar,* no. 8300, 26
       April 1872, written from the Philippines; see *Expression of the Emo-
       tions,* 274. For Gibbs, see *Calendar,* no. 5479, 31 March 1867.

160   For Howitt, see Butcher, "Darwin's Australian Correspondents,"
       148. For Dawson, an Australian farmer, see *Calendar,* no. 13192, 3
       June 1881 (draft). Moseley gave Darwin a Japanese book illustrating
       expression of the emotions; see *Calendar,* no. 10661, 3 November
       1876, and no. 11761, 26 November 1878. The edition of *Expression
       of the Emotions* published by Francis Darwin in 1890 is not con-
       sidered here.

161   Charles Darwin and Francis Darwin, *The Power of Movement in
       Plants* (London: John Murray, 1880), 82; *Calendar,* no. 12553, Rat-
       tan to Asa Gray, 29 March 1880; no. 12792, Darwin to [Rattan],
       3 November 1880.

162   *Calendar,* no. 12408, 6 January 1880; Darwin's last studies on *Dros-
       era* are reported in *CP,* 2: 236–256, 256–276.

163   Darwin, *Vegetable Mould,* 147.

164   Ibid., 122. *Calendar,* no. 8930, Darwin to [Krefft] [June? 1873]; no.
       8975, Darwin to [Krefft], 12 July [1873]; no. 9002, Krefft to Darwin,
       8 August 1873; no. 9037, Darwin to [Krefft] [September 1873].

165   *Voyage,* 391.

166   *Calendar,* no. 8428, Gulick to Darwin, 27 July 1872, *APS,* 421; no.
       8431, Darwin to Gulick, 28 July 1872, *APS,* 422, published in Addi-
       son Gulick, *Evolutionist and Missionary: John Thomas Gulick* (Chi-
       cago: University of Chicago Press, 1932), 233; no. 8453, Gulick to
       Darwin, 6 August 1872, DAR 165; no. 8457, Darwin to [Gulick],
       8 August [1872], *APS,* 423, in A. Gulick, *Evolutionist and Mission-
       ary,* 234.

167   Darwin learned of Edwards through Benjamin Walsh, a Cambridge
       contemporary cum Illinois entomologist, who sent him data from
       Edwards on the sex ratios of butterflies; *Descent,* 267.

168   Edwards' first and second letters to Darwin are lost; Darwin's replies
       are *Calendar,* no. 8978, published in Sir Gavin de Beer, "Further
       Unpublished Letters of Charles Darwin," *Annals of Science* 14
       (1958): 83–115, 87; and no. 9216.

169   Edwards' letter to Darwin is *Calendar,* no. 10328. Darwin's reply is
       no. 10411, *APS,* 486. See *Descent,* 331, on dimorphism in Lycaenae
       (butterflies).

170   Butler's books include *Erewhon* (1872), *Life and Habit* (1877), *Evo-
       lution Old and New* (1880); his correspondence with Darwin is sum-
       marized in *Calendar,* nos. 4904, 8305, 8318, 8361, 8859, 11152,
       11254, 12393, 12438 (1875–1880); see also Tee, "Darwin's Corre-
       spondents in New Zealand," 375–376.

171   *Calendar,* no. 10663, 5 November 1876; no. 10665, 7 November
       1876.

172   *Calendar,* no. 10947, 1 May 1877; no. 11026, 30 June 1877; Paulus
       P. Hoek from the Netherlands classified the cirripedes after Darwin
       reviewed Hoek's earlier work; *Calendar* nos. 9883, 10334, 11016.

173   *Calendar,* no. 11533, Darwin to Nash on Nash's book *Oregon: There
       and Back* (London: Macmillan, 1878; reprint Corvallis: Oregon State
       University Press, 1976); no. 12400, Nash to Darwin, from Corvallis.

174   *Calendar,* no. 8177, 24 January 1872.

175   *Calendar,* no. 8104, 10 December 1871.

176   *Calendar,* no. 7039, 31 December 1869.

177   *Calendar,* nos. 10036, 10887, in 1875 and 1877.

178   *Calendar,* no. 13059, 1881, quoted in Glenn, *Botanical Explorers of
       New Zealand,* 61.

179   *Origin,* 6th ed., 1: 203.

180   *CP,* 2:235.

181   Darwin's principle of diversity is now called adaptive radiation.

182   Coan communicated to Darwin through his son, Titus Coan, Jr. See
       contributors to *The Descent of Man.*

183   Plews, "Hawaiian Sex Ratios," 37.

184   James West Stack (1835–1919) was a missionary in New Zealand in 1860–1898; the *Calendar* lists the wrong James Stack, who returned to England in 1847.

185   Other examples are William Henty (1808–1881), an English civil servant in Tasmania from 1857 to 1862 (Henty wrote to Darwin in 1868 but not about Pacific science [*Calendar,* nos. 5900 and 6203], so is omitted from appendix 2) and Louis Bouton (1799–1878), a naturalist on Mauritius (*Calendar* nos. 1961 and 7961; omitted from appendix 1 because Mauritius is in the Indian Ocean, not the Pacific).

186   Burkhardt, "England and Scotland," 52.

187   Moyal, *Scientists in Nineteenth-Century Australia,* 191.

188   George Bentham of Kew Gardens insisted on classifying them, to Mueller's chagrin; Michael Hoare, "Botany and Society in Eastern Australia," in *People and Plants in Australia,* ed. Carr and Carr, 183–219, esp. 212.

189   *Calendar,* no. 8331, Krefft to Darwin, 15 May 1872; no. 8416, Darwin to Krefft, 17 July 1872. Butcher, "Darwin's Australian Correspondents," 146.

190   The sources for this list are the *Calendar* and the published volumes of the *Correspondence,* except where otherwise noted (see n. 12). Parentheses ( ) around a number indicate that no letters are listed in the *Calendar.*

191   Two officers of the *Beagle* with whom Darwin had extensive correspondence were Robert FitzRoy (during the period 1831–1850) and Bartholomew Sulivan (1832–1881), but I found no discussions of Pacific-area science in their letters to Darwin; hence they are not listed.

KEITH R. BENSON

7 The Darwinian Legacy in the Pacific Northwest

Seattle's Young Naturalists' Society, P. Brooks Randolph, and Conchology

Despite the commonplace and accurate assumption that Charles Darwin played a central role in nineteenth-century natural history, the determination of the extent of Darwin's influence or the influence of evolution theory upon the theory and practice of late-nineteenth-century naturalists in the Pacific Northwest is fraught with difficulties.[1] First, although Darwin spent from May 1834 through March 1836 in the Pacific, he reached no farther north than the Galapagos Islands. As the remainder of his Pacific voyage was decidedly southern, there is no doubt that Darwin had no direct experience with the natural history of the northern Pacific Ocean, in particular that of the temperate coastal region of North America. Consequently, Darwin could not have directly inspired others to work in the Northwest based on his own experiences.

Second, Darwin's famous trip, popularized in nineteenth-century exploration literature as the third volume of *Narrative of the Surveying Voyages of His Majesty's Ships* Adventure *and* Beagle, *between the Years 1826 and 1836, Describing Their Examination of the Southern Shores of South America, and the* Beagle's *Circumnavigation of the Globe,*[2] was sandwiched between the two best known American expeditions to the Northwest,[3] Meriwether Lewis and William Clark's overland trip from 1804 to 1806 and the country's first scientific expedition, the U.S. Exploring Expedition of 1838–1842, led by Charles Wilkes. The naturalists on both expeditions collected specimens and sent these collections to museums in a number of U.S. cities between Chicago and New York, but there is no documentary evidence that the Northwest observations or collections of any of these naturalists were directly influenced by Darwin.

For Lewis and Clark, of course, this is obvious because they completed their work before Darwin was born. But although Darwin returned to London before Wilkes and his "scientifics" departed on their voyage, the published account of the *Beagle* was not available to the Americans until after they returned in 1842. The only examples of any connection between the two sets of voyagers, albeit tangential connections at best, are two: in 1840 James Dwight Dana read a report of Darwin's forthcoming work on coral reefs (*Structure and Distribution of Coral Reefs,* 1842), which "called forth feelings of peculiar satisfaction, and of gratefulness to Mr. Darwin," for Dana was also working on the coral reefs of the South Pacific;[4] and the actual route that Wilkes selected retraced much of the route of the *Beagle,* adding to the English ship's itinerary important excursions to Antarctica, Hawaii, and the Pacific Northwest, during its circumnavigation. But there are no other indications from Wilkes' expedition or from any other major American expedition to the Northwest that naturalists were influenced directly by Darwin's experiences aboard the *Beagle.*

Similarly, subsequent influences from the *Origin of Species* and evolution theory on American naturalists working in the West do not appear to be direct ones. Reports from the War Department surveys of California and Oregon, the surveys associated with routing railroad lines to the West, the Northwest Boundary Survey, and the work of the Coast Survey—all of which sent naturalists to the western shores and returned natural history specimens to eastern museums— are notable for their lack of reference to Darwin or evolution theory. Only at the end of the nineteenth century and during the early twentieth century are there specific examples of naturalists who directly incorporated Darwinian explanations in their work. For example, William Emerson Ritter, working at the University of California at Berkeley and the Scripps Institute of Biological Research (later the Scripps Institution of Oceanography), and David Starr Jordan, the first president of Stanford University, overtly expressed their debt to Darwin in their many publications relating to the faunistic characteristics of the West Coast (primarily California).

Fourth, there was not a well-developed institutional nexus for naturalists in the West until late in the nineteenth century. The California Academy of Sciences, founded in 1853, did not begin a systematic natural history collection until George Davidson headed the organization in 1872, and it lacked an adequate exhibit hall until its museum was built in 1892.[5] Similarly, plans for a museum at the University of California at Berkeley, called for in the report establishing the university in 1864, were not completed until the twentieth century. Jordan's

Stanford University, started in 1891, shared the same plight. To the north, Thomas Condon and the Reverend Plutarch S. Knight established the Oregon School and College Natural History Society in 1876, an organization with a natural history museum and a part-time curator in Salem.[6] In Seattle, the first organization to collect from the natural world was an organization begun by amateurs, the Young Naturalists' Society, started in 1879 and occupying its own museum building by 1885.[7] It is important to stress, however, that none of these western organizations represented natural history museums with the same level of sophistication or the same size as those in Chicago, Philadelphia, Boston, New York, and Washington, D.C. In fact, the natural history museums in the Northwest can best be described as "proprietary" museums established for the enjoyment of their amateur members; full-time professional curators and staff members were not hired until the twentieth century.

Despite the attendant difficulties in assessing Darwin's direct influence on natural history in the Northwest, there are other ways to document his importance. For example, during most of the nineteenth century, information concerning species variation and its relationship to geographical distribution became part and parcel of natural history. Initiated at the beginning of the century by Alexander von Humboldt through his romantic tales in *Voyage to the Equinoctial Regions of the New World, made in 1799–1804,* and continued by other naturalists such as Darwin in the 1830s and T. H. Huxley and Joseph Dalton Hooker in the 1840s and 1850s, observations of geographic variation also inspired the Americans.[8] Charles Pickering, one of the naturalists on the U.S. Exploring Expedition, was led from descriptive natural history to the study of biogeographical distribution by his observations relating the fauna and flora of islands distant from continents and eventually published his own views on the subject in *Geographical Distribution of Animals and Plants* in 1854.[9] Meanwhile, Asa Gray's work on the geographical distribution of the botanical specimens from the Wilkes Expedition "readied him for Darwin."[10] Indeed, by the end of the century the need to document the variability of species and the range of species over a geographical region was as critical to the enterprise of natural history as the urge to collect "new species to science." Hence, an early goal of the California Academy of Sciences was the "mapping and inventorying [of] their new surroundings," a goal occupying most naturalists who visited new regions of the world.[11]

Admittedly, and characteristic of many American naturalists, these goals were usually realized with little, if any, reference to theoretical

concerns or any direct reference to Darwin. But the first task for naturalists working in a new region was to collect material for processing
and documenting by specialists in the museums that sponsored or
organized the expedition. Not surprisingly, therefore, it was uncom-
mon for naturalists to append to their observations any speculations
concerning the causes for geographical patterns in the natural world;
but many naturalists did document the reality of species variation and
divergence over space and time, accepting as a given that the globe
consisted of innumerable regional assemblages of indigenous fauna
and flora.

With the publication of the *Origin of Species* in 1859, a new theoretical framework to explain variation and geographical distribution
became available. In the United States, these new ideas were given an
additional, theistic meaning. Under the influence of the devout Harvard botanist Asa Gray,[12] Darwinian theory became a record of God's
creative agency, natural selection, almost as often as it was greeted as
the first naturalistic account of speciation events in nature. Even as
naturalists at the end of the century became increasingly skeptical
about the role of natural selection, most read the "development of
species" into their work.[13] Indeed, adherence to Gray's theistic brand
of evolution theory and concomitant lack of reference to Darwin
characterized most American naturalists at century's end.

Methodologically, the impact of evolution theory did not directly
alter the taxonomic work associated with natural history. Instead, it
provided a readily acceptable naturalistic explanation for the hierarchical nature that characterized systematics by the midnineteenth
century.[14] Earlier notions of "common plan," "definite archetype,"
"doctrine of types," and "community of organization" were simply
redefined by Darwin's work. His notion of the community of descent
made theoretical sense of ideas that, before 1859, lacked any comprehensive underpinning. But this did not alter significantly the taxonomic approaches of the naturalists. By the 1860s, studies of
variation and geographic distribution already had an implied and
accepted method, and "younger taxonomists who fully accepted evolution, like Walter Faxon, could also continue the tradition of their
predecessors with no significant change of method."[15]

Darwin's contribution to the Americans, therefore, was not to
direct their work in the field; his influence was to provide a unifying
rationale to what they observed from the field. But despite the lack of
direct influence, the Darwinian legacy did cast an important shadow
over the developing natural history community on the West Coast,
especially as these naturalists complied with requests from their east-

ern colleagues who, perhaps more sensitive to the theoretical implications of evolution theory, were eager to expand their examples of
variation and geographical distribution. The exchanges between Seattle's P. Brooks Randolph and museum-based naturalists in the East
bear testimony to this connection.

Natural History in the West

When Lord Lister visited Seattle at the end of the nineteenth
century, he asked to meet the naturalist Trevor Kincaid.[16] There are
no historical records to document what happened at the meeting
between the two men. But the English visitor from the Royal Society
may have been slightly taken aback when he learned that Kincaid was
but an undergraduate student at the University of Washington.
Despite his youth and educational background, Kincaid had already
established himself internationally through his extensive collections of
Northwest insects, which he exchanged with other naturalists and
museum collectors to help build the museum collection of the Young
Naturalists' Society (YNS). In fact, Lister may have been even more
surprised to realize that essentially all the natural history work in
Seattle was done under the auspices of the amateur-dominated YNS,
located in its own museum on property leased from the Territorial
University of Washington.

Unfortunately, historical knowledge of Seattle's *fin-de-siècle* natural
history community and the natural history tradition in the Northwest
has not improved dramatically since Lister's visit.[17] What little work
has been done has emphasized expeditionary natural history. The
explorers cum naturalists Meriwether Lewis and William Clark
returned to the eastern seaboard in 1806 with tales, drawings,
and specimens selected from the vast region of the Columbia River
drainage basin. Much of this material is now available in the form of
annotated journals, but little attention has been given to the actual
natural history practices of these men.[18] The U.S. Exploring Expedition has received some attention. Books by William Stanton, William
H. Goetzmann, and Herman J. Viola and Carolyn Margolis have
detailed various aspects of America's first scientific exploration,
which also made the initial investigation of the Puget Sound area
when Wilkes and his men entered Admiralty Inlet in 1841.[19] The collections that survived the expedition, including an impressive selection of mollusks, were extremely important to American natural
history because they served as the base for the new U.S. National
Museum (Smithsonian), while the botanical collections "forced the

creation of a national herbarium in Washington."[20] Unfortunately, much less is known about any natural history work conducted by the numerous War Department surveys of California and Oregon, the Pacific railroad surveys, the Northwest Boundary survey, and several marine surveys under the auspices of the Coastal Survey.[21] One additional study by Goetzmann and Kay Sloan provides a much-needed narrative account of Edward H. Harriman's expedition to Alaska aboard the *George W. Elder* during the summer of 1899.[22] Complete with Noachian pairs of geologists, botanists, zoologists, artists, and so on, Harriman dedicated the trip to the natural history of Alaska, eventually commissioning a thirteen-volume work (edited by C. Hart Merriam) documenting the accomplishments of the trip. However, little beyond the Merriam volumes is known about the natural history work conducted on this important voyage.

While many of these studies address explorers who visited the Northwest, there has been virtually no work done on the natural history conducted by resident naturalists within the area.[23] Therefore, we know little about the practice of naturalists working in Oregon and Washington. This is not surprising, however, given the poor institutional development of the field and the fact that most of the work was done by isolated individuals with only an avocational interest in natural history. Additionally, there are few archival sources with materials for the historian that bear on the subject. Nevertheless, a few recent studies, when reconstructed as a montage, provide us with a better understanding of what naturalists did in the Northwest and how they may have responded to the new ideas from Darwin.

Nancy Rockafellar has written a remarkable essay about the career of the Harvard-educated physician Dr. Albert Chase Folsom, who escaped family troubles in the East by moving to Snohomish City (present-day Monroe, Washington), where he started a medical practice in 1872.[24] Folsom's interest in natural history led him to establish the Snohomish Athenaeum Society, with the help of his attorney friend Eldridge Morse, in 1873. By 1874, Morse boasted that the society had already created a unique opportunity for the residents of Snohomish City because there was "no place in this Territory affording better chances for a young man to educate himself than by means of an [sic] library and the museum connected with it."[25]

Folsom not only contributed to the society through his natural history projects, he also popularized the subject through his oratorical skills and a number of published essays concerning science. In an essay in the late 1870s, he commented on evolution theory:

It is too early yet to predict the verdict of science on the subject of what is popularly known as Darwin's theory. Of one thing we are certain; he has opened up a channel for research that mere assertion cannot gainsay. Nothing but stubborn fact now satisfies the inquiring scientific mind. Darwin does not claim to have proven his theory. He explains it in unmistakable language untrammeled by his belief, his hopes, or his aspirations; cites well-known and long-established facts as proof in fact of its truth, points out channels for future investigation and invites the cooperation of the scientific world to establish its correctness or its error.[26]

Through his remarks, Folsom illustrates that the openness of naturalists to Darwin did not require an overt acceptance of Darwin's ideas. In addition, by underscoring the need for "future investigations" Folsom helped point other naturalists to the study of nature in an attempt to explicate Darwin's theoretical claims.

A similar openness to Darwin and evolution theory can be seen in the work of Oregon's state geologist, Thomas Condon. Having received a copy of the *Origin* from O. C. Marsh in 1871 and having been exposed to evolutionary ideas through his reading of Charles Lyell, James McCosh, Asa Gray, and Alpheus Packard, Condon often addressed evolution and related topics during his lectures at Pacific University, University of Oregon, and the Oregon School and College Natural History Society in Salem. Adopting an orientation to evolution that was similar to Gray's, Condon referred to Darwin's ideas as the "doctrine of theistic evolution" which "declares evolution to be God's process of creation [and] is taught by all the higher colleges of our country."[27] Through his own work in geology, Condon continually emphasized how observations from the natural world demonstrated the validity of the "development of species."

In their time Folsom and Condon were among the leading naturalists in the Northwest. Both men addressed audiences of naturalists and the lay public alike, so it is reasonable to suppose they helped acquaint others with Darwin's ideas. And because there are no indications that these ideas created any problems or engendered any reaction, it may be safe to assume that Darwinian evolution theory became easily incorporated into the natural history tradition in the Northwest, at least in the guise of the historical development of species. As evidence, when Charles Keeler of the California Academy of Sciences and a member of the Harriman expedition delivered the Fourth of July (1899) address in Dutch Harbor, Alaska, his topic was Darwinism.[28] Nonetheless, despite the implicit and facile incorporation of evolution theory, most naturalists did not deal with theoretical issues in their writings. In fact, as Goetzmann and Sloan illustrate in their study of the Harriman Expedition, the biological writings from the trip "amounted to compilations and lists. . . . Virtually none of the biological works ventured into the realm of theoretical speculation except that of Addison Emery Verrill. . . . In studying starfish, he found a long evolutionary sequence from the primitive Devonian five-pointed starfish to extremely complex starfish."[29] Such was the overt nature of the appeal to Darwin.

A case might be made that the sheer enormity of the task of collecting specimens from the diverse fauna and flora of the Northwest was sufficient to occupy the interests of these naturalists. Certainly this characterized the work of other prominent American naturalists who visited the Northwest during the last half of the nineteenth century, including Alexander Agassiz (as a member of the Coast Survey), Othniel C. Marsh, Edward Drinker Cope, William H. Dall, David Starr Jordan, and E. B. Wilson (with a group of biologists from Columbia University who established a summer location near Port Townsend). In most cases, the only written records they left concerning their visits to the Northwest related to their collections. As a result, additional examinations of the work of resident naturalists is even more important if we are to understand exactly what occurred in the practice of natural history in the Northwest.

Fortunately, especially in light of the relative poverty of sources in Northwest natural history, the amateur naturalist P. Brooks Randolph maintained his correspondence records dating from his days as head of the conchology collection of the Young Naturalists' Society.[30] This material affords a glimpse into the practice of natural history in the Northwest and provides some indication of how naturalists were influenced by Darwinian theory.

Seattle, the University of Washington, and the Young Naturalists' Society

The citizens of the new Washington Territory, which was formed and named as such after Oregon became a state in 1859, established the region's first university two years after Charles Darwin published the *Origin* and almost thirty years before statehood. Situated in the pioneer lumbering town of Seattle—a provincial settlement that lacked any semblance of an educational institution until 1861—the Territorial University of Washington was hardly a university, even according to lax nineteenth-century American standards. Originally designed to serve as a preparatory school for Seattle's adolescent population, because many of these students completely lacked

any education, the school was frequently plagued by financial instability and poor public support, a thinly stretched and poorly trained
faculty, and the lack of clearly defined academic programs, especially
in the sciences.[31] In fact, natural history, the midcentury antecedent to
biology, was conspicuously absent until 1882, when Orson Bennett
Johnson replaced Frank Gilman, the first natural scientist on the faculty, appointed in 1880. Seattle's relative isolation from other urban
centers with academic communities exacerbated the problem; indeed,
there were few educational institutions west of Minneapolis or north
of San Francisco until the twentieth century. As a result, the rapid
development of an American community of biologists that characterized midwestern and eastern cities did not occur along the shores of
Puget Sound.

At the same time, because the Northwest contains an unquestionably rich and diverse fauna and flora, an observation that had been
noted and documented by naturalists accompanying the numerous
expeditions sent to explore the area since the end of the eighteenth
century, it offered almost unparalleled opportunities for those interested in pursuing these interests. Consequently, museums and collectors throughout the United States knew of the region's potential as
a source of natural history specimens. However, until Professor
Johnson's appointment the new university was unequipped academically and institutionally to address these needs; after Johnson's
appointment, the Young Naturalists' Society merged forces with the
territorial university to yield a growing cadre of naturalists and a
growing cabinet of natural history specimens.

In many ways, the Young Naturalists' Society provides another
example of the important connection between a natural history society annexed to a university and subsequent developments within a
more academic setting.[32] But in this case, the YNS museum represented a facility where nonprofessionals first attempted to create a
sophisticated museum, then a professional collection was added to
create an institution in which natural history could be taught, and
finally the museum became amalgamated within the university. These
themes cannot all be treated here; instead, I will examine how Randolph's work in the Young Naturalists' Society epitomized the practice of natural history in the northwest corner of the United States.

Randolph and Conchology

Much like similar institutions in the East that developed earlier
in the century, the YNS began as a group of amateurs who innocently
believed that the study of natural history offered the opportunity for

social intercourse and mental stimulation. P. Brooks Randolph, a self-styled naturalist and court bailiff by training, developed an early interest in collecting molluscan shells, or conchology as it was referred to in the nineteenth century,[33] and was often the elected curator of conchology for the society during the 1890s. Randolph illustrates nicely many facets of the natural history tradition, including the implicit acceptance of evolution theory and the workings of the natural history exchange network. He was nineteen in 1879 when he joined with three companions "to organize a chess club, but on mature deliberation it was found that the interest in such a society would soon wane, and they cast about them for some society that would stand the test of time and become a perpetual source of pleasure and instruction, and the only society which would answer their purpose was one in which the study of natural history could be pursued."[34] The new amateur organization represented Seattle's initial venture into natural history. Not surprisingly, early minutes of meetings reveal the almost painfully naive interests of its members. Archival records list presentations on "The Skunk," debates on "Resolved that deer shed their horns every year is false," and essays like G. Walter Boardman's that claimed the bat to be "half quadruped and half bird and is neither one or the other it is a kind of monster."[35]

In a progressive vein, the society soon began to organize a museum in the back of the home of A. A. Denny, the original benefactor of the society and father of one of its initial members. Randolph was appointed to be the curator of entomological specimens, the first "department" identified by the society. Soon thereafter, the young men established a department of conchology. Lacking the expertise to organize the accumulating collections, they started a library, purchasing the fourth edition of S. P. Woodward's classic, *A Manual of the Mollusca* (1880), and inscribing the title page "This our book." A second reference in the library was George W. Tryon's *Manual of Conchology* (1879) in which the author stated in the "advertisement" the value of the book for the young naturalists. "I feel that the work I propose to undertake is a worthy one; that its completion will enable the Conchologist *for the first time* to identify and to learn the history of all the species in his cabinet."[36] Here is a good example of how an author provided implicit evolutionary claims as he sought to teach the "history of all the species." Similarly, Woodward claimed in the preface to the book that "portions of the work have been treated in most detail which throw light on . . . great natural history problems, such as the value of species and genera, and the laws of geographical and geological distribution."[37] Again, without direct mention of Darwin,

reference is made to the laws Darwin provided in 1859; young naturalists absorbed these ideas as they learned the methods of systematics.

At the same time, conchology in Woodward's tradition also promised to meet the social and educational expectations of the YNS members. In the preface to the book, the author noted the value of the
study of shells:

> The recreations of the young seldom fail to exercise a serious influence on
> afterlife; and the utility of their pursuits must greatly depend on the spirit
> in which they are followed. If wisely chosen and conscientiously prose-
> cuted, they may help to form habits of exact observation; they may train
> the eye and mind to seize upon characteristic facts, and to discern their real
> import; to discriminate between the essential and the accidental and to
> detect the relations of phenomena, however widely separated and appar-
> ently unlike.[38]

In addition, this tradition of conchology paralleled the peculiarly
American tie of natural history to the natural theology framework
that followed Gray's popularization of Darwin and Louis Agassiz's
popularization of nature study. "For to the thoughtful and earnest
investigator, nature ever discloses indications of harmony and order,
and reflects the attributes of the Maker."[39] Tryon, who was a conchologist at the Academy of Natural Sciences, emphasized a similar
orientation:

> We might perhaps answer, that its great merit consists in affording an inno-
> cent recreation to the mind of men. But there is surely a nobler object to
> be gained by the study of conchology. God, who created man in His own
> image, has also placed around us a host of living things, each after its own
> kind, an exemplification of divine wisdom, in the admirable adaptation
> of means to ends, as shown in their organism and mode of life; and who
> shall say that it is profitless for man to examine these animals, endeavor to
> indicate among them groups approaching each other in various degrees of
> relationship, and to learn, as far as we may know it, the plan of the Creator
> in their formation. As God has not considered these animals unworthy of
> His attention, surely they are worthy of our earnest study.[40]

It is easy to see, therefore, how naturalists in the Northwest could
adopt a natural history with its implicit developmental model and its
explicit theistic overtones.

Conchology became one of the most popular departments of natural history in nineteenth-century America, eventually gripping the
country in what was called "shell fever."[41] Tryon's numerous publications were intended to meet the demand of both professional natural-

ists and amateur aficionados. In fact, he even started one of the earliest U.S. natural history periodicals, *American Journal of Conchology*, in 1865, more than twenty years before the first specialty journal in the biological sciences. While it met its demise in 1872 because of financial problems (Tryon published it with his own money), it was quickly succeeded by Henry Augustus Pilsbry's *Nautilus*, a monthly periodical published under the auspices of Philadelphia's Academy of Natural Sciences and Wagner Free Institute. These and other publications carried articles about new species, advertisements concerning materials necessary to collect shells, and lists of naturalists and museums requesting exchanges. It was in this latter category that the amateur audience contributed most dramatically, "furnishing *materiél* to our authors, and by the distribution of specimens, much aided the progress of the science."[42]

By 1882 the fledgling natural history society in Seattle had developed to the stage that it could begin to contribute to the natural history community in the United States. Professor Johnson, who with the Oregon geologist Thomas Condon represented the entire professional natural history community in the Pacific Northwest at this time, brought with him to Seattle "his entire collection consisting of over twenty thousand specimens." Using the collection as a base, the naturalists reorganized their existing collection according to the "departments" of natural history in Johnson's cabinet. Four years later, the society constructed its own building on university property, housing a museum collection that Randolph claimed was known "all over the territory" and containing a respectable library with holdings that included natural history journals, textbooks, and taxonomy manuals. By 1895 the society had emerged as a natural history organization with amateur and professional members and a clear direction. Its newly revised constitution revealed the change: "The objects and purposes of this corporation shall be and is [*sic*] the promotion and diffusion of scientific knowledge, by the reading and publication of original papers, by the maintenance of a library and museum, and by other means calculated to arouse and stimulate scientific investigation."[43] The YNS had matured to become the center of natural history in the Northwest.

Randolph's role in the society and position in the conchology community in the United States reveal this same maturation process. While he maintained a catholic interest in natural history throughout his life, by the early 1890s he had chosen to specialize in mollusks and had become responsible for the excellence of the society's collection. Typical of many of his conchological correspondents, Randolph was largely self-educated, though he did, of course, receive professional guidance from Professor Johnson. Another guide for amateurs was Woodward's easily understood manual. In addition, Johnson donated his own copy of Tryon's *Structural and Systematic Conchology* to the society, and Randolph used it extensively. Tryon's opus addressed a critical need of American naturalists, to include descriptions of native mollusks.

> Besides this [the need of a conservative taxonomic work], it had occurred to me that no conchological textbook, except translations of elementary works, had been published in this country; and that a work in which especial prominence should be given to the description and illustration of American genera would be found very useful by our students, as well as by many conchologists in other countries who are interested in American mollusks.[44]

With the Tryon work as its foundation, Randolph's "education" was supplemented by the society's subscription to the *Nautilus,* its purchase of several volumes of Tryon's short-lived *Journal of Conchology,* and its selection of the entire first series of Tryon and Pilsbry's *Manual of Conchology.*[45] In other words, Randolph had before him the essential literature in molluscan systematics and taxonomy. More important, it was in a form completely understandable to the literate amateur and layperson. With this solid background, Randolph turned his attention to shells; and by the time he began his written record in the mid-1890s, he had become a well-schooled conchologist.

The base of the collection housed in the new hall of the YNS was Johnson's Oregon collection plus the materials collected informally by the YNS members during the 1880s. By the early 1890s, the society organized its own collecting efforts. In addition to weekend expeditions and summertime collecting trips in the Northwest, it sponsored annual marine dredging excursions in Puget Sound. Dredging was a new and exciting method for collecting mollusks in the Northwest and enabled the society to make substantial additions from the local subtidal and benthic fauna to its collection. Included in these dredges were many specimens of brachiopods, not a common group to American conchologists, but a group that raised interesting historical questions. The result of these activities in the 1890s was the continual addition to a growing and impressive museum.

Naturally, the society's reputation spread as its collection and species exchanges grew. William Emerson Ritter, the professor of zoology at Berkeley who introduced laboratory instruction in zoology to the

University of California, wrote to the YNS explaining the value of its collection for his work. "How to get material from your locality has been a question with me for some time, so your collection already made is timely, and I trust I may have further help, both by way of material, and of data on distribution, habits, etc., from members of your Society."[46] Similar attitudes were echoed by professional collectors who wrote to Randolph requesting specimens for collections at the Smithsonian and the Academy of Natural Sciences in Philadelphia. William H. Dall, then the curator of mollusks at the Smithsonian, visited Seattle and the YNS museum in 1895, a year after he had written Randolph that "energetic collecting ought to produce good results and possibly some new forms in your vicinity."[47] Then in 1896, Dall exhorted Randolph to continue sending specimens to the National Museum: "I shall be glad to see any new or interesting finds, dredged last summer as I am convinced that Puget Sound is likely to afford quite a number of additions to the w. coast fauna. I hope the Society is keeping a record of the species and will eventually print a list of them."[48]

Pilsbry, the editor of the *Nautilus* and curator of mollusks at the Academy of Natural Sciences, was another ardent supporter of both the YNS and Randolph. In a humorous exchange concerning the collection of slugs, an impressive and ubiquitous Northwest mollusk, Pilsbry conveyed his excitement to Randolph. One of the early letters included Pilsbry's suggestion that Randolph kill the slugs "by drowning, as they are well extended then."[49] In 1896 he wrote: "I received the last lot of slugs, and was greatly pleased with them. . . . If you know of any resident collectors who could be induced to gather slugs, at any of these locations, I would be greatly indebted to you for information regarding them."[50] With characteristic zeal, Randolph set about collecting more material for Pilsbry. For his part, Pilsbry continued to provide encouragement. In June 1896 he wrote Randolph that one of the slugs he had received from Seattle was a new species. Because he was preparing a paper on slugs, he told Randolph the new slug was to be named *Prophysaon randolphi*. Later, he waxed eloquent about another Randolph specimen: "Your *Pisidium idahoense* is a wonder! Much larger than any other known species."[51]

Randolph's correspondence is equally represented by letters to amateurs. Here, too, there is the same appreciation and encouragement for the work of the Young Naturalists. George H. Clapp, an engineer by training and an amateur conchologist who collected for the Carnegie Museum in his native Pittsburgh, wrote Randolph often, sometimes expressing envy. "Was out collecting this afternoon, usual luck, *same old things*. I wish I was near enough to join you in some of your collecting trips as I would like to have the pleasure of finding something new and have the chance of, perhaps, picking up a new species."[52] In the same letter, Clapp encouraged Randolph to collect "geographic suites" of mollusks because they demonstrated an "immense amount of variation." Henry Hemphill, perhaps the best known amateur conchologist on the West Coast, wrote to Randolph after he received word from Clapp that Randolph had discovered a new species of slug. Later, he mentioned the value of the exchange of specimens to his San Diego collection. "The shells were very acceptable to me as they closed some gaps in my collection and are of especial interest on account of their northern habitat."[53] Both Clapp and Hemphill illustrate the evolutionary bias through their remarks concerning variation and geographical distribution. Hemphill also illustrates the implicit Darwinian attitude of these conchologists when he states that "a close study of the series cannot help but be instructive. The process of species making by nature is well illustrated and so plain that the most casual observer can see it."[54] Typical of other late-nineteenth-century naturalists, he felt that the developmental pattern was clearly demonstrated by geographic variation.

The exchange network played an important role in circulating Northwestern forms throughout the country. Access to the network was varied; the *Nautilus* was undoubtedly an important source of information. After all, it was the leading "monthly devoted to the interests of conchology." The journal included numerous articles describing new species and depicting new methods (several issues contained information on new marine dredges). Additionally, each issue concluded with a section entitled "Exchanges," which listed names and desiderata of conchologists throughout the world. The typical exchange notice was similar to the one of H. E. Sargent, an amateur conchologist from Woodville, Alabama: "Wanted.—To Exchange Northern Alabama and Freshwater Shells for shells from other locality. Send lists and receive mine."[55]

Because many of Randolph's exchanges were with individuals who advertised in the *Nautilus,* he may have used this source to begin his correspondence. Included in this group were Sargent, Clapp, and Walter F. Webb ("Jobber in Natural History Specimens and Curiosities, Artificial Glass Eyes, Bird Skins, Bird Eggs, Moths, Butterflies, Indian Relics, Minerals, Fossils, Corals, Cabinet and Show Shells"). Several exchanges began with requests for specific mollusks, again an indication of the response to a published notice. A. H. Gardner from Long Island, New York, was interested in the YNS collection because many of the shells were new to him.[56] Sargent repeated this theme: "It is quite exceptional to get a list with so many desirable things upon it as yours has. Nearly all of the species are new to me and the others I should like for locality."[57] Webb specified Northwest examples of *Helix,* the slug. From Georgia, C. H. Turner asked for more specimens of Puget Sound ostracods because Randolph's exchange lists piqued his interest. "There is one thing about your collection that made it quite interesting. Altho there are several species of *Erpetocypris* known to science, no one seems to have found any males: but in the collection you sent me almost all were males. This latter fact makes me anxious to secure additional specimens."[58] The director of the provincial museum of British Columbia, C. F. Newcombe, offered to exchange lists of marine shells in an effort to strengthen both the Seattle collection and the Victoria museum. Charles W. Johnson, the curator at the Wagner Free Institute and coeditor of the *Nautilus,* desired exchanges to fill "some of the gaps in my collection of North American land shells."[59] A final example of specific requests is a letter from Olaf O. Nylander. Nylander, a recent immigrant with limited skills in his adopted language, developed an impressive reputation as a conchologist. He wrote to Randolph for brachiopods, an enigmatic group for the nineteenth-century conchologist: "I wold like very much to obtain specimens of Terebratulina ungricula Cpr & Terebratella caurina Gld—if only a singel god specimens could bi hade—ther is number of odors alsa, and I vill send you a list of my duplicates in the later part of the summer to gatter with my desiderat from your marin shells."[60] Nylander's message, which may not be clear from his prose, was to seek exchange specimens from the YNS.

Randolph's correspondence also includes letters from neophyte naturalists and less established conchologists. Fred H. Andrus, a self-styled "Collecting Naturalist" from Elkton, Oregon, used the exchange with Randolph to begin his mollusk collection. Mrs. Mary P. Olney, an elderly woman from Spokane, Washington, who despite her years was the secretary of the "Juvenile Section of the Agassiz Club," exchanged with Randolph "to do what I can in conchological work to help pass the lonely hours" after her husband of forty-nine years had died.[61] Another amateur, Minnie Taylor from Los Angeles, wanted to exchange Southern California specimens for Puget Sound forms. While she desired shells, she offered to send Randolph more exotic choices: "Do you care to have Calif. curios, such as a stuffed horned toad or a tarantula? I have received thirteen species for a horned toad mounted on orange wood, and eleven species for a tarantula mounted on card board."[62] J. D. Mitchell from Victoria, Texas, eagerly corresponded and exchanged with Randolph because he enjoyed "collecting more than anything else & I exchange for the purpose of comparisons & study."[63] A. G. Wetherby of Magnetic City, North Carolina, was another collector anxious to maintain contact with the YNS because he felt he was a kindred spirit to Randolph: he "sympathize[d] with you [Randolph] in your isolation." Wetherby was another self-styled conchologist, advertising himself on his letterhead as the founder of the "Zoological and Geological Laboratory of A. G. Wetherby & Son." He thanked Randolph for the shells from the Northwest because they have "given me the greatest pleasure. . . . This little lot is *very, very* acceptable."[64]

The collegial attitude among American conchologists evident in Randolph's correspondence also may have aided in making the exchange network wider and more efficient. Often collectors exchanged names of colleagues as well as specimens. For example, the Oakland, California, lawyer and noted collector Fred Button wrote to the Young Naturalists at the suggestion of William Dall.[65] George Hubbard of St. Cloud, Minnesota, exchanged specimens with Randolph and then asked if Randolph could "give me a few names of collectors with whom you have made satisfactory exchanges?"[66] Others, like J. J. White of Rockledge, Florida, provided Randolph with names. Randolph's marginalia in the letter included "checks" by the names with whom he corresponded.[67]

Many collectors were willing to cooperate because they considered themselves to be joined in a common effort: the building of shell collections. Wetherby epitomized this spirit by declaring, "*Let us help each other!* This is the naturalists [*sic*] spirit, and the one that I trust animates me in all my correspondence with those who are not mercenary."[68] Clapp shared the same perspective when he welcomed Randolph's return to Seattle after a brief sojourn to Alaska, exhorting him to be "ready to take up shells with newness of vigor and interest as *we need you* to continue your good work in Wash[ington]."[69]

From all available evidence, the exchange network was effective in creating communication channels among many American conchologists, both amateur and professional. The benefits for the participants were obvious: collections expanded, information was shared, and colleagues in isolated areas were brought into contact with peers. Professional naturalists in university museums and natural history societies especially benefited. They faced a number of difficulties in building museum collections: expeditions were expensive and funding sources limited; the vastness of the United States practically prohibited individually supervised surveys; and many of the museums were far from areas with extensive molluscan populations. The presence of amateur collectors throughout the country helped ameliorate these problems. Amateurs, for their part, benefited from the expertise of professionals. Despite the availability of textbooks to aid them, amateurs still experienced many problems with precise identification. Randolph, for example, relied almost exclusively upon Dall at the Smithsonian and Pilsbry at the Academy of Natural Sciences. His correspondence with these men is replete with lists indicating the correct species names for specimens sent to them from Seattle. On several occasions, the mollusks he sent represented new species, and Dall and Pilsbry, in part to recognize their Northwestern colleagues, offered to honor various Young Naturalists by naming species after them. In 1895 Dall honored Professor Johnson, the territorial university naturalist who played such a vital role in the maturation of the local natural history community. "Perhaps it would please Prof. Johnson, who has done so much to promote an interest in the mollusks of Puget Sound, if this little species was named after him, so, if you have no objection I will call it *V. [Vitrea] Johnsoni.*"[70]

In the Northwest, Randolph was the expert for local collectors and, as such, was frequently consulted on systematic and taxonomic issues. Fred Andrus wrote from Oregon, accepting Randolph's offer to help identify his finds: "You see I accept your offer of help as I am compelled to rely on some one for the identity of my shells not having the necessary work of refference [*sic*] myself."[71] Randolph was also the arbiter when Andrus consulted two "authorities" and received two different opinions. In his position, therefore, Randolph played a similar role to amateurs in the Northwest that Pilsbry and Dall played at the national level to amateur conchologists like Randolph—he provided valuable information to his less-informed colleagues.

While the exchange network operated marvelously to increase communication among naturalists, it also pointed out one of the gravest problems with the mix of amateurs and professionals in conchology. Because of their positions of prominence in two of the largest museums in the country, Pilsbry and Dall usually represented the final opinion on species identification. However, there were several other major collectors with impressive reputations who often identified new specimens, sometimes at variance with Pilsbry and Dall. Acting to complicate this problem were the many amateurs who anxiously searched to collect species "new to science," thereby securing their place in conchological perpetuity. In a few cases, Randolph was drawn into the debate, usually unwittingly, because several specimens collected by the Young Naturalists were either new species or were varieties of species not observed previously. The general lines of the debate, as expected for these issues, were formed about the classic taxonomic arguments of "lumpers" and "splitters"; in other words, should existing species be expanded to include new varieties or should new species be designated?

Randolph became most involved in this issue in 1895, when he sent several specimens to Victor Sterki, a physician in New Philadelphia, Ohio, who was originally from Switzerland and who shared the European tendency to split species. He was also an expert on North American *Pisidia,* working on this group as the assistant conchologist in Pittsburgh's Carnegie Museum and as associate curator of mollusks in the Ohio Academy of Science.[72] Sterki identified species from Randolph and offered, as a postscript, a thorough discussion detailing his taxonomic position.[73] When Randolph relayed this information to Dall, he received a critical evaluation of Sterki's work including a discussion about the issue of "lumping" and "splitting."

> A *propros* of Sterki, I sent him some of your shells but did not say where they came from and he then called them *binneyana.* The *simplex* and *edentula* are synonymous, only the former was given to the american [sic] shell and the other to the European. I have *(entre nous)* caught Sterki twice this way. He is a good fellow and very careful, but he has the foreign way of drawing the lines of distinction too taut, and so misses it occassionally [sic]. I am not sure that it is not a better way than "lumping" things which are distinct.[74]

Not surprisingly, many amateurs took exception with Dall and preferred more exact distinctions between species, à la Sterki. Edward W. Roper of Colorado Springs wrote to Randolph that in his opinion the new species identified by Sterki were correct.[75] The well-known San Francisco collector John Rowell agreed. In his own *Pisidia* work, he sided with the Ohio-based naturalist: "I have no patience with our modern conchologists who fight against multiplication of species, but create genera, on far less differences than they allow to justify new species."[76]

Randolph was left to ponder how he was to define a species. The Reverend George Taylor of St. Alban's Rectory in Nanaimo (Vancouver Island), British Columbia, provided an accurate précis of Randolph's dilemma when he responded to Randolph's questions by concluding that "some of the names seem to me to be incorrect but there is so much difference of opinion as to the species in some genera that one hardly knows what to believe."[77] Fortunately, Randolph's more established colleagues offered some help. George Clapp opposed the views of his fellow curator Sterki and advised Randolph to choose Dall's identification every time. Clapp accepted a more nominalistic and Darwinian position concerning species: "In a great many cases Genera and species are only artificial groups gotten up for 'our own convenience'—Nature does not draw such hard and fast lines as we claim."[78] He continued to express similar ideas after he examined a number of Northwest slugs. After "studying them you begin to wonder if there is such a thing as 'species' in nature—Hemphill says there is not and I more than half agree with him."[79] Later in the same year, Clapp vented his spleen against his colleagues and told Randolph, "I can do as well as Sterki; in fact do it *better* as I am *not* a *'species maker'* and will not make a new species all on account of locality."[80]

The species debate was the most visible problem facing nineteenth-century conchology at century's end. Of course there were many other minor problems, most relating to personality conflicts among collectors. Several letters to Randolph warned him of possible exchange problems associated with specific conchologists. Clapp, a veritable wellspring of information on any issue, wrote Randolph that Pilsbry was notorious for his poor record as a correspondent. Randolph, however, did not experience this problem; he and Pilsbry corresponded extensively in the 1890s. Clapp also advised Randolph to *"not send the shell to Dr. Sterki* as you may never see it again."[81] Other amateurs, forced to earn their living in other professions, complained to Randolph that time to pursue their avocational interest was limited. Wetherby's engineering business was too time consuming, while J. H. Ferriss, editor of the *Monthly Sentinel* and *Daily News* and president of "The News Company" of Joliet, Illinois, complained that his "newspaper interferes so much with my shell business it bothers me to keep up."[82] Finally, there is some evidence that Randolph experienced problems with certain correspondents. A Mr. W. Miller from Grand Rapids, Michigan, exchanged specimens with the YNS but was disappointed with the quality of shells he received. When Randolph conveyed his own dissatisfaction with the shells Miller sent west, Miller replied angrily that despite his recent exposure to the exchange network, his problems with the YNS were unprecedented; his experience with Randolph was enough to cause him to abandon conchology.[83] Apparently the dispute was never resolved amicably.

With the exception of these few problems, which should be expected given the highly personal nature of natural history studies, the exchange network served effectively as a conduit for nineteenth-century natural history materials and information. Randolph's correspondence provides us with a valuable window to glance into the American conchological community at the end of the nineteenth century. In particular, the correspondence provides the base for a classic case study of an amateur naturalist, living far from established centers in natural history and largely self-trained, who became an integral cog in the natural history community. Randolph's involvement as a collector of shells, communicator, museum curator, and exchange participant placed him in a unique role to serve professionals and amateurs interested in the study of shells. Moreover, he is a striking example of why historians of American science must not overlook the contribution of amateur natural historians in the maturation of American biology. These often indefatigable naturalists played crucial parts in popularizing science in a country lacking a rich scientific legacy and in building the museum collections of universities and natural history societies.

Conclusion

By the end of the nineteenth century, evolution theory had become an acceptable and nonproblematic working principle for American biologists. These ideas percolated into the amateur natural history community, where P. Brooks Randolph and his colleagues in the Young Naturalists' Society adopted them implicitly. Working in the northwest corner of the United States, these naturalists helped to document the ubiquity of variation in the natural world and the regional character of the fauna and flora. Exchanging specimens, providing new observations from the natural world, and serving as valued collaborators to trained specialists in the east, members of the YNS made important contributions to the beginnings of natural history in the Northwest. They adopted arguments for the developmental history of faunal groups, they accepted the genealogical relationships between taxa, and they grasped the tenuous nature of species, all ideas traceable to Darwinian evolution theory. And while their pronouncements concerning the natural world may have lacked extensive references to Darwin, the debt of the naturalists to the formulator of evolution theory is clear.

Notes

1   I appreciate the suggestions of Bruce Hevly in helping me to understand how to document influence when direct evidence is lacking. Professor Hevly, however, does not shoulder any of the blame for deficiencies in my argument.

2   Darwin titled the third volume of the series first published in 1839,

Journals and Remarks, 1832–1836. When it was published as a separate work in 1845, the title grew to *Journal of Researches into the Natural History and Geology of the Countries Visited during the Voyage of H.M.S. "Beagle" round the World under the Command of Capt. FitzRoy, R. N.* Later editions were shortened to the present title, *The Voyage of the "Beagle"* (see edition edited by Leonard Engel [Garden City, NJ: Anchor Books, 1962], xvi–xvii).

3   In this paper, "the Northwest" refers to that area of the United States encompassing the present states of Oregon, Washington, Idaho, and western Montana, or the area previously known as the Oregon Territory.

4   Herman J. Viola and Carolyn Margolis, eds., *Magnificent Voyagers: The U.S. Exploring Expedition, 1838–1842* (Washington, DC: Smithsonian Institution, 1985), 91. There is one other obscure reference to a connection between Wilkes and Darwin. Evidently Wilkes arranged to meet Darwin in 1836 when he traveled to London to buy supplies for the expedition. The evidence for such a meeting comes from a letter Darwin wrote to Wilkes (7 November 1836) suggesting that the two men meet "on Wednesday between 12 and 1 o'clock." There is no other indication that the meeting actually took place. I thank the anonymous reviewer for pointing out that this reference is in *The Correspondence of Charles Darwin,* ed. Frederick Burkhardt and Sydney Smith, 10 vols. (Cambridge: Cambridge University Press, 1985–1994), 1:517–518.

5   The most recent material on the California Academy of Sciences is in Michael Smith, *Pacific Visions: California Scientists and the Environment* (New Haven: Yale University Press, 1987), 108–120.

6   Robert D. Clarke, *The Odyssey of Thomas Condon* (Portland: Oregon Historical Society, 1989), 296.

7   Keith R. Benson, "The Young Naturalists' Society and Natural History in the Northwest," *American Zoologist* 26 (1985): 351–361 and idem, "The Young Naturalists' Society: From Chess to Natural History Collections," *Pacific Northwest Quarterly* 77 (1986): 82–93.

8   William H. Goetzmann, *New Lands, New Men: America and the Second Great Age of Discovery* (New York: Viking, 1986), 190.

9   Viola and Margolis, eds., *Magnificent Voyagers,* 40–41; and William Stanton, *The Great United States Exploring Expedition of 1838–1842* (Berkeley: University of California Press, 1975), 340.

10   Viola and Margolis, eds., *Magnificent Voyagers,* 38.

11   Smith, *Pacific Visions,* 49.

12   For an excellent biography of Gray, including his treatment of evolution theory, see A. Hunter Dupree, *Asa Gray, 1810–1888* (Cambridge: Harvard University Press, 1959). A companion source that also illustrates the gradual acceptance of evolution or developmental ideas is

Edward Lurie, *Louis Agassiz: A Life in Science* (Chicago: University of Chicago Press, 1960; reprint, Baltimore: Johns Hopkins University Press, 1988).

13   Clarke, *Thomas Condon*, 257.

14   This theme is pervasive in the work of Polly Winsor. See Mary P. Winsor, "Barnacle Larvae in the Nineteenth Century: A Case Study in Taxonomic Theory," *Journal of the History of Medicine and Allied Sciences* 24 (1969): 294–309; idem, *Starfish, Jellyfish, and the Order of Life* (New Haven: Yale University Press, 1976); idem, "The Impact of Darwinism upon the Linnaean Enterprise, with Special Reference to the Work of T. H. Huxley," in *Contemporary Perspectives on Linnaeus,* ed. John Weinstock (Lanham, MD: University Press of America, 1985); and idem, *Reading the Shape of Nature: Comparative Zoology at the Agassiz Museum* (Chicago: University of Chicago Press, 1991).

15   Winsor, *Reading the Shape of Nature*, 248.

16   Muriel L. Guberlet, *The Windows to His World: The Story of Trevor Kincaid* (Palo Alto, CA: Pacific Books, 1975), 117.

17   The only published works are two studies of the Young Naturalists' Society by Benson (n. 7).

18   There are a number of works that include the journals and some reference to the natural history on the expedition. The classic texts are Meriwether Lewis, *History of the Expeditions under the Command of Lewis and Clark, to the Sources of the Missouri River, thence across the Rocky Mountains and down the Columbia River to the Pacific Ocean, Performed During the Years, 1804–5–6, by Order of the Government of the United States,* ed. Elliott Coues, 3 vols. (New York: Francis P. Harper, 1893); Meriwether Lewis, *Original Journals of the Lewis and Clark Expedition,* ed. R. G. Thwaites (New York: Dodd, Mead, 1904–1905); R. D. Burroughs, *The Natural History of the Lewis and Clark Expedition* (East Lansing: Michigan State University Press, 1961); and P. R. Cutright, *Lewis and Clark: Pioneering Naturalists* (Urbana: University of Illinois Press, 1969). For an example of a correction to the classic literature see Keith R. Benson, "Herpetology of the Lewis and Clark Expedition, 1804–1806," *Herpetological Review* 9 (1978): 87–91.

19   See Stanton, *Great United States Exploring Expedition;* Goetzmann, *New Lands, New Men;* and Viola and Margolis, eds., *Magnificent Voyagers.*

20   Goetzman, *New Lands, New Men,* 289.

21   Secondary treatments of these expeditions are few. See William H. Goetzmann, *Army Exploration of the West, 1803–1863* (New Haven: Yale University Press, 1959); idem, *Exploration and Empire: The Explorer and Scientist in the Winning of the West* (New York: Knopf,

1966); and John A. Moore, "Zoology of the Pacific Railroad Surveys," *American Zoologist* 26 (1986): 331–341. The source book for information about all these expeditions is Max Meisel, *A Bibliography of American Natural History: The Pioneer Century, 1769–1865* (Brooklyn, NY: Premier, 1924–1929; reprint, 3 vols., New York: Hafner, 1967). The information about the early Coast Survey visits to Puget Sound is scant.

22 William H. Goetzmann and Kay Sloan, *Looking Far North: The Harriman Expedition to Alaska, 1899* (Princeton: Princeton University Press, 1982).

23 Benson, "Young Naturalists' Society: From Chess to Natural History Collections."

24 Nancy Rockafellar, "Progress, Pleasure, and Science in the Intellectual Wilderness: Dr. Albert Chase Folsom in Snohomish City, W. T., 1872–1885" (Paper, University of Washington, 1985) (unpaginated).

25 Ibid.

26 Ibid.

27 Clarke, *Thomas Condon.*

28 Goetzmann and Sloan, *Looking Far North,* 151.

29 Ibid., 200–201.

30 The Randolph correspondence collection includes 373 letters.

31 For the early history of the university, see Charles M. Gates, *The First Century at the University of Washington, 1861–1961* (Seattle: University of Washington Press, 1961).

32 For information on museums, natural history societies, and early American biology, see Toby A. Appel, "Science, Popular Culture, and Profit: Peale's Philadelphia Museum," *Journal of the Society for the Bibliography of Natural History* 9 (1980): 619–634; Sally Gregory Kohlstedt, "Henry A. Ward: The Merchant Naturalist and American Museum Development," *Journal of the Society for the Bibliography of Natural History* 9 (1980): 647–661; idem, "Museums on Campus: A Tradition of Inquiry and Teaching," in *The American Development of Biology,* ed. Ronald Rainger, Keith R. Benson, and Jane Maienschein (Philadelphia: University of Pennsylvania Press, 1988); and Margaret Rossiter, "Benjamin Silliman and the Lowell Institute: The Popularization of Science in Nineteenth-Century America," *New England Quarterly* 44 (1971): 602–626.

33 In the nineteenth century, studies of Mollusca were divided into conchology, the study of shells, and malacology, the study of molluscan animals. Generally speaking, conchology was more fashionable among amateur naturalists, especially in the United States. See Peter Dance, *Shell Collecting: An Illustrated History* (Berkeley: University of California Press, 1966), 270–273.

34   Speeches and writings, 20 January 1882, Young Naturalists' Society,
      70-68 (4–8), University of Washington Libraries, University Archives.

35   Minutes, 12 March 1881, Young Naturalists' Society, 70-68 (2–4),
      University of Washington Libraries, University Archives.

36   George W. Tryon, *Manual of Conchology; Structural and Systematic
      with Illustrations of the Species* (Philadelphia: Academy of Natural
      Sciences, 1879).

37   S. P. Woodward, *A Manual of the Mollusca*, 4th ed. (London: Crosby
      Lockwood, 1880), iv.

38   Ibid., v.

39   Ibid.

40   George W. Tryon, "A Sketch of the History of Conchology in the
      United States," *American Journal of Arts and Science and Arts* 33
      (1862): 180.

41   Despite its popularity in the continental United States, conchology
      (and its practitioners) has received little historical attention. In addi-
      tion to Peter Dance's work, *Shell Collecting*, most of the work has
      been done by Ralph Dexter. See Ralph Dexter, "Some Interesting
      Molluscan Records of George J. Streator, 1881–1909," *Sterkiana*,
      no. 12 (1963): 9–14; idem, "Dr. Victor Sterki as a Malacologist,"
      Sterkiana, no. 26 (1967): 7–9; idem, "George W. Dean (1820–1901),
      Amateur Malacologist in Ohio," *Sterkiana*, no. 33 (1969): 1–3; idem,
      "Benjamin Tappan, Jr. (1773–1857) as a Naturalist and Malacolo-
      gist," *Sterkiana*, no. 41 (1971): 45–49; idem, "Dr. Sterki and Some of
      His Malacological Correspondence," *Sterkiana*, nos. 63–64 (1976):
      65–76; idem, "Dr. Jared P. Kirtland, Cleveland's First Malacologist
      and Some of His Correspondence," *Sterkiana*, nos. 65–66 (1977):
      11–13; idem, "Some Correspondence of Victor Sterki, M.D., Noted
      Physician and Malacologist of New Philadelphia," *Bulletin of the
      Pittsburgh Shell Club*, Bulletin of 1978 (1979): 1–3. An article con-
      cerning conchology in the Pacific is E. Alison Kay and William J.
      Clench, "A Bibliography of William Harper Pease, Malacologist of
      Polynesia," *Nemouria*, Occasional Papers of the Delaware Museum
      of Natural History, no. 16 (1975).

42   Tryon, "History of Conchology," 180.

43   Historical features, 8 March 1895, Young Naturalists' Society, 70-68
      (1–1), University of Washington Libraries, University Archives.

44   George W. Tryon, Jr., *Structural and Systematic Conchology: An
      Introduction to the Study of the Mollusca*, 2 vols. (Philadelphia:
      Published by the author, 1882), 1: v.

45   For information on Tryon's *Journal of Conchology* and Tryon and
      Pilsbry's *Manual of Conchology*, see Dance, *Shell Collecting*, 186–
      188. *Nautilus* was published as a joint venture of the Academy of
      Natural Sciences and the Wagner Free Institute.

46 W. E. Ritter to P. Brooks Randolph, 27 August 1895, Young Naturalists' Society, 70-68 (1–29), University of Washington Libraries, University Archives.

47 W. H. Dall to P. B. Randolph, 14 November 1894, Washington State Museum, Burke Memorial, Randolph collection.

48 Dall to P. B. Randolph, 14 February 1896, Randolph collection.

49 Henry Augustus Pilsbry to Randolph, 11 December [n.d.], Randolph collection.

50 Pilsbry to Randolph, 29 May 1896, Randolph collection.

51 Pilsbry to Randolph, 18 December 1898, Randolph collection.

52 George G. Clapp to Randolph, 16 May 1897, Randolph collection.

53 Henry Hemphill to Randolph, 24 September 1896, Randolph collection.

54 Dexter, "Dr. Sterki and Some of His Malacological Correspondence," 73.

55 *Nautilus,* advertisement section.

56 A. H. Gardner to Randolph, 5 December 1895, Randolph collection.

57 H. E. Sargent to Randolph, 5 April 1895, Randolph collection.

58 C. H. Turner to Randolph, 19 December 1898, Randolph collection.

59 Charles W. Johnson to Randolph, 12 May 1899, Randolph collection.

60 Olaf Nylander to Randolph, 15 July 1896, Randolph collection. Spelling in quotation is taken from the original.

61 Minnie Taylor to Randolph, 25 May 1895, Randolph collection.

62 Mary P. Olney to Randolph, 9 March 1899, Randolph collection.

63 J. D. Mitchell to Randolph, 27 May 1897, Randolph collection.

64 A. G. Wetherby to Randolph, 4 April 1899, Randolph collection.

65 Fred L. Button to Randolph, 12 December 1895, Randolph collection.

66 George C. Hubbard to Randolph, 30 September 1895, Randolph collection.

67 J. J. White to Randolph, 23 May 1895, Randolph collection.

68 Wetherby to Randolph, 3 May 1899, Randolph collection.

69 Clapp to Randolph, 10 August 1898, Randolph collection.

70 Dall to Randolph, 6 May 1895, Randolph collection.

71 Fred H. Andrus to Randolph, 9 October 1895, Randolph collection.

72 See Dexter's articles on Sterki, "Dr. Victor Sterki as a Malacologist," "Dr. Victor Sterki and Some of His Malacological Correspondence," and "Some Correspondence of Victor Sterki" (n. 41).

73 Victor Sterki to Randolph, 5 February 1896, Randolph collection.

74 Dall to Randolph, 13 May 1896, Randolph collection.

75   Edward W. Roper to Randolph, 30 November 1895, Randolph
     collection.

76   John Rowell to Randolph, 10 February 1896, Randolph collection.

77   George Taylor to Randolph, 17 January 1896, Randolph collection.

78   Clapp to Randolph, 12 February 1896, Randolph collection.

79   Clapp to Randolph, 3 September 1896, Randolph collection.

80   Clapp to Randolph, 22 December 1896, Randolph collection.

81   Clapp to Randolph, 1 April 1897, Randolph collection.

82   J. H. Ferris to Randolph, 13 October 1899, Randolph collection.

83   W. Miller to Randolph, 12 October and 4 November 1895, Randolph
     collection.

PAULINE PAYNE

8 "Science at the Periphery"
Dr. Schomburgk's Garden

In the years 1830–1850, a number of naturalists visited Australia, including Charles Darwin, Thomas Huxley, Joseph Hooker, John and Elizabeth Gould, and James Dwight Dana. These were among the most important of many naturalists whose scientific careers developed after a lengthy expedition, the "big science" of its day in costs and equipment, requiring teams of workers and government support. Naturalists examined flora, fauna, and geological phenomena and produced substantial publications. Many followed successful careers on their return. The young Darwin left Australia without regrets, convinced that the "splendid" climate and opportunities for material advancement in the Australian settlements were outweighed by the "very low ebb of literature," poorly stocked bookshops, and the taint of convict settlement.[1] However, there were a few European naturalists who decided to settle in Australia and whose work would create distinctive traditions for Australia in the life sciences. While earlier scientific visitors had made collections and observations of the environment and indigenous people, the period 1855–1885 saw the establishment and expansion of colonial museums and universities, with positions available for permanent, paid work in science. These naturalists arrived to take full advantage of these new opportunities. They did so in part by introducing plants to a landscape that had no Aboriginal tradition of agriculture or horticulture. This chapter will focus on the work of one such naturalist, about whom relatively little is known—Richard Moritz Schomburgk (1811–1891, figure 8.1), younger brother of the botanist and explorer Sir Robert Schomburgk, and second director of the Adelaide Botanic Garden between 1865 and 1891.

Adelaide, the capital of South Australia, was founded in 1836, the year of Darwin's visit to Australia. Its botanic garden was established nineteen years later, under the directorship of George William Francis (1800–1865). With the importation and acclimatization of new

8.1 Richard Moritz
Schomburgk, 1884
(photo by S. Solomon,
Adelaide). Courtesy of
the Botanic Garden of
Adelaide.

plants, Adelaide's garden developed as a center for scientific endeavor
and reflected the particular kind of contribution that scientists could
make in a new settlement. Over a half century, Schomburgk's work
would reveal much about the intellectual climate that shaped colonial
natural history, with its utilitarian, localized profile, and its close
working relationships with colleagues overseas. Those colleagues,
while frequently part of the British imperial network,[2] could also
include vital "extraimperial" contacts, whose friendship and expertise
proved vital in facilitating transfers of knowledge and material.

An Expedition and Its Aftermath

For a young naturalist in early-nineteenth-century Europe,
embarking upon an expedition of exploration offered both adventure
and fame. Richard Schomburgk was a naturalist for whom an expedition established a scientific career. The third son of an assistant Luth-
eran pastor in Saxony, he was apprenticed at fourteen as a gardener
at Merseburg. Before he saw military service in the Royal Guard,
his apprenticeship provided good career prospects at a time when
German gardeners enjoyed a high reputation throughout Europe.[3]

Through Robert Schomburgk, his eldest brother, Richard soon made his mark. While on business in the United States and the West Indies, Robert had established a reputation for producing navigational charts for the British Admiralty and for expeditions he led to the interior of British Guiana. These attracted the notice of Alexander von Humboldt, the distinguished naturalist, who had been to the upper reaches of the Orinoco River on his own expedition to South and Central America (1799–1804).[4] When the British, Brazilian, and Venezuelan governments required fresh information to arbitrate their boundary disputes, Robert was asked to lead a geographical expedition under the joint auspices of the British government and the Royal Geographical Society.[5] He arranged that Richard was attached as naturalist and historian for the Prussian government, with instructions to collect for scientific institutions in Berlin.

Embarking on a major government expedition at the age of twenty-nine—an opportunity made possible by Humboldt's association with the Prussian court—would make an excellent start to a career. Accidental wounds, exposure, snakebite, infections from the bites of insects, and encounters with piranhas led to illness, injury, and the death of a colleague, but the travels of the Schomburgks in British Guiana between 1840 and 1844 established their reputations. Richard survived yellow fever, and the brothers returned to Europe with a wealth of botanical and zoological material as well as astronomical and physical measurements.[6] Robert, knighted by a grateful British government, embarked on a diplomatic career, becoming British consul in Siam. Richard returned to Berlin, where he wrote a three-volume account of the expedition, *Reisen in Britisch Guiana,* which was sold to major libraries throughout Europe.

In South America, Schomburgk met tropical flora new and exciting to European eyes. There was also the risk of death or permanent injury. Buchan and Parkinson had perished on Captain Cook's first voyage, as had John Gilbert and Ludwig Leichhardt on expeditions within Australia. However, if a young man survived, an account of his travels could both be marketable and bring him scientific notice. Through the production of *Reisen,* Schomburgk, whose formal training in science was limited, came into contact with botanists of the calibre of Nees von Esenbeck and August Grisebach and the naturalist Christian Gottfried Ehrenberg.[7] Richard warmly acknowledged his debt to Alexander von Humboldt. Through the "friendly consideration" of Humboldt, "whose name like a guiding star will lead the way in Science for all time," Richard noted, "I was enabled with my slender resources to add my contribution to the knowledge of the surface structure of our planet though only as a collector of material for the further study of the subject."[8] Susan Faye Cannon has emphasized the distinctive character of Humboldtian science which, with its empirical, quantitative, synthetic ambitions, fails to fit into twentieth-century boundaries.[9] Humboldt's plant geography was centrally concerned with vegetation, its character, distribution, and relation to environmental parameters.[10] Scientific travel and field work were required to gain accurate measurements of phenomena that previous travelers had merely described.[11] And while Humboldt acknowledged the importance of individual plants and species, his approach was generally holistic and influenced Schomburgk greatly.[12]

Living with his brother Otto in Berlin, Schomburgk spent four years writing up his South American observations and experiences. Then, amid the political upheavals of 1848, the two brothers helped form a South Australian Colonization Society. They sailed from Hamburg on the *Prinzess Louise* in March 1849.[13] Richard Schomburgk recalled that he and Otto were "black sheep" after the revolution and that Humboldt used his position at court and among his scientific friends to help the young men begin overseas a new life that would provide both political freedom and economic opportunity.[14]

Establishing a farm, vineyard, and orchard on fertile land thirty kilometers from Adelaide, the Schomburgks pioneered a small settlement, named Buchsfelde after Leopold von Buch, the renowned geologist and friend of Humboldt who had also helped them. They took an active part in local government and community organizations, became involved in a German-language newspaper, and were much concerned with scientific agriculture. Richard, in the capacity of honorary curator of a local natural history museum, began collecting, and in the manner of the period, sent significant collections of reptiles and amphibians for identification to Professor Peters at Berlin.[15] The brothers also remained in contact with Berlin and Humboldt by establishing a meteorological recording station at Buchsfelde and sending observations to Europe.[16]

Following Otto's death in 1857, Richard farmed at Buchsfelde until 1865, when he was appointed second director of the Adelaide Botanic Garden. His letter of application states he held the title of Doctor of Philosophy from the Deutsche Akademie der Wissenschaften in Berlin[17] and was a member of the Leopoldina, the kaiserliche Leopoldinisch-Carolinische deutsche Akademie der Naturforscher—honors that resulted from his British Guiana research. He later said he had taken the botanic garden position to provide for his six children's education. This it did, with a substantial house in the gardens and a salary rising to £600. The gardens also gave him the opportunity to develop plant science, using his extensive contacts with the German scientific community.

There he served economic botany and the applied sciences of horticulture, agriculture, viticulture, and forestry in ways appropriate to colonial needs. In Australia, as in other British colonies, economic growth was linked to the production of staple export products. Colonial governments supported investigation in order to further resource development—to understand in order to use and control.[18] The scientific culture established by European intellectuals, while providing where possible for social and cultural interests, was necessarily concerned with practical needs.[19] Schomburgk's career led him to be "a big fish in a small pond" concerned with the applications of botany. He farmed and established a position in the local community, experience that helped gain acceptance for his later projects. Darwin had left Australia "without sorrow or regret."[20] But for Schomburgk and his botanical counterpart in Melbourne, Ferdinand von Mueller, a fellow German, Australia would be home for life. Both were naturalized as British subjects and never returned to Europe. As one of Schomburgk's friends from the *Prinzess Louise* explained, "We have left all that behind."

Schomburgk's twenty-five-year career in Adelaide saw him develop four distinctive aspects of a successful scientific life. First, he struck a successful balance between different aspects of the work of the botanic garden, essential to obtain the necessary resources for the garden's development. Second, he used the institution, with its generous funding, as a beachhead for the development of scientific culture. Third, he inspired cooperation with European scientists and settlers to introduce plants and to develop agriculture and horticulture in a European tradition. Finally, he gave a pragmatic approach to an institution that, while owing much to its British origins, created important links for the colony with the United States, the Pacific, and continental Europe.

A Balanced Approach

Schomburgk's first projects reflected the approach that typified his administration. If he gave too much attention to the scientific aspects of the work of the botanic garden, he would lose popular support. If, on the other hand, he merely provided a recreation ground, the opportunity was lost to provide a scientific service. Early in his directorship Schomburgk worked with his board to provide features of popular appeal. He developed walks winding through shrubberies—of the kind admired by Darwin in Sydney's Botanic Gardens.[21] Avenues of trees together with statues, fountains, and flower beds planted in the fashionable geometrical patterns of the day, along with a rosery and improved greenhouses for the orchid collection, all added to the popularity of the gardens.[22]

One ambitious project was the Victoria House built for the *Victoria regia (V. amazonica)* water lily. While some in government considered this an extravagance, growing a "vegetable wonder" that won worldwide attention proved a great coup. Newspapers in 1868 printed hour-by-hour descriptions of the opening of the flowers;[23] and at a time when the population of the colony was only 163,000, the gardens attracted 7,500 visitors on a Sunday and 300,000 in a year. The *Victoria* was associated with the Schomburgk brothers, who had seen the plant in Guiana and who were instrumental in having it identified and named after Queen Victoria.[24] If one did not have Darwin's wealth, a capacity for diplomacy and entrepreneurship were useful adjuncts to a love of botany. It was not enough for a botanic garden director to be capable and diligent or creative and innovative in using plant material. He needed also to bring prestige to the institution and glory to his colonial masters.

In 1877 Schomburgk opened a new Palm House—imported, prefabricated, from Bremen[25]—for the display of his large collection of palms and orchids. In Adelaide, glasshouses, like shrubberies and garden beds, served a recreational function that kept pace with the scientific and educational work of the garden. Early projects of a utilitarian nature included a nursery for trees suitable for civic planting and an experimental ground for "medicinal, industrial, and fodder plants," plots of interest to farmers and merchants. Schomburgk also proposed a system garden in 1866, with plants laid out according to their botanical classification. Aware that a system garden, while important to botanists, would be of interest to few visitors, he postponed the work until 1871, when other projects with more popular appeal had been completed.

The new positions in government service that opened in the 1850s and 1860s enabled men like Schomburgk, von Mueller, Krefft, and Selwyn to maintain collections, with support staff. However, government employees had few of the freedoms of scientific workers with independent means. Salaried scientific officers had to maintain good relations with the boards of their institutions and with politicians. The risks of death or disease on an expedition were replaced by the risks of being fired or publicly humiliated. Schomburgk's talent for maintaining excellent relations with his masters can be contrasted with the sad plight of Gerard Krefft, dismissed from the curatorship of the Australian Museum in Sydney,[26] and the removal of Ferdinand von Mueller from his directorship of the Melbourne Botanic Garden in 1873.[27] Even Sir Joseph Hooker had his share of controversy at Kew.[28]

There was one area of controversy in science in which Schomburgk might have become embroiled—the controversy that followed the publication of Darwin's *Origin of Species*. Krefft commented on Darwinian views, as did von Mueller and Professor Frederick McCoy of the University of Melbourne.[29] But Schomburgk remained silent. His only recorded statement on the subject is ambiguous.[30] In 1875 he wrote of a gibbon in his zoological collection that had died of an illness akin to pneumonia: "Her sufferings, and her behaviour ...reminded me so much of that of a human being...that it is no wonder if I became an adherent to Darwin's theory."[31] At a time when it was widely believed that human beings were specially created in the Garden of Eden,[32] Schomburgk gave cautious approval to the *Descent of Man,* published in 1871.

The Botanic Gardens as a Focus for Scientific Culture

If circumstances were propitious, a botanic garden could provide both a recreational and educational service and a focus for scientific culture. Some scientific activities were of value in themselves, such as the herbarium, with its dried plants labeled and filed for reference and research. Other activities gave science standing in the community. In 1881 Schomburgk opened a Museum of Economic Botany, modeled on the museum at Kew and similarly dedicated to showing how plant products could be used for food and beverages, paper, textiles, adhesives, dyes, cordage, and medicines. At the same time, the Museum of Economic Botany provided storage for the herbarium.[33]

Schomburgk's research interests lay in economic botany and horticulture rather than in taxonomy. He rarely made field trips, but he acted as patron and promoter of others. Through his influence, the botanist Frederick Schultze was included in Goyder's 1870 expedition to the Northern Territory. Similarly, his interest in the acclimatization of tropical plants led him to support a botanic garden in the Northern Territory. As director, he acted as a scientific spokesman. Thus, after years of campaigning about pollution in the streams of the gardens, he was invited to give evidence to the Sanitation Commission.[34] He spoke out on environmental issues such as the destruction of native pasture grasses and forest trees and the soil degradation that resulted.[35] Just as Darwin had seen some of the Australian vegetation as "desolate and untidy" or "monotonous," Schomburgk admitted to finding some South Australian vegetation—for example, that in the mallee areas—as "monotonous" and "depressing." Like other Europeans, he saw Australian vegetation through European eyes and with European stereotypes. Yet he did promote the use of indigenous plants, such as the taller species of eucalypts and other native trees and shrubs. His catalogues of 1871 and 1878 reveal that 13 percent of species in the botanic garden were indigenous to Australia.[36] He demonstrated the use of trees and shrubs that would grow locally and provided suitable trees for planting by local corporations and district councils, distributing up to twelve thousand trees per annum. Within Adelaide Botanic Garden and in nearby Botanic Park, an area planted between 1873 and 1876 as a landscape garden and arboretum, avenues of trees in the European tradition helped provide visual interest to an otherwise flat site. A balance between exotic and indigenous plants and a pragmatic attitude to the selection of plants were important elements of his approach. His interest in silviculture led him to become involved in the creation of South Australia's State Forest Service. He served on the first Forest Board, established in 1875, well before its counterparts elsewhere in Australia and the first of its kind in the British Empire.[37] Along with other German-born colleagues, such as F. E. H. W. Krichauff, he brought ideas on forestry management from continental Europe to the British settlement.

Serving on a commission on agricultural and technical education, which recommended the creation of a chair of agriculture and model and experimental farms, Schomburgk played a part in the establishment of Roseworthy Agricultural College in 1883—the first college of its kind established in Australia. He hoped to see an increasing interest in botany—perhaps "in the younger generation"—after the University of Adelaide was established in 1874 with a foundation chair in natural history. The system garden provided a valuable facility for botany students at the new university. The university (established when the population of South Australia was only 185,000), followed those in Sydney and Melbourne.[38] Bookshops flourished in a way that would have delighted Darwin; and Schomburgk's new colleague, the energetic professor of natural history Ralph Tate, infused the local Philosophical Society (later the Royal Society) in South Australia, to which Schomburgk belonged, with new spirit.[39] Schomburgk reinforced his practical philosophy with papers to the local Chamber of Manufactures on crops that could be grown in the colony. The authority of the directorship gave him status in supporting new ventures, such the Central Bureau of Agriculture, formed in 1888.

Individuals, organizations, and government approached Schomburgk for information and support. Sir Joseph Hooker offered some wise advice on this aspect of colonial botany when he wrote to James Hector in Wellington: "I am heartily glad you have started the Museum at Wellington; there is nothing like a Museum and Gardens to screw money out of the public for science."[40] With considerable skill at doing just this, Schomburgk created at the garden a focus for the practical applications of natural history.

The Introduction of Plants

Australia is very unusual in being a country where, with very few exceptions (such as the macadamia nut), every edible cultivar and every crop plant is or has been derived from an introduction. This is also the case with most of the ornamentals, lawn grasses, and sown pasture species.[41] Australian botanic gardens played a role in plant introduction, as acclimatization centers, working in conjunction with commercial nurserymen and private enthusiasts. In an era when there was a profound belief in the desirability of exploiting natural resources, a completely new economic flora was introduced to a country in which agriculture and horticulture had not been practiced. While providing ornamental displays, Schomburgk was at pains to show his botanic garden as both educational and economic. It was "not a mere colonial show got up for the purpose of attracting the colonists or strangers who may honor South Australia with a visit." Instead,

> it is really an educational institution, by means of whose operation instruction may be spread over the colony, as to the constitution, habits, and mode of culture of introduced plants, not solely for the profit of individuals who may be engaged in the culture of the soil, but for the ultimate benefit of the whole community which furnishes funds for that purpose.[42]

To this end, Schomburgk imported, tested, and distributed plants that could be used in orchard, farm, and pasture. He distributed grafts of the sultana vine (Thompson's seedless), medicinal herbs, almond trees, and mulberry trees to foster a sericulture industry and helped to foster the production of wattle bark for the tanning industry.[43] He experimented with forage plants and plants yielding fiber and oil (such as sunflower, sesame seed, and flax) and reported on pulses such as chick-peas, lentils, lupin, and vetch—all the subject of crop trials in Australia today. There were attempts to foster local production of imported goods: mustard, chicory, dried fruit, and medicinal herbs. He worked on cereals (annual grasses cultivated for their grains) and what one might broadly call pasture grasses. South Australia was on the way to becoming the "breadbasket" of Australia, but there remained a need for varieties better suited to local conditions.[44] Schomburgk's experiments, and his American contacts, led to the importation of the wheat variety Du Toits, which proved of great commercial importance.[45]

There were also experiments on conditions causing rust in wheat—a major problem for wheat growers—and trials of pasture grasses.[46] Overstocking, droughts, and clearing had destroyed native grasses. Introduced grasses were difficult to establish. Schomburgk's annual *Reports* record trials of 220 grasses between 1867 and 1890.[47] Some proved commercially useful for pasture; others, such as lawn grasses, were valuable for domestic and civic planting.[48] After testing plants at the garden, Schomburgk sent seed to farmers for trials. The response could be disappointing, as when seven hundred packets of seeds were distributed and only one reply returned.[49] Settlers had still to learn how to cope with hot, dry summers and with wide variations in rainfall. Seed from overseas was sometimes mislabeled, and some needed special cultivation. Nevertheless, trials focused attention on the problems of farming and horticulture and encouraged the public to see the garden as a center for the exchange of information on new plants. These came from such varied sources as American agricultural institutions, acclimatization societies, commercial nurserymen, and colonists traveling overseas.[50] Meanwhile, blessed by the enthusiasm of staff and the efficiency of the nineteenth-century postage system, catalogs were distributed to other institutions, thus stimulating exchanges and helping to increase Adelaide's collections.[51]

Special skills were needed for agricultural extension work, and it is not surprising that Schomburgk, operating from the city, met some resistance from farmers and orchardists in the introduction of crops. However, the garden brought a commitment to proper trials of new materials. During Schomburgk's directorship, Adelaide Botanic Garden became the major plant introduction agency for the colony. At the time of the 1878 *Catalogue*, it had one of the largest living plant collections in the world. R. H. Pulleine (1869–1935) believed that "in point of species, he [Schomburgk], through the gardens must be regarded as the greatest plant introducer we have ever had";[52] there is little doubt that Schomburgk "was probably the greatest plant introducer to have operated in Australia."[53]

Lucile Brockway has represented the process of plant distribution as contributing to worldwide transfers of energy, human resources, and capital.[54] Given the importance to colonial expansion of the materials Schomburgk received, it is illuminating to examine their sources. The records of botanic garden exchanges, extending over a quarter of a century, reveal much about the network Schomburgk used.[55] Plant material from Europe came in two general categories: donated specimens, by exchange, and plants purchased from commercial nurseries. Material from Kew was available because of the extensive exchange system of which Kew was the center. Predictably, the Royal Botanic Gardens at Kew was the single most important institution for gifts[56] and was recorded as a source of donations in twenty-two of twenty-four years.[57] Hooker also contributed extensively to the Museum of Economic Botany. Schomburgk might be sent plants or seeds of South African origin from Kew rather than directly from Natal or Cape Town. The botanic gardens of Mauritius and Singapore provided material in twelve and eleven years, respectively. In approximately half the garden's annual *Reports*, three other regions in the empire are represented—the South African colonies, Jamaica and Trinidad, and the Indian subcontinent. Natal and the Cape Colony, where climatic conditions were similar to those of South Australia, were important sources, and Jamaica provided plants, despite its very different climatic conditions.[58] Interest in economic botany drove exchanges with the government gardens of India, with donations mostly arriving in the period 1878–1889. There was considerable contact with the garden at Saharanpur (eleven years of twenty-four, and every year from 1879 to 1889).[59] Afforestation in South Australia was almost certainly influenced by the active program in India.

From elsewhere in Australia, Sydney's Botanic Gardens—with whose director, Charles Moore, Schomburgk was on friendly terms—was the second most important British donor institution (twenty years out of twenty-four).[60] Material came from Melbourne Botanic Gardens during eighteen years,[61] from Brisbane Botanic Gardens in seventeen (in addition to donations from the Brisbane Acclimatisation Society in eight years), and from the Botanic Gardens of Hobart in eleven.

The Adelaide Botanic Garden records demonstrate that the exchange was not only through Kew and the network of British botanic gardens. A very pragmatic approach developed, in which exchanges of plant material used non-British institutions, the commercial network, and a widely dispersed group of enthusiastic amateurs. St. Petersburg provided donations in twenty-one of twenty-four years—in one year, six hundred packets of seeds are recorded, a remarkable number.[62] St. Petersburg, which became the center of Russian botanical science under E. L. Regel, had sources that included not only central Asia and the Far East, but also Chile and Brazil, where St. Petersburg had a satellite garden.[63] Also of importance were the donations from the botanic garden at Buitenzorg, Java, part of the Dutch colonial network, acknowledged in seventeen of twenty-four annual *Reports*. Dr. R. H. C. Scheffer, director of Buitenzorg (well staffed with as many as thirteen Europeans by 1892), was an important source of tropical plant material for the glasshouses.[64]

For economic plants, a further extremely important channel was the U.S. Department of Agriculture. Donations were received in fourteen years of the twenty-four recorded, principally in the period 1872–1886, with Commissioner F. Watts (1801–1889) playing an important role.[65] Augmenting this link were the New York Agricultural Station; the New York seed merchants Bliss and Sons; and agricultural researchers such as J. Hagenauer of Monticello, Florida, and C. G. Pringle, a leading plant breeder and collector of Vermont. Schomburgk also maintained regular contact with scientists in Germany, France, Italy, Russia, and the United States. Through the Leopoldina, he was linked with some 650 naturalists interested in botany, chemistry, physics, geology, geography, and medicine. By 1886, thirty Leopoldina members were directors of botanic gardens, professors of botany, or holders of dual positions.[66] Schomburgk was one of only five Australasian members: with von Mueller and the Victorian government astronomer, Robert Ellery; and from New Zealand, James Hector, director of the Geological Survey, and Julius von Haast of the Canterbury Museum.[67]

Finally, Schomburgk was a member of many scientific organizations, botanical, horticultural, and geographical; these memberships helped maintain his links with Europe and the United States. Annual *Reports* document contacts with the secretary of the California State Board of Forestry in San Francisco, the Department of Agriculture in Washington, D.C., and the New York Agricultural Station, all of which were sources of plant material. Through such contacts came accounts of research into the effect of vegetation on climate carried out in France and Germany and American research into what new strains of wheat and sorghum and phylloxera-resistant vinestock might come to Adelaide, together with accounts of forestry management and agricultural education.[68]

A Successful Career at "the Periphery"

Schomburgk provided a channel for scientific ideas coming from Europe and the Americas to Australia. He lived at a time of important changes in colonial science and colonial development.

Between 1851 and 1881, Australia's population expanded from 437,665 in 1851, to 1,151,947 in 1861, and to 2,250,194 in 1881; in South Australia the population increased from 63,700 in 1851 to 276,414 in 1881.[69] Australian science benefited from this expansion and its accompanying high level of urbanization. As early as 1851 some 40 percent of the Australian population lived in cities, compared with 14 percent in the United States and 12 percent in Canada. Capital cities, such as Adelaide, Melbourne, and Sydney, contained one quarter of the total population in 1871.[70] A city like Adelaide, with its merchants and professional people, its concentration of people with ideas, its early self-government and its ideal of being a "model city of a model colony,"[71] provided an ideal setting for new institutions and services. Colonial legislatures could see the potential for science to contribute to economic expansion. Australia was developing market-minded farmers rather than self-sufficient peasants, and European farming practices were modified to suit conditions of regular dry seasons and soils of middling fertility.[72] The botanist who contributed to crop research typified the ideal of the "practical man"[73] in science in an era when there were high hopes that developments in science and technology would lead to progress and prosperity.

The efforts of naturalists were complemented by enthusiastic involvement in acclimatization activities and land exploration by government and general public alike.[74] Schomburgk's sturdiness, confidence, and administrative skills suited a situation where observation leading to action was prized much more highly than observation leading to theory. Well-educated and prosperous Adelaide businessmen and property owners already active in the support of institutions such as the library, the natural history museum, the university, scientific and cultural societies, and health and welfare bodies[75] recognized his skills as an administrator. Schomburgk could say in later life that he had become "the people's pet."[76] He enjoyed great personal success. Adelaide Botanic Garden became known as "Dr. Schomburgk's garden." He was called upon to give evidence to government committees on matters ranging from sanitation to rust in cereals and served on the Forest Board and the Central Agricultural Bureau. In 1884 a group of leading businessmen and politicians presented a portrait of the elderly director to the botanic garden, the inscription recording that the gift was in appreciation of the "zeal, energy and skill which he had devoted to rendering the Botanic Gardens an ornament to the City of Adelaide and the pride of the province of South Australia."

Overseas, Schomburgk's work was acknowledged by the Grand Duchy of Hesse and the kings of Italy and Prussia. Although these awards were earned on the basis of work in British Guiana rather than research in Australia, his plant material from Adelaide helped to complete collections in Britain and continental Europe. To Darwin, Huxley, or Hooker at the "center," he might have seemed peripheral. In the "center" of South Australia, however, he was pivotal. Botanists like Schomburgk provided a mechanism for European expansion. Supporting that scientific enterprise was a network of scientific and professional bodies and an active group of individuals. Schomburgk's career epitomizes both the demands made on scientists in settler society and the potential for Australian colonial scientists to make a contribution to an increasingly urban population. "Dr. Schomburgk's Garden" was in effect a cultural center at the periphery.

Notes

I would like to acknowledge the help of Professors Roy MacLeod, Fritz Rehbock, Austin Gough, and Ian Inkster and of Ms. Gaye Denny, Ms. Sara Maroske, and Mr. David Symon in the preparation of this article. Some material on which this essay is based has previously appeared in my article, "Richard Moritz Schomburgk: Second Director of the Adelaide Botanic Garden, 1865–1891," in *The German Experience of Australia 1833–1938,* ed. Ian Harmstorf and Peter Schwerdtweger (Adelaide: Australian Association of Humboldt Fellows, 1988), 69–92; and in " 'Picturesque scientific gardening': Developing Adelaide Botanic Garden 1865–1891," in *William Shakespeare's Adelaide, 1860–1930,* ed. Brian Dickey (Adelaide: Association of Professional Historians, 1992.)

1   *Charles Darwin's "Beagle" Diary,* ed. Richard Darwin Keynes (Cambridge: Cambridge University Press, 1988), 397.

2   Lucile Brockway, *Science and Colonial Expansion: The Role of the British Royal Botanic Gardens* (London: Academic Press, 1979).

3   J. C. Loudon, *An Encyclopaedia of Gardening,* rev. ed. (London: Longman, Rees, Orme, Brown, Green and Longman, 1835), 132, 224. The second son of the Schomburgk family, Otto, went to university at Halle, where he studied theology, and subsequently practiced medicine.

4   W. T. Stearn, "Humboldt and Bonpland's Travels in America," in *Humboldt, Bonpland, Kunth, and Tropical American Botany,* ed. W. T. Stearn (Stuttgart: Cramer, 1968), 45–47; and J. Rodway, "The 'Schomburgks' in British Guiana," *Timehri,* n.s., 3 (8) (June 1889): 1–29.

5   *Proceedings of the Royal Geographical Society* 9 (1864–1865): 208.

6   The "Schomburgk line" helped establish the boundary of British Guiana, Venezuela, and Brazil—and provided controversy for many years to come.

7   Richard Schomburgk, *Travels in British Guiana*, 2 vols., translation
     by W. Roth of *Reisen in Britisch Guiana*, 3 vols. (Leipzig, 1847–1848;
     Georgetown: Daily Chronicle Office, 1922), 1: Preface. Grisebach
     (professor at Göttingen, 1841–1879) published works on the West
     Indies and South America, regions with which Robert and Richard
     Schomburgk were associated. Grisebach, Ehrenberg, and Humboldt
     all had connections with Darwin. Ehrenberg was a source of informa-
     tion on infusoria (microscopic animal life) for Darwin in 1844–1846.

8   Ibid.

9   S. F. Cannon, *Science in Culture: The Early Victorian Period* (New
     York: Dawson and Science History Publications, 1978), 73–110. See
     also Von Hanno Beck, "Das Ziel der grossen Reise Alexander von
     Humboldts," in *Humboldt, Bonpland, Kunth, and Tropical American
     Botany*, ed. Stearn, 49, reprinted from *Erdkunde* 12 (1958): 42–50;
     L. Kellner, *Alexander von Humboldt* (London: Oxford University
     Press, 1963), 166. Valuable information on Humboldt has been sup-
     plied by Professor Kurt-R. Biermann, Berlin-Buch.

10   Malcolm Nicolson, "Alexander von Humboldt, Humboldtian Science
     and the Origins of the Study of Vegetation," *History of Science* 68
     (June 1987): 169.

11   Cannon, *Science in Culture*, 77.

12   Ibid., 171–178.

13   Pauline Payne, "Richard Moritz Schomburgk: Second Director of the
     Adelaide Botanic Garden 1865–1891," in *The German Experience of
     Australia 1833–1938*, ed. Harmstorf and Schwerdtfeger, 72.

14   Letter to Mrs. Manget, reprinted in *Timehri* 1 (2) (1882): 294–297.
     Although Raoul Middelmann's account in *Australian Dictionary of
     Biography* questions the political motivation for emigration, Schom-
     burgk's own account makes it clear that the brothers needed to make
     a life elsewhere, notwithstanding farewell gifts from the royal patrons
     (who may have been quietly relieved at the young men's departure).
     See *Australian Dictionary of Biography*, 13 vols. (Melbourne: Mel-
     bourne University Press, 1976), 6:91–92.

15   They included *Tiliqua occipitalis* (Peters, 1863), the Western blue-
     tongued lizard; *Tiliqua adelaidensis* (Peters, 1863), the common blue-
     tongued lizard; and *Lygosoma schomburgkii*, now *Ctenotus schom-
     burgkii* (Peters, 1863). See *Zoological Catalogue of Australia*, vol. 1,
     Amphibia and Reptilia (Canberra: Australian Government Printing
     Service, 1983), 157; and Michael Tyler in *Mitteilungen der Zoologis-
     ches Museum in Berlin* 61 (2) (1985): 335–337. Otto Schomburgk
     had worked with Peters on veterinary experiments into the effect of
     curare, specimens of which were brought back from British Guiana.

16   For example, the brothers continued to correspond with von Hum-
     boldt and von Buch after emigrating to Australia.

17   Adelaide Botanic Garden Archival Collection. Schomburgk's letter of
      application for the Adelaide Botanic Garden directorship, 11 August
      1865.

18   J. M. Powell, *Environmental Management in Australia, 1788–1914,
      Guardians, Improvers, and Profit: An Introductory Survey* (Mel-
      bourne: Oxford University Press, 1976), 45.

19   Ian Inkster and Jan Todd, "Support for Scientific Enterprise, 1850–
      1900," in *Australian Science in the Making*, ed. R. W. Home (Mel-
      bourne: Cambridge University Press, 1988), 102.

20   *Charles Darwin's "Beagle" Diary*, ed. Keynes, 413; F. W. and
      J. M. Nicholas, *Charles Darwin in Australia* (Sydney: Cambridge
      University Press, 1989), 102–103.

21   *Charles Darwin's "Beagle" Diary*, ed. Keynes, 397.

22   This was at a time when orchids were much prized in the gardening
      world, and in Britain £300 might be paid for a prized specimen. See
      Payne, "Richard Moritz Schomburgk," 74. The £300 was equivalent
      to six months of Schomburgk's final salary of £600 per annum.

23   *Adelaide Advertiser*, 2 October 1868; *Examiner and Daily Telegraph*,
      30 September 1868.

24   Payne, "Richard Moritz Schomburgk," 75, and " 'Picturesque Scien-
      tific Gardening,' " 130.

25   One of the finest Victorian glasshouses still extant in Australia and
      thought to be the only remaining example in the world of this type
      of German cast iron/wrought iron conservatory architecture of its
      period. See LeMessurier Architects, *The Palm House, Adelaide
      Botanic Garden: Draft Conservation Plan* (Adelaide, 1991).

26   Schomburgk's apprenticeship in the working world included not only
      his gardening apprenticeship but having to work in British Guiana
      under the leadership of an older brother who, while capable and effi-
      cient, was also subject to the "abominable tempers" described by the
      young artist Goodall, who accompanied the boundary expedition. See
      "Edward Goodall's Diary," *Journal of the British Guiana Museum
      and Zoo* 36 (1962): 55, 56. It is significant that the premier of New
      South Wales, Henry Parkes, wrote to Krefft, "You must learn to keep
      a cool temper & respectful bearing even to a gentleman who may be
      opposed to you"; quoted in G. P. Whitley and Marina Rutledge,
      "Johann Ludwig (Louis) Gerard Krefft," *Australian Dictionary of
      Biography*, vol. 5 (1851–1890), 45.

27   Schomburgk was actually offered the directorship of the Melbourne
      Gardens (which he refused) before Guilfoyle was appointed.

28   See W. Blunt, *In for a Penny, a Prospect of Kew Gardens: Their Flora,
      Fauna and Falballas* (London: Hamish Hamilton in association with
      the Tryon Gallery, 1978), 164–170.

29   A. Moyal, *"A Bright and Savage Land": Scientists in Colonial Australia* (Sydney: Collins, 1986), 144–147.

30   There is limited information on Schomburgk's correspondence, and no diaries or notebooks have survived.

31   R. Schomburgk, *Report on the Progress and Condition of the Botanic Garden during the Year 1875* (Adelaide: Government Printer, 1876), 9. (Report titles varied slightly from year to year and will be referred to subsequently as *Report.*)

32   D. R. Oldroyd, *Darwinian Impacts: An Introduction to the Darwinian Revolution* (Sydney: New South Wales University Press, 1980), 146.

33   And made room for twelve busts of famous scientists, including Newton, Linnaeus, Sir Joseph Banks, Humboldt, von Liebig, Faraday, Virchow, Leopold von Buch, C. L. Willdenow, Jöns Jacob Berzelius, Johannes Müller, and de Jussieu.

34   *Report of the Sanitation Commission,* South Australian Parliamentary Papers, no. 18 (Adelaide: Government Printer, 1876), 89–92. His eldest daughter, Antonia, died of typhoid fever, thought to have been caused by polluted water in the well near their house; but he survived an attack.

35   It was difficult to regenerate native pasture grasses once they were destroyed by pastoralists overstocking their runs. This was especially the case in semiarid areas when stock numbers were increased during years of fairly good rainfall.

36   E. Caldicott, Department of Geography, University of Adelaide, notes this figure was maintained in the next *Catalogue,* that of 1955. The most recent *Catalogue* (1988) shows 21 percent indigenous plants (personal communication).

37   N. B. Lewis, *A Hundred Years of State Forestry, 1875–1975* (Adelaide: Woods and Forests Department, 1975), 14; L. T. Carron, *A History of Forestry in Australia* (Canberra: Australian National University Press, 1985). After preliminary moves in 1876 and 1884, Victoria's state forestry service was not properly established until 1907. In New South Wales, limited resources were provided before 1909.

38   The universities of Sydney and Melbourne were established in 1850 and 1852, respectively. In 1871 the population of New South Wales was 502,000, that of Victoria, 730,000. See Wray Vamplew, ed., *Australians: Historical Statistics* (Sydney: Fairfax, Smith, and Weldon, 1987), 26.

39   C. R. Twidale et al., *Ideas and Endeavours: The Natural Sciences in South Australia* (Adelaide: Royal Society of South Australia, 1986), 169–170.

40   Quoted in Winsome Shepherd and Walter Cook, *The Botanic Gar-

den, Wellington: A New Zealand History, 1840–1987 (Wellington: Millwood Press, 1988), 10.

41   R. L. Burt and W. T. Williams, "Plant Introduction in Australia," in *Australian Science*, ed. Home, 252.

42   *Report . . . 1888*, 6.

43   For example, see R. Schomburgk, "Capabilities of the Various Districts of the Colony," in *Papers Read before the Chamber of Manufactures* (Adelaide: Government Printer, 1873), 103–104.; idem, *Wattle Farming* (Adelaide: Government Printer, 1884).

44   See E. Dunsdorfs, *The Australian Wheat-Growing Industry, 1788–1943* (Melbourne: Melbourne University Press, 1956), 121, 186; D. W. Meinig, *On the Margins of the Good Earth: The South Australian Wheat Frontier, 1869–1884* (London: Association of American Geographers, 1962), 22, 48, 204.

45   From Du Toits were selected three varieties that were to dominate the Australian wheat belt after 1900. See C. W. Wrigley and A. Rathjen, "Wheat Breeding in Australia," in *Plants and Man in Australia*, ed. D. J. Carr & S. G. M. Carr (Sydney: Academic Press, 1981), 96–100.

46   In Europe, intensive farming predominates, and there is a relatively small area under permanent grassland. In Australia, Asia, the Americas, and Africa, native and naturalized permanent pasture provide the bulk of food for grazing animals.

47   The list of 220 is based on species referred to in the *Catalogue of Plants in the Government Botanic Garden Adelaide* of 1871 and that of 1878 and in the annual *Reports*.

48   For example, he promoted *Dactylis glomerata* (European cocksfoot), an important agricultural grass, in the cooler, higher-rainfall areas. *Lolium perenne* (rye grass) is widely used in moister parts of South Australia. Its importance has increased in recent years with the introduction of Mediterranean ecotypes. Some are of minor significance, such as *Festuca pratensis* (meadow fescue) and *Lagurus ovatus*, widespread along the South Australian coastline. Lawn grasses include buffalo and couch.

49   *Report . . . 1887*, 5.

50   On one occasion a German compatriot living in a small township more than 300 kilometers from Adelaide sent Schomburgk an item about Japanese clover that had appeared in the *Rural Californian* newspaper; *Report . . . 1885*, 5. Another example is extracts from the *New Caledonia Moniteur* sent by an Adelaide resident; see *Report . . . 1878*, 4. See also *Report . . . 1886*, 6.

51   Preparation of material for exchange was time consuming, and Schomburgk's exchanges indicate that he spent more time on the task than did many of his fellow directors. Guilfoyle complained soon after his appointment at Melbourne Botanic Garden that "much time

is lost in selecting, packing, directing and forwarding plants from this garden to various institutions." See R. T. M. Pescott, *W. R. Guilfoyle, 1840–1912, Master of Landscaping* (Melbourne: Melbourne University Press, 1974), 81.

52   R. H. Pulleine, "The Botanical Colonization of the Adelaide Plain," *Proceedings of the Royal Geographical Society of Australasia, S.A. Branch*, 35 (1935): 46. It is not clear whether Pulleine was referring to South Australia specifically or to Australia generally.

53   Peter Kloot, "Studies in the Alien Flora of the Cereal Rotation Areas of South Australia" (Ph.D. dissertation, University of Adelaide, 1985), 7. Commercial nurserymen imported species they knew could sell and would have imported plant material for "repeat orders" of popular varieties. It is unlikely that they imported such a variety of species as Schomburgk. However, nurserymen worked closely with Adelaide Botanic Garden, and Schomburgk regarded cooperation with them as of great importance. This is apparent in surveys made by both Kloot and Robert Swinbourne of the catalogues of the leading South Australian nurserymen. Schomburgk also worked closely with local nurserymen on committees of the Royal Agricultural and Horticultural Society.

54   Brockway, *Science and Colonial Expansion*, 6.

55   This set of annual *Reports* is unique in colonial Australia, not only in respect to length but in the number of consecutive years for which the *Reports* are available.

56   Other botanic gardens in the British Isles, such as Edinburgh, Glasgow, Belfast, Dublin, and Birmingham, appear to be of very minor importance as far as direct exchanges with Adelaide Botanic Garden were concerned.

57   Schomburgk's first *Report* was for 1866, his last, for 1889.

58   Contact with Jamaica was helped by the interest and energy of Daniel (later Sir Daniel) Morris (1844–1933), director of public gardens, 1879–1886, who had served at the botanic gardens in Peradeniya, Ceylon, 1877–1879. He became an assistant director of Kew, 1886–1898.

59   Saharanpur had a considerable area planted with utilitarian vegetables and plants.

60   Some material would have come to the Sydney gardens from overseas institutions such as Kew, but records do not establish the details of transfer.

61   This is indicated by a letter from Schomburgk to Bentham in 1872. Royal Botanic Gardens, Kew, archival collection.

62   Today the botanic garden staff would view fifty packets from one institution in a year as a large amount.

63   P. I. Lapin, *Botanical Gardens of the U.S.S.R.* (Moscow: Kolos, 1984),
      31.

64   Dr. Rudolph Herman Christian Carel Scheffer (1844–1880) was
      director of the Buitenzorg (Bogor) Botanic Gardens, 1868–1880, and
      founded the Economic Garden and the Agricultural School. Dr.
      J. E. Teijmann was curator between 1831 and 1868. Frans A. Stafleu
      and Richard S. Cowan, *Taxonomic Literature: A Selective Guide to
      Botanical Publications and Collections with Dates, Commentaries,
      and Types,* 2d ed., 7 vols. (The Hague: Scheltema and Holkema,
      1979), 5:123, 201. See also James Veitch, *A Traveller's Notes: Notes
      of a Tour through India, Malaysia, Japan, Correa, the Australian Col-
      onies, and New Zealand during the Years 1891–1893* (London: pri-
      vately published by James Veitch and Sons, 1896), 83. Veitch (visiting
      in 1892) admired the "system and thoroughness" of the institution,
      noting that five of the staff were doctors of science.

65   Watts was renowned for supporting the applications of science to
      farming and of agricultural education and forestry. See Claribel R.
      Barnett, "Frederick Watts," *Dictionary of American Biography,* 20
      vols. (New York and London: Humphrey Milford–Oxford University
      Press, 1936), 19:556.

66   Members included Professor Phillipi in Chile, Dr. Regel of St. Peters-
      burg (both sources of plant material for Schomburgk), and Charles
      Martins of Montpellier. Outside Germany there were six each in Bel-
      gium, Holland, and Denmark; thirteen in France; eighteen in Great
      Britain (including Sir Joseph Hooker at Kew); eighteen in Italy; eleven
      in North America (including Asa Gray at Harvard and the director of
      the Smithsonian Institution); and four in Asia. *Leopoldina: Amtliches
      Organ der kaiserlichen Leopoldino-Carolinischen deutschen Akade-
      mie der Naturforscher* 22 (January 1886): 1–2, 6–19.

67   Georg von Neumayer, Ellery's predecessor at the Melbourne
      Observatory before his return to Germany, was also a member. Julius
      von Haast (1824–1887), born in Bonn, became government geologist
      in Canterbury, New Zealand. Robert Ellery (1827–1908), von
      Neumayer, and H. C. Russell, government astronomer of New
      South Wales, were key figures in the extension of colonial meteo-
      rology.

68   Schomburgk referred in his *Reports* to receiving information on
      phylloxera research done by the Department of Agriculture and Com-
      merce in Montpellier, by the French National School of Agriculture,
      and by Professor Hilgard in California. *Report . . . 1882,* 4.

69   Vamplew, ed., *Australians: Historical Statistics,* 26.

70   L. Frost, *Australian Cities in Comparative View* (Melbourne:
      MacPhee Gribble, 1990), 15–16.

71   Tony Denholm, "Adelaide: A Victorian Bastide?" in *The Origins of*

Australia's Capital Cities, ed. P. Statham (Melbourne: Cambridge University Press, 1989), 190.

72 Frost, *Australian Cities,* 9.

73 See discussion in Roy MacLeod, " 'The Practical Man': Myth and Metaphor in Anglo-Australian Science," *Australian Cultural History,* no. 8 (1989): 24–49.

74 Helen M. Cohn, "Some Foundations of Science in Victoria in the Decade after Separation" (M.A. thesis, University of Melbourne, 1990), 7.

75 Inkster and Todd provide an account of these bodies in *Australian Science,* ed. Home, 108–109.

76 Letter to Mrs. Manget, reprinted in *Timehri* 1 (2) (1882): 294–297.

PART THREE

Natives, Colonials, and Anthropologists

JANET BROWNE

9   Missionaries and the
    Human Mind
    Charles Darwin and Robert FitzRoy

Few historians need to be reminded that the last decade has seen an avalanche of publications, both popular and scholarly, about Charles Darwin, covering in minute detail the life and work of this important figure in the history of biology.[1] However, the briefest glance at some of this voluminous literature will reveal curious omissions and gaps in our understanding of Darwin and Darwinism. Despite considerable research, for example, little is known about Darwin's larger social opinions to set against the well-documented systems laid out by direct contemporaries like Herbert Spencer or Alfred Russel Wallace, or about how much Darwin followed the tangled course of late-Victorian politics in which his own name featured so prominently. Nor has the application of his biological views to scientific projects and in geographical locations far removed from the cozy world of Down House in Kent been investigated much beyond the confines of Europe and America: this new book on Darwin and Darwinism in the Pacific region provides a welcome indicator of fresh avenues for historical inquiry. Other noteworthy topics undoubtedly remain untouched by the literature.

Even the well-known history of the *Beagle* voyage (1831–1836) can, on reexamination, disclose several unexpected twists and turns. Much of the story has been built up inside a scaffolding of historical images—potent images of Darwin as a solitary traveler, a picturesque and romantic figure alone on the *Beagle*'s deck, moving through strange seas of thought, like Isaac Newton, or an intrepid Victorian hero, grappling with the facts of nature, his eyes freshly opened to phenomena that could only be explained by a great leap into the scientific unknown.

Without wishing to deny the importance of images such as these—for fame is constructed on convenient fictions that embody the deeply

263

held beliefs of contemporary life—they do tend to obscure other significant features that deserve at least some passing attention. In part the
problem arises because Darwin himself created many of these powerful pictures. His version of the *Beagle* voyage, at first given in letters
sent home to his family,[2] then repeated in his *Journal of Researches*[3]
and eventually in an autobiography written late in life,[4] was necessarily subject to the literary and scientific conventions of the time. These
texts tell us a great deal about the preconceived ideas of the brambles
and roses around the pathway to Victorian eminence, but not as much
as we would hope about Darwin's life as it happened.[5]

The purpose of this essay is to take one particular image found
in Darwin's *Autobiography*, one that is often repeated in modern
accounts of the *Beagle* voyage, and try to edge it toward voluntary
retirement by telling quite a different story about the combined experiences of Darwin and his captain, Robert FitzRoy, particularly in
relation to the work of missionaries in the Pacific and elsewhere. Darwin's and FitzRoy's travels in the Pacific area seem to have dramatically altered and intensified their idea of aboriginal peoples. En route,
the paper will touch loosely on some of the interrelations among
geography, nature, and exploration as they were expressed in Darwin's and FitzRoy's views about the natural condition of humanity in
the southern hemisphere.

Historians and biographers alike are accustomed to claim that Darwin and FitzRoy were intellectually and theoretically at odds during
the *Beagle* voyage, the one coming from a liberal, free-thinking, professional background, the other patently aristocratic and Tory in sentiment. Much is made of the idea that Darwin's early thoughts about
politics, slavery, aboriginal humanity, and perhaps even some of his
nascent views about the evolutionary origins of human beings, were
first formulated in opposition to those assumed to emanate from
FitzRoy. Certainly, Darwin did possess strong views about these
issues. Certainly, the two came from widely disparate backgrounds.
But it seems that Darwin, far from differing from his companion in
his philosophical beliefs, largely followed the same general principles
as FitzRoy. During the *Beagle* period there was little divergence of
views between them over the question of the human race. Together
they thought about the origins and possible geographical dispersal of
the aboriginal races encountered during the expedition and eagerly
discussed ethnographic questions relating to tribal habits, language,
and behavior. They were greatly interested in the social philosophies
of native races, intrigued by cultural differences in ideas of beauty and
commercial value.

Most of all, under FitzRoy's particular guidance, they concerned themselves with the concept of progress, the belief that savage races could be improved through the endeavors of missionaries. It is often forgotten that Darwin and FitzRoy composed a joint letter to be sent to a South African newspaper about the work of Anglican missionaries in Tahiti and New Zealand. Their letter was published in the *South African Christian Recorder* in 1836, just before the *Beagle* returned to England, and was both Darwin's and FitzRoy's first conscious attempt to publish a statement of their opinions.[6]

FitzRoy's First Voyage

FitzRoy was four years older than Darwin. Like him, he carried the name of a famous family, in his case the noble line of the dukes of Grafton, originally stemming from the illegitimate children of Charles II and Barbara Villiers. The Graftons owned vast estates and were, one and all, prominent Torys and members of the royal court.[7] FitzRoy was a snob about his relations, perhaps with some justification. In marked contrast to this state of affairs, there were no titles or obvious snobbery in the Darwin line. Indeed, the family shared a stout Midlands disdain for the trappings of aristocracy, resolutely believing people forfeited their freedom by courting titles and privileges. Though the Darwins moved freely among the lower reaches of the socially elect, they never wished to move higher: Erasmus Darwin, the doctor, poet, and enlightenment philosopher, rejected the opportunity of advancement by refusing to become physician to George III;[8] his son, Robert Waring Darwin (Charles Darwin's father), was wealthy and famous enough as a physician in Shrewsbury to make himself available for the same kind of offer if he had desired; none of Charles Darwin's four sisters sought an aristocratic marriage, and they were intelligently scathing—in full Jane Austen style—about those among their Shropshire circle who did. Politically, the family was Whig and staunchly reformist in their principles.

This stolid belief in the intrinsic worth of the landed professional classes, which was an important part of Charles Darwin's character and social background, dictated many of his later actions and governed the development of his views on human society. It made him different from FitzRoy in several ways, most notably on the slavery question—a difference that led to at least one violent clash of opinion on the *Beagle* voyage[9]—but their differences, in the main, were never completely insurmountable and often the subject of good-natured jokes.[10] Much later on, after FitzRoy's scandal-dogged parliamentary career and disastrous term of office as governor of New Zealand, his

and Darwin's political views diverged so drastically that there could
be no middle ground for discussion. On the *Beagle* there was much
more room to maneuver.

FitzRoy's interest in the work of Anglican missions had always
been pronounced. Before meeting Darwin, he had been almost wholly
concerned with the care of three aboriginals from Tierra del Fuego.
These Fuegians were brought back to England by FitzRoy after a pre-
vious expedition of the *Beagle* which, under the overall command of
Phillip Parker King, surveyed the South American coast in 1826.[11]
FitzRoy joined that first expedition in 1828, as a temporary captain,
when the original captain, Pringle Stokes, committed suicide.[12] Fitz-
Roy was sent off by King to complete Stokes' survey of Tierra del
Fuego.

There, while carefully charting the western approaches of the Beagle Channel, he was involved in an incident only too familiar to the
Admiralty at that time. A small boat, essential for surveying the shal-
lows, was stolen by a group of Fuegians from a camp site on shore.
Convinced that the boat was being hidden somewhere, FitzRoy took
several local hostages, all of whom escaped except one young girl and
two men who seemed quite content to remain on board (figure 9.1).[13]
Giving up his boat as a lost cause, FitzRoy conceived the grand plan
of taking the three Fuegians to England, educating them in the ways
of the Church of England, and bringing them back, at his own
expense if necessary, with sufficient equipment to set up a small mission. Never one to do things by halves, the captain flung himself into
the experiment with autocratic enthusiasm. Another Fuegian, a youth
from a neighboring tribe, was further purchased for a single mother-
of-pearl button, prompting the crew to call him Jemmy (James) Button, and FitzRoy began to compile a vocabulary of Fuegian words.
This study of local dialects was, in fact, the first to be carried out in
Tierra del Fuego.[14]

Yet when the *Beagle* returned to England in 1830, the Admiralty
would have nothing to do with FitzRoy's plans. Nor would the
Church Missionary Society interest itself in the project, for their eyes
were almost exclusively turned toward West Africa, the antipodes,
and the Far East.[15] The London Missionary Society, with its strong-
holds in the Pacific and South Africa, might perhaps have been a
better proposition if FitzRoy had approached it; but the Congregationalist tone of this society was altogether too low-church for
FitzRoy.[16] His aristocratic background and religious inclinations gave
him a natural affiliation with the former association which was, after
all, an official wing of the established Church of England. Unfortu-

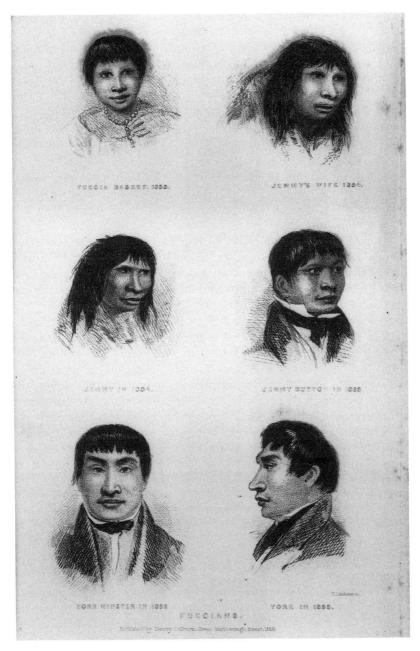

FUEGIA BASKET. 1833.   JEMMY'S WIFE 1834.

JEMMY IN 1834.   JEMMY BUTTON IN 1833.

YORK MINSTER IN 1832.   YORK IN 1833.

FUEGIANS.

Published by Henry Colburn, Great Marlborough Street, 1838.

9.1 The three Fuegians whom Captain Robert FitzRoy took to England in 1828 and returned to Tierra del Fuego in 1833 (drawings by R. FitzRoy). From R. FitzRoy and P. P. King, eds., *Narrative of the Voyage of the "Beagle,"* 1839. Courtesy of the Wellcome Institute Library, London.

nately, the Church Missionary Society was chronically short of funds and could only refer FitzRoy to a likely looking private arrangement with the National Society for Providing the Education of the Poor in the Principles of the Established Church. Through the latter, and by now in some personal desperation, FitzRoy arranged for his Fuegians to lodge with and be educated by an infant-school teacher while he investigated the possibility of hiring a merchant ship out of his own pocket. The death from smallpox of one of the four, despite FitzRoy's medical precautions, undoubtedly made a bad situation seem worse. At last, in December 1830, the remaining Fuegians were settled in their teacher's home in Walthamstow, at that time a small village just outside London.

During their ten-month stay in England, these Fuegians retreated into almost total oblivion except for one brilliant, highlighted episode when there came a summons for FitzRoy to show them to the king and queen.[17] The publicity, though unwelcome to FitzRoy, clearly did no harm. He was, by then, distractedly arranging to hire a ship privately on which he would accompany the Fuegians back to Tierra del Fuego for the completion of his evangelizing plans: as he said, he felt "too much bound to these natives" to send them back without him. And the Admiralty had let him down: "Finding to my great disappointment . . . that there was no intention to prosecute the survey," he wrote unhappily, "I naturally became anxious about the Fuegians." However, the royal audience brought his plight—and his project— into public view. A few weeks later, just as FitzRoy was about to finalize his private shipping contract to sail south, Francis Beaufort of the Hydrographer's Office—who took a professional interest in FitzRoy's surveying career—and FitzRoy's influential uncle, the fourth duke of Grafton, managed to persuade the Admiralty Lords that Captain King's survey of Tierra del Fuego was still incomplete.[18] Accordingly, at the end of July 1831, FitzRoy was commissioned to finish the work of the previous voyage and given special dispensation to take his Fuegians, a volunteer missionary, and equipment for a mission station with him.

The roundabout route by which the *Beagle* was brought back into active service did not, of course, mean that FitzRoy failed to take his official surveying duties seriously. An inspired surveyor—keen, meticulous, and talented—he was one of Beaufort's favored men in the task of bringing the Admiralty charts up to date and introducing scientific and technical advances to the civil wing of the navy. But the fate of the Fuegians and the desire to set them back in their community as the first step in a program of gradual Christianization of South America were intensely important personal commitments that have, for the most part, been ignored by historians.

The Mission at Woollya Sound

Darwin, naturally enough, did not fully recognize the visions dancing in FitzRoy's head until the *Beagle* arrived in Tierra del Fuego. Before then, with the comfortable liberalism of upper-class English Whigs, he found the polite manners and cheerful, open disposition of Jemmy Button and the other English-speaking Fuegians completely unremarkable. The shock of seeing genuine wild humans as the *Beagle* ran down the eastern tip of the continent never thereafter left him: "The sight of a naked savage in his native land is an event which can never be forgotten."[19] Naively, he recounted his surprise that Jemmy was almost another species of human compared with those who were his literal relatives. Of all Darwin's varied experiences, this sudden awareness of the acquired nature of civilization and the extraordinary contrast of human habits and lifestyles around the world moved him the most. "I could not have believed," he wrote, "how wide was the difference, between savage and civilized man. It is greater than between a wild and domesticated animal, in as much as in man there is a greater power of improvement."[20]

Like FitzRoy, he followed the fortunes of the new mission camp with great interest. FitzRoy had brought with him on the *Beagle* a volunteer missionary, a "catechist" as yet untrained. This young man, Richard Matthews, was independently financed by subscriptions raised by members of the Church Missionary Society and amply provided with stores and equipment given by well-meaning friends of FitzRoy's. Anglican missions were almost always run on practical lines, and this one was to be no exception. Matthews was to try to establish a tiny core of Christianity in Woollya Sound by showing Jemmy Button and his tribe how to farm the land and build permanent houses, giving the people clothes, promoting cleanliness, and, if all went well, teaching some basic English and the precepts of the Protestant church.

The practical, paternalistic bias in nineteenth-century missionary work is well known, and it is not necessary to go far into it here. "The Bible and the plough" was an expression so familiar at the time that it could easily have served as the motto for any of the numerous missionary societies proliferating in London and the other major cities of Britain. FitzRoy was evidently only one of many philanthropic aristocrats who sincerely believed that Christianity was indistinguishable from English civilization and that the inculcation of one would inevitably lead to the other: cultivation of the land would lead to cultivation of the mind; clothes inexorably brought savage races closer to Christ. The point of educating other races in English farming techniques, housing, language, and the words of the Bible was, it was thought, primarily to facilitate an advance in aboriginal culture toward northern values.

These unsophisticated, chauvinistic convictions, so widespread in early-nineteenth-century British life, were necessarily underpinned by a strong commitment to the idea of progress. Progress, as many historians have pointed out, was the theme of the age. In all areas of daily and national life, people had come to believe in a universal and inbuilt tendency toward, or potential for, improvement and felt it their responsibility to provide the means of similar improvements to groups who plainly could not effect it for themselves. For FitzRoy and Darwin, such a concept of progress was made real during the *Beagle* voyage in the most dramatic and obvious fashion imaginable. Three Fuegians were turned into virtual Europeans in the space of two years. Jemmy Button oiled his hair and used suspenders on his trousers; Fuegia Basket, now a young woman, wore a ring and bonnet given to her by Queen Adelaide. The ability to change like this, to advance from a state of savagery to the world of English manners, was to Darwin and FitzRoy, as it was to many others in pre-Victorian society, an outstandingly important feature of the human condition. "What a scale of improvement is comprehended between the faculties of a Fuegian savage & a Sir Isaac Newton," wrote Darwin in his diary with amazement.[21] A voyage such as the *Beagle's,* which took them to strange, remote countries inhabited by races scarcely known in Europe, brought the notion home with a vengeance.

Darwin's interest in the possibility of change in human beings has, naturally enough, been seen by several scholars as a crucial step toward his later conversion to evolutionary theory.[22] But Darwin's attention to the contrast between savage and civilized humanity may also have been in the same league as FitzRoy's progressive, philanthropic sentiments. To be impressed by the difference between two states of humanity is not quite the same thing as espousing evolution; to liken Fuegians to wild animals and their Anglicized relatives to domesticated species was a common enough response, made familiar through the ready naturalism of late-eighteenth-century travelogs and early ethnographic texts and brought into contemporary prominence in the 1820s and 1830s by the publication of James Cowles Prichard's work on the primitive history of humankind.[23] The difference was one of degree, epitomized by the Enlightenment and turn-of-the-century conviction that human beings were all brothers and sisters under the skin.[24]

What Darwin's response does seem to indicate is that he, like FitzRoy, believed in a single origin for the human race. In this belief, the two men followed Prichard in thought if not always in actual name. Prichard considered that human beings had spread out from a single, biblical point of creation. Wherever different groups had come to rest, they had adapted and changed to accommodate themselves to the new conditions, particularly in cultural terms. Though Prichard took care to dissociate himself from any obvious environmental determinism, his readers tended to stress this aspect of the scheme, elaborating on the older eighteenth-century view that human beings were closely attuned to their geographical situation.

Most important, Prichard's followers, with FitzRoy among them, felt that the minds and social customs of individual races were also part of an environmentally based system: the human mind was a malleable instrument that absorbed and expressed the surrounding geography and climatic conditions in the sense that fertile, pleasant regions would foster social virtue and intellectual development, whereas an inhospitable, barren place led to nothing but savagery. Bracing mountains had produced the austere race of Scots, the desert its Nubians, Polynesia its untutored children of nature. For FitzRoy, the harsh desolation of Tierra del Fuego could create only barbarity in its inhabitants—a view he spelled out in his private notes and later in the *Narrative* of the *Beagle* expedition.[25]

In this way, the mental and moral characteristics of aboriginals were correlated to the natural world and were held to be only ephemeral: if the conditions changed, as FitzRoy believed he had demonstrated with the three Anglicized Fuegians, the human mind improved. Other advances in health, physique, and manners would also come in due course as the advantages of education became absorbed. Missionaries were therefore not just trying to claim or reclaim lost souls for the church. Under this wider environmentalist scheme, they were seen as front-line agents in a scientifically and biblically harmonized program of amelioration and progress. Geography and the quality of natural resources were here closely intermingled with scientific questions relating to the races of humankind and ideas about the moral realm, a powerful mixture of concepts that intoxicated thinkers from all walks of life in early-nineteenth-century Britain. Education, philanthropy, science, and religion worked together to improve the conditions and minds of human beings. The future condition of humanity was at stake.

The Mission's Collapse

Unfortunately, FitzRoy's South American project did not live up to these elevated ideals. Matthews soon wanted to return to the *Beagle*. He was intimidated by what he called a "large number of Fuegians" who flooded into the area, stealing mission property and making him fear for his life with "unconcealed signs of dislike." The settlement, he felt, had to be abandoned before he was killed. The English-speaking Fuegians had returned to their families and did not wish to rejoin the ship. Bitterly disappointed by this unexpected turn of events, FitzRoy took Matthews back on board and left the remainder to their fate. He nevertheless hoped that some benefit, however slight, might result from the mingling of Jemmy Button and the others with their people. The first hesitant step toward civilization had been made, he dejectedly claimed.

The failure of FitzRoy's attempts to set up a mission should not be allowed, however, to eclipse the magnitude of the task he had set himself. These areas of South America were not brought into the Christian fold until the closing years of the nineteenth century, and South America as a whole was generally considered, by Anglicans at least, to be the "neglected continent." Fuegians were genuine primitives in that they had few of the traditional skills of other South American or Pacific peoples, as in, for example, the construction of canoes or the making of shelters. Although they had long had the use of fire (Tierra del Fuego was so named by Magellan from the multitude of fires seen on the islands), the Fuegians did not cook any food and despised the hot offerings made them by *Beagle* crewmen. They were virtually unclothed and unhoused, with no obvious tribal structure. Moreover, both Darwin and FitzRoy were horrified (if gullible) to hear that Fuegians were perhaps occasional cannibals. Various tribal elders told them gruesome stories, translated by Jemmy Button, about the disposal of unwanted children and old women.[26]

Subsequent missionary activity in the area tended only to confirm the impression of barbarism. During the 1850s two expeditions sponsored by a newly established London-based "Patagonian Mission" ended in disaster, the first (under Allen Gardiner) resulting in the entire party's starving to death, the second (under Captain Parker Snow) being abruptly terminated by the murder of all except one of the missionaries and their helpers.[27] FitzRoy's wistful hope that Jemmy Button's children would be prompted to kind deeds by the "traditions they will have heard of men of other lands" remained unfulfilled.

Before leaving Tierra del Fuego for other waters, the *Beagle* returned once or twice to Jemmy's cove in Woollya Sound and found Jemmy well, though naked and thinner, and still capable of speaking English and using a knife and fork.[28] Reports from sealers and whalers in the district during the next decade or two indicated that he and Fuegia Basket were occasionally seen. Jemmy went on to help with the establishment of the ill-fated Patagonian missions. He lived, it is thought, until 1863.[29]

Tahiti

After the *Beagle* left America in 1835, the supreme interest for FitzRoy and Darwin lay in Tahiti. Both men had been reading the travels of Otto von Kotzebue, who last visited Tahiti in 1824, eleven years before the arrival of the *Beagle*. But in his book *A New Voyage round the World* (1830), Kotzebue came down heavily against the Society Islands missionaries. He accused them of narrowness of outlook, of having killed the natural, innocent gaiety of the Tahitians, of an unscrupulous thirst for power, and even of having been the direct cause of internecine strife in the islands.[30] Furthermore, he singled out the rashness and impropriety of Britain in having allowed the administration of church activities to fall into the hands of what he called uneducated sailors, a direct hit at the London Missionary Society's policy of deploying "mechanic" missionaries who were not in divine orders or university educated.[31]

FitzRoy and Darwin had a more generous opinion of Charles Wilson, who ran the mission at Matavai—with the help of George Pritchard and Henry Nott, the Bible translator—from 1801. The London Missionary Society had been involved with the Society Islands since the days of its foundation in 1795 and took considerable pride in the way their men, mechanics or no, had overcome a succession of difficulties.[32] Yet Kotzebue claimed the Tahitians had become a gloomy race and lived in fear of the English.

Instead of discontent, the *Beagle* travelers found, to all appearances, a happy, merry throng. They were united in outrage at Kotzebue's apparently groundless attacks. In particular, FitzRoy, who had been commissioned to exact payment of a fine from the new queen of the Society Islands, found both the queen and her chiefs politely at ease with the missionaries and willing to pay their dues to the British government. The captain subsequently invited Queen Pomare II to a dinner party on board the *Beagle*. He and Darwin independently recorded their impression that her behavior and that of her party were "extremely correct: their habits and manners perfectly inoffensive." Indeed, the group had absorbed evangelical preachings so completely that they were disapprovingly puzzled by the "merry comic

songs" sung for them by the sailors. Some hastily devised "grave performances" were greeted with more approbation.[33]

FitzRoy plainly believed that a mission education provided the
queen and her elders with European manners suited to their social
standing. Ordinary Tahitians, on the other hand, were perceived as
cheerful, unruly children. FitzRoy described—with amusement—how
difficult it was to make chronometric measurements for surveying
purposes while crowds of interested spectators jostled to look inside
his instrument tent. Darwin, on his part, was full of admiration for
the statuesque beauty of Tahitian men, their firm observation of Sunday rituals, the prayers they offered up during an expedition into the
interior. He concluded that Kotzebue's criticism of the missionaries'
rule was unjustified, probably stimulated by disappointment that the
celebrated licentiousness of Tahitian women was no longer evident. It
is useless to argue against such men, he asserted. "They expect the
Missionaries to effect what the very Apostles failed to do."[34]

Full of romanticized images of noble savages and of a stable, hierarchical, pastoral England, Darwin and FitzRoy were enchanted by
what they found. The missionaries had succeeded in turning the settlement of Matavai into something like a country village in Shropshire. The hymn singing was "decidedly pretty," the church "filled to
excess by tidy clean people of all ages & sexes." FitzRoy even compared two chiefs of inferior rank with "respectable English farmers."[35] "A more orderly, quiet inoffensive community I have not seen
in any other part of the world," he further wrote.[36] English moral
values and an approximation toward English social structure were
evidently exactly what mission work was expected to achieve. The
efforts of several worthy missionaries within an environment ideal for
fostering self-improvement had brought these people to the brink of
civilization. Tahiti was to them a success story. Seeing such success
reinforced FitzRoy's belief that his attempts in Tierra del Fuego were
justifiable.

The captain's unthinking assumption that civilization meant an ide-
alized form of British behavior was echoed by Darwin in his diary.
Nor were these joint assumptions dented by the next port of call. In
New Zealand, FitzRoy had few official responsibilities to carry out,
and he and Darwin were free to travel inland together to see how the
missions were working.

New Zealand and the Cape Colony

New Zealand was the religious property, so to speak, of the
Church Missionary Society. Whereas the London Missionary Society,

the senior body, and the Wesleyan Missionary Society dominated missionary activity in the South Pacific from Tahiti westward to Fiji,[37] the Church of England, by contrast, was confined to a single diocese—the diocese of Australia, which embraced the rudimentary British colonies of New South Wales and New Zealand. The *Beagle,* however, arrived in the area several years before George Augustus Selwyn was sent out to become the first primate of New Zealand. Before that time, there were only one or two, admittedly flourishing, missions in the North Island, around the Bay of Islands, dating from Christmas Day 1814, when the Reverend Samuel Marsden preached the first sermon that a tattooed Maori assembly had ever heard.[38] Once again, the two travelers read about the missions before arriving, this time in Augustus Earle's book *A Narrative of Nine Months Residence in New Zealand* (1832). Since Earle was briefly employed as the *Beagle*'s artist from 1831 to 1832, his remarks were especially pertinent. But he too, like Kotzebue, fiercely attacked the missionaries. And once again, Darwin and FitzRoy were indignant. The situation seemed to them utterly different.

The first and largest settlement was at Paihai. Several hundred Europeans lived there. Darwin found the settlement a pleasing reminder of home, with English garden flowers climbing over the verandahs and all the Maori huts discretely sited on the outskirts of town.[39] Yet walking over to pay a visit to Kororarika, he and FitzRoy were shocked to find English people living in squalor as filthy as that of the Maoris. These poor white émigrés were perceived by them to be drunkards, addicted to all kinds of vice. A great number were the very refuse of society, complained Darwin.[40] Proper laws, he said, were quite unknown. Furthermore, by introducing the local inhabitants to drink, money, and what FitzRoy called "the most abandoned, profligate habits," this unruly element in the settlers' community (escaped convicts for the most part) wiped out many of the successes they believed attributable to Christian improvement.

The travelers' equilibrium was restored by an expedition to Waimate, where the missionaries William Williams, brother of the more famous Henry, and Richard Davis lived in an English-style farming community. "I looked at it as a fragment of Old England," wrote FitzRoy complacently, "small indeed, but apparently genuine."[41] Here FitzRoy finally said goodbye to his *Beagle* missionary, Richard Matthews, whose brother had lived in Waimate for some years. The men stationed here were gratifyingly interested to hear of FitzRoy's work among the Fuegians and insisted that, instead of courting failure, he had shown remarkable enterprise.[42] FitzRoy was deeply touched and from then on a close and admiring friend of the New Zealand missions, a relationship that was insignificant in 1835 but that put him in an awkward position when he later returned as governor and was faced with the land crisis brought about by the infamous Treaty of Waitangi. FitzRoy's wish to satisfy all the parties concerned led him to bankrupt the country with two bloody massacres along the way—the settlement of Kororarika among them.[43]

As recounted by FitzRoy during this first visit, Williams and the other professionals freely acknowledged that the missionary system in New Zealand needed different procedures from those already established in Tahiti, Sierra Leone, and South Africa. The Maoris, they said, were hard to handle and accustomed to a fierce native government. Progress was slow and uncertain. FitzRoy was nevertheless impressed to find English tea served in the midst of men who had once eaten human flesh. He and Darwin took their leave of these workers in the field full of admiration at the courage and humility with which they faced the difficult, dangerous, thankless tasks of the church.

But it was the Cape Colony that really set FitzRoy and Darwin thinking about the adversities suffered by missionaries in New Zealand. Missionaries at the Cape, they found, with John Philips, the prominent political activist at their head, seemed similarly besieged from every quarter. They were charged with exacerbating racial conflict between Dutch and British settlers and the Bantus; criticized for their lack of secular control over supposed converts; and accused of lining their own pockets by taking advantage of a close relationship with aborigines to buy land at cheap prices and then sell it at a profit to Europeans. Much of the blame for the turmoil of the 1830s—the economic hardship following on from slave emancipation in 1833, the Sixth Frontier War of 1834, the Great Trek of 1835, even the disturbances that accompanied legislation detailing the civil rights of Hottentots—was laid at the doors of the African mission houses.[44]

Fresh from their South Pacific and American experiences, FitzRoy and Darwin felt the criticism was unwarranted. In June 1836, after a short stay in Cape Town, they composed "a letter, containing remarks on the moral state of Tahiti, New Zealand, &c," a brief notice describing the favorable impressions they had received of mission activity in New Zealand and Tahiti.[45] They had seen, they said, missionaries working hard under difficult conditions with never a thought for self-advancement. Charles Wilson of Tahiti, they reported, had the "sincere and naturally impressive manner of a kind-hearted honest man earnestly performing his duties." The Williams family in Waimate, New Zealand, had "superior characters," an "air of honesty and that outward tranquillity which is the result of a clear conscience and inward peace." Credit should be given, they thought, for what had been achieved against almost insuperable odds. Moreover, added Darwin darkly, repeating a thought that FitzRoy earlier expressed in relation to Tierra del Fuego and not far removed from their own nautical circumstances, some shipwrecked sailor of the future would no doubt be thankful for even the slightest moral improvement in races renowned for murderous behavior. Who could deny dutiful servants of God and the promoters of English moral values the opportunity of buying a smallholding for the maintenance of their families? There is land enough for everyone, they declaimed; must a missionary seek out only the worst?

Conclusion

Even though Darwin and FitzRoy's joint paper was only a letter to a minor colonial newspaper, itself established just one year previously and directed exclusively to the evangelical community, it reveals that a remarkable accord had built up between the two men during the course of the voyage. Despite arguments at times and a quiet irritability with each other that increased as the voyage wore on, they felt pretty much the same way about the missionaries they met and wanted the merits of such men to be more widely recognized.

Apart from this, their paper also represented the culmination of a set of discussions, experiences, disappointments, excitements, and developing opinions they had shared. Their interest in mission activity was, to be sure, only one aspect of a long and predominantly friendly association on board the *Beagle*. Yet the interest was hardly negligible. It brought to a focus important issues concerning human origins, questions about the relationship of a human being with the natural environment, and moral themes of progress and improvement. By wishing to give credit to missionaries for taking the first and hardest steps in spreading European values throughout the world, they were subscribing to a particular view of humanity—a view clearly based on the concepts of unity and a capacity for cultural progress through education and the alleviation of inhibiting or unpropitious circumstances. Darwin's opinions reflected the emancipationist, liberal views of his father and grandfather before him. FitzRoy came to the same conclusions for rather different reasons. FitzRoy—like his father and grandfather before him—believed in the high-Tory, Christian ethic in which paternalism provided the motive for supplying direct economic and practical aid to primitive societies. United nonetheless by their mutual concern for these aboriginal groups and steeped in the same kind of European cultural chauvinism, Darwin and FitzRoy met on the common ground of British philanthropy at a time when optimism and high-minded ideals had not yet been completely submerged by the cruel exploitations of the high-Victorian era.

Ideas like these had become important to FitzRoy and Darwin only during the *Beagle*'s voyages. Before they sailed, neither had any practical knowledge of races other than their own. What at first was a solely theoretical interest, based on personal and emotional considerations drawn from their individual family backgrounds and a wide spectrum of British upper-class politics, was thus given objective reality as they traveled round the world. By the time they reached Cape Town in 1836, both FitzRoy and Darwin truly believed in progress and the unity of the human race.

Of course, these beliefs were not new to the nineteenth century. The point that needs stressing here, rather, is that the act of traveling through the southern hemisphere; working in and around Tierra del Fuego; and visiting New Zealand, Tahiti, and other Pacific islands made previously abstract thoughts concrete for these two men. Without the opportunities offered by the *Beagle* expedition, they could not have felt the full force of contemporary opinion in the way they did. And though their future lives diverged dramatically—FitzRoy becoming cemented into his Tory paternalism and Darwin moving in other far more heterodox directions—both men continued, each in his own way, to call on concepts relating to humankind that had taken shape on the voyage. Missionaries and the human mind—the hope of civilizing the uncivilized, in the terminology of the time—were subjects that had drawn them together and affected them more deeply than we are accustomed to acknowledge.

Notes

1   A notable benchmark in Darwin studies is the collection of papers issued to commemorate the centenary of Darwin's death: see David Kohn, ed., *The Darwinian Heritage* (Princeton: Princeton University Press, 1985).

2   *The Correspondence of Charles Darwin,* ed. Frederick Burkhardt and Sydney Smith, 10 vols. (Cambridge: Cambridge University Press, 1985–1994), vol. 1, covering the years 1821–1836.

3   Charles Darwin, *Journal of Researches into the Geology and Natural History of the Various Countries visited by H.M.S. "Beagle"* (London, 1839), reprinted with an introduction by Janet Browne and Michael Neve, eds., *Voyage of the "Beagle": Charles Darwin's "Journal of Researches"* (Harmondsworth: Penguin Books, 1989).

4   *The Autobiography of Charles Darwin, 1809–1882, with Original Omissions Restored,* ed. Nora Barlow (London: Collins, 1958).

5   See, particularly, Anthony O. J. Cockshut, *The Art of Autobiography in Nineteenth- and Twentieth-Century England* (New Haven: Yale University Press, 1984); Avron Fleishman, *Figures of Autobiography: The Language of Self-writing in Victorian and Modern England* (Berkeley and London: University of California Press, 1983); George P. Landow, ed., *Approaches to Victorian Autobiography* (Athens, Ohio: Ohio University Press, 1979); Linda H. Peterson, *Victorian Autobiography: The Tradition of Self-interpretation* (New Haven: Yale University Press, 1986), 156–165. See also Janet Browne, "The Charles Darwin–Joseph Hooker Correspondence: An Analysis of Manuscript Resources and Their Use in Biography,"*Journal of the Society for the Bibliography of Natural History* 8 (1978): 351–366.

6   Robert FitzRoy and Charles Darwin, "A Letter, containing Remarks on the Moral State of Tahiti, New Zealand, &c." *South African Christian Recorder* 2 (1836): 221–238, reprinted in *The Collected Papers of Charles Darwin,* ed. Paul H. Barrett, 2 vols. (Chicago and London: University of Chicago Press, 1977), 1: 19–38. Strictly speaking, Darwin had been involved with two earlier papers, but these had been composed without his knowledge from extracts from his *Beagle* letters. John Stevens Henslow, Darwin's mentor at Cambridge University, compiled a paper to read at a meeting of the Cambridge Philosophical Society in November 1835. This was subsequently privately printed and distributed among Henslow's and Darwin's friends (see *Correspondence,* ed. Burkhardt and Smith, 1: 239 et seq.). Another shorter paper was read at a meeting of the Geological Society of London, also in November 1835. The latter paper was not published until 1838; see *Collected Papers,* ed. Barrett, 1: 3–19. The letter to the *South African Christian Recorder* was the first piece of work deliberately to be composed and forwarded for publication by Darwin.

7   Harold Edward Leslie Mellersh, *FitzRoy of the Beagle* (London: Rupert Hart-Davis, 1968).

8   Desmond King-Hele, *Erasmus Darwin* (London: Macmillan, 1963), 32.

9   *Autobiography,* ed. Barlow, 73–74.

10   See, for example, a letter from Darwin to FitzRoy, 6 October 1836, just after Darwin had returned home from the *Beagle* voyage, in which Darwin teased FitzRoy that even though his father, Robert Waring Darwin, had come round to the Tory view far enough to have a picture of George IV in his sitting room, Darwin's own views are as "wisely founded as ever they were" (*Correspondence,* ed. Burkhardt and Smith, 1: 507).

11   Robert FitzRoy, ed., *Narrative of the Surveying Voyages of H.M.S.*

"Adventure" and "Beagle" between the Years 1826 and 1836, 4 vols. (London: H. Colburn, 1839), vol. 1; Mellersh, *FitzRoy*, 30–49.

12   FitzRoy, ed., *Narrative*, 1: xiv, 188; Mellersh, *FitzRoy*, 30–49.

13   FitzRoy, ed., *Narrative*, 1: 386–416, 444, 458.

14   Ibid., Appendix, 135–136.

15   C. Hole, *The Early History of the Church Missionary Society* (London, 1896), and Eugene Stock, *The History of the Church Missionary Society: Its Environment, Its Men and Its Work*, 2 vols. (London, 1899).

16   Richard Lovett, *The History of the London Missionary Society, 1795–1895*, 2 vols. (London: H. Frowde, 1899).

17   FitzRoy, ed., *Narrative*, 2:12–13. My attempts to build a dossier on the Fuegians during their residence in England have been interestingly unsuccessful.

18   Ibid., 2: 6–18. See also Alfred Friendly, *Beaufort of the Admiralty: The Life of Sir Francis Beaufort, 1774–1857* (London: Hutchinson, 1977), 144–146; Mellersh, *FitzRoy*, 58–60.

19   *Autobiography*, ed. Barlow, 80.

20   *Voyage of the "Beagle,"* ed. Browne and Neve, 172.

21   *Charles Darwin's "Beagle" Diary*, ed. Richard Darwin Keynes (Cambridge: Cambridge University Press, 1988), 223.

22   Sandra Herbert, "The Place of Man in the Development of Darwin's Theory of Transmutation," *Journal of the History of Biology* 7 (1974): 217–258; 10 (1977): 155–227. See also Howard E. Gruber, *Darwin on Man: A Psychological Study of Scientific Creativity. Together with Darwin's Early and Unpublished Notebooks Transcribed and Annotated by Paul H. Barrett* (London: Wildwood House, 1974).

23   James Cowles Prichard, *Researches into the Physical History of Mankind* (London, 1813), edited with an introductory essay by George W. Stocking (Chicago and London: University of Chicago Press, 1973).

24   See John C. Greene, *The Death of Adam: Evolution and Its Impact on Western Thought* (Ames: Iowa State University Press, 1959), and George Stocking, *Victorian Anthropology* (New York: Free Press; London: Collier Macmillan, 1989). For a resume of abolitionist literature see Ronald Rainger, "Philanthropy and Science in the 1830's: The British and Foreign Aborigines' Protection Society," *Man*, n.s., 15 (1980): 702–717.

25   FitzRoy, ed., *Narrative*, 2: 129–143, 175–201. In the penultimate chapter of this book, FitzRoy discussed the biblical origins and subsequent dispersal of human beings (Ibid., 641–656).

26   The point about cannibalism has been controverted by E. L. Bridges, *Uttermost Part of the Earth* (London: Hodder and Stoughton, 1948), 33–34. However, FitzRoy reported it in good faith in FitzRoy,

ed., *Narrative*, 2: 189. Darwin repeated the stories in *Journal of Researches*, 2d ed. (London: John Murray, 1845), 214; see Darwin, *The Voyage of the "Beagle"* (London: Dent, 1959), 204.

27   Mellersh, *FitzRoy*, 236–255.

28   FitzRoy, ed., *Narrative*, 2: 323–327; Mellersh, *FitzRoy*, 109.

29   Mellersh, *FitzRoy*, 295.

30   Otto von Kotzebue, *A New Voyage round the World in the Years 1823, 1824, 1825, and 1826* (London, 1830). William Ellis, the famous South Sea islands missionary, rebuffed Kotzebue's claims in *A Vindication of the South Seas Missions from the Misrepresentations of Otto von Kotzebue* (London, 1831). Both Kotzebue's *Voyage* and Ellis's earlier work (*Polynesian Researches, during a Residence of Nearly Six Years on the South Sea Islands* [London, 1829]) were in the *Beagle* library (see *Correspondence*, ed. Burkhardt and Smith, 1: 560, 561).

31   Niel Gunson, *Messengers of Grace: Evangelical Missionaries in the South Seas, 1797–1860* (Oxford and Melbourne: Oxford University Press, 1978), 31–41.

32   Lovett, *London Missionary Society*, 1: 117–325.

33   FitzRoy, ed., *Narrative*, 2: 544–545.

34   *Diary*, ed. Keynes, 377.

35   FitzRoy, ed., *Narrative*, 2: 511.

36   *Collected Papers*, ed. Barrett, 1: 23.

37   Gunson, *Messengers of Grace*; David Hilliard, *God's Gentlemen: A History of the Melanesian Mission, 1849–1942* (St. Lucia: University of Queensland Press, 1978). For the earliest activity of the London Missionary Society in the area, see James Wilson, *A Missionary Voyage to the Southern Pacific Ocean, 1776–1798,* introduced by Irmgard Moschner (New York, Washington, and London: Praeger, 1980).

38   Stock, *Church Missionary Society*, 1: 203–215. See also J. M. R. Owens, *Prophets in the Wilderness: The Wesleyan Mission to New Zealand, 1819–1827* (Oxford and Auckland: Oxford University Press and Auckland University Press, 1974), and Eric Ramsden, *Marsden and the Missions: Prelude to Waitangi* (Sydney: Angus and Robertson, 1936).

39   *Diary*, ed. Keynes, 381–387.

40   Ibid., 395.

41   FitzRoy, ed., *Narrative*, 2: 601.

42   Ibid., 2: 601, 605; Mellersh, *FitzRoy*, 164.

43   Mellersh, *FitzRoy*, 197–235. FitzRoy attempted to justify his actions in a book published after his ignominious return. See Robert FitzRoy, *Remarks on New Zealand in 1846* (London, 1846).

44   There are many texts on mission activity in the Cape Colony: see
      particularly C. P. Groves, *The Planting of Christianity in Africa* (Lon-
      don: Butterworth, 1948–1958), vol. 1. Other useful sources are
      D. K. Clinton, *The South-African Melting-pot: A Vindication of Mis-
      sionary Policy, 1799–1836* (London: Longmans, Green, 1937), and
      Andrew Ross, *John Philip (1775–1851): Missions, Race, and Politics
      in South Africa* (Aberdeen: Aberdeen University Press, 1986). The
      case for the missionaries was put in R. Godlonton, *Case of the Colo-
      nists of the Eastern Province of the Cape of Good Hope, in Reference
      to the Kaffir Wars of 1835–1836 and 1846* (Grahamstown, 1846).
      Events of the 1840s and 1850s are described in Richard Grove,
      "Scottish Missionaries, Evangelical Discourses, and the Origins of
      Conservation Thinking in Southern Africa, 1820–1900," *Journal
      of Southern African Studies* 15 (1989): 163–187. See also Rainger,
      "Philanthropy and Science."

45   *Collected Papers,* ed. Barrett, 1: 19–38.

NIEL GUNSON

10 British Missionaries and Their Contribution to Science in the Pacific Islands

> ... Darwin's self conversed with men like these
> While at Tahiti's kindred isle he stayed.
> There he explored the bush-clad mountains high,
> What time Charles Wilson kept glad open house
> For strangers from the homeland distant far;
> Nor knew the fame his eager guest would win
> When he that book should write which men have
> hailed Chief book of all the teeming century!
> —G. B. STALLWORTHY, "Darwin at Tahiti,"
> *Legends of Samoa*

Protestant missionaries living in the Pacific Islands at the time of Charles Darwin's visit in 1835–1836 derived from two distinct traditions in their relation to scientific endeavors. The more recent tradition, that of the Evangelical Revival, emphasized the saving nature of the Christian gospel over the role of education. If the lives of gardeners and carpenters could be changed by reading the Bible, missionaries could be drawn from this class of "godly mechanics."[1] Such missionaries needed only the most basic practical training, and their minds might well be closed to secular learning. In contrast, many of the early founders and supporters of missions had been educated at Dissenting academies, which carried on the tradition of providing a well-disciplined secular education as well as theological training.[2] This essay looks at the attitudes to science of the first Protestant missionaries in the Pacific, then explores their relationship with visiting naturalists, and finally assesses the contribution of the later scientifically aware missionaries after the publication of Darwin's *Origin of Species*.

Attitudes to Science in the Missionary Background

Throughout the eighteenth century the most progressive Dissenting academies were the serious rivals of the universities, producing such distinguished natural philosophers as John Eames, F.R.S., and Joseph Priestley.[3] When the Missionary Society (later, London Missionary Society) was founded in 1795 there was a serious debate between the Methodist (i.e., Evangelical) party and the Presbyterian (i.e., traditional Dissenting) party regarding missionary education.[4] The outcome was a compromise. All missionaries regarded as "godly mechanics" were required to attend Gosport Academy for a period of intensive training while a select few were prepared for the ministry as regular theological students.

While the course at Gosport under the conservative "Presbyterian" principal, Dr. David Bogue, was much more theological in orientation than, for instance, that at Warrington, where Priestley had studied, the strict academic discipline was seen as suitable training for future self-improvement. The outlines of the 386 lectures the students were expected to copy and expand included not only strictly theological subjects but also metaphysics and logic, the history of philosophy, and the general principles of astronomy.[5] Perhaps the most interesting lectures were those designed for students entering the seminary and those leaving it.[6]

Those leaving were told that "six hours application to study in a day is little for the first seven years, eight hours moderate, ten hours good work, twelve hours hard study."[7] They were advised to apply their time to languages (Latin, Greek, Hebrew, and French) and the sciences (Logic, Moral Philosophy, Natural Philosophy, Mathematics, and the General Principles of Law), belles lettres, and history.[8] Although other branches of inquiry such as natural history were not specified, it was assumed that some individual choice would prevail. Of course missionaries in the field would have less time for self-improvement than ministers at home, but it was still expected that a portion of each day be given over to study.

As well as being taught to continue their studies on a broader base after completing their courses, missionary candidates were early exposed to the Evangelical periodicals of the day. These were largely designed to broaden the secular as well as sacred knowledge of the laity: natural history, astronomy, and geography featured largely in them. Thus, the *Youth's Magazine or Evangelical Miscellany* for 1816 listed nine eclipses of the sun—"the quantity of which exceeds nine digits, or three quarters of the solar disk"—that would be visible in Great Britain for the remainder of the century.[9] Of Darwinian relevance was the great attention paid to the fossils of prehistoric creatures, which appeared in all their skeletal magnificence even in the *Missionary Sketches.*[10]

In the decade 1830–1840 the *Youth's Magazine* published a series of articles, fully illustrated, on such extinct species as the Megatherium, the Great Mastodon, the Arctic Elephant, the Dinotherium, and the Anoplotherium.[11] While the articles were partly designed to show "how wisely the Creator has always fitted his creatures to the circumstances in which they were to be placed,"[12] the language comes close to suggesting some measure of evolution. Readers were told that the Dinotherium "appears to have formed a connecting link between the tapir and the mastodon, and to have presented in the form of the joint at the back of the head, some analogy to the *cetacea* or whale tribe."[13] Indeed, many of the natural history articles in periodicals published by the Religious Tract Society suggest that the writers already accepted some degree of evolution in the natural world, providing "man" was seen as a separate creation.

An article on "Sponges and Zoophytes" in the *Visitor, or Monthly Instructor, for 1842* stated that "nature does nothing *per saltum:* in other words, that the Almighty has been pleased to show his power in the establishment of a plan of creation, founded upon an increase in the gradual developement of organization."[14] While marine biology and botany[15] were favorite subjects for the study of "gradual developement," the human species was not omitted from the process. An article "On the Teeth of Mammalia" in the same journal for 1838 stated that "at the head of the omnivorous mammalia, stands our own species."[16] To the inquiring religious mind the challenging part in Darwin's thesis twenty years hence would be the role of natural selection—the survival of the fittest—and the emphasis on mechanistic determinism.

While many of the first missionaries to the islands had access to this periodical literature and all were more or less engaged in continuous self-improvement, the ordained artisans were often not too far removed from a flat-earth mentality. William Henry—a former carpenter and itinerant preacher and one of the first missionaries to sail to Tahiti (on board the *Duff* in 1796)—was typical of those who did not have a Gosport education, though he had been given some tuition by the noted mathematician and theologian Dr. John Walker at Trinity College, Dublin. Henry's explanation of the formation of coral illustrates his conservative cast of mind even when confronted with the observations of French savants who visited the Society Islands in the *Coquille* in 1823.[17]

In October 1825 Henry complained to the directors of the LMS about the account of the island of Tahaa in number 31 of the *Quarterly Chronicle of the Transactions of the Missionary Society* in which "the Worthy Deputation" (Daniel Tyerman and George Bennett) had referred to the reef that surrounded Tahaa and Raiatea as being "the work of a tender insignificant insect":[18]

> A wonder working insect indeed! Although gentlemen of a refined understanding & superior intelligence, yet I know they were carried away with the comparatively novel, and truly ridiculous opinion of the French naturalists & others, who refer all coral productions to the animal tribe, and suppose the coral to be the work of a small insect: and of course as the reefs which incompass the greater part of the islands in these seas, are *white coral,* or perhaps more properly *Madrepora,* that they conceived *them* also to be the work of that supposed insect, (which they have never been able to discover during their residence among the islands, and, I am persuaded, never will discover) yet I could not have imagined that they would have so confidently affirmed a thing they knew to be so contrary to the general opinion of the greatest naturalists & philosophers, and also which the[y] knew would be laid before the public, without offering the smallest proof in support of it.[19]

Henry's position was based on his own observation and that of countless people before him: "The natives of these islands have no other idea than that the Coral grows like a plant or vegetable." He had also studied the coral through a microscope and was able to describe six distinct varieties of white coral or Madreporaria. The missionaries used the variety called *toapu* or *pua* for the walls of their chapels and other European-style buildings. Henry's view of the formation of coral islands is not without interest:

> The reefs of these islands & of the others in these seas, were most probably formed by large quantities of broken coral being rolled by the sea towards them, in some places going nearer, & in others farther from them as it met with hinderances: and on these bodies of coral, other coral growing and being thrown down by the agitation of the sea from storms, and on that other coral growing, then falling & more growing upon that, & so on until the reefs reached the surface of the sea; and the whole being cemented by a kind of calcine or limy substance, produced by the coral itself, & mixed with other substances becoming one mass. This appears to me to be the most natural & rational way to account for the formation of coral reefs, and also of Coral Islands.[20]

Unfortunately, we have no record of Henry's reaction to Darwin's own theories of the origin of coral atolls.[21] Henry was so obsessed with the nonexistence of the coral insect that he took Dr. John Dunmore Lang to task for writing a poem about the creature.[22] It is perhaps relevant that Henry and some of his colleagues were also convinced that the Society Islands shamans or *taura* were able to plunge their arms into solid rock or earth up to their elbows and perform other miracles (supposedly through the devil's instrumentality) whereas the Gosport graduates regarded such performances as trickery and sleight of hand and went to great lengths to expose them.[23]

The later missionaries not only had greater respect for secular education than their predecessors, but their philosophical outlook was more geared to scientific change and innovation than, for instance, the ideological preoccupations of the Anglican establishment. Evangelical nonconformists generally distrusted the universal polity classics of the episcopal church—not just the *Ecclesiastical Polity* of Richard Hooker but also the anonymous *Whole Duty of Man* and especially William Paley's *Natural Theology* which, more than any other work, by elaborating the Argument from Design, confirmed the religious and educational foundations of the pre-Darwinian world.[24] Nonconformists were essentially advocates of an alternative culture: they generally favored homeopathy and hydropathy over traditional medicine, and they were among the first to embrace the principles of higher criticism in biblical scholarship formulated on the Continent.[25]

Missionaries in the field read Paley and no doubt approved the Argument from Design, but they also read more challenging and disturbing works.[26] They knew from experience that the world was full of contradictions and blind pathways. The missionary J. M. Orsmond had read the works of the Scottish philosopher Thomas Dick, who sought to reconcile the world of science with that of religion and who even argued for the "plurality of worlds," that is, the existence of life on other planets in the universe.[27] Though Dick's works argued the omnipotence of the deity, the emphasis in his theology was on a universe made for the arcane purposes of the creative intelligence (that is, the mind behind the universe), not on a universe made for man. The only design of any theological consequence was the creation of human intelligence so that the creature could appreciate and stand in awe of the grand creation. There is a terrible, savage, experimenting reality about the god of the Old Testament and the god of Calvinism, a reality far removed from the benevolent, anthropomorphic god of the natural theologians.

The nonconformist and Reformed clergy were in a frame of mind receptive to the intellectual challenges of contemporary science. They had little difficulty in rejecting biblical literalism in favor of new theories that accommodated science. Hugh Miller's view that the six days of creation represented six ages or eons of geological evolution reduced Archbishop Ussher's age of the world to pious mythology.[28] Indeed, Dick writing much earlier saw no conflict between the earth's being millions of years old and the Mosaic history, though he supposed "the first appearance of man upon the face of the globe, or, at least, the renewal of the human race after some great catastrophe, cannot be referred to a period farther back than 5,000, or 6,000 years from the present time."[29]

Cooperation with Visiting Scientists

The era of the 1820s and 1830s saw close cooperation between the missionaries in the Pacific and visiting scientists. The missionaries who arrived after 1815 were more generally innovative and adaptive than their seniors, introducing coral lime buildings, improvising oil lamps for their chapels and houses, and introducing technical skills such as printing.[30] This era also produced the first generation of significant missionary ethnographers.[31] One such, Charles Barff, missionary to the Society Islands, deserves a significant place in the history of Pacific science (figure 10.1). Although most of his own writings were lost at sea,[32] his urbanity, tolerant outlook, and hospitality won him the approval of numerous visitors. He was host to naval commanders, world travelers, and pious beachcombers alike, and at times his mission house must have resembled a tourist hostelry. Joseph Smith, a young adventurer, later a planter in Tahiti, lived for about a year in the family "and became convinced that if any man in the world, pursued a main object intelligently intently and unblameably," it was Barff.[33]

Besides the scientists who traveled on official expeditions,[34] many free-lance naturalists and geologists came in whaling or pearling ships, and one came in his own schooner. Nearly all spent longer periods in the islands than those in naval vessels, and they depended on the missionaries for information about guides and localities. Many probably could never have collected so much without drawing on the knowledge and even the collections of particular missionaries.

Samuel Stutchbury (1797–1859) was one of the first of the roving naturalists to have close relations with the missionaries.[35] In 1825 he traveled on board the Pacific Pearl Fishing Company's vessel the *Sir George Osborne* as a "collector in natural history." He took a significant collection of shells back to England[36] and anticipated Darwin in studying the formation of coral islands.[37] He early became friendly with the Anglican missionaries of the Church Missionary Society

10.1 (Above, left) Reverend Charles Barff (1792–1866), missionary at Huahine, Society Islands, and friend of scientists, 1816 (London Missionary Society miniature). Courtesy of Council for World Mission Archives, London.

10.2 (Above) Hugh Cuming (1791–1865), shell collector and friend of missionaries (engraving by Reeve, Benham, and Reeve, 1840). Source unknown.

10.3 (Left) Reverend Lorimer Fison (1832–1907), missionary and pioneer anthropologist, ca. 1900. Courtesy of the National Library of Australia.

going out to New Zealand in the *Sir George Osborne*[38] and while in Australia, New Zealand, and the Society Islands saw much of the CMS, Wesleyan, and LMS missionaries. His closer contacts were with the better-educated Williams brothers in New Zealand and the more urbane missionaries such as John Williams and Barff in the Society Islands, though other missionaries were helpful. As with most of those who made expeditions to the interior of Tahiti, he was assisted by the planter-trader Samuel Henry, son of the missionary, and he probably obtained his guides through Charles Wilson, the missionary at Matavai.[39]

Williams and Charles Pitman took Stutchbury on a mountain-climbing expedition in Raiatea,[40] and at most of the stations he shot birds and collected shells. Naturalists were mostly eager "specimen hunters" and saw no harm in their refined sporting activities. When it is recalled that most officers, chaplains, and scientists engaged in wanton shooting of exotic specimens throughout the nineteenth century, it is little wonder that many species became extinct.

Hugh Cuming (1791–1865) was perhaps the greatest of the collecting naturalists of the period, though he was much criticized in his day for his carelessness in assigning exact provenance (figure 10.2).[41] A gifted amateur, he began life as a sailmaker but was taught the rudiments of classification by his patron, Colonel Montagu, author of the *Testacea Britannica*, and at the age of twenty-eight he left his native Devon for South America. At Valparaiso he continued his studies in natural history encouraged by Nugent, the British consul, and several officers of the Royal Navy including Lieutenant Frembly and the officers of the surveying ships serving under Captains King and FitzRoy.[42] When he retired from sailmaking in 1826, he built a schooner "expressly fitted for the collection and storage of objects of Natural History" and embarked on a voyage in the eastern Pacific. He left in December 1827 equipped for a twelve-month voyage.[43]

Most of Cuming's time was spent in the Society Islands, the Austral Islands, and the Tuamotus. Although he was an eager searcher for new plants, most of his discoveries were in conchology. He recorded in his journal the various types of seashells and the new discoveries he made.[44] Although at first critical of the missionaries, particularly for not substituting new forms of relaxation for the old ones that they considered indecent, he generally supported their work. Again Barff and Williams were probably the most helpful to him. Barff acted as interpreter for him and no doubt took an intelligent interest in his collecting. Cuming spoke of Barff as "the most indefatigable man" he had ever seen or known as a minister[45] and wrongly concluded that he had received "a classical Education and was intend[ed] for they [*sic*] Establish'd Church."[46]

Barff recruited collectors and divers for Cuming at Huahine; Wilson remained the best contact for recruiting divers and guides at Matavai Bay. In the Austral Islands, where he collected "a variety of strange plants,"[47] Cuming's scientific pursuits were further assisted by the Tahitian teachers. On Rurutu he collected "several Cryptogamia, of much Interest to the Botanist,"[48] and on Rapa he "procured a number of Botanical specimens new to me, amongst which several species of Laurels and some beautiful Mosses & Ferns."[49]

The specimens brought back to Britain by Stutchbury and Cuming formed the basis of valuable collections.[50] They were described for the Royal Botanic Gardens at Kew and the Zoological, Linnean, and Geological Societies of London and brought both men into contact with Dr. William Hooker of Kew and Richard Owen, F.Z.S., then assistant conservator of the museum of the Royal College of Surgeons in London.[51]

The next important naturalist to be assisted by the missionaries was the surgeon George Bennett (1804–1893), a close friend of Owen, who joined a scientific expedition to the Pacific as surgeon-naturalist in 1829. Bennett made many discoveries on this voyage (1829–1831), not least that of the living animal of the pearly nautilus at Marakini or Dillon's Bay, Erromanga, in the New Hebrides on 24 August 1829. His itinerary included Tanna in the same group, Rotuma, Tongatapu, New Zealand, the Society Islands, and Hawaii. His papers on kava and "the mode of preparing heads among the New Zealanders" owed much to the missionaries. Although his stay in Tahiti in 1829 was brief, he saw much of the island with the help of the Henry and Wilson families and examined its botanical species. On Moorea he found Alexander Simpson to be "a most intelligent missionary."[52] In Hawaii, though mainly with Richard Charlton, the British consul, he saw much of Oahu and described the variety of its flora. Of particular interest to him was "a species of hawk moth *(sphinx pungens)* [which] flitted about like the puny humming-bird, thrusting its proboscis into every flower to extract the nectar."[53] Bennett, who made a more publicized visit to New South Wales in 1832,[54] was later to settle in Sydney. He was there during the visit of Charles Darwin in January 1836, a matter unrecorded by Darwin in both his private and public journals, a surprising fact in view of their mutual associates and Darwin's later acknowledgment of Bennett's information.[55]

Yet another naturalist to receive help from the missionaries and whose information was used by Darwin was David Douglas (1799–1834), said to be "the most extraordinary and most prolifically successful botanist of all time."[56] His principal host in Hawaii was Charlton, but he had close associations with two of the American Board missionaries, Joseph Goodrich and John Diell, who were also amateur geologists. Goodrich, the missionary at Hilo, felt honored to have a guest of Douglas' scientific reputation and arranged a climbing party of sixteen guides and baggage carriers to escort Douglas to the peak of Mauna Kea. Goodrich himself had ascended the extinct vol-

cano twice before and was also the missionary who witnessed the
chiefess Kapiolani returning from her defiance of the volcano goddess
Pele on Kilauea.[57] Douglas also ascended Kilauea with Goodrich's
help and in turn acted as a guide to Diell, the newly appointed missionary to seamen, on his visit to the active volcano. Between these
expeditions he collected more than two thousand botanical specimens
as well as climbed the lesser peaks.

Douglas' short scientific life formed an interesting prologue to Darwin's Pacific voyage. Douglas had actually studied the flora of the
Galapagos early in 1825 but was alienated by what he saw, perhaps
subconsciously feeling it challenged the notion of fixed species.[58]
Then, while in Honolulu in 1832, Hooker sent him a copy of Charles
Lyell's *Principles of Geology,*[59] the same volume J. S. Henslow had recommended Charles Darwin to read on the eve of his voyage in the
Beagle and which was to have a profound influence on the formulation of Darwin's evolutionary theories.

An air of mystery surrounds Douglas' death on the slopes of
Mauna Kea, where he was gored to death by a bull in a pit made to
trap wild cattle. Had he stumbled in, perhaps preoccupied with Lyell's
challenge to his comfortable religious views recently reinforced by a
mystical experience at the crater of Kilauea; or had he been killed by
the pit owner, an escaped convict from New South Wales, and
thrown into the pit as some people suspected? He had seen some of
the evidence for Darwin's theories, but he was eliminated from the
field of potential discovery.

Darwin reached Tahiti following his own momentous visit to the
Galapagos Islands. Unlike Douglas, his eyes had been opened to the
remarkable variation of species concentrated in the latter group. Like
naturalists before him, Darwin was reasonably impressed by the missionaries and appeared to approve their "civilizing" role, notwithstanding the strictness of some of the local laws.[60] Charles Wilson, as
usual, provided guides for Darwin's excursion in the mountains. Darwin thought him more like a "good natured quiet trader" than a gentleman but believed that his exterior hid "a great deal of most
unpretending excellent merit."[61] Darwin later met the veteran missionary Henry Nott and George Pritchard, not yet an internationally
known figure, whom he saw as a "sensible agreeable gentleman &
good man."[62] Darwin and Captain FitzRoy dined twice with the Prit-
chards, and Darwin regretted he did not have time to become better
acquainted with his host.[63]

In New Zealand Darwin was equally impressed by the missionaries, though he preferred the mission policy in Tahiti of "religious

instruction & . . . the direct improvement of the mind" to the practice in New Zealand of introducing the "arts of civilization."[64] In the scale of human evolution he placed the Tahitian above the New Zealander.

Between Darwin's visit and the publication of the *Origin of Species* in 1859 the missionaries encountered other scientists. Most naturalists, however, were connected with official expeditions. The U.S. Exploring Expedition under Charles Wilkes spent much time in the region and had good relations with the mission personnel. The linguist Horatio Hale acquired much ethnographic and linguistic material from missionaries, and probably the natural scientists benefited also, although little was recorded in the mission journals.[65]

During this period many of the missionaries had established routines that enabled them to spend more time developing linguistic and ethnographic interests, while a few explored more technical avenues. Rudolph Krause, who served the LMS in the Cook and Society Islands, built an observatory at his mission station on Bora Bora where he trained his theological students in astronomy.[66] He also had a dark room in the late 1850s and was one of the first missionaries to record island life photographically (figure 10.4).[67]

Meanwhile the tradition of missionary cooperation with scientific expeditions continued. Berthold Seemann (1825–1871), the eminent botanist who accompanied Colonel Smythe on their government mission to Fiji in 1860, was greatly assisted in his collecting expeditions, which resulted in the publication of his monumental *Flora Vitiensis.*[68]

Evangelicals and the Post-Darwinian Impetus to Science

Far from being hostile to evolutionary views, as some historians have supposed, Evangelicals were often in the forefront of the scientific advance.[69] Those who resisted Darwin's ideas with vigor were more likely to be High Church (not Anglo-Catholic) Anglicans brought up on Paley or biblical literalists (later called fundamentalists and creationists). The founders of the great scientific societies of the nineteenth century were not necessarily agnostic or even Broad Church. Some, such as William Vernon Harcourt, a founder of the British Association for the Advancement of Science, held conservative religious views; Harcourt's views placed him in the Evangelical tradition even if he did not identify himself as an Evangelical.[70]

The most significant scientific traveler to visit the Pacific Islands just before the publication of Darwin's *Origin of Species* was an Evangelical: William Henry Harvey (1811–1866), celebrated for his *Sea-Side Book* of 1849, which contributed substantially to the popu-

10.4 Residence of the Reverend E. R. W. Krause at Bora Bora,
showing octagonal building with observatory behind house
(lithography by Snyder, Black, and Sturn, New York). From Edward
T. Perkins, *Na Motu* (New York, 1854), facing p. 287.

larization of science in Victorian times.[71] His visit in 1855 was note-
worthy for both missions and science. In Sydney he had stayed with
George Bennett and no doubt heard Bennett's reminiscences of the
islands of twenty years earlier. A devout Church of Ireland convert,
Harvey traveled to Tonga and Fiji in the Wesleyan mission ship *John
Wesley.*[72]

Harvey affirmed that he usually did not support the work of "dissenters," but he was so impressed by that of the Wesleyan missionaries that he established the Polynesian Medical Aid Society, designed to
provide them with an annual contribution of medicines.[73] He spent
his time collecting specimens in the Tongan archipelago while the
John Wesley was absent in the Samoan group.

Harvey became one of the transitional figures in accommodating
Darwin's views. At first he reacted in skeptical good humor with a
privately printed lecture to the Dublin University Zoological and
Botanical Association—*An Inquiry into the Probable Origin of the
Human Animal.*[74] He also opposed Darwin's theory in two reviews,
one in the *Edinburgh Review* (1860), another in the *Dublin Hospital
Gazette* (1861). Nevertheless, he told his friend Asa Gray that he had
no objection to a doctrine of derivative descent.

Why should I? or why should any man? *One* mode of creation is as feasable to the Almighty as another, &, *as put by you,* such a scheme is very consonant to sound doctrine. But—I still think that, as put by Darwin, a very different sort of grape may be gathered from the thistle. He certainly has a proclivity—as you say—to the positivism of the day—or he would not have been so reticent as he is. But, we [who] have no proclivity—may read his mystery in our own way—& so read, we can accept much of his book as an explanation of natural evolution.[75]

Harvey found much of value in Darwin's views on geographical distribution and on the "geological geogr[aphical] distribution, successing through ages." He exchanged views with Darwin on some points and voiced his reservations on others:

A good deal of Darwin reads to me like an ingenious dream—& some of it reads like *bosh*—e.g. the whole passage explaining why plants on Islands become trees—and sundry such explanations, here & there, that I can hardly call other than whimsical—if not childish.[76]

Although so much was "admirable," he felt Darwin to be obsessive: "He seems to be unable to look at *any thing,* that cannot at once be *solved* by his *single* solvent—the *one* idea of Nat. Selection." Harvey's view of Darwinism was more prophetic than he realized. He felt that Darwinism and Newton's law of gravity were but approximations to the true scientific situation and that *"duality* of law" lay at the "base of the structure of the Universe."[77]

After 1860 interest in the sciences in the mission field was probably more marked than before. Those who, like Professor Harvey, accommodated their religious beliefs to evolution became even more interested in what they saw, while those who took what has become known as the "creationist" position were eager to discover natural phenomena that supported the Argument from Design. Indeed, Christian evolutionists themselves still recognized that argument in regard to the human species and its place in evolution.

The atmosphere of the 1860s was one of scientific awareness rather than heated debate. Naturalistically minded Evangelicals and nonconformists were inclined to accept or reject evolutionary theories on their own merits but naturally seized on information that tended to modify the Darwinian position in so far as it appeared to minimize the need for a creative intelligence. Thus, while a reviewer in the *British Quarterly Review* in 1860 treated Darwin's work sympathetically if critically, a decade later the same journal published an article claiming that there were many gaps in Darwin's evidence.[78] Indeed, Darwin himself appears to have been only too well aware of some of these gaps. In 1861 he wrote to his friend Thomas Davidson of Brighton, the palaeontologist,

> I do not know whether you have read my "Origin of Species." In that book I have made the remark, which I apprehend will be universally admitted, that, as a whole, the fauna of any formation is intermediate in character between that of the formation above and below. But several really good judges have remarked to me how desirable it would be that this should be exemplified and worked out in some detail, and with some single group of beings. Now everyone will admit that no one in the world could do this better than you with Brachiopods. The result might turn out very unfavourable to the views which I hold; if so, so much the better for those who are opposed to me. But I am inclined to suspect that on the whole it would be favourable to the notion of descent with modification.[79]

Davidson carried out the study and concluded that brachiopods did not show "the formation of species by modification of form in a long course of descent." He informed the Geologists Association in 1877 that Darwin's "tempting and beautiful theory of descent with modification" was likely to remain a theory: "we are still and shall probably for ever remain in the dark, or within the regions of suppositions, with respect to so important a question."[80] Nevertheless, he believed it was "a far more exalted conception than the idea of instant independent creations." Davidson's opinions were eagerly relayed to the thousands of readers of the Religious Tract Society's publication, the *Leisure Hour*.[81]

Missionaries may not have had access to the scientific journals, but they would have seen the variety of Christian responses to Darwin's theories in the *Leisure Hour*, the *British Quarterly Review*, and the *Eclectic Review*.[82] At least one missionary tackled the question head on. S. J. Whitmee and his wife took a large number of books to read on the voyage from Britain to Samoa in 1863:

> I had taken as scientific pabulum Darwin's "Origin of Species", determined to make a thorough study of it. This I did, and made a digest which was so full that from it I afterwards prepared a lecture on "The Darwinian Theory," which was subsequently delivered to Foreign residents in Samoa, and afterwards to audiences in Australia, England and Ireland.[83]

On furlough in 1879 he delivered on behalf of the Congregational College in Melbourne a prelection entitled "The Relation of Science to Revelation" in which he argued that since nature and revelation were both from God there could be no antagonism between them and that where they were said not to agree "it is because one or the other has been inaccurately interpreted, or perhaps both more or less misunderstood."[84]

A singular feature of the post-*Origin* period was the important role of clergymen as collectors and scientific or descriptive writers. One of the most successful, the Reverend Julius Brenchley (1816–1873), vicar of Maidstone, Kent, made several visits to the Pacific. In 1850 he accompanied the French naturalist Jules Remy in Hawaii, but it was in 1865 that he made his most significant sortie, visiting Tonga, Fiji, the New Hebrides, New Caledonia, and the Solomons. He obtained many natural history specimens and large quantities of ethnographic material and in 1873 published *Jottings during the Cruise of H.M.S. "Curaçao" among the South Sea Islands in 1865*. His collection, now mostly held in the British and Maidstone Museums, contains more than a thousand artifacts from the Solomons alone.[85]

While in the Solomons Brenchley and his colleagues were considerably helped by Bishop Patteson, who was visiting his mission stations in that group in the *Southern Cross*.[86] The newly arrived missionary R. H. Codrington also assisted[87] and probably began his own inquiries, which led to his own major work on the Melanesian peoples.[88] At the other missions Brenchley was inclined to look down on "dissenters," but he accepted their cooperation.

Another great clerical collector of the post-*Origin* era, although he did not visit the Pacific, was the Reverend John George Wood (1827–1889), best known as a popularizer of scientific subjects.[89] His numerous books published between 1851 and his death made natural history intelligible to nonscientific minds. Not least among his works was *The Natural History of Man*,[90] which contained much material derived from missionaries, particularly engravings taken from early photographs and pen drawings of weapons and other artifacts from his own collection.

But it was the missionaries themselves who began to take the initiative in scientific collecting in this period. The LMS missionaries had always taken an interest in the natural objects of their island homes ever since William Shelley inscribed his name and the date 1797 on a magnificent Tahitian cowrie shell he sent home to one of the society's directors.[91] But it was not until the Reverend William Wyatt Gill of Mangaia in the Cook Islands began to write a series of articles for the *Sunday at Home, Leisure Hour,* and other religious periodicals that the missionaries' own contribution to natural history became apparent.[92] Some of Gill's natural history articles were republished in *Jottings from the Pacific* in 1885.

Much of Gill's natural history writing concerned the newly opened mission field of New Guinea. The LMS missionaries showed a talent for exploration, and many of them contributed New Guinea flora to Ferdinand von Mueller's herbarium in Melbourne in the period 1875–1896, as well as assisting scientific expeditions in the region.[93] One of the most assiduous LMS "specimen hunters" was Whitmee. Most of the zoological specimens in his collection were obtained for him by Samoans.[94] Unlike many clerical collectors, he did not like shooting birds and had the back verandah of the mission house at Upolu converted into an aviary, which he could enter from his study and from which he could observe their habits.[95]

Whitmee's principal scientific interest, however, was botany, and whenever he returned from another district by horseback he would collect specimens in a special container attached to the front of his saddle.[96] He also went on regular camping expeditions, accompanied by the pastor and male members of each mission village in rotation, traveling as far afield as Savaii, where on one occasion he climbed the highest peak and discovered a climbing fern, which was named after him. He believed he had discovered about 30 new species of ferns and had 158 species in his own collection.[97] After sending his first collection of plants to Melbourne, Whitmee sent eleven large consignments to Dr. Hooker at Kew via British men-of-war. On his return to England in 1879 he visited Kew and arranged for the disposal of seven duplicate sets of two hundred or more pieces and several smaller sets.[98]

Whitmee soon built up a large circle of scientific correspondents including Hooker and Owen and distinguished amateurs such as Canon Tristram of Durham. One of the most enthusiastic was George Rolleston (1829–1881), Linacre Professor of Anatomy and Physiology at Oxford. In 1865 Whitmee had sent a rare bird[99] preserved in metholated spirits to Rolleston at his request, and soon Rolleston was asking for other specimens for the museum at Oxford such as a Nautilus cephalopod and specimens of Polynesian crania.

Whitmee had acquired a botanical assistant, a young Dane named Jensen who lived in the family and helped with the collections.[100] At his own expense Whitmee arranged for Jensen to travel in the mission ship *John Williams* on its round of the Cook and Society groups and the Tokelau, Ellice, and Gilbert Islands. Jensen carried letters in English and Samoan explaining that the skulls would be preserved and would be valuable in studying the human races. Jensen returned with several representative skulls (paid for with Rolleston's money) and a collection, thought to be complete, of the plants of the Tokelau, Ellice, and Gilbert Islands, which was forwarded to Kew.

Although the Wesleyan Methodists came from a tradition that discouraged worldly pursuits, many of the midcentury Methodist missionaries were deeply appreciative of science. Thomas Adams of Tonga had brothers who became eminent astronomers,[101] and John Whewell was a relation of the eminent Master of Trinity, William Whewell, whose review of Lyell's work reflected his debt to Paley.[102] James Egan Moulton of Tonga was another great missionary advocate of science. Member of a large family distinguished for scholarship, he founded Tupou College, an advanced educational institution on Tongatapu, in 1866. Besides mathematical subjects his curriculum included chemistry and astronomy. A telescope not only served the students but also enabled Moulton to follow one of his favorite pastimes, scanning the heavens.[103] A daily meteorological record was carefully kept. Moulton was also an innovative linguist and introduced many new conceptual forms into the Tongan language, creating composite words from existing terms to convey abstract meanings.[104]

One of the greatest Methodist "specimen hunters" was George Brown of Samoa and New Britain, who became an avid collector of butterflies and other natural history objects.[105] Brown's story highlights the way in which the missionary contribution to science was often overlooked. During his fourteen years in Samoa he built up a valuable collection of botanical and zoological specimens and was "especially proud of some birds he had shot, skinned or preserved."[106] He augmented this collection with specimens from Rotuma including some rare birds he had shot on a shooting trip across the island. In 1874 one of the most prestigious of the British scientific expeditions to the Pacific arrived in Fiji in HMS *Challenger*. Brown's biographer records that Charles Wyville Thomson (1830–1882), the distinguished professor of natural history at Edinburgh University who led the scientific team selected by the Royal Society, had a lengthy interchange of information with Brown on board the *Challenger* and even persuaded Brown to part with his valuable collection of natural history specimens. While the experience encouraged Brown to continue his studies, it remained a sore point with him that Wyville Thomson never officially acknowledged the specimens, never acknowledged their source in his report of the expedition, and never gave public recognition to the missionary's assistance.[107]

Brown was almost as avid a collector as Brenchley and Whitmee and built up a unique collection of "South Sea native work in fighting weapons, artistic work of various kinds, and models of . . . sailing craft," a collection he eventually sold to the Bowes Museum in his birth town of Barnard Castle. This collection, which was of considerable ethnographic importance, contained, among other items from New Britain, "two small baskets woven from fern so artistically but so closely that they will hold water."[108]

But it was not all butterflies and baskets. The post-*Origin* period also saw a renewal of interest in fossils and extinct or dying species. The LMS missionary George Turner and his son-in-law S. J. Whitmee described the Samoan *manu mea* or "little dodo,"[109] while the CMS missionaries in New Zealand were among the foremost authorities on the extinct moa, which was first brought to public attention in 1838. Shortly afterward, several of the missionaries including William Colenso and Richard Taylor became absorbed by the moa quest. Colenso published an article on the subject in the *Tasmanian Journal of Natural Science* in 1846,[110] while Taylor's *Te Ika a Maui* of 1855 contained further material in addition to several chapters on geology, natural history, and botany.[111] From 1873 on, Taylor, Colenso, J. W. Stack, and J. F. H. Wohlers all contributed papers to the *Transactions of the New Zealand Institute* on the subject.

Certainly by the end of the century missionaries had become prominent as collectors and popularizers of natural and geological science. But there was another field in which they were preeminent. Despite the fascination of natural history, ethnography was the primary interest of those with a scientific bent and the field in which they made their greatest contribution.

The Birth of Anthropology

Although many of the first missionaries to the islands had been "godly artisans" with a smattering of learning, the directorate of the Missionary Society included a number of men who either moved in learned circles or had contacts in the scientific world. The society had been organized largely on class lines: the directors tended to be from the middle and upper classes while the missionaries, even though members, were regarded more as servants of the society. Dr. Thomas Haweis, recognized as the father of the South Sea Mission, corresponded with Sir Joseph Banks and moved in circles that gave him access to the world of patronage and learning.[112] His colleague, the Reverend Samuel Greatheed, was probably the leading scholar in the directorate. A military engineer by training, he was a linguist, ethnographer, and prehistorian by inclination. He had the task of preparing ethnographic histories of all the island groups to which the society expected to send missionaries. He also compiled a Polynesian grammar and vocabulary that became the model for the grammars prepared by the missionaries themselves. His studies of the ancient population movements and linguistic changes of Europe earned him a Fellowship of the Society of Antiquaries.[113]

The scientific objectivity of Greatheed's work is clear from the careful questioning of his sources. After reading the original voyage narratives of the explorers (and later the missionaries)—which he annotated and cross-referenced—he cross-examined those who had firsthand knowledge of the islands. Diet, sexual customs, geographical factors, linguistic differences all received minute attention. In the field of ethnography the missionaries built on Greatheed's researches. W. P. Crook, his principal informant, took three manuscript volumes of Greatheed's account of the Marquesas to the mission field and greatly expanded the work.[114] John Davies expanded the Polynesian Grammar into the first Tahitian Grammar.[115]

William Ellis, one of the few missionaries to become a director, compiled his influential *Polynesian Researches* partly as a record of missionary achievement, partly as a contribution to ethnography.[116] Ellis' contemporaries were equally motivated to gather indigenous material. J. M. Orsmond, initially prompted by Ellis and Dr. Lang of Sydney, collected a vast amount of ethnographic, linguistic, and historical material in the Society Islands.[117] Charles Barff also collected for Ellis but, as mentioned earlier, lost most of his own papers in a shipwreck. L. E. Threlkeld was one of the first serious scholars of Australian Aboriginal ethnography and languages.[118] And Robert Thomson compiled histories of the Marquesas and Society Islands.[119]

The Wesleyans were also pioneers in Pacific ethnography. John Thomas wrote an extensive history and mythology of Tonga and supplied much of the descriptive material for Mrs. Farmer's *Tonga and the Friendly Islands*.[120] Thomas Williams and James Calvert, also pioneers, combined to write the two parts of *Fiji and the Fijians*, which contains much ethnographical and descriptive material.[121]

From the middle of the nineteenth century a new type of cooperation took place between the missionaries and scientists, particularly in ethnography. Ethnologists, folklorists, and other professional students of so-called primitive culture who rarely left the confines of universities and private studies began to build their theories around the primary documentation supplied by missionaries. The Ethnological Society of London and the British Association for the Advancement of Science sent questionnaires to missionaries in the field.[122] Some of the missionaries who went beyond the range of the questions were rewarded with honorary memberships and fellowships.[123]

Cells of ethnographic scholars became linked in correspondence among themselves and with their missionary informants. One group included Friedrich Max Müller, Edward Tylor, J. G. Frazer, J. J. Lister, and J. Estlin Carpenter. Max Müller took an interest in Wyatt Gill's work and wrote the preface to his *Myths and Songs from the South Pacific....*[124] Tylor encouraged George Turner of Samoa to refine and expand his notes on Samoan ethnography originally published in the *Samoan Reporter*.[125] He wrote the preface to Turner's *Samoa a Hundred Years Ago ...*, which was published as an ethnographic text without the usual chapters devoted to missionary achievement. Similarly, Gill presented his "historical sketches" of Mangaia to two separate audiences, one version—*From Darkness to Light in Polynesia*—containing additional chapters of pious history.[126] His Samoan colleague S. J. Whitmee also wrote on both natural history and ethnological subjects. Largely encouraged by Rolleston of Oxford, Whitmee wrote extensively on the Polynesians and rapidly became the accepted authority on the subject after publishing an article in the *Contemporary Review* criticizing the views of Alfred Russel Wallace.[127] Wallace is alleged to have admitted to Sir John Lubbock (afterward Lord Avebury) that he conceded to Whitmee's views.[128] Whitmee also corresponded with Max Müller and the comparative philologist A. H. Sayce. Max Müller, Sayce, and others tried to obtain a fellowship for Whitmee to work on the Polynesian languages but came up against the Oxford prejudices against nonconformity.[129]

George Brown, Martin Dyson, and Lorimer Fison were among the foremost Wesleyan missionary ethnographers. Fison, a Cambridge graduate, wrote with great authority about the Pacific (figure 10.3). His work in conjunction with A. W. Howitt on the Australian Aborigines and his Fijian studies were of major importance to colonial policy as well as to science.[130] Fison was brought to the attention of Lewis H. Morgan, the noted anthropologist, by Professor Goldwin Smith about 1870 and from then on became an important informant.[131] He also collaborated with Dr. R. H. Codrington, who served in the Melanesian Mission from 1863 to 1887 and made a substantial contribution to the new science.[132] Codrington's material was the chief source for the influential *mana* theory of the origin of religion associated with Robert Marett, Tylor's disciple and successor at Oxford.[133] That Tylor, Marett, and others were "armchair" theorists and got it wrong is no reflection on the outstanding contribution of the missionaries.

The university orientation of the Anglican missionaries of the

Melanesian Mission was particularly noteworthy. Ethnographic material supplied by Codrington, Alfred Penny, and others was deposited in the Pitt-Rivers Museum at Oxford and described by J. Edge-Partington. C. E. Fox and Walter George Ivens carried on the mission's anthropological tradition. Ivens, in particular, who served in Melanesia between 1896 and 1909, was to devote the remainder of his life to linguistic and anthropological studies. He was appointed to a research fellowship at the University of Melbourne in 1924.[134] Another trained linguist, S. H. Ray, used material supplied by Codrington, Chalmers of the LMS in Papua, and William Gunn and William Grey of the Presbyterian Mission in the New Hebrides. This sort of partnership also took place in the Methodist mission field. Edward Gifford, one of the first accredited anthropologists to work in Tonga, drew heavily on the writings and ethnographic contacts of the Methodist missionary E. E. V. Collocott.

The principal LMS missionaries in Papua formed their own group. Though primarily explorers, they were a great source of information and assistance to scientific expeditions.[135] They were particularly fortunate in their links with the Cambridge anthropologist Alfred Cort Haddon, who was also of Congregational/Baptist background. A zoologist turned anthropologist, Haddon had become increasingly critical of missionary activity.[136] Following his celebrated Cambridge anthropological expedition to the Torres Strait, New Guinea, and Sarawak in 1898–1899, he took an active role in promoting anthropological training for missionaries at the same time as W. H. R. Rivers was exerting a similar influence on the Anglicans.[137]

For these "Christian evolutionists" the so-called primitive religions were not perversions of old cultures or even the inferior off-castings of cultural evolution[138] but religions to be respected for their place in preparing humankind for higher religion. The missionary John Henry Holmes was a convert to the new order and, after working with the anthropologist C. G. Seligman in 1898, became one of Haddon's valued correspondents, making his own contribution with information, papers, and cultural artifacts.[139]

Perhaps the most organized group of corresponding missionaries and scholars during the last two decades of the nineteenth century centered on the lay Presbyterian ethnographer Dr. John Fraser (1834–1904) of Maitland, New South Wales. Fraser had developed close ties with missionaries in the field who supplied him with material; he also kept in close contact with the retired LMS missionaries living in Sydney. He was a prominent member of the Royal Society of New South Wales and a founding member of the Australasian Association for the

Advancement of Science and the Polynesian Society. The missionaries who published learned papers in the journals of these societies either in their own right or edited by Fraser included Daniel Macdonald of the New Hebrides; George Pratt, Samuel Ella, and J. B. Stair of Samoa; and W. W. Gill of the Cook Islands.[140] Unlike the missionaries with strong university links, some of those in Fraser's circle—like some of their colleagues in the Polynesian Society—were attracted to exotic and bizarre theories. Fraser himself and Macdonald in particular were apt to draw conclusions that could not be supported by the evidence.[141]

Cultural Degeneration or Social Darwinism?

Although missionaries were given some training in anthropology and comparative religion from about 1900, this was not seen as an urgent requirement in the late nineteenth century. Missionaries believed that they were recording details about primitive peoples who were about to disappear from the earth. They had been conditioned to accept the doctrines of social Darwinism, that various peoples of the earth were the losers in the progress of evolution and that these people were to be found on the periphery of advanced societies doomed to give way to the advances of the fittest of the human species.

In the pre-Darwinian era the prevailing theological theory was one of degeneration of culture, that the so-called primitive societies of the earth had retrogressed from a higher state. These views were particularly associated with the Oxford philosopher Richard Whately (1787–1863), sometime Archbishop of Dublin, and were embraced by Bishop Russell in his study of the Polynesians.[142] The evolutionists, on the other hand, especially Tylor, Lubbock (Lord Avebury), and G. H. L. F. Pitt-Rivers argued that decline was exceptional and that the human species was involved in an upward movement in which the least fit were pushed to the periphery of civilization, where they would eventually die out. Both schools of thought regarded the Pacific peoples as being well down the ladder of progress.

Missionaries embraced both positions, agreeing that all Pacific Islanders had little hope of competing with the so-called advanced races. Perhaps the most vivid picture of social Darwinism expressed by any missionary was that by Lorimer Fison, who wrote in his journal in 1867 that

> [the Fijians] seem to be utterly incapable of social & political improvement. That they are capable of a *moral* improvement is an established fact; & therefore they can be made fit for Heaven: but they cannot be made fit

for Earth. It is useless to say that such as they *are*, our forefathers *were*. They are made of different stuff. . . . They live in a different mind-world, out of which it seems utterly impossible to bring them. They oppose a dull apathy to all social & political improvement: their houses are no better than they were in ye old heathen times: their gardens are tilled in ye same primitive style: their canoes are in no one point improved: their habits are as filthy as ever: in short they show themselves (with very, very few exceptions—few & far between) to be utterly incapable of better things: & therefore do I feel assured that they must perish from off ye face of ye earth.[143]

This pessimistic outlook was to affect mission policy well into the twentieth century. Thus mission literature as late as 1918 contained sentiments like the following:

It is also argued that, as the Islanders are a dying people, or at least a people who have not a world-future, it is not true economy to spend upon them what can be spent to much better advantage upon people with a future. But what if we can keep them from dying out?[144]

For those who believed in degeneration of culture there was probably more hope. George Douglas Campbell, Duke of Argyll, denounced the theories of the evolutionists. A notable polemicist who was not afraid to take on Spencer and T. H. Huxley, he also sought to revive the degenerationist theories of Whately. He believed that progress and evolution were planned and directed by "mind." Those holding these views believed there was some hope for the primitive peoples if they could be taught industrial crafts and given new educational opportunities. There was no need for them to wither away or give up their lands to so-called superior races. For the missionaries, however, these different theoretical positions were not critical: they were in the business of making souls "fit for Heaven," and for that there was always a sense of urgency.

One missionary who actually entered the debate was Donald Macdonald of the Presbyterian Mission in the New Hebrides. He tackled Lubbock's *Origin of Civilisation,* claiming to be objective:

Thus it will be seen that his view is in harmony with the Darwinian or development theory, leading us back not to human beings, but to "hairy quadrupeds," as the progenitors not only of savages but also of civilised men. Although this seems repugnant, *yet if it is true we are bound to accept it;* and the fact that a man of Sir John Lubbock's eminence advocates it shows that something can be said in its favour.[145]

Macdonald argued in favor of cultural degeneration, refuting Lubbock's claims that no fragment of pottery and no architectural remains
had been found in the Pacific. To him the Pacific peoples were "not in
their spring, but in their winter or second childhood . . . the hopelessness and languor of senile decrepitude. Hence the mournful and
widely if not universally entertained conviction that they are 'dying
out.' "[146] What is extraordinary, however, is that Macdonald believed
he had refuted more fundamental principles of Darwinism: "The gulf
between us and the 'hairy quadruped' is, therefore, as unabridged as
ever; and this surely is a comforting truth. The link is missing to complete the development chain."[147]

The recognition of anthropology as a major discipline that missionaries felt obliged to study was one outcome of the decline of social
Darwinism. Indigenous cultures came to be recognized as having their
own inherent qualities worthy of preservation and study.

The Missionary Contribution

Although many articles on natural history, geography, and ethnography were published by missionaries in religious periodicals for
the edification of the public at large, other, more detailed articles
were contributed to the journals of learned societies and so made a
direct contribution to scientific advance. From the late 1860s there
was a steady flow of specialized articles ranging from vulcanology to
linguistics. Some were written in collaboration with secular experts.[148]
These articles, written largely as a result of the impetus given to science by the researches of Darwin, continued beyond the 1930s, by
which time the missionaries were ceasing to be the main source of
empirical data in the islands.

This survey has shown that, despite the conservative religious legacy of eighteenth-century revivalism, most Protestant missionaries of
all denominations who served in the Pacific were sympathetic to scientific pursuits and that after the publication of Darwin's *Origin of
Species* (1859) and his *Descent of Man* (1871), missionaries themselves became collectors, recorders, and protagonists in the evolutionary debate. Several of the missionaries played key roles in extending
contemporary knowledge of the natural world, and a larger number
were influential in pioneering modern anthropology. Although not all
Darwin's views were accepted, his *Origin* was still seen as the "chief
book of all the teeming century," and scientific truth was seen to lie
somewhere between his writings and a nonliteral understanding of
the Bible.

Notes

1   See Niel Gunson, *Messengers of Grace: Evangelical Missionaries in the South Seas, 1797–1860* (Melbourne/New York: Oxford University Press, 1978), 31–33.

2   For the curricula of the academies see J. W. Ashley Smith, *The Birth of Modern Education: The Contribution of the Dissenting Academies, 1660–1800* (London: Independent Press, 1954).

3   Ibid., 95–96, 152–159; Irene Parker, *Dissenting Academies in England: Their Rise and Progress and Their Place among the Educational Systems of the Country* (Cambridge: Cambridge University Press, 1914).

4   Gunson, *Messengers of Grace*, 36–37.

5   A nine-volume set of Bogue's Lectures totaling about five thousand pages copied by J. Lowndes was held by New College, London, and is now in Dr. Williams's Library, London.

6   Those entering were taught to "throw off all vulgarisms and provincialisms," "guard against loud and boisterous behaviour," avoid special friendships, adopt moderation in eating and drinking, avoid too great an intimacy with poorer Christians, and avoid being alone with young women. (Ibid.)

7   David Bogue, A Lecture, as an Appendix to Those on the Pastoral Office: Studies of a Young Minister after Leaving the Seminary, in Bogue's "Lectures on the Pastoral Office" (Lowndes copy above), 457–467.

8   Ibid., 467. "Unless when necessity, duty or health require, never leave home till after dinner [i.e., early afternoon]."

9   *Youth's Magazine* 11 (1816): 422.

10 *Missionary Sketches*, no. 15, displayed the skull and horns of a species of rhinoceros apparently extinct "supposed to be the unicorn of scripture" together with that of a common rhinoceros.

11 See *Youth's Magazine*, 3d ser., 9 (1836): 306; 4th ser., 1 (1838): 134 and 3 (1840): passim.

12 *Youth's Magazine*, 4th ser., 3 (1840): 73–74.

13 Ibid., 109.

14 *Visitor*, 1842, 5.

15 See, for instance, *Visitor*, 1838, 53ff.

16 Ibid., 418.

17 For the cooperation between the missionaries and the scientists sailing with Louis-Isidore Duperrey, see John Dunmore, *French Explorers in the Pacific*, 2 vols. (Oxford: Clarendon Press, 1969), 2: 125ff.

18 The deputation also commented on coral formation in their public

journal: "each poor worm, among millions which perhaps an angel could not count, is merely performing the common functions of its brief existence." *Voyages and Travels round the World, by the Rev. Daniel Tyerman and George Bennet . . .* , ed. James Montgomery, 2d ed. (London: John Snow, 1840), 56.

19   W. Henry to W. Alers Hankey, October 1825, London Missionary Society, South Sea Letters, Council for World Mission Archives, School of Oriental and African Studies Library, University of London (hereafter LMS, SSL).

20   Ibid.

21   See Charles Darwin, *The Structure and Distribution of Coral Reefs* (London: Smith, Elder, 1842).

22   "The poem upon the Imaginary Creature the Coral Insect, is very ingenious and spiritual, but, in my opinion, is not founded in truth. The old opinion that the Coral is a sea plant or production, is certainly correct." W. Henry to J. D. Lang, 10 January 1828, Mitchell Library, Sydney, Lang Papers, vol. 15.

23   On the credulity of the older missionaries see, for instance, William Ellis, *Polynesian Researches . . .* , 2d ed., 4 vols. (London: Fisher, Son, and Jackson, 1831), 1:361–362.

24   See generally Lynn Barber, *The Heyday of Natural History, 1820–1870* (London: Jonathan Cape, 1980), 22 et passim.

25   Opposition to higher criticism or "Germanism" was probably more controversial than opposition to Darwinism.

26   For the disillusionment of Evangelical theologians with Paley, see Boyd Hilton, *The Age of Atonement: The Influence of Evangelicalism on Social and Economic Thought, 1795–1865* (Oxford: Clarendon Press, 1988), esp. 170–179.

27   Thomas Dick, *Works*, 7 vols., vol. 2, *The Christian Philosopher; or the Connection of Science and Philosophy with Religion* (Philadelphia: Edward C. Biddle, 1840), 193–194.

28   It was a nonconformist theologian, John Pye Smith, who "did more than any other British theologian of his day to bring the exegesis of Genesis into accord with geological fact." *Dictionary of National Biography.* For Miller's role, see Barber, *Natural History,* 225–238.

29   Dick, *Christian Philosopher,* 166.

30   These "civilizing" innovations were described particularly by the missionaries John Williams and L. E. Threlkeld of Raiatea in their letters and publications.

31   *Australian Reminiscences and Papers of L. E. Threlkeld, Missionary to the Aborigines, 1824–1859*, ed. Niel Gunson, 2 vols. (Canberra:

Australian Institute of Aboriginal Studies, 1974), 1: v. For the fruits of their ethnography, see below, "The Birth of Anthropology."

32 C. Barff wrote that on 17 May 1864 he lost all his manuscripts in a shipwreck, "the labour of many years in collecting"; unpublished MS in LMS, Miscellaneous Folder 9, South Seas, Council for World Mission Archives, School of Oriental and African Studies, Library, University of London.

33 Joseph Smith, "Sentimental Reminiscences, [1826–1844]." TS and original, formerly called "Ross MS," Bernice P. Bishop Museum Library, Honolulu, TS 12.

34 The most notable scientific voyage of this period was that of Captain F. W. Beechey. See his *Narrative of a Voyage to the Pacific and Beering's Strait, to Co-operate with the Polar Expeditions . . .* 2 vols. (London: Colburn, 1831).

35 Samuel Stutchbury, "Observations Made During a Voyage to New South Wales and the Polynesian Isles in the Pacific Pearl Fishery Comp^ys Ships Sir George Osborne and Rolla in the Years 1825, 26, & 27." MS, Turnbull Library, Wellington.

36 Many of the shells brought back to Britain by Stutchbury are referred to by W. J. Broderip in his descriptions of species in the *Transactions of the Zoological Society of London* from 1834.

37 See his articles "An Account of the Mode of Growth of Young Corals of the Genus *Fungia,*" *Transactions of the Linnean Society of London* 16 (1833): 493–498; and "On the Formation and Growth of Coral Reefs and Islands," *West of England Journal of Science and Literature* 1 (1836): 45–56.

38 William Williams and James Hamlin and their wives. For missionaries and travelers in New Zealand see J. R. H. Andrews, *The Southern Ark: Zoological Discovery in New Zealand 1769–1900* (Honolulu: University of Hawaii Press, 1986), 101–122.

39 Stutchbury, "Observations," 91. Wilson was mentioned by most of the visiting scientists.

40 Ibid., 78.

41 S. Peter Dance, *Shell Collecting: An Illustrated History* (London: Faber and Faber, 1966), 167.

42 J. C. Melvill, "An Epitome of the Life of the Late Hugh Cuming, F.I.S., C.M.Z.S., &c," *Journal of Conchology* 8 (1895): 59–60.

43 *Athenaeum,* 19 August 1865, 247. See also S. Peter Dance, "Hugh Cuming (1791–1869), Prince of Collectors," *Journal of the Society for the Bibliography of Natural History* 9 (4) (1980): 478.

44 Hugh Cuming, "Journal of a Voyage from Valparaiso to the Society and the Adjacent Islands Perform'd in the Schooner *Discoverer* Sam-

uel Grimwood Master in the Years 1827 and 1828." MS, Mitchell Library, Sydney.

45   Ibid., TS copy in author's possession, 86.

46   Ibid.

47   Ibid., 115.

48   Ibid., 106.

49   Ibid., 122.

50   The institutions that benefited most were the British Museum of Natural History and the Royal Botanic Gardens, Kew, but Cuming sold widely to private collectors. See Edward Edwards, *Lives of the Founders of the British Museum; with Notices of its Chief Augmentors and Other Benefactors, 1570–1870,* 2 vols. (London: Trübner, 1870).

51   Some of Cuming's correspondence with Hooker has been published. See Elmer D. Merrill, "Hugh Cuming's Letters to Sir William J. Hooker," *Philippine Journal of Science* 30 (1926): 153–184.

52   George Bennet[t], "Notes on the Island of Tahiti, and on the Sandwich Islands, Southern Pacific Ocean," *The Schoolmaster, and Edinburgh Weekly Magazine* 2 (1833): 309.

53   Ibid., 310.

54   See his *Gatherings of a Naturalist in Australasia . . .* (London: John Van Voorst, 1860).

55   "It is curious that we find no mention of Bennett by the young Darwin, who gave vivid impressions of Sydney and Australia during the voyage of the *Beagle* in 1834." *Plarr's Lives of the Fellows of the Royal College of Surgeons of England* (Bristol: John Wright and Sons, 1930), 89. See also *Charles Darwin's "Beagle" Diary,* ed. Richard Darwin Keynes (Cambridge: Cambridge University Press, 1988), 395–407.

56   William Morwood, *Traveller in a Vanished Landscape: The Life and Times of David Douglas* (London: Gentry Books, 1973), publisher's blurb.

57   Kapiolani's heroic gesture as a testimony of her Christian convictions was much publicized in missionary and other pious literature throughout the world.

58   Morwood, *David Douglas,* 47–49.

59   Ibid., 213–215. This would be the first volume (of three), which appeared in 1830. Darwin's copy was given to him by Captain FitzRoy.

60   *"Beagle" Diary,* ed. Keynes, 376–377.

61   Ibid., 367. This was scored out in the original.

62   Ibid., 376.

63   Ibid., 380.

64   Ibid., 390.

65   Although the missionaries were mentioned in Wilkes' official account, they are ignored in modern accounts of the expedition. Hale expressed his debt to William Pascoe Crook and Charles Stewart.

66   Edward T. Perkins, *Na Motu: or, Reef-rovings in the South Seas: A Narrative of Adventures at the Hawaiian, Georgian and Society Islands . . .* (New York: Pudney and Russell, 1854), 288. The observatory is illustrated facing 287.

67   E. R. W. Krause forwarded photographs taken on Aneiteum to the directors on 30 December 1859. LMS, SSL.

68   See Berthold Seemann, *Viti, an Account of a Government Mission to the Vitian or Fijian Islands, 1860–1861* (Cambridge: Macmillan, 1862).

69   See particularly Hilton, *Age of Atonement*, 22 n. 66 et passim.

70   Ibid., 30.

71   Barber, *Natural History*, 47, 81, 127, 292.

72   *The Contented Botanist: Letters of W. H. Harvey about Australia and the Pacific*, ed. Sophie C. Ducker (Melbourne: Melbourne University Press, 1988), 11.

73   W. H. Harvey to N. B. Ward, 29 July 1855 in ibid., 241; *Missionary Notices*, 3d ser., 3 (1856): 24–28.

74   *Contented Botanist*, ed. Ducker, 14.

75   W. H. Harvey to Asa Gray, 3 November 1860, in *Contented Botanist*, ed. Ducker, 330.

76   Ibid., 331.

77   Ibid., 332.

78   See R. Tudur Jones, *Congregationalism in England 1662–1962* (London: Independent Press, 1962), 262.

79   Letter dated 26 April 1861 quoted in the *Leisure Hour* 25 (1877): 614.

80   Ibid.

81   The article "The Darwinian Theory tested by Science" was signed S. R. P.; ibid., 613–616.

82   Tudur Jones, *Congregationalism*, 262. In 1874 a contributor to the *British Quarterly Review* could see no reason why Darwin's main theory could not be acceptable to orthodox Christians.

83   Samuel James Whitmee, "Recollections of a Long Life [1917]." TS in author's possession, 32.

84   Ibid., 140.

85   See Deborah B. Waite, *Artefacts from the Solomon Islands in the*

Julius L. Brenchley Collection (London: British Museum Publications, 1987).

86   Ibid., 13. See also chap. 11.

87   Ibid., 90.

88   Codrington's major works were *The Melanesian Languages* (Oxford: Clarendon Press, 1885) and *The Melanesians: Studies in Their Anthropology and Folklore* (Oxford: Clarendon Press, 1891). See also below.

89   His books carried such titles as *Common Objects of the Country* and *Common Objects of the Microscope*. See Barber, *Natural History,* passim.

90   Published in two volumes (London: Routledge, 1870), "being an account of the manners and customs of the uncivilized races of men," the second volume being devoted to Australia, New Zealand, and Polynesia.

91   Shown to me in London in 1959 by Mrs. Aris, granddaughter of the Reverend John Arundel.

92   Most of the natural history articles were published in the *Leisure Hour* between 1872 and 1884.

93   David G. Frodin, "The Natural World of New Guinea: Hopes, Realities, and Legacies," in *Nature in Its Greatest Extent: Western Science in the Pacific,* ed. Roy MacLeod and Philip F. Rehbock (Honolulu: University of Hawaii Press, 1988), 129–130 n.33.

94   Whitmee, "Recollections," 144. Chap. 17, devoted to zoology, is missing from the manuscript.

95   Ibid., 152. For his dislike of shooting Australian parrots, even though pests, see ibid., 41.

96   Ibid., 144.

97   Ibid., 149.

98   Whitmee kept the second set, afterward given to Trinity College, Dublin. The other sets went to the British Museum, Oxford, Cambridge, Edinburgh, the United States (to Asa Gray), and Copenhagen (to Jensen). The smaller sets went to Canon Tristram of Durham and other private botanists.

99   The *manu mea* (see below). Whitmee gives a detailed account of this bird in "Recollections," 151–154.

100   Ibid., 155–156.

101   John Adams was the discoverer of Neptune. G. Elsie Harrison, *Methodist Good Companions* (London: Epworth Press, 1935), 91.

102   William Whewell was professor of moral philosophy at Cambridge. He and the "Trinity sages" set out "systematically to denigrate Paley as a mere utilitarian egoist." Hilton, *Age of Atonement,* 171.

103 J. Egan Moulton, *Moulton of Tonga* (London: Epworth Press, 1921), 56. He wrongly believed it to be "the first observatory in the network of islands in the Pacific."

104 Personal communication from Nigel Statham (Tongatapu, 1970), who studied Moulton's original MS notebooks at Tupou College.

105 "[I]t was commonly asserted that Mr Brown cared more about his name being given to a new snake, bird, or insect than he did for all the souls of the New Britain people put together.. . . Mr Brown had not only helped to open up the place to such men [naturalists], but had made many important discoveries. And they envied him." *In Wild New Britain: The Story of Benjamin Danks, Pioneer Missionary,* ed. Wallace Deane (Sydney: Angus and Robertson, 1923), 76.

106 C. Brunsdon Fletcher, *The Black Knight of the Pacific* (Sydney: Australasian Publishing Company, 1944), 106.

107 Ibid., 107.

108 Ibid., 17. The collection has since been dispersed.

109 S. J. Whitmee, "Rare Bird from Samoa," *Leisure Hour* 19 (1870): 568; "Notes on Didunculus and Pareundiastes," *Proceedings of the Zoological Society* (1874): 183–186. Although J. B. Stair claimed to be instrumental in obtaining the first specimen of the *manu mea* for the Zoological Society, it was evidently obtained from a Samoan chief and forwarded by George Brown in 1864. Fletcher, *Black Knight,* 108–111.

110 W. Colenso, "An Account of Some Enormous Fossil Bones of an unknown Species of the Class Aves, lately discovered in New Zealand," *Tasmanian Journal of Natural Science, Agriculture, Statistics, etc.* 2 (1846): 81–107; R. Taylor, letter to Owen [1844] in Richard Owen, "On *Dinornis,* part 2," *Transactions of the Zoological Society* 3 (4) (1846): 327. See also Andrews, *Southern Ark,* 123–140.

111 Richard Taylor, *Te Ika a Maui; or, New Zealand and Its Inhabitants . . . together with the Geology, Natural History, Productions, and Climate of the Country,* 2d ed. (London: William Macintosh; Wanganui: H. Ireson Jones, 1870). Colenso also published articles on the botany of the North Island of New Zealand in 1845 and 1865.

112 See Niel Gunson, "Co-operation without Paradox: A reply to Dr. Strauss," *Historical Studies, Australia and New Zealand* 11 (1965): 513–534.

113 Although a Dissenter, Greatheed mixed in a circle that included the poet Cowper, John Newton, "Blake's Hayley," and the artist George Romney. He spoke several languages and was one of the first to designate the "Australian" or Austronesian group.

114 Crook to directors, 25 May 1825, LMS, SSL.

115   John Davies, *A Grammar of the Tahitian Dialect of the Pre-Polyne-sian Language* (Tahiti: Mission Press, 1823); idem (with D. Darling), *A Tahitian and English Dictionary . . . and a Short Grammar of the Tahitian Dialect* (Papeete: London Missionary Society, 1851).

116   The first edition of *Polynesian Researches* appeared in two volumes in 1829 (London: Fisher, Son, and Jackson), the second in four volumes in 1831. Besides his own notes Ellis relied heavily on contributions from the missionaries Barff and Orsmond and possibly on the papers of George Bennett, member of a Society deputation to the LMS mission fields.

117   Lang sought material from Orsmond for his *View of the Origin and Migrations of the Polynesian Nation . . .* (London: Cochrane and McCrone, 1834) and encouraged Orsmond to collect in his own right. See Gunson, *Messengers of Grace,* 211.

118   See *Australian Reminiscences of L. E. Threlkeld,* ed. Gunson.

119   See Robert Thomson, *The Marquesas Islands: Their Description and Early History,* Introduction and Notes by Robert D. Craig (Laie: Institute for Polynesian Studies, 1978). The excellent history of the Society Islands remains unpublished.

120   Sarah S. Farmer, *Tonga and the Friendly Islands; with A Sketch of their Mission History, Written for Young People* (London: Hamilton, Adams, 1855), contains both natural history and ethnographic material. Thomas' own works are presently being prepared for publication.

121   *Fiji and the Fijians,* ed. George Stringer Rowe, 2 vols. (London: Alexander Heylin, 1858). Williams, who compiled the ethnographic volume, also kept a journal (published in two volumes in 1931), which is a valuable ethnographic source.

122   Dr. James Cowles Prichard (1786–1848), regarded as the pioneer of ethnology, had drawn up his *Manual of Scientific Enquiry* (1849), which was revised as a *Manual of Ethnological Inquiry.* In 1851 a subcommittee of the British Association for the Advancement of Science consisting of Richard Cull and Thomas Hodgkin was appointed to prepare a new edition of "the questions concerning the human race." Other editions of the questionnaire followed, culminating in *Notes and Queries on Anthropology* issued by the British Association.

123   The veteran missionary L. E. Threlkeld was honored with a diploma as Corresponding Member of the Ethnological Society in 1854 in recognition of his "linguistic researches into the dialects of Australia." *Australian Reminiscences of L. E. Threlkeld,* ed. Gunson, 2: 298.

124   William Wyatt Gill, *Myths and Songs from the South Pacific* (London: King, 1876).

125   See George Turner, *Nineteen Years in Polynesia . . .* (London: John

Snow, 1861), 173. Turner "followed the order of a list of queries respecting the human race, drawn up a number of years ago, by a committee of the British Association for the Advancement of Science."

126   William Wyatt Gill, *Historical Sketches of Savage Life in Polynesia, with Illustrative Clan Songs* (Wellington: Government Printer, 1880); *From Darkness to Light in Polynesia, with Illustrative Clan Songs* (London: Religious Tract Society, 1894).

127   *Contemporary Review* 21 (1873): 389–407. He contributed the article on Polynesians to the *Encyclopedia Britannica*.

128   Whitmee, "Recollections," 154–155.

129   Ibid., 159.

130   Peter France, *The Charter of the Land: Custom and Colonization in Fiji* (Melbourne: Oxford University Press, 1969), 117ff. Fison was president of the anthropology section of the AAAS at Hobart in 1892, and Brown was president of the AAAS Congress at Sydney in 1902.

131   Lewis H. Morgan, "Systems of Consanguinity and Affinity," *Contributions to Knowledge* (Washington, DC: Smithsonian Institution, 1870), 17: 568; France, *Charter of the Land*, 117.

132   See obituary of Codrington with bibliography by S. H. Ray in *Man* 22 (1922): 169–177. For his major works see above, n. 88.

133   Eric J. Sharpe, *Comparative Religion: A History,* 2d ed. (La Salle, IL: Open Court, 1986), 69.

134   *Pacific Islands Monthly,* October 1940, 29. Ivens was also traveling secretary in the Pacific for the Melanesian Mission before pursuing an academic career in Melbourne and London. Fox was "converted" to ethnology by W. H. R. Rivers in 1908. See his obituary by David Hilliard, *Journal of Pacific History* 13 (1978): 74.

135   MacLeod and Rehbock, eds., *Nature in Its Greatest Extent,* 101.

136   See James Urry, "From Zoology to Ethnology: A. C. Haddon's Conversion to Anthropology," *Canberra Anthropology* 5 (2) (1982): 58–85.

137   R. E. Reid, "John Henry Holmes in Papua: Changing Missionary Perspectives on Indigenous Cultures, 1890–1914," *Journal of Pacific History* 13 (1978): 179, 185.

138   See below, "Cultural Degeneration or Social Darwinism?"

139   See generally Reid, "J. H. Holmes," 173–187.

140   Macdonald, Stair, and Gill all published full-length works. Ethnographic articles by the missionaries W. W. Gill and J. M. Orsmond were published posthumously by G. Newell and Miss Teuira Henry respectively.

141   "Aryan" and "Turanian" theories were the order of the day. Mac-

donald maintained a Semitic or Arabian origin for the Austronesians, whom he termed Polynesians. D. J. Mulvaney has referred to papers that "skirted the lunatic fringe" and to the propagandist nature of many of the missionary papers at the early meetings of the AAAS. See his "Australian Anthropology and ANZAAS: 'Strictly Scientific and Critical,'" in *The Commonwealth of Science: ANZAAS and the Scientific Enterprise in Australasia, 1888–1988*, ed. Roy MacLeod (Melbourne: Oxford University Press, 1988), 199–200.

142   M. Russell, *Polynesia: or, an Historical Account of the Principal Islands in the South Sea, including New Zealand . . .*, 3d ed. (Edinburgh: Oliver and Boyd, 1845), 99–100.

143   Lorimer Fison, 26 March 1867, journal, letters, memos, etc., Microfilm 120, Records Room, Division of Pacific and Asian History, Australian National University.

144   Alexander Don, *Light in Dark Isles: A Jubilee Record and Study of the New Hebrides Mission of the Presbyterian Church of New Zealand* (Dunedin: Foreign Missions Committee, P.C., N.Z., 1918), 175. The same author quotes another writer concerning Fiji: "He must be taught to work out his own salvation in physical and mental toil; and, if he is not taught, or if he will not learn the lesson set him, there is no alternative—he will go to the wall and we shall have another illustration of the survival of the fittest" (164).

145   Macdonald, "The Antecedents of Existing Savages: Sir John Lubbock versus Archbishop Whately and the Duke of Argyll," *Victorian Review* 7 (1882–1883): 241. Italics added.

146   Ibid., 246.

147   Ibid.

148   More than 200 articles were published by British missionaries in the Pacific in scientific journals between 1868 and 1900, more than 130 articles between 1901 and 1930. Other scientific articles by missionaries were published in religious periodicals.

S A R A   S O H M E R

11 The Melanesian Mission and Victorian Anthropology

A Study in Symbiosis

Since the 1970s, a revival of interest in the Christian missionary movement in general and the relationship between missionaries and anthropologists in particular has considerably enhanced our understanding of cross-cultural encounter. The scholarship of historians and anthropologists has substantially revised the stereotypic image of unbending zealots uniformly determined on "Christianity and Civilization" by carefully examining the goals of particular mission organizations and the practice of individual missionaries in the field.[1] Reappraisals of the relationship have moved beyond the examination of the conflicts and tensions between the two groups to consider the contributions each made to the work of the other and to recognize that both groups imposed their cultural values on the indigenous peoples they encountered.[2]

To date, however, the intellectual context of the missionary movement in the nineteenth century has, unfortunately, been neglected. The degree of involvement with the main currents of the intellectual life of their age varied widely among both individual missionaries and mission organizations. But at a time when changes in print technology and a global communication/transportation network made books and periodicals available to literate men and women in the remotest corners of the mission field, this context must be considered. Missionaries may have been isolated, but by the second half of the nineteenth century they did not live in an intellectual vacuum. A consideration of developments in Victorian intellectual life, for example, can prove useful in any attempt to analyze the complex patterns of identity and tension that characterized missionaries' interaction with indigenous peoples and with anthropologists. In the particular case of the Melanesian Mission of the Church of England, an awareness of and affinity for much of that development on the part of its highly educated leadership may be the single most important factor in the easy, cooperative relationship the mission maintained with the emerging science of anthropology.

It would be difficult to imagine a time and place more problematic for that relationship than England in the second half of the nineteenth century. The common ground that science, ethics, and religion had shared in English intellectual life was rapidly disappearing. The old certainties, whether defined by biblical prescription or rationalism, fell prey to new discoveries in many scholarly disciplines. The Darwinian revolution that made human beings subject to the same forces that governed the rest of the biological world was the most dramatic example of this intellectual disjuncture. But thoughtful Victorians also had to absorb new perceptions of language introduced by comparative philology, a new understanding of time precipitated by Lyell's work in geology, and the limitations of the Euclidean geometry that had underlain the work of Descartes and Newton.

The demise of a priori truths in so many areas created a crisis of meaning. Scientific naturalism provided a rigorous approach to the investigation of the natural world. Yet by its very insistence on limiting truth to matters amenable to investigation and experimentation, it could not furnish a satisfactory paradigm for the more transcendent issues of religion and ethics. Few Victorians were prepared to give up the search for meaning simply because it had become more elusive. The more extreme manifestations of that search are well known. Some Victorians, rejecting out of hand the evidence that science and other scholarly disciplines presented, retreated into the security of fundamentalist Christianity and biblical literalism. Others denied the reality of religion in the light of the new truth of science. Our understanding of Victorian intellectual life is not, however, well served by this sort of polarization. Thoughtful individuals seldom found a single discourse sufficient for the thornier problems of interpretation and meaning.

An examination of the discourses available to a particular mission in the Pacific, the Melanesian Mission of the Church of England, and of the influence these discourses had on mission policy and practice leads to a reappraisal of the missionary's role in cultural contact and the supposedly dichotomous relationship of the sacred and the secular—of religion and science—in Victorian intellectual life, for the interaction between the missionaries of the Melanesian Mission and the pioneer figures of British anthropology was characterized by a symmetry of values that allowed for a working relationship far more symbiotic than competitive. Ironically, the Pacific region, a source of empirical data for the developments in Darwinian science that helped precipitate the Victorian crises of meaning, also provided critical data for those engaged in formulating new definitions of meaning in human experience.

The Melanesian Mission

The nature of the missionary-anthropologist relationship was in many respects conditioned by the development of the Melanesian Mission in the years before anthropological inquiry began to focus on Melanesia. The mission's founder, George Augustus Selwyn (1809–1878), the first Anglican bishop of New Zealand, saw the colonial church and the mission field as golden opportunities for the revitalization of the moribund Church of England. Despite the press of his duties in New Zealand, he determined on "some definite system for the evangelization of western Polynesia [Melanesia] including all the 'News'—New Caledonia, New Hebrides, New Britain, New Ireland, New Hanover, and New Guinea—where, if it please God, I hope in ten years to shake hands with the Bishop of Borneo."[3]

Selwyn's strategy for achieving this grand vision, however, was dictated by the hard reality of insufficient human resources and money. Recognizing the infeasibility of resident European missionaries for such a large, linguistically diverse, and dangerous field, Selwyn formulated a plan for a mission ship to collect young Melanesian "scholars" and bring them to the boarding school he had established in Auckland in 1843. The scholars were to spend spring and summer engaged in Christian education and industrial/agricultural training and then return to their home islands when the approach of colder weather in New Zealand put their health at risk. The rotation would continue until a scholar was deemed ready for baptism and knowledgeable enough to return to his island as a permanent teacher. In this manner, a small, dedicated English staff on the mission ship and at the boarding school could become, to use a phrase beloved by the mission staff, "white corks upholding a black net."[4]

Selwyn and his most important recruit for the mission, John Coleridge Patteson (1827–1871), had a very specific view of the background and character of the individuals they hoped would comprise the European staff. This differed markedly from the assumption of the great evangelical mission societies at the beginning of the nineteenth century that "humble men full of zeal" could fill the missionary role.[5] The ideal recruit for the Melanesian Mission, by contrast, was to be a paragon of education, resourcefulness, common sense, athletic prowess, and piety who could only have come from a public school, university background much like that of Selwyn and Patteson themselves. "A very few men," Patteson wrote, "well-educated, who will really try to understand what heathenism is and will seek . . . to work honestly without prejudice and without an indiscriminating admiration for all their own national tastes and modes of thought. We need only a few."[6]

In 1849 Selwyn began his grand enterprise, covering, on his first voyage, some three thousand miles in largely uncharted waters. He returned with five Melanesian scholars.[7] By 1854 the school and the rotation voyages had reached proportions that required more attention than Selwyn alone could give them. He recruited Patteson, who would, in 1861, be consecrated as the first missionary bishop of Melanesia. Patteson shared Selwyn's devotion to the concept of a revitalized Anglican church; but, unlike the dynamic bishop, he possessed a thoughtful, scholarly nature and a special gift for languages. Within a few years, he emerged as the principal architect of the mission's methodology. His concept of Melanesian Christianity—a doctrinally and theologically sound Anglicanism that could be sustained within the context of Melanesian culture—can be linked to both his intense interest in Melanesian languages and his commitment to the earliest possible establishment of an indigenous clergy.[8]

When the Reverend Robert Codrington (1830–1922) joined the mission staff as headmaster of the Norfolk Island school in 1867, the continued influence of Patteson's ideas was assured. Codrington, another linguistically gifted Oxford graduate, worked very closely with Patteson and shared his respect for Melanesian culture. Although he refused appointment as the second bishop of Melanesia, Codrington served as acting head of the mission for six years following Patteson's death and remained as headmaster of the boarding school until 1887. Like Patteson before him, he personally trained the Melanesian and the European clergy and teachers who served the mission.

From the time of Bishop Patteson, this small mission[9] in the southwest Pacific maintained an attitude toward the peoples it served atypical in many respects of the Victorian missionary movement. Sentiments such as those expressed by the quintessential Victorian missionary hero, Dr. David Livingstone, were far more common.

> We come among them [the heathen], [Livingstone maintained,] as members
> of a superior race and servants of a government that desires to elevate the
> more degraded portions of the human family. We are the adherents of
> a benign holy religion and may by consistent conduct and wise, patient

efforts become the harbingers of peace to a hitherto distracted and trodden race.[10]

It would, however, be misleading to consider the missionary ideal developed by the leadership of the Melanesian Mission as nothing more than an interesting oddity. Similar perspectives can be found in the Universities Mission to Central Africa (hereafter the UMCA), organized in 1857, and the Anglican Mission to Papua, an Australia-based mission founded in 1894. Like the Melanesian, these missions had associations with the High Church party within the Anglican communion. And like it, too, they attracted a higher percentage of university graduates than their evangelical counterparts. Almost half of those serving the Melanesian Mission in the nineteenth century were graduates of either British or colonial universities.[11] In the same period, university graduates made up about one third of the UMCA staff.[12] Although the leadership of the Anglican Mission to Papua was university-educated, most of the rank and file were not; only about 16 percent of its European staff were degree holders in 1920.[13]

The most obvious connection among these missions was a common adherence to a missionary ideal that eschewed the Christianity = civilization formula. "We have," wrote Bishop Steere of the UMCA,

> . . . from the first steadily set our faces against any denationalization of the people of Africa. For this purpose, we have been anxious to teach them in their own language, to accustom them to their own style of food and dress, as far as we could, in order to raise up a race of people who should not feel that they were strangers amongst their brethren.[14]

The Collaborative Tradition

Significantly, a number of prominent Victorian scholars and colonial officials recognized the merit of this alternative missionary ideal and found in its adherents trustworthy informants and collaborators. By the turn of the century, positive appraisals of the Melanesian Mission by those outside the ranks of the church usually noted not only the "enlightened" concepts developed by Patteson but also the mission's use of the new discipline of anthropology. Everarad Im Thurn, governor of Fiji from 1904 to 1910, praised the mission for its skillful blend of missionary zeal and anthropological methods.[15] The pioneer anthropologist William Halse Rivers saw in the mission's culturally sensitive evangelization a possible cure for the psychological malaise he believed to be the root cause of the depopulation of the region.[16] In the course of his field work in Melanesia (1898, 1908) and by correspondence from Cambridge, Rivers worked closely with

Walter J. Durrad, W. C. Ferrall, Arthur I. Hopkins, and Charles Fox, all members of the Melanesian Mission who produced important ethnographic studies of their own.

This collaborative tradition can be traced to the earliest development of anthropological inquiry in Victorian England. Friedrich Max Müller (1823–1900), Oxford professor of modern languages, translator of the Vedic classics, and a recognized authority on comparative mythology, corresponded with both Bishop Patteson and the Reverend Robert Codrington. As his philological studies broadened into a search for the theoretical origins of religious systems, he sought data on Melanesian religious practices and languages. His contention, in *Lectures on the Origin and Growth of Religion* (1878),[17] that all religion rests on the universal ability of the human mind to grasp the Infinite, for example, owed a great deal to Codrington's descriptions of the Melanesian concept of *mana*.[18]

Codrington, the author of important studies of Melanesian languages and custom,[19] also exchanged views with Edward Tylor (1832–1917), who held the readership in anthropology created at Oxford in 1884 and was a central figure in the first generation of evolutionary social theorists. Again, Codrington's data proved important in the formulation of theory: Tylor's views on exogamy and classificatory relationships relied on it as did the revision of his theory of the evolution of religious forms devised by his pupil and colleague, R. R. Marett (1866–1943).[20]

Despite their profound distrust of all biblical or religious perspectives for the study of human culture, Victorian anthropologists frequently used information provided by the missionaries—a situation not as strange as it might at first appear. The staff of the Melanesian Mission consisted for the most part of educated men disposed by both their particular vision of Christian mission and their long association with Melanesians to regard indigenous culture with respect. There was little inherent reason to distrust the objectivity of a missionary source. Besides, the use of reasonable, trustworthy informants had pragmatic advantages. Until the 1890s British anthropology remained largely the anthropology of the study, if not the armchair.[21] The legitimacy of comparative inquiry based on data collected by travelers, missionaries, and colonial administrators enjoyed wide acceptance. In evaluating informants, some scholars, like the early ethnologist Dr. James C. Prichard (1786–1848), preferred data from long-resident missionaries familiar with the nuances of native language.[22] Descriptions provided by such sources could, Edward Tylor thought, provide the scholar of culture with patterns and comparisons needed to form a proper theoretical framework[23]—a view apparently agreeable to Darwin, who used information from Patteson's writings as the source for his speculations on population patterns in Melanesia in the second edition of *The Descent of Man* in 1874.[24]

The more compelling question is why the staff of the Melanesian Mission—this particular group of determined Christians—felt so much affinity for the new science of humankind. The answer lies in the nature of Victorian anthropology itself. While its proponents confidently declared the complete feasibility of the scientific study of humankind,[25] in fact the second half of the nineteenth century constituted a period of uncertainty and confusion for the infant social science. The strong empirical bent of British science and the impact of evolutionary, developmental concepts undoubtedly formed the basis for anthropological inquiry in this period. But this framework was not enough to deliver the discipline from the confusion created by the demise of the old intellectual certainties. However determined one might be to study humanity scientifically, no one really knew how to go about it.[26] And, like many of their contemporaries, some Victorian anthropologists required reassurance that human life on earth meant something more than the end product of random Darwinian processes. The methodology of German idealist thought—the comparative historical method derived from philology and the concept of progressive stages of development—proved to be particularly attractive in their search for a view of human beings that was simultaneously "scientific" and "progressive," as indeed it was for their thoughtful contemporaries engaged in theological speculation.[27]

The early leaders in the field, moreover, were not, and indeed could not be, specialists. Men like Sir Henry Maine and Edward Tylor were the products of an educational system designed to produce men broadly educated for the professions and service with the state or the Church. In a very real sense, they were amateurs vis-à-vis the discipline they were constructing. Anthropology had only tenuous claims as an academic discipline in the British university system until the turn of the century.[28] Throughout its formative period, British anthropology was characterized by "role hybrids," that is to say, by individuals who began their professional lives in other fields and came to anthropology only as their interest in more speculative matters grew.[29] A. C. Haddon, who held the first readership in ethnology at Cambridge and organized the Torres Strait Expedition, worked originally as a zoologist. W. H. R. Rivers began his professional life as a neurologist, and Jane Harrison, the source of critical ideas on the interrelationship of myth and ritual in culture, was a classicist.[30]

There is little here to suggest that the intellectual concerns of the early Victorian anthropologists represented a radical departure from those of other educated, thoughtful Victorians. In searching for new answers, anthropology exhibited the eclectic, unspecialized, and unsystematic methods that characterized Victorian intellectual life in general.[31] In their training, the problems that interested them, and the methodology they employed, its early practitioners shared common ground with other serious, critically minded men, including the members of the Melanesian Mission of the Church of England. If, as J. W. Burrow has suggested, Sir Henry Maine approached the study of society, not as a professional scientist with a formula for inquiry, but as a classical scholar with direct experience in a country with a culture alien to its governors,[32] then his vantage point did not differ markedly from that of the Reverend Robert Codrington or Bishop John C. Patteson.

One of their most important shared concerns centered on the origin and development of civilization. For the European staff of the Melanesian Mission, attempting to come to terms with the "uncivilized" islanders and to sort out the relationship between a theoretically universal faith and its parent civilization, this was a critical issue. The speculations of anthropology offered the comforting possibility of clarification or even exegesis for men who had to balance the civilized and the primitive in their daily affairs.

George W. Stocking has suggested that the fascination of anthropology with the question of civilization reflects both the unease and the self-confidence of the Victorian era. Civilization in a sense formed the only possible cushion from the inexorable forces of a new Darwinian nature. Although humans had their origins in nature and remained part of it, civilization put them at some remove from its forces and gave them some control over it.[33] By the midnineteenth century, an expansive economy, a functioning empire, and a sense of confidence rooted in both Evangelical and Utilitarian fervor combined to convince Victorian society of the efficacy of civilization as a buffer against the arbitrary forces of nature. The most problematic feature of civilization lay less in its failures and discontents than in an inadequate explication of its origins and development. Anthropological inquiry focused to a considerable degree on this need. Gradually, the natural history of humankind began to be interpreted less in terms of movement in space and more as development in time. Methodological and conceptual innovations in both history and the natural sciences—for example, historicism, uniformitarianism, and evolution—reinforced this change.[34]

This emphasis on what Stocking calls the "cultural evolutionary ladder"[35] determined the Victorian approach to the study of primitive cultures. As functioning social systems with complex, interrelated cultural features, they merited passing interest at best. But as exemplars of the stages and processes of human cultural development, they proved invaluable. "No one who can see," wrote Tylor, ". . . how direct and close the connexion may be between modern culture and the condition of the rudest savage, will be prone to accuse students who spend their labour on even the lowest and most trifling facts of ethnography, of wasting their hours in the satisfaction of a frivolous curiosity."[36] Those who recognized the importance of this connection for the study of the origin and development of civilization were also fairly confident that they understood how it functioned. The paramount place of religion in that development, the uniformity of human cultural response across time and space, and the presence of "true progress" in human history were largely assumed.

None of these intellectual assumptions was a likely source of conflict for missionaries committed to both the universal and the transcendent. In the case of the Melanesian Mission, common assumptions were reinforced by a common methodology. For at least the first thirty years after the emergence of anthropology as an independent discipline, both groups utilized a comparative historical approach derived primarily from philology to comprehend primitive culture. This commonality of interests is nowhere more apparent than in the relationship between Max Müller and Bishop Patteson and the Reverend Robert Codrington.

Language and Myth: The Comparative Approach

Max Müller was, by 1860, undisputedly the foremost authority on language and myth in Great Britain. Thoroughly versed in German idealist philosophy and philology, he introduced comparative philology at Oxford, translated the Indian classics, and became a sought-after lecturer. Like many scholars, he used his specialized interests as a springboard to the study of broader issues. Language became the key to an understanding of the function of religion and the origin of social structures. "Language," he wrote, "stands in the system of the intellectual world as light stands in the system of the physical world, comprising all, and revealing all."[37] In a lecture entitled "On the Stratification of Language" given in 1868, he further developed the thesis that in philology, as in geology, stratifications forming chronological series could be observed. By studying these stratifications, philologists could analyze the development of language from its inception.[38] Thus the scientific study of language became the best possible approach to the study of human prehistory. Müller indeed argued at Oxford that philology should be numbered as one of the natural sciences.[39]

In keeping with his view that language study constituted a science, Müller stressed the importance of data collection and classification followed by theoretical extrapolation.[40] For the first two steps, he required the assistance of those in direct contact with the languages and mythological systems of contemporary primitive cultures. He turned to Bishop Patteson and Robert Codrington, both of whom he had known at Oxford before they went to Melanesia. It was, he wrote to Patteson in 1865, only through "savage" languages that one could hope to understand fully the mysterious process of change in language, as literary languages could be completely misleading on this point.[41]

Given the demands on his time and energy, Patteson appears to have done his best for Müller. He had, he replied to Müller's queries, to learn languages for very practical reasons and simply could not spend a great deal of time informing the literati at home of the fine points of dialectic variation.[42] But his comments elsewhere indicate an interest in language study that went far beyond the pragmatic. His own training was extensive, encompassing German and Hebrew as well as the standard Greek and Latin. In Melanesia he worked on at least twenty languages in his rather brief lifetime. The process of trying to derive accurate meanings fostered a profound respect for the complexity and expressiveness of "primitive" language and a highly cautious approach to translation.[43] "Don't," he warned, "attempt to use words as [assumed] equivalents of abstract ideas."[44] It is hardly surprising that he read Müller's work on languages with interest.[45]

Codrington shared Patteson's appreciation of Melanesian languages. Writing on the philology and ethnology of Melanesia in 1875—and complaining of a lack of time to pursue these interests— he pointed out that a Melanesian language spoken on a small island by only a thousand or so people had, nonetheless, a vocabulary and grammar of such complexity that a person of average education and intelligence would require a long period to master it. Patteson, he recalled, used to become angry with those who maintained that the speech of savages could not properly be called language. Codrington himself thought it worth notice that "there is a great deal of scholarship in a savage tongue. Why is it, again, that among savages in an uncultivated and unwritten language, you never find anyone who says anything incorrect . . . ? And are people properly savages whose language is so exact?"[46]

For Patteson and Codrington—or for Max Müller—the answer

was a definitive no. "The language of a savage People," Codrington maintained, "is the most conspicuous product of their mental power. People in the least advanced condition as to civilization have language; and their language is never found in a condition corresponding to the backward state of their arts of life."[47] Recognition of Melanesian speech patterns as full-fledged languages entailed a corresponding recognition of the place of Melanesians "as members of the common brotherhood, partakers in the aspirations and capacities which other races have been enabled to develop and exercise, not always by better qualities but by better fortune."[48]

In the case of language, the convergence among the missionaries' own observations in the field, their theological proclivities, and the theoretical direction of early Victorian anthropology proved almost perfect. Christianity incorporated "the other" into the human family through its recognition of the immortal human soul. The recognition of the completeness of all human language provided in part by Victorian anthropology served to confirm that place. The Melanesian Mission, persuaded that Melanesians could both comprehend the fundamental universal truths of the faith and incorporate them in a meaningful manner into their own culture, welcomed the "proof" of mental and spiritual distinction provided by language.

Language was far from the only means of assigning Melanesians and other primitive peoples a place in the human brotherhood. For Edward Tylor and Sir Henry Maine, this inclusive view could be further supported by a developmental concept of human progress and the use of comparative historical methods. Bishop Patteson read the works of both scholars while in Melanesia. Tylor himself approached the study of human development with a certain missionary zeal.[49] By finding evidence that all rational human beings will give essentially the same response to the same conditions he sought to combat the popular, but in his view pernicious, degeneration theory of primitive culture. The universality of particular myths seemed a case in point.[50] "The facts collected," he wrote in his *Researches into the Early History of Mankind and the Development of Civilization,* "seem to favour the view that the wide differences in the civilization and mental state of the various races of mankind are rather differences of development than of origin, rather of degree than of kind."[51]

For Sir Henry Maine (1822–1888) the mythological record contained the moral and metaphysical conceptions that influenced all successive developments, including his special interest, the law. "These rudimentary ideas are to the jurist," Maine said, "what the primary crusts of the earth are to the geologist."[52] The observation of contemporary primitive societies—whose existence he, like Tylor, attributed to different rates of human social development—provided the best means of establishing the basis of the social state. This invaluable resource for understanding social order had, regrettably, been neglected out of fear, religious prejudice, and the very use of the terms *civilization* and *barbarian*. As long as observers perceived primitive cultures in terms of differences in kind and not degree, they would fail to grasp the significance of what they saw.[53]

Maine could not have complained of the Melanesian Mission on this score. Its founders clearly viewed Melanesian culture in comparative and developmental terms. As Bishop Patteson came to know island languages, he compared them to Hebrew. The central though often overlooked fact of Hebrew, he wrote to the bishop of Salisbury in 1871, is that it was basically the spoken language of an illiterate people, written down eventually without manipulation by an educated elite. To approximate the meaning of the ancient Hebrews required shedding many modes of thought and expression that characterize a "civilized" mentality. Many contemporary peoples, including the islanders of Melanesia, thought and spoke in the manner of the ancient Hebrews.[54] Both groups revealed the mode of expression of people still in a fairly early stage of cultural development.[55] Yet it would hardly have occurred to Patteson or his contemporaries to question the profound spiritual insights contained in the Old Testament.

Patteson also identified in contemporary European civilization survivals of earlier practices, an idea used by Tylor as well. Hence the custom of ladies withdrawing at the end of a meal had some relationship to Melanesian "tapus" on dining with women, while the Odd Fellows, trade unions, and Freemasons stemmed from the same impulse as primitive secret societies.[56] And while Patteson would hardly have been prepared to view the Last Supper as a mere survival, he did understand its relationship to the feast as it existed in primitive culture. "The Last Supper," he wrote in 1867,

> whatever higher and deeper meanings it may have, has this simple but most significant meaning to the primitive of feasting or of a child with his brothers and sisters at his Father's Board. . . . This privilege of membership, strengthening the tie, a familiarizing oneself more and more with the thoughts and custom of that Heavenly Family—this surely is a very great deal of what human instincts as exhibited in almost universal customs required.[57]

Insofar, then, as a developing anthropology focused on the common elements in the dizzying diversity of human culture, its affinity with the mission is readily apparent. R. R. Marett wrote of his mentor, Edward Tylor: "The need of his age was to proclaim that mankind is a many in one, with the emphasis on the one."[58] While the "one" was defined for the Melanesian Mission primarily in terms of the Christian universalist ideal, the reinforcement provided by anthropology was most welcome. The mission's leadership, however, parted company with those early anthropologists who saw human cultural development in terms of strict determinist and racialist patterns. Patteson read *The Plurality of Race*,[59] by the French scholar George Pouchet, "with much dispute" in 1866.[60] Pouchet, a physician, a member of the Anthropological Society of Paris, and a corresponding member of the Anthropological Society of London, insisted on speciation within the human race. Intellectual inequality figured prominently in his concept, a position he supported by citing missionary reports concerning the total lack of religious perception among Australian Aborigines, Africans, and Eskimos. "We must," he proclaimed, "distrust those minds which begin by declaring *a priori* the universality of beliefs, hopes, and fears among mankind, as a natural consequence of the primitive unity of the human species."[61] It is small wonder that Patteson, who as early as 1856 had "quite learnt to believe that there are no 'savages' anywhere, at least among black or coloured people,"[62] read Pouchet with distrust.

The same distrust is apparent in Robert Codrington's response to the conclusions of another scholar of evolution, Sir John Lubbock (later Lord Avebury). Lubbock had much closer connections to evolutionary biology than Tylor or Maine, and his view of the human social condition contained decidedly hierarchical and determinist overtones. He believed that civilized and uncivilized races exhibited marked differences in almost every respect. Primitive language, for example, lacked the means of expressing abstract concepts. In his *Prehistoric Times* (1865), Lubbock cited the futile efforts of the St. Petersburg Bible Society to translate basic Christian texts into the language of Siberian indigenes, a failure caused by "the language being entirely deficient in words to express new and abstract ideas, and partly for want of letters to convey the variety of strange and uncouth sounds of which the language itself consists."[63] This inability to form abstractions also led Lubbock to question whether primitives were capable of creating anything that could properly be called religion. "How...," he asked, "can a people who are unable to count their own fingers possibly raise their mind so far as to realize the difficult problems of religion?"[64]

As if this pessimistic view of primitive abilities was not enough, Lubbock assured his readers that "their real condition is even worse and more abject than that which I have endeavoured to depict,"[65] a condition he attributed ultimately to natural selection: "The great principle of natural selection which in animals affects the body and seems to have little influence on the mind, in man affects the mind and has little influence on the body. In the first, it tends mainly to the preservation of life; in the second, to the improvement of the mind, and consequently to the increase of happiness."[66] For Lubbock, the evolutionary, the ultimately progressive process of human development had passed the savage by. A study of primitive culture might provide some insight into prehistory and had a certain utility for the proper management of indigenes in the British Empire, but it could hardly inform civilized society.

That articles by Codrington and Lubbock appeared in the same learned journal on at least one occasion forms an interesting commentary on the unsettled character of Victorian anthropology,[67] for they could hardly have been further removed from each other in their view of primitive culture. "I confess," Codrington wrote in 1875, "that the savage of books does not come my way. As I read Sir John Lubbock . . . and find that such and such is the case with savages, I come to the conclusion that our people [Melanesians] are not savages."[68] The language of Melanesians not only had the same complexity and subtlety of civilized tongues but possessed a strong aesthetic appeal as well. The Psalms *could* be translated into Mota, the chief language of the mission, and those translations, to Codrington's ear, were "as lofty in their diction and as harmonious in their rhythm . . . as anything . . . in any language."[69]

As for religion, the very practices that Lubbock cited as proof of inferiority provided Codrington with proof of the universality of human religious response and hope for the eventual success of the Christian message. The Melanesian, he noted, lived on easy terms with the invisible world, certain that the body did not represent all of the individual and confident of the ability of human beings to communicate with unseen powers and enlist their aid.

> It is not wise for any teacher of true religion to neglect or despise, even if he must abhor them, the superstitious beliefs and rites of those whom he would lead from darkness to light. It is far better, if it be possible, to search for and recognize what is true and good among wild and foul superstitions; to find the common foundation, if such there be, which lies in human nature itself, ready for the superstructure of the Gospel. It may surely be said that no missionary who knows and loves his people will ever fail to find this foundation, even among the lowest races of mankind, or find him-

self utterly unable to say to them: "Whom ye ignorantly worship, Him I declare unto you."[70]

Without the "common foundation," the truth of the Christian message, Codrington thought, would not be recognized and consequently would have no influence. However morally limited indigenous belief systems might be,

> there is the belief, found among all savage people, in the existence of the soul, and in its continued existence after death; there is the feeling, over and above the desire to obtain what will be useful in this world from spirits, that communication with the unseen world is a thing to be desired in itself. A savage people, if such are to be found, who have no appetite for intercourse with the invisible, would fail to supply to a missionary a fulcrum by which, when it exists, they may be raised to a higher level. The man who believes he has a soul, and that death is but a change of existence, and that unseen spiritual influence is at work upon him, is in a more receptive condition as regards Christianity than one whose whole thought is to eat and drink for tomorrow he dies.[71]

The disagreement between Lubbock and Codrington over the religious capabilities of primitive peoples reflects both the widespread interest in the subject and the innovative approaches to its study that appeared in the nineteenth century. Once Christianity was removed from the sphere of the sacred and the unquestionable, the study of religion as a whole shifted from a simple division of the true and the false to the comparative and the developmental. The methodology applied to religion, in short, paralleled that utilized in the study of other human institutions.

By far the most prominent theoretical constructs applied to religion were developmental. Tylor, for example, saw religion as evolving "upwards from the simplest theory which attributes life and personality to animal, vegetable and mineral alike . . . up to that which sees in each department of the world the protecting and fostering care of an appropriate divinity, and at last of one Supreme Being ordering and controlling the lower hierarchy."[72] Thus the human religious experience could be marshaled into a fairly tidy order, beginning with the attribution of vitality to all natural phenomena—the process Tylor called animism—proceeding through polytheism and ending in the rationalization that produced the concept of monotheism.[73]

Although Tylor had formulated his construct from data supplied by Codrington, the missionary-ethnographer could not agree. The source of his disagreement was certainly theological in part. If any single principle could be said to account for the goals and methods articulated by the Melanesian Mission, the best choice would be the belief in the universality and fundamental uniformity of human religious response, a belief deeply rooted in particular High Church traditions and reinforced by the more liberal Anglican responses to the intellectual crises Christianity faced in the nineteenth century. But Codrington's exception to Tylor's development scheme had an empirical basis as well. His own observation of Melanesian religious belief and practice led to the first authoritative expression of the concept of *mana*. As Codrington saw it, the Melanesian mind was entirely possessed by its belief in a supernatural power or influence affecting everything beyond the ordinary power of human beings or the common processes of nature. This power, known throughout Melanesia as *mana*, was not fixed in anything and could be conveyed to almost anything. *Mana* itself had a purely impersonal nature, although it could only be made manifest through some person or spirit that directed it. Thus all Melanesian religious practice centered on acquiring *mana* and using it for one's own benefit.[74]

Ernst Cassirer has suggested that Codrington erred in designating *mana* a spiritual as well as a magical power. In Cassirer's view, *mana* must be regarded as a very generalized, undifferentiated concept—so undifferentiated, in fact, that it cannot properly be treated as either a noun or a verb. Codrington, in short, may have confused the Indefinite with the Infinite.[75] But the important consideration here is not that Codrington may have reached incorrect conclusions or that his data confirmed his theological proclivities. It is rather that his scholarly contemporaries valued his contribution as a respectable endeavor subject to the same scholarly criteria as that of anyone else in the field. No one dismissed his evaluation of *mana* as a mere configuration of his clerical status. A review of *The Melanesians* (1891) published in *Internationales Archiv für Ethnographie* praised Codrington as "a keen observer, cautious in drawing inferences, free from any kind of dogmatism and, what is most important, kind in his feelings towards fellow men in a backward state of civilization commonly and vulgarly called savages."[76]

Codrington had credibility as an independent theorist as well as a reliable collector of data. The perspective on the study of Melanesian language and culture that he and Patteson created was gradually incorporated into the methodology of anthropological field work. Stocking has suggested that the prototype for the essentials of the intensive method (long residence, linguistic expertise, and firsthand observation) was developed first by the best of the missionary ethnographers and later absorbed by field anthropologists. W. H. R. Rivers, for example, began his field work by confining himself to survey work based on information provided by informants. Through his elaboration of the methods for ferreting out intricate kinship/genealogical arrangements, he made a major contribution to the scientific approach to ethnological observation. Using Rivers' methods, the trained scientific observer could, in a comparatively short time, collect pertinent information that had escaped even long-term residents. The observer would have, in other words, the means of establishing the basic structure of any indigenous society.

Gradually, however, Rivers became aware of the need for intensive study and long-term residence. The advantage of this approach lay in the addition of the empathetic, detailed, and penetrating knowledge that characterized the work of some missionary ethnographers. His own work revealed a growing sensitivity to the difficulties of cultural translation—however effective the methodological models the investigator employed—and the necessity of the intensive method in overcoming them. Thus when the British Association for the Advancement of Science asked for Rivers' help in the revision of *Notes and Queries,* originally published in 1881 to provide guidance for missionaries, government officials, and other nonprofessionals engaged in gathering anthropological data, he emphasized the critical need to acquire indigenous language, the danger of posing questions that had no logic in the culture of indigenous informants, and the role of tact, sympathy, and patience.[77] It does not seem unreasonable to suggest that Rivers (and through him British field anthropology) may have been influenced by the particular expertise of the members of the Melanesian Mission he encountered in the field and with whom he collaborated closely. Those missionaries (Durrad, Fox, Ferrall, and Hopkins), however appreciative they might be of Rivers' science, were first and foremost the heirs and perpetuators of a mission philosophy that had from the time of Bishop Patteson granted indigenous culture its own worth and validity and, perhaps even more significantly, its own complexity.

Conclusion

The basis of the Melanesian Mission's easy, almost symbiotic, relationship with anthropology appears to reflect an intellectual flexibility among at least some educated, inquiring Victorians originating in common intellectual reference points, shared ethical concerns, and a less rigid view of the division between amateur and professional than is presently the case. The concept of a chasm between religion and science—including the science that sought to examine and explain human development—may have had some relevance for more rigid minds at either end of the intellectual spectrum. But for Codrington and Patteson, or for that matter, Tylor and Müller, the issue remained more a matter of dialog than of conflict. In the renewed interest in the relationship between the only two groups of Europeans—anthropologists and missionaries—who consistently brought intellectual assumptions to their encounter with indigenous peoples, it is well to keep this Victorian example in mind. As James Clifford pointed out in his study of the missionary-ethnologist Maurice Leenhardt, "to the extent that the two positions [religion and science] are maintained in opposition as an either/or choice, a whole range of political or cultural action *with* others is precluded."[78]

Notes

1   For the Pacific mission field other than Hawaii see Hugh Laracy, *Marists and Melanesians: A History of Catholic Missions in the Solomon Islands* (Canberra: Australian National University Press, 1976); David Wetherell, *Reluctant Mission: The Anglican Church in Papua New Guinea* (St. Lucia, Australia: University of Queensland Press, 1977); David Hilliard, *God's Gentlemen: A History of the Melanesian Mission 1849–1942* (St. Lucia, Australia: University of Queensland Press, 1978); Niel Gunson, *Messengers of Grace: Evangelical Missionaries in the South Seas, 1797–1860* (Melbourne: Oxford University Press, 1978); Diane Langmore, *Missionary Lives: Papua, 1874–1914* (Honolulu: University of Hawaii Press, 1988); Mary T. Huber, *The Bishops' Progress: A Historical Ethnography of Catholic Missionary Experience on the Sepik Frontier* (Washington, DC: Smithsonian Institution Press, 1988). For Hawaii see Sandra Wagner, "Sojourners among Strangers: The First Two Companies of Missionaries to the Sandwich Islands" (Ph.D. dissertation, University of Hawaii, 1986); Nancy Morris, "Hawaiian Missionaries Abroad, 1853–1909" (Ph.D. dissertation, University of Hawaii, 1987); Patricia Grimshaw, *Paths of Duty: American Missionary Wives in Nineteenth-Century Hawaii* (Honolulu: University of Hawaii Press, 1989); Mary Zwiep, *Pilgrim Path: The First Company of Women Missionaries to Hawaii* (Madison: University of Wisconsin Press, 1991). For Africa see David Neave, "Aspects of the History of the Universities' Mission to Central Africa, 1885–1900 (M.A. thesis, University of York, 1974); Robert Strayer, *The Making of Mission Communities in East Africa: Anglicans and Africans in Colonial Kenya, 1875–1935* (Albany: State University of New York Press, 1978); Jean Comaroff and John Comaroff, *Of Revelation and Revolution: Christianity, Colonialism, and Consciousness in South Africa* (Chicago: University

of Chicago Press, 1991), vol. 1. For a perceptive statement of the necessity of reexamining the missionary movement, see T. O. Beidelman, "Social Theory and the Study of Christian Missions in Africa," *Africa* 46 (1974): 235–249.

2   For examinations of the relationship between missionaries and anthropologists, see Claude E. Stipes, "Anthropologists versus Missionaries: The Influence of Presuppositions," *Current Anthropology* 22 (1980): 165–179; Daniel Hughes, "Mutual Biases of Anthropologists and Missionaries," and Kenelm Burridge, "Missionary Occasions," in *Mission, Church, and Sect in Oceania*, ed. James A. Boutilier, Daniel T. Hughes, and Sharon W. Tiffany (New York: University Press of America, 1978); Paul G. Hiebert, "Missions and Anthropology: A Love/Hate Relationship," *Missiology* 6 (1978): 167–179; Frank A. Salomone, "Anthropologists and Missionaries: Competition or Reciprocity," *Human Organization* 36 (1977): 407–412.

3   Letter to William Ewart Gladstone, July 1853, Gladstone Papers, series 44–299ff., British Library, London.

4   Hilliard, *God's Gentlemen*, 10.

5   Sarah Potter, "The Making of Missionaries in the Nineteenth Century: Conversion and Convention," *Sociological Yearbook of Religion in Britain* 8 (1975): 103–124.

6   J. C. Patteson to his cousin, Derwent Coleridge, 8 August 1863, in *Life of John Coleridge Patteson, Missionary Bishop of Melanesia*, ed. Charlotte Yonge, 2 vols. (London: Macmillan, 1874), 2:67.

7   The school relocated to the relatively more salubrious climate of Norfolk Island in 1867, but the system of rotating between boarding school and island remained a fundamental aspect of the mission until the end of World War I.

8   This goal was realized in 1868 when George Sarawia, a Banks Islander, became the first Melanesian to receive holy orders. Hilliard, *God's Gentlemen*, 61.

9   A list in the Blencowe Collection of Papers pertaining to the Melanesian Mission puts at forty-four the number of Europeans serving the mission in any capacity between 1850 and 1900. Australian Joint Copying Project, Microfilm nos. M802–M806.

10   *The Zambezi Expedition of David Livingstone, 1858–1863*, quoted in *The Victorian Crisis of Faith*, ed. Anthony Symondson (London: SPCK, 1970), 65.

11   Blencowe Collection.

12   David Neave, "Aspects of the Universities' Mission to Central Africa, 1869–1900" (M.A. thesis, University of York, 1974).

13   Langmore, *Missionary Lives*, 25–28. For a discussion of the educational backgrounds of evangelical missionaries, see Sarah Potter, "The

Making of Missionaries in the Nineteenth Century: Conversion and Convention," *Sociological Yearbook of Religion in Britain* 8 (1975): 103–123; and C. P. Williams, " 'Not Quite Gentlemen': An Examination of 'Middling Class,' Protestant Missionaries from Britain, c. 1850–1900," *Journal of Ecclesiastical History* 31 (1980): 301–315.

14   Alan C. Cairns, *Prelude to Imperialism: British Reactions to Central African Society, 1840–1890* (London: Routledge and Kegan Paul, 1965), 219.

15   Everarad Im Thurn, in *Essays on the Depopulation of Melanesia,* ed. W. H. R. Rivers (Cambridge: Cambridge University Press, 1922), vi.

16   Ibid., 94–110.

17   Max Müller, *Lectures on the Origin and Growth of Religion* (London, 1878).

18   Ernst Cassirer, *Language and Myth* (New York: Harper, 1946), 80.

19   See Robert Codrington, *The Melanesians: Studies in their Anthropology and Folk-lore* (Oxford: Clarendon Press, 1885), and idem, *The Melanesian Languages* (Oxford: Clarendon Press, 1885).

20   George W. Stocking, *Victorian Anthropology* (New York: Free Press, 1987), 317–320.

21   J. W. Burrow, *Evolution and Society: A Study in Victorian Social Theory* (Cambridge: Cambridge University Press, 1966), 85.

22   Stocking, *Victorian Anthropology,* 79.

23   Edward Tylor, *The Origins of Primitive Culture* (1871; New York: Harper Torchbooks, 1958), 9.

24   Charles Darwin, *The Descent of Man* (New York: D. Appleton, 1883), 185.

25   Burrow, *Evolution and Society,* 119.

26   Ibid., 132–133.

27   Stocking, *Victorian Anthropology,* 325.

28   Oxford established its first readership in anthropology in 1884, with the position becoming a chair in 1896. Cambridge University did not follow suit until the first decade of the twentieth century, even though both the Torres Straits Expedition (1898) and the Percy Slade Trust Expedition (1907), the earliest British anthropological expeditions, had been organized under its auspices. Richard Slobodin, *W. H. R. Rivers* (New York: Columbia University Press, 1978), 130.

29   Ian Langham, *The Building of British Social Anthropology: W. H. R. Rivers and His Cambridge Disciples in the Development of Kinship Studies, 1898–1931* (London: D. Reidel, 1981), 51.

30   Slobodin, *W. H. R. Rivers,* 27, 28.

31   Morse Peckham, *Victorian Revolutionaries: Speculations on Some Heroes of a Cultural Crisis* (New York: George Braziller, 1970), 209.

32   Burrow, *Evolution and Society*, 158.

33   Stocking, *Victorian Anthropology*, 325.

34   Ibid., 77.

35   Ibid.

36   Tylor, *Primitive Culture*, 159.

37   Max Müller, quoted in Nirad C. Chaudhuai, *Scholar Extraordinary: The Life of Professor the Rt. Hon. Friedrich Max Müller* (London: Chatto and Windus, 1974), 82.

38   Ibid., 185–186.

39   Ibid., 82.

40   Ibid., 188.

41   Letter from Müller to Bishop Patteson, 1865, series 29, Codrington Collection, Rhodes House, Oxford. Müller felt that the earliest written languages reflected a degree of development and complexity that limited their usefulness in illuminating the origins and early structures of language.

42   Yonge, *Patteson*, 2:187.

43   Ibid., 135.

44   Ibid., 191.

45   Patteson diary for 1866, papers relating to Bishop John C. Patteson, Selwyn College Library, Cambridge.

46   Printed letter to Mr. Freeling, 1875, Codrington Collection, series 9.

47   Printed article, "The Language of a Savage People," Codrington Collection, series A.

48   Ibid., 2.

49   Peckham, *Victorian Revolutionaries*, 186.

50   Abram Kardiner and Edward Preble, *They Studied Man* (New York: Mentor Books, 1961), 59–60.

51   Edward Tylor, *Researches into the Early History of Mankind and the Development of Civilization* (1865; Chicago: University of Chicago Press, 1964), 232.

52   Sir Henry Maine, *Ancient Law* (1861; London: Dorset, 1989), 2.

53   Ibid., 99–100.

54   Yonge, *Patteson*, 2:504.

55   Ibid., 475.

56   Patteson Papers, 1867, Rhodes House, Oxford.

57   Ibid.

58   Marett, *Tylor*, 48; quoted in Burrow, *Evolution and Society*, 251.

59   George Pouchet, *The Plurality of Races* (London: Publishing Committee of the London Anthropological Society, 1866).

60   Patteson diary, entry for 31 August 1866, Selwyn Collection.

61   Pouchet, *Plurality*, 69.

62   Yonge, *Patteson*, 1:301.

63   Sir John Lubbock, *Prehistoric Times* (1865; Oosterhout, The Netherlands: Anthropological Publications, 1969), 566.

64   Ibid., 573.

65   Ibid., 577.

66   Ibid., 593.

67   *Journal of the Anthropological Institute* 10 (1880–1881).

68   Printed letter to Mr. Freeling, 1875, Codrington Collection, series 9.

69   Miscellaneous Papers relating to the Melanesian Mission, Tempest Papers, National Library of Australia and the Library of New South Wales, Australian Joint Copying Project, Microfilm nos. M802–M806.

70   Robert Codrington, "Religious Beliefs and Practices in Melanesia," *Journal of the Anthropological Institute* 10 (1880–1881): 312.

71   Ibid., 313.

72   Edward Tylor, "The Religion of Savages," *Fortnightly Review 6,* (1866): 71–86. Quoted in Stocking, *Victorian Anthropology,* 192.

73   S. G. F. Brandon, "Origins of Religion," in *Dictionary of the History of Ideas: Studies of Selected Pivotal Ideas,* ed. Philip P. Wiener, 5 vols. (New York: Charles Scribner's Sons, 1973), 4: 94–95.

74   Codrington, *The Melanesians*, 118–119.

75   Cassirer, *Language and Myth,* 66–80.

76   Review from *Internationales Archiv für Ethnographie,* 1892, 98, Codrington Collection, series A.

77   George W. Stocking, "The Ethnographer's Magic," in *Observers Observed: Essays on Ethnographic Fieldwork,* ed. George W. Stocking (Madison: University of Wisconsin Press, 1983), 87–91.

78   James Clifford, *Person and Myth: Maurice Leenhardt in the Melanesian World* (Berkeley: University of California Press, 1982), 126–127.

HENRIKA KUKLICK

12 The Color Blue

From Research in the Torres Strait to an Ecology of Human Behavior

Between April and November of 1898, a cluster of islands in the waters between Australia and New Guinea was the site of a research project that significantly affected anthropology and psychology: the Cambridge Anthropological Expedition to the Torres Strait. The expedition was conducted by a team of seven men organized by A. C. Haddon, a zoologist-turned-anthropologist who would hold Cambridge's first full-time position in anthropology.[1] Conceived to realize Haddon's "long felt" expectation that anthropology could make "real advance" only if it adopted psychological research methods, the expedition surpassed Haddon's earlier efforts to put Francis Galton's psychological tests to anthropological purposes because it was genuinely interdisciplinary—that is, it was designed to correct errors built into the practices of both disciplines.[2] In two important ways, its corrective measures entailed use of a Darwinian approach. First, it embraced the method of the field naturalist. Second, it applied Darwin's evolutionary ecological framework to the phenomena it observed.

For psychologists, the Torres Strait researchers addressed the discipline's then crystallizing problem—the specification of individual differences in response to all types of stimuli. But they did so in anthropological terms, recognizing that the socialization individuals received as members of particular cultural groups shaped their psychological reactions. In the controlled conditions of European laboratories, cultural factors were ignored, and subjects' responses were effectively treated as simple functions of innate endowments. The Cambridge researchers determined that psychologists could appreciate the importance of culture only if they took their laboratory practices into the field, performing their tests on culturally exotic populations such as the Torres Strait islanders, whose distinctive responses to psychological tests could be understood through ethnographic observation.

For anthropologists, too, the expedition was intended to challenge existing methodology. The leading anthropologists of the day were so-called armchair scholars, men such as the Oxford professor of anthropology E. B. Tylor and Haddon's Cambridge colleague and anthropological mentor, J. G. Frazer (who resisted the temptation to break the habits of a lifetime spent in his study and join Haddon's team).[3] They and their kind did not collect their own data, but generalized from evidence provided by all manner of informants, only some of whom were knowing collaborators in anthropological research—travelers, missionaries, colonial agents, and traders. Haddon and his colleagues rejected their predecessors' procedures, insisting that anthropology would not become truly scientific until its theorists did their own field research. Viewed as an exercise in anthropological method, the expedition was revolutionary. The next generation of anthropologists was to make a fetish of field work, to make a prolonged period of residence among an exotic people an essential stage in an anthropologist's career.

From a theoretical standpoint, the expedition contributed to an intellectual change occurring in both anthropology and psychology. The data accumulated in the Torres Strait repudiated the model of human behavior, predicated on Lamarckian biology, that had informed much of nineteenth-century social science. Not only were the human sciences in Britain much affected by the expedition's findings, but their analogs elsewhere (especially in the English-speaking world) were also to a degree impressed by the truly novel research undertaken in the Pacific. But the expedition did not inspire increased cooperation between anthropology and psychology. Despite Haddon's hopes, his project contributed to the rationale for increasing disciplinary differentiation.

British Anthropology before the Torres Strait Expedition

Before 1898 some important anthropological studies had been done by men who had considerable personal contact with various indigenous peoples of the British Empire, researchers such as the colonial official E. H. Man and the missionary R. H. Codrington.[4] Furthermore, anthropologists such as Tylor and Galton had as young men journeyed through non-Western societies. But anthropology's central theoretical problems were posed by armchair scholars, and experience in the field was irrelevant to the achievement of disciplinary eminence. Anthropology preserved a division of scientific labor that was blurred earlier in other branches of natural history such as botany, zoology, and geology.

To be sure, nineteenth-century field naturalists continued to supplement the results of their own investigations with material they found or solicited; Charles Darwin, for example, built his theoretical edifice on evidence from diverse sources. Naturalists of all persuasions believed their procedure to be viable because they believed that facts were not necessarily theory-laden, that the acts of data collection and interpretation could be entirely distinct.[5] But armchair anthropologists were vehement in their defense of the division of scientific roles. J. G. Frazer, for example, maintained that it fostered scientific impartiality: because the man in the field, collecting data for anthropologists' use, had no theoretical bias, he was not tempted to report only such evidence as supported some preconceived hypothesis; and because the scholar had not gathered his data himself, he could be dispassionate in his consideration of the material available to him.[6]

The complete fusion of the roles of data collector and interpreter in the single person of the scientific investigator was a consequence of professionalization in all the disciplines that sustained natural history's tradition of generalization based on field research. As the structure of universities changed in the late nineteenth century, admitting new academic subjects and creating more opportunities for remunerated scholarly careers pursued over working lifetimes, academically employed theoreticians went into the field and freed themselves from dependence on their amateur collaborators. By the era of World War I, the expectation that the scientist was necessarily a field worker became a commonplace throughout the natural history disciplines.[7] The Torres Strait expedition heralded the emergence of professional anthropology, and not coincidentally it discredited the theories prevalent during the discipline's amateur era.

Nevertheless, it would be wrong to see the intellectual revolution the expedition provoked as a simple product of careerist ambition to demonstrate the superiority of professional over amateur work. Nineteenth-century anthropological theory was a functional adaptation to the occupational ecology of the day. It represented a framework within which material collected by amateurs could be used productively. When the leaders of anthropological opinion took to the field themselves, they were able to dispense with the theoretical certainties their predecessors required to make sense of data that could not be contextualized specifically—neither related to the peculiar cultures of given peoples nor evaluated with reference to the reliability of given observers.

The central problem of nineteenth-century anthropology was historical: the specification of the course of human development.

Although the field depended on evolutionary theory, it was more Lamarckian than Darwinian. When anthropologists described social progress as the product of biologically driven human efforts to cope with the natural environment, they charted a teleological course of evolution, a realization of humankind's innate potential that environmental conditions could either retard or encourage. Conceiving physical and cultural evolution to be interdependent, anthropologists represented the distinctions among individuals and peoples as matters of degree rather than kind: throughout all recorded time, individuals and societies had matured along the same path, and the developmental journey of each individual and each society recapitulated the history of the human race. Because individuals and societies developed at varying rates, their differences represented different stages of evolution, and all individuals and peoples judged deficient by the standards of educated Western male society were comparable: all were examples of the incomplete realization of human potential. Equating rationality and morality, nineteenth-century anthropologists judged the pattern of human history to constitute the progressive triumph of reason over instinct, the transformation of human beings from creatures of passion and animal cunning into persons whose conduct was governed by the objective standards exemplified in modern scientific norms—into the people they believed themselves to be. In sum, anthropologists understood evolution to follow a line of ascent up a single developmental ladder, rather than displaying the branching, nondirectional pattern Darwin described.

Their unilinear evolutionary scheme allowed armchair anthropologists to make efficient use of whatever information came their way. Adopting the "comparative method," anthropologists could use any evidence about a given population judged to be in a specific stage of biological/cultural evolution to inform their analysis of any other population considered to be in a comparable stage of development. Their method was extraordinarily economical, given that they were prepared to equate the contemporary peoples they termed "primitives" with the classical ancients of Greece, Rome, and Egypt; with the ancestors of modern Europeans; and with people in their own society who were judged somehow deficient—women, children, social and mental deviants, rural residents, and the urban underclass. For example, they could explain the development of modern British children as the recapitulation of the history of the human race, assuming that their children's forebears were essentially identical to the peoples then living in materially simple conditions, the peoples they termed "primitives." As modern children negotiated the moral stages of past ages, they naturally found archaic material culture appealing, playing with the bow and arrow of the hunter and the rattle of the witch doctor; as modern children matured physically, they passed through stages in which they resembled primitives, with flat noses, forward-opening nostrils, wide-set eyes, large mouths, and undeveloped frontal sinuses. Reasoning along these lines, anthropologists also argued that the lower orders in Britain displayed physical capabilities of strength and endurance that their social superiors had lost during the course of their maturation into rational beings.[8]

Unilinear evolutionist anthropological reasoning could not be sustained unless physical and cultural development were interdependent, and anthropologists relied on the mechanism of the inheritance of acquired characteristics to explain the linkage of physical and cultural advance. But the Lamarckian premise of evolutionist anthropology came under increased scrutiny during the last third of the nineteenth century. In many quarters of the scientific community, support for Lamarckism grew in an explicitly anti-Darwiniam reaction. By the 1880s, however, some biologists were mounting a fully articulated case against the Lamarckian model of heredity. In these debates, anthropologists were divided according to their primary disciplinary interests. Those who had come to anthropology from the biomedical sciences, whose research stressed the physical aspect of human evolution—men such as Francis Galton and A. C. Haddon—were inclined to identify themselves as Darwinians and to welcome the anti-Lamarckian arguments of August Weismann and others. Anthropologists whose primary concern was the explanation of cultural evolution, however, whose position had been most starkly outlined by the social scientific polymath Herbert Spencer, felt that their data were incomprehensible without explanatory recourse to the inheritance of acquired characteristics. Writing in 1887, for example, Spencer stressed the necessity of explaining the accelerating rate of change from the past to the present, arguing that a consistent interpretation of all social progress made since the beginning of time required a Lamarckian account of inheritance.[9]

Certainly, even those who embraced new biological notions, such as Francis Galton, did not do so wholeheartedly. The popularizer of the distinction between nature and nurture, Galton followed his cousin Charles Darwin in resorting to Lamarckian explanations when he described the development of humankind's higher mental qualities, for example identifying "inherited conscience" as "the organized result of the social experiences of many generations."[10] When Galton contemplated most aspects of evolution, however, he assumed that human traits were unaffected by environmental factors. Like Spencer, he thought that the rapidity of recent social change was telling evidence indeed, but his account of the dynamic of history was altogether different from Spencer's. "[S]udden eras of great intellectual progress cannot be due to any alteration in the natural faculties of the race," Galton wrote in 1883, "because there has not been time for that"; rather, altered circumstances elicited productive application of inherited aptitudes that had not been exploited previously. Moreover, we can easily recognize that Galton's formulation of the relationship between inherited nature and cultural circumstances had antecedents in Darwin's work (which was itself informed by anthropological research). Indeed, Darwin had in *The Descent of Man* (1871) produced what he believed to be especially persuasive evidence of the importance of circumstances to the expression of human potential—the capacity to adapt to British behavioral norms demonstrated by individuals removed to Britain from Tierra del Fuego, where they had behaved as "the lowest barbarians."[11]

It is not surprising that Galton was instrumental in raising the funds that supported the Torres Strait expedition, since its research was designed to substantiate arguments like his. That is, Haddon's team undertook to demonstrate that culturally different peoples behaved as they did because their respective circumstances favored selective expression of innate characteristics common to all humankind. If, as travelers to exotic parts had long reported, the residents of simple societies had formidable physical skills—the ability to hear sounds and see sights imperceptible to Europeans, as well as the capacity to endure discomforts Europeans found unbearably painful—aborigines' behavior did not indicate that they were less evolved members of the human species, closer to the lower animals than Europeans were. Their behavior reflected learning, not inheritance. Lamarckian explanations were not accurate: physical and cultural evolution were not concomitant. In essence, the arguments made by the Torres Strait researchers depended on an ecological model of the variability of the human species and were, as such, fundamentally Darwinian.

Taking the Laboratory into the Field

The proximate cause of Haddon's choice of venue for his expedition was familiarity: he had been there before. He had made his first trip to the Torres Strait in 1888, when he was professor of zoology at the Royal College of Science at Dublin. He had gone to the islands to study the coral reefs and marine zoology of the area. Once there, however, he had become fascinated by the local culture—to which his attention had possibly been directed in the first instance by his friend J. G. Frazer, who charged him with collecting information. Resolving that he would dedicate himself to anthropology thereafter, Haddon determined that he would approach his new intellectual problems as he did his work in marine biology, not as the mere agent of an arm-chair theorist. And his initial experience in the Torres Strait predisposed him to return there for anthropological research. On his first trip, Haddon had of necessity cultivated a network of missionaries, colonial officials, and indigenous informants, upon whom he depended for the safe conduct of his biological and ethnological investigations, a network that served him well when he returned in 1898 (indeed, he was to return again in 1914, and maintained contact with his old friends throughout his career). Because Haddon envisioned scientific anthropology as the product of collaborative research, it took him some time to raise the funds necessary to support his return to the Torres Strait accompanied by a team of colleagues—and the Cambridge expedition was so named because the university supplied the largest single contribution (and provided additional funds when the project ran over budget).[12]

Haddon was no pioneer in the Torres Strait, however. The islands were hardly *terra incognita* to natural historians. After the British settled Australia, a series of expeditions explored the human and natural resources of the land and water of the area. To wit, investigations were conducted by the personnel of the *Isabella* in 1836; of the *Fly* and the *Bramble* in 1844–1845; and of the *Rattlesnake* and the *Bramble* in 1848–1849—in whose company was found Thomas Huxley (who was later helpful in securing Haddon funds for his first trip to Torres Strait). These ventures were conducted for economic as well as scientific purposes. But for natural historians, they represented opportunities to study the diverse life forms of the antipodes, which for centuries had been believed to be among the most primitive—if not *the* most primitive—forms on earth.

To anthropologists, in particular, the hallowed legends of life in the antipodes suggested that there they might find living fossils, peoples who in every particular retained the characteristics of the human species at the earliest stages of its evolution. To be sure, other peoples—such as Darwin's Fuegians—were put forth as exemplars of the lowest form of humanity, but the habit of seeing antipodean peoples as specimens of humankind in an unadulterated state of nature was persistent.[13] This habit in large measure explains why antipodean peoples figured so prominently in the important anthropological works of the late nineteenth and early twentieth centuries, from J. G. Frazer's *Golden Bough* (1890) to Emile Durkheim's *Elementary Forms of the Religious Life* (1912)—which secured a truly international audience—to Bronislaw Malinowski's *Argonauts of the Western Pacific* (1922). In the first decades of the twentieth century, the peoples of the Pacific gained increased attention because so many of them were island peoples. As we will shortly understand, anthropologists' fascination with island peoples was significantly enhanced by the findings of the Torres Strait expedition, and it indicated a (if not *the*) high point of Darwinian thinking in anthropology.

When Haddon was planning his first trip to Torres Strait, he was urged by Alfred Russel Wallace to go instead to the West Indies, where he would have been "able to work in a comfortable house and with civilized surroundings."[14] In truth, however, the anthropologist who came to the Torres Strait islanders expecting to find a population uncontaminated by Western culture was grossly mistaken—as one of the members of Haddon's team was to observe some years after the Cambridge expedition took place.[15] (And the greatest discomfort suffered by Haddon's team was apparently sunburnt feet).[16] The Torres Strait islanders had been exposed to European influences at least since the seventeenth century, when Dutch, Spanish, and British ships began to sail through their waters. In the subsequent centuries, the islanders were increasingly drawn into the world economy, as suppliers of the goods (largely pearls and pearl shell) colonialists wanted. From 1863 they were subjected to formal Anglo-Australian rule of increasing specificity. And from 1871 they suffered the attentions of missionaries. By the time the Cambridge expedition reached the islands, most of the inhabitants had converted to Christianity and learned some English—facilitating communication with the researchers.

Nevertheless, at the time of the expedition it seemed that the population of the islands was sufficiently diverse to provide the basis for the sort of comparative analysis central to the researchers' project. Because the islands had been differentially integrated into the colonial economy, the islanders were acculturated to Western norms in varying degrees, permitting the researchers to measure the effects of civilization on individual perceptions. Because the islands were inhabited by a racially heterogeneous population, albeit of various types of Melanesians—the islands nearest the Australian mainland had residents akin to Australian Aborigines, while the more remote islands were peopled by purer Papuan strains—the researchers could test the hypothesis that individuals' perceptions were functions of their racial endowments.

The Torres Strait expedition collected vast quantities of evidence. Its published reports eventually ran to six volumes, most devoted to the sort of material armchair anthropologists found useful—straightforward descriptions of diverse customs. Indeed, because the published reports used information sent to Britain from the islands after 1899, they were examples of old-style anthropology in part. The most significant findings of the expedition, however, were those generated by its psychological research, and these were produced because Haddon secured the services of his Cambridge colleague W. H. R. Rivers, then the university's lecturer in physiological and experimental psychology. A physician, Rivers was the preeminent psychological experimentalist of his day, the man who headed Britain's first university psychological laboratories, those established in 1897 at both Cambridge and University College, London, and whom British psychologists have continued to acknowledge as their first scientific experimentalist.[17] Other natural scientists with medical training also joined the group: Rivers' Cambridge students William McDougall and Charles S. Myers and Myers' friend Charles G. Seligman.[18] The expedition team also included Sidney Ray, an expert on the languages of Melanesia who spent his entire career as a primary school teacher, as well as Anthony Wilkin, then still a Cambridge undergraduate, whose promising anthropological career ended with his early death in 1901.

Rivers designed the expedition's psychological experiments. He also developed an innovative research technique, his "genealogical method," which permitted the investigators to consider in other ways the questions addressed by their psychological research. As conceived by Rivers, the genealogical method was an instrument of survey research, useful to investigators spending only a brief time in the field.[19] Consisting of the compilation of informants' family histories, the method permitted rapid accumulation of social and vital statistics—patterns of marriage alliances; differential birth and death rates; and the incidence of aptitudes, disease, and congenital deformities among the population. Indeed, it may be appropriate to see both the team organization of the Cambridge expedition and the results obtained by the genealogical method as akin to the surveys of the British poor, which took the family (or household) as the basic unit of analysis. The first of these inquiries were mounted in the 1880s by Charles Booth and Seebohm Rowntree, and although they were intended to serve very different purposes from Rivers' inquiries—to explain the cause of poverty so that effective remedial strategies could be formulated—their approach to understanding the behavior of their subjects was identical to Rivers'. That is, poverty research was also designed to disaggregate the effects of biological nature and cultural conditioning on individuals' conduct.[20] Such a comparison would not have seemed odd to Rivers, who, like so many of his contemporaries, viewed aboriginal peoples as akin to the British underclass.[21]

More important, Rivers' genealogical method bears an intellectual family resemblance to the investigatory approach followed by Francis Galton, who compiled pedigrees to support his hereditarian views. Rivers was certainly familiar with Galton's genealogical research, although he did not cite it in descriptions of his method; and he developed his techniques to serve some purposes quite different from Galton's. Nevertheless, Rivers intended his method to resolve issues that concerned Galton. For example, investigators who used the genealogical method as Rivers intended would take care to distinguish biological from adopted children; thus, they could weigh the relative importance of heredity and environment in the determination of individual characteristics. Whatever Galton's precise relationship to Rivers, however, the work of both derived from intellectual habits encouraged in both by their medical training. And when anthropologists took up the genealogical technique, they were appropriating the medical practice of taking patients' histories. Rivers' anthropological method was presaged by medical research he had undertaken before his trip to Torres Strait, in the family histories he had compiled while analyzing individuals' defects of color vision. Indeed, Rivers later conceptualized the anthropological analysis of culture as a task analogous to that of medical diagnosis.[22]

With the equipment they had brought to Torres Strait, Rivers and his associates created a psychological laboratory in the field (figure 12.1). For four months, Rivers, Myers, and McDougall lived and worked on Murray Island, one of the eastern islands in Torres Strait, chosen as the site of intense study because it was relatively unaffected by European influence. With Seligman's assistance, Rivers supplemented the results of the Murray Island research with some comparative data. The two men spent a month on one of the western islands in Torres Strait, which was an area integrated into the colonial economy, as well as a week on the island of Kiwai, part of British New Guinea.[23]

Generating quantifiable data that could be compared with the results of experiments done in European laboratories, the expedition's psychological tests measured the so-called special senses of sight, hearing, smell, and touch, using introspective and objective procedures. In large part, these were aptitude tests, comparable to those later used by Myers when he turned his talents to the tasks of vocational guidance and selection after World War I.[24] The researchers'

12.1 The Torres Strait expedition: Cambridge scientists adapt
to their island surroundings. Seated: A. C. Haddon. Standing,
left to right: W. H. R. Rivers, C. G. Seligman, S. Ray, A. Wilkin.
Missing: W. McDougall, C. S. Myers. From A. H. Quiggin, *Haddon,
the Head Hunter: A Short Sketch of the Life of A. C. Haddon*
(Cambridge: Cambridge University Press, 1942).

procedures enabled them to distinguish between aptitudes and
achievements, between individuals' sensory capacities and the level to
which they had developed their natural talents. The tests were
intended to determine if people who had only primitive social and
technological culture did indeed have highly refined sensory skills and
whether their skills were learned or manifestations of their physical
endowments.

Rivers and his associates did not simply replicate European experiments in novel settings. Because they were able to observe their subjects both under experimental conditions and in everyday life, they
were able to differentiate among the various factors that affected the
islanders' performances in psychological tests. In some respects, individuals' performances varied from day to day, modified by transitory
conditions such as fatigue. In other respects, individuals' performances were consistent. Subjects consistently varied from one another
because of their individual differences of maturity, personality, and
innate capacity—visual and auditory acuity, age, temperamental char-

acteristics, and ethnic backgrounds (which the researchers classified as biological factors). And the test results displayed general patterns, products of cultural factors that had shaped subjects' trained perceptions as well as their receptivity to any given experimental task they were set.

By the standards employed in the Torres Strait research, then, the experimental research done in European laboratories was inadequately controlled, for European psychologists were usually ignorant of the array of personal and cultural factors that affected test responses. Thus, the Torres Strait experiments conveyed lessons as much methodological as substantive and had implications for future research in both anthropology and psychology. To anthropologists, the experiments refuted conventional wisdom about primitives' sensibilities. To psychologists, they demonstrated the unreliability of laboratory research conducted in ignorance of subjects' social situations; when scientists evaluated and reported their results, they were obliged to specify the different situations in which they performed their experiments. For example, Rivers himself subsequently did this when he described his studies of the effects of ingesting noxious substances on individuals' experiences of potentially fatiguing tasks, which he conducted with the assistance of McDougall and others.[25]

Contrary to the Torres Strait researchers' (professed) anticipations, the islanders' performances on psychological tests were not very different from those of Europeans. Yet when they were going about their daily activities, the islanders displayed formidable sensory skills, correctly identifying faint sounds and distant objects that were imperceptible to Europeans. They also seemed more tolerant of pain and less interested in aesthetic matters than Europeans. Thus, the patterns of behavior observed among the islanders seemed to confirm the evolutionist hypothesis that peoples who possessed only primitive cultural institutions were also at a primitive stage of physical development—of necessity, because they could not live off the land without at least some of the sensory skills possessed by the lower animals. How were the researchers to reconcile the apparently contradictory evidence they had collected—their measurement of the islanders' unexceptional sensory endowments and their observation of the islanders' extraordinary perceptual powers? The researchers postulated that if tests of the islanders failed to reveal consistent differences between their natural endowments and those of Europeans, whatever variations were found between the sensory skills of primitives and Europeans had to be products of cultural conditioning.

Rivers set out to obtain compelling evidence of the importance of cultural conditioning to sensory skills by tests of the islanders' vision and hearing. By objective measures, his team found that the islanders' vision was generally superior to that of Europeans: few were deceived by the psychologists' optical illusions, which usually fooled Europeans; and few of them suffered from myopia, astigmatism, or color blindness. Nonetheless, the islanders were somewhat more sensitive to red and less sensitive to blue than Europeans. Rivers explained that the slight insensitivity to blue was congenital, a consequence of the intense pigmentation of the macula lutea in the retina, but he also observed that this localized region of perceptual deficiency was practically insignificant—the islanders readily recognized blue on the peripheral retina. In contrast to their vision, the islanders' hearing was not as acute as Europeans'—or, at least, it was inferior to that of the researchers—perhaps in consequence of injury sustained in repeated pearl diving. But the islanders were highly responsive to both visual and auditory stimuli; this finding demonstrated that their sensory skills were learned, not simple functions of their aptitudes.

The team concluded that by virtue of their established habits of close attention to minute stimuli in a familiar environment, the islanders had developed skills necessary to survival. If they were transported to another location, they would certainly be no more capable of observational feats than Europeans would be if they found themselves in equally novel circumstances. The expedition thus resolved a debate that had raged in anthropological circles—and in other quarters of the scientific community—during the 1880s, and confirmed a judgment Galton had reached on impressionistic evidence.[26]

The Color Blue

From the work the expedition did in Torres Strait on color vision, in particular, we can best appreciate the model of human adaptive behavior the researchers were attempting to document, as well as the relation between the specific research projects the expedition's psychologists executed and issues their scientific colleagues in Britain considered of the greatest importance. Moreover, the team's approach to analysis of the islanders' color sensibilities exemplifies the fusion of anthropological and psychological method the expedition sought. Had the anthropologists not performed psychological tests, they might have taken the islanders' language as an index to their perceptual capacities and assumed that the islanders were congenitally incapable of making refined distinctions among colors. Instead, the researchers concluded that the islanders could discriminate among colors just as Europeans did. Had they not been able to observe the islanders' behavior, they might have disregarded some of their results. The aesthetic preferences the islanders expressed during testing seemed unlikely, suggesting that the experimenters had given inadequate pretest instructions to their subjects. Yet when the island-ers were dressed in the finery they chose to wear to church, they expressed the same color preferences they had articulated under ques-tioning. Finally, the islanders' relative insensitivity to blue could be interpreted only with reference to comparative data on the color sen-sibilities of other peoples, primitive as well as civilized. Primitives everywhere were insensitive to blue, and this finding was symptom-atic of a general phenomenon: unlike Europeans, primitives had little aesthetic interest in nature, which was held to be indicative of their lack of higher mental development overall.

In the study of vision, Rivers was a recognized master. Indeed, nearly half a century after he contributed an essay on vision to E. A. Schäffer's 1900 *Textbook of Physiology,* Erwin Ackernecht observed that his article was "still regarded as one of the most accu-rate and careful accounts of the whole subject in the English lan-guage."[27] Rivers' work in the Torres Strait enabled him to consolidate his position of authority in this field, and it was in his day a very important field indeed. Answers to vital questions posed by diverse scholars and policy makers turned on elucidation of the mechanisms of color vision.

The classicists who figured prominently in the anthropological community, concerned to establish parallels between the peoples of the ancient world and contemporary primitives, asked the question first posed by the future prime minister W. E. Gladstone in 1858: did the vagueness of color terminology used by the ancient Greeks indi-cate that they were at a lower stage of physical evolution than modern Europeans and congenitally incapable of refined color discrimina-tions? To them, Rivers responded that although the color terms used by Homer were equivalent to those of the least advanced of the peo-ples studied by the Torres Strait researchers, the very slight deficiency in the islanders' color sensitivity was insufficient to account for their crude color nomenclature. Furthermore, such ancient peoples as the Egyptians evidently possessed a fully developed color sense, although the fact that they did was not directly relevant to the case of the Greeks. In sum, although there were obvious cultural parallels between peoples of the ancient world and contemporary primitives, and although color terminology was associated with cultural develop-ment, there was no causal link between sensitivity to color and the physical evolution of the human species per se.[28]

Far more important to policy makers and a congeries of scientists alike were the studies of color vision prompted by concerns about the safe conduct of vital occupations. The last quarter of the nineteenth century witnessed a veritable explosion in studies of individual variability of color perception. These were conducted by practicing physicians, physiologists, experimental psychologists, and anthropologists all over Europe. Research on color vision had a recognizable impetus: in April 1876 a catastrophic railroad accident occurred in Sweden because a color-blind railway employee misperceived a signal, and the investigations that followed the accident showed that the culpable employee was by no means the only railway worker who suffered from color blindness.[29]

In Britain, concern over the occupational hazards posed by color blindness prompted the Royal Society to appoint a Committee on Colour-Vision in 1890. The committee included men who had in the 1880s led the scientific debate on the etiology of visual acuity among primitive peoples—its chairman, the future Nobel laureate physicist Lord Rayleigh (whose research accomplishments included explanation of the reasons the sky appeared to be blue), Francis Galton, and R. Brudenell Carter, an ophthalmic surgeon—as well as Michael Foster, the Cambridge professor of physiology who actively advanced the university careers of Haddon and Rivers (among others). Taking extensive testimony from men involved in railway traffic and navigation, clinicians, and other interested parties, the committee was in the first instance concerned to establish the very existence of color blindness, which many employers refused to recognize. In particular, officials of the mercantile marine and the navy expected youths unhappy at sea to feign the disorder so that they might gain release from service and so chose to deny the reality of color blindness to prevent any unwanted loss of personnel.

The committee's conclusions were unambiguous: the testimony they had heard, as well as the ample available scientific literature, indicated that color blindness was a genuine disorder and was fairly widespread. They recommended mandatory testing for all workers whose responsibilities required accurate color discrimination. They judged that of the available tests for color blindness Holmgren's colored wool test was superior, since it tested perceptual skills per se, rather than knowledge of color names (which was often rudimentary among persons of the lower classes and nonexistent among foreign workers). This was the test the Torres Strait researchers adopted. But the Torres Strait expedition was linked to the committee by more than procedural agreement.

To us, it is especially significant that the Royal Society committee's findings indicated that color blindness could be temporary as well as congenital. Temporary perceptual disability could be caused by disease, fatigue, mental shock, psychological depression, or excessive consumption of tobacco (particularly injurious if coupled with heavy alcohol use). When witnesses testified to the existence of temporary color blindness, they were sympathetically questioned by Michael Foster, Rivers' Cambridge ally. The committee as a whole endorsed his view that defective color vision could result from situational factors.[30]

The Torres Strait researchers translated the findings of the Royal Society committee into anthropological terms, arguing that perceptions were affected by conditions that might obtain throughout a culture, as well as by the stressful circumstances in which specific individuals might find (or place) themselves. As we will shortly see, the psychologists of the Torres Strait expedition were at a later stage of their careers to extend this argument further, determining that under stressful conditions civilized Europeans could fall into behavior patterns similar to those of primitive peoples.

In the model of individual adaptation embraced by Rivers and his colleagues, each person constituted a bounded economy with limited resources. Individuals' resources could be expended to develop only some of their physical or mental talents, and their social situation determined how their resources would be allocated. Rivers explained that the residents of simple societies possessed innate capacities little different from those of Europeans, but because they devoted so much of their attention to developing their powers of acute sensory observation, they cultivated their sensory capacities at the expense of their intellectual skills. Exclusive concentration on the concrete particulars of their lives was necessarily "a distinct hindrance to higher mental development," he wrote, allowing that this might seem paradoxical, since "the growth of intellect depends on material which is furnished by the senses, and it therefore at first sight may appear strange that elaboration of the sensory side of mental life should be a hindrance to intellectual development." But individuals could not develop every one of their potential skills, since they did not have infinite personal energies, and "if too much energy is expended on the sensory foundations, it is natural that the intellectual superstructure should suffer."[31]

The findings of the Torres Strait expedition could not be reconciled with the Lamarckian theory on which evolutionist anthropology had been premised; they indicated that the correlations anthropologists had been accustomed to make among race, environment, and culture were spurious. Clearly, the Torres Strait islanders exercised their sensory capacities to an extraordinary degree, but there was no evidence that their long-established habits had altered their natural endowments. Nor did environment affect physical characteristics, for if it had done so, physical variation would have been greater among groups than within them. Instead, when a given human endowment, such as vision, was studied in different populations, such as Englishmen and Murray Islanders, the range of variation in each population was virtually identical, although the frequency distribution of degrees of visual acuity possessed by members of each population could be rather different.

Certainly, the innate capacities of individuals that social structures selectively developed were legacies of the phases of the biological evolution of the human species and represented stratified layers of individual personality. Children could not distinguish colors until they were nearly two, for example, and learned to recognize red before blue, indicating that the sociobiological development of the child recapitulated the history of the race.[32] Moreover, evolutionist anthropologists had correctly arrayed various sorts of social structures on a hierarchical developmental scale of civilization. But the evolutionists had been wrong to see biological nature and cultural nurture as simple functions of one another: the residents of simple societies were as members of the human species no less evolved than Europeans were. Close investigation of their psychological processes, Rivers was to write, "leads us into no mystical dawn of the human mind, but introduces us to concepts and beliefs of the same order as those which direct our own activities."[33]

The Legacy of the Torres Strait Expedition

The members of the Cambridge Expedition—Haddon, Rivers, and Seligman in particular—spawned distinguished lines of professional descendants. At Cambridge, Haddon and Rivers trained some future leaders of anthropology, most notably A. R. Radcliffe-Brown (the first recipient of the studentship established to memorialize Anthony Wilkin), who after a peripatetic career at Cape Town, Sydney, and Chicago became in 1937 the first occupant of the established chair in anthropology at Oxford; indeed, Radcliffe-Brown was something of an anthropological missionary, for he inaugurated the teaching of anthropology in South Africa and Australia when he became in turn the first occupant of the professorships established at Cape Town and Sydney, in 1921 and 1925 respectively. At the London School of Economics, Seligman became the first professor of anthropology (styled "ethnology") within the University of London, where he was

one of the teachers of Bronislaw Malinowski; Malinowski became
Seligman's colleague at the London School of Economics, and the two
men together trained most of the leading anthropologists who came
to intellectual maturity during the interwar period. Radcliffe-Brown
and Malinowski claimed—and were given—joint credit for founding
the functionalist school of anthropology, the school that became dominant in British universities after World War I and influenced anthropologists throughout the English-speaking world. Modern British
social anthropologists trace their intellectual pedigree to the Torres
Strait expedition, obviously with considerable justification.

It is equally appropriate to see the expedition as a watershed in
the history of British psychology. When Rivers returned to Cambridge
after going on the expedition, he continued to teach psychology.
While he offered lectures in anthropology—gratis—his primary contributions were to psychology. With James Ward, Cambridge's professor of moral philosophy, he founded the *British Journal of Psychology*
in 1904, creating a vehicle for self-conscious discipline building; until
1948, the editorship of the journal remained in the hands of Rivers or
one of his students. The existence of this platform surely helped Rivers' school to become recognized as "the modern British school of
academic psychology," as one observer wrote in 1922, the year of
Rivers' death.[34] And the line of academic descendants Rivers and
Myers engendered at Cambridge enabled their school's influence
to persist into the next generation. Most notably, they trained
F. C. Bartlett, who became the first professor of experimental psychology at Cambridge and guided a remarkable number of the discipline's
subsequent leaders.[35]

Another of the Torres Strait researchers, William McDougall, also
established a professional lineage in psychology. McDougall did not
fulfill his earlier promise after he left Britain in 1920 for the United
States, where he was employed first at Harvard and then at Duke. But
before his military service in World War I, McDougall had been from
1904 Oxford's Wilde Reader in Mental Philosophy and had worked
with a number of graduate students who later achieved some eminence in British psychology. Conspicuous among them was the man
generally identified as Britain's "first professional psychologist," the
immensely influential and posthumously notorious Cyril Burt, who
was also linked to the Cambridge network through Myers, serving
briefly (1912–1913) as Myers' assistant in the Cambridge Psychological Laboratory and later working for the National Institute of Industrial Psychology Myers helped found in 1921.[36]

If students of the Torres Strait researchers figured prominently in the next generation of British anthropologists and psychologists, how much of their work sustained the intellectual legacy of their mentors? The Torres Strait expedition was as much an end as a beginning, and it indicated some intellectual directions that were not taken. As the classicist-anthropologist J. L. Myres pointed out, it marked the end of an era for British natural history: there were to be no more large-scale ventures mounted by naturalists of any variety, expeditions on which each member was expected to contribute a specialized skill to a complex research project.[37] And research of the sort done in Torres Strait was not to be replicated precisely. Perhaps Rivers' formulation of the genealogical method served to intensify social anthropologists' already considerable concern with kinship. In the future, however, social anthropologists would not conduct genealogical research in order to elucidate patterns of biological inheritance. And they were more concerned to translate into formal terms the social rules for contracting kinship alliances than they were to follow Rivers' method to specify the degrees to which practices departed from professed rules. Nor was the research done in Torres Strait much imitated by later psychologists.[38] Post-expedition developments in anthropology and psychology bespoke the increasing differentiation of the disciplines, which veterans of the expedition deplored in prescriptive writings and public addresses, arguing that academic specialization could only lead to incomplete explanations of varieties of human behavior.[39]

Anthropology and psychology became almost mutually exclusive after 1920 because their practitioners made very different uses of findings such as had been accumulated in Torres Strait. Both disciplines described human beings as creatures engaged in evolutionary adaptation to circumstances. Both accepted the dichotomy between nature and culture that the Torres Strait expedition had documented. But each discipline chose a different unit of analysis: for the anthropologists it was to be the group joined by common culture, which dictated individuals' lives; for the psychologists it was to be individuals, who varied considerably within populations. In consequence, each discipline provided a distinctive account of human adaptation.

Anthropologists solved the problem of explaining the relation of human social organization to biological survival by defining it as nonsensical. Led by the functionalists, they took to extremes the argument the Torres Strait researchers had made—that culture shaped the expression of human potential—perhaps because their major theorists, the Polish émigré Malinowski and the peripatetic Radcliffe-Brown, each spent most of his working life outside his native society. We can assume that Malinowski and Radcliffe-Brown were predisposed to social determinism because each knew from experience that the behavioral skills specific to each alien culture were not natural but learned—and essential to survival. In functionalist theory, the individual as such became epiphenomenal, a creature of cultural conditioning. The functionalist anthropologist was "not interested in what A or B may feel *qua* individuals . . . only in what they feel *qua* members of a given community."[40]

Functionalists posited that any society that survived in its environment did so because its institutions satisfied the basic biological requirements of self-preservation. They allowed that general human biological characteristics limited the variability of cultural forms to a degree. Every society had to contrive means of regulating individuals' sexual drives. And every kinship structure had to cope with the needs women had during pregnancy and childbirth. But functionalists reasoned that the biological characteristics of the individual members of a society were not as such critical to the group's capacity to survive in its environment. Successful environmental adaptation was a product of social organization and could be achieved in many ways. And social organization rigorously shaped the expression of humankind's innate endowments.[41]

Considered as an account of adaptation, this twentieth-century anthropological scheme was closer to Darwinian explanation than nineteenth-century evolutionary anthropology had been, indicating that social change had no preordained direction. And following the Torres Strait expedition, anthropologists took up the naturalists' methodology that had facilitated Darwinian observation, insisting that human variation could not be understood unless anthropologists examined diverse cultures *in situ*. Moreover, because post-expedition anthropologists could not explain cultural variation as differential expression of a single innate pattern of human behavior, twentieth-century anthropologists instead undertook to document the extreme possibilities of human plasticity. In pursuit of understanding the potential variability of social forms, they turned for preference to the study of (largely Pacific) island peoples, expressing in their choice of research venues the Darwinian theme of the importance of geographical isolation to speciation. When in the late 1920s it became far easier for anthropologists to obtain funds for field work in Africa than in the Pacific, they preserved—however inappropriately—the analytic habit of treating the predominantly African peoples they studied as isolated populations, describing in the static terms of the "ethnographic present" the stable cultures they believed to have existed before the disruptive colonial presence introduced traditional societies to outside influences.[42]

Nevertheless, when anthropologists determined that biological traits did not dictate culture, and thereby established a division of labor between those of their company who studied human physical variation and those concerned with social behavior, they jettisoned a significant portion of the Darwinian project, effectively ignoring evolutionary adaptation as such. They simply postulated that every group's social organization constituted a functional adaptation to its environment and was of necessity sufficiently flexible to permit appropriate accommodation to circumstantial change—unless, as Radcliffe-Brown observed while contemplating the indigenous peoples of Australia, change was of the catastrophic sort brought by particularly oppressive colonialism.[43]

By contrast, British psychologists remained concerned to specify the mechanisms of human adaptation to diverse situations, but virtually ignored the situations themselves. The Torres Strait expedition had briefly turned them into field naturalists, but thereafter they rarely considered systematically the importance of social structural factors in individual behavior. Instead, they elicited information from their subjects in situations they contrived—the experimental conditions of the laboratory and the test room. To be sure, Bartlett and his disciples in British universities pursued investigations of psychological phenomena with an eye to understanding the social contexts of perception and learning, sometimes even venturing into the field to test their hypotheses among exotic peoples; but their cross-cultural explanations were more simplistic than those of their predecessors.[44] Moreover, psychology's growth area after the war was outside academe, in the applied fields of educational and industrial consultancy. The clients of the likes of Cyril Burt and C. S. Myers were not interested in learning how to restructure schools and factories to elicit individuals' potential (much though Myers wished his National Institute for Industrial Psychology to be consulted for this purpose); rather, they hired psychologists to give aptitude tests, assuming that individuals' capacities to master educational and occupational tasks were simple functions of their innate endowments. The results of the Torres Strait expedition had, of course, indicated that this was not the case.[45]

Indeed, the most important legacy of the Torres Strait expedition was to be found outside academe, in the changed outlook of large numbers of the general public. The lessons Rivers and his associates had learned in the Pacific were brought to the attention of a wide audience because all of the medically trained participants in the Torres Strait expedition—Rivers, McDougall, Myers, and Seligman—served in World War I as psychiatrists to the many soldiers who suffered from "shell shock," the psychological disorder named by

Myers. To Rivers and his associates, shell shock victims' behavior confirmed their earlier assertions; Riversians conceptualized the most severe form of military psychosis as regression to an infantile mental state—less developed than that of peoples in the simplest of societies—and argued that less afflicted soldiers perceived their surroundings much as primitives did. The war demonstrated the importance of social conditions to individual behavior: whatever the soldier's prior experience and hereditary predisposition, he was susceptible to breakdown if he was placed in sufficiently stressful circumstances. In essence, the soldier's psychological economy was identical to that of the Torres Strait islander. That is, if he was attempting to cope with the exigencies of survival at the most fundamental level, he could lose command of his higher rational faculties.[46]

Conclusion

By the scientific standards of Rivers and his colleagues, the Torres Strait expedition was a partial failure. Their work during and after the expedition disaggregated the effects of nature and culture on human behavior but did not lead to the creation of a unified human science. Nevertheless, an audience much larger than the scientific community was primed to listen to Riversians during the war years. The general public and government officials alike were prepared to believe the Torres Strait researchers' diagnosis of shell shock—that it betrayed neither congenital deficiency nor failure of courage but situational stress—not the least because significant numbers of shell shock victims fell in the field of battle in the early stage of the war, before Britain introduced conscription.[47] After the war, Riversian psychiatry gained legitimacy in scholarly and public circles alike, and Rivers himself won popular recognition because he was a hero in some of the most celebrated memoirs of literary soldiers.[48] Furthermore, on the home front, the expanded wartime economy had depended on many persons previously thought to be congenitally incapable of functioning as productive members of society; they proved competent to hold jobs when the opportunity to secure them was presented. Individuals' responses to diverse wartime conditions served to justify the expansion of British social services and the creation of the welfare state, designed to protect those incapable of caring for themselves by virtue of their position in the social order.[49] In post–World War I Britain, then, the view that individuals' lives were constrained by their social ecology became commonplace in liberal politics.

From Rivers' own behavior, we can judge that he welcomed this permutation of the argument he had been making since his days in the Torres Strait: at the time of his death, he had embarked on a political career and was standing as a Labour candidate for Parliament. This projected step in his career was really a logical development of the path he had been following since he first ventured into anthropology, rather than the abrupt change it might seem. Rivers was effectively proposing to use his knowledge to serve as physician to his society.

Moreover, the liberalism of the post–World War I era shaped anthropology's general orientation. It may be fairly said that the influence Rivers had on educated opinion was as important to the development of the discipline as were the particular methods he advocated. Born out of events that suspended belief in the old certain hierarchies of class and culture, postwar liberalism engendered the cultural relativism that anthropologists made their formal creed (although they suffered occasional lapses from doctrinal orthodoxy). No longer would anthropologists look to such peoples as Pacific islanders to find biocultural fossils of the earliest stages of the development of the human species, for, as the war had demonstrated, human nature at its most infantile and base could readily be observed at home, among the apparently civilized. In the future, anthropologists frequently were to find among simple societies virtues technologically advanced peoples lacked. The conceptual shift the Torres Strait expedition initiated was complete: the category of "primitive" had a changed meaning.

Notes

1   Alfred Cort Haddon (1855–1940), who took a First in the Natural Sciences Tripos at Cambridge, was at the time of the expedition professor of zoology at the Royal College of Science at Dublin and a part-time lecturer in physical anthropology at Cambridge. In 1900 the post of University Lecturer in Ethnology was created for him at Cambridge, and he resigned his Dublin chair. In 1909 he was promoted to a university readership.

2   See A. C. Haddon, ed., "Introduction," *Reports of the Cambridge Anthropological Expedition to Torres Straits,* 6 vols. (Cambridge: Cambridge University Press, 1901–1935), 1:xii. Francis Galton (1822–1911) opened his anthropometric laboratory, Britain's first psychological laboratory, in 1884; Haddon undertook investigations like his in Ireland, helped by Galton's "greatest encouragement and . . . fullest assistance." See D. J. Cunningham and A. C. Haddon, "The Anthropometric Laboratory of Ireland," *Journal of the Anthropological Institute* 21 (1891): 35.

3   E. B. Tylor (1832–1917) was the occupant of Britain's first university post in anthropology, the readership created in 1884 at Oxford; in

1896 he was given a personal professorship. J. G. Frazer (1854–1941), a classicist-turned-anthropologist, was a Fellow of Trinity College, Cambridge, and was certainly Britain's most widely read anthropologist in the first decades of the twentieth century. On Frazer's relationship to Haddon and his interest in participating in the Torres Strait expedition, see Robert Ackerman, *J. G. Frazer, His Life and Work* (Cambridge: Cambridge University Press, 1987), esp. 121–122, 147. Tylor and Frazer were each knighted in recognition of their scholarly achievements, as was Galton.

4   See George W. Stocking, Jr., *Victorian Anthropology* (New York: Free Press, 1987), 236–237, 259, 319.

5   For one illustration of anthropologists' efforts to elicit information, see J. G. Frazer, "Questions on the Manners, Customs, Religious Superstitions, &c of Uncivilized and Semi-Civilized Peoples," *Journal of the Anthropological Institute* 18 (1888): 431–439. For the general structure of natural history research, see Roy Porter, "Gentlemen and Geology: The Emergence of a Scientific Career, 1860–1920," *Historical Journal* 21 (1978): 809–836. On the intellectual foundation of this structure, see, e.g., Richard Yeo, "An Idol of the Marketplace: Baconianism in Nineteenth-Century Britain," *History of Science* 23 (1985): esp. 284–285.

6   See J. G. Frazer, "Obituary: Canon John Roscoe," *Nature* 130 (1932): 918.

7   See David Elliston Allen, *The Naturalist in Britain* (London: Allen Lane, 1976), 238.

8   The most schematic presentations of evolutionist argument were those offered by anthropologists who were determined to reject it. See, e.g., W. H. R. Rivers, "The Ethnological Analysis of Culture," Presidential Address to Section H (anthropology) of the British Association for the Advancement of Science, reprinted in *Nature* 87 (1911): 356–360. Convinced practitioners of the genre also offered cogent summaries of its method, however. See, e.g., G. Lawrence Gomme, "On the Method of Determining the Value of Folk-Lore as Ethnological Data," in *Fourth Report of the British Association for the Advancement of Science Committee on the Ethnographical Survey of the United Kingdom* (London, 1896), Appendix, 626–656. For further discussion of evolutionist anthropology, see my *The Savage Within* (New York: Cambridge University Press, 1991), 75–118.

9   For one account of the Lamarckian reaction to Darwinism, see Peter J. Bowler, *Charles Darwin: The Man and His Influence* (Oxford: Basil Blackwell, 1990), 175–176. For Haddon's appreciation of the value of anti-Lamarckian argument to his cause, see his account of the history of anthropology—written with obvious polemical intent shortly after the Torres Strait expedition. A. C. Haddon, *History of Anthro-*

pology (London: G. P. Putnam's Sons, 1910), 76–77. For Spencer's views in particular, see Robert M. Young, *Darwin's Metaphor* (Cambridge: Cambridge University Press, 1985), 51.

10   Francis Galton, *Inquiries into Human Faculty* (London: Macmillan, 1883), 212.

11   Ibid., 179. And see chapter 3 of Darwin's *Descent of Man.*

12   See David R. Moore, *The Torres Strait Collections of A. C. Haddon* (London: British Museum, 1984), 11–12. For Haddon's own account of his initial foray into anthropology and his efforts to organize the Cambridge expedition, see his *Headhunters Black, White, and Brown* (London: Methuen, 1901), vii–xiv. For details of the financial negotiations over the expedition, see Haddon's account books; the letter written on behalf of the Royal Society by J. Keltie to Haddon, 14 October 1897; the proceedings of the Cambridge University Senate meeting of 9 November 1899—all in the Haddon Papers, Cambridge University Library, Envelopes 1921 and 1049. Lesser contributors to the expedition were the British Association for the Advancement of Science, the Royal Geographical Society, the Royal Dublin Society, the colonial government of Queensland, and the Royal Society—in whose deliberations the recommendations of Frazer and Galton were important.

13   See Pauline Turner Strong, "Fathoming the Primitive," *Ethnohistory* 33 (1986): 175–194. For one illustration of evolutionist anthropologists' identification of antipodean peoples as truly primitive, see E. B. Tylor, "On the Tasmanians as Representatives of Paleolithic Man," *Journal of the Anthropological Institute* 23 (1893): 150.

14   Wallace's letter to Haddon is quoted in A. H. Quiggin and E. S. Fegan, "Alfred Cort Haddon, 1855–1940," *Man* 40 (1940): 99.

15   W. H. R. Rivers, "A General Account of Method," in *Notes and Queries on Anthropology,* ed. B. Friere-Marreco and J. L. Myres, 4th ed. (London: Royal Anthropological Institute, 1912), 124.

16   Haddon, *Headhunters,* 5.

17   On the place of Rivers (1864–1922) in British psychology, see, e.g., L. S. Hearnshaw, *A Short History of British Psychology, 1840–1940* (New York: Barnes and Noble, 1964), 134–135.

18   William McDougall (1871–1938), Charles Samuel Myers (1873–1946), Charles Gabriel Seligman (1873–1940).

19   Rivers' anthropological methods were generally designed to facilitate speedy research and were admired by the anthropological community for this reason. See, e.g., A. M. Hocart's review of Rivers' *History of Melanesian Society,* which praises its factual accuracy while questioning some of its conclusions. *Man* 15 (1915): 89–93.

20   For one account of the British social survey, see Raymond Kent, "The Emergence of the Sociological Survey, 1887–1939," in *Essays on the History of British Sociological Research,* ed. Martin Bulmer (Cam-

bridge: Cambridge University Press, 1985), 52–69. See also
A. W. McBriar, *An Edwardian Mixed Doubles* (Oxford: Oxford University Press, 1987), 268–274, 342. Members of the anthropological community were certainly familiar with the British social surveys. See, e.g., Francis Galton's 1902 Huxley Memorial Lecture to the Anthropological Institute, "The Possible Improvement of the Human Breed," reprinted in his *Essays in Eugenics* (London: Eugenics Education Society, 1909), 9–11.

21   See W. H. R. Rivers, *Dreams and Primitive Culture* (Manchester: Manchester University Press, 1918), 16–21.

22   For some discussion of the genesis of the "genealogical method" and the possible influence of Galton on Rivers, see Ian Langham, *The Building of British Social Anthropology* (Dordrecht: Reidel, 1981), 67–71. In the published reports of the Cambridge expedition to Torres Strait, Rivers does not describe the method as he applied it on the expedition but refers the reader to his "Genealogical Method of Collecting Social and Vital Statistics," *Journal of the Anthropological Institute* 30 (1900): 74–82, which contains no acknowledgments. For the sort of (rather disparaging) references Rivers made to Galton, see W. H. R. Rivers, "Introduction," in *Reports of the Cambridge Anthropological Expedition to Torres Straits* (Cambridge: Cambridge University Press, 1903), 2: 5. On anthropological inquiry as an extension of medical diagnosis, see Rivers, *Dreams and Primitive Culture*, 16.

23   Unless otherwise noted, the description of the Torres Strait work that follows summarizes A. C. Haddon, ed., *Reports of the Cambridge Anthropological Expedition to Torres Straits* (Cambridge: Cambridge University Press, 1901, 1903), 2: esp. 1–6, 25–26, 40–48, 64, 70, 83, 95, 127, 130–131, 148, 177–182, 192–195.

24   See, e.g., "Vocational Guidance and Selection," a report on a lecture given by Myers, *Lancet* 1920 (2): 1014–1015.

25   W. H. R. Rivers, *The Influence of Alcohol and Other Drugs on Fatigue,* The Croonian Lectures Delivered at the Royal College of Physicians in 1906 (London: Edward Arnold, 1908).

26   See, e.g., the notes and letters in *Nature* 31 (1885) headed "Civilisation and Eyesight": 12 February, 340; 19 February, 359–360; 26 February, 386–388; 5 March, 407–408; 12 March, 433–434; 19 March, 457–458; 2 April 503–504; 16 April, 552–553. See also R. Brudenell Carter, "The Influence of Civilisation Upon Eyesight," *Journal of the Society of Arts* 33 (1885): 239–250; minutes of the meeting of the Anthropological Institute on 25 March 1885, Francis Galton, president, in the chair, *Journal of the Anthropological Institute* 15 (1885): 113–131; Galton, *Inquiries into Human Faculty,* 132.

27   Erwin H. Ackerknecht, "In Memory of William H. R. Rivers, 1864–1922," *Bulletin of the History of Medicine* 11 (1942): 478–479.

28 W. H. R. Rivers, "Primitive Color Vision," *Popular Science Monthly* 59 (1901): 44–58.

29 R. Steven Turner, "Paradigms and Productivity: The Case of Physiological Optics, 1840–94," *Social Studies of Science* 17 (1987): 52–53.

30 Royal Society Committee on Colour-Vision (Lord Rayleigh, Lord Kelvin, R. Brudenell Carter, A. H. Church, J. Evans, R. Farquharson, M. Foster, F. Galton, W. Pole, G. G. Stokes, W. de Abney), "Report of the Committee on Colour-Vision," *Proceedings of the Royal Society of London* 51 (March–May 1892): esp. 290, 293, 296, 298, 311, 328–335, 339, 343.

31 Rivers in *Expedition to Torres Straits*, 2: 44–45. Shortly after their trip to Torres Strait, Rivers and Myers did more work of the same kind. See W. H. R. Rivers, "The Color Vision of the Natives of Upper Egypt," *Journal of the Anthropological Institute* 31 (1901): 229–247; W. H. R. Rivers, "Observations on the Senses of the Todas," *British Journal of Psychology* 1 (1905): 321–396; Charles S. Myers, "The Taste Names of Primitive Peoples," *British Journal of Psychology* 1 (1904): 117–126.

32 Rivers, "Primitive Color Vision," 55.

33 W. H. R. Rivers, "Medicine, Magic and Religion," the Fitzpatrick Lectures to the Royal College of Physicians, Lecture 1, *Lancet*, 1916 (1): 65.

34 A. G. Tansley, "The Relations of Complex and Sentiment," *British Journal of Psychology* 8 (1922): 120.

35 Myers secured an appointment as Rivers' assistant at Cambridge in 1902, rising in the academic ranks until he became reader in experimental psychology in 1921; in that year he cofounded a London-based consulting firm, the National Institute of Industrial Psychology, and subsequently left Cambridge. F. C. (Sir Frederick) Bartlett (1896–1969) left an extraordinary legacy to psychology upon his retirement in 1952; in 1960, most of the occupants of chairs of psychology in British universities had been Bartlett's students. For their careers and appraisals of the importance of the Torres Strait expedition to psychology, see Hearnshaw, *Short History of British Psychology* 172–173; Edwin G. Boring, *A History of Experimental Psychology* (New York: Appleton-Century Crofts, 1950), 491.

36 On (Sir) Cyril Burt (1883–1971) and his audience, see Gillian Sutherland, *Ability, Merit, and Measurement* (Oxford: Oxford University Press, 1984), esp. 121, 130–148.

37 J. L. Myres, "The Science of Man in the Service of the State," *Journal of the Royal Anthropological Institute* 59 (1929): 50.

38 F. C. Bartlett, "Psychological Methods and Anthropological Problems," *Africa* 10 (1937): 403.

39 See, e.g., W. H. R. Rivers, "The Unity of Anthropology," presidential

address, *Journal of the Royal Anthropological Institute* 52 (1922): 12–25; C. G. Seligman, "Anthropology and Psychology: A Study of Some Points of Contact," presidential address, *Journal of the Royal Anthropological Institute* 54 (1924): 13–46; William McDougall, *Anthropology and History,* the Robert Boyle Lecture (London: Oxford University Press, 1920).

40 Bronislaw Malinowski (1884–1942), Alfred Reginald (originally Brown) Radcliffe-Brown (1881–1955). The quotation is from Bronislaw Malinowski, *Argonauts of the Western Pacific* (London: Macmillan, 1922), 23.

41 See, e.g., Bronislaw Malinowski, "Parenthood—the Basis of Social Structure," in *The New Generation,* ed. V. F. Calvertan and Samuel D. Schmalhausen (New York: Horace Liveright, 1930), esp. 117–119, 132–133, 154; Bronislaw Malinowski, "Psychoanalysis and Anthropology," *Nature* 112 (1923): 650–651; A. R. Radcliffe-Brown, "The Methods of Ethnology and Social Anthropology," in *Method in Social Anthropology,* ed. M. N. Srinivas (1923; Chicago: University of Chicago Press, 1958), 3–38; A. R. Radcliffe-Brown, "The Social Organization of Australian Tribes," *Oceania* 1 (1930): 30.

42 The foundation of the International African Institute in 1926 prompted the shift of anthropological attention to Africa. The creation of an international (but primarily British) coalition of colonial officials, missionaries, and scholars, the IAI was intended to provide useful knowledge for the still-nascent bureaucracies of African colonial rule; and the funds at its disposal (largely contributed by the Rockefeller philanthropies) provided the first secure base for anthropologists' research support, thus ensuring that the anthropologists of the interwar years—the first truly professional generation of anthropologists—were largely Africanists. For an extended discussion of these developments, see my *Savage Within,* esp. 205–216. On the convention of treating anthropology's subjects as participants in stable, isolated societies, see John W. Burton, "Shadows at Twilight: A Note on History and the Ethnographic Present," *Proceedings of the American Philosophical Society* 132 (1988): 420–433.

43 See, e.g., A. R. Radcliffe-Brown, "On the Concept of Function in Social Science," reprinted in his *Structure and Function in Primitive Society* (1935; New York: Free Press, 1952), 183.

44 See F. C. Bartlett, *Psychology and Primitive Culture* (New York: Macmillan, 1923); idem, *Remembering* (Cambridge: Cambridge University Press, 1932); idem, "Anthropology in Reconstruction," Huxley Memorial Lecture, *Journal of the Royal Anthropological Institute* 73 (1943): 9–15. See also D. B. Broadbent, "Frederick Charles Bartlett," *Biographical Memoirs of Fellows of the Royal Society* 16 (1970): 1–13.

45   See Sutherland, *Ability*. See also C. S. Myers, *Man and Work* (London: University of London Press, 1920), 27–30, 163–167, 190. And see Eric Farmer, "Early Days in Industrial Psychology: An Autobiographical Note," 32; C. R. Frisby, "The Development of Industrial Psychology at the NIIP," 37–39; Winifred Raphael, "The NIIP and Its Staff, 1921–1961," 68—all in *Occupational Psychology* 44 (1970).

46   See, e.g., William McDougall, "The Nature of Functional Disease," *American Journal of Psychiatry*, n.s., 1 (1922): 339–340; Charles S. Myers, "Contributions to the Study of Shell Shock," *Lancet*, 1916 (1): 467, 609 and (2): 464; W. H. R. Rivers, *Instinct and the Unconscious* (Cambridge: Cambridge University Press, 1922), 209.

47   See, e.g., the speech in the House of Commons by William Brace, parliamentary undersecretary at the War Office, 17 June 1915, reported in "Treatment of Mental Strain in Soldiers," *Lancet*, 1915 (1): 1377. See also *Lancet*, 1915 (1): 352, 412, 1059. And see Martin Stone, "Shellshock and the Psychologists," in *The Anatomy of Madness*, ed. W. F. Bynum, Roy Porter, and Michael Shepherd (London: Tavistock, 1985), 2: 253–254.

48   See, e.g., Dean Rapp, "The Reception of Freud by the British Press: General Interest and Literary Magazines, 1920–1925," *Journal of the History of the Behavioral Sciences* 24 (1988): 191–201; Siegfried Sassoon, *Sherston's Progress* (New York: Literary Guild of America, 1937), pt. 1, "Rivers," 3–92.

49   See, e.g., McBriar, *Mixed Doubles*, 358.

PART FOUR

Social Darwinisms

B A R R Y   W.   B U T C H E R

13 Darwinism, Social Darwinism, and the Australian Aborigines

A Reevaluation

Two propositions will be argued in this essay. First, because recent scholarship suggests that the traditional distinction drawn between Darwinism and Social Darwinism is historically untenable, there is a need to reevaluate the manner in which scholars have deployed these terms when analyzing the history of race relations in Australia. Second, this reevaluation will lead to a reassessment of the way in which Australia's contribution to evolutionary anthropology has been perceived. Far from being merely a quarry to be mined for value-free and ideologically untainted ethnographic resources, Australia exported information in the human sciences which was tightly constrained by a set of social values and political ideology.

Historians have often commented on European settlers' use of Darwinian rhetoric as part of the agenda for justifying racial supremacy and land dispossession in Australia.[1] They have often sought to make sense of that rhetoric by applying to an Australian context a series of propositions widely accepted as part of nineteenth-century social theory and political ideology. Although rarely spelled out in detail, these propositions invariably focus on the supposed misapplication of Darwin's biological theory of evolution by natural selection (with all its metaphorical allusion to struggle, fitness, and survival) to social development and racial fitness. Since Richard Hofstadter's pioneering study of Social Darwinism in America was first published in 1944, the concept has been taken to apply to two areas of study:[2] on the one hand it has been used in analyzing right-wing, individualist philosophy; on the other, in understanding the spread of European imperialism in the second half of the nineteenth century.

It is in the first sense that Australian scholars have applied the concept when detailing the tragic consequences of the collision of European and Aboriginal cultures. In essence they have seen Social

Darwinian rhetoric as part of a conservative ideology invoked to uphold the claims of a pastoral elite in their struggle for land and political power. Bernard Smith, for instance, in his Boyer Lectures for the Australian Broadcasting Corporation in 1980 said that Darwin's theory of natural selection

> was a biological theory. . . . It offers no explanation except by analogy for social change. But in the hands of popularisers of the theory of natural selection such as Herbert Spencer, social analogies were seized upon. A man with a gun was fitter to survive than a man with a spear; the murderer was fitter than his victim.[3]

The invocation of Spencer's name has long been part of the established demonology of scholars of Social Darwinism; to Spencer is usually attributed the perversion of the pure Darwinism said to be expounded in the *Origin of Species*. Defending that supposed purity has been the occupation of many historians of biology in the past century, and the historical trash can of Social Darwinism has proven to be a popular receptacle for all the ideological impurities found at the door of Spencer and his friends.[4]

In recent times there has been a decided shift away from the Hofstadter line outlined above. In the 1960s Robert M. Young suggested that both the form and content of Darwin's theory depended on a complex collection of social and cultural ideas that existed as part of the dominant ideology of nineteenth-century Britain. In particular, Young pointed to the work of political economists such as Adam Smith and Thomas Malthus, which along with the natural theology of William Paley and the psychology of Dugald Stewart helped create a "common context" of intellectual life in which Darwin was situated.[5] Young's attempt to show that, as he later termed it, "Darwinism is social," was extended by the sociologists Barry Barnes and Steven Shapin in a provocative paper published in 1979. They argued that the purported purity of Darwin's theory was an artifact created by historians for the purpose of distinguishing the legitimate domain of natural selection—biology and the natural world—from its illegitimate extension to social theory and political philosophy.[6]

In 1986 the historian James Moore brought together these ideas, and through the simple expedient of looking at what Darwin actually said about humans and human biological and social history made the point that the distinction between Darwinism and Social Darwinism would have been lost on Darwin himself. As Moore makes clear, both the *Descent of Man* and the *Expression of the Emotions* resonate with supposedly Social Darwinian terms and expressions, and Darwin showed no reluctance to apply the findings he put forward in the *Origin* to human development, physical or social. Put briefly, the revised view of Darwin's own attitude toward the application of his theory of evolution by natural selection to social affairs suggests that he would not have seen the distinction between the social and natural realm as having much, if any, validity. As Moore makes clear, it was all of a piece in his thinking, an integrated whole.[7]

This revision of what may be termed the standard view has opened the way for a reevaluation of the use of Darwinian theory in the context of nineteenth-century Australian history. If, after all, there is no clear distinction between Darwinism and Social Darwinism, then the type of comment made by Bernard Smith is based on a misconception and must be rejected. Further, the work of Young, Barnes, Shapin, and Moore has made it possible to look again at the manner in which Darwin used resources to construct his theoretical picture of human biological, social, and cultural development. Australian material played an important role in that process, but with the insights provided by the reevaluation of the scholarship in the area it is possible to go beyond merely listing and cataloging those resources to examine to what extent Australian anthropological materials were already framed within an ideological context that could be slotted into a Darwinian view of human physical and social evolution.

Before Darwin: Ideology, Race, and the Ethics of Conquest

The settlement of Australia after 1788 quickly led to conflict between the European invaders and the native aboriginal population. Despite occasional protests from the British authorities, there was little local pressure to come to a peaceful arrangement between the conflicting cultures. The spread of pastoralism from the 1820s on saw the emergence of what might be termed a myth of legitimation designed to justify the appropriation of the land from the Aborigines. In 1849 the prominent pastoralist James Macarthur expounded the essential features of this myth when declaring that

> the worthless, idle Aborigine has been driven from the land that he knew not how to make use of, and valued not, to make room for a more noble race of beings, who are more capable of estimating the value of this fine country. Is it not right that it should be so?[8]

Macarthur's vision of the onward march of civilization, represented by hard-working Europeans destined to supplant a primitive, unreflective race of natives, was neither original nor unusual. It was based on a long and continuing tradition in British social thought; John Locke had elaborated the view that unutilized land could be colonized, and down to the present day "unutilized" has meant "not brought within the confines of European modes of agriculture and pastoral use."[9]

Using land in the traditional Aboriginal manner—usually for hunting and gathering—counted for little when judged against the cultural values of the European invaders of Australia. In the 1830s the *Sydney Morning Herald* berated the defenders of the native population as obstacles to progress: "it is the right of civilised men to occupy country in a state of nature. . . . If this were not so the great end of civilisation could never be effected."[10] Bernard Smith quotes a commentator in 1847 as saying that "regret concerning the disappearance of the Aborigines is hardly more reasonable than it would be to complain of drainage of marshes or the disappearance of wild animals."[11] Smith describes this attitude as the ethos of the pastoral life, the outcome of distorted cultural values, while Michael Roe terms it "the squatter theory of value."[12] Implicit in this fundamentally ideological position was the belief that Aboriginal culture, judged from a European perspective, was primitive and destined to disappear. Smith and the historian Henry Reynolds both emphasize the functional aspect of this ideology, which in Reynolds' words "cleared the conscience just as the superior arms of the whites cleared the land."[13] But Smith's point that it was the result of distorted cultural values brings the issue closer to the interests of this chapter. While Australian culture was largely a dependent one, in a frontier, rural, and agricultural environment, imported ethics were transmuted. Enlightenment ideals of human equality were lost sight of, and necessity led to the invention of an ethical system more congenial to colonists' needs. Conquest and the takeover of Aboriginal lands were justified by invoking a set of social values based on utilitarianism and a work ethic based on a growing belief in social progress. Smith convincingly argues that this ethic was home grown, an original Australian construction, albeit built on elements drawn from political and social philosophies devised elsewhere.[14]

The assumption that the Aborigines belonged to an inferior race that must inevitably disappear when confronted by a "superior" one was popularized in the writings of explorers and naturalists in the early decades of the nineteenth century. The botanist Allan Cunningham, for instance, assured readers of his published journal that the natives were "at the very zero of civilisation, constituting in a measure the connecting link between man and the monkey tribe."[15] Written in 1834, these words seem to presage a later Darwinian attitude, but in reality they probably refer back to the old notion of the "great chain of being" where racial hierarchies were accepted as part of an ideal set of relationships emanating from divine thought rather than as real genetic affinities. While there was some protest against the type of thinking characterized in Cunningham's description, it was clearly in line with the interests of the majority of Europeans.

Other historical and cultural factors were also involved in the process of classifying the Aborigines. Bernard Smith points to the role of the biblical myth of the separation of the races as the guiding metaphor of pre-Darwinian racist ideology, but of increasing importance was the influence of scientific ideas, especially those associated with the rise and development of phrenology.[16] Henry Reynolds quotes the important British publicist for phrenology, George Combe, as saying that the Australian Aborigines had great deficiencies in the moral and intellectual organs and therefore were unsuited for and indeed incapable of civilization.[17] Phrenology seems to have been something of a fascination for the early explorers of Australia. The naturalist George Bennett complained that the Aborigines distrusted his attempts to administer phrenological tests, which they apparently took to be a form of witchcraft,[18] while Charles Sturt and John Lort Stokes applied phrenological principles when attempting to describe the Aborigines' physiognomical configuration for their readers. Stokes, who was usually well disposed toward the natives, painted a particularly menacing picture:

> They have very overhanging brows, and retreating foreheads, large noses, full lips. . . . The unfavourable impression produced by their physiognomy is confirmed if their phrenological conformation is taken into consideration; and certainly if the principles of that science are admitted to be true, these savages are woefully deficient in all the qualities which contribute to man's moral superiority.[19]

Sturt agreed with this analysis but made the somewhat ambivalent remark that "in a savage state the higher intellectual faculties . . . are seldom called forth."[20] In the 1850s the Victorian colonial government took evidence from a phrenologist who declared the Aborigines to be "beyond permanent improvement. . . . The sides of the forehead offer the greatest possible contrast with the Grecian or artistic skull."[21] Thus phrenology, "the first science of man," achieved a degree of official recognition in the Australian colonies, but more important, it provided scientific support for an ideology congenial to the invading European culture. Phrenology explained why the native population did not use the land or show any inclination to, and it did this by entrenching that explanation in a strongly deterministic biological theory. When Darwin visited Australia in 1836 he found the ethic of conquest firmly ensconced in the ideology of colonial expansion. Nor did it remain within the confines of the Australian colonies. In Britain and Europe, the journals and accounts of Australian explorers, naturalists, and pastoral settlers were widely read, and with few exceptions they carried the message that the Aborigines were a low and doomed race. One cynical commentator quipped at the time that "the recipe for an Australian novel was a quick read through Stokes, Grey, Sturt and Eyre followed by a quick visit to the Royal Gardens at Kew for a quick review of Australian plant life."[22] It might be said with equal validity that precisely the same ingredients went into the creation of scientific knowledge about the Australian continent, including its human inhabitants.

The best of the explorers' accounts often exhibited an ambivalence toward the natives. Sturt wrote in the early 1830s that he doubted whether they had any idea of a "superintending providence," which in the context of the time was a clear sign of "savagery," and added that he believed them to be at the bottom of the scale of humanity.[23] Some years later, with the benefit of more direct experience, he altered his opinion, suggesting that they should not occupy "so low a place in the scale of human society as that which has been assigned to them." Against the trend of current opinion, Sturt went on to point out that the culture of the Aborigines, not their biological make up, presented the chief obstacle to their becoming fully civilized.[24] Sturt's *Journal* remained unpublished for more than a century, robbing potential readers of the benefit of his mature and revised reflections on the nature of the Aborigines. Thomas Mitchell agreed in the main with Sturt, explaining the decline of the natives as being due to the encroachments of pastoralism and the disappearance from the traditional hunting grounds of their staple food, the kangaroo.[25] Such straightforward observation-based explanations were in the minority however. Increasingly the trend was toward attributing the low status and poor prospects of the Aborigines to fixed biological laws. Representative of this view was Paul Strzelecki's explanation of the ill effects of interracial sexual union on the fertility of Aboriginal women. According to Strzelecki, inferior native breeding was incompatible with that of the superior European.[26] George Bennett, pushing the phrenological case to its logical conclusion, quoted the French scholar Lesson to the effect that "judged by external appearances and intellect [the Aborigine] has been degraded from the true rank of man and approaches the nature of the brute."[27]

In summary, there are good reasons for believing that long before the appearance of the *Origin of Species* the European settlers considered the Australian Aborigines as biologically ill-equipped to sustain their lifestyle and culture in the face of an invasive "superior" race and culture. According to Henry Reynolds, Darwin contributed a dynamic aspect to this picture, providing a naturalistic law to explain Aboriginal inferiority.[28] While no doubt correct, there is an element missing from this account. Before Darwinism became part of the process of legitimation for colonial expansion in Australia, it was itself informed by the image of the Aborigines described above. There is thus a fascinating feedback process at work that casts doubt on any attempt to interpret the relationship of Darwinian theory to social theory as one of the simple, additional input of science into prevailing social and political ideology.

Darwinism and the Aborigines

Fortunately there is direct evidence of Darwin's own appreciation of the nature and status of the Australian Aborigines. In his *Journal of Researches,* he thought them higher in the scale of humanity than the inhabitants of Tierra del Fuego, though this said little in their favor.[29] Later he turned, like every other person interested in matters Australian, to the exploration literature. His notebooks make it clear that he was an avid reader of the works of Sturt, Mitchell, and Grey. In his two books on human evolution, *The Descent of Man* and *The Expression of the Emotions in Man and Animals,* there are numerous references to the Australian natives, and in *Emotions* he made extensive use of replies to questionnaires sent to Australia.[30] In neither of these works is there direct evidence that Darwin took over the ideological views of his correspondents when formulating his theoretical ideas. That they were implicit in his thinking, however, can be seen from other available evidence. The best example of this brings together the two founders of the theory of natural selection. While they differed on key points, this exchange makes it clear that they shared certain assumptions about the relationship between the human races and accepted prevailing attitudes toward the effects of cultural collision.

In 1864 Alfred Russel Wallace published a paper entitled "The Development of Human Races under the Law of Natural Selection." In this he claimed that

> it is the same great law of "the preservation of the favoured races in the struggle for life" which leads to the inevitable extinction of all those low and mentally undeveloped populations with which Europeans come into

contact. The Red Indian in North America and in Brazil; the Tasmanian, Australian and New Zealander in the southern hemisphere, die out not from any one special cause, but from the inevitable effects of an unequal mental and physical struggle.[31]

"The preservation of the favoured races in the struggle for life" is of course the subtitle of the *Origin of Species,* and Wallace removed any doubt about the extent to which he was applying the principles of natural selection to the human realm when he added later that the native races die out and are replaced "just as the weeds of Europe overrun North America and Australia, extinguishing native productions by the inherent vigour of their organisation, and by their greater capacity for existence and multiplication."[32]

Darwin's response to Wallace's paper illustrates the extent to which he was prepared to go in allowing his theory to incorporate human history and development. Commenting on Wallace's discussion of natural selection, he sought to strengthen the point by alluding to his own reading of the Australian literature: "when reading Sir George Grey's account of the constant battles of Australian savages, I remember thinking that natural selection would come in."[33]

It is surprising that this striking and, by Darwin's standards, unambiguous application of natural selection to human evolution has not excited more attention among scholars debating the extent to which Darwin was a Social Darwinist.[34] The text of this letter to Wallace, and the context in which it occurs, would seem to suggest that at this relatively late stage—four years after the first appearance of the *Origin*—Darwin was comfortable with the extension of his theory to include human social evolution. Indeed, a plain reading of the text makes it clear that the distinction between the natural and social worlds was simply not an issue. Such an interpretation supports a point made by Dov Ospovat in his seminal work, *The Development of Darwin's Theory,* that bears quoting in full:

> In the second and subsequent editions of the *Origin* Darwin argued that the equation "more fit = higher" is generally correct. Those who later took Darwin's theory as a basis for ideologies of progress and the natural dominance of "higher" over "lower" human races were not required to distort it to serve their purposes. The theory itself already contained elements of such an analysis.[35]

Ospovat remained unsure of the extent to which Darwin shared the social attitudes his theory was validating, but the letter to Wallace (and what follows below) strongly supports James Moore's point that

Darwin would have seen no difficulty in applying his theory to human social evolution. In any event, Ospovat's claim that regardless of his personal attitude Darwin "was building his theory out of ideologically loaded concepts" can hardly be denied in the light of the available evidence.[36]

We know that Darwin changed his position on the question of "higher" and "lower" organisms before the second edition of the *Origin* appeared. From first determining not to talk in such terms, he moved to accepting the view that, as Ospovat says, "higher" equals "more fit." Throughout the 1850s, in a debate with Joseph Hooker over the relationship of the floras of eastern and western Australia, Darwin argued that his new position was supported by the manner in which the plants of the northern hemisphere were overrunning those in the south. Wallace's weed analogy therefore had impeccable credentials.[37]

However, one can go back even earlier to find Darwin arguing, within an Australian context, the same point—and this time in relation to human beings and the relative fitness of different cultures. The example illustrates the reemergence of the old ideology of conquest and the "pastoral ethic" in the guise of Darwinian scientific theory. In 1870 the Australian writer and historian James Bonwick published an important book detailing the destruction of aboriginal culture in Tasmania. Of that destruction he wrote,

> Such will sadly demonstrate Mr Darwin's philosophy that "the varieties of man seem to act on each other in the same way as different species of animals; the stronger always extirpates the weaker."[38]

Compare this with the following quotation taken from Swedish naturalist Carl Lumholtz's description of his travels in Queensland, published in 1889:

> When civilised nations come into contact with barbarians that struggle is but short, excepting where a dangerous climate helps the native race, says Mr Darwin, and history corroborates his statement.[39]

The essential similarity of these two references is indisputable, and the two authors quoting them did so in the full expectation that their readers would understand the force of giving a scientific explanation for disturbing sociocultural phenomena.

What is interesting now, however, is the provenance of the two Darwinian quotations. Lumholtz was making use of the *Descent of Man,* and, to the extent that it was a post-*Origin* reference, it was unproblematic as a case of standard Social Darwinian rhetoric, one of many that historians have uncovered.[40] The Bonwick quotation, however, is much more intriguing, for it comes not from the *Descent* nor indeed from any of Darwin's explicitly anthropological works; it can be found in the *Journal of Researches,* published in 1839, twenty years before the theory of natural selection was presented to the world. And an analysis of the source of the reference shows that the initial observations on which it was based were made by Darwin in New South Wales in 1836, during the *Beagle* voyage.

> Wherever the European has trod, death seems to pursue the aboriginal. We may look to the wide extent of the Americas, Polynesia, the Cape of good hope, and Australia, and we shall find the same result. . . . The varieties of man act on each other; in the same way as different species of animals—the stronger always extirpate the weaker.[41]

Two important points emerge from all this. First, any plain reading of Darwin's words makes it clear that he held views that were later to be encapsulated in the phrase *Social Darwinism* before he had clearly worked out the theory of natural selection. At the risk of belaboring the point, there are grounds for believing that these views were to some extent formed in the light of his observations and experiences in Australia, where he was exposed to the "squatter theory of value" and the "pastoral ethic" first hand. And Darwin, as we know, spent some time partaking of the hospitality of some of Australia's pastoral elite, including a section of the Macarthur clan, one of whom, William Macarthur, he met and dined with in London in the 1850s.[42] Later, of course, his ideas on the comparative fitness of cultures were strengthened by his reading of the scientific and exploration literature emanating from Australia. This suggested to him ways in which the mechanism of natural selection might apply in the case of human beings—as his letter to Wallace makes clear.

The second point that emerges from this discussion is that Bonwick's use of a Darwinian reference that predates the development of Darwin's ideas on evolution shows the extent to which the case for Darwin's theory having been constructed out of commonly understood ideologically loaded elements is proven. The polemical words of James Macarthur and the *Sydney Morning Herald* quoted earlier were transformed into the language of science and made the basis of belief in a natural law which determined that "when civilised nations come into contact with barbarians the struggle is but short." As scientific truth this could now be reintegrated into the governing ideology as justification for the destruction of native culture or, as in the cases of Bonwick and Lumholtz, as an explanation for it. The consequences that could be derived from this scientized version of an old ideology were all articulated in the philosophy of post-*Origin* Social Darwinism. "Pitiless nature" guaranteed that the destruction of the Aboriginal population was both inevitable and amoral, for it was a result of the forces of destiny. Efforts to intervene in the process were a "malign influence," a hindrance to the further evolution of the higher European races. From the standpoint of human sensibilities, the "passing of the Aborigines" was no more than a minor drawback to a larger good—the evolution of a higher race that would emerge from the white colonizers of the continent.[43]

Reimporting the Ideology: Hearn to Baldwin Spencer

Henry Reynolds describes the totality of evolutionary philosophy as it was applied to the Australian Aborigines as "flourishing racism." Social Darwinism carried a message of struggle, competition, and violence; it swept away philanthropy, multiracial creation, and the like in favor of "inevitable natural law."[44] The word "social" can now be removed from this analysis and some recognition made of the fact that the idea of "inevitable natural law" did not need Darwin's imprimatur in relation to the decline of the Aborigines, although the general acceptance of Darwinism certainly gave new force to the concept. Once bolstered with the scientific authority of Darwinian theory, the colonial picture of the Aborigines became part of the attempt to construct an evolutionary anthropology.

Armchair theorists in Europe and America called on their Australian correspondents for information and received a wealth of detail that in broad terms supported a picture of social evolution in which "lower races" were assumed to be remnants of earlier stages in the rise of humanity. This process has generally been seen as part of the patron/client web of relationships that existed between scientific center and periphery. Those working in the latter were supposed to be sending back factual data; those in the center turned the data into theory. This may accord with some earlier, cruder interpretations of the spread of Western science, but it does no justice to the facts. The armchair theorists worked on material that was already heavily value- and theory-laden and added further scientific value to it before reexporting it. Australian contributors were important figures in the scientific landscape, not mere servants at the periphery tyrannized by distance and isolated from intellectual contact with their European colleagues. Their work, as culturally constructed as any could be, was crucial to the development of the anthropological sciences, which evolutionary theory influenced significantly in the second half of the nineteenth century.[45]

Those responsible for providing an evolutionary interpretation of

Australia's native population after 1860 came from a wide spectrum of colonial society. Many were academics engaged in university work, while others were missionaries, government officials, or popular writers. Their numbers were small but, insofar as their influence extended beyond the colonial setting, significant. Defining the place of the Aborigines in nature and colonial society often meant redefining old material through the medium of social-evolutionary philosophy, if not always specifically Darwinian theory.

The legal status of the Aborigines within the jurisdiction of British law remained a matter of debate until 1967, when they were finally granted full citizen rights and included in the national census. The doctrine of *terra nullius* under which James Cook took possession of the continent in 1769 made it difficult for the British authorities to include the native population within the law as anything other than property. To the ordinary European settler, they were part of the natural realm of the continent; their failure to use land in European style left them open to the charge that they should give way to those who would. As governments after midcentury began to grapple with the question of dealing with the remaining native groups, legal opinion concerning their status took on some importance. In Victoria, the internationally renowned scholar William Edward Hearn (1826–1888) sought to clarify the issue in his textbook *The Theory of Legal Duties and Rights,* published in 1883. According to Hearn, the natives were outside the sanction of the law except where their interests impinged in some way on the interests of third parties who were included within its ambit. They were "the objects to which the prescribed forbearances apply, but they are not the third parties for whose benefit the forbearance is intended." The duties of the law toward the Aborigines were to be understood as a branch of "Absolute Duties," defined by Hearn as "duties performed for the benefit of the population at large, not the parties to which the duties are addressed."[46] Hearn then elaborated on the implications:

> These duties are commands given for the purposes of public policy to all persons, requiring them to observe certain forbearances in respect to these natives. That is, the Aborigines are the objects to which the prescribed forbearance is intended. They are thus in the same position as those lower animals in whose behalf the law in certain circumstances thinks fit to interpose. Duties are cast upon the owners of cattle. . . . It would be absurd to say that these animals, whether tame or wild, had rights. They are simply the secondary objects of absolute duties.[47]

Hearn's equating the social situation of the Aborigines with the ownership of cattle should not be taken as an example of a legal nicety only, because his ideas on the evolution of society required that the "savage races" of the world be understood as vestiges of an earlier and more primitive period of human history. In his book *Plutology,* published in 1863, he had compared primitive societies with the modern industrial state:

> In the complexity of its social structure, and in the definite character of its several organs no less than in its actual bulk, the English nation exceeds an Aboriginal tribe at least as much as one of the higher mammals exceeds a zoophyte.[48]

Hearn gave it as a maxim that "between the laws of nature and the laws of the Queen there is no resemblance and no means of comparison,"[49] but he was nonetheless prepared to resort to biological analogies to illustrate points relating to social matters. Furthermore, the discussion of social development in *Plutology* was carried on within a framework of biological terminology strongly influenced by the organic development theories of Herbert Spencer, who was given as the source of much of Hearn's material. Social change was implicitly assumed by Hearn to follow analogous patterns to change in the organic realm. *Plutology* was a work of political economy much admired by William Stanley Jevons, Leslie Stephen, and Herbert Spencer for its original manner of incorporating economics into an evolutionary theory of social development.[50] It remained a set text for generations of Hearn's pupils at the University of Melbourne, where it made a lasting impression on several who were to make their mark on colonial life.

One such was Alexander Sutherland (1852–1902), a writer on numerous scientific and social topics, including the evolution of the moral instinct. Sutherland constructed a hierarchical racial tree that was still in use well into the twentieth century. The Aborigines were placed among the middle rank of "savages" where they inhabited a twilight zone between the lower animals and civilization. Writing in the 1880s and 1890s, Sutherland had the benefit of Hearn's earlier writings to guide him, along with the contemporary literature emanating from Europe. He had no firsthand knowledge of the Aborigines but had no qualms about pointing to the "inadequately developed brain" and the "misery" of their mode of living when describing their inevitable decline. Sutherland claimed that they placed little value on human life, and although affectionate toward children they allowed to survive, had no compunction about killing at birth those they did not want. Extending Hearn's invocation of biology to illustrate the chasm between Aboriginal culture and that of the higher races, Sutherland asserted that "we must be content to look upon their customs, their moral notions, as so many biological facts without presuming to try them by laws which they do not own and have never dreamt of."[51]

Given the deterministic nature of this analysis, it is not surprising that Sutherland denied that there were any ethical issues involved in the demise of the Aborigines. Indeed, their passing was a positive step in the further evolution of the higher races: "to the sentimentalist it is undoubtedly an iniquity; to the practical it represents a distinct step in human progress involving the sacrificing of a few thousand of an inferior race."[52]

Another who made a name locally and internationally was the Oxford don and Australian radical Charles Henry Pearson (1830–1894).[53] In his influential book *National Life and Character,* Pearson praised the extension of Anglo-Saxon culture around the globe, using the Australian case as an example of its virtues:

> Australia is an unexampled instance of a great continent that has been left for the first civilised people that found it to take and occupy. The natives have died out as we approached; there have been no complications with foreign powers; and the climate of the South is magnificent.[54]

There is more than a whiff of manifest destiny here, and it appears to be one involving both a providentialist teleology—note how the natives mysteriously died out before they actually made any contact with their conquerors—and a biological imperative—superior races supplanting inferior ones. Such a peculiar blend of science and religion was not unusual—even Sutherland had made reference to the "divine law."

Social theorists like Hearn, Sutherland, and Pearson won a wide audience at home and abroad, but a more lasting influence emerged with the earliest generation of Australian anthropologists. Social evolutionary theory provided the direct stimulus for much of this early work, as the case of Alfred Howitt demonstrates. In 1880 Howitt and his collaborator Lorimer Fison produced one of the most important contributions to anthropology ever written in Australia. *Kamilaroi and Kurnai* dealt with group marriage, elopement, and kinship among the two Aboriginal groups named in the title. The authors' most important overseas correspondent was the American anthropologist Lewis Henry Morgan, and on the basis of their own field work they sided with him in his disputes with Andrew Lang, John Lubbock, and, to a lesser extent, Edward Tylor. The book was dedicated to Morgan, who agreed to write a prefatory note. This "note" ran to twenty pages, and in it Morgan described the Aborigines as "melting away before the touch of civilisation even more rapidly than the American aborigines." He continued:

> In a lower ethnical condition than the latter, they have displayed less power of resistance. They now represent the condition of mankind in savagery better than it is elsewhere represented on the earth—a condition now rapidly passing away, through the destructive influence of superior races.[55]

Morgan protested against the worst excesses of the Europeans against the natives, but it is abundantly clear that he shared his Australian correspondents' belief that they represented a relic from an earlier age. Morgan did not stipulate in this note the extent to which he believed that biology determined the Aborigines' condition, but Howitt provided a bleak picture of the likelihood that they could raise themselves to a higher stage:

> According to my experience, the young Kurnai can learn with great facility. He has great imitative powers and therefore often acquires an excellent handwriting; but he also unlearns with great facility. In this we must recognise mental powers naturally good but not fixed by hereditary training. We must say, I think, that his mind develops quickly, and perhaps fully up to the standard of that of a white child of twelve or fourteen, but there stops.[56]

Trapped in a backwater of cultural evolution according to Morgan's scheme of human history, the Aborigine was equally caught in Howitt's analysis (which is distinctly deterministic) in a state of mental underdevelopment. Biology prevents the development of the Aboriginal mind beyond the level of the child. Decline was brought about not by European practices, the introduction of alcohol, or disease, but by the operation of an inevitable law of which Europeans were but agents. The observations of Sturt and others that suggested sociocultural reasons for the decline of the natives gave way to a belief in what Howitt described in a letter to Morgan as "the principle of Evolution."[57]

Metaphysical principles blended into natural law to such an extent that even those possessed of some sympathy for the Aborigines accepted it. Recall the references from Bonwick and Lumholtz, both of whom spoke out against ways in which Europeans were seeking to destroy native culture. The picture of the Aborigines as a low if pitiable race soon found its way into the popular culture. Notable overseas visitors to Australia quickly assessed the hopelessness of the Aborigines' cause. Anthony Trollope said in 1872 that trying to assist the Aborigines was "not worth the candle. . . . The race is doomed, and is very quickly encountering its doom."[58] The Australian poet Henry Lawson put into verse his own memories of the racist indoctrination commonly heard in the schoolroom:

> And Ireland?—that was known from the coast line to Athlone,
> But little of the land that gave us birth;
> Save that Captain Cook was killed (and was very likely grilled)
> And "our blacks are just the lowest race on earth".
> And a woodcut in its place, of the same degraded race,
> More like camels than the blackmen that we knew.[59]

It was the work of Walter Baldwin Spencer (1860–1929) that proved the most fruitful for the armchair theorists of Europe. Spencer studied under Edward Tylor and assisted in the transfer of the Pitt-Rivers ethnological museum to Oxford. In 1867 A. H. Pitt-Rivers had described the Aborigines as "living representatives of our common ancestors" whose material culture stood in the same relation to that of prehistoric Europe as "the mollusca of recent species to the mollusca of the primary geological period."[60] Spencer imbibed these images, and the results are to be found scattered throughout his many volumes on the Aborigines written between 1898 and 1926. In the first and most important of these, he invoked a rather poorly defined "necessity" to account for the decline of Aboriginal culture:

> However kindly disposed the white settler may be, his advent at once and of necessity introduces a disturbing element into the environment of the native, and from that moment degeneration sets in, no matter how friendly may be the relations between the Aborigines and the newcomers.[61]

Settlement was thus a tool of an inevitable historical process that destined the natives to disappear; put strongly, it was a factor in human evolution. Nearly three decades later when summarizing his years of anthropological investigation, Spencer described Australia as the home of creatures

> crude and quaint, that have elsewhere passed away and given place to higher forms. This applies equally to the Aboriginal as to the platypus and kangaroo. Just as the platypus, laying its eggs and feebly suckling its young, reveals a mammal in the making, so does the Aboriginal show us, at least in broad outline, what an early man must have been like before he learned to read and write.[62]

Visitors to the Museum of Victoria who might not have been expected to read Spencer and Gillen's voluminous publications were given the message nonetheless, for Spencer repeated the description in his guidebook to the Aboriginal material in the National Museum of Victoria, still in print in 1922.[63]

The Later British Darwinians and the Aborigines

The manner in which scientific understanding of the Aborigines developed throughout the nineteenth century is reminiscent more of the workings of trade and industry than of the rules of method, philosophy, or logic. This essay has suggested how ideas have been exported, reimported, and then exported again from Australia with value being added at each step. From the colonial picture of the Aborigines as an inferior race destined for extinction because of their failure to utilize the land to the Darwinian image of the same race as a biological and cultural relic, a living fossil, the ideological component remained largely intact. But just as Australia's natural products are exported as raw materials, so its scientific materials are said to be exported raw and unfinished, with no value added. The case of the Aborigines demonstrates how simplistic this view is. Pre-Darwinian attitudes toward the Aborigines depended on value judgments and cultural interpretations about what place in the scheme of things "primitive races" held. European theorists from Darwin and Wallace to Morgan and beyond used colonial resources as they received them, wrapped in a package of sociocultural ideology, and then reprocessed those resources into a more refined but essentially similar product. Imported back into Australia, the post-Darwinian picture of the Aborigine became the framework within which anthropologists and sociologists on the spot carried out their work, adding more value to the developing product. Exported once again it became valuable source material for another generation of social commentators— Edward Tylor, John Lubbock, and James Frazer being perhaps the best known.

Toward the end of the century, the interest in evolutionary theory as an explanatory framework reached its height. Every facet of human life and endeavor was subsumed beneath the banner of evolutionary progress. Science itself became incorporated into the process; as anthropologists and sociologists sought to unravel the development of society and its institutions, so theorists sought to incorporate the history of science into an evolutionary scheme. William Stanley Jevons, for example, while denying that historical and cultural development could be understood through the application of scientific principles, still turned to a form of argument that depended on the assumption of an advancing human knowledge and industrial civilization when making his case:

> No one can safely generalise upon the subtle variations of temper and emotion which may arise in a person of ordinary character.. . . Character grows more many sided. Two well educated Englishmen are far better distinguished from each other than two common labourers and these are better distinguished than two Australian Aborigines.[64]

The evolutionary connection in this passage may seem vague until it is remembered that the type of differentiation Jevons is describing was a central factor of Spencer's notion that evolution was exemplified by the growth of heterogeneity, or for that matter, Darwin's ideas on the diversity brought about in the natural world by natural selection. Implicit in Jevons' words is the belief that the well-educated Englishmen were at a higher stage of development than laborers and Aborigines.

When Karl Pearson came to write his classic text *The Grammar of Science* in 1892, evolution provided the backdrop against which the merits of scientific claims were assessed. The complete Darwinian, Pearson expounded often on the application of evolutionary principles to past, present, and future states of humanity. For example, in 1901 he wrote that "the path of progress is strewn with the wreck of nations; traces are everywhere to be seen of the hecatombs of inferior races. . . . Yet these dead people are in very truth the stepping stones on which mankind has risen."[65] Henry Reynolds used this quote to draw attention to Pearson's social Darwinian attitude toward "primitive" races, and in that respect the case is unproblematic. In *The Grammar of Science,* however, Pearson was setting down the principles and methods of science, a study of the "foundations," the "fundamental concepts of modern science . . . free from metaphysics."[66] Since its publication it has become a recognized classic, setting out the principles of scientific methodology, the facts of science, natural law, cause and effect, time, motion, matter, and the laws of life. In the first edition, in a chapter entitled "Life," Pearson wrote:

> It cannot be indifferent to mankind as a whole whether the occupants of a country leaves its fields untilled, and its natural resources underdeveloped. It is a false view of human solidarity, a weak humanitarianism, not a true humanism, which regrets that a capable and stalwart race of white men should replace a dark-skinned tribe which can neither utilise its land for the full benefit of mankind, nor contribute its quota to the common stock of human knowledge.[67]

Pearson's claim to be dealing in the objective factors of science appears on first sight to be at odds with this statement. On reflection, however, it becomes evident that Pearson saw the Aborigines and

their impending demise as factual elements in an evolutionary understanding of life. Rather than indulging in subjective analysis of a
humanitarian problem, Pearson was making the strong claim that the
Aborigines were themselves so much scientific data. In a footnote to
this paragraph, he stressed that his words were not to be taken as justification for deliberately destroying life, because "the anti-social
effects of such a mode of accelerating the survival of the fittest may go
far to destroy the preponderating fitness of the survivor." Nonetheless, the historical trend was clear: "At the same time there is cause
for human satisfaction in the replacement of the aborigines throughout America and Australia by races of a far higher civilisation."[68]

From being a mere impediment to European settlement, the
Aborigine had become an object of scientific inquiry, a salutory
reminder of the inevitability of human social and intellectual
progress, and a sign that such progress could be understood by applying scientific principles. The Aborigine's incorporation into the evolutionary world view of post-Darwinian Western culture was to all
intents and purposes the completion of a process of classification that
had begun nearly a century before.

Conclusion

Jim Moore has argued that the historiography of Darwinism
and Social Darwinism has until recently been seen in terms of good
and bad lines of historical descent, with pure lines emerging from the
work of Charles Darwin himself and impure ones traceable to Herbert Spencer and his followers. However, as Young, Barnes, Shapin,
and Moore himself have argued, this dichotomy is more the product
of particular approaches to historiographical discourse than the
reflection of historical reality. Some of the strongest defenders of the
purity of Darwin's thought are now conceding his "progressionist"
tendencies in relation to human physical and cultural evolution, so
the revisionists' case is clearly a strong one.[69] As this essay has suggested, the roots of some of Darwin's ideas on human evolution are to
be found in his use, over a period of some thirty years, of material
sent to him from Australia. By incorporating this material, with all its
ideological wrapping, into his anthropology, Darwin was providing
scientific credence to an ideological position that had for decades
been the basis of European and Aboriginal relationships in Australia.
In a very strong sense, the mold into which the Australian Aborigines
were cast by European settlers was essentially the same at the end of
the nineteenth century as at the beginning. What had changed was the
manner of its legitimation. Nineteenth-century anthropological sci-

ence, strongly influenced by evolutionary doctrines, was a product of ideologically loaded resources, and much of that ideology was of Australian colonial origin.

Notes

I would like to thank Monica MacCallum, Wade Chambers, Max Charlesworth, and Rod Home for their assistance with this essay. Numerous others at Deakin University have assisted with its presentation, and I take this opportunity to thank them all. Fritz Rehbock and Roy MacLeod have shown their usual patience with an at times errant author, and I thank them once again.

1   See Henry Reynolds, *Frontier* (Sydney: Allen and Unwin, 1987); Charles Rowley, *The Destruction of Aboriginal Society* (Melbourne: Penguin Books, 1972); Andrew Markus, *Fear and Hatred: Purifying Australia and California* (Melbourne: Hale and Iremonger, 1979); Noel McLachlan, *Waiting for the Revolution: A History of Australian Nationalism* (Melbourne: Penguin Books, 1989).

2   Richard Hofstadter, *Social Darwinism in American Thought, 1860–1915* (Philadelphia: University of Pennsylvania Press, 1944).

3   Bernard Smith, *The Spectre of Trugganini* (Sydney: Australian Broadcasting Commission, 1981), 20.

4   See, for example, Ernst Mayr, *The Growth of Evolutionary Thought* (Cambridge: Harvard University Press, 1982), 386. "Spencer's ideas contributed nothing positive to Darwin's thinking; on the contrary they became a source of considerable subsequent confusion. . . . Worst of all it was he who became the principal spokesman for a social theory based on a brutal struggle for existence, misleadingly termed social Darwinism." Mayr gave Hofstadter for his source. A somewhat softer line is taken by Michael Ruse, but the same element of blame is evident when he asserts that "these various doctrines [associated with Social Darwinism—B. B.] owed as much to Herbert Spencer as to Charles Darwin, if not more." Ruse does go on to point out the ambiguity evident in Darwin's writings when it came to the application of natural selection to man; see Ruse, *The Darwinian Revolution* (Chicago: University of Chicago Press, 1979), 264–265.

5   Robert M. Young, *Darwin's Metaphor* (Cambridge: Cambridge University Press, 1985), esp. chap. 2, "Malthus and the Evolutionists: The Common Context of Biological and Social Theory." See also idem, "Darwinism *Is* Social," in *The Darwinian Heritage,* ed. David Kohn (Princeton: Princeton University Press, 1985), chap. 21.

6   Barry Barnes and Steven Shapin, "Darwin and Social Darwinism: Purity and History," in *Natural Order: Historical Studies of Scientific*

Culture, ed. Barry Barnes and Steven Shapin (Beverley Hills: Sage, 1979), 125–142.

7   Jim Moore, "Socialising Darwinism: Historiography and the Fortunes of a Phrase," in Science as Politics, ed. Les Levidow (London: Free Press, 1986), 38–80.

8   Quoted in Michael Roe, Quest for Authority in Eastern Australia, 1835–1851 (Melbourne: Melbourne University Press, 1965), 67.

9   John Locke, Two Treatises of Government: A Critical Edition with an Introduction and Apparatus Criticus by Peter Laslett, 2d ed. (Cambridge: Cambridge University Press, 1970). Locke's views on colonization and the utilization of unoccupied land are set out in a number of places throughout this work, but see esp. bk. 2, 313–318.

10   Quoted in Roe, Quest for Authority, 27.

11   Quoted in Smith, Spectre of Trugganini, 17.

12   Ibid., 15–16 ; Roe, Quest for Authority, 67.

13   Reynolds, Frontier, 104.

14   Smith, Spectre of Trugganini, 17–18.

15   Quoted in Reynolds, Frontier, 110.

16   Smith, Spectre of Trugganini, 19–20. Debate over the scientific merits of phrenology was much in evidence in the 1830s and 1840s in Edinburgh, the stronghold of the movement in Britain, and at the early meetings of the British Association for the Advancement of Science. See Steven Shapin, "Phrenological Knowledge and the Social Structure of Early-Nineteenth-Century Edinburgh," Annals of Science 30 (1975): 219–43; and Jack Morrell and Arnold Thackray, Gentlemen of Science: Early Years of the British Association for the Advancement of Science (Oxford: Clarendon Press, 1981), 276–281.

17   Reynolds, Frontier, 113.

18   George Bennett, Wanderings in New South Wales, Batavia, Pedir Coast. . . , 2 vols. (London: Richard Bentley, 1834), 242–243.

19   John Lort Stokes, Discoveries in Australia (London: T. W. Bone, 1846), 89.

20   Charles Sturt, Journal of the Central Australian Expedition, 1844–1845 (Perth: Caliban Books, 1984), 255.

21   Victorian Legislative Council, Report of the Select Committee on Aborigines, Session 1858–1859 (Melbourne: Government Printer, 1860), 46–48.

22   Quoted in J. J. Healy, Literature and the Aborigine in Australia, 1770–1975 (St. Lucia: University of Queensland Press, 1978), 26.

23   Charles Sturt, Two Expeditions into the Interior of Southern Australia . . . , 2 vols. (London: Smith, Elder, 1833), 1:107.

24   Sturt, *Journal,* 252.

25   Thomas Mitchell, *Journal of an Expedition into the Interior of Tropi-
      cal Australia* (London: Longman, Brown, Green & Longmans, 1845),
      328–329.

26   Paul E. de Strzelecki, *Physical Description of New South Wales and
      Van Diemans Land* . . . (London: Longman, Brown, Green and Long-
      mans, 1845), 343.

27   Bennett, *Wanderings,* 1: 171–172.

28   Reynolds, *Frontier,* 129.

29   Charles Darwin, *Journal of Researches into the Geology and Natural
      History of the Various Countries Visited by H. M. S. "Beagle".* . .
      (London: Henry Colburn, 1839), 519.

30   See Barry W. Butcher, " 'Adding Stones to the Great Pile?' Charles
      Darwin's Use of Australian Resources, 1837–1882," *Historical
      Records of Australian Science* 8 (1) (1989): 1–14.

31   Alfred Russel Wallace, "The Development of Human Races under the
      Law of Natural Selection," in his *Contributions to the Theory of Nat-
      ural Selection: A Series of Essays,* 2d ed. (London: Macmillan, 1871),
      318–319.

32   Ibid., 319.

33   Darwin to Wallace, 28 May 1864. Quoted in *Alfred Russel Wallace:
      Letters and Reminiscences,* ed. James Marchant, 2 vols. (London:
      Cassell, 1916), 1: 153–154.

34   An important exception to this neglect can be found in an essay by
      John C. Greene, "Darwin as a Social Evolutionist," first published in
      the *Journal of the History of Biology* 10 (1977): 1–27 and reprinted
      in *Science, Ideology, and World View* (Berkeley: University of Califor-
      nia Press, 1981), 95–127. Greene does not mention the reference to
      Grey, however. Wallace responded to Darwin by pointing out some
      rather obvious faults of reasoning:
          With regard to the constant battles of savages leading to selec-
      tion of physical superiority, I think it would be very imperfect, and
      subject to so many exceptions and irregularities that it could pro-
      duce no definite result. For instance, the strongest and bravest men
      would lead and expose themselves most, and would therefore be
      most subject to wounds and death. . . . Again, superior cunning,
      stealth and swiftness of foot, or even better weapons, would often
      lead to victory as well as mere physical strength.
      Wallace to Darwin, 29 May 1864, in *Alfred Russel Wallace,* ed.
      Marchant, 1:154.

35   Dov Ospovat, *The Development of Darwin's Theory* (Cambridge:
      Cambridge University Press, 1981), 232–233.

36   Ibid., 233.

37   For a discussion of the "higher" and "lower" problem in relation to
      the Australian fauna and the Darwin-Hooker correspondence on the
      case, see Butcher, "Adding Stones," 6–9.

38   James Bonwick, *The Last of the Tasmanians* (London: Sampson Low,
      Son, and Marston, 1870), 377.

39   Carl Lumholtz, *Among Cannibals: An Account of Four Years' Travel
      in Australia . . .* (London: John Murray, 1889), 376.

40   Moore, "Socialising Darwinism," 63–64.

41   Darwin, *Journal of Researches,* 520.

42   Darwin mentions his meeting with Macarthur in a letter to his former
      shipmate and servant Syms Covington, who was by then settled in
      Pambula, New South Wales. Darwin to Covington, 22 February
      1857, in *The Correspondence of Charles Darwin,* ed. Frederick
      Burkhardt and Sydney Smith, 10 vols. (Cambridge: Cambridge Uni-
      versity Press, 1985–1994), 6:345.

43   For a general discussion of the influence of Darwinian themes in pop-
      ular social theory in Australia, see Beverley Kingston, *Glad, Confi-
      dent Morning,* vol. 3 in *The Oxford History of Australia* (Melbourne:
      Oxford University Press, 1988), chap. 2, "Belief."

44   Reynolds, *Frontier,* 129.

45   For a discussion of the relationship of Australian scientists to their
      patrons in Europe see Ian Inkster, "Scientific Enterprise and the Colo-
      nial 'Model': Observations on Australian Experience in Historical
      Context," *Social Studies of Science* 15 (1985): 677–704.

46   William Edward Hearn, *The Theory of Legal Duties and Rights*
      (Melbourne: John Ferres, 1883), 60.

47   Ibid.

48   William Edward Hearn, *Plutology, or The Theory of the Efforts to
      Satisfy Human Wants* (London: Macmillan, 1864 [1863]), 385.

49   Hearn, *Legal Duties and Rights,* 8.

50   For Hearn's career see John La Nauze, *Political Economy in Australia*
      (Melbourne: Melbourne University Press, 1949), chap. 3, "Hearn and
      Economic Optimism."

51   Alexander Sutherland, *Victoria and Its Metropolis,* 3 vols. (London:
      McCarron, Bird, 1888), 2: 22.

52   Ibid., 29.

53   For Pearson's career see John Tregenza, *Professor of Democracy: The
      Life of Charles Henry Pearson, 1830–1894* (Melbourne: Melbourne
      University Press, 1968).

54   Charles Henry Pearson, *National Life and Character—a Forecast*
      (London: Macmillan, 1893), 16.

55   L. H. Morgan in Lorimer Fison and Alfred Howitt, *Kamilaroi and Kurnai* (Melbourne: George Robertson, 1880), 2–3.

56   Ibid., 260.

57   Howitt to Morgan, 27 July 1877, in Bernard J. Stern, "Selections from the Letters of Lorimer Fison and A. W. Howitt to Lewis Henry Morgan," *American Anthropologist*, n.s., 32 (1930): 264.

58   Quoted in Noel McLachlan, *Waiting for the Revolution*, 121.

59   Henry Lawson, "The Old Bark School," reprinted in *In the Days When the World Was Wide* (Victoria: Lloyd O'Neil, 1970), 309.

60   Quoted in D. J. Mulvaney, "The Darwinian Perspective," in *Seeing the First Australians,* ed. Ian Donaldson and Tamsin Donaldson (Melbourne: George Allen and Unwin, 1985), 69.

61   Walter Baldwin Spencer and Frank Gillen, *The Native Tribes of Central Australia* (London: Macmillan, 1898), 7.

62   Walter Baldwin Spencer and Frank Gillen, *The Arunta: A Study of a Stone Age People,* 2 vols. (London: Macmillan, 1927), 1: vii.

63   Walter Baldwin Spencer, *Guide to the Australian Ethnological Collections Exhibited in the National Museum of Victoria,* 3d ed. (Melbourne: Albert J. Mullett, 1922), 9–13.

64   William Stanley Jevons, *The Principles of Science: A Treatise on Logic and Scientific Method* (London: Macmillan, 1883), 734.

65   Reynolds, *Frontier,* 125.

66   Karl Pearson, *The Grammar of Science* (London: Walter Scott, 1892), Preface.

67   Ibid., 438.

68   Ibid., 438.

69   For an example of a scholar moving from the older to the newer position, see Michael Ruse, "Molecules to Men: Evolutionary Biology and Thoughts of Progress," in *Evolutionary Progress,* ed. Mathew H. Nitecki (Chicago: University Press, 1988), 97–126.

JOHN STENHOUSE

14 The Darwinian Enlightenment and New Zealand Politics

To many modern minds the intellectual revolution associated with the name of Charles Darwin represents the glorious fulfillment of the promise of the Enlightenment. This great eighteenth-century intellectual movement had promised to liberate the human mind from the darkness of "stupidity, Christianity and ignorance," as the Scottish philosopher David Hume put it. Yet the light failed to dispel the surrounding shadows. In the middle of the following century the *Origin of Species* (1859) was hailed by many as the final nail in the coffin of darkness, theology, and obscurantism. Thanks to Darwin, enlightenment, science, and progress would prevail.

Everywhere people proclaimed the dawn of a bright new day. As Ernst Haeckel, the German biologist, wrote in 1868, "Evolution is henceforth the magic word by which we shall solve all the riddles that surround us."[1] The American millionaire Andrew Carnegie described the impact of Darwin and Spencer like a religious conversion, during which "light came in as a flood and all was clear. Not only had I got rid of theology and the supernatural but I had found the truth of evolution. 'All is well since all grows better' became my motto, my true source of comfort."[2]

These experiences of illumination were echoed in the wave-lapped islands of the South Pacific. Darwin's theory, declared a popular New Zealand periodical in 1863, had cast a whole "new light" not merely on biology but on such political questions as British colonization and Maori-*pakeha* relations.[3] Robert Stout, who abandoned Christian theology as eagerly as Carnegie and became New Zealand's premier in 1884, declared that it illuminated especially the problem of the poor.[4]

This essay examines the relationship between evolution and politics in New Zealand, and in particular the ways in which scientific ideas were employed to shape attitudes toward Maori and toward the colonial underclass. This is not a detailed examination of particular pieces of legislation; rather it is a study of the way in which scientific ideas shaped and were shaped by political concerns. My argument is two-fold. First, evolutionary concepts were commandeered as political weapons by eager New Zealanders to establish and consolidate their power against other groups, especially the two identified above, who threatened their vision of a new and better Britain in the South Pacific. Second, despite the rhetoric of scientific enlightenment, this *pakeha* ideology had racist, elitist, and totalitarian dimensions. In New Zealand the Darwinian enlightenment had a distinctly dark side.

Edward Gibbon Wakefield and the New Zealand Dream

Unlike the founding fathers of the United States, most British colonists coming into New Zealand in the 1840s and 1850s had not come to build the New Jerusalem. Edward Gibbon Wakefield, the chief theorist of the first New Zealand settlements, wanted to create a new and better Britain (although of course many Englishmen believed that "merrie England" was the nearest that humans had yet come to the kingdom of God).[5] Wakefield attempted to transplant a vertical slice of English society into the colony. Aristocracy and gentry would buy land at a "sufficient price" from Wakefield's New Zealand Company, establish towns as nuclei of prosperous agricultural settlements, and inject capital for economic development. Natural political leaders, they would also set an appropriate cultural tone. Deferential skilled workmen and rural laborers would supply the muscle for development and after a few years of hard work would be able to afford to buy their own piece of land, achieving the kind of secure and independent existence as small farmers impossible to attain in Britain.

One group would be conspicuous by its absence from this green and pleasant land: those paupers, vagrants, criminals, and moral failures who formed the underclass that periodically threatened the established order in the mother country and had, in the opinion of many, doomed Australia from penal beginnings. The dregs of the Old World were to be carefully filtered out. Wakefield's planned and systematic approach to colonization would, he hoped, solve the problems of population dispersion and lawlessness that had dogged the American frontier as well as Australia. New Zealand would solve the problems that plagued the Old World and jeopardized colonization in the New.

From the beginning, then, a powerful moral idealism fueled the New Zealand dream. New Zealand was to be a better society than

elsewhere. Immigrants were to be carefully selected by New Zealand
Company agents in Britain. Only the best of British stock—respectable, upright, and hard-working persons—would do. Placed in a land
of natural abundance, led by benevolent social superiors, they would
by hard work and self-sacrifice—crucial virtues both—fashion an
antipodean utopia. The company's agents in Britain were instructed
to avoid accepting persons of doubtful "character," for moral character was held to be the key to economic and social success. The equation was simple. Hard work, self-sacrifice, and self-discipline would
lead (eventually) to prosperity and social respectability. Sloth, indisci-
pline, and profligacy would lead to the gutter. Stock New Zealand
with people displaying the former characteristics and it must succeed.

Reality fell some distance short of these ideals. The first three settlements established early in the 1840s—Wellington, New Plymouth,
and Nelson—did not develop as well as Wakefield had hoped. Lecher-
ous rakes and violent drunkards had not all been weeded out by conscientious immigration agents, and some spoiled the voyage out for
respectable folk. Land was neither as fertile nor as abundant as the
settlers had been promised. Maori were neither as eager to sell their
land nor to become brown-skinned, claret-sipping Englishmen as
Wakefield believed. Indeed, they showed an infuriating disposition to
hang on to the best and most fertile areas (such as the Waitara block
in Taranaki and the Wairau valley near Nelson) and where necessary
forcibly defended them. Missionaries defended Maori land rights
under the Treaty of Waitangi and criticized the dubious land purchase
tactics of the New Zealand Company. Government Land Commissioner William Spain considerably reduced its land claims. There were
insufficient men of means to inject capital for economic development
in the settlements. British speculators, who should in theory have
been deterred by the "sufficient price" safeguard, rushed in to make a
quick profit. The lower orders were distressingly egalitarian and
assertive, not nearly as deferential as Wakefield had hoped.

He turned his thoughts toward religion. Inspired by accounts of the
founding of New England by Puritans a couple of centuries earlier,
Wakefield decided that the missing ingredient in his recipe for successful colonization was Christianity. The Otago and Canterbury settlements established in 1848 and 1850 respectively would therefore be
settled by god-fearing churchgoers: Otago to be Scottish and Presbyterian, Canterbury English and Anglican. Even here Wakefield valued
religion not as an end in itself but rather as a means. To transplant the
churches and schools of home would attract the cultured men of capital essential to economic success; in Canterbury this plan succeeded

relatively well; in Otago less so. Practicing Christians, it was hoped, would be trustworthy employers; honest, submissive workers; decent husbands; devoted wives and mothers; and obedient children. Religion would ensure the settlements' moral health and social cohesion. By making churchgoing a criterion for accepting prospective immigrants, the leaders of the Otago and Canterbury settlements hoped also to exclude the rebellious riff-raff who had plagued the earlier settlements from the start.

This modified plan certainly had some of its intended effects. Presbyterian Otago, for example, was remarkably free of serious crime in its early years. Yet circumstances were probably more important than planning or religion in the success of these two settlements. The local Maori were much less numerous and obstructive than those farther north, and race relations were smoother as a result. The Canterbury plains and central Otago were ideal for sheep farming and gave a good economic base. Both these factors were crucial in accounting for the relative success of these two settlements.

If Wakefield valued religion simply as a means to the end of establishing thriving, prosperous colonies, many of the incoming immigrants gave it even less place than that. Charles Torlesse, an early Canterbury settler, noted that his fellow settlers, even in this putative church settlement, tended quickly to jettison principles that might prove an embarrassment to their headlong economic progress.[6] Most immigrants' minds were occupied with material realities, not religious ideals. They wanted power—the ability to do what they liked in the new land, the chance to get on. And they wanted land as a means to those ends.

Settlers versus Maori and Missionaries

But the settlers were faced with a problem. The Maori, especially on the North Island, had both land and power. And the Treaty of Waitangi, signed in 1840 by Governor Hobson as the queen's representative and more than five hundred Maori chiefs, guaranteed them full rights of ownership of their lands, forests, and fisheries and granted them the rights and privileges of British subjects. In return, the chiefs ceded to Britain the sovereignty of New Zealand and gave the Crown an exclusive right of preemption of such lands as the Maori wished to sell. By fully recognizing Maori rights the treaty had made it difficult for *pakeha* simply to shoulder Maori aside in their quest to take over the new land.[7]

Religion contributed substantially to this situation. The Treaty of Waitangi was inspired by the early-nineteenth-century humanitarian movement, which owed its strength chiefly to evangelical Christianity. At their peak of influence in the 1830s, evangelicals emancipated slaves, campaigned against the exploitation of child labor, and established the Aborigines Protection Society, designed to protect indigenous peoples against the depredations of unscrupulous Europeans. The Church Missionary Society, an Anglican body that saw New Zealand as a mission field, had been so concerned about Maori welfare that it petitioned the British parliament in 1838 against granting Wakefield's New Zealand Association a charter, which would permit that body to colonize the country. "European Colonization," the CMS argued, had "uniformly" produced "disastrous consequences to the Aborigines of uncivilized countries, in their rights, their persons, their property, and moral condition."[8] The petition failed and the Association (soon renamed the New Zealand Company) got its charter. Company officials and missionaries remained at loggerheads. Wakefield, for example, savaged them for attempting to establish a " 'Theocracy' and 'Levitical Republic'."[9]

Christian humanitarians continued to uphold Maori rights and welfare in the following decades, as the trickle of British immigrants swelled to a flood. Robert FitzRoy, for example, a staunch evangelical Anglican who had been Darwin's captain on board HMS *Beagle,* in 1843 became the second governor of New Zealand. The only early governor who was a zealot for Maori welfare, he was determined to protect their rights in accordance with the Treaty of Waitangi.[10] He was accordingly despised by many colonists, who demanded his recall.[11] Conflict came to a head in the late 1850s with the formation of the Maori King movement, an attempt to unite the various tribes under a single king with the aim of halting further land sales. Then in 1860 fighting broke out in Taranaki province. The Taranaki war was the spark that ignited the New Zealand Wars, fought mostly in the North Island, which lasted throughout the 1860s and beyond. The wars were cataclysmic events in New Zealand race relations, which had until that time been relatively peaceful and economically advantageous for both races.

The main group to oppose the policies of the government and settlers in Taranaki were Church of England missionaries and their lay supporters, led by Bishop Selwyn and Archdeacon Octavius Hadfield. Selwyn had for some time been warning Taranaki settlers that their unprincipled demand for Maori land must be abandoned or else it would lead them to commit "the sin of murder as the direct consequence of the sin of covetousness."[12] This warning went unheeded and so, in 1860, battle was joined. Its immediate cause outraged the

Anglican hierarchy. Governor Gore Browne had commanded troops forcibly to expel Maori chief Wiremu Kingi for resisting *pakeha* attempts to occupy the Waitara block, which Kingi believed belonged to him and his Ati Awa tribe. Archdeacon Hadfield, CMS missionary at Otaki and Waikanae to the south of Taranaki, was an acknowledged expert on Maori land tenure, knew Wiremu Kingi well, and was sure, rightly as it turned out, that government officials had not adequately investigated the ownership question. He united the Anglican hierarchy in condemning the actions of Governor Gore Browne and his government as stupid, unjust, and, from a Christian point of view, hypocritical.[13] Not surprisingly, he was hated by many settlers. These Church of England leaders represented the largest denomination in the colony. If they were anything to go by, Christianity upheld the rights of Maori.

Not surprisingly, politicians complained about the way evangelicals pushed Maori rights "to a preposterous extreme," as Henry Sewell, first premier of the country put it.[14] Prevailing political wisdom proved more useful than Christianity in legitimizing the subjugation of Maori. Again and again in the colonial parliament in the early 1860s it was insisted that, whatever the rights and wrongs of the Waitara purchase, war was justified because the Taranaki Maori were rebels against the legitimate authority of the Crown. For example, during the parliamentary session of 1860 Hugh Carleton, who had deep misgivings about the Waitara purchase, moved to appoint a Parliamentary Committee of the Whole House to inquire into the circumstances that led to the Taranaki war. William Sefton Moorhouse, member for Akaroa district near Christchurch and superintendent of the Canterbury province, was not interested. "We should go on and conquer the belligerent Natives, and have nothing to say to any motion like the present until we should have completely prostrated the rebellion," he declared.[15] Invoking the hallowed concept of the supremacy of the state as guarantor of civil order evidently overrode all such minor considerations as justice, the facts of the Waitara case, Maori rights, and the Treaty of Waitangi. Self-interest motivated Moorhouse as well; he was one of a number of South Island members who disliked having to pay for expensive wars on the North Island.

This concept of the sanctity of the state, though rejected by churchmen like Selwyn and Hadfield, who placed their duty to God and Maori above their loyalty to the *pakeha* government, was no spur-of-the-moment invention of colonial politicians. It had much traditional political wisdom on its side, and in particular that of the philosopher Thomas Hobbes. In the seventeenth century, England had executed its king and been torn apart by civil war, all inspired to a great extent by religious enthusiasm. The answer to all this blood-shed and strife, decided Hobbes, was to elevate the sovereignty of the state above all competing authorities (including that of religion). Bet-ter to enjoy the safety and security of civil order even under a domi-neering sovereign than to be riven by internecine strife and civil war. Rebellion was never justified; even tyranny was better than anarchy in Hobbes' view.

Later in the century, John Locke introduced a more liberal element into the essentially secular political theory of Hobbes. A sovereign violating the life or property of his subjects had broken the social con-tract and could therefore be overthrown. Locke's ideas were invoked to justify the Glorious Revolution of 1688 and the American Revolu-tion of the following century. They could readily have been appealed to by Wiremu Kingi and pro-Maori *pakeha* to justify Kingi's resort to arms. Was Kingi not a British subject legitimately defending his prop-erty against the arbitrary encroachments of the state? Octavius Had-field offered exactly this defense of Kingi's resistance, but he was not taken seriously.[16] When Lockean political theory supported Wiremu Kingi and "rebellion" in New Zealand in 1860, it was ignored.

Most colonial politicians invoked the spirit of Hobbes rather than that of Locke. The paramount consideration stressed by speaker after speaker in the New Zealand parliament during the debates following the outbreak of the Taranaki war was the necessity of upholding her majesty's supremacy, which meant *pakeha* power. The security of the state was the *summum bonum* before which all other consider-ations—the Treaty of Waitangi, Maori rights, Christian humanitarian principles—paled into insignificance. This is most strikingly illus-trated by the argument of Alfred DeBathe Brandon, member of the House of Representatives for Wellington Country. In the session of 1860 he actually blamed the governor and his ministers for starting the Taranaki war. Yet despite these misgivings about the justice of *pakeha* actions, he called for all-out warfare against the Maori until Wiremu Kingi had laid down his arms and "it had been made mani-fest to the Natives that further fighting was useless, and that the pake-has would be the conquerors."[17] The reestablishment of civil order was more imperative than investigating the justice of the Waitara pur-chase. This scale of values, ranking civil order and state power above justice and Maori rights, was widely shared. Crosbie Ward, M.H.R. for Lyttelton, was one of a number who called for the government to "prosecute the appeal to arms in support of Her Majesty's suprem-acy." It was crucial, he declared that "British sovereignty was vindicated, and its force understood throughout the Island" in order that "the lesson once taught by arms might be well understood for ever."[18]

Might is right had become the effective political theory of many *pakeha*, who found ultraconservative Hobbesianism the most expedient ideology to invoke to subjugate Maori. The paradox here is that Hobbes' approach to politics was originally designed to avert civil war; in New Zealand in 1860 it helped to cause it. This *pakeha* elevation of the power of the state above justice and Maori rights had clear racist and totalitarian dimensions.

Science and *Pakeha* Racial Ideology

The use of science as well as politics to rationalize racism and imperialism had a long history. In sixteenth-century South America, for example, the natural philosophy of Aristotle—his idea that certain groups of people were slaves by nature—was invoked by Spanish colonists to justify enslaving Indians.[19] Science was bent to similar ends by *pakeha* in New Zealand. During the *Beagle's* visit to New Zealand in 1835, Darwin noted that introduced European species often supplanted indigenous ones. "The common Norway rat," he recorded in his journal, "in the short space of two years, annihilated in this northern end of the island the New Zealand species."[20] Aggressive *pakeha* elevated this observation into a law of nature, which applied as surely to human races as to plants and animals. "The Maori race is doomed wherever the Anglo-Saxon appears," announced the *Taranaki Herald* in 1852 with scarcely veiled delight. "The fire-water or blanket, the small-pox or musket ball, do the work of extermination. Hereafter the green *mere* [club], or a half-obliterated mound, will be the only trace of them."[21]

Philosophical materialism—the doctrine that reality consisted of matter in motion and nothing more—underpinned Hobbes' politics. It was designed to safeguard political stability by disposing of the supernatural realm of spirit appealed to by religious enthusiasts. Although philosophical materialists were few in New Zealand, many settlers found a kind of crude materialism or naturalism almost irresistible when it came to describing Maori. Any trace of the theological conviction that inspired the missionaries—that Maori were God's creatures, redeemable in Christ—was conspicuous by its absence from most descriptions. "Nigger," "black," and "savage" were common. One Taranaki settler, who described Maori as "niggers" and "horrid wretches," suggested a policy of having "the heads of every Maori we catch stuck up on a pole." He signed himself "One Who Has Gentlemanly Feeling At Least."[22]

Maori were believed to be poorly endowed intellectually. As a result of careful measurements with tapes and compasses, army surgeon Dr. A. S. Thomson concluded that Maori heads were smaller than *pakeha* heads and that Maori were inferior in mental capacity. "It is only natural," he observed, "that generations of mental indolence should lessen the size of brains." Some doubted whether such an inferior race was capable of improvement or elevation at all. "Until in his coffin, no Native can ever be civilized" declared the *Auckland Examiner*.[23] Such attitudes were by no means confined to the uneducated. Christopher William Richmond was a cultivated intellectual, a lawyer by profession, member of the House of Representatives for Taranaki and native minister from 1856. The responsibilities of office did not deter him from describing Maori on occasion as "a pack of contumacious savages" or a "mob" of "begging animals."[24]

Into this climate of opinion came Darwin's *Origin,* published in 1859, just before the New Zealand Wars. Darwin's book had cast a whole "new light" on the colonization process, declared the *Southern Monthly Magazine* in 1863.[25] Lawyer, politician, and scientist William Travers was captivated by the "light" that evolution threw on racial questions.[26]

What was so illuminating about Darwinism? Analysis of the arguments of New Zealand commentators reveal a number of attractive aspects. First, its metaphysics were compelling. The *Origin of Species* explained the history of living beings on earth in terms of natural laws and processes, not divine intervention. The two or three passing references to the Creator were to a dim, distant deity who, having created the first organic forms, stepped out and let Nature do the rest. These vestiges of deism disappeared from Darwin's book on human evolution, *The Descent of Man* (1871), and nature, not the transcendent Christian God, reigned supreme. As already indicated, a crude naturalism dominated *pakeha* descriptions of Maori before 1859. Afterward, thanks to Darwin, naturalism became respectable and scientific. Consequently—and this was not the least of its attractions—it disposed of that infernal nuisance, the God of the missionaries.

A number openly attacked the theological anthropology of the missionaries and bestialized the Maori, depicting them as nothing but savages or animals. "The bubble is burst," announced the Auckland periodical the *Southern Cross* in 1863. "The Maori is now known to us as what he is, and not as *missionaries and philanthropists* were willing to believe him." He was "ignorant and savage, loving darkness and anarchy... bloodthirsty, cruel, ungrateful, treacherous."[27] Robert Creighton had become editor of the *Southern Cross* in 1861 and greatly increased its popularity by inflammatory writing in favor of a policy of war against Maori.[28] His open antagonism toward the missionary defenders of Maori rights was echoed by the *Taranaki Herald:* "The [missionary] policy of elevating the savage and degrading the European must cease. Are we, the sons of the greatest nation of the earth, for ever to knuckle under to a parcel of savages?"[29]

Occasionally the authority of Darwin was explicitly invoked to justify the rejection of the humanitarian approach that was proving so annoying. The *Southern Monthly Magazine* announced that Darwin had shone a bright "new light" on British colonization. It condemned Christian ideas about elevating and preserving the Maori race as "fallacious philanthropy." From now on "all rights and obligations" would be based on "the fitness of things." The writer soon made clear what this phrase meant. There was "no fitness" in allowing Maori to retain their land in a barren state, and it was therefore legitimate for *pakeha* to confiscate unused land by force. "Our war is essentially a war of colonization," the writer concluded, "and justifiable on that ground."[30]

Dr. A. K. Newman (1849–1924) provides a clear example of the ideological advantages the new scientific naturalism could confer. He was a medical doctor and a successful politician, well acquainted with Darwin's works, who read a number of papers to the Wellington Philosophical Society on topics mainly connected with health. One of a handful of avowed philosophical materialists in New Zealand, he believed that only matter existed; the transcendent Christian God did not. In 1882 Newman read a paper to the society entitled "A Study of the Causes Leading to the Extinction of the Maori." He began by citing a host of statistics to show that "the race is rapidly dying out." In fact, the extinction of indigenous races was occurring throughout the Pacific. The North American Indian, the "Ainos" of Japan, the Eskimo, the Australian Aborigine, and the Moriori of the Chatham Islands would soon vanish. Only the "Anglo-Saxon race" was everywhere "rapidly progressing."[31] Why were Maori dying out? According to Newman, change in living conditions was all important. In recent years they had left their "sunny and airy" *pa* (fortified places) and were now living near bush or swamp in "low-lying, damp, ill-drained spots." This caused widespread consumption (tuberculosis). The intelligent *pakeha* could eliminate such a disease by refraining from marriage when ill, by medicine, nursing, and change of climate. However, "of these the Maori knows nothing." Maori consumptives married and produced sickly offspring who soon died. The "close fetid air of their tiny *whares*" (houses) caused them to "breathe and rebreathe each others' unhealthy breaths," and so "the naturally healthy catch the disease in large numbers."

Their decline was entirely the Maori's own fault. Newman rejected what modern historians call the "fatal impact" theory, that the incoming *pakeha* were responsible for falling numbers. The white man's diseases caused little Maori mortality, asserted Newman, who had "not been able to detect any evils" resulting from syphilis, for example. Alcohol and tobacco may have had some effect, but a couple of inherent racial characters were more important. Maori "laziness" and aversion to hard work, for instance, generated "a host of evils" and contributed to their declining numbers. While not going quite so far as to argue that *pakeha* ought to enslave Maori, Newman did observe that in the United States "negro slaves kept at work increased in numbers, whilst freed negroes steadily decreased."

Their other great problem was sterility; the Maori race was "singularly infertile." Here again the *pakeha* bore no responsibility. Imported diseases like syphilis contributed little to the sterility of Maori females, Newman asserted. The chief source of infertility, he declared, was inbreeding. Too many Maori married into their own or an adjacent tribe. He cited Darwin's *Variation of Animals and Plants under Domestication* (1868) to prove that inbreeding was "the chief cause of the barrenness of the race."

Another contributing factor was the abundance of European food, which the Maori enjoyed. This was *"infinitely more nutritious"* than their traditional diet; meat, wheat, and potatoes contained "far more nutriment" than "treble or quadruple the quantity" of shellfish, fern root, or convolvulus root. However, Maori turned the horn of plenty proffered by the *pakeha* into Pandora's box. Maori women, fed on such a rich diet and drinking beer, milk, and tea instead of water, grew fat and lazy. As "all breeders of domestic animals recognize," a condition of "fatness and general plethora" led in Maori women, "as in all the lower animals," to a "lessened fertility, and . . . absolute sterility."

One obvious solution presented itself. Why not simply cross the Maori with "the more vigorous fertile white race?" The resulting half-castes ought to prove considerably more fertile than the pure Maori. The idea was fine in theory but, said Newman, it just did not work in practice. Half-castes, though often "handsome and well-made," were so "delicate" and shallow-chested that "they all die young," especially of consumption.[32] The dream of mere "theorists" that the two races might amalgamate was idle. What was sure to happen instead was "the utter effacement of the Maori race." His conclusion was plain: "Taking all things into consideration," he proclaimed, "the disappearance of the race is scarcely subject for much regret. They are dying out in a quick, easy way, and are being supplanted by a superior race."[33]

This conclusion illustrates the ideological advantages scientific materialism offered *pakeha* thinkers like Newman. With matter in motion the only reality, the Christian view that humans transcended nature and had significance and value as creatures of God disappeared. Maori extinction, a prospect Anglican clergy had decried as a tragedy and a crime, became for Newman a fact of nature to be accepted with aplomb.

Racial Fitness and the New Zealand Wars

Given the philosophical influence of Darwinism, I want to examine in detail the second area of impact, the idea of interracial struggle. The following discussion selects and conflates eight *pakeha* analyses of racial fitness over a thirty-year period. Individual arguments are not set each in its own particular context, but rather in contrast with the outlook of the humanitarians and evangelicals, an outlook the racial analyses supplanted. Neither has any attempt been made systematically to distinguish between the "pseudo-scientific" propaganda of the *Southern Monthly Magazine* and the "respectable" racial analyses of Darwinians like Sir Walter Buller, F.R.S, the famous ornithologist. Without suggesting that any scientists involved were consciously twisting science to justify *pakeha* supremacism, there is no doubt that their analyses were expedient. Perhaps they were even more effective in this respect than the obviously propagandistic *Southern Monthly,* thanks precisely to their studied air of impartiality and objectivity.

The *Origin's* subtitle, *The Preservation of Favoured Races in the Struggle for Life,* lent itself perfectly to the colonists' needs. It told them with all the authority of science that, as the *Southern Monthly Magazine* put it, "a weak and ill-furnished race will necessarily have to give way before one which is strong and highly endowed."[34] In the 1860s and 1870s, the decades of warfare, it was hardly surprising that *pakeha* took considerable interest in assessing the relative fitness of the warring races.

There were certain initial problems. A number of observers were forced to admit that on purely physical grounds Maori might have some advantages over *pakeha*. John Turnbull Thomson, an explorer, surveyor, and leading light of the Otago and Southland institutes, noted that their physical strength, or "brute force" as he preferred to put it, was substantial.[35] During and after the wars, Maori physical courage was widely remarked on and admired.

In addition to bodily advantages, many were prepared to admit that Maori were not without certain instinctive skills and abilities. *Pakeha* were forced to explain what qualities their opponents possessed to enable them so skillfully to stave off defeat at the hands of the much larger, technologically superior British army. Most of the abilities adduced in this explanation were little more than animal instincts, however. They had the capacity to "burrow like rabbits through the high fern," declared one observer. "Anyone who knows what it is to shoot a snipe or a rat when running, can form some idea of the motion of a native in the bush." The Maori, noted one British veteran, "like other vermin, were partial to underground holes, and once concealed in these could not possibly be ferreted out. Now all this puzzles an English soldier; he is a match for an army of men, but he feels at a loss with an army of rats."[36]

Pakeha commentators were prepared to impute not only uncanny animal instincts but also "lower" mental qualities to explain the good show their foes had put up. The Maori were good at bush fighting. They were capable and at times clever guerrillas. Their courage and chivalry were widely admired. Of course, it was easier to marvel at Maori heroism than to credit the Maori with the higher military talents, like discipline, the capacity to think strategically, and to intelligently coordinate in battle, as James Belich has argued. The Victorian racial stereotype that the British had a monopoly on the higher faculties held firm.[37]

Many of the colonists agreed with the *Otago Witness* when it observed that "those best acquainted with the natives confirm that they are deficient in the higher qualities of the human mind."[38] The mental characteristics that, according to Darwin, set the Briton even above other Europeans were conspicuous by their absence in Maori, according to *pakeha* analysts. A number of themes were repeated again and again. The first might be characterized as racial vigor. In *The Descent of Man*, Darwin had employed this argument, contrasting the energy of "the frugal, foreseeing, self-respecting, ambitious Scot" with the lassitude of "the careless, squalid, unaspiring Irishman." He ascribed "the remarkable success of the English as colonists, compared to other European nations" to their "daring and persistent energy" and asserted that this was well illustrated by the fact that Canadians of English extraction were more successful than those of French extraction.[39]

New Zealander William Travers contrasted the "vigorous races of

Europe" with the "aimless" Maori.[40] According to J. T. Thomson the "Anglo-Saxon" was triumphing over dark races everywhere in the world, including New Zealand, because he was "progressive and aggressive."[41] The Anglo-Saxon race was "newer and fresher" said A. K. Newman, whereas the Maori was "effete" and "worn out."[42]

Economic productivity was also believed to be a criterion of race fitness. From the beginning of settlement, Maori economic behavior had been a source of extreme annoyance to eager settlers. Land was normally communally rather than individually owned, making it difficult for *pakeha* to know who the owners were before buying it. To Native Minister C. W. Richmond such "beastly communism" indicated that Maori were trapped in the "slough of barbarism."[43] In addition, they worked only when they needed to. According to Dr. Morgan S. Grace, who had been a surgeon in the British Army during the New Zealand Wars, such laziness was the main reason the race was declining: "If it were possible to make the Maoris do a fair share of work for their existence the race would improve."[44] William Travers contrasted Maori and European productivity in the starkest fashion:

> Instead of the miserable "pahs" and "kaingas" of an uncivilized and utterly barbarous race, we have, in most of the great ports of the country, flourishing towns, each inhabited by thousands of Europeans, and many of them possessing buildings which present all the characters of wealth and durability. . . . Instead of our great tracts of native pasture lying idle . . . they are now roamed over by and maintain large herds of cattle and flocks of sheep. . . . Instead of the narrow bush track, along which the savage travelled on his mission of revenge, we have roads penetrating the country in all directions . . . essential to the progress of the community in wealth and civilization.[45]

The *Southern Monthly Magazine* argued that since the Maori were not using their land productively they were unfit to possess it. "There is no fitness or propriety whatever in allowing him, like the dog in the manger, to retain in a barren state the land which is the gift of providence to the human race." The *pakeha* ought, it concluded, "to have taken and held by force any land not actually held by the natives" from the very beginning of colonization.[46]

As well as being more productive, the *pakeha* considered themselves to be better organized, another significant indicator of racial quality. Well-organized and "disciplined soldiers," said Darwin, have an immense advantage in battle over "undisciplined hordes."[47] The *Southern Monthly Magazine* asserted that a single criterion was sufficient to decide whether the English race or the Maori was superior: "Which presents the highest perfection of human organization?"[48] Walter Buller told the Wellington Philosophical Society that an "aboriginal race" must inevitably give way before a "more highly organized" one.[49] By contrast to rational British regimen the Maori, according to the Auckland *Southern Cross,* had a pronounced "hatred of intelligence and order."[50]

These first three criteria of racial fitness—energy and vigor, economic fruitfulness, and organization and discipline—ought to be examined in a little more detail. All three, commentators agreed, *pakeha* had in abundance and Maori lacked. All were cardinal virtues in the moral economy of capitalism. While it would be going too far to reduce racial prejudice to "nothing but" class prejudice, it is plain that with respect to Maori, capitalist values and race prejudice reinforced each other. Maori were considered racially inferior not just because of the color of their skin but also because they were believed to reject the work ethic prized by the colonists. If they did not work their land long and hard, day in and day out, then despite what Genesis said about the creation of all humans in the image of God, Maori were scarcely human and had no right to unused land. Sloughing off all past connection with Christian theology, the work ethic was becoming an autonomous, secular standard by which to measure human worth.

Many saw science and technology as another indicator of racial fitness. In *The Descent of Man,* Darwin argued that among primitive humans technological innovation—the invention of a new trap or weapon—gave the tribe possessing it an advantage in the struggle for existence over other tribes.[51] The same principle was believed to hold good for racial contests in the nineteenth century. J. T. Thomson told the Otago Institute that the reason the white race was triumphing in North America and New Zealand was the Anglo-Saxon monopoly of science. Steam technology powered both industry and the merchant and royal navies, paving the way for British economic dominance and imperial expansion. "Science in this era more than ever supplies your necessities and protects your race," he concluded.[52]

Thomson made the negative implication plain. All those races that had "mere brute force and no science" would succumb in the struggle for existence.[53] That the Maori was one of these was confirmed by William Travers. In the centuries-long "night time" leading to the arrival of the European, New Zealand "gave birth to no science," he concluded at the end of his 1869 lecture explaining the demise of the Maori.[54]

Closely allied to these themes of vigor, productivity, organization, and science in explaining British superiority was the motif of progress. J. T. Thomson emphasized how "progressive" the Teutonic Anglo-Saxon was.[55] William Travers contrasted the "progressive civilization" of the European colonists with the "unprogressive" state of the Maori.[56] According to Christine Bolt, Victorian anthropologists "were generally agreed on the conservatism of primitive peoples."[57] Because they lacked the higher mental faculties, stasis was all one could expect.

That the British race was considerably more intellectually advanced was an article of faith among many *pakeha*. According to Darwin, "civilized nations" were "everywhere supplanting barbarous nations" mainly "through their arts, which are the products of the intellect."[58] William Travers contrasted the "arts and letters, the matured policy, and the ennobling impulses" of the European with the Maori, who "had accomplished so imperfectly every object of man's being" by failing to produce any science, philosophy, or moral teaching.[59]

And if it was said once it was said a hundred times, the European was more civilized. Darwin systematically contrasted the "western nations of Europe" standing "at the summit of civilization" with the "lower races." "The grade of their civilization," he reflected, "seems to be a most important element in the success of competing nations."[60] William Travers spoke of the "wise policy" and "generous statesmanship" of the "progressive civilization" of the incoming Europeans.[61] Walter Buller declared it to be a "law of Nature" that a "more civilized" race supplant an aboriginal one.[62]

By contrast the "dark races" were "barbaric," said Edward Tregear.[63] For William Travers not only Maori but also the Mori-ori of the Chatham Islands, whose traditions and customs he outlined in a paper read to the Wellington Philosophical Society, were an "inferior" and "uncivilized people."[64]

Maori were considered deficient not only in the higher qualities of the human mind but, and especially, in moral virtue. A clear distinction between the two was seldom made. Indeed, if we look at Maori mental disadvantages as outlined above it is striking how regularly they include moral flaws. The failure of Maori society to produce any systematic "moral teaching" was evidence to William Travers of moral as well as intellectual inferiority.[65] Many of the predicates used to describe Maori were loaded with moral freight. "Barbaric," "savage," "uncivilized," and so on implied at once intellectual inferiority and moral degradation.

By contrast, virtue and ability were conjoined in the Briton. "True industry and virtue," said Dr. Morgan Grace, were characteristic of European civilization.[66] The *Southern Monthly Magazine* spoke of the "higher moral instincts" of the English, of their "virtues of humanity and chivalrous courtesy."[67] John Turnbull Thomson insisted that it was not just superior science that enabled the Anglo-Saxon to triumph over dark races, but also superior "humanity."[68]

Thomson's argument ought to be examined in more detail. A Fellow of the Royal Geographical Society in Britain, in 1874 he was elected president of the Otago Institute. In his retiring address of that year, Thomson dealt with the fate of the Maori. It was well known that the pre-Christian Maori were cannibals, and Thomson cited Augustus Earle's 1833 description of the killing, cooking, and eating of a young Maori girl by fellow Maori. This, said Thomson, was "the shadow of coming events, an allegory of the certain fate of so inhuman a race." The outstanding feature of the "Anglo-Saxon . . . of the Teutonic race," by contrast, was "humanity."

This was not just racial arrogance on Thomson's part, though it was certainly that. His contention that the white Anglo-Saxon was triumphing over dark races thanks to superior "humanity" was thoroughly Darwinian. In *The Descent of Man,* which Thomson had carefully read, Darwin argued that the moral instincts had developed in humans because they were useful. Groups that encouraged virtues like loyalty, courage, and cooperation would succeed better in the struggle for existence than groups fragmented and weakened by selfishness, cowardice, and infighting. Hence, natural selection, selecting the most moral and cohesive groups, accounted for the origin and development of the moral sense in the human species.[69] Thomson was convinced that the Maori race was doomed precisely because, as its penchant for cannibalism illustrated, it had not developed these altruistic instincts to the same level as the Anglo-Saxon. The superior "humanity" of the Teutonic Anglo-Saxon—the capacity for cooperation, self-sacrifice, and altruism—made for a cohesive, stronger, more successful race.[70]

Darwin: A Social Darwinist?

How much did the arguments of these colonists owe to Darwin? Were they fair interpretations or tendentious distortions of Darwin's ideas? It has been popular for some time to distance the gentle and sensitive sage of Down from the rabid racism and pseudo-science of his followers. This began with the classic work on Social Darwinism, Richard Hofstadter's *Social Darwinism in American Thought,* first published in 1944. "Intrinsically," Hofstadter argued, Darwinism "was a neutral instrument, capable of supporting opposing ideologies."[71] Many subsequent writers have agreed. According to James Joll's standard text *Europe since 1870,* Darwin "had not himself devoted much attention to any social implications his ideas might have had."[72] Some neo-Darwinian scientists, for whom Darwin is a patron saint, have gone even further. According to Sir Andrew Huxley, president of the Royal Society and grandson of Darwin's bulldog, T. H. Huxley, Darwinism as expressed in *The Descent of Man* was concerned only with human "bodily features" and not with "mental phenomena," including social ones.[73] Australasian commentators concur. According to the Australian anthropologist Derek Freeman, Darwin had nothing to do with Social Darwinism.[74] New Zealand historian Kerry Howe refers to "the myths and half-truths of 'social Darwinist' beliefs."[75] The most extreme position of all is taken by the American historian Robert C. Bannister, who not only exonerates Darwin from the charge but virtually denies the existence of Social Darwinism, conceived as ruthless competitive struggle, altogether.[76]

Three observations are relevant. The first is that Darwin himself often disagreed with the uses some of his so-called followers made of his ideas. In a letter to the geologist Sir Charles Lyell, for example, he wrote: "I have received, in a Manchester newspaper, rather a good squib, showing that I have proved 'might is right', and therefore that Napoleon is right, and every cheating tradesman is also right."[77] Second, it is clear that at least some *pakeha* propagandists selected from Darwin's works only what suited their purposes. "Whatever may be thought of Mr. Darwin's views concerning natural selection and the origin of species," said the *Southern Monthly Magazine,* "no-one will be disposed to deny the existence of that struggle for life which he describes, or that a weak and ill-furnished race will necessarily have to give way before one which is strong and highly endowed."[78] Plainly this writer liked not the scientific merits of evolution but the ideological utility of the concepts of competitive struggle and the triumph of superior races. However, and this is my third point, not all were crude racists. Others, like Travers, Thomson, and Buller, were capable scientists who became convinced evolutionists after reading Darwin. They found in Darwin's works, especially *The Descent of Man,* the idea repeatedly discussed that races were unequally endowed in the struggle for existence and that Britons were especially well equipped for success. Almost every criterion they used to account for the triumph of the *pakeha* over the Maori race can be either paralleled in or plucked directly from *The Descent of Man.* Darwin supplied plenty of grist for the *pakeha* supremacist mill.

Darwin himself discussed the decreasing population of "Maories," as well as other Pacific peoples, in chapter seven of the *Descent*, "The Extinction of Races."[79] Using F. D. Fenton's census of the Maori, published in New Zealand in 1859, he accepted Fenton's argument that introduced diseases, alcoholism, and musket warfare were insufficient causes, and that low birth rate, as well as high infant mortality, were the critical factors. What caused the decrease in fertility? Maori themselves believed, and both Fenton and Darwin concurred, that it was "changed conditions." This was true of other races as well. Melanesians died in large numbers when taken to New Zealand to be trained as missionaries, Darwin noted. Hawaiians, Tasmanians, Andamanians, and Nepalis suffered similarly when their lifestyles changed rapidly. "Many of the wilder races of man are apt to suffer much in health when subjected to changed conditions or habits of life," Darwin argued. Civilized races could "resist with impunity the greatest diversities of climate and other changes," but "man in his wild condition seems to be in this respect almost as susceptible as his nearest allies, the anthropoid apes, which have never yet survived long, when removed from their native country." Savage races, like wild animals, stopped breeding if conditions changed quickly: "if savages of any race are induced suddenly to change their habits of life, they become more or less sterile . . . in the same manner and from the same cause, as do the elephant and hunting-leopard in India, many monkeys in America, and a host of animals of all kinds, on removal from their natural conditions."

The immediate cause of changing conditions and falling fertility for indigenous peoples in the nineteenth century was of course "the immigration of civilised men." But this was almost incidental. "Any cause, such as the inroad of a conquering tribe" of their own race would probably have the same effect, Darwin argued. The decrease and ultimate extinction of human races was a highly complex problem, he concluded, depending on a variety of causes, which operated differently in different places at different times. But in principle it did not differ from the problem of the extinction of one of the higher animals, like the fossil horse of South America, which was displaced by the Spanish horse. The Maori was conscious of this parallel between animal and human extinction, Darwin noted, "for he compares his future fate with that of the native rat now almost exterminated by the European rat." This analogy—comparing the native rat supplanted by the European rat with the Maori exterminated by the *pakeha*— was widely held in New Zealand and had become proverbial among Maori. "The inroads of conquering tribes" needed to supply only a small additional check to the checks on human populations normally operating to send "wild races" plummeting to extinction, Darwin concluded.

The racial ideology of these *pakeha*, then, was consonant with Darwin's own ideas. Admittedly Darwin's tone was neutral and detached on the whole, as befitted a naturalist. But he did not decry the prospect of the extinction of "wild" races as a bad thing, to be reversed at all costs. His concept of the evolutionary progress of humanity, shared by these *pakeha*, was largely responsible. He believed that progress, though not inevitable, "has been much more general than retrogression" and that "man has risen, though by slow and interrupted steps, from a lowly condition to the highest standard as yet attained by him in knowledge, morals and religion."[80] It was difficult to see the extinction of savage races lagging considerably behind this "highest standard" as anything but acceptable. Feelings of sympathy and humanity, which the sensitive Darwin certainly possessed, might have made such conclusions repugnant. But since these feelings were themselves products of evolution, and since evolution was not necessarily progressive, they might, if followed blindly, lead to the degeneration of humankind. It was difficult to see why they should be considered paramount, not disregarded as evolutionary excrescences.

Certainly New Zealand commentators disregarded them and had little but criticism for the "fallacious philanthropy" shown Maori by Anglican clergy. Darwinism, then, served *pakeha* purposes in a variety of ways. Its philosophical naturalism made Christianity look obsolete, which was all to the good since nobody wanted to listen to philo-Maori Christians like Selwyn and Hadfield. It confirmed, using criteria from the hottest new scientific theory, what *pakeha* had always known, that they were superior beings. And it legitimized the New Zealand Wars. Nobody saw them as holy wars. A small, vocal minority had doubts about their being just wars. In stepped these social Darwinists to show that they were natural wars. *Pakeha* conquest and Maori extinction were all in accord with the great law of natural selection. Pulverized by *pakeha* cannon, the last rites of the Maori were intoned by *pakeha* science.

Science and "Unfit" *Pakeha*

In passing from science and Maori to science and *pakeha*, I emphasize continuities rather than differences. The apostles of progress were as eager to be rid of unfit whites as of Maori. Some attacked Christianity even more overtly and systematically than had the antimissionary racists of the 1860s. And just as the *pakeha* gov-

ernment had unjustly wielded its power to subjugate Maori, there was
a totalitarian tinge to the ideas of those we shall examine below. The
target groups differed, but beneath the high-flown scientific language
the same brew of greed, rapacity, and lust for power continued to
bubble.

By the end of the 1860s, considerable progress had been made as
far as many *pakeha* were concerned. Huge areas of Maori land had
been confiscated from "rebels" during the wars and were being resold
to settlers. Substantive rather than merely nominal sovereignty had
been imposed on Maori. Land and power were becoming locked in
pakeha hands. Yet problems remained. The economy prospered in fits
and starts. Some immigrants, lured by the promise of cheap land and
the chance to get on, found getting on more difficult than they hoped.
How could the New Zealand dream be preserved from contamination
by failures, who might drag others down with them? What was to be
done with those who went to the wall in the intra-*pakeha* struggle
for existence?

Robert Stout, a lawyer and ardently liberal politician, answered
that question in Dunedin in 1870: nothing. Poverty and suffering
among the working classes was an inevitable part of the "struggle for
existence," he declared. The "unfit" ought to be "weeded out" in
order to "purify" the race.[81] Stout was well acquainted with the evolutionary ideas of Darwin and Spencer. On the question of poverty
his approach was classical laissez-faire liberalism dressed up in the
latest scientific rhetoric. Spencer, the hugely popular philosopher of
evolution, had argued in *Social Statics* that the "unfit" ought to be
left unaided by the state to die out. "It seem [*sic*] hard that a labourer
incapacitated by sickness from competing with his stronger fellows,
should have to bear the resulting privations. It seems hard that wid-
ows and orphans should be left to struggle for life or death. Nevertheless, when regarded . . . in connexion with the interests of universal
humanity, these harsh fatalities are seen to be full of beneficence."
He called on "spurious philanthropists" to accept the fact that
"under the natural order of things society is constantly excreting its
unhealthy, imbecile, slow, vacillating, faithless members." For the
"paupers' friends" to interfere with this process simply because of
"the wailings it here and there produces" would be a dreadful
"curse" on humanity.[82]

Darwin was more ambivalent in the *Descent*. He went some of the
way with Spencer. "We civilized men . . . build asylums for the imbecile, the maimed, and the sick; we institute poor laws" and thus "the
weak members of civilised societies propagate their kind. No one who

has attended to the breeding of domestic animals will doubt that this must be highly injurious to the race of man."[83] But to check our sympathy, he warned, would result in the "deterioration in the noblest part of our nature. . . . If we were intentionally to neglect the weak and helpless, it could only be for a contingent benefit, with an overwhelming present evil." There is no doubt that Darwin held this opinion sincerely, although undoubtedly, sensitive as he always was to public opinion, this was politic as well. But exactly why he should regard sympathy for the weak as so self-evidently "the noblest part of our nature," not as an originally adaptive trait gone to seed (like the horns of the Irish elk), was not clear. This ambivalence was evident in his conclusion: "We must therefore bear the undoubtedly bad effects of the weak surviving and propagating their kind."[84]

Robert Stout was not so equivocal. Elected premier of New Zealand in 1884, he refused to accept government responsibility for social welfare during the economic depression of the decade.[85] If the government refused to coddle the "unfit," nature would surely cull them.

Stout also exemplifies a continuing stream of antagonism against theology. In an 1881 speech, he insisted that the theory of evolution had made the Christian idea of God incredible to all thinking people and that Christianity would soon become a relic of humanity's benighted past. "To me it seems that the truly religious man is he who refuses to worship a book," Stout declared, "but who in looking around him, in peering into stellar space, or endeavouring to understand the functions of the millions of creatures with which we are surrounded . . . gets an idea of the immensity of Nature, of the grandeur of her laws." A scientific understanding of nature was "a real and true revelation and guide of life of greatly increased clearness and range."[86] For Stout there was no God but nature, and Darwin and Spencer were its prophets.

Stout argued, in the spirit of the Enlightenment, that one of the chief defects of Christianity was that it was built on the doctrines of the Fall and Original Sin. Christian teaching was based on the concept of human "degeneracy," he charged, and was too pessimistic. Evolution was a much better creed since it "teaches us to look to the future with hope, with a belief that progress is the law of existence," and leads to "paradise."[87] It was an optimistic creed nicely calculated to appeal to New Zealanders determined to avoid the degeneracy and social problems of the rest of the world.

Fellow freethinker Duncan MacGregor outlined similar views in a series of articles published in 1876 entitled "The Problem of Poverty in New Zealand."[88] First professor of mental and moral philosophy at the University of Otago, his chair had been endowed in 1870 by the local Presbyterian synod, some of whose members soon became disturbed by MacGregor's teaching. He was influential nonetheless; Stout and other political leaders were numbered among his students.

Julius Vogel's Immigration and Public Works Act of 1870 gave government assistance to British immigrants otherwise unable to afford the passage to New Zealand. Not all immigrants, however, were equally welcome. The arrival of a boatload of poor Irish Catholic girls at Dunedin's Port Chalmers, for example, caused many to fear that the sewers of the Old World had been directed south.

Duncan MacGregor argued along neo-Malthusian lines that misguided philanthropy exacerbated the problem of poverty. Excessive charity, as well as mistaken ideas about the sanctity of individual freedom, were preventing Nature from weeding out the unfit. MacGregor defined this class more precisely; it included the "ignorant," the "stupid," and the "thriftless." Such people lacked the intellectual and moral qualities to succeed in the economic struggle for existence, which had supplanted the brute physical struggle of more primitive days. Instead of being productive citizens such persons lapsed into disease, vice, and crime until eventually they became the "sewer of society." By draining off taxpayers' money to support the prisons, hospitals, and charitable aid institutions that kept them going, they ate "like a cancer into the vitals of society." MacGregor's solution was to curtail such persons' freedom, because otherwise they would breed and their offspring would swell the ranks of the "degenerate." Since nature was being prevented from doing its job, the state should step in to incarcerate such "waste products":

> The time is coming when the law must extend its definition of insanity, so as to include hopeless drunkards, hopeless criminals, and hopeless paupers, adjudged to be such after a sufficient number of trials and failures. They must be made to work for their own support, and deprived of liberty until death, in order to prevent their injuring society by their crimes or by having children to inherit their curse.[89]

MacGregor would seem to have been advocating some sort of permanent labor camp solution to the problem of poverty.

Though his views were more extreme than most, he found support among others who had abandoned Christianity for the progressive evolutionary creed. Concerned about Anglo-Saxon racial purity, Edward Tregear echoed MacGregor when he suggested that "worship of the liberty of the individual" would soon lead to "the ruin of mankind." The practice of allowing people released from asylums to "marry and propagate children of infected and tainted blood" ought to be stopped, he insisted.[90] As first secretary of labor in the Liberal government of the 1890s, Tregear was determined to keep casual laborers and wandering swaggers in regular work. With German examples to guide him, he advocated compulsory work camps for the lazy and shiftless.[91]

As the twentieth century opened, Robert Stout, who would soon become both chief justice of the Supreme Court and chancellor of the University of New Zealand, was still bewailing the dangers of granting state aid to the "unfit," much as he had in 1870. Yet he could also envisage a more active role for the state in solving the problem of the underclass in the science of eugenics. This had first been developed in Britain by Darwin's step-cousin Francis Galton. He believed that in civilized societies natural selection, the engine of Darwinian evolution, was not being allowed to "weed out" defective stock. Therefore the state should step in to lend a helping hand. It should encourage able people to breed (positive eugenics) and discourage the subnormal from breeding (negative eugenics).

From the beginning of settlement, New Zealanders had been determined to create a better society than anything that existed elsewhere in the world. Maori had effectively been shunted aside, but still the residuum threatened. In the early twentieth century eugenics became popular with middle-class professional groups: doctors, lawyers, biologists, academics, politicians, and some clergy.[92] In 1903 New Zealand-born surgeon and politician W. A. Chapple published a scientific study *The Fertility of the Unfit.* In this he defined the unfit in much the same way as had Stout, MacGregor, and Tregear: "The unfit in the state include all those mental and moral defectives who are unable or unwilling to support themselves according to the recognised laws of human society." Since the fittest were not breeding fast enough, Chapple proposed to prevent the unfit from breeding by programs of compulsory sterilization. If that did not work, he suggested a more stringent, and final, solution. Mental defectives, epileptics, habitual drunkards, insane criminals, most murderers, nocturnal housebreakers, and other incorrigible antisocial persons should be given a medical examination administered by the state: "The painless extinction of these lives would present no practical difficulty," he observed, because "in carbonic acid gas we have an agent which would instantly fulfil the need."[93] Robert Stout was so impressed by Chapple's book that he offered to assist its publication in Britain. He became a leading figure in the eugenics movement in New Zealand.

Whether by minimizing or by maximizing state intervention, he was determined to get rid of the underclass.

Conclusion

By this time the New Zealand dream had lost the conservative, hierarchical dimensions of the early Wakefield ideal. The "Britain of the South" had become a more egalitarian society, personified by the premier, the rough-and-ready and enormously popular former publican Richard "King Dick" Seddon. His Liberal government of the 1890s had promised to break up the great estates of the land monopolists and redistribute them to small and middling farmers. The Liberals' advanced labor legislation was designed to give the working class a fairer deal and to ensure an efficient economy unhampered by strikes. If the Liberals promised more than they delivered, they made a fine and popular start. This legislation was designed to ensure a rough equality of opportunity for all. These extraordinary "state experiments" taking place in the "social laboratory of the world" attracted international attention.

Yet equality of opportunity was by no means the same thing as equality of outcome. The dominant *pakeha* ideology was as ready as ever to get rid of those who squandered fine opportunities, who failed the struggle for existence. There was considerable consistency in attitudes to Maori and the *pakeha* residuum. Economic criteria were crucial. Maori worked only when they had to, were "beastly" communists, owned vast areas of land that they failed to exploit and would not sell to eager *pakeha*. "Degenerate" *pakeha* ignored the work ethic, failed to contribute to the economy, and cost decent taxpayers money. Intellectual criteria were important also. Both Maori and poor whites were believed to be too stupid to succeed in the modern struggle for existence. Finally, both groups lacked the moral prerequisites for success. Maori were "savage," "barbarous," and uncivilized; the *pakeha* underclass was thriftless, undisciplined, and immoral. It was clear to these New Zealand Social Darwinists that for the sake of the progress of the human race, both groups ought to fade out.

It would, of course, be easy to exaggerate the popularity of the eugenics movement. Public opinion lagged some considerable way behind that of advanced thinkers like Robert Stout, who had to confine his activities to propagandizing rather than sterilizing, desexualizing, or gassing. New Zealanders were, on the whole, less troubled about consigning the Maori race than unfit *pakeha* to extinction. This was not new; white Anglo-Saxons had always tended to confine their tender humanitarian feelings to fellow whites. But there is a further explanation for the lack of public support for eugenics. The prolonged, colonywide depression of the 1880s had made most *pakeha* conscious of their own vulnerability. Another depression, poor wool prices, or just a bit of bad luck, and they might find themselves plunged down into the underclass. Next, if the eugenists had their way, might come the work camp, the surgeon's scissors, perhaps even the gas chamber. Maori might be allowed to follow the native rat into oblivion, but this all came too close to the bone for most *pakeha* to accept.

It is not difficult to guess who was the fittest in the evolutionary economy of these analysts: the hardworking, productive, able, upright *pakeha*. The white, middle-class, Anglo-Saxon professional—a person, coincidentally, just like these Social Darwinists themselves—turned out to be the most perfect being yet evolved. The race and class prejudice and latent totalitarianism of this ideology reveal that the "Darwinian enlightenment" in New Zealand had a dark side. This is not to deny that Darwin's science produced genuine scientific progress. Most New Zealand scientists welcomed the theory of evolution as a magnificent insight into the origins and development of organic beings.[94] But science has never existed in splendid isolation from the totality of other forces shaping society. The anxieties, greed, and will-to-power of *pakeha* bent on creating a better Britain determined which elements of Darwinism they chose to emphasize.

If Christian thinkers criticized their arguments, this was of little concern. Christian theology, evangelical aspiration, humanitarian concern, the Treaty of Waitangi, Maori rights, social justice—all were thrust firmly aside when they ran counter to *pakeha* hubris and self-interest. The dominant *pakeha* ideology commandeered traditional political wisdom and the latest scientific knowledge to thrust Christianity, Maori, and the "unfit" into the outer darkness, outside the mainstream of intellectual and political life.

Notes

1   Ernst Haeckel, *Natürliche Schöpfungsgeschichte,* 8th ed., 2 vols. (Berlin, 1889 [1868]) 1: Vorwert, quoted in John R. Durant, "The Great Debate: Evolution and Society in the Nineteenth Century," in *Charles Darwin 1809–1882: A Centennial Commemorative,* ed. Roger G. Chapman and Cleveland T. Duval (Wellington: Nova Pacifica, 1982), 133.

2   Quoted in Richard Hofstadter, *Social Darwinism in American Thought,* rev. ed. (Boston: Beacon Press, 1955), 45.

3   "Our Colonization and Its Ethics," *Southern Monthly Magazine* 1 (10) (1863): 548–551. *Pakeha* is the Maori term for Caucasians.

4   Robert Stout, *State Education* (Dunedin: Mills, Dick, 1870), passim.

5   On Wakefield and the New Zealand Company see Patricia Burns, *Fatal Success: A History of the New Zealand Company* (Auckland: Heinemann Reed, 1989).

6   C. O. Torlesse to his mother, 5 May 1854, Torlesse Papers, Canterbury Museum Library, quoted in David Herron, "Alsatia or Utopia? New Zealand Society and Politics in the 1850's," *Landfall* 13 (1959): 324–342, 331.

7   The best introduction to the Treaty of Waitangi and its history is Claudia Orange, *The Treaty of Waitangi* (Wellington: Allen and Unwin, 1987).

8   *Proceedings of the Church Missionary Society for Africa and the East, 1838–1839,* 142–146. Substantial excerpts from this petition, from which these quotations are taken, are published in Allan K. Davidson and Peter J. Lineham, eds., *Transplanted Christianity: Documents Illustrating Aspects of New Zealand Church History* (Auckland: College Communications, 1987), 52–55.

9   Burns, *Fatal Success,* 96.

10   Keith Sinclair, *The Origins of the Maori Wars* (Wellington: New Zealand University Press, 1961), 225.

11   Raewyn Dalziel, "The Politics of Settlement," in *The Oxford History of New Zealand,* ed. W. H. Oliver with B. R. Williams (Wellington: Oxford University Press, 1981), 90.

12   G. A. Selwyn, *Extracts of Letters from New Zealand on the War Question* (London, 1861), 83–84, 86–87, quoted in Davidson and Lineham, *Transplanted Christianity,* 120–121.

13   See Hadfield's published pamphlets: *One of England's Little Wars* (London: Williams and Norgate, 1860); *A Sequel to "One of England's Little Wars"* (London: Williams and Norgate, 1861); *The Second Year of One of England's Little Wars* (London: Williams and Norgate, 1861).

14   *New Zealand Parliamentary Debates* (hereafter NZPD), 1862, 689.

15   *NZPD,* 7 August 1860, 236.

16   Hadfield, *A Sequel,* 14–15.

17   *NZPD,* 16 August 1860, 322.

18   Ibid., 7 August 1860, 211. For similar arguments see ibid., 3 August 1860, 201 (Weld), 7 August 1860, 251–253 (Fox), 15 August 1860, 317 (J. C. Richmond), 16 August 1860, 338 (Gillies).

19   See, for example, Stephen Neill, *A History of Christian Missions* (Harmondsworth: Penguin, 1964), 171–172.

20   Charles Darwin, *The Voyage of the "Beagle"* (London: Everyman, 1959), 404–405.

21   *Taranaki Herald,* 20 October 1852.

22   *Taranaki Punch,* 21 November 1860, 8.

23   For these and similar examples see Sinclair, *Maori Wars,* 1–12.

24   Quoted in ibid., 133; *NZPD,* 1858–1860, 266.

25   "Our Colonization and Its Ethics," 549. This article is unsigned, and it is difficult to be sure exactly who wrote it or who edited the magazine at this time. It was published by Robert Creighton, who also edited the *Southern Cross,* and we shall examine his views in more detail below. Both organs reflected the views of Auckland politicians, businessmen, and settlers who wanted to get their hands on large areas of Maori land surrounding Auckland, particularly in the Waikato to the south. The tone of the papers was antimissionary (since missionaries defended Maori land rights), anti-Maori, and in favor of a government policy of war against Maori "rebels," followed by confiscation of their lands.

26   W. T. L. Travers, "On the Changes Effected in the Natural Features of a New Country by the Introduction of Civilized Races," *Transactions and Proceedings of the New Zealand Institute* (herafter *TPNZI*) 2 (1869): 299–313, 300.

27   *Southern Cross,* 7 August 1863.

28   *Auckland Weekly News,* 3 June 1893, 15.

29   Quoted in Sinclair, *Maori Wars,* 128.

30   "Our Colonization and Its Ethics," passim.

31   These and the following quotations are from Alfred K. Newman, "A Study of the Causes Leading to the Extinction of the Maori," *TPNZI* 15 (1882): 459–477.

32   Other commentators concurred. Walter Buller, for instance, noted that when half-castes married Maori, the offspring had "no stamina" and "seldom reached maturity." *TPNZI* 17 (1884): 446.

33   Newman, "Causes," 476–477.

34   "Waitara and the Native Question," *Southern Monthly Magazine* 1 (5) (1863): 215.

35   J. T. Thomson, "Presidential Address to the Otago Institute," *TPNZI* 6 (1873): 440–445, 446.

36   These examples are quoted in James Belich, *The New Zealand Wars and the Victorian Interpretation of Racial Conflict* (Auckland: Auckland University Press, 1986), 315, 329–330.

37   Ibid., 315–320.

38   *Otago Witness,* 20 October 1860.

39   Charles Darwin, *The Descent of Man and Selection in Relation to Sex,* 2d ed. (London: John Murray, 1913 [1871]), 138, 142.

40   Travers, "On the Changes," 313.

41   Thomson, "Presidential Address," 445.

42   Newman, "Causes," 464.

43   *NZPD,* 1858–1860, 186.

44   *TPNZI* 14 (1881): 539.

45   Travers, "On the Changes," 311–312.

46   "Our Colonization and Its Ethics," 549.

47   Darwin, *Descent,* 130.

48   "Our Colonization and Its Ethics," 549.

49   Walter L. Buller, "Presidential Address to the Wellington Philosophical Society," *TPNZI* 17 (1884): 443–445, 444.

50   *Southern Cross,* 7 August 1863.

51   Darwin, *Descent,* 127–128.

52   Thomson, "Presidential Address," 445–446.

53   Ibid., 446.

54   Travers, "On the Changes," 313.

55   Thomson, "Presidential Address," 445.

56   Travers, "On the Changes," 313.

57   Christine Bolt, *Victorian Attitudes to Race* (London: Routledge and Kegan Paul, 1971), 25.

58   Darwin, *Descent,* 128.

59   Travers, "On the Changes," 313.

60   Darwin, *Descent,* 141, chap. 5 passim, 183.

61   Travers, "On the Changes," 313.

62   Buller, "Presidential Address," 444.

63   Edward Tregear, "Presidential Address to the Wellington Philosophical Society," *TPNZI* 24 (1891): 687.

64   W. T. L. Travers, "Notes of the Traditions and Manners and Customs of the Mori-oris," *TPNZI* 9 (1876): 15–27, 15.

65   Travers, "On the Changes," 313.

66   *TPNZI* 14 (1881): 539.

67   "Waitara and the Native Question," 215; "Our Colonization and Its Ethics," 552.

68   Thomson, "Presidential Address," 445.

69   For Darwin's discussion of the origin and development of the moral sense see *Descent,* 97–133.

70   Thomson, "Presidential Address," 445.

71   Hofstadter, *Social Darwinism,* 201.

72   James Joll, *Europe since 1870* (Harmondsworth: Penguin, 1976), 102–103.

73   Andrew Huxley, "How Far Will Darwin Take Us?" in *Evolution from Molecules to Men,* ed. D. S. Bendall (Cambridge: Cambridge University Press, 1983), 3–19, 14, 16.

74   Derek Freeman, "The Evolutionary Theories of Charles Darwin and Herbert Spencer," *Current Anthropology* 15 (3) (1974): 211–237.

75   K. R. Howe, *Race Relations: Australia and New Zealand: A Comparative Survey, 1770s–1970s* (Wellington: Methuen, 1977), 43.

76   Robert C. Bannister, *Social Darwinism: Science and Myth in Anglo-American Social Thought* (Philadelphia: Temple University Press, 1979).

77   *The Correspondence of Charles Darwin,* ed. Frederick Burkhardt and Sydney Smith, 10 vols. (Cambridge: Cambridge University Press, 1985–1994), 8: 188–189.

78   "Waitara and the Native Question," 215.

79   The following analysis and quotations are taken from *Descent,* 184–192.

80   Ibid., 145.

81   D. A. Hamer, "The Law and the Prophet: A Political Biography of Sir Robert Stout (1844–1930)," (M.A. thesis, University of Auckland, 1960), 57.

82   Herbert Spencer, *Social Statics,* abridged and rev. (New York: D. Appleton, 1896), 150–151.

83   Darwin, *Descent,* 133–134.

84   Ibid., 134.

85   A. H. McLintock, ed., *An Encyclopaedia of New Zealand* (Wellington: Government Printer, 1966), 3: 322.

86   Robert Stout, *Inspiration* (Dunedin: Joseph Braithwaite, 1880), 8.

87   Robert Stout, *The Future* (Dunedin: Guardian Printing Company, 1875), 8; idem, *Evolution and Theism* (Christchurch: Telegraph and Standard Offices, 1881), 7. For a full discussion of Stout's social, scientific, and religious views, see John Stenhouse, "Science versus Religion in Nineteenth-Century New Zealand: Robert Stout and Social Darwinism," *Pacifica: Australian Theological Studies* 2 (1) (1989): 61–86.

88   D. MacGregor, "The Problem of Poverty in New Zealand," *New Zealand Magazine* 1 (1) (1876): 60–75; 1 (2) (1876): 207–216; 1 (3) (1876): 310–32.

89   Ibid., 1 (3) (1876): 317, 320.

90   *TPNZI* 31 (1898): 616.

91   P. J. Gibbons, " 'Turning Tramps into Taxpayers': The Department of Labour and the Casual Labourer in the 1890's" (M.A. thesis, Massey University, 1972), 80–89.

92   Philip J. Fleming, "Eugenics in New Zealand, 1900–1940" (M.A. thesis, Massey University, 1981).

93   W. A. Chapple, *The Fertility of the Unfit* (Melbourne: Whitcombe and Tombs, 1903), xv–xvi, 102, 118–123.

94   John Stenhouse, " 'The Wretched Gorilla Damnification of Humanity': The 'Battle' between Science and Religion over Evolution in Nineteenth-Century New Zealand," *New Zealand Journal of History* 18 (2) (1984): 143–162.

15 Environment and Race

Geography's Search for a Darwinian Synthesis

Following the publication of *On the Origin of Species,* natural selection came under attack from two sides—first by those who leaned toward a Lamarckian perspective, which preserved the notion of purpose in nature's laws, then by those who, after the rediscovery of Mendel's theories of hybridization, argued for an internalist mechanism to account for large mutations unexplained by the fossil record. By the late nineteenth century, Darwin's once unifying theoretical framework had become fragmented into an array of evolutionary theories. Only during the 1930s and 1940s, through the work of R. A. Fisher, J. B. S. Haldane, and Julian Huxley in Britain and of George Gaylord Simpson, Thomas Hunt Morgan, Sewell Wright, and Ernst Mayr in the United States, was a new Darwinian synthesis achieved. This synthesis brought together the once antagonistic theories of Mendelians and Darwinians by establishing genetic factors as the means by which variation and natural selection operate.[1] Without the aid of modern genetics, Darwin could only postulate that struggle eliminated the unfit and in responding to his critics on this crucial matter could only fall back upon Lamarckian theories of use and disuse, of variation resulting from direct adaptation to the environment.

As twentieth-century biologists saw it, this new Darwinian "orthodoxy" effectively routed the last vestiges of Lamarckism and its associations with idealist morphological speculations that organisms were selected according to adaptation to an "ideal plan."[2] George Gaylord Simpson, the American paleontologist, reasserted Darwin's emphasis upon evolution as a random process of local but imperfect adaptation against biologists who claimed to find direct, causal relationships between an organism's structure, function, and the environment.[3] Likewise, Julian Huxley maintained, as had Darwin, that natural selection was the product of blind forces and created neither purpose nor progress, only functional advantage.[4] However, even while disavowing any link between biology and ethics and asserting that science dealt merely with material phenomena, both Simpson and Huxley, like Darwin himself, could not escape the ideological and value-laden implications of science. Simpson concluded that the "new evolution" embraced a world view that included the cosmic and spiritual,[5] while Huxley saw evolutionary process as progressive, acting "as a guide in formulating our purpose in the future," whereby human beings gained control of nature.[6]

Because the Darwinian synthesis became an orthodoxy, most discussions of twentieth-century biological science delineate a direct trajectory from Darwin, to Mendel, to modern sociobiology.[7] Indeed, the modern synthesis has effectively rewritten all evolutionary thought in its image so that non-Darwinian mechanisms of evolutionary change are deemed minor relative to the impact of natural selection. Recently, however, John C. Greene, Robert M. Young, Peter Bowler, and Robert Richards have challenged natural selection,[8] arguing that while many accepted evolution as early as the 1860s, most rejected natural selection as the chief mechanism of evolution, favoring instead theories such as orthogenesis or Lamarckism, which stressed inner vitalist or direct environmental influences and which preserved a more orderly and purposeful image of nature.

Indeed, even the modern Darwinians, Simpson and Huxley, could not entirely rid themselves of a need to seek in nature for moral and social principles to guide human action in place of biblical revelation.[9] The complexity of Darwin's original statement and his subsequent revisions to the *Origin of Species* bequeathed a much richer, more complex, and often contradictory constellation of ideas that enabled many to claim allegiance to Darwinism while still ignoring the irritant of natural selection. Although it is generally accepted that Darwin drew heavily upon Thomas Malthus' equation between a diminishing food supply and the increase of competition between individuals for survival in arriving at his theory of natural selection, contemporary facts of biogeography and the problem of geographical distribution functioned as equally important catalysts. Indeed, two chapters of the *Origin* were devoted to a discussion of geography and its relationship to variation within a species. In the first decades of the twentieth-century this environmentalist dimension of Darwin's thinking was appropriated and developed by botanists, zoologists, and geographers who wished to refurbish the field naturalist tradition. In his famous "entangled bank" passage in the *Origin*, Darwin reverentially etched the delicate interrelationship of the organism with both the organic and the inorganic environment. This holistic conception of the natural world as a seamless web became the basis of an ecological modern synthesis. While sharing the focus upon intraspecies competition with the hereditarians, it argued against natural selection, viewing external factors such as the environment and climate as the determining mechanisms of species variation and organic evolution.

The career of Griffith Taylor (1880–1964), a geographer who established departments of geography at the University of Sydney in 1920 and the University of Toronto in 1935 and who taught at the University of Chicago between 1928 and 1935,[10] spanned the transitional decades between the breakdown of the nineteenth-century Darwinian framework and the creation of the modern Darwinian synthesis of the 1940s. Taylor's evolutionary viewpoint demonstrated that there was no one Darwinian orthodoxy. Like Darwin, Taylor recognized the value of Malthus' views on moral economy and incorporated notions of struggle and dominance into his theories of human origins and racial distribution. Following Darwin, Taylor asserted a strenuously materialistic interpretation of the natural world in order to disavow what he viewed as the mystical and unscientific reversion to idealist and spiritual explanations of nature that were eventually harbored by once "pure" Darwinians such as T. H. Huxley and Alfred Russel Wallace. However, Taylor never fully embraced natural selection. Instead, building upon Darwin's biogeographical perspective and correlating geographical distribution with evolution, Taylor emphasized the direct response of the organism to its changing environment. His evolutionary perspective owed much to Lamarckism, but while he opposed the modern hereditarians, his interest in populations also owed much to Mendelism. From this came a theory of racial classification that yoked polygenist physical anthropology to modern Darwinism by positing a "zones and strata" theory of climatic change and geographical migration. This theory offered, for the first time, a coherent causal explanation accounting for common origins and subsequent racial variation within and among the human species.

Paleontology and the Influence of Haeckel

Griffith Taylor first encountered Darwinism through his father, a chemist and government metallurgist of New South Wales, who introduced him to the writings of Asa Gray, America's leading Darwinian and professor of natural history at Harvard University. Gray offered a theistic interpretation of Darwinism that harmonized natural selection with natural theology. Thus while he accepted Darwin's notion of natural selection, Gray likewise maintained that this mechanism operated not at random but according to "designed" natural laws which, through a series of minute adaptations, created positive improvement toward a higher state.[11]

As a student at Sydney University between 1899 and 1904, Taylor studied geology with T. W. (later Sir) Edgeworth David, an avowed Darwinian. Famous as one of the codiscoverers of the south magnetic pole on the Shackleton Antarctic expedition of 1907–1909, David greatly enhanced the prestige of Australian colonial science when, between 1896 and 1904, after failed attempts by British geologists, he led two expeditions to Funafuti that threw new light on Darwin's theory of the origin of coral atolls.[12] Following his mentor, Taylor's first professional field work took him to the Great Barrier Reef off the coast of Queensland.[13] In a 1907 paper on coral reefs to the Australasian Association for the Advancement of Science (AAAS), Taylor defended Darwin's theory of subsidence against Louis Agassiz's more stationary and antievolutionary view of geological formation and articulated what was to become the hallmark of his mature scientific work—the interrelationship of biology, geology, and geography.[14] Deeply influenced by physiography—what David termed the "mapping of nature"—Taylor conceived of nature in holistic terms.[15] He concluded that the morphology of any organism—in this case, coral—could be explained only in relation to geographical location and environment. In this paper Taylor also began to revise Darwin by viewing evolution in cyclical terms, in which geological succession was the outcome of periodic fluctuations in the earth's climate.[16]

In an era when, in Australia as elsewhere, the universality of scientific knowledge was giving way before disciplinary, laboratory-based specialization,[17] David approached the study of nature in a manner reminiscent of his Victorian predecessors. His course on physiography, which formed the intellectual foundation of the new discipline of geography, broadly focused upon the interaction of the inorganic and organic, and in it he lectured on geology, climate, the importance of the ice ages in the Paleozoic age, paleontology, the origins of humankind, and mammalian and human evolution. It was here that Griffith Taylor derived his eclectic approach to Darwin, evolution, and race. David was highly critical of several aspects of Darwin's thought, and remarkably, given his general evolutionist outlook, continued to insist upon degeneration as a scientifically viable hypothesis.[18] David accepted Huxley's fossil evidence regarding the horse's hoof as proof that evolution proceeded incrementally from lower to higher forms, but he did not wholly share Darwin's theory that similarity of type was an argument for common origin. Offering the echidna and British hedgehog as evidence of similarity and persistence of type—an argument favored by natural theologians of the early nineteenth century—David became an advocate of parallel evolution.[19] This perspective he shared with Lamarckians such as the American paleontologist Edward Drinker Cope, who sought to portray evolution as a process of regular embryological growth and thus argued that similarities between species were the result of each passing through a similar pattern of growth.[20]

The idea that the embryological growth of each individual organism recapitulated the regular sequence of fossil forms found its most explicit rendering in the work of the German biologist Ernst Haeckel. Best known as Darwin's principal apologist in Germany, Haeckel championed an evolutionism that combined Darwinian, Lamarckian, and idealist evolutionary theories. Beginning as a materialist, Haeckel soon relegated natural selection to a secondary role, favoring the Lamarckian principle of direct adaptation to the environment, a principle that more easily accorded with ideas adapted from Goethe, that evolution was a progressive and creative process.[21] In utilizing the individual's passage through birth, maturity, and death as an analogy for the evolution of species, Haeckel was also one of the first to describe progress in terms of a pattern of cyclical growth.[22] His Lamarckian tendencies were best expressed in the theory that "ontogeny recapitulates phylogeny"; in other words, he concluded that each modern embryo must pass through the embryological forms that represent past stages of evolution.[23] Haeckel's Darwinian-Lamarckian synthesis was translated into popular English textbooks and became immensely influential among biologists, psychologists, and paleontologists. David's views on evolution and human races owed much to it and like the German Darwinian, he combined a materialist approach to organic nature with a vestigial idealism. Moreover, Haeckel had coined the term *ecology,* and his environmentalist perspective appealed greatly to David, who was himself actively transforming the now more specialized practice of geology into a comprehensive geographical study of humankind. Indeed, David's conclusions regarding human evolution and racial divergence totally replicated those of Haeckel. David, an expert on glaciation and one of the first to argue that there had been multiple ice ages both before and during the Pleistocene,[24] easily accepted Haeckel's argument for the great antiquity of human beings. Like Huxley, Haeckel believed that human lineage lay with the apes although, unlike Darwin and Huxley, he believed that the Asian apes, the orang and gibbon, were the closest human ancestors.[25] Moreover, Haeckel was always more sanguine than Darwin about the gaps in the fossil record, insisting that because there was more struggle within a species, many fossil remains had been obliterated. As a result Haeckel believed that the missing links in the fossil records could be filled in through comparative anatomy, and thus he predicted that one would find in the Pleistocene formations an apelike creature—whom he called Pithecanthropus—that might confirm the linear evolution of human beings. The skull of this ostensible "missing link" was discovered by the Dutch naturalist Eugene Dubois in Java in 1891 and named *Pithecanthropus erectus*. Very few paleontologists accepted this discovery as confirmation of human evolution, except Haeckel and Edgeworth David and Griffith Taylor in Australia.[26] This new emphasis upon the great antiquity of human origins, however, further confused the old debate between monogenists and polygenists, and in fact, by pushing human origins back thousands of years, provided scientific grist for racialists who wished to see modern racial groups as separate species. Indeed, in keeping with his views on parallel evolution, Haeckel himself concluded that each contemporary race had emerged from separate anthropoid stocks. For his part Edgeworth David sat on the fence, though he left the door open for Griffith Taylor to develop a crypto-polygenist position by concluding in 1899 that because of their ancient divergence from apes in the Pleistocene, modern human "types" evolved "from the common stock or stocks" of humankind.[27]

On the flyleaf of his lecture book, Taylor wrote that David's course on physiography had not only earned him a university prize, but also became the intellectual catalyst for his life work.[28] Undoubtedly, Taylor's conception of geography as the interaction between organisms and their environment, which later developed into what he called *human ecology*, derived from David's example. One can trace almost all of the animating concepts concerning geology, paleontology, human evolution, and racial classification to David at Sydney. The importance of the Tertiary ice age in the evolution of modern humans; the idea of linking human fossil remains with modern races; and the fusion of anthropology, archeology, geology, and biology into a new geographical or ecological synthesis owed their inspiration to the fertile mind of David.

In his first public lecture on ethnology, delivered to the Sydney University Science Society in 1906, Taylor, a science demonstrator for David, spoke on "The Antiquity of Man." Humankind, he argued, was at least seven thousand years old, having evolved by "slow and very gradual changes" from the Asian anthropoids. As taught by David, Taylor noted that there was a parallel between human ontog-

eny and corresponding organisms in the "scale of life"; he accepted
Haeckel's emphasis upon intraspecies struggle to account for gaps in
the fossil record; and, in viewing Java Man as Haeckel's missing fossil
link between the apes and human beings, he advanced a linear interpretation of evolution.[29] Darwinism and Lamarckism converged in
Taylor's evolutionism. But unlike David and Haeckel, who sought to
preserve a moral dimension within natural law, Taylor eviscerated all
moral concern from his scientific endeavors. Thus, he retained the
Lamarckian emphasis upon regular patterns of development and the
action of the environment as the primary mechanism of organic
change but shed the original idealist preoccupation with evolution as
a moral process.[30] As a devotee of both Darwin and Huxley,[31] he postulated that the mode and stages of human development were identical to those of animals, and in thus rejecting arguments for the
perfectibility of man, Taylor attached himself to a materialist position—the principle that all spiritual endowments are the product of
merely physical phenomena—in a way that Darwin could not have
attempted in the 1860s.[32] Taylor endorsed Lamarckism's orderly,
progressive, and linear conception of organic evolution and with it
combined a Darwinian emphasis upon the mechanism of struggle.

Taylor continued to elaborate upon Darwin's "great scheme of bio-
genesis"[33] when, in 1907, he won an 1851 Exhibition Scholarship to
study paleontology at Cambridge, to pursue a problematic fossil from
the lower Cambrian called *Archeocyanthinae*. Taylor's interest in
paleontology dated from Edgeworth David's expedition to the Flinders
Ranges in South Australia in 1904. These contained some of the rich-
est limestone coral specimens from the Cambrian period. At this time
interest in Cambrian and pre-Cambrian rocks had been stimulated by
the work of British geologists, including Thomas G. Bonney, professor of geology at University College, London, and Andrew Ramsay,
director general of the Geological Survey of the United Kingdom, who
challenged Lyell and Kelvin's shortened time span for the age of the
earth and sought in ancient Cambrian rocks evidence for a definite
rather than a relative dating of geological time.[34] The diversified
explosion of life during the Cambrian saw both the first appearance
of multicellular organisms and the rapid extinction of many species.[35]
The explosion of species was particularly problematic for Darwinians
because without fossil evidence of a common ancestor in the pre-
Cambrian, antievolutionists could point to the richness of life in the
Cambrian as evidence of God's handiwork. Darwin clearly saw the
importance of locating a precursor, and in the *Origin* called upon
paleontologists to discover "in a fossil state numerous intermediate

gradations."[36] The discovery in 1865 in the Precambrian rocks of the Canadian Shield of a giant Foraminifera named *Eozoon canadense* by the Canadian naturalist and antievolutionist Sir William Dawson reawakened hope among Darwinians that a common ancestor before the "explosion" could be located. However, following a lengthy debate about whether this fossil indeed represented organic material, scientists in the early twentieth century concluded it was not the supposed "dawn animal."[37]

Edgeworth David was among the geologists who doubted the paleontological significance of *Eozoon canadense,* and he pressed Taylor to search the Flinders limestones for other transitional fossils. By 1906 Taylor's good friend, the geologist and Antarctic explorer Douglas Mawson, was sending him limestone specimens of *Archeocyanthinae,* which looked like a sponge but functioned like Algae and was thought to be a possible link between plants and animals.[38] One of the first specimens had been collected in 1861 by Elkanah Billings, a paleontologist with the Geological Survey of Canada, who placed it among the sponges (Porifera).[39] Later Sir William Dawson declared it a relative of his *Eozoon canadense,* and for the next forty years it slid back and forth between the sponges and algae.[40]

After two years spent at Cambridge painstakingly slicing his specimens to discover their internal structure, Taylor was the first to place the *Archeocyanthinae* in a new genus, which it still occupies.[41] Relying upon Haeckel's recapitulation hypothesis, Taylor stated that *Archeocyanthinae* represented the larval stage of past Cambrian corals and thus was "a new contribution to the phylogeny of the marine Invertebrates."[42] By classifying it as a species between the corals and sponges, Taylor believed that he had indeed located one of the "fine, intermediate, fossil links"[43] that Darwin needed to prove his theory of evolution. Because of these fossils, he stated, one could "hope for much for evolution."[44] However, Taylor had larger aspirations than simply filling in gaps in the invertebrate fossil record, for he believed that his discovery of a transitional fossil among the lower animals held implications for all the "subdivisions of the Animal Kingdom," including human beings. With deductive logic Taylor concluded: "As man is in some respects intermediate between the Orang and the Chimpanzee—a study of the common features leading one to a knowledge of the primeval Pithecanthropus—may not the *Archeocyanthinae* be descendants of that Proto-coelenterate from which also are derived the sponges and corals?"[45]

Taylor's supervisor at Cambridge, T. G. Bonney, then professor of geology, a Fellow of St. John's College, and an expert on glacial theory and coral reefs,[46] astutely judged that Taylor's scientific memoir on "the structure and relations of these anomalous and very ancient organisms" would make his mark in paleontology.[47] It brought Taylor to the attention of W. J. Sollas, professor of geology at Oxford, with whom he began to exchange coral fossil specimens.[48] Sollas, a contemporary of Edgeworth David and a veteran of the British expedition to Funafuti,[49] directed Taylor's attention to the importance of racial migrations in human evolution.[50] Although, like Taylor, he maintained that there was a linear progression from the Neanderthals to modern humans, Sollas was also a confirmed Darwinian who thought tribal struggle was a central factor in human evolution.[51] Taylor's geographic inclinations were further reinforced by the anthropogeographical approach of A. C. Haddon, the first university lecturer in anthropology in Britain, whose Cambridge lectures on physical anthropology Taylor attended. Like Sollas, Haddon leaned toward Lamarckism, but while Taylor became fascinated by eugenics and Mendelism,[52] he was not diverted from environmentalism. However, Mendelism pushed Taylor away from the traditional Darwinian concern with individual variation toward the study of divergence within a larger population or racial group.

It was difficult to escape the Darwinian heritage at Cambridge in 1909, for that year marked the centenary of Darwin's birth and occasioned a flood of Darwinian literature and exhibits.[53] Indeed, it was at the Darwinian Reception held at the Fitzwilliam Museum that Taylor met Charles Doolittle Walcott. Best known for locating the Burgess Shale, an outstanding fossil discovery in which a diverse range of the rarest, soft-bodied organisms of the Cambrian "explosion" were preserved, Walcott was a leading expert on fossil trilobites and Cambrian geology.[54] Just weeks before ascending above Field, in British Columbia, where he discovered the Burgess Shale, Walcott had proclaimed Taylor's *Archeocyanthinae* the finest specimen in the world and his Cambridge memoir as "a classical one on the subject," and he asked Taylor to send a collection of his Cambrian fossils to the Smithsonian Institution.[55]

Even as Darwin's centenary was being celebrated, scientists were further fragmenting the original nineteenth-century Darwinian synthesis by arguing that experimental investigation must proceed within specialized fields, which had been spawned from the older natural history tradition. Although Taylor's microscopic investigations of *Archeocyanthinae* conformed to the rigorous empiricism required by modern science, his paleontological publications belied his restiveness with current orthodoxies. Certainly Taylor enjoyed his new-found authority, but he believed that empiricism lacked direction unless wedded to a larger theoretical purpose and so looked to the universalism of the older natural history tradition.[56] Similarly T. G. Bonney viewed modern geology as an evolving synthesis that continued to include paleontology, zoology, and botany as it expanded to incorporate the newly developed discipline of geography—all under the umbrella of Darwinism. Commenting in 1919 on the status of geology, he wrote:

> Since the publication of the "Origin of Species," which antedated that of *Nature* by ten years, scientific palaeontology may almost be said to have been born. Missing links in the chain of living creatures have been found, gaps in knowledge have been filled in, difficulties which raised opposition from not a few good naturalists have been removed; evolution has passed from a stage of hypothesis to that of theory, and extended from natural history to other branches of science and into yet wider fields. The pedigree of not a few forms of life has been constructed, so that "zoning" by fossils has greatly aided the stratigrapher, and the zoologist finds it possible in many cases to retrace the steps of that pedigree until, in the tree of life, the twigs are followed down into the branches, and the branches to the primary stems.[57]

Bonney was also subtly reminding his readers that Darwin's theory of evolution owed little to morphology, being rather a synthesis written by a geologist whose observations of nature were made through biogeographical and ecological lenses.

And because of the traditional affinities between natural selection and geographical distribution, when geography emerged as a scientific discipline at the turn of the twentieth century, it drew upon both Darwin's evolutionary hypothesis and his synthetic perspective. William Morris Davis, professor of physical geography at Harvard University, was one of the first to apply Darwinian and biological principles to the study of landforms. Borrowing from Haeckel the description of geological formations in terms of the life cycle of the individual, he even borrowed the German's terminology by calling his approach "physiographic ontogeny."[58] Like Haeckel, Davis saw physiographic evolution as both a linear and cyclical process that followed a regular pattern of birth, adolescence, maturity, and decay; he integrated a pre-Darwinian view of cyclical time derived from James Hutton with the linearity of Darwinian evolutionism,[59] combining a largely uniformitarian model of geological formation with a minor catastrophism allowing for smaller intervals of rapid geological process.[60] This mirrored the work of biologists who had come to include periods of rapid evolutionary change within a generally Darwinian concept of incremental adaptation and variation. Davis also drew upon Darwinian biogeography to transform physiography, which was principally physical geography, into what he called "ontography"— the ecological study of the evolving relationship of the earth and its inhabitants.[61] By building on Haeckel's holistic concept of nature as the study of the reciprocity between inorganic and organic, Davis sought to transcend the dualism between humans and nature characteristic of older geographical investigations. At the same time, the Darwinian framework provided the "new geography" with scientific rigor it had lacked when geography consisted largely of descriptive accounts collected by traveling soldiers and missionaries.[62]

In 1908 Taylor accompanied Davis on a field trip to the Swiss Alps to study glacial topography.[63] By the meeting of the British Association for the Advancement of Science (BAAS) in 1909, Taylor had been converted to Davis' theories on glacial erosion.[64] This field trip also secured Taylor's appointment as senior geologist on Captain Scott's ill-fated Antarctic Expedition of 1910–1913. Taylor's expeditionary field notes show that he fully assimilated Davis' biological approach to physiography. Heeding Davis' anti-Baconian injunction to practice Darwin's method of "deductive imagination" in plumbing the geological series of Antarctica,[65] Taylor investigated the continent's physiographic features according to "a comprehensive theory on the line of Evolution."[66] Taylor's descriptions of his surroundings were rife with biological metaphors, testifying to his use of the Darwinian evolutionary framework to link paleontology, geology, botany, and physiography. Thus, Taylor described the weather in Antarctica as an "organic" heart which pumped "streams" back to Australia "to revivify regions of vital importance to man."[67] In "the struggle for existence," Taylor observed that plankton followed a "cycle of life" from birth to death, just as the glacial valleys he mapped passed like organisms through a regular "sequence of changes" from youth to old age and could be classified depending upon their stage of development.[68] Where Darwin used contemporary geological theories to help unlock his developmental hypothesis, Taylor with similar deductive insight enlisted organic evolution to decipher physiographic succession. "Charles Darwin," Taylor wrote,

> advised young naturalists to seek for evidence of evolution in a given group
> of organisms among the specimens themselves. If enough samples are
> present there are, said he, likely to be many different stages represented.
> Applying the same principle to Antarctica, I believe that I can see varying

stages in the evolution of the topography of the Taylor Valley indicated in adjacent landforms.[69]

In the opening decades of the twentieth century, when laboratory investigation challenged the field method of the natural history program, Taylor continued to perpetuate the view held by Victorian evolutionists that organic nature was a seamless whole. He shared with Haeckel and Huxley the belief that evolutionism would explain "the whole domain of human knowledge."[70] By 1919 Taylor, once he had discovered the great climatic stimulus of successive ice ages, which he believed explained rapid organic adaptation to the environment, postulated a new evolutionary synthesis that reunited geology, paleontology, glaciology, climatology, and anthropology. As he informed his father:

> I really think I can explain the causes of the Ice Ages, and of the origin of the human races, the stages in the evolution of life, and the periods when life evolved so rapidly. It explains coal formation, mountain building, salt deposits, and gives a good clue to the actual periods occupied in the geological succession. . . . It is curious how my cogitation on *Archeocyanthinae* Corals, on the Ice Ages . . . , on the migrations of man, and on the desert climate of Ooldea, &c. should weld together into this coherent whole.[71]

This environmentalist and climatic interpretation of human evolution and racial distribution first appeared in a series of lengthy articles for the *Geographical Review,* edited by the American geographer Isaiah Bowman. These in turn were drawn together into a broader narrative, published under the editorship of Sir Arthur Keith, the British anatomist and promoter of Piltdown Man, entitled *Environment and Race.*[72] As one reviewer stated, *Environment and Race,* because it had isolated climate as the mechanism of variation, conclusively established "the general theory of organic evolution" as it related to humankind.[73]

For the next three decades, following his appointment to the chair of geography at the University of Sydney, Taylor expanded his Darwinian umbrella to cover anthropology, philology, sociology, history, and urban planning.[74] He described geographical subspecialties in terms of Darwin's branching tree and interpreted urban growth as an "evolving organism." Just as Darwin had reconstructed the creation of coral atolls, the geographer could study a village to understand the evolution of the city.[75] In an age when cultural anthropologists of the Boasian school were attempting to dislodge culture from biological determinism, Taylor campaigned to reduce the humanities to hand-

maids of science and relegated all thought and endeavor to epiphe-
nomena of climatic and environmental laws. He championed the
most revolutionary and problematic implication of Darwinian evolution—the notion that human beings are subject to the same organic
laws as plants and animals[76] to such an extremity as to leave no scope
for independent action of the human mind. In 1938 he explained the
biological bases of culture to the BAAS:

> To the geographer interested in culture-spreads it seems likely that the out-
> standing fact has often been neglected by sociologists. It should be clear
> that as long as man was controlled primarily by the same factors as the
> higher mammals his evolution is likely to proceed along somewhat similar
> lines. We should find that in many fields of research that we are dealing
> with the same phenomena, i.e. with progressive stages of evolution devel-
> oping in the Old World "cradle". The concept can be illustrated in
> Mammals, Human Race and Human Culture alike.[77]

By the 1890s even T. H. Huxley had drawn back from Darwin's
insistence upon the predominance of natural law and from the idea,
enunciated most cogently by Herbert Spencer, that ethics could be
founded wholly upon natural law.[78] In his Romanes Lecture of 1893,
"Evolution and Ethics," Huxley posited an inherent conflict between
civil and natural history and between humanistic values and science.
With nature as the realm governed by brute force, morality must be
wrested away from the ironclad laws of evolution and made once
again the purview of human choice.[79] Huxley abandoned the equation
between natural law and human perfection, but Taylor remained
unerringly confident that "Nature"[80] was an infallible guide of human
progress. The renewal of Spencer's optimistic naturalism represented
the mainstream of twentieth-century evolutionary thinking. Although
Taylor was an atheist and disparaged things of the spirit (because they
could not be quantified),[81] scientific evolutionism became his new cat-
echism, for it offered the assurance of providential predictability.[82]
Evolution should become mandatory within schools, Taylor maintained, because only through its study would students "know man
evolved from lower animals and give hope that we will continue to
evolve to something higher."[83]

True to Spencer, Taylor equated material progress with an ethical
good. He believed that geography, the scientific study of Nature's patterns, was the guardian of modern spiritual values, not only because it
integrated science and human values, but also because it could forecast
the evolutionary trajectory of human society.[84] If Nature necessarily
worked toward an ultimate good, human departure from natural law

was evil, for the ultimate survival of the white race depended upon adherence to "the *logical order* of material development" described in Nature. Humankind suffered, Taylor concluded, whenever people tried to disobey "the laws of [N]ature."[85] Hence Taylor vehemently campaigned against settlement in Australia's desert interior because "Nature" had decided against it; likewise, he opposed the "White Australia" policy because it was a form of social reform that interfered with natural processes, which he believed would ultimately amalgamate the white and Asian races.[86] Like Spencer, Taylor believed that government intervention was necessary only in the early stages of social development and that with the perfect "equilibrium"[87] evolution would bring about, the state would wither away. Despite claiming to be a Fabian socialist, Griffith Taylor was a nineteenth-century laissez-faire liberal who stood staunchly for free trade.

Perhaps because of his own background in physics, Taylor's conception of nature was reminiscent of the rational, mechanical universe of Isaac Newton.[88] While humans were illogical, Nature was balanced. The land masses of the eastern and western hemispheres were in perfect equilibrium, and nature was always beneficent. Any lack of one economic resource was compensated by the abundance of another.[89] Thus Nature was an "ever-logical" hidden hand.[90] Taylor called Nature "the evolution key" and saw its development as a largely teleological and progressive unfolding through regular and predictable patterns.[91] Natural law operated in Taylor's world view with Paleyite regularity, but Nature was technocratic, elitist, and efficient, and its laws were to be administered by a new priesthood of expert geographers and social scientists, who could interpret the predictive patterns of nature for social engineering and national planning.[92] While Nature might govern according to the laws of the common good, it often provided an alienating aspect to the individual. Taylor disavowed the reverential Victorian naturalist sense of communion—that "oneness with Nature," as Sollas called it.[93] Taylor's universe was ultimately amoral and verged toward a Darwinian randomness and futility:

> Though evolution is governed by fixed laws, these laws have little regard for the individual and not much more for the race. Mighty consequences for good or evil have resulted from what seemed to be trivial occurrences in the life of a race, such as the direction of a migration. These appeared of such small importance at the time indeed that the tribe could not possibly have controlled them, and yet one path led to empire and the other to extinction.[94]

Taylor was fond of quoting H. G. Wells that evolution was still in progress for humankind and that individuals were living factors within it. However, the notion that human beings could act alongside natural law as part of "the mechanism of evolution" was qualified within Taylor's geographical determinism: humans were ultimately not free agents.[95] Only those with expert knowledge of the mysteries of nature, namely, geographers, could work "right on the battlefront in man's progress towards a higher type of civilization."[96]

Historians have portrayed the course of Darwinian thought as an inversion of Darwin's metaphor of the branching tree, whereby the great variety of evolutionary theories that so characterized the post-1870 debates[97] became extinct among the next generation, who found a more specialized synthesis in the form of post-1940 Darwinism. I would argue, however, that the intellectual structure of twentieth-century Darwinism developed by a process of parallel evolution and of convergence, whereby separate strands of Lamarckian and ortho-genic theories emerged out of rather non-Darwinian perspectives but after 1930 began to acquire some of the features of Darwinism, namely, the emphasis upon struggle for survival. Thus the diversity of evolutionary thought that contributed to the revival of Lamarckism during the late nineteenth century was preserved by geographers and paleontologists well into the midtwentieth century, as Taylor's career illustrates.[98] As John C. Greene has observed, although evolution in its most general form had become the established biological paradigm by the 1860s, the popular revival of neo-Lamarckian ideas after the 1880s militated against the theory of natural selection becoming scientific orthodoxy until the 1930s.[99] At Cambridge, Taylor had flirted with Mendelism and during the 1920s held an equivocal attitude toward eugenics, seeing it rather as a faddish and unscientific palliative in an "age of social stress."[100] He opposed natural selection in part because its emphasis upon local and imperfect adaptation did not necessitate a definite end-point of evolution. His main objection, however, was that it functioned as a conservative force; for hereditarian principles, while explaining the preservation of the species, could not adequately address the future progress of human civilization.

For the most part, Taylor's evolutionism was both derivative and eclectic; it manifested varieties of Darwinism, Lamarckism, orthogenesis, and theories of racial recapitulation. Taylor used Haeckel's concept that the "individual recalls the evolution of the race"[101] to confirm his contention that the Chinese were the latest race to evolve. "The recapitulation theory would demand that the Mongol child would show criteria somewhat resembling those of the white man.

The white child again is more doliocephalic than the adult and resembles the negro. The black child resembles the apes."[102] Taylor even defended the orthogenism of the anatomist Sir Arthur Keith, who advanced the vitalistic view that the pituitary and thyroid glands were selective mechanisms and that deficiency disorders in them were responsible for degenerative negroid features.[103] Like most geographers of his day,[104] Taylor relied upon a Lamarckian viewpoint. "Evolution," wrote Taylor, "has been the constant readjustment of organisms to geographical environments that are themselves changing."[105] While accepting Darwin's analogy of the branching tree, in reality he agreed with Spencer in denoting only one major trunk "the line of evolution," which "line" described one organic process that proceeded "from the primitive to the more complex."[106] As late as 1946, knowing that his position was anathema to the now orthodox Darwinian theory of genetic selection, Taylor expounded the Lamarckian line, declaiming that skin color, which according to Lamarckian theory was environmentally determined, was a prime example of "the inheritance of acquired characteristics."[107]

Taylor's Racial Ecology

In 1922 Harlan H. Barrows, of the University of Chicago, told the Association of American geographers that the new "scientific" geography had taken human ecology as its most distinctive model. Because ecology studied the mutual relations between organisms and their environment and thus investigated the natural world as a whole, geography was the "mother of all the sciences."[108] Two years before, Barrington Moore, editor of the newly founded journal *Ecology*, had proclaimed geography a new universal science that, through its ecological study of relationships, had effected a reunification of all the biological sciences and thus reaffirmed the true Darwinian synthesis.[109]

Taylor had been studying Australian settlement patterns and racial .classification in terms of "human ecology" well before Barrows' famous address of 1922.[110] Certainly his studies of the influence of climate upon race were instrumental in winning an appointment to Barrows' department of geography at the University of Chicago in 1928. Taylor offered a more deterministic interpretation of the harmonious interrelations of human beings and their environment than Barrows, but he saw nature as a great continuum. Claiming that "we are all parts of a complex whole,"[111] he became a frequent contributor to *Ecology*. When, in *Environment and Race,* he correlated plant, animal, and human distribution and conceived of racial migrations in terms of geographical zonation, the struggle for group dominance, and adjustment to a new environment, Taylor's name was placed among major contributors to the study of ecology in the United States, such as Ellsworth Huntington and Roland Dixon in anthropo-geography and Robert Park, Ernest W. Burgess, and R. D. McKenzie in sociology.[112] The influence of ecological thought became increas-ingly important throughout his career, and by the time he founded the Department of Geography at the University of Toronto in 1935, the study of human distribution had become its central organizing concept. "Evolution can be learnt from Ecology," wrote Taylor. "In settlement, race, cities, nations and linguistics we gain a great deal if we plot our distributions. Following Matthew—the biologist—I believe that ecology (i.e. geographical distribution) often enables us to decide which is the real explanation on many vexed questions."[113]

Although Wallace maintained that the study of the distribution of plants and animals had not become a branch of natural history until Darwin,[114] its roots were pre-Darwinian. Alexander von Humboldt was one of the first naturalists to break free of morphological studies of individual plants and their forms to investigate whole populations of plants in terms of their geographical distribution. These migrations were in turn correlated to both environmental and climatic factors.[115] Ecological studies became popular in Britain during the 1830s with the biogeography of Edward Forbes, who along with Humboldt introduced Darwin to the importance of geographical distribution, and during this period the ethnologist James Cowles Prichard was the first to relate plant and animal migration to the problem of racial dif-fusion.[116] By midcentury the ecological tradition had firmly taken hold in Britain: both Hooker and Wallace had invested their scientific writ-ings with the problem of geographic distribution, and Charles Lyell related the dispersal of species to climatic and geological change.[117] Darwin himself had given renewed impetus to ecological investiga-tion, for it was the very problem of how organisms respond once they have migrated to a new environment that led Darwin to believe in the transmutation of species.[118] Thereafter Darwin noted the relationship between time and space. Quoting Edward Forbes, Darwin observed in the *Origin of Species* that "there is a striking parallelism in the laws of life throughout time and space: the laws governing the succession of forms in past time being nearly the same with those governing at the present time the differences in different areas."[119] However, any systematic correlation between evolution in time with geographical distribution had to await twentieth-century polymaths such as W. D. Matthew and Griffith Taylor.

Darwin viewed nature as one integrated ecological system, as a "web of life" in which all parts are bound together by interdependent linkages.[120] Darwin's vision of "an entangled bank" is evocative of nature's complexity and harmonious interrelatedness. However, within this vision of "grandeur," Darwin made a telling reference to "the war of nature" for survival.[121] Because Darwin did not believe that each organism was perfectly adapted to its environment, he emphasized the way in which migrant organisms could dominate and expel indigenous species.[122] To the more descriptive and harmonious ecological studies of Humboldt, Forbes, and Hooker, Darwin added the factor of intraspecies competition. Thus the modern study of ecology—whose name was coined in 1866 by Ernst Haeckel—was an amalgam of both the pre- and post-Darwinian traditions.[123] Taylor's own major ecological treatise, *Environment and Race,* was influenced by a plant geographer, J. C. Willis, and a zoogeographer, W. D. Matthew, who represented these two intellectual poles: Willis argued a strongly pre-Darwinian, almost Paleyite position, while Matthew, a Lamarckian environmentalist, leaned further than any of his fellow paleontologists toward a Darwinian orthodoxy.[124]

In 1922 J. C. Willis wrote *Age and Area,* a study of the geographical distribution of plants around the world, as a corrective to Darwin's theory of natural selection and in the hope that it would help resuscitate the works of Charles Lyell and Joseph Hooker. Willis was an evolutionist, but he also believed in teleological explanations; and in language reminiscent of the natural theology of William Paley, Willis concluded that the "evolutionary clock was wound up to run on a very definite plan."[125] Willis approved of Darwin's conclusion that natural laws had similarly guided both evolution and geographical distribution of species, but as an advocate of parallelism, he insisted that natural selection could not account for uniformity of expression among species.[126] According to Willis, only when a new plant was coming into existence for the first time did it have to pass through "the sieve of natural selection." Once established, a new plant species became widely diffused not because it was dominant, as Darwin had postulated,[127] but through the simple principle of age. Thus, Willis established the axiom that the older the plant, the wider its distribution. Willis believed he had thereby circumvented the problem of adaptation. If a plant was confined to a particular area, this was because it was too young to have spread further. If there was a causal force behind plant invasions, this was to be found in the direct influence of the environment, especially climatic conditions whose cooling and warming cycles moved plants equatorward or northward respectively. One of the most important aspects of Willis' work on plant migrations was that he shifted the study of plants away from the process of individual adaptation favored by Darwin to one that focused on "societies" or groups of plants. He also undertook to analyze correlations in time and space with mathematical models created in contemporary genetic research by the Mendelians Hugo DeVries and William Bateson.[128]

While Willis' *Age and Area* showed Taylor how to study the influence of climate upon the distribution of whole populations of plants on a global scale, the work on mammalian evolution by W. D. Matthew, one of America's leading vertebrate paleontologists, was decisive in shifting Taylor's embryonic theories of geographical dispersal toward a more Darwinian framework. Matthew first presented his theories in 1911 to the New York Academy of Sciences. After receiving a copy of Matthew's *Climate and Evolution*, Taylor commented that it was "the most stimulating research" he had ever read.[129] In 1895 Matthew had been appointed by his graduate supervisor, Henry Fairfield Osborn—probably the most famous vertebrate specialist of his day and best known for his work on the Triassic period—to the Department of Vertebrate Paleontology within the American Museum of Natural History in New York. There, he cataloged the massive fossil collections of the Lamarckian Edward Drinker Cope. But Matthew's early scientific training had been in geology. A Canadian, born in St. John, New Brunswick, Matthew studied under his father, George F. Matthew, an outstanding amateur geologist and paleontologist who, as an expert on fossil plants and amphibian footprints, frequently collected for the Geological Survey of Canada. The elder Matthew was one of the founding members of the Royal Society of Canada and was awarded the Murchison Medal from the Royal Geographical Society for his prolific scientific publications on Acadian geology.[130] This early Canadian training served as the basis of many of the younger Matthew's early professional publications. His 1894 doctoral dissertation at Columbia University concerned the classification of igneous rocks in New Brunswick, and he wrote a series of papers on botanical classification, trilobites, and other Cambrian fossils from his native province.[131] Matthew's scientific training was remarkably similar to that of Taylor in that it bridged geology and paleontology. They were led simultaneously to the idea that geology could be reoriented to amplify theories of biological evolution.

The pivot upon which Matthew's interpretation of mammalian migration turned was an adaptation of the geological conclusions of T. C. Chamberlain, the chairman of Chicago's geology department. Chamberlain disagreed with the older notion, usually associated with catastrophism,[132] that the earth has been progressively cooling. Holding instead to the view that continental masses were permanent, Chamberlain developed a theory of climatic cycles—actually an adumbration of Lyell's uniformitarian system of geological cycles whose fluctuations operated within a generally permanent earth structure—to account for periodic shifts in sea level throughout geological time.[133] Matthew applied Chamberlain's geological theories to the evolution of land vertebrates by demonstrating that the regular cycle of alteration between warm-moist and cool-arid climates was the major causal factor behind the radial dispersal of animals that had evolved along "concentric external circles"[134] outward from a common point of origin. Having trained under Osborn, the leading advocate of orthogenesis, Matthew had earlier argued that there was an innate principle at work, which produced a directed and linear development of the horse. Chamberlain was therefore instrumental in directing him toward external stimuli as mechanisms of evolutionary change. "Broadly speaking," wrote Matthew, "geography has played the most important part in mammalian distribution. Climate and environment become relatively more and more important as we go down the scale. . . . Evolution, migration and extinction are thus conditioned by a changing environment."[135]

This renewed emphasis upon climatic change as the primary factor in evolution led Matthew to look to the harshest and most dramatic period of climatic change, the ice ages, as the pivotal age of vertebrate evolution. A major stumbling block for Darwinians was the absence of any fossil remains of humans in Europe during the Tertiary period. From this Wallace had argued a priori that the human species had not spread widely upon the earth and was of recent origin. Since fossil remains had been located only in the tropics, Wallace concluded that these warm climes had been the cradle of human evolution.[136] Matthew took Wallace's dictum that "the natural sequence of the species by affinity is also geographical" and his assumption that the more progressive species are produced in the temperate zones[137] to state his own "holarctic" or north polar theory of human evolution.[138] Like Wallace, Matthew agreed that gaps in the fossil record were indeed problematical, but instead of following the Darwinians in looking to minute mutations, he posited migration as an explanation for the lack of ancient fossil remains in northern regions. Matthew argued that the higher mammals and human beings had originated in northern Asia during the Tertiary period and that each subsequent ice age impelled a migration outward toward the tropics. Following Hooker's observation that few plant species returned to their northern origins after the climate had again warmed,[139] Matthew argued that the southern continents became the refuge "of the less adaptable and progressive types."[140] "At any one time, therefore, the most advanced stages should be nearest the centre of dispersal, the most conservative stages farthest from it. It is not in Australia that we should look for the ancestry of man, but in Asia."[141] For those more adaptable species hardy enough to reinvade their northern homeland, the successive periods of stimulating cold produced successively higher stages of development, and at the same each of these concentric circles of migration pushed the less evolved organisms progressively toward the periphery, to marginal lands farthest from the original point of dispersal or origin.

Although Matthew maintained that progressive evolution was the outcome of environmental change, he nevertheless did not see this as a total explanation of modification. Matthew's theories of geographical distribution owed much to contemporary ecological thought. He rejected its emphasis upon perfect adaptation, however, and viewed the process of migration in clearly Darwinian terms of invasion, struggle, dominance, and extinction. "Throughout all the evolutionary history of the vertebrates," Matthew declared, "we see numerous examples of races which, having become adapted to a higher plane of life, have re-invaded a lower plane." Matthew's conception of nature did not involve harmonious adaptation to one's surroundings; evolution was the outcome of struggle between species in which "the higher organization and greater activity acquired in the higher plane have caused them to become dominant, and spread widely in the absence of efficient competition."[142]

Although Taylor claimed to have used *Climate and Evolution* in a merely suggestive way, his "racial ecology" bore a striking resemblance to Matthew's interpretation.[143] Matthew knew of the implications of his theory for human racial distribution and had himself cited the climatic eruptions of the Pleistocene as the point of divergence between the "pre-human stage" of anthropoid apes and modern human beings.[144] However, before reading Matthew, Taylor had agreed with Darwin that there was no discontinuity between the higher mammals and humans. Humans and all the modern races were of great antiquity, according to Taylor; thus "early man of such a primitive type can surely be considered as obeying the same laws of migration as the higher mammals."[145] Like Matthew, Taylor rejected the continental drift theory of Alfred Wegener and believed that the earth's temperature, which had consistently tended toward increasing warmth, had been punctuated by cycles of rapid cooling, represented by the aberration of the ice ages.[146]

However, in seeing the various cycles of rapid climatic change in each ice age as almost discrete epochs or "catastrophic periods" that in turn produced accelerated organic variation,[147] Taylor had almost returned to the catastrophism of Cuvier, who likewise believed that the plant and animal life of each geological stage was a closed system unto itself. Although Taylor attempted to back away from the obsolete theory of catastrophism, by claiming that "all Nature's processes are processional rather than paroxysmal," at the same time he contended that each period of climatic instability had caused "decisive geological breaks" that produced "new forms."[148] Life began in the Cambrian; the Devonian produced the "birth of the vertebrates"; the Permian saw the emergence of mammals; and humans appeared in either the Pliocene or the Pleistocene.[149] "In conclusion it may be stated," said Taylor in 1921, "that the uniformitarian theory of geological evolution, though true enough through most of the record, applies only in modified form to the Pliocene and Pleistocene epochs."[150] Taylor traced an ancient lineage for the division of humankind and thereby established a vast divergence of racial character. Because Taylor believed in the ancient divergence of human beings into separate races, he was ambivalent on the question of monogenism versus polygenism. By producing an almost discontinuous variation in the sequence of organic life, accelerated evolution during the ice ages systematically explained the great divergence of racial types without surrendering the Darwinian orthodoxy concerning common origins. Thus Taylor was able to combine Darwin's evolution by minute variations with the modern Mendelian emphasis upon rapid and dramatic mutations.[151]

According to Taylor, humans evolved in the Pliocene, either in Sumeria or Turkestan—ironically, the very location of the biblical Garden of Eden—where open parkland forced them to walk upright and the cool climate engendered the energy and invention that separated them from their apelike ancestors.[152] A cyclical series of four ice ages had "exercised perhaps paramount influence on the evolution of life" and in each of their "striking breaks in the biological succession" had created the four human races: the Negrito, Mediterranean, Nordic, and Alpine types.[153] This process was largely linear, for Taylor rejected Darwin's branching tree of life in tracing a direct line from Neanderthal to modern humans.[154] Taylor contended that the traditional "ethnological tree" should ideally be replaced by geographical block diagrams, which could visually correlate horizontal and vertical movement. His vision of racial evolution, however, owed more to geology than to biology. Each of the races occupied a particular "ecological stratum" composed of layers of racial and cultural evidence which were deposited according to the law of "geological superposition."[155] With each period of climatic cooling a new and higher racial type was spawned, which in turn forced out the weaker and less evolved "species" toward more remote migration zones. The racial groups that geographically ranged farthest from the center, closer to the periphery—for example, the Australian Aborigines—similarly occupied a lower level on the scale of evolution. Thus, the strongest held to the common cradleland of frigid temperatures, which continued to stimulate human evolution toward broader heads, straighter hair, and rounder eyes. The first ice age produced the Negrito and Negro types, which comprised two wings of migration from a common origin; the second glacial epoch was cooler and therefore stimulated the growth of "civilization and intellect" represented by the Australian and Mousterian culture; the third brought about another "break in the continuity of descent" in creating the Eskimo and Bushmen of Africa; and the highest races, those with a cephalic index over 76, were the Nordic-Mediterranean and Alpine peoples.[156]

Because each climatic stage produced two separate migrations of a common stock—the Nordics traveled northward and thus became "blonder" while the Mediterraneans remained dark-haired as they spread to southern Europe, Indonesia, and the Americas[157]—Taylor drew into one biocultural zone peoples who had traditionally been organized by anthropologists into inferior and superior races. The Fuegians, whom Darwin described as almost inhuman,[158] Taylor classified as "ethnologically akin" to the "sturdy Scotch race" because they dispersed in the same wave of migration.[159] However, when Taylor's environmentalism failed to account for the convergence between skin color and level of culture—notably the Botocudo in Brazil, who were of exceedingly light coloring but had a culture "lower" than that of the Australian Aborigines—he resorted to Darwin's theory of sexual selection to fill in gaps in his general theory.[160]

By identifying the environment as the crucial factor in human evolution, Taylor inveighed against the racialist argument that race was an immutable category. He leaned toward the purely Darwinian idea that each human race could be ranked only according to its degree of adaptation and survival in a particular environment and concluded that throughout human history any race could be dominant at any particular time. If the culture of a particular race was inferior—like that of the Fijians, who shared a biological zone with the British—the inferiority was due to the unfortunate circumstance of migrating to a less hospitable and rigorous environment.[161] Once-superior races like the Chinese civilization had degenerated to their present backwardness as a result of an increasingly arid environment. "It is shown that environment is more important than heredity," observed Taylor in 1921. "As the environment changes so does the civilization wax and wane, and so different races rise to eminence and then sink into oblivion."[162] Taylor did not believe that the white race was innately superior and in fact argued consistently that the Mongolian or Alpine race would one day dominate.[163] Yet, while his novel racial configuration invited many "inferior" groups—namely the Polynesian, Mongolian, and Amerind peoples—into the mainstream of Western civilization, he believed that the black races were confined to perpetual inferiority and might even constitute a distinct species. Thus Taylor failed to abstract himself from Victorian racialism, and although he preached a more progressive environmentalism, he still saw the tropics as a bastion of cultural stagnation. As Taylor explained it, the "negro" races had developed little beyond the Neanderthal because "however stimulating the tropics regions are to lowly organisms, Man does not experience in the tropics those daily integrations of energy which in the long run produce evolution."[164]

Taylor believed that his racial ecology argued against the current argument that there were two precursors of modern humans, the Neanderthal and the proto-Negro. His idea that, during each migration, twin races departed from a common cradleland and headed either for the Atlantic or Pacific land masses was a middle ground between Darwinian monogenism and the older, racialist polygenism. That Taylor preserved racial classification within an evolutionist framework supports George Stocking's view that despite the preeminence of the monogenist position after Darwin, a vestigial polygenism persisted well into the twentieth century.[165] In *Environment and Race,* Taylor set about to revise orthodox racial classification; but despite his insistence upon the plasticity of racial characteristics under the impact of a changing environment, his methods—which measured the cephalic index, hair type, and skin color—tied him to the older, racialist science. Moreover, his conclusions depended heavily upon the work of the American sociologist William Z. Ripley; the physical anthropologist from Harvard University Roland Dixon; A. H. Keane, emeritus professor of Hindustani at University College, London; and the racial categories of Alfred C. Haddon, the Cambridge anthropologist and zoologist, all of whom accepted the relative stability of racial traits.[166]

Because cultural anthropology presently occupies the mainstream of that discipline, many historians have given pride of place to the ethnological tradition of Edward Tylor and Sir John Lubbock. However, in part because of the naturalistic approach inspired by Darwinism, racial classification reached its zenith in the late nineteenth and early twentieth centuries. In 1876 a committee devoted to the study of racial classification was established within the British Association for the Advancement of Science and spawned a vast number of anthropometric surveys.[167] Well into the 1920s, physical anthropology was invested with greater scientific prestige than the Boasian school in the United States largely because of the support of the National Research Council.[168] The savaging by Ruth Benedict, a student of Boas, of Taylor's *Environment and Race* can be better understood in the context of this rivalry for professional dominance.[169] Taylor was a vociferous critic of Boas' studies of head shapes of immigrant children. Because these so patently demonstrated the immediate variability of head shape in a new environment, they thoroughly undermined the usefulness of the cephalic index and thus were viewed by physical anthroplogists as a direct challenge to the scientific validity of racial classification. Ironicially, both Boas and Taylor were in fundamental agreement insofar as they both believed they were challenging orthodox racial hierarchies and upholding a more pluralist conception of culture because they saw no absolute division between savagery and civilization. Like Taylor, Boas had trained as a geographer and similarly considered ecological conditions as the determinants of racial differences, even terming the separate human stocks "ecotypes."[170]

Taylor's interest in the origin of racial stocks had its roots in the pre-Darwinian ethnological questions posed by James Cowles Prichard. Using a historical and linguistic rather than a natural scientific approach, Prichard in his search for common human origins was animated by a desire to confirm the biblical narrative. His biblical anthropology of racial migration and diffusion of culture[171] gave way by the 1850s to a naturalistic approach, once Darwinian evolution confirmed that human beings must be studied as part of the animal world. If humans constituted a single species, Prichard's argument for common origins must be anatomically confirmed. Thus in 1863 Huxley argued that the similarity and unity of the human races must be founded upon a more scientifically rigorous zoological study of hair type, skin color, and skull shape. Huxley determined that the human species was made up of no fewer than eleven semipermanent stocks who were still undergoing natural selection.[172] However, by positing an ancient origin for race formation and concluding that natural selection no longer affected human physicial variation, Darwin and Wallace confirmed the polygenist belief in the fixity of races. Darwin's hypothesis on the variation of species reinvigorated the debate over racial classification. His belief that racial traits were nonadaptive and therefore stable led him to ignore the question of human differentiation, even in *The Descent of Man*.[173] But Darwinism bequeathed a mixed legacy to the study of human differentiation. In many respects, Darwin had reconciled the conflict between monogenists and polygenists by demonstrating how one species could through natural selection evolve into present racial diversification. However, in the absence of human fossil remains, Darwinians had no tangible evidence for either a common human origin or mutation. Not wishing to surrender to the polygenists, who were generally chary of evolution, Darwinians evaded applying evolution to the human races.

Thus by 1900 a gulf persisted between evolutionary biologists, who avoided the implications of their theories for human evolution, and physical anthropologists, who did not believe in evolution. As late as 1919, in a paper to Section H of the BAAS—"The Differentiation of Mankind into Racial Groups"—Sir Arthur Keith reiterated the vexatious problem of human origins. As he stated, most anthropologists had come to accept the notion that human varieties may have stemmed from a common ancestor, but there still remained no systematic scientific theory for the causes of racial diversity.[174] It must have been with some gratification, therefore, that Keith edited and published Taylor's *Environment and Race,* the first study to bring racial classification under the rubric of evolutionary biology. As the Harvard anthropologist Roland Dixon affirmed, Taylor was the first to articulate a scientific causal explanation for both "racial origins and development." In his view, anthropologists had too long shirked the larger problem of human evolution. In a laudatory letter to Taylor in 1925, Dixon noted that racial studies "have rarely tried to visualize the problem as a whole in space and time." To anthropology Taylor had at last offered a purely naturalistic framework in which to investigate "problems of racial distribution in mankind, on the same bases as biologists do for animals, taking also into account the known and possible topographic changes in the world's surface which have occurred since man began to spread."[175]

In one very important respect Taylor's "great general racial plan of mankind," as Ellsworth Huntington called it,[176] was a significant departure from orthodox interpretations of racial evolution. Where previously William Z. Ripley and Roland Dixon had favored hybridization of the European races, Taylor now extended racial intermixture to include all indigenous peoples of the world, excepting the black races of Africa, which would thus ultimately reconnect biologically the world's peoples into a common unity.[177] His aim was to use his own scientific ethnology to denigrate the pseudo-science of the eugenicists who preached the message of racial purity. As Taylor attempted to demonstrate in his racial anthropology, racial migration and intermixture were themselves natural imperatives of the evolutionary process and as such formed the very basis of modern human development and civilization. "Surely, in view of the considerable racial mixture which has produced two of the most enterprising nations of our times," observed Taylor of Britain and Japan, "it is folly to quote that dictum as to the 'vices of half-castes' which we still hear on all sides!"[178] In exact inversion of the comte de Gobineau, the notorious inventor of the myth of Nordic supremacy, who also insisted that racial mixture produced degeneration, Taylor encouraged open immigration, claiming that isolation and the lack of group struggle endangered the future progress of civilization. In Taylor's view, the backward Australian Aborigines were telling evidence of the perils of national and racial isolation, and he encouraged Australia to open its doors to the Chinese, who as part of the most highly evolved Alpine race, would elevate them "biologically."[179] According to Taylor, racial mixture was a universal phenomenon and the only antidote to both "race repugnance" and "racial degeneration," which followed the laws of nature.[180] True to Spencer, Taylor continued somewhat naively to believe that there was no need for interventionist social policies: the hidden hand of natural law through the workings of the environment would promote the ultimate unity of the human race and create a final equipoise of "World Brotherhood." "Given time and goodwill," wrote Taylor, "the most diverse races will amalgamate, as the whole history of man demonstrates."[181] Taylor made it clear, however, that one still had to distinguish scientifically between the primitive and advanced races. In this respect his racial thought did not radically advance beyond the views of the pioneer of craniometry, Paul Broca, who expounded limited intermarriage between closely related races.[182]

Taylor's conception of the mutual interdependence of human life—what he termed the "web of civilization"[183]—was greatly qualified by his own commitment to preserving the integrity of the British Empire and the hegemony of the Western world. The very raison d'être of Taylor's racial theories was to provide a scientific rationalization for the general amalgamation of all the progressive Alpine, Nordic, and Mediterranean stocks to combat the rising black and colored races, who had learned all too well the lessons of empire building from their white overlords and who were, according to Taylor, on the brink of making a play for the world's dwindling resources.[184] Like most ecologists, Taylor eschewed warfare and frequently proclaimed pacifist credentials. However, his conception of Nature and the world order hinged on struggle as the guiding principle of progress and the survival of Western civilization.[185] If Taylor advocated racial cooperation among certain races, this was but a strategy in the larger struggle between races and nations for control of economic resources.

In essence, Taylor was a modern-day Malthusian. As a moral injunction, Malthus placed great emphasis upon the limitations to population growth; and by positing a birthrate that would naturally outstrip the food supply, he identified struggle as a positive moral force, because in evangelical terms it placed the burden on the individual to practice moral restraint and cultivate a work ethic.[186] From reading Malthus Darwin concluded that a struggle for existence inevitably followed from the naturally high rate at which organic individuals reproduced.[187] As the world population increasingly moved toward the saturation point, as the "backward races" prolifically reproduced, Taylor's admonitions were no less moralistic than those of Malthus, for Taylor believed that victory and survival would fall inevitably to the "thrifty and sober."[188]

Although Taylor believed that struggle was a positive force propelling human progress, unlike Darwin and Malthus he saw struggle in terms of groups rather than between individuals. "But however energetic a race may be, it has not much chance in the struggle for existence if natural resources are wanting."[189] Moreover, Taylor did not envisage fitness for survival in terms of reproductive success, as did Darwin; rather he saw scientific survival deriving from the efficient management of agricultural settlement and control of natural resources. The eugenic solution of birth control was a last resort, to be attempted only if the science of geographical nation planning failed to buttress the organizational supremacy of the white nations.[190]

For Taylor, science and Darwinian evolution were moral imperatives. Despite his environmental determinism, Taylor believed that racial ecology and the science of geography must reawaken the pioneering and competitive spirit in each individual so that preeminence in the struggle would not be wrested from the European nations. Despite the patina of twentieth-century scientism, the core of Taylor's thought testified to cardinal tenets of natural theology—that the study of nature enjoined prescriptions for human behavior.

Conclusion

Although Taylor's major geographical and anthropological work addressed the increasing pressure of population and international economic competition flowing from the changing balance of power after World War I, his central question—how to explain the progress and retrogression of human civilization—found its roots in the preoccupations of nineteenth-century social theorists. In fashioning his ecological synthesis, Taylor drew selectively upon Malthus, Lamarck, Spencer, Darwin, Huxley, and Haeckel, and like them he believed that evolution must become the central and all-encompassing intellectual framework through which to investigate nature holistically. Taylor thus construed geography as the modern scientific vehicle for preserving the Victorian naturalist tradition by making its focus the general study of the interaction of organisms with their environment. Just as the *Origin of Species* had offered a unifying theory describing the developing web of life, Taylor presented his ecological zones and strata theory as a modern, integrative interpretation of the "web of civilisation." In this way, Taylor considered himself a true successor to Darwin, even though much of his conception of the development of life owed more to ostensibly non-Darwinian principles of order, regularity, and linearity. Taylor, however, was not simply a scientific "antiquarian," for he was clearly abreast of all recent geological, paleontological, and biological theories and accepted the modern authority of scientific expertise. And although his generally environmentalist interpretation of human evolution was intended to combat the growing influence of hereditarianism, Taylor's interest in studying entire populations, his insistence upon rapid, discontinuous mutations within a particular race, and his increasing reliance upon Darwinian notions of interspecies competition and dominance foreshadowed many of the dimensions of the modern biological synthesis of the 1940s.

Perhaps the most significant influence upon the direction of Taylor's geographical thought was the early professional training he received in Australia, on the periphery of the empire of science. His environmental determinist position was the immediate consequence of studying extremities of climate first in Australia and Antarctica, later in the inhospitable northern regions of Canada. Taylor grew up in Sydney, which was the metropolitan hub of the southwestern Pacific. His proximity to Asia, together with Australia's history of intermarriage between whites and Aborigines, inspired him to construct a novel reinterpretation of racial classification which, for the first time, attributed primary importance both to the Aborigines and all peoples of the Pacific, including the Chinese and Japanese, in relation to the development of the European peoples and which upheld racial intermixture as a positive ideal. Indeed, racial unification became the very *leitmotif* of Taylor's program for a new world order. Writing from the margins, far from the centers of world population, Taylor in his zones and strata theory focused upon successive evolutionary waves of migration from the center to the periphery. Moreover, the experience of studying science in a young nation whose scientific establishment continued to tilt toward the British metropolis and whose institutional structures had not fully matured was instrumental in perpetuating Taylor's holistic evolutionary outlook. In these new societies, where divisions between amateurs and professionals remained weak, the Victorian naturalist tradition took special hold. The paucity of university chairs in science necessitated that Edgeworth David become a scientific polymath and that his perspective be bequeathed to his student Griffith Taylor, who as the only professor of geography easily perpetuated its holistic bias both at Sydney during the 1920s and at Toronto well into the 1940s. Moreover, it was significant that Taylor's most acclaimed evolutionary synthesis, *Environment and Race*, consciously drew upon and resembled the biogeographical theories of the Canadian William Diller Matthew, who likewise had grown up in a new society, where he had trained in the dominant naturalist outlook that combined geology, paleontology, biology, and anthropology under the aegis of the Geological Survey of Canada. It was this very universalist evolutionary tradition, emboldened in ecological geography, that preserved in these new societies a more harmonious relationship between the human and the natural sciences.

Notes

1   Peter J. Bowler, *Evolution: The History of an Idea* (Berkeley and Los Angeles: University of California Press, 1984), 250–264. For the best overview of modern Darwinian biology, see Ernst Mayr and William B. Provine, eds., *The Evolutionary Synthesis* (Cambridge: Harvard University Press, 1980). For the impact of modern population genetics upon theories of race, see Nancy Stepan, *The Idea of Race in Science: Great Britain, 1800–1960* (Hamden, CT: Archon Books, 1982).

2   Julian Huxley, *Evolution: The Modern Synthesis* (London: George Allen and Unwin, 1942), 449, 459, 460–461.

3   George Gaylord Simpson, *The Meaning of Evolution* (New Haven: Yale University Press, 1967), 121, 269.

4   Huxley, *Evolution*, 412, 445, 466–467.

5   See John C. Greene, *Science, Ideology, and World View* (Berkeley and Los Angeles: University of California Press, 1981), 173; Simpson, *Meaning of Evolution*, 349.

6   Huxley, *Evolution,* 577–578. For Huxley's view that evolution must
        be used to provide purpose for human society, see John C. Greene,
        "The Interaction of Science and World View in Sir Julian Huxley's
        Evolutionary Biology," *Journal of the History of Biology* 23 (1990):
        39–55.

7   For this linear interpretation of evolutionary thought, see Sharon
        Kingsland, "Evolution and Debates over Human Progress from Dar-
        win to Sociobiology," in *Population and Resources in Western Intel-
        lectual Traditions,* ed. Michael S. Teitelbaum and Jay M. Winter
        (Cambridge: Cambridge University Press, 1989). Although Kingsland
        notes the work of Richards and Bowler, both of whom have resur-
        rected the Lamarckian or environmentalist perspective to the main-
        stream of evolutionary thought between 1870 and 1930, she virtually
        ignores the importance of ecology in twentieth-century biology, favor-
        ing the linkages between eugenics and sociobiology.

8   Robert M. Young, *Darwin's Metaphor* (Cambridge: Cambridge Uni-
        versity Press, 1985); Greene, *World View;* Bowler, *Evolution;* Peter J.
        Bowler, *Theories of Human Evolution: A Century of Debate, 1844–
        1944* (Baltimore: Johns Hopkins University Press, 1986); Robert J.
        Richards, *Darwin and the Emergence of Evolutionary Theories of
        Mind and Behavior* (Chicago: University of Chicago Press, 1987).

9   Greene, "Interaction," 40.

10   For a more complete discussion of Taylor's contribution to geographi-
        cal thought, the ecological basis of his social scientific views, and the
        institutional context of his career, see Nancy J. Christie, " 'Pioneering
        for a Civilized World': Griffith Taylor and the Ecology of Geogra-
        phy," in *Dominions Apart,* ed. Roy MacLeod and Richard Jarrell
        (Toronto: Scientia Press, 1994).

11   Australian National Library (ANL), Griffith Taylor Papers, 1003/5/
        56, Taylor to Pal, 31 January 1931. For Asa Gray, see Young, *Dar-
        win's Metaphor,* 107; Michael Ruse, *The Darwinian Revolution*
        (Chicago: University of Chicago Press, 1979), 249; Bowler, *Evolu-
        tion,* 210.

12   For a thorough discussion of the Funafuti expeditions, see Roy
        MacLeod, "Imperial Reflections in the Southern Seas: The Funafuti
        Expeditions 1896–1904," in *Nature in Its Greatest Extent: Western
        Science in the Pacific,* ed. Roy MacLeod and Philip F. Rehbock
        (Honolulu: University of Hawaii Press, 1988). For David, see T. G.
        Vallance and D. F. Branagan, "Sir Edgeworth David," *Australian Dic-
        tionary of Biography* 8:218–221; Vallance and Branagan, "The Earth
        Sciences: Searching for Geological Order," in *The Commonwealth of
        Science: ANZAAS and the Scientific Enterprise, 1888–1988,* ed. Roy
        MacLeod (Oxford: Oxford University Press, 1988), 136.

13   David supported Darwin's hypothesis that the shape of coral atolls,

with their characteristic wedge pointing downward, was the product of coral growth outward. Sydney University Archives (SUA), Griffith Taylor Papers, Accession no. 979, series 1, item 1, "Lecture Notes on Physiography," lecture on Origin of Atolls. For Darwin's views on the formation of coral atolls, see Charles Darwin, *On the Structure and Distribution of Coral Reefs; also Geological Observations on the Volcanic Islands and Parts of South America Visited during the Voyage of H.M.S. "Beagle"* (London: Ward, Lock, 1842).

14   Griffith Taylor and C. Hedley, "Coral Reefs of the Great Barrier, Queensland: A Study of Their Structure, Life-Distribution, and Relation to Mainland Physiography," *Report of the Australasian Association for the Advancement of Science (AAAS)* 11 (1907): 405.

15   SUA, Acc. no. 979, "Lecture Notes on Physiography." The biogeographical dimensions of Darwinism that so predominated in Taylor's thinking were further enhanced by his association with Baldwin Spencer, professor of biology at the University of Melbourne and a professed Darwinian, who studied alongside the celebrated British geographer Halford Mackinder while at Oxford. See D. J. Mulvaney, "Patron and Client: The Web of Intellectual Kinship in Australian Anthropology," in *Scientific Colonialism: A Cross-Cultural Comparison,* ed. Nathan Reingold and Marc Rothenberg (Washington, DC: Smithsonian Institution, 1987), 67. Spencer also influenced Taylor's ideas on race. For the importance of Spencer's role in promoting Australian science, see MacLeod, *Commonwealth of Science.*

16   Taylor, "Great Barrier," 405. Taylor seems to have been influenced by the work of the American geologist T. C. Chamberlain, professor of geology at the University of Chicago and a thorough Darwinian. Taylor's career reinforces the conclusion of David Stoddart that the real impact of Darwin upon the discipline of geography occurred just prior to World War I, among the generation who taught well after World War II. See David R. Stoddart, "Darwin's Influence on the Development of Geography in the United States, 1859–1914," in *The Origins of Academic Geography in the United States,* ed. Brian Blouet (Hamden, CT: Archon Books, 1981), 268–270.

17   For the Australian scientific reaction to specialization and the breakdown of Victorian natural history, see Baldwin Spencer, "Presidential Address," *Report of the British Association for the Advancement of Science (BAAS),* 89 (1921): lvii.

18   SUA, Griffith Taylor Papers, Acc. no. 979, "Lecture Notes on Physiography," lecture 30, Evolution.

19   SUA, Griffith Taylor Papers, Acc. no. 979, "Lecture Notes on Physiography."

20   Bowler, *Evolution,* 247–249.

21   For Haeckel's evolutionary theories, see Wolf-Ernst Reif, "Evolution-

ary Theory in German Paleontology," in *Dimensions of Darwinism*, ed. Marjorie Grene (Cambridge: Cambridge University Press, 1983), 179–182; Paul Weindling, "Ernst Haeckel, Darwinismus, and the Secularization of Nature," in *History, Humanity, and Evolution*, ed. James R. Moore (Cambridge: Cambridge University Press, 1989), 318–326; Bowler, *Evolution*, 187–190; Richards, *Darwin*, 64, 522.

22   Reif, "Evolutionary Theory," 179.

23   Ernst Haeckel, *The Evolution of Man: A Popular Exposition of the Principal Points of Human Ontogeny and Phylogeny* (New York: D. Appleton, 1879), xxv.

24   Vallance and Branagan, "Sir Edgeworth David," *Australian Dictionary of Biography* 8: 218–221.

25   See Haeckel, *Evolution of Man,* 101. T. H. Huxley's argument that humans descended from apes was first iterated in 1863 in *Man's Place in Nature.*

26   Bowler, *Human Evolution,* 67, 218; Peter J. Bowler, *Fossils and Progress* (New York: Science History Publications, 1976), 138; SUA, Griffith Taylor Papers, Acc. no. 979, "Lecture Notes on Physiography," Lecture 1. Huxley rejected the idea that this Neanderthal man formed an intermediary between humans and the anthropoids. See Ruse, *Darwinian Revolution,* 244.

27   SUA, Griffith Taylor Papers, Acc. no. 979, "Lecture Notes on Physiography," Lecture 1.

28   Ibid.

29   SUA, Acc. no. 979, Group 163, series 2, item 1, "The Antiquity of Man," 2–3, 10–11. Taylor also promoted the view, supported by Haeckel, Darwin, and Alfred Russel Wallace, that humans had achieved their upright position and thus diverged from their ape-ancestors upon the open plains and that this process in turn stimulated tool use and the subsequent development of the brain. On this debate regarding the evolution of the human brain, see Bowler, *Human Evolution,* 158–162.

30   Bowler, *Evolution,* 212–213, 247–249.

31   SUA, Acc. no. 979, "The Antiquity of Man," 11.

32   On Darwin and materialist philosophy, see Richards, *Darwin,* 152–153.

33   Griffith Taylor, "Preliminary Note on Archeocyanthinae from the Cambrian Corals of South Australia," *Report of the AAAS* 11 (1907): 423.

34   See Beryl M. Hamilton, "British Geologists' Changing Perceptions of Pre-Cambrian Time in the Nineteenth Century," *Earth Sciences History* 8 (1989): 146–147.

35   Stephen Jay Gould, *Wonderful Life: The Burgess Shale and the Nature of History* (New York: W. W. Norton, 1989), 55, 60, 64.

36   Charles Darwin, *On the Origin of Species,* rev. ed. (London: Penguin, 1968 [London: John Murray, 1859]). 306–307, 313.

37   For the debate over this fossil, see Charles F. O'Brien, *"Eozoön Canadense:* The Dawn Animal of Canada," *Isis* 61 (1970): 206–223, 513–514; Bowler, *Evolution,* 192; Ruse, *Darwinian Revolution,* 222.

38   ANL, Griffith Taylor Papers, 1003/1/46–49, Mawson to Taylor, 28 September 1905. To locate a transitional organism between plants and animals formed a central problem in Darwin's invertebrate coral studies of the 1830s. See Phillip R. Sloan, "Darwin's Invertebrate Program, 1826–1836: Preconditions for Transformism," in *The Darwinian Heritage,* ed. David Kohn (Princeton: Princeton University Press, 1985). This problem preoccupied late-nineteenth-century paleontologists.

39   Taylor, "Preliminary Note on Archeocyanthinae," 423; E. Billings, *Palaeozoic Fossils* vol. 1, *Silurian Rocks, 1861–1865* (Montreal: Dawson, 1865), 5.

40   Taylor, "Preliminary Note on Archeocyanthinae," 423.

41   Gould, *Wonderful Life,* 314–315.

42   SUA, Griffith Taylor Papers, Acc. no. 979, Group 163, series 1, item 3, "Working Notes at the Sedgewick Museum, Cambridge, as 1851 Exhibition Science Research Scholar," 1908.

43   Darwin, *Origin,* 306–307.

44   Taylor, "Preliminary Note on Archeocyanthinae," 437. In his C notebook, Darwin had concluded that although "there can be no animal at present time having an intermediate affinity between two classes— there may be some descendant of some intermediate link." Quoted in Howard E. Gruber, *Darwin on Man* (Chicago: University of Chicago Press, 1974), 197. Darwin used the analogy of the branching tree to show how humans and the primates were distantly related to a common ancestor, thus, according to Darwin, obviating the need to find a "missing link."

45   Taylor, "Preliminary Note on Archeocyanthinae," 437.

46   For Bonney's role in solving Darwin's coral reef problem, see MacLeod, "Imperial Reflections," 164–65. See also David R. Oldroyd, *The Highlands Controversy: Constructing Geological Knowledge through Fieldwork in Nineteenth-Century Britain* (Chicago: University of Chicago Press, 1990), 179, 252.

47   ANL, Griffith Taylor Papers, 1003/1/41–46, T. G. Bonney, letter of reference, 15 March 1910.

48   ANL, Griffith Taylor Papers, 1003/1/70, W. J. Sollas to Taylor, 14 June 1909.

49   See MacLeod, "Imperial Reflections."

50   For Sollas' theme of racial migration, see his *Ancient Hunters and Their Modern Representatives* (London: Macmillan, 1911). Like

Edgeworth David, Sollas believed that the mind played a role in evolution. Although Taylor disagreed with this dimension of Sollas' thought, he adopted most of Sollas' ideas regarding human evolution into his later work, including Sollas' view of natural laws as inherently progressive. Like David, Sollas also emphasized the Pleistocene, with its dramatic climatic fluctuations, as the center of human evolution. This emphasis upon the ice ages was further encouraged by the work of Archibald Geikie, who was an expert on the Scottish Cambrian and whose younger brother James Geikie penned *The Great Ice Ages* (1874), which argued for a series of ice ages rather than for one singular ice age. Taylor was introduced to Archibald Geikie by his supervisor, Bonney. See ANL, Griffith Taylor Papers, 1003/1/158, Bonney to Taylor, 5 December 1907.

51   For Sollas' views on human evolution see Bowler, *Human Evolution*, 85–87, 97, 225.

52   ANL, Griffith Taylor Papers, 1003/1/40–45, Taylor to Mick, 27 January 1909; SUA, Griffith Taylor Papers, Acc. no. 979, series 4, item 3, "With Scott: The Silver Lining," 1. For Mendel's impact upon later population studies, see Garland Allen, "Genetics, Eugenics and Society," *Social Studies of Science* 6 (1976): 108.

53   Michael T. Ghiselin, "The Failure of Morphology to Assimilate Darwinism," in *Evolutionary Synthesis*, ed. Mayr and Provine.

54   For Walcott's career see Gould, *Wonderful Life*, 242–245, 257–258.

55   ANL, Griffith Taylor Papers, 1003/1/4, Taylor to Mater, n.d.; 1003/1/71, Walcott to Taylor, 9 July 1909. In 1912 Walcott published on organisms similar to Taylor's fossil specimen. Gould, *Wonderful Life*, 245.

56   For Taylor's views of the scientific expert, see Christie, "Civilized World."

57   Professor T. G. Bonney, "The Expansion of Geology," *Nature* 104 (6 November 1919): 213. It is significant that Bonney was asked to write for the fiftieth anniversary issue of *Nature*.

58   Stoddart, "Darwin's Influence," 272.

59   For the resurrection of Huttonian geology in the late nineteenth century, see Cecil J. Scheer, "Geology, Time, and History," *Earth Sciences History* 8 (1989), 103–105. See also Stephen J. Gould, *Time's Arrow, Time's Cycle: Myth and Metaphor in the Discovery of Geological Time* (Cambridge: Harvard University Press, 1987).

60   Davis was a student of the American geographer Nathaniel Shaler, who allowed for a certain degree of catastrophism within his development approach to physiography. See David N. Livingstone, *Nathaniel Southgate Shaler and the Culture of American Science* (Tuscaloosa: University of Alabama Press, 1987), 220.

61   Richard Hartshorne, "William Morris Davis—The Course of Devel-

opment of His Concept of Geography," in *Academic Geography,* ed. Blouet, 142–144.

62 For Davis' ecological ideas, see D. R. Stoddart, *On Geography and Its History* (Oxford: Oxford University Press, 1986), 159, 163–167. For the amateur status of geography in the nineteenth century, see Robert A. Stafford, *Scientist of Empire: Sir Roderick Murchison, Scientific Exploration and Victorian Imperialism* (Cambridge: Cambridge University Press, 1989).

63 Griffith Taylor, *Our Evolving Civilization* (Toronto: University of Toronto Press, 1946), viii.

64 ANL, Griffith Taylor Papers, Taylor to Jeff, 9 September 1908.

65 ANL, Griffith Taylor Papers, 1003/1/1–4, W. M. Davis to Taylor, 19 March 1910.

66 SUA, Griffith Taylor Papers, Acc. no. 979, series 3, item 2, "Antarctic Sledge Diary, 1911–1912," entry for 20 December 1911, 106.

67 University of Toronto Library (UTL), Griffith Taylor Papers, MS 20, Box 21, *Antarctic Adventure* (New York: D. Appleton, 1931), 7.

68 SUA, Griffith Taylor Papers, Acc. no. 979, series 3, item 1, "Notebook: Cape Evans, May 1911." In this notebook Taylor made particular note of Davis' article "The Alps in the Glacial Period." Ibid., series 4, item 3, "With Scott: The Silver Lining."

69 UTL, Griffith Taylor Papers, MS 20, Box 21, *Antarctic Adventure,* 126. For Darwin's geological contributions to his later thought see James A. Secord, "The Discovery of a Vocation: Darwin's Early Geology," *British Journal for the History of Science* 24 (1991), 133–158; Sandra Herbert, "Charles Darwin as a Prospective Author," *British Journal for the History of Science* 24 (1991): 159–192. For the equally important anti-Baconian tradition in British science, see Philip F. Rehbock, *The Philosophical Naturalists: Themes in Early-Nineteenth-Century British Biology* (Madison: University of Wisconsin Press, 1983). Darwin combined both inductive and deductive methods. See Greene, *World View,* 51; James R. Moore, *The Post-Darwinian Controversies* (Cambridge: Cambridge University Press, 1979), 154; J. W. Burrow, "Introduction," in Darwin, *Origin,* 42.

70 Ernst Haeckel, *The History of Creation* (New York: D. Appleton, 1874), 2. For Huxley's belief that evolutionism was broader than the theory of natural selection, see Greene, *World View,* 150. In the twentieth century, the Victorian naturalist tradition was generally preserved by scholars like Taylor who studied ecology. See Donald Worster, *Nature's Economy: A History of Ecological Ideas* (Cambridge: Cambridge University Press, 1977), 183.

71 ANL, Griffith Taylor Papers, 1003/4/127/80B, Taylor to Pater, 1 August 1919.

72 Griffith Taylor, *Environment and Race* (Oxford: Oxford University

Press, 1927). This volume was later expanded as *Environment, Race, and Migration* (Toronto: University of Toronto Press, 1937).

73   ANL, Griffith Taylor Papers, 1003/5/114, R. A. Goodwin, "Review of *Environment and Race*," *Chicago Evening Post*, 30 March 1928. For a lengthier analysis of the international reception of Taylor's work, see Christie, "Civilized World."

74   UTL, Griffith Taylor Papers, Box 23, "Correlations and Culture: A Study in Technique," Presidential Address, Section E, *Report of the BAAS* 32 (1928); ibid., Box 23, "Environment and Nation," *American Journal of Sociology* 40 (1934): 21–33; ibid., Box 23, "Environment, Village, and City: A Genetic Approach to Urban Geography," *Annals of the Association of American Geographers* 32 (1942); *Our Evolving Civilization* (Toronto: University of Toronto Press, 1946); ANL, Griffith Taylor Papers, 1003/4/127/71C, Taylor to Mater, 20 April 1920; ibid., 1003/6/196 Taylor to Mawson, 12 January 1944; Taylor, *Canada: A Study of Cool Continental Environments and Their Effect on British and French Settlements* (London: Methuen, 1947).

75   See UTL, Griffith Taylor Papers, Box 21, "Geography and Education for Citizen Responsibilities," presidential address to the American Society of Geographers, 1942, 7; ibid., Box 23, "Environment, Village and City," 54, 59.

76   For Darwin's belief that organic evolution applied equally to animal species and human races, see Darwin, *The Descent of Man* (London: John Murray, 1871). See also Ruse, *Darwinian Revolution,* 181; Stepan, *Idea of Race,* 51–53. Even among scientists such as Darwin and Wallace the natural theological partition between nature and morality had not been completely breached, and they recoiled from interpreting human culture in strictly biological terms. For the continued prominence granted the role of human agency in evolution among Victorian scientists, see Young, *Darwin's Metaphor,* 142–143. Though a strong exponent of natural selection, even Wallace argued that a supernatural agency undergirded human evolution. See Bowler, *Evolution,* 207.

77   Taylor, "Correlations and Culture," 109.

78   On the convergence of organic and social evolution brought about largely through Spencer's philosophical naturalism, see Bowler, *Evolution,* 207; Greene, *World View,* 132. For the best study that resurrects Spencer as a central figure in the Victorian debate on Darwin and human psychology, see Richards, *Darwin,* 243–294. Many of what passed as "Darwinian" theories concerning human evolution were in fact derived from Spencer. Darwin, who knew little of psychology, depended heavily in *The Descent of Man* upon the work of Spencer, whom he greatly admired.

79   For an excellent discussion of Huxley's revolt against Spencer's evolu-
       tionary ethical system, see James Paradis and George C. Williams,
       eds., *Evolution and Ethics* (Princeton: Princeton University Press,
       1989), 3, 39. See also Bowler, *Evolution,* 231.

80   Like Darwin, Taylor capitalized the word *nature,* and in doing so was
       consciously suggesting an intelligent force within natural law. For the
       Victorian scientific debate over Darwin's use of language, see Young,
       Darwin's Metaphor, 100.

81   Griffith Taylor, "The Distribution of Future White Settlement,"
       Geographical Review 12 (1922): 390.

82   UTL, Griffith Taylor Papers, Box 23, "European Migration: Past,
       Present and Future," Camden College, *Livingstone Lectures* (Sydney,
       1928), 6.

83   ANL, Griffith Taylor Papers, 1003/4/489, "Ascent of Man," speech
       to conference of secondary teachers. Taylor believed that Nature
       replaced Providence; see Griffith Taylor, *Australia: A Study of Warm
       Climates and Their Effect upon British Settlement* (London: Meth-
       uen, 1940), 478–479.

84   UTL, Griffith Taylor Papers, Box 23, "Geography: The Vital Study of
       Our Age," *Secondary Teacher* 14 (1919): 14–15.

85   UTL, Griffith Taylor Papers, Box 23, "Correlations and Culture,"
       134.

86   UTL, Griffith Taylor Papers, Box 23, "Environment, Village and
       City," 3; ibid., Box 23, "The Frontiers of Settlement in Australia,"
       Geographical Review 16 (1926): 25; ANL, Griffith Taylor Papers,
       1003/4/127/98B, Taylor to Professor Carslaw, 13 September 1919.

87   Spencer believed that the evolutionary process would result in an ulti-
       mate stage of perfect equilibrium. Taylor applied this Spencerian view
       of evolution to Canadian cities, thus concluding that Charlottetown
       had reached a mature stage of development and was thus in "equilib-
       rium." See Taylor, *Our Evolving Civilization,* 221.

88   Greene, *World View,* 14.

89   Taylor, *Warm Climates,* 15; UTL, Griffith Taylor Papers, Box 23,
       "A Correlation of Contour, Climate, and Coal: A Contribution to the
       Physiography of New South Wales," *Proceedings of the Linnean Soci-
       ety of New South Wales* 31 (1906): 517–529.

90   Taylor, *Our Evolving Civilization,* 227.

91   UTL, Griffith Taylor Papers, Box 23, "Environment, Village, and
       City," 65. Taylor referred to "King Coal, King Frost, and King
       Drought" as "those anthropomorphic servants of the environment"
       and more important than Charlemagne in determining the growth of
       nation-states in Europe.

92   UTL, Griffith Taylor Papers, Box 23, "Future Population in Canada:

A Study in Technique," *Economic Geography* 88 (1946): 67, 70–71, 74. See also Christie, "Civilized World," for a discussion of Taylor's scientist views of geography and their usefulness in social planning.

93   SUA, Edgeworth David Papers, 1/24, series 32, Box 43, William Sollas to David, 29 April 1933.

94   Griffith Taylor, "The Evolution and Distribution of Race, Culture, and Language," *Geographical Review* 11 (1921): 102.

95   ANL, Griffith Taylor Papers, 1003/6/423, Taylor to George Tatham, University of Toronto, 5 August 1948; Griffith Taylor, ed., *Geography in the Twentieth Century* (New York: Philosophical Library, 1949), 11, 14. By this time Taylor had softened his environmental determinism somewhat and stated that Nature provided the plan and humans acted as agents. However, Taylor still refused to grant humans an independent role in determining social policy.

96   UTL, Griffith Taylor Papers, Box 21, "Geography and Education for Citizen Responsibilities," 16–17.

97   Moore, *Post-Darwinian Controversies,* 141.

98   In *Human Evolution,* 269, Peter Bowler has presented a similar argument, effectively demonstrating that the linear image of evolution so characteristic of Lamarckism animated the thought of almost every human evolutionist of the twentieth century.

99   Greene, *World View,* 53.

100   ANL, Griffith Taylor Papers, 1003/1/76, Taylor to Mater, 30 July 1908, in which Taylor notes viewing a display on Mendelism at the South Kensington Museum in London that led him and his Canadian classmate to begin "catching Beetles for Mendelian Purposes"; 1003/4/489, Taylor, "Review of Ellsworth Huntington's *West of the Pacific,*" *Sydney Morning Herald,* 13 February 1926, in which Taylor uncritically accepts its eugenic message largely because it appealed to his own class bias. In *The Character of Races* (New York: Charles Scribner's Sons, 1924), vii, Huntington saw human civilization as the product of three forces: the influence of the physical environment, natural selection, and historical development. Later in his career, Huntington softened his defense of natural selection; see ibid., 1003/9, Box 5, Huntington to Taylor, 11 September 1945. For Taylor's most vehement criticism of Huntington's reliance upon natural selection, see Taylor, "Review of Ellsworth Huntington's *The Character of Races,*" *Ecology* 6 (1925): 453–457.

101   Taylor, *Environment, Race, and Migration,* 60. See Haeckel, *Evolution of Man,* 3. For the popularity of orthogenesis in the early twentieth century, see Peter J. Bowler, "Holding Your Head Up High: Degeneration and Orthogenesis in Theories of Human Evolution," in *History, Humanity, and Evolution,* ed. Moore.

102   SUA, Griffith Taylor Papers, Acc. no. 979, series 2, item 3, "The Evo-

lution of Culture and Language," 29 March 1920, 8; UTL, Griffith Taylor Papers, Box 23, "Climatic Cycles and Evolution," *Geographical Review* 7 (1919): 300; ANL, Griffith Taylor Papers, 103/4/127/67B, Taylor to Dr. Currell, n.d.

103   Taylor, *Environment, Race, and Migration,* 266–269. See also Sir Arthur Keith, "The Differentiation of Mankind into Racial Groups," *Nature* 104 (11 September 1919): 36–37. Keith actually believed that humans with thyroid deficiencies should be classed as separate human species. For Keith's hormonal interpretation of evolution, see Bowler, *Human Evolution,* 207. Interestingly, Keith's theories regarding the orthogenic role of the pituitary gland also found their way into Julian Huxley's views of selection. See Huxley, *Evolution,* 506.

104   There had been a long tradition of Lamarckian geographers. See Livingstone, *Nathaniel Southgate Shaler,* 60, 63. By the twentieth century the foremost among these were W. M. Davis, Patrick Geddes, Archibald Geikie, H. J. Fleure, A. H. Keane, and Sir William Herbertson. See J. A. Campbell and D. N. Livingstone, "Neo-Lamarckism and the Development of Geography in the United States and Great Britain," *Transactions of the Institute of British Geographers,* n.s., 8 (1983): 267–294; D. N. Livingstone, "Natural Theology and Neo-Lamarckism: The Changing Context of Nineteenth-Century Geography in the United States and Great Britain," *Annals of the Association of American Geographers* 4 (1984): 19–23. Like Taylor, H. J. Fleure, the famous anthropogeographer from the University of Aberystwyth, best known for his anthropometrical survey of Wales, combined Darwinism and Lamarckism. See Harold Peake and Harold John Fleure, *Apes and Men* (New Haven: Yale University Press, 1927), 37; H. J. Fleure, "Geography and Evolution, Presidential Address," *Geography* 34 (1949): 2, 9.

105   UTL, Griffith Taylor Papers, Box 22, "The Teaching of Geography"; ANL, Griffith Taylor Papers, 1003/4/489, "Professor's Plain English," *Sunday News,* 1 May 1927.

106   Taylor, *Environment, Race, and Migration,* 8–9. Taylor's Lamarckian views did not necessarily make him antagonistic to Darwinism; rather, like Fleure and the paleontologists Henry Fairfield Osborn and William Diller Matthew, Taylor posited an integrated Darwinian-Lamarckian perspective. In response to his critics, Darwin himself began to lean increasingly upon Lamarck's inheritance of acquired characteristics in later versions of the *Origin.* For Darwin's Lamarckian tendencies, see Greene, *World View,* 52; Ruse, *Darwinian Revolution,* 184, 195; Gruber, *Darwin on Man,* 193; Richard W. Burkhardt, Jr., "Lamarckism in Britain and the United States," in *Evolutionary Synthesis,* ed. Mayr and Provine, 417; Secord, "Discovery of a Vocation," 136. By 1862 Darwin wrote Hooker that he was believing more firmly in the direct action of the environment as a mechanism of

evolution in addition to natural selection. See Young, *Darwin's Metaphor,* 116. Thus for later evolutionists like Taylor, Darwin offered a more pluralistic approach to organic variation.

107   Taylor, *Our Evolving Civilization,* 61.

108   Harlan H. Barrows, "Geography as Human Ecology," *Annals of the Association of American Geographers* 12 (1922): 2–7. Barrows had studied with Frederick Jackson Turner at the University of Wisconsin and later taught at the University of Chicago. In 1928 he hired Griffith Taylor, the expert on human ecology and racial migrations, to join his department. For Taylor's important role in developing the study of ecology at the University of Chicago, see Christie, "Civilized World."

109   Barrington Moore, "The Scope of Ecology," *Ecology* 1 (1920): 3–4; J. W. Redway, "Human Ecology: Review of Ellsworth Huntington and Sumner W. Cushing, *Principles of Human Geography,*" *Ecology* 2 (1921): 229. For the relationship between geography and ecology, and the influence of Darwin and Haeckel, see Stoddart, *On Geography,* 163, 167.

110   UTL, Griffith Taylor Papers, Box 23, "Food and Population Problems on the Pacific Basin," *Proceedings of the Institute of International Relations* 6 (1930): 207.

111   UTL, Griffith Taylor Papers, Box 21, "The Geographer's Aid in Nation-Planning," *Report of the BAAS,* September 1931, 27. For Taylor's interdependent conception of nature, see Walter P. Taylor, "What Is Ecology and What Good Is It?" *Ecology* 17 (1936): 338.

112   See E. S. Craighill Handy, "Review of *Environment and Race,*" *American Anthropologist,* October 1928. Handy was curator of the Bishop Museum, Honolulu. For Taylor's contribution to the study of ecology in the United States, see Charles C. Adams, "The Relation of General Ecology to Human Geology," *Ecology* 16 (1935): 318–320, 329. For the influence of geography upon the study of human ecology among sociologists, see R. D. McKenzie, "The Field and Problems of Demography, Human Geography, and Human Ecology," in *The Fields and Methods of Sociology,* ed. L. L. Bernard (New York: Long and Smith, 1934).

113   ANL, Griffith Taylor Papers, 1003/6/343, Taylor to Mr. Osborne, Registrar, University of Canberra, 17 January 1948. In *The Science of Social Redemption: McGill, the Chicago School, and the Origins of Social Research in Canada* (Toronto: University of Toronto Press, 1987), Marlene Shore has argued that the center for the study of human ecology in Canada was McGill University and in so doing has wholly neglected its deep roots at the University of Toronto, where it was taught in geography, political economy, and biology. For a discussion of human ecology at the University of Toronto see Christie, "Civilized World."

114 Alfred Russel Wallace, *Natural Selection and Tropical Nature* (London: Macmillan, 1891), 469.

115 Margaret Bowen, *Empiricism and Geographical Thought: From Francis Bacon to Alexander von Humboldt* (Cambridge: Cambridge University Press, 1981), 213–232; Clarence J. Glacken, *Traces on the Rhodian Shore* (Berkeley and Los Angeles: University of California Press, 1967), 709; Haeckel, *Evolution of Man*, 13. See also Janet Browne, *The Secular Ark* (New Haven: Yale University Press, 1983).

116 Rehbock, *Philosophical Naturalists*, 123–149. For Prichard, see Greene, *World View*, 98; George W. Stocking, *Victorian Anthropology* (New York: Free Press, 1987), chap. 2.

117 Ruse, *Darwinian Revolution*, 227; Rehbock, *Philosophical Naturalists*, 141, 154.

118 Moore, *Post-Darwinian Controversies*, 129; Young, *Darwin's Metaphor*, 86; John R. Durant, "The Ascent of Nature in Darwin's *Descent of Man*," in *Darwinian Heritage*, ed. Kohn, 649; Bowler, *Evolution*, 235.

119 Darwin, *Origin*, 395.

120 Ibid., 126, 320, 459. On Darwin's interpretation of the "web of life," see Haeckel, *History of Creation*, 47.

121 Darwin, *Origin*, 459.

122 Gruber, *Darwin on Man*, 283.

123 Haeckel, *Evolution of Man*, 114. See also G. E. Nichols, "Plant Ecology," *Ecology* 9 (1928): 268. "Oecologie" was coined in Haeckel, *Generalle Morphologie der Organismen*, 1866.

124 Taylor also said he was influenced by the age and area concept of the American anthropologist Clark Wissler, although his contact with Wissler came during the mid-1920s when his own zones and strata thesis had already been asserted. Since Wissler worked at the American Museum of Natural History as did W. D. Matthew, it is possible that his ideas were derived from this famous evolutionist, as were Taylor's. For Wissler's age and area thesis see George W. Stocking, "The Scientific Reaction against Cultural Anthropology," in *Race, Culture, and Evolution*, ed. George W. Stocking (New York: Free Press, 1968), 218.

125 J. C. Willis, *Age and Area: A Study in Geographical Distribution and Origin of Species* (Cambridge: Cambridge University Press, 1922), 198, 204, 231.

126 Ibid., 206.

127 Darwin, *Origin*, 328.

128 Willis, *Age and Area*, 2, 7, 20, 26–27, 61, 82, 206.

129 Taylor, *Our Evolving Civilization*, 55; Griffith Taylor, *Journeyman Taylor* (London: Hale, 1958), 139. So impressed with Matthew was Taylor that after Matthew told him that he firmly disagreed with

Wegener's thesis of continental drift, Taylor recanted his adherence to the Gondwana-land theory. See ANL, Griffith Taylor Papers, 1003/4/127/180, W. D. Matthew to Taylor, 19 July 1920.

130   See Edwin H. Colbert, "W. D. Matthew's Early Western Fieldtrips," *Earth Sciences History* 9 (1990): 42; W. K. Gregory, "A Biographical Sketch of William Diller Matthew, 1871–1930," in *Climate and Evolution,* ed. W. D. Matthew (1915; New York: New York Academy of Sciences, 1939), vii.

131   Ronald Rainger, "W. D. Matthew, Fossil Vertebrates, and Geological Time," *Earth Sciences History* 8 (1989): 159.

132   Bowler, *Evolution,* 114, 194–195. Lord Kelvin was the last to support the cooling-earth theory in order to demonstrate the recent origin of the earth, thus negating the basis of Darwin's theory of evolution.

133   Matthew, *Climate and Evolution,* 4.

134   Ibid., 32–33.

135   Ibid., 181, 184. For the early orthogenic bias in Matthew's paleontological investigations, see Huxley, *Evolution,* 498.

136   Wallace, *Natural Selection and Tropical Nature,* 180.

137   Ibid., 5.

138   For the affinities between Matthew's and Wallace's northern origins theories, see Henry Fairfield Osborn, *The Origin and Evolution of Life* (New York: Charles Scribner's Sons, 1918), 257. See also Bowler, *Human Evolution,* 175. Osborn was greatly influenced by his student and by the 1920s was himself advocating central Asia as the cradle of human origins. He also accepted that the general trends of human evolution were coordinated with mammalian evolution and that Osborn's concept of "adaptive radiation" was very similar to Matthew's definition of evolution and dispersal in concentric circles outward from the pole. See Bowler, *Human Evolution,* 173–174, 177–179. Matthew's theories of Asian origin also influenced another Canadian, Davidson Black, who in 1925 discovered Peking Man. See Bowler, *Human Evolution,* 179.

139   Ruse, *Darwinian Revolution,* 226.

140   Matthew, *Climate and Evolution,* 8. For a similar conclusion see Haeckel, *History of Creation,* 366–367.

141   Matthew, *Climate and Evolution,* 10.

142   Ibid., 13. Rainger has argued that Matthew, unlike most of his fellow paleontologists, was a Darwinian who foreshadowed the modern Darwinian synthesis. See Ronald Rainger, "Just Before Simpson: William Diller Matthew's Understanding of Evolution," *Proceedings of the American Philosophical Society* 130 (1986): 453–474. Matthew's thought was very similar to that of one of Taylor's mentors, W. J. Sollas, who saw evolution as basically progressivist and linear but also

emphasized struggle as an important factor stimulating migration. See Bowler, *Human Evolution,* 91.

143   Taylor, *Our Evolving Civilization,* 52.

144   Matthew, *Climate and Evolution,* 42–44.

145   Darwin, *Descent,* 219; ANL, Griffith Taylor Papers, 1003/4/127/27C, Taylor to Tucker, April 29, 1920; UTL, Griffith Taylor Papers, Box 22, "The Zones and Strata Theory—A Biological Classification of Races," draft of speech delivered at the University of Toronto, 4.

146   Taylor, *Our Evolving Civilization,* 261. Taylor preferred the permamentist interpretation of the Irish physicist, John Joly, who penned *The Surface History of the Earth* (Oxford: Oxford University Press, 1925). For the debates over the continental drift theory, see Ursula B. Marvin, "The British Reception of Alfred Wegener's Continental Drift Hypothesis," *Earth Sciences History* 4 (1985): 145; H. E. LeGrand, *Drifting Continents and Shifting Theories* (Cambridge: Cambridge University Press, 1988), 57. Edgeworth David, Taylor's professor at Sydney University, began to lean toward the drift theory in 1928. The acceptance of Wegener's thesis as scientific orthodoxy necessitated a total reassessment of the role of geographical distribution and its relation to evolution. On this point, see Huxley, *Evolution,* 609.

147   Taylor, *Environment, Race, and Migration,* 16; *Our Evolving Civilization,* 16.

148   UTL, Griffith Taylor Papers, Box 23, "Climatic Cycles and Evolution," *Geographical Review* 7 (1919): 319.

149   UTL, Griffith Taylor Papers, Box 23, "Climatic Cycles and Evolution," *Geographical Review* 8 (1919): 320.

150   Taylor, "Evolution and Distribution of Race, Culture, and Language," 61.

151   For William Bateson's views on discontinuous variation, see Bowler, *Evolution,* 242. Bateson was particularly influential in Australia, having visited there in 1914 as part of the British Association for the Advancement of Science meetings. His ideas were soon absorbed into Australian biology. See Baldwin Spencer, "Presidential Address," *Report of the AAAS,* 34 (1921): lvii.

152   Taylor, *Environment, Race, and Migration,* 158; Taylor, "Climatic Cycles and Evolution," 303.

153   Taylor, "Climatic Cycles and Evolution," 289–290.

154   In the twentieth-century debate over human origins, whether one saw Neanderthal man as a direct ancestor of modern human beings or as a minor side branch indicated whether one accepted a largely linear and Lamarckian view of evolution or leaned toward Darwin's analogy of the branching tree. Taylor's mentor at Cambridge, W. J. Sollas, was the last major exponent of the link between Neanderthal man and

modern living races. See Bowler, *Human Evolution,* 87. Taylor frequently refers to Sollas' *Ancient Hunters* in his analysis of racial migration, and like Sollas, and Fleure, he believed there were modern remnants of Neanderthal man in modern Wales and drew a connection between Cro-Magnon Man and modern Eskimos and Algonkian Indians of North America. See Taylor, *Environment, Race, and Migration,* 159, 162.

155   Taylor, *Environment, Race, and Migration,* 261; UTL, Griffith Taylor Papers, Box 21, "The Ecological Basis of Anthropology," 13–14.

156   Taylor, "Climatic Cyles and Evolution," 303–311.

157   UTL, Griffith Taylor Papers, Box 22, "Zones and Strata Theory," 20.

158   For Darwin's first observations of the Indians from Tierra del Fuego, see Gruber, *Darwin on Man,* 10, 182–183.

159   Taylor, "Evolution and Distribution of Race, Culture, and Language," 62; ANL, Griffith Taylor Papers, 1003/4/227, "The Human Race," *Sydney Morning Herald,* 21 June 1923, in which Taylor concluded that Robert Louis Stevenson's black cook was higher "ethnologically" and consequently more intellectual than its author. Needless to say, comments such as these infuriated the Australian public. For the public debate on Taylor's iconoclastic racial views, see Christie, "Civilized World."

160   Taylor, "Evolution and Distribution of Race, Culture, and Language," 80.

161   ANL, Griffith Taylor Papers, 1003/4/127/57C, Taylor to W. L. Joerg, *Geographical Review* 10 (27 March 1920); ibid., 1003/4/127/82C, Taylor to Joerg, 17 May 1920.

162   Taylor, "Evolution and Distribution of Race, Culture, and Language," 55.

163   SUA, Griffith Taylor Papers, Acc. no. 979, series 2, item 3, "Climate and Dispersal of Man," August 1916.

164   UTL, Griffith Taylor Papers, Box 21, "The Ecological Basis of Anthropology," 30.

165   George W. Stocking, Jr., "The Persistence of Polygenist Thought in Post-Darwinian Anthropology," in *Race, Culture, and Evolution,* ed. Stocking.

166   See ibid., 62; Stepan, *Idea of Race,* 83, 89, 90.

167   Haddon undertook a survey of Britain, and Fleure conducted a similar investigation of Wales. Taylor used the 1908 handbook published by the Anthropometric Committee of the BAAS to study Australian Aborigines. See UTL, Griffith Taylor Papers, Box 21, "The Richmond River Kyogle"; Taylor and F. Jardine, "Kamilaroi and White, a Study of Racial Mixture in New South Wales," *Journal and Proceedings of the Royal Society of New South Wales* 58 (1925): 268–288. These

early anthropological studies were fairly typical in that they concluded that following natural law, the aborigines would be fully
extinct in thirty years. Taylor's early views on aborigines also well
demonstrate his Spencerian laissez-faire views against government
intervention. In contrast to A. R. Radcliffe-Brown, who occupied
the first chair of anthropology at Sydney University, Taylor opposed
social welfare for the Aborigines. See ANL, Griffith Taylor Papers,
1003/4/227, debate in *Sydney Morning Herald,* 29 October 1924, in
which Taylor opposed the intervention of the Aborigines Protection
Department on the grounds that it would hasten their death. "All we
can do is treat them fairly during the last chapters of their history." At
the 1923 Pan-Pacific Conference in Sydney, Taylor sat on the committee that was active in promoting the establishment of Australia's first
chair in anthropology. See Tigger Wise, *The Self-Made Anthropologist: A Life of A. P. Elkin* (Sydney: Allen and Unwin, 1985), 40.

168 Stocking, "Scientific Reaction," 287.

169 For Benedict's review of Taylor's *Environment and Race,* see Christie,
     "Civilized World."

170 Taylor's racial ideas had much in common with Boas' early anthropo-
     logical thought. See Franz Boas, "New Evidences in Regard to the
     Instability of Human Types" (1916), in Franz Boas, *Race, Language,
     and Culture* (Chicago: University of Chicago Press, 1940), 77. Boas
     generally supported anthropometry and only objected to using the
     cephalic index without other physical evidence such as hair type, etc.
     This was exactly the position held by Taylor, although he stressed the
     cephalic index more than Boas. See Boas, "Review of William Z.
     Ripley's *The Races of Europe,*" in ibid., 159.

171 Stocking, *Victorian Anthropology,* 45–57.

172 Stepan, *Idea of Race,* 79. Although Darwinians rejected the polygen-
     ist identification of ability with race, there was a continued scientific
     defense of skull measurement as a general index of intelligence. See
     Douglas A. Lorimer, *Colour, Class, and the Victorians* (Leicester:
     Leicester University Press, 1978), 137.

173 Darwin, *Descent,* 225; Thomas Huxley, *Evidence as to Man's Place
     in Nature* (London: Williams and Norgate, 1863), 153–154; Stepan,
     Idea of Race, 64–66, 86; Roger Smith, "Wallace: Philosophy of
     Nature and Man," *British Journal of the History of Science* 16
     (1972): 177–199; Herbert H. Odom, "Generalizations on Race in
     Nineteenth-Century Physical Anthropology," *Isis* 58 (1967): 14.

174 Sir Arthur Keith, "The Differentiation of Mankind into Racial
     Groups," *Nature* 104 (11 September 1919): 36–37.

175 ANL, Griffith Taylor Papers, 1003/4/406, Roland Dixon to Taylor,
     8 March 1925.

176 ANL, Griffith Taylor Papers, 1003/5/112, Ellsworth Huntington,

"Review of *Environment and Race,*" *Saturday Review,* 1 October 1927, 48.

177 UTL, Griffith Taylor Papers, Box 22, "Race and Nation in Europe," *Australian Journal of Psychology and Philosophy* 4 (1926); 6; ibid., Box 23, "European Migration: Past, Present, and Future," Camden College, *Livingstone Lectures* (Sydney, 1928), 38.

178 Taylor, *Environment, Race, and Migration,* 218. For the eugenicist position on the purity of race, see Daniel J. Kevles, *In the Name of Eugenics* (New York: Knopf, 1985), 97.

179 Taylor, *Environment, Race, and Migration,* 370; UTL, Griffith Taylor Papers, Box 22, "Race and Nation in Europe," 5; Taylor, "Evolution and Distribution of Race, Culture, and Language," 76. For Gobineau, see Lorimer, *Colour, Class, and the Victorians,* 139.

180 Taylor, "Evolution and Distribution of Race, Culture, and Language," 115; ANL, Griffith Taylor Papers, 1003/5/105, "Racial Mixture and the World," Sydney University Extension Board Lecture, n.d. Taylor particularly admired James Bryce's positive assessment of racial mixture in South America. Indeed, Taylor saw modern Brazil and Switzerland as models for world racial harmony.

181 ANL, Griffith Taylor Papers, 1003/4/127/82C, Taylor to Joerg, 17 May 1920; Taylor, *Environment, Race, and Migration,* 49.

182 Nancy Stepan, "Biological Degeneration: Races and Proper Places," in *Degeneration: The Dark Side of Progress,* ed. J. Edward Chamberlain and Sander L. Gilman (New York: Columbia University Press, 1985), 110. In 1920 Baldwin Spencer, professor of natural science at the University of Melbourne, instructed Taylor to read Broca's *Anthropologiques Generale.* See ANL, Griffith Taylor Papers, 1003/4/127/28D, Baldwin Spencer to Taylor, 3 August 1920. On Spencer's biological and anthropological ideas, see Derek John Mulvaney and J. H. Caleby, *"So Much That Is New": Baldwin Spencer, 1860–1929: A Biography* (Melbourne: Melbourne University Press, 1985).

183 Taylor, *Environment, Race, and Migration,* 7.

184 Taylor, "Geographers and World Peace: A Plea for Geopacifics," *Australian Geographical Studies* 1 (1963): 7–8; UTL, Griffith Taylor Papers, Box 23, "Correlations and Culture: A Study in Technique," 115.

185 For the identification of ecology with pacifism, see D. P. Crook, "Peter Chalmers Mitchell and Anti-War Evolutionism in Britain during the Great War," *Journal of the History of Biology* 22 (1989): 325–356. In contrast, Sir Arthur Keith saw evolutionary struggle in terms of overt tribal warfare, while Taylor believed there was an initial process of racial conflict during periods of migration but that this was resolved through the relatively peaceful and benign process of "racial incorporation" through intermarriage. See Sir Arthur Keith,

Evolution and Ethics (New York: Putnam, 1946); Taylor, *Environment, Race, and Migration*, 223; Taylor, *Environment and Nation* (Toronto: University of Toronto Press, 1936), 129–34.

186 Greene, *World View,* 139; Paradis and Williams, *Evolution and Ethics,* 9–11.

187 Ruse, *Darwinian Revolution,* 189; Young, *Darwin's Metaphor,* 23–55.

188 Taylor, *Environment, Race, and Migration,* 457.

189 Ibid., 423.

190 ANL, Griffith Taylor Papers, 1003/4/363, Taylor to Isaiah Bowman, 2 March 1928; 1003/4/227, "Population and Pessimism," 10 October 1923, lecture to Prohibition Conference; Taylor, *Environment, Race, and Migration,* 3; Taylor, "Future White Settlement," 375, 381.

JOHN LAURENT

16 Varieties of Social Darwinism in Australia, Japan, and Hawaii, 1883–1921

A fascination with Darwinism characterized late-nineteenth- and early-twentieth-century intellectual life in the West in a way perhaps unparalleled before or since. The 1908 Nobel Prize winner for literature, Rudolph Eucken of Germany, referred to this interest in his bestselling book, *Main Currents of Modern Thought* (published in 1912 and read in translation in Japan before the end of 1913 with "much interest").[1] Eucken spoke of his era as one "intoxicated" with the idea of evolution. Darwinism was "a tendency which has carried the age," and the "whole idea of evolution . . . permeates the modern world."[2] Darwin's theories were by then half a century old. According to Eucken, "[r]eligion and speculation [had become] mere shadows of their former selves and for many people non-existent, [while] their product, the belief in progress, has remained."[3] For many people, organic evolution implied progress as the natural order of things, an idea that seemed to find confirmation in the achievements of science—in medicine, for example (where the discovery of radium was widely heralded as the "cure" for cancer), and in transport and communications. And just as the advance of science was seen as epitomizing this evolutionary progress, so too was the discovery of the principle of the evolution of life by natural selection itself seen as the crowning achievement of science, signaling the final demise of religion and superstition.

Social Darwinism was concerned with the application of Darwin's theories to human society, a subject that gained much attention in the West around the turn of the century.[4] And this interest quickly spread to countries as widely dispersed as Australia, Japan, and Hawaii. This essay examines some of the various forms assumed by Social Darwinism in these countries, ranging from extreme laissez-faire—even rac-

474

ist—versions, to socialist and internationalist interpretations. We will look at first Australia, where, it will be seen, both ends of the spectrum of Social Darwinist ideas could find a home, then Japan, where Marxist interpretations of Darwinism seem to have found widest appeal, and finally Hawaii, where internationalist interpretations were ultimately to find concrete expression in the Pan-Pacific movement of the years immediately following World War I.

Australia: "White Labor's Paradise"?

The substitution of evolution for traditional religion by many people in the West is illustrated by the rapid growth of the Secularist movement. Founded by George Jacob Holyoake and Charles Bradlaugh in England and by Colonel Robert Ingersoll in the United States, the Secularist (or "Free Thought") movement gained a rapid adherence from the late 1870s.[5] In Australia, support for Secularism grew considerably following visits by Free Thought lecturers such as the American Moncure Conway, who arrived in 1884. A perusal of newspaper reports of Conway's lectures shows just how prominent a theme Darwinian evolution had become. In Brisbane, for example, where Conway addressed a "crowded" audience in the Gaiety Theatre, Conway explained that "[t]hus far the most momentous achievement of the nineteenth century was to have produced the scientific generalization called 'Evolution'" and that "the discovery of Charles Darwin had wrought a revolution in the thoughts of men."[6] At about the same time another visiting (and ultimately resident) lecturer, Wallace Nelson, was debating the topic "Creation or Evolution?" with a Baptist minister in the pages of the Queensland *Gympie Miner,* Nelson not only taking upon himself Darwin's defense, but also contending that "Herbert Spencer... is regarded by all cultured persons as England's greatest philosopher and the world's greatest evolutionist."[7]

Herbert Spencer is mainly remembered today, however, for his Social Darwinist views. The phrase "survival of the fittest," popular even today among "New" Right economic theorists and which for many people captures the essence of Darwinism, was of course Spencer's (though Darwin was happy to adopt it in the fifth edition of the *Origin of Species*), and it readily lent itself to socioeconomic interpretations. Essentially the idea endorsed a laissez-faire society in which the "fittest" individuals would be most likely to succeed in the "struggle for existence" and so ensure the continuance of material advancement. Spencer did provide much of the philosophical foundation for such views. In *Social Statics* he wrote, "The poverty of the incapable, the distresses that come upon the imprudent, the starvations of the idle ... are the decrees of a large, far-seeing benevolence. ... Under the natural order of things society is constantly excreting its unhealthy, imbecile, slow, vacillating, faithless members."[8] However, the most extreme type of Social Darwinism—that advocating genocide, in effect—seems to have stemmed not so much from Spencer's writing as from that of certain prominent *scientists,* beginning, as far as I can determine, with the eminent British biometrician Karl Pearson.

Pearson was also another early Free Thought lecturer, and in a National Secular Society pamphlet (available in Australia through local branches of the society), Pearson had the following to say:

> The struggle for existence involves not only the struggle of individual man against individual man, but also the struggle of individual society against individual society. ... I think there is cause for human satisfaction in the replacement of the aborigines throughout America and Australia by white races. The Society for the Protection of the Aborigines may usefully act as a brake, but it would be harmful as a check on the extermination of the inferior human races.[9]

Such opinions were seriously held in British and American scientific circles, so it is not difficult to appreciate how they could be taken up by the general community in an era of widely and firmly held notions of white superiority. With regard to the Australian Aborigines, perhaps some of the most notorious remarks in this connection were those reported to have been made by a "learned university professor" (unnamed in the newspaper item from which this information is taken) in a lecture on climatology in Melbourne in 1921:

> We in Australia have the curse of the aboriginal inhabitants; but these creatures are not so virile as the negro, or even the American Indian. That they will gradually disappear, at least from the greater part of the continent, is the verdict of those most competent to give an opinion. If that be so, their disappearance will be lamented only by the anthropologists. An abundant native population, like a giant slum in a city, is a reservoir of diseases, which are continually escaping into the homes of the civilized.[10]

The Tasmanian Aborigines had already disappeared in one sense (Truganini, the last "full-blooded" member of her race, died in 1876), but this does not seem to have been regarded altogether as a tragedy—unless from the point of view of the anthropologist—by another scientist of standing, Ronald Hamlyn-Harris, director of the Queensland Museum from 1910 to 1917. In a public lecture on "Primitive Man" in May 1914, Hamlyn-Harris explained that the Tasmanian Aborigines "had now followed the prevailing law that when a lower race of mankind came in contact with a race of higher mental and physical abilities, the former invariably disappeared."[11] In a later lecture at the University of Queensland, Hamlyn-Harris appealed for public support of anthropological research such as he was engaged in: "Civilization evolved from savagery," Hamlyn-Harris explained, and "a study of such [is] necessary to the understanding of the evolution of humanity. The early history of mankind [is] full of gaps, and these [can] only be imperfectly bridged by the comparative study of the still-existing savage races."[12]

The rationale behind this argument was that "primitive" people, like the Aborigines, represented "remnants" of an earlier stage in human evolution—a concept that (as has been recently noted by the Australian anthropologist John Mulvaney)[13] reflected racialist Social Darwinist beliefs at the time. It is not now regarded as a valid concept, but it was a popular one in some circles at the time. Thus, the leader of a Swedish scientific expedition to the Kimberleys in 1911, Dr. J. Mjoberg, told a reporter from the Melbourne *Argus* that he had "found a striking likeness between the Aboriginals and the old Neanderthal race, which [became] extinct in Europe centuries ago." The similarity, Mjoberg explained, consisted principally in the "low, receding forehead, a reduced volume of skull, and a small brain capacity, while there were a number of smaller points common to the two races."[14]

But, as already indicated, there were other kinds of Social Darwinism as well. One, which, curiously (since it was mainly used by socialists), also owed a great deal to the writing of Herbert Spencer, underlined the "society-as-organism" concept. As Eucken explained, this concept was used principally by Spencer as a means of "fitting the individual into the social whole." The idea, according to Eucken, seemed "peculiarly adapted to serve as a means for reconciling the respective claims of society and the individual." In a "real body," Eucken went on, "the more each limb develops its own character and strength, the more useful it is for the whole; the whole, on the other hand, stands higher, the more highly differentiated are its several parts."[15] In its more strictly *evolutionary* sense, this concept seems to have been first proposed by Spencer, in *Social Statics* (though as a literary device it goes back at least to St. Paul).[16] In the original (1851) version of *Social Statics* (later much changed in conformity with Spencer's antipathy toward socialism), Spencer wrote as follows:

Progress . . . is not an accident, but a necessity. Instead of civilization being artificial, it is part of nature; all of a piece with the development of the embryo or the unfolding of a flower. The modifications mankind have [*sic*] undergone, and are still undergoing, result from a law underlying the whole of organic creation; and provided the human race continues, and the constitution of things remains the same . . . so surely must the human faculties be moulded into complete fitness for the social state.[17]

It would appear that Spencer conceived this ideal state of things to have been achieved—in industrialized Victorian England.[18] But whatever the case, his concept readily lent itself to utopian interpretations and was accordingly taken up by socialists, who argued for the evolution of society *beyond* its Victorian laissez-faire form to something more in keeping with their own visions. One of the first to utilize this device was the American Henry George, who specifically cited Spencer as the authority for his theory:

> In short, to use the language in which Herbert Spencer has defined evolution, the development of society is, in relation to its component individuals, the passing from an indefinite, incoherent homogeneity [George is citing Spencer's *First Principles*] to a definite, coherent heterogeneity. The lower the stage of social development, the more society resembles one of those lowest of animal organisms, which are without organs or limbs, and from which a part may be cut and yet live. The higher the stage of social development, the more society resembles those higher organisms in which functions and powers are specialized, and each member is vitally dependent on the others.[19]

Such arguments became commonplace in socialist propaganda in the late nineteenth and early twentieth centuries. Their plainly analogical nature is obvious enough, but this did not deter their promulgation by prominent socialist and Labor-movement leaders—such as William Morris Hughes, Labor prime minister of Australia from 1915, who, in 1907, when shadow attorney general, explained in a paper read before a meeting of the Australasian Association for the Advancement of Science (AAAS) in Adelaide that

> the modern State, considered as an organism, exhibits those marks which invariably accompany higher development. It responds more readily to stimuli, it specializes functions, and it has evolved new organs, or, what is the same thing, rudimentary organs have developed until they perform functions entirely new, or formerly very imperfectly performed by the individual.[20]

Later in his paper, Hughes attempted to buttress this argument for a socialist state by introducing another Social Darwinist theme, this time laying at least some claim in Darwin's own writing. The "facts of the case," Hughes contended, were as follows:

Competition is no doubt a law of nature, but so is co-operation; and the one is as general and as important as the other.... Competition, perhaps, is the primary law of life, but co-operation is certainly that of society. Amongst primitive communities the State generally protects the individual but slightly. With civilization the restraint of the individual for the benefit of the community becomes more marked. Life and property are protected from the strong and unscrupulous. The weaker individuals by co-operation prevent the stronger from exercising their strength against the rest of the community.[21]

What Hughes appears to be attempting here is to combine those elements in Spencer he finds useful (Spencer's name is mentioned elsewhere in the paper) with some arguments Darwin set forth in *Descent of Man*. These should now be looked at in some detail.

In the second (1874) edition of *Descent of Man*, Darwin devoted a whole chapter (chapter 4) to a discussion of what he called "the moral sense," which, he noted, is traditionally "summed up in that short but imperious word *ought,* so full of high significance."[22] Darwin went on to explain that this great subject "has been discussed by many writers of consummate ability, and my sole excuse for touching on it, is the impossibility of here passing it over; and because, as far as I know, no one has approached it exclusively from the side of natural history."[23] This, then, Darwin attempted to do. The theory he arrived at stems from a familiar observation of naturalists: the tendency for various species of animals to congregate. As Gilbert White had noted in his *Natural History of Selborne* (one of Darwin's favorite books from his student days): "There is a wonderful spirit of sociality in the brute creation, independent of sexual attachment.... Oxen and cows will not fatten by themselves; but will neglect the finest pasture that is not recommended by society."[24] Darwin assumed that there must be selective advantages in this phenomenon, and he suggested various possibilities, partly gleaned from further observations by naturalists:

Animals ... render ... important services to one another: thus wolves and some other beasts of prey hunt in packs, and aid one another in attacking their victims. Pelicans fish in concert. The Hamadryas baboons turn over stones to find insects, etc.; and when they come to a large one, as many as can stand round, turn it over together and share the booty. Social animals mutually defend each other. Bull bisons in North America, where there is danger, drive the cows and calves into the middle of the herd, whilst they defend the outside.[25]

It is not difficult to see how such apparently mutually beneficial behaviors would be preserved and passed on to offspring through natural selection operating at the *group* level. That is to say, animal communities that engaged in such behaviors would be at a selective advantage over those that did not. This, anyway, was Darwin's argument, and it is apparently what Karl Pearson, in the pamphlet referred to above, was alluding to, in the human sphere, when he referred to the "struggle of individual society against individual society." (Indeed, Pearson regarded himself as a socialist, and the title of his pamphlet is "The Positive Creed of Freethought with Some Remarks on the Relation of Freethought to Socialism.") Darwin took the argument further, however, by suggesting that such behaviors can be seen to be based in instincts for "sympathy," or "affection," between members of a troup, pack, and the like and that these instincts, in turn, would be selected for since "those communities which included the greatest number of the most sympathetic members would flourish best and rear the greatest number of offspring."[26] And such principles, according to Darwin, have probably been operating in human evolutionary history. As he notes: "Every one will admit that man is a social being." He summarizes his argument as follows:

> The social animals which stand at the bottom of the scale [he is employing the *scala natura* idea, with "Man" at the apex] are guided almost exclusively, and those which stand higher in the scale are largely guided, by special instincts in the aid which they give to the members of the same community. . . . Although man . . . has no special instincts to tell him how to aid his fellow-men, he still has the impulse, and with his improved intellectual faculties would naturally be much guided in this respect by reason and experience.[27]

Actually, the "man-is-a-social-animal" idea, and the apparent difficulties this posed for "social contract" theories (as in Hobbes and Rousseau, with their "state of nature" thesis and its "war of all against all"), had earlier been argued by Marx, in an essay originally intended to be an introduction to his *Contribution to the Critique of Political Economy* (1859). Marx (a correspondent of Darwin) had written these lines:

> The further back we trace the course of history, the more does the individual . . . appear to be dependent on and belong to a larger whole. . . . Man is a *Zoon politikon* in the most literal sense: he is not only a social animal, but an animal that can be individualized only within society. Production by a solitary individual outside society . . . is just as preposterous as the development of speech without individuals who live *together* [Marx's emphasis] and talk to one another.[28]

By the time W. M. Hughes addressed the AAAS meeting in Adelaide, Darwin's, Spencer's, and other evolutionists' ideas were well known in Australia. Newspaper items on evolution and related subjects were frequent, and these were often from a Social Darwinist perspective of some sort. In the same year as Hughes' address (1907), the *Adelaide Advertiser* featured items on "Man's Descent: Professor Haeckel on Humanity's Past and Future," "The Oldest Picture in the World" (on the recent discovery of cave paintings in the south of France), and "Improving the Race"[29]—an item on some of the ideas on eugenics of Luther Burbank, the well-known plant breeder in California. Burbank is reported to have said that he "would prohibit in every State in the Union the marriage of the physically, mentally and morally unfit" and that "when we blend two poisonous plants we get a third even more virulent, a vegetable degenerate. A similar thing happens when two degenerate human beings are united."[30] Besides such items, which suggest a perceived interest in evolution among the reading public, there are also advertisements for books, including novels, on evolutionary themes. Among these would be Jack London's *Before Adam*, which is prominently announced on the front page of the *Adelaide Advertiser* of 30 July 1907 as being available from a local bookseller. London was a socialist, and his novel, set in prehistoric times (he had some of his characters living in trees), conveys his socialistic interpretation of Darwin's concept of the place of cooperation and altruism in human evolution: for example, one of the "cave people" in the story assists another at personal risk in the face of danger, which conduct London (as narrator) takes as "a foreshadowing of the altruism and comradeship that have helped make man the mightiest of the animals."[31]

Books and pamphlets on evolutionary themes were also regularly listed in the Melbourne *Socialist* as available from the newspaper's office. Lists in the 20 July and 28 December 1907 numbers, for example, contain C. W. Saleeby's *Heredity* and *Organic Evolution,* J. A. Hobson's *Evolution of Capitalism,* Enrico Ferri's *Socialism and Positive Science* (which is subtitled "Darwin-Spencer-Marx"), a pamphlet by the Irish socialist Jim Connell titled *Socialism and the Survival of the Fittest,* and "Works by Spencer, Mill, H. G. Wells, Darwin, Haeckel, Huxley, etc., each : 6d." All of the latter (except Wells?) were probably the paperback reprints offered at that price by the British Rationalist Press Association, which had been established in 1899 by the National Secular Society.[32] Also listed in these two issues of the *Socialist* were Robert Blatchford's *God and My Neighbour* and *Not Guilty,* both of which have lengthy discussions on

Darwinism,[33] and Jack London's *War of the Classes* and "What Communities Lose by the Competitive System." The latter (a pamphlet) further outlines London's views on the relevance of evolutionary theory to socialism:

> Man's primacy in the animal kingdom was made possible, first, by his manifestation of the gregarious instinct; and second, by becoming conscious of that instinct and the power within it which worked for his own good and permitted him to endure. Natural selection, undeviating, pitiless, careless of the individual, destroyed or allowed to perpetuate, as the case might be, such breeds as were unfittest or fittest to survive. In this sternest of struggles man . . . early learned the great lesson: that he stood . . . unaided in a mighty battle wherein all the natural forces and the myriad forms of organic life seethed in one vast, precarious turmoil. From this he drew the corollary, that his strength lay in numbers, in unity of interests, in solidarity of effort—in short, in combination against the hostile elements of his environment.[34]

It is not difficult to see, from this treatment of Darwin's concept of the value of cooperation by London, how the concept could be made to appeal to people in the trade union and labor movement (a powerful force in Australian politics at the turn of the century, Australians electing the world's first national Labor government in 1904). Another important writer who made effective use of Darwinian metaphors was the *Socialist*'s editor, Tom Mann. Mann's booklet "Socialism," for example, which was also available through the newspaper's office, has much Darwinian argument.[35] Mann was also in demand as a lecturer, and his topics—such as "Evolution in Nature, Industrialism and Politics," "Communism Amongst Animals," "Man's Place in Nature"[36]—attest to his interest in Darwinism and evolution. In 1908–1909, Mann acted as organizer for the miners' unions in a protracted dispute with the Broken Hill Proprietary company in the mining center of Broken Hill in far western New South Wales and also gave a number of lectures on evolution. In an address on "Human Progress—The Laws That Govern It," for example, which was given before a packed audience in the Broken Hill Town Hall after settlement of the dispute, Mann explained that "the law of mutual interdependence was just as true as the struggle for existence. . . . When after food wolves were prepared to hunt together and enjoy the food together. The same with mankind. Had man not been able to cooperate they would not have been able to attain what they had attained."[37] (The outcome of the strike was a qualified victory for the unions.)

Mann is important in any discussion on Social Darwinism in Australia in another respect as well. In this same lecture in Broken Hill, Mann explained that "Hindus, Europeans, Medes and Persians" were probably all descended from an original Asian stock (Darwin argues this in *Descent of Man*),[38] so that "this was the race from which we sprang. Australians came from the same race as the Hindus . . . and they [the audience] should remember that fact."[39] Mann was alluding to the racialist element that also lurked in the Australian Labor movement at the time (figure 16.1) and that had found occasional expression in crimes committed against Afghan camel drivers in Broken Hill. Indeed, a colleague of Mann, R. S. Ross, a former editor of the Broken Hill *Barrier Truth*, had once fired what historian Brian Kennedy has described as "a salvo of Darwinian rhetoric" at one Afghan's plea for tolerance: "*Truth* [i.e., *Barrier Truth*] is not opposed to colour because it is colour, but because to object to intermarriage with aliens is a Fundamental Instinct to protect the species; because it is socially, economically, racially ruinous to tolerate an alien people in a white community."[40] Such attitudes no doubt stemmed from xenophobic fears of wholesale immigration of cheap labor, such as in items like the following, from the *Australian Workman* in 1891: "The Hindoos are monopolizing potato digging in the Grafton [Northern New South Wales] district this year."

Mann, however, was consistently and strenuously opposed to such attitudes; he saw them as fundamentally in conflict with his socialist internationalism, with its "Workers of the World, Unite!" and "Bond of Brotherhood" idealism, which he believed he could support with a Darwinian argument as well (see below). Just how significant a place racialism had in the early Australian Labor movement remains unclear. The Labor historian Verity Burgmann considers it very significant;[41] Geoffrey Serle questions this;[42] but whatever the case, it was undeniably there. And Mann's efforts to oppose racialism took other forms as well as lectures: in 1905 during a visit to Charters Towers, Queensland, for example, Mann made a point of personally congratulating Bungie, a local Aborigine who had won one of the races at the May Day sports carnival being held at the time.[43]

Whatever the place of racialism in the Australian Labor movement, it was prominent enough under the Commonwealth's first national governments, the Barton and Deakin governments of 1901–1903, under which immigration restriction bills based on "White Australia" policies were enforced.[44] The British writer J. H. Curle, who visited Australia sometime before World War I, recorded his thoughts on this policy in these words:

16.1 "Up for Vagrancy: What May Soon Happen in
Queensland," (*The Worker*, 1899; reproduced
in the 100th Anniversary Issue, 1986).

Australia has set out on a great experiment. Her aborigines are dead, or dying out fast. The Chinese, who came out in the early mining days, are mostly gone away. The Kanakas, brought in to work the sugar fields of Queensland, have been sent back to the Islands, and this great continent is now solely the heritage of whites. Australians have determined it shall remain so.

. . . A fine ideal!—and yet not without alloy. Our natives of British India may not enter here. And amongst the races on whom exclusion falls are the Japanese. But the Japanese are a powerful people, and to avenge contumely of this sort are capable of blowing the Australian cities to bits.[45]

These prophetic words were written in 1921—twenty-one years before the Japanese bombing of Darwin, ironically named after the man from whom Social Darwinism liked to take its name. Ironically, too, it would appear that it was socialist interpretations of Darwinism that found widest appeal in Japan, as will be discussed shortly.

In Australia, then, a range of Social Darwinist ideas had gained currency by about 1910. But even in the Labor movement these ideas could vary from the internationalism of people like Tom Mann, based on the so-called brotherhood of the human species, to the racialism represented in, for example, some of the utterances of R. S. Ross. We should now look at some of the distinctive contributions to Social Darwinist thought made by Japanese thinkers during the period with which we are concerned.

Japan: Darwinism and Marxism

In a lecture in Broken Hill, Tom Mann mentioned his friendship with the Japanese socialist and trade union organizer Sen Katayama. Katayama had introduced himself following an address by Mann to a crowd of dockers in the East End of London in the early 1890s. "It is my intention to inaugurate trades unionism and the Socialist movement in my own country," Katayama (who spoke English) had said.[46] By 1908 these movements were well under way in Japan, notwithstanding continued harassment from the government (especially during socialists' opposition to the 1904–1905 Russo-Japanese war). "These Japs were waging the class war," Mann said, and were "asking their fellow-workers in Broken Hill to fraternize with them."[47]

In an interview in the *Japan Times* in April 1903, Katayama claimed that Japanese workers were "imbibing socialistic ideas" and that "whereas ten years ago socialistic doctrines awakened no sympathetic chord among our working men, the latter now form the most enthusiastic part of the audience at any lecture meeting where such doctrines are expounded."[48] Japanese workmen were also, according to Katayama, welcoming "with the utmost eagerness all printed matter containing socialistic writing."[49] There is good evidence that this interest involved Darwinian ideas. Eikoh Shimao, in an article on "Darwinism in Japan, 1877–1927," has argued that for roughly the first half of that period "people's interest in Darwinism consisted in its social and political implications rather than in a biological theory," since "[i]t was only in the 1910s that modern biology emerged in Japan."[50] Similarly, Jiro Kikkawa, professor of zoology at the University of Queensland, has assured me that Darwin's ideas had "no" impact on Japanese biology during this time but much influence on political and social thought and that Darwinism was "introduced through Marxism."[51]

It is true that Darwinism seems to have first been introduced into Japan by biologists, notably the Americans Edward Sylvester Morse (in a series of public lectures at the newly established Tokyo University in the 1870s) and John Thomas Gulick, a Christian missionary as well as evolutionary biologist (in a number of lectures in Kyoto and elsewhere from about 1883).[52] But these introductions seem to have been largely interpreted in a social sense. As Naohide Isono has recently pointed out, by the time Morse's lectures were translated into Japanese, under the title *Dobutsu shinkaron* (The theory of animal evolution) in 1885, Herbert Spencer's ideas were also beginning to "spread rapidly" in Japan, and Spencer's publications were utilized "not only by conservatives but also by liberals, for his ideas were so broad that they could be interpreted in various ways."[53] Naohide argues that it is "highly likely" that Morse's lectures, especially in their translated form, were "rather intentionally utilized for the authorization of the latter" (i.e., these various interpretations of Spencer).[54] In Gulick's case, there seems little doubt that the social "implications" of Darwinism would have intruded and that this would have been from a socialistic perspective: Gulick was a Christian Socialist who later turned increasingly toward Marxist ideas. Examples of his later publications include "The General Laws of Evolution as Seen in Social Evolution" in the *International Socialist Review,* and "Socialism in a Nutshell" in the Honolulu *Friend.*[55]

Whatever the case, one certainly finds plenty of reference to Darwinism and evolution in the pages of the *Japan Times* from about the time of Katayama's remarks, and virtually all of this is in sociopolitical contexts. For example, a leader on "Socialism in Japan" in the

Japan Times of 8 April 1903 criticized the "vigorous manner" in which the police had recently broken up a "gigantic labour meeting" organized by the *Niroku shimpo* (a newspaper sympathetic to the labor cause). While the votaries of socialism "appear to be increasing in number and importance," the leader continued, this was to be welcomed, since

> happily or unhappily, according to the way in which the matter is looked at, the struggle for existence here has none of that sharp and unfeeling intensity which is calculated to engender in the breasts of its unfortunate victims in the West a deep and sullen hostility to the present order of things. Society here has, for centuries, been constructed on principles fundamentally different from those obtaining in the West. Our society is more communistic in its character than theirs.

It is interesting to compare these remarks with those quoted from a Professor Kenzo Wadagaki of Tokyo University in Sen Katayama's 1918 book *The Labor Movement in Japan:* "Japan as a nation is socialistic. The Japanese are of socialistic character."[56]

In a similar vein, an article in the *Japan Times* headed "Progress or Degeneration" in February 1909 argued that the "great problem of the future" will be whether Western civilization can find a place for "the humanitarian basis of socialism."[57] The West could learn from Japan, it is suggested, whose dramatic defeat of Russia had been "inspired by a wonderful patriotism with the solidarity of the nation behind her."[58] This article goes on to cite Benjamin Kidd's 1898 volume *Social Evolution,* in which, it is argued, Kidd "points to social instinct and feeling and its realisation as to the one element in which western civilization maintains itself as superior to preceding civilizations." The *Japan Times* article concludes: "May it not be that progress *means* the growth of social instinct, the realization of human solidarity?"[59]

Be all this as it may, there seems reason to believe that such ideas were beginning to find a fairly wide audience in Japan. While no doubt there were few worker-intellectuals like Katayama (of peasant parentage, he had worked his way through college in the United States), English had been part of the elementary school curriculum since the 1890s, and by 1910 former prime minister Shigenobu Okuma was claiming that "[t]he effect of the acquisition of the English tongue on the mental habits ... of our people is incalculable."[60] Among English authors mentioned by Okuma as those whom "many Japanese minds have come under the spell of" were Spencer, Huxley, and the author of the famous materialistic Belfast Address,

John Tyndall.[61] Lists of books available from booksellers in the *Japan Times* may also attest to an interest in Darwinian ideas among English-reading Japanese. In any event, such works are prominent. A list offered by Maruya and Company of Yokohama in April 1903, for instance, includes Darwin's *Origin of Species, Descent of Man,* and *Naturalists' Voyage Around the World* and Francis Darwin's *Life and Letters* of his father.[62] In March 1907 the same bookseller was offering Malthus' *Principles of Population;* Haeckel's *Evolution of Man, History of Creation,* and *Last Words on Evolution;* as well as A. R. Wallace's *Malay Archipelago, Contributions to the Theory of Natural Selection, Tropical Nature, Island Life,* and *Darwinism.*[63] Lists in February 1909 include R. H. Lock's *Variation, Heredity, and Evolution* and the complete set (twenty-nine volumes) of Walter Scott's Contemporary Science Series, nearly half of which (thirteen) are works on evolution and related subjects.[64]

The greatest number of titles from Wallace may be not insignificant. Darwin could hardly be described as a socialist—he once wrote to Baron Von Schezer in Germany: "What a foolish idea seems to prevail in Germany on the connection between socialism and evolution through natural selection"[65]—but Wallace certainly can, having been drawn to this social philosophy ever since hearing Robert Owen's ideas expounded in a London "Hall of Science" in his younger days.[66] He became president of the British Land Nationalization Society and on at least two occasions wrote chapters in books on socialism whose contributors included Tom Mann.[67] In fact, it is quite possible that Wallace's "incipient socialism" had some influence on his friend Darwin's theory of the selective value of cooperation in *Descent of Man.*[68] Such ideas, in any case, are adumbrated in Wallace's earlier book, *Contributions to the Theory of Natural Selection,* which is in the above list:

> In proportion as ... physical characteristics become of less importance, mental and moral qualities will have increasing influence on the well being of the race. Capacity for acting in concert for protection, and for the acquisition of food and shelter; sympathy, which leads all in turn to assist each other ... are all qualities, that from their earliest appearance must have been for the benefit of each community, and would, therefore, have become the subjects of "natural selection."[69]

To whatever extent such books were being read, that they were so substantially from a sociopolitical perspective would seem to be reinforced by the titles of other books in English being made available at the same time. These included, for example, W. E. Blackman's *The*

Making of Hawaii: A Study of Social Evolution, J. H. Hollander's *American Trade Unionism,* V. S. Clark's *The Labour Movement in Australia,* R. Hunter's *Socialists at Work,* J. A. Hobson's *Evolution of Modern Capitalism,* S. Patten's *Heredity and Social Progress,* and Major Leonard Darwin's *Municipal Trade.*[70]

But quite apart from the availability of such books in English, there is convincing evidence for the association of Darwinism and socialistic ideas in Japan in terms of the books in this general area being translated into Japanese. Notable instances would be the translation of Darwin's *Origin of Species* (in 1914) and Kropotkin's *Mutual Aid: A Factor of Evolution* (1917) by Sakae Osugi, a socialist intellectual and early member of the Yuaikai (Friendly Society), an organization founded in 1912 with the original object of mediating in labor disputes but which became increasingly radical with time.[71] Osugi himself (who was eventually—in 1923—beaten to death by the police) was strongly imbued with anarcho-syndicalist ideas and with "theories of evolution which suggested that society, like the natural world, changed constantly."[72] The title of Kropotkin's book—which really only extends on Darwin's ideas in *Descent of Man* (which Kropotkin fully acknowledges)[73]—should indicate its content; but perhaps some lines from it will serve to further underscore this Darwinian element in Japanese socialist thought:

> As soon as we study animals—not in laboratories and museums only, but in the forest and prairies, in the steppe and the mountains—we at once perceive that though there is an immense amount of warfare and extermination going on amidst various species—there is, at the same time, as much, or perhaps even more, of mutual support, mutual aid, and mutual defence amidst animals belonging to the same species or, at least, to the same society. Sociability is as much a law of nature as mutual struggle.[74]

And Kropotkin was equally certain that this law applied to human society: "Therefore combine—practise mutual aid! That is the surest means for giving to each and to all the greatest safety, the best guarantee of existence and progress, bodily, intellectual, and moral. That is what nature teaches us . . . and that is why man has reached the position upon which we stand now."[75]

Other early socialists in Japan who, according to Eikoh Shimao, "took a deep interest in Darwinism," were the journalists Shusui Kotoku and Toshiaki Sakai.[76] Kotoku and Sakai had been closely associated with Katayama since the founding by the latter of the Shakai shugi kyokai (Socialist Association) in 1901, and the subjects of lectures by each—such as "Socialist Ethics" by Kotoku (which more than likely drew on Darwin's concept of the "moral sense" as elaborated in publications like Kropotkin's pamphlet "Anarchist Morality")[77] and "The Origin of Society" by Sakai—attest to this interest.[78] Another of Katayama's associates, a certain Reverend Garst, was an enthusiast for Henry George's ideas and published a pamphlet on these ideas in Japanese.[79] Among other works mentioned by Katayama in *The Labor Movement in Japan* as having been translated into Japanese by the Shakai shugi kyokai was Emile Vandervelde's *Collectivism and Industrial Evolution*. This work argues that "socialism is nothing else than the ideal projection as well as the organic culmination of present tendencies"; that the socialist state will be a "powerful organism of co-operation"; and that

> more and more in proportion to the extension of the collective domain, the necessity will increase for a differentiation of the economic and the political functions—a differentiation as complete as that which exists in the individual organism between nutrition, digestion and circulation on the one side and the functions of the nervous system, of life in its larger relations, on the other side.[80]

As mentioned earlier, Eucken's *Main Currents of Modern Thought* was also translated into Japanese during this period; so, too, were Bergson's *Creative Evolution* (Osugi was also much impressed by this author)[81] and G. B. Shaw's evolutionary *Man and Superman*. According to the *Japan Times*, translations of works on "Syndicalism" also "caught the attention of the public."[82]

One "ardent admirer of Kropotkin's ideas" at this time was Ichizo Yamamoto, a twenty-three-year-old student who committed suicide in November 1913 after having been hounded by the police for his socialist and antiwar views.[83] This episode, as well as Osugi's death, cautions us from thinking that socialist views had become orthodox in Japan by this time, which we might be led to infer from the enthusiastic accounts of Katayama. Notwithstanding remarkable gains in earlier years, beginning with Katayama's organization of the first trade union in Japan—the Japan Iron Workers' Union, in 1897—government suppression, particularly following socialist opposition to the Russo-Japanese War, was beginning to have an effect.[84] And while Marxist doctrines continued to find a considerable hearing in Japan,[85] they tended to be oriented toward a nationalistic, rather than an internationalist, framework of thinking. This nationalism came through strongly, moreover, in other versions of Social Darwinism, which also found a hearing in Japan. Thus an item in the *Japan Times* in November 1913 headed "Race Suicide in Japan!" expresses concern that "many women resort to artificial means to disqualify themselves as good mothers" (that is, practice contraception).[86] Similar ideas were of course current in other parts of the world around this time also. The novelist H. Rider Haggard, for instance, is quoted in the *Japan Times* as having drawn the attention of a British National Birthrate Commission to the "dangers of artificially keeping down births, which is now a widespread practice in every western nation." Haggard is reported to have gone on to say that "unless a startling change happened to the western races within the next two centuries they would be submerged beneath the teeming myriads of the East."[87] In Australia, Octavius Beale, a Victorian piano manufacturer and close friend of Prime Minister Alfred Deakin, is said to have convinced the latter that "new-fangled birth control devices were ruining prospects of the British-Australian race."[88]

Yet internationalist views found a sympathetic hearing in Japan, too, and these were sometimes also expressed in Darwinian terms. Thus, in a letter in response to an editorial headed "Struggle for Existence" in the *Japan Times* of 22 November 1912 in which it was contended that "it is wrong . . . to take for granted that national armament is a product of human perfidy, avarice, and brutality" and that "armament is but a scheme to hold out in the struggle for existence, and is that which maintains peace," the correspondent ("Asio") wrote:

> If the struggle for existence is, as we suppose, to secure the survival of the fittest, it is our duty to struggle to overcome those difficulties such as hunger, pestilence *and war* [emphasis in original] which obstruct our path. . . . If you persist that fratricide (all men are brothers) is a necessary part of the scheme of life then I will give you the names of three who were very famous exponents of the art of destroying their own species, and I will set up against them three other names and ask your readers to decide which three they consider have done most for the welfare of the human race.[89]

"Asio" then went on to list Attila, Genghiz Khan, and Napoleon on the one hand, and Jenner, Lister, and Kitisato (the Japanese bacteriologist and one of the founders of immunology) on the other.

The following month, at a well-attended meeting of the Japan Peace Society held at the Kanda YMCA, a Dr. Nitobe argued that "war deprives a nation of its strong and stalwart men and only weak people are left behind to transmit their blood to posterity. This means the destruction of the law of natural selection and the consequence is the retrogression of the nation both in mind and body."[90]

Here we have an interesting association, expressed in Darwinian language, of nationalist views (the welfare of Japan's "blood" seems to be the issue) with peace initiatives aiming at the avoidance of international conflict. This argument was also being used by another prominent peace campaigner of the time, the American biologist and president of Stanford University David Starr Jordan. In his 1907 book *The Human Harvest,* Jordan had similarly argued that "the survival of the fittest in the struggle for existence is the primal cause of race progress and race-changes. But in the red field of human history the natural process of selection is often reversed. The survival of the unfittest is the primal cause of the downfall of nations."[91] This argument appears to have first been proposed as early as 1872, by the Christian Socialist and naturalist friend of T. H. Huxley, the Reverend Charles Kingsley, in a lecture at the Birmingham and Midland (Mechanics') Institute in England, where the young Tom Mann was an evening student at the time. Kingsley had said:

> War is, without doubt, the most hideous physical curse which fallen man inflicts upon himself; and for this simple reason, that it reverses the very laws of nature, and is more cruel even than pestilence. For instead of issuing in the survival of the fittest, it issues in the survival of the less fit: and therefore, if protracted, must deteriorate generations yet unborn.[92]

Whatever the origins of these ideas, there is no doubt that a strong antiwar movement—very much centered on the concept, as described by Tom Mann in the Melbourne *Socialist,* of a "world-wide Brotherhood and Sisterhood" of the human family[93]—had begun to emerge before World War I and that this movement was finding expression in Australia and Japan. But in some ways the movement was to find its most effective expression in the Pan-Pacific movement in Hawaii, to which country we now turn.

Hawaii: "Hands-around-the-Pacific"

The first Pan-Pacific Science Conference in Hawaii in 1920 was a direct outcome of the Pan-Pacific movement, itself largely the brainchild of an American journalist, Alexander Hume Ford (1868–1945), who visited Hawaii briefly in 1899 and settled there in 1907.[94] But another key figure in the negotiations leading up to the congress (listed also as a vice-president of Ford's Hands-around-the-Pacific Club in 1912)[95] was David Starr Jordan. Jordan had had a long-standing interest not only in internationalism, but also in Hawaii, having made a study of the fish of the Hawaiian archipelago in 1901–1902, which resulted in his 1905 book *The Shore Fishes of Hawaii.*[96]

Another most effective publicist for the Pan-Pacific idea was Jack London, who was a close friend of both Jordan (whom he had first met in Oakland, California, in the 1890s, following a university extension lecture on evolution given by Jordan)[97] and Ford. In 1907, while on a visit to Hawaii during what was intended to be a round-the-world voyage on his yacht, the *Snark*, London gave a series of lectures on socialism, and these attracted Ford's attention. Their first discussion of the Pan-Pacific concept shortly afterward is described by London's wife, Charmian:

> Under the algarobas at Pearl Harbour, in 1907, one day he [London] and Mr. Ford were discussing socialism—upon Ford's initiative. "Well," the latter concluded, "I can't 'see' your socialism. *My* idea is, to find out what people want, help them to it, then make them do what you wish them to do; and if it is right, they *will* do it—if you keep right after them! . . . Now, I'm soon leaving for Australia and around the Pacific at my own expense, to see if there is a way to get the people to work together for one another and for the Pacific."
>
> "That's socialism—look out!" [London replied]. "I don't care if it is," retorted his friend, "that won't stop me. Walter Frear has just been appointed Governor of Hawaii, and I've interested him, and carry an official letter with me. Hawaii, with her mixture of Pacific races, yet with no race problems, should be the country to take the lead. I'm going to call a Pan-Pacific Convention here."
>
> "Go to it, Ford, and I'll help all I can," [London] approved.[98]

The immediate outcome was a lecture by London at the University Club the following week. By 1918, according to Mrs. London, "The Pan Pacific Club grows apace, with headquarters at the University Club in Honolulu, in the room where Jack first fulfilled his pledge to speak on the subject."[99] Ford himself acknowledges his debt to London in his *Mid-Pacific Magazine* that year: "[T]his movement was born during Jack London's first stay in Hawaii, and with Jack London and Joseph Platt Cooke [a Honolulu financier], the Pan Pacific Union is closely identified."[100] Earlier, in 1915, London was again in Hawaii for an extended stay, and according to Ford,

> In Hawaii Jack London has been preaching the doctrine of a Patriotism of the Pacific, and now some three hundred people of every race and creed known to Pacific lands gather together [at the Pan-Pacific Club] to demonstrate to the legislators of the American Republic that the people of every race and creed of the Pacific can and do get together and work together for the good of one and all.[101]

Before discussing the question of how London was able to argue for this "Patriotism of the Pacific" from a Darwinian point of view, it should be noted that Ford's description of Hawaii as a country "with no race problems" is more an expression of Ford's idealism than of reality. In 1887, twenty years before Ford's arrival, the then hereditary ruler of the islands, King Kalakaua, who was described as having "strong English predilections,"[102] was humiliatingly forced by U.S. property interests to dismiss his ministry and agree to a new constitution greatly limiting his powers. There was also pressure from the U.S. government on the king to surrender Pearl Harbor for the use of the U.S. Navy. However, Kalakaua was said to have been "averse" to this cession since he believed it would be "looked upon by many persons as the first step towards the annexation of the islands to the United States."[103] Kalakaua was of course perfectly correct—the islands were annexed eleven years later. In the meantime, in 1893, a "revolution" ousted Hawaii's last monarch, Queen Liliuokalani, and replaced her with what one contemporary newspaper described as "a grotesque Government having at its head a Californian sugar broker, and for its executive a crowd of American speculators."[104]

The newspaper report from which this comment is taken also revealed a Social Darwinist perspective. Thus, the report concludes: "Then, the spectacle is a sorry one for Christian morality, and a bitter lesson to feeble races of what they have to expect when the interests of civilized Powers come into collision."[105] Charmian London, too, seems to have been unable to avoid this kind of language when she described Queen Liliuokalani's overthrow in *Our Hawaii:* "As far as I can figure it, she was tricked and trapped by brains for which her brain, remarkable though it be, was no match. . . . There is no gainsaying that truism, 'the survival of the fittest' in the far drift of the human, and the white indubitably has proved the fittest; but our hearts are all for this poor old Queen-woman."[106]

By the time of Mrs. London's writing (1917), the original Hawaiian race was fast disappearing. Darwin had noted, in *Descent of Man,* that between Captain Cook's visit to the islands in 1778 and a census in 1872, the native population had decreased from some 300,000 to 51,531. Darwin had attributed this primarily to the destructive effects of European contact (for example, declining fertility associated with the spread of venereal disease).[107] By 1898 the native Hawaiian population had fallen to 30,975, and by 1910, to 26,041;[108] and as the American sociologist J. K. Goodrich remarked, "If Nature is still promoting the survival of the fittest . . . it seems an awkward commentary upon the advancing and all-conquering Caucasian race that its vices are largely responsible for the disappearance of the Malayo-Polynesian race, to which group the Hawaiians belong."[109]

Thoughtful Hawaiians were acutely aware of this decline in their numbers. A Mr. James Keola for instance, who is described in the *Honolulu Star-Bulletin* in February 1918 as a "prominent Hawaiian of Maui,"[110] suggested that much of the problem could be attributed to the lack of a sense of racial identity among his people. In a plea for "race regeneration," Keola contended that "the great majority of the youths of today of both sexes pride themselves on the fact that they know a 'little English' and less Hawaiian and nothing else" and that "the pidgin English that is being spoken by them in their homes and on the highways would make one of Darwin's monkeys blush for very shame."[111] Other commentators, however, saw matters differently. An American writer a decade previously, for example, who was urging that "for the protection and progress of Americanism Hawaii needs Americans," believed that while "[r]acially [the Hawaiian] will become obsolete," this loss was not to be bewailed since "[s]o have almost all races of men." In any case, this writer argued, the Hawaiian, in losing racial identity, "greatly enriches the cosmopolitan man now in the evolutionary alembic."[112]

But probably the most significant factor making for racial tension in Hawaii was the presence of large numbers of Japanese. From 1886, when permission was granted by the Japanese government, thousands of Japanese emigrated to Hawaii to work on the sugar plantations, for which they were recruited under a contract system. By 1910, of Hawaii's total population of 191,909, Japanese numbered 79,674 and were the largest single ethnic group, notwithstanding many having left (more than 10,000 in 1905 alone) for the American mainland.[113]

Appalling working conditions on the plantations were not only to lead to a number of widespread strikes but also to violent confrontations between the Japanese labor unions and the Hawaiian Sugar Planters' Association. Racist rhetoric, which carried Darwinian overtones, frequently accompanied this confrontation. At Lahaina, Maui, in 1905, when seventeen hundred Japanese demonstrated against labor conditions on the Pioneer Sugar Company's plantation, the planters' association enlisted the police, who broke up the demonstration, killing one Japanese laborer and injuring several others.[114] The following year, after another strike, on Oahu, the planters' newspaper, the *Pacific Commercial Advertiser*, advised maintaining a labor surplus, playing race against race: "To discharge every Jap and put on newly-imported laborers of another race would be a most impressive object lesson to the little brown men on all the planta-

tions. . . . It would subdue their dangerous faith in their own indis-
pensability."[115] In 1909 a major month-long strike broke out on
several large Oahu sugar plantations in protest over the fact the Caucasians earned a third more than Asian field hands for the same
work; and in 1919–1920 a bitter and at times violent five-month
strike was fought on the islands of Oahu, Maui, Hawaii, and Kauai
over various demands, including the right to receive overtime pay on
Sundays and legal public holidays. Again the planters took a racist
stance: "What we face now is an attempt on the part of an alien
race to cripple our principal industry and to gain dominance of the
American territory of Hawaii," the *Pacific Commercial Advertiser*
warned,[116] to which the *Honolulu Star-Bulletin* added that Hawaii
must remain "in the hands of Anglo-Saxons whose brains and means
have made the Territory what it is."[117]

That such sentiments were finding a hearing among Hawaii's leading circle is suggested by other items in Hawaiian newspapers. Thus,
the *Honolulu Star-Bulletin* of 27 October 1919, under the heading
"Bishop's Sermon Sounds Warning of Yellow Peril," reported an
address by the Episcopal bishop of Honolulu, the Reverend Henry
Restarick: "if the English speaking race is to maintain its position in
the world it must do it by toil." The bishop went on: "untold millions
of men in the Orient are gaining knowledge every day as to modern
business methods and will eventually capture trade if men in English
speaking lands insist on working five days a week and six hours a
day." In Ford's own *Mid-Pacific Magazine* an article entitled "The
Pan-Pacific Racial Problem," by George Bronson Rea, warned that
the "races of Asia are now multiplying twice as rapidly as the white
races" and that "the future looms dark for western civilization"
unless "plagues and pestilence, floods and famines and other visita-
tions of a merciful Nature [*sic*] which in the past have placed a check
on the increase" can be relied upon to have their effect.[118] (In a note at
the beginning of the article Ford explained that "the *Mid-Pacific
Magazine* sets before its readers these . . . assertions made by Mr. Rea,
and invites helpful and constructive criticism."[119])

There are also numerous more trivial hints in passing allusions in
newspapers of a "survival of the fittest" Social Darwinist mentality
pervading Hawaiian society at this time. The *Honolulu Star-Bulletin* of
12 February 1918, for example, has the following intriguing piece of
intelligence: "The people of Honolulu will recall with pleasure the
Eugenic Marriage that took place in Honolulu some years ago.
Rumour has it that there will soon be another marriage of this kind."
Even advertisements are suggestive: an advertisement for Doan's Back-

ache Kidney Pills in January 1918 assures readers of the *Star-Bulletin* that this product will help them "Keep Fit for the Daily Struggle."[120] In 1917–1918 the United States was, of course, at war with Germany, and Social Darwinist notions were a conspicuous feature of the rampant propaganda associated with this venture also—as encapsulated in the cartoon (figure 16.2) featured in the *Star-Bulletin* of 7 January 1918. The belief that the war was an expression of the inevitable struggle for existence between races and nations (with the reassurance in this case that Germans, being lower in the evolutionary scale, were bound to be defeated) was well summed up by David Starr Jordan (who, as might be expected, totally repudiated the view) in his book *Democracy and World Relations,* published the same year: "Social Darwinism applies the law of survival to races and nations, and makes it a national duty to assist evolution by war and conquest.... According to [this doctrine], if a nation succeeds in the vigorous and ruthless struggle for existence, its might has thereby become right."[121]

But Ford did have some basis for believing that Hawaii could be the center of a Pan-Pacific movement that would overcome racial barriers. Early-twentieth-century internationalist philosophies, often linked to socialist views, had their sympathizers in Hawaii too. Among them were the lawyer (and apiculturist and botanist) L. L. Burr, who was interviewed by the *Honolulu Star-Bulletin* in February 1918 after being nominated by President Woodrow Wilson as judge of the Maui circuit court. Burr, who before qualifying in law had worked in construction and had "received ... his education ... in public libraries in various cities throughout the United States,"[122] was reported to have said that "the socialists have in the past, and are today [*sic*] advocating a number of good things" and "even the Syndicalists, as exemplified by the I.W.W.s on the Pacific Coast, are not without some good features, for as Herbert Spencer says, 'there must be some truth in things erroneous, otherwise there would be nothing to commend them to the minds of men.' "[123]

J. T. Gulick has already been mentioned in connection with Japan. Gulick, born to missionary parents on Kauai in 1832, returned to Hawaii in 1906, settling in Honolulu, where he remained till his death in 1923. An article on Gulick in the *Mid-Pacific Magazine* in January 1912 describes him as the "foremost scientist of the Pacific;"[124] and indeed, his study of Hawaiian land shells, which had led to a highly original theory of the importance of reproductive isolation in evolution, had been described by A. R. Wallace in *Island Life* as being of "especial interest."[125] And like Wallace, Gulick was a socialist as well as evolutionist; in fact, if one is to go by the views

DRAWN BY C. R. MACAULEY

16.2 "The Nemesis of the Beast"
(*Honolulu Star-Bulletin,* 7 January 1918).

expressed in his article "Socialism in a Nutshell" in the Honolulu
Friend in May 1916, he could probably more accurately be described
as a syndicalist:

> A cure must be found, for each country now fights for new markets and
> colonies over the sea where their goods may be sold. . . . Their factories
> close, having more than their people can buy. . . . If tools are producing
> so much that the laborers starve, let the laborers rise and combine for the
> owning of tools, and the owning of all that the tools they now use may
> produce.[126]

One could also mention, in connection with socialist and internationalist interpretations of Darwinism in Hawaii, the physician and poet Dr. Edward S. Goodhue. Goodhue, a friend of Jack and Charmian London, was applauded in Ford's magazine for his "universality full of . . . the brotherhood of his race."[127] In 1913 he reviewed London's autobiographical and socialistic novel *Martin Eden* (which London had apparently largely written when staying with Goodhue at Kona, on the Big Island, in 1907) in the *Mid-Pacific Magazine,* praising the book highly and drawing readers' attention to some of London's other volumes, including *The Iron Heel* and *The House of Pride and Other Tales of Hawaii.*[128] The latter (which is among a list of the "100 Most Important Books on Hawaii" published in the *Honolulu Star-Bulletin,* along with Gulick's *Evolution, Racial and Habitudinal*[129]) contains an autobiographical chapter by London in which he explains that "the writers who have influenced me most are Karl Marx in a particular, and Spencer in a general, way."[130] In *The Iron Heel* London again, as in "What Communities Lose by the Competitive System" and *Before Adam,* spells out his theory (derived from Darwin) of the value of cooperation and the "Union Is Strength" principle in human evolution: Socialism, in the words of the novel's hero, Ernest Everhard,

> is the fiat of evolution. It is the word of God. Combination is stronger than competition. Primitive man was a puny creature hiding in the crevices of the rocks. He combined and made war upon his carnivorous enemies. They were competitive beasts. Primitive man was a combinative beast, and because of it he rose to primacy over all the animals.[131]

But the question remains, how was London able to argue for his and Ford's "Patriotism of the Pacific"—that is, their internationalism—from a Darwinian point of view? The clue, I think, can be found in some further lines in *Descent of Man,* following Darwin's discussion of his concept of the role of "sympathy" and "affection" in human social evolution (with its provision for a large place for the human intellect):

> As man advances in civilization, and small tribes are united into larger communities, the simplest reason would tell each individual that he ought to extend his social instincts and sympathies to all the members of the same nation, though personally unknown to him. This point being reached, there is only an artificial barrier to prevent his sympathies extending to the men of all nations and races.[132]

That this idea lay behind London's universalism (and there is good evidence that he read Darwin's volume: in 1899 he wrote to his friend, the journalist Cloudsley Johns, "Why, take the enormous power for human good contained in Darwin's *Origin of Species* and *Descent of Man*"[133]) seems clear enough from another of his prehistoric tales, "The Strength of the Strong," a short story written in Tasmania in January 1909 at the end of the *Snark* voyage. (The round-the-world cruise had to be abandoned in Australia because of London's poor health). In this story, an allegory of unionism and socialism first published in *Hampton's Magazine* in 1910 and later reprinted as a socialist pamphlet, Hair Face, a member of the tribe of Fish Eaters, tries to teach the young men the value of unity and cooperation by telling them about a time when the tribe consisted of families hostile to each other, each fending for itself. They learned the value of cooperation when a unified tribe, the Meat Eaters, of whom it was said "each . . . had the strength of ten for the ten had fought as one man," attacked them. The war continued, but Hair Face is trying to get the young men to see that their real enemies were not the Meat Eaters but their own rulers, who were perpetuating the war for their own ends, and that they should overthrow the latter and make common cause with the Meat Eaters:

> Before, we lived in trees my brothers, and no man was safe. But we fight no more with one another. Then let us fight no more with the Meat-Eaters.
> Let us add our strength and their strength together, the Fish-Eaters and the Meat-Eaters. . . . In that day we will be so strong that all the wild animals will flee before us. . . . [N]othing will withstand us, for the strength of each man will be the strength of all men in the world.[134]

It is perhaps worth noting that during his time in Australia (November 1908–April 1909) London corresponded frequently with Tom Mann, who was in Broken Hill (London wrote an article supporting Mann's union activities there in the Sydney *Star*);[136] and Mann used similar arguments. During the visit to Australia of the U.S. Great White Fleet in August 1908, for instance, Mann had written the following lines in *The Socialist*: "Time was when a tribesman would hate and fight the members of every tribe but his own. The ignorant villager would speak contemptuously of those belonging to other villages. . . . But a better knowledge tells us the residents of one village are the same of those of other countries."[136] In any event, that London's "Patriotism of the Pacific" incorporated this kind of thinking is evident enough in his remarks in Ford's *Mid-Pacific Magazine* in June 1915: members of the Hands-around-the-Pacific Club were,

London said, "learning to understand the language of each others' tribes."[137]

And for a time, anyway—especially in the period of optimism surrounding the Treaty of Versailles and the launching of the League of Nations—these ideas were reaching a wider audience. Certainly London's books were being read (there is a full-page article on him in the *Honolulu Star-Bulletin* of 29 November 1919 and interviews with Charmian London, on the occasion of the third anniversary of his death), whether through purchase or through the library. Among other authors whose works were announced in the *Honolulu Star-Bulletin* as available in the library of Hawaii (and presumably considered of interest to readers) were Rudolph Eucken, Karl Liebknecht (*Militarism*), G. B. Shaw, and H. G. Wells.[138] In November 1919 Wells' *The Undying Fire* is included in a list of "best sellers" in a discussion of the Christmas book trade in the *Honolulu Star-Bulletin*.[139] Wells presents arguments similar to London's, speaking of the "elaborate futility and horror into which partial ideas about life, combative and competitive ideas of life, thrust mankind" and making a plea for the idea of "a single human community" based on the "blood brotherhood [of] all men."[140] Wells observed, *pace* Pearson and others, that "there is a kind of crazy belief that killing, however cruel, has a kind of justification in the survival of the killer; we make that our excuse, for instance, for the destruction of the native Tasmanians who were shot whenever they were seen, and killed by poisoned meat left in their paths."[141] Wells also spoke of a time when "men" might become "alive to the facts of their common origin."[142] Certainly a general fascination with evolution seems to have been as conspicuous in Hawaii at this time as elsewhere. At another level, this may have even extended to a feeling of relatedness to the other creatures. When the movie *Tarzan of the Apes* was showing at the Honolulu Bijou Theatre in January 1919, the *Star-Bulletin* noted its great popularity and enthusiastically spoke of the "rare combination" of educational and absorbing entertainment the film offered, "showing the relationships and closeness of the human family to the vertebrate animals of primeval days."[143] Social Darwinism, from being the last refuge of scoundrels in racialist nationalism, had, for some people at least, evolved into a universal kinship.

Afterword

By December 1919 A. H. Ford was claiming that the "Pan-Pacific Idea [Was] Said to Be Gripping [the] Imagination of People of All Nations": "Dr. H. E. Gregory is already lining up the biggest sci-

entists of the Pacific for the Honolulu conference in July," Ford
explained in an article in the *Star-Bulletin,* and "Dr. Hovey... of the
museum of natural history in New York tells me he is coming to that
conference and will bring some wonderful slides and films. He sees
wonderful possibilities for a series of Pan-Pacific scientific congresses
held in Honolulu where men of his class may meet conveniently and
compare notes."[144] This first science congress did of course meet, and
it continues to do so, very successfully. So in a real sense the Pacific
Science Association is a concrete and enduring outcome of Ford's
vision of a meeting together of many peoples for the exchange of
ideas. But it is not all that Ford had in mind; indeed, Ford seems to
have had only a limited interest in science.[145] A consideration of some
of the various forms of Social Darwinism that existed around the
Pacific, each with its scientific advocates, serves to remind us of the
inevitable cultural and ideological dimensions of scientific theories.
But just as Ford's vision was able to incorporate the Mertonian scientific ideal of universality, yet could apparently extend beyond this
to any meetings making for "mutual inter-racial understanding and
co-operation,"[146] so may not decision makers, even today, learn
something from this broader perspective?

Notes

Among the many who generously assisted me in my research for this chapter,
I should make special mention of Roy MacLeod, Ian Inkster, Morris Low,
and Jiro Kikkawa, who initially gave me useful leads; Margaret Campbell,
Roger Morris, Chris Illert, Pam Falkenburg, Laurie Neill, David Burch, and
Ian Lowe, with whom I have had helpful discussions; and Russ Kingman, Jim
Thompson, and Masao Watanabe, who sent me helpful information. I am
also grateful to the staff of the libraries of Griffith University, the University
of Queensland, Bond University, and the University of New South Wales as
well as the New South Wales, Queensland, and Hawaii State Libraries, the
Mitchell Library, and the library of the Queensland Museum. I also wish to
express my thanks to my brother, Robert Laurent, for sending me the cartoon
from the centenary edition of the Queensland *Worker,* and to Jim Leary for
the item from *Barrier Truth.*

1   *Japan Times,* 1 January 1914.

2   Rudolph Eucken, *Main Currents of Modern Thought* (London:
       T. Fisher Unwin, 1912), 255–256, 263.

3   Ibid., 263.

4   For a good general discussion on Social Darwinism see Greta Jones,
       Social Darwinism and English Thought (Brighton: Harvester, 1980).

5   For an informative history of the Secularist movement see Edward

Royle, *Radicals, Secularists, and Republicans: Popular Free-thought in Britain, 1866–1915* (Manchester: Manchester University Press, 1980).

6   Undated (1884) and unnamed newspaper cutting pasted in the back of a copy of Edward Aveling's *Student's Darwin* (London: Freethought, 1881) in the Biosciences Library, University of Queensland.

7   Ibid.

8   Quoted in Science as Ideology Group of the British Society for Social Responsibility in Science, "The New Synthesis Is an Old Story," *New Scientist,* 13 May 1976, 346–348, quoted at 348.

9   Karl Pearson, *The Positive Creed of Freethought with Some Remarks on the Relation of Freethought to Socialism* (London: William Reeves, 1888), 10–11, 14.

10   *Leader* (Melbourne), 1 October 1921.

11   *Post* (Cairns), 27 May 1914.

12   Undated (1916?) and unnamed newspaper cutting in volume of same in Queensland Museum Library, 73.

13   Interview in *Talking History* program, January 1991 (Australian Broadcasting Commission Radio Tapes).

14   *Argus* (Melbourne), 19 August 1911.

15   Eucken, *Modern Thought,* 342–343.

16   I Corinthians 12:12–13.

17   Quoted in Robert J. Richards, *Darwin and the Emergence of Evolutionary Theories of Mind and Behavior* (Chicago: University of Chicago Press, 1987), 266.

18   In *First Principles* (London: Williams and Norgate, 1870), Spencer wrote: "[T]he evolution which, beginning with a tribe whose members severally perform the same actions, each for himself, *ends* [my emphasis] with a civilized community whose members severally perform different actions" (345–346).

19   Henry George, *Progress and Poverty* (London: Kegan Paul, Trench and Co., 1884), 363–364.

20   William Morris Hughes, "The Limits of State Interference," in *Report of the Eleventh Meeting of the Australasian Association for the Advancement of Science* (Adelaide, 1908), 622–632, quotation at 624.

21   Ibid., 627.

22   Charles Darwin, *The Descent of Man and Selection in Relation to Sex* 2d ed. (London: John Murray, 1874 [1871]), 97.

23   Ibid.

24   Gilbert White, *The Natural History of Selborne* (London: J. M. Dent and Sons, 1912), letter 24.

25   Darwin, *Descent,* 101.

26   Ibid., 107.

27   Ibid., 109.

28   Karl Marx, *A Contribution to the Critique of Political Economy* (Moscow: Progress Publishers, 1977), 189.

29   *Advertiser* (Adelaide), 29 July, 3 August, 7 September 1907.

30   Ibid., 3 August 1907.

31   Jack London, *Before Adam,* in *Jack London, Series II,* ed. C. Booss and P. J. Horowitz (New York: Avenel, 1982), 312. While London's idea of people living in trees may now be viewed as erroneous, it reflects thinking at the time. See, for example, F. Wood Jones, *Arboreal Man* (London: Edward Arnold, 1918).

32   Royle, *Radicals, Secularists, and Republicans,* 166. Among the "etc." would have been Samuel Laing's *Human Origins,* originally published by Chapman and Hall (London) in 1892, and Edward Clodd's *Story of Creation,* originally published by Longmans in 1898. For an excellent discussion of Ferri's ideas, see G. Pancaldi, *Charles Darwin: "Storia" ed "Economia" Della Natura* (Florence: La Nuova Italia, 1977), 163–198.

33   In *God and My Neighbour* (London: Clarion Press, 1903), Blatchford writes (160):

    It is not to revelation that we owe the ideal of human brotherhood, but to evolution. It is because altruism is better than selfishness that it has survived. . . . From the love of the animal for its mate, from the love of parents for their young, sprang the ties of kindred and the loyalty of friendship; and these in time developed into tribal, and thence into national patriotism. And these stages of altruistic evolution may be seen among the brutes. It remained for Man to take the grand step of embracing all humanity as one brotherhood and one nation.

    Not Guilty (London: Clarion Press, 1914) has chapters on "Where Do Our Natures Come From?" "How Heredity and Environment Work," "The Origin of Conscience," and "The Beginnings of Conscience," all of which draw considerably on Darwin's "moral sense" chapter (chap. 4) in *Descent.*

34   Jack London, "What Communities Lose by the Competitive System," in *The Social Writings of Jack London,* ed. P. S. Foner (Secaucus, NJ: Citadel, 1964), 419–430, quotation at 419.

35   Tom Mann, *Socialism* (Melbourne: "Tocsin" Office, 1905), 34–35.

36   *Socialist* (Melbourne), 4, 19 May, 1 October 1906.

37   *Barrier Daily Truth* (Broken Hill), 4 June 1909.

38   Darwin, *Descent,* 192.

39   *Barrier Daily Truth,* 4 June 1909.

40 Cited in Brian Kennedy, *Silver, Sin, and Sixpenny Ale: A Social History of Broken Hill* (Melbourne: University of Melbourne Press, 1978), 91. It should be noted, however, that such isolated outbursts hardly do justice to the full range of Ross' thinking, which was substantial and contained in a prolific journalistic output. See Edgar Ross, *These Things Shall Be! Bob Ross, Socialist Pioneer—His Life and Times* (West Ryde, NSW: Mulavon Publishing, 1988).

41 Verity Burgmann, "Racism, Socialism, and the Australian Labour Movement, 1887–1917," *Labour History,* no. 47 (November 1984): 39–54.

42 Geoffrey Serle, untitled paper read at Labour History Conference, University of Sydney, 3 December 1989.

43 Verity Burgmann, *"In Our Time": Socialism and the Rise of Labor, 1885–1905* (Sydney: George Allen and Unwin, 1985), 192.

44 See Andrew Markus, *Fear and Hatred: Purifying Australia and California, 1850–1901* (Sydney: Hale and Iremonger, 1979), Introduction.

45 J. H. Curle, *This World of Ours* (London: Methuen, 1921), 48.

46 *Barrier Truth,* 23 October 1908. (This newspaper became a daily, and changed its name accordingly, later the same year).

47 Ibid.

48 *Japan Times,* 26 April 1903.

49 Ibid.

50 Eikoh Shimao, "Darwinism in Japan, 1877–1927," *Annals of Science* 38 (1981): 93–102, quotes at 93. For the latter part of this period, see also Kazuo Sibuya, "Present-day Evaluation of the Ecological Aspects of Darwin's Theories in Japan," *Japanese Studies in the History of Science* 1 (1962): 117–124. Sibuya notes that the "introduction of Marx-Engels' views on Darwin's theories . . . was done chiefly in the form of translation of their two books [*sic*—both books are actually by Engels]: *Anti-Duhring* and *Dialectics of Nature*" (117).

51 Jiro Kikkawa, conversation with author, 20 November 1990.

52 Masao Watanabe, "John Thomas Gulick: American Evolutionist and Missionary in Japan," *Japanese Studies in the History of Science* 5 (1967): 140–149.

53 Isono Naohide, "Contributions of Edward S. Morse to Developing Young Japan," in *Foreign Employees in Nineteenth-Century Japan,* ed. Edward R. Beauchamp and Akira Iriye (Boulder, CO: Westview, 1990), 193–212, quotes at 203. On Morse, see also James R. Bartholomew, *The Formation of Science in Japan* (New Haven and London: Yale University Press, 1989), 64–66.

54 Naohide, "Contributions," 203.

55 Watanabe, "John Thomas Gulick," 148.

56 Sen Katayama, *The Labor Movement in Japan* (Chicago: Charles H.

Kerr, 1918), 73. More recently, outgoing Singapore prime minister Lee Kuan Yew has been similarly quoted as saying that Japan's economic success has been based primarily on its "strong communitarian values" (*Australian Financial Review,* 7 December 1990).

57   *Japan Times,* 28 February 1909.

58   Ibid.

59   Ibid.

60   Count Shigenobu Okuma, *Fifty Years of New Japan* (London: Smith, Elder, 1910), 474. The paleontologist and later sexologist Marie Stopes, who spent some time researching in Japan in 1907–1909, made the following observation in her *Journal from Japan* (London: Blackie and Son, 1910): "It was interesting to notice some native Indians studying here, and to find that they, and one or two others who could not speak Japanese, had special classes held in English and given by a Japanese teacher for the various subjects" (175). There are advertisements for English lessons by Japanese teachers in the *Japan Times* over this period (e.g., 20 April 1897, 4 March 1903, 11 March 1907, 12 December 1912).

61   Okuma, *Fifty Years of New Japan,* 474.

62   *Japan Times,* 2 April 1903.

63   Ibid., 19 March 1907.

64   Ibid., 3, 24 February 1909.

65   Quoted in *The Australian Higher Education Supplement,* 3 August 1986.

66   Alfred Russel Wallace, *My Life: A Record of Events and Opinions* (London: Chapman and Hall, 1905), 1: 87. See also Wallace's *Wonderful Century* (London: Swan Sonnenschein, 1898), 21–22, 378–389.

67   Wallace and Mann have chapters in *Vox Clamantium,* ed. A. Reid (Melbourne: Melville, Mullen, and Slade, 1894), and in *Forecasts of the Coming Century,* ed. E. Carpenter (Manchester: Labour Press, 1897).

68   Eveleen Richards, "Darwin and the Descent of Woman," in *The Wider Domain of Evolutionary Thought,* ed. David Oldroyd and Ian Langham (Dordrecht: Reidel, 1983), 57–111, quotation at 66.

69   Alfred Russel Wallace, *Contributions to the Theory of Natural Selection* (London: Swan Sonnenschein, 1870), 312–313.

70   *Japan Times,* 13 March 1907, 30 January 1909.

71   Shimao, "Darwinism in Japan," 96; Stephen S. Large, *The Rise of Labor in Japan: The Yuaikai, 1912–1919* (Tokyo: Sophia University Press, 1972). On the Yuaikai, see also Oswald White (H.M. vice-consul at Osaka), *Report on Japanese Labour* (London: His Majesty's Stationery Office, 1920).

72 Thomas A. Stanley, "Osugi Sakae (1885–1923)," in *Kodansha Encyclopaedia of Japan* (Tokyo: Kodansha, 1983), 6: 127–128.

73 See John Laurent, *Tom Mann's Social and Economic Writings* (Nottingham and Sydney: Spokesman and A.M.W.U., 1988), Introduction.

74 Peter Kropotkin, *Mutual Aid: A Factor of Evolution* (London: Heinemann, 1903), 5.

75 Ibid., 75.

76 Shimao, "Darwinism in Japan," 96.

77 Peter Kropotkin, *Anarchist Morality* (London: Freedom Pamphlettes, n.d.).

78 Katayama, *Labor Movement in Japan,* 122.

79 Okuma, *Fifty Years of New Japan,* 511.

80 Emile Vandervelde, *Collectivism and Industrial Evolution* (Chicago: Charles H. Kerr, 1904), 12, 128–129, 182.

81 Stanley, "Osugi Sakae," 127.

82 *Japan Times,* 1 January 1914.

83 Ibid., 8 November 1913.

84 Katayama, *Labor Movement in Japan,* 38; Andrew Gordon, *The Evolution of Labor Relations in Japan: Heavy Industry, 1853–1955* (Cambridge: Harvard University Press, 1985), 30, 47–49.

85 A useful recent discussion on the influence of Marxist ideas in early Japanese economic thinking can be found in Martin Fransman, review of Tessa Morris-Suzuki, *A History of Japanese Economic Thought* (Cambridge, London, and Oxford: Routledge and Nissan Institute for Japanese Studies, 1989), *Prometheus* 8 (1990): 387–389.

86 *Japan Times,* 7 November 1913.

87 Ibid., 16 October 1919.

88 Michael Cannon, *Australia: A History in Photographs* (South Yarra, Victoria: Viking O'Neil, 1988), 162.

89 *Japan Times,* 29 November 1912.

90 Ibid., 17 December 1912.

91 David Starr Jordan, *The Human Harvest: A Study of the Decay of Races through the Survival of the Unfit* (Boston: American Unitarian Association, 1907), 54.

92 Charles Kingsley, "The Science of Health," in idem, *Health and Education* (London: Daldy, Isbister, 1875), 1–25, quotation at 6.

93 *Socialist,* 31 July 1908.

94 See Philip F. Rehbock, "Organizing Pacific Science: Local and International Origins of the Pacific Science Association," in *Nature in Its Greatest Extent: Western Science in the Pacific,* ed. Roy MacLeod and Philip F. Rehbock (Honolulu: University of Hawaii Press, 1988), 195–221.

95   *Mid-Pacific Magazine* 3 (May 1912), unpaginated announcement.

96   David Starr Jordan, *The Shore Fishes of Hawaii* (Washington, DC: U.S. Government Printing Office, 1905).

97   David Starr Jordan, *The Days of a Man: Being Memoirs of a Naturalist Teacher and Minor Prophet of Democracy* (Yonkers-on-Hudson, NY: World Book, 1922), 1: 460.

98   Charmian K. London, *Our Hawaii* (New York: Macmillan, 1917), quoted in *Mid-Pacific Magazine* 16 (1918), 328.

99   Charmian K. London, *Jack London and Hawaii* (London: Mills and Boon, 1918), 298.

100   *Mid-Pacific Magazine* 16 (1916): 327.

101   Ibid., 9 (1915), unpaginated announcement. For an account of London's activities in Hawaii, see also R. Kingman, *A Pictorial Life of Jack London* (New York: Crown, 1979).

102   Undated (1887) and unnamed newspaper cutting in unpaginated volume in Mitchell Library, Sydney (Cat. no. Q988/N).

103   Ibid.

104   Ibid. (1893).

105   Ibid.

106   London, *Our Hawaii,* 57.

107   Darwin, *Descent,* 186–187. On this topic see also John H. R. Plews, "Charles Darwin and Hawaiian Sex Ratios; or, Genius Is a Capacity for Making Compensatory Errors," *Hawaiian Journal of History* 14 (1980): 26–49.

108   Jean A. Owen, *The Story of Hawaii* (London and New York: Harper, 1898), 216; Joseph King Goodrich, *The Coming Hawaii* (Chicago: A. C. McClurg, 1914), 84.

109   Goodrich, *Coming Hawaii,* 136.

110   *Honolulu Star-Bulletin,* 23 February 1918.

111   Ibid.

112   Willard French, "Hawaii: Our Forgotten Key to the Pacific Ocean," in *America across the Seas: Our Colonial Empire,* various authors (New York: C. S. Hammond, 1909), 37–47, quotes at 42, 46.

113   Goodrich, *Coming Hawaii,* 84; Lawrence H. Fuchs, *Hawaii Pono: A Social History* (San Diego and New York: Harcourt Brace Jovanovich, 1983), 209.

114   Fuchs, *Hawaii Pono,* 209.

115   Ibid., 210.

116   Ibid., 216.

117   *Honolulu Star-Bulletin,* 4 February 1920.

118   *Mid-Pacific Magazine* 17 (1917): 139–143, quotations at 142.

119   Ibid., 139. These events and expressed sentiments did not go unno-

ticed in Japan. The *Japan Times* of 13 March 1907 has a two-column report on a "mass meeting" of Japanese in Hawaii protesting a bill then currently before Congress prohibiting Japanese emigration to the United States. Such a measure, various speakers were reported to have said, "enslaves us permanently to Hawaii's capitalists" and "was totally opposed to the doctrine of the equality of man" (the bill was defeated, but a similar one was passed in 1917). On 23 February 1909, the *Japan Times* carried an item on "Anti-Japanese Feeling in Hawaii" in which a Mr. Saito, the Japanese consul in Hawaii, is reported to have expressed concern about the possibility of certain "anti-Japanese measures" being introduced into the Hawaiian legislature "in view of the fact that a movement for the increase of wages for Japanese has of late been prevailing in the islands."

120   *Honolulu Star-Bulletin,* 11 January 1918.

121   David Starr Jordan, *Democracy and World Relations* (Yonkers-on-Hudson, NY: World Book, 1918), 52. In an earlier item in the *New York Times* (3 October 1915) Jordan is cited (in a review of another of his books, *War and the Breed*) as similarly repudiating this theory by referring to the "survival of the unfittest" concept (above) and by enlisting Leonard Darwin in support:

> Major Leonard Darwin, son of Charles Darwin and President of the Eugenics Education Society of London, is quoted in a vigorous protest against the connecting of his father's name with the pseudo-scientific theory of "social Darwinism" and its glorification of "the will of the stronger." Major Darwin cites *The Descent of Man* to prove his point, and adds that England's fittest are dying by thousands in this war.

122   *Honolulu Star-Bulletin,* 16 February 1918.

123   Ibid.

124   *Mid-Pacific Magazine* 3 (1912): 89.

125   Alfred Russel Wallace, *Island Life, or, The Phenomena and Causes of Insular Faunas and Floras* (London: Macmillan, 1911), 317.

126   John T. Gulick, "Socialism in a Nutshell," *The Friend* (Honolulu), May 1916, 111.

127   *Mid-Pacific Magazine* 3 (1912): 595.

128   Ibid., 6 (1913): 359–363. In March 1914, Goodhue sent London a copy of his book of poetry, *Verses from the Valley* (Oakland, CA: Pacific Press, 1888), with the inscription: "I think you have not seen this book of mine, penned the most of it over thirty years ago. . . . ' The Clock and the Owl'—'The Throne,' 'Psyche' are . . . socialism, and for the rest accept them from a friend" (cited in D. Mike Hamilton, *"The Tools of My Trade": The Annotated Books in Jack London's Library* [Seattle and London: University of Washington Press, 1984], 83).

129 *Honolulu Star-Bulletin,* 1 February 1919.

130 Jack London, *"The House of Pride" and Other Tales of Hawaii*
     (London: Mills and Boon, 1916), 155–156.

131 Jack London, *The Iron Heel* (New York: Macmillan, 1907), 132.

132 Darwin, *Descent,* 122.

133 Jack London to Cloudsley Johns, 10 August 1899, in *Letters from
     Jack London,* ed. K. Hendricks and I. Shepard (London: MacGibbon
     and Kee, 1966), 51.

134 Jack London, *The Strength of the Strong* (New York: Macmillan,
     1914), 30–31.

135 *Star* (Sydney), 14 January 1909.

136 *Socialist,* 28 August 1908.

137 *Mid-Pacific Magazine* 9 (1915): 567.

138 *Honolulu Star-Bulletin,* 23 March 1918. The Library of Hawaii
     appears to have been well used—at least the territory's superintendent
     of public instruction, Vaughan MacCaughey, thought so. In a letter to
     the *Star-Bulletin* (20 February 1919), MacCaughey claimed that "no
     other single educational institution reaches continuously throughout
     the year, as many people, of all classes and ages, as does the Library
     of Hawaii." Public lectures on subjects like "The Library and How to
     Use It" were given at venues like the Honolulu YWCA, and organiza-
     tions such as the Humane Society and the Honolulu branch of the
     Pacific Co-operative League (organized on "Rochdale principles")
     held their meetings at the library (*Honolulu Star-Bulletin,* 3 January
     1918; 19 November, 8 December 1919).

139 *Honolulu Star-Bulletin,* 29 November 1919.

140 H. G. Wells, *The Undying Fire* (New York: Cassell, 1919), 181, 186.

141 Ibid., 180.

142 Ibid., 210.

143 *Honolulu Star-Bulletin,* 15 January 1919. The author of *Tarzan of the
     Apes* (first published 1914), Edgar Rice Burroughs, apparently had a
     deep personal interest in evolutionary theory, and according to one
     author, "Darwinism is so pervasive in Burroughs that it cannot be
     ignored" and "Tarzan was the ideal vehicle for developing his
     thoughts on this subject" (Erling B. Holtsmark, *Tarzan and Tradi-
     tion—Classical Myth in Popular Culture* [Westport, CT: Greenwood
     Press, 1981], 144–145). The 1918 film is said to have "followed the
     Burroughs story in most respects" (Irwin Porges, *Edgar Rice Bur-
     roughs: The Man Who Created Tarzan* [Provo, UT: Brigham Young
     University Press, 1975], 274).

144 *Honolulu Star-Bulletin,* 6 December 1919.

145 Rehbock, "Organizing Pacific Science," 208.

146 *Honolulu Star-Bulletin,* 6 December 1919.

Contributors

R O N   A M U N D S O N   is professor of philosophy at the University of Hawai'i at Hilo. He specializes in the history and philosophy of science, especially evolutionary biology and experimental psychology. He is currently studying historical debates surrounding adaptational and morphological explanations of biological form.

K E I T H   R .   B E N S O N   is professor at the University of Washington, where he teaches the history of biology in the Program in the History of Science, Technology, and Medicine. With Jane Maienschein and Ron Rainger, he has edited two volumes, *The American Development of Biology* and *The Expansion of American Biology*.

J A N E T   B R O W N E   is a lecturer in history of biology at the Wellcome Institute for the History of Medicine, London. She works mainly in the life sciences and is a former editor of the *Correspondence of Charles Darwin*. She has recently published (with Michael Neve) a new edition of Darwin's *Voyage of the "Beagle"* and is currently preparing a biography of Darwin.

B A R R Y   W .   B U T C H E R   is a lecturer in the social studies of science at Deakin University, Geelong, Victoria. He is interested in the colonial reception of Darwinism and has published several articles on the relation of science and colonialism, with special emphasis on the reception of Darwinism in Australia.

J A N E   R .   C A M E R I N I   is a postdoctoral fellow in science studies at the University of California, San Diego. Her research is on the role of visual representations in the development of scientific theories. She is currently writing a book, *Mapping Nature,* on the emergence and establishment of distribution mapping in evolutionary biology.

N A N C Y   J .   C H R I S T I E   has taught at the universities of Manitoba and Winnipeg and was Webster Fellow in the Humanities at Queen's University, Kingston, Ontario. She has worked on the impact of Darwin on Canadian and Australian culture and is currently writing a history of the social sciences at the University of Toronto.

J A N E T   G A R B E R is a retired professor of biology at Los Angeles Harbor College and an independent scholar. She holds a doctorate in history from UCLA and is currently preparing for publication her dissertation, "Charles Darwin as a Laboratory Director."

N I E L   G U N S O N is senior fellow in Pacific history at the Australian National Univesity. He has specialized in contact and religious history. His books include *Messengers of Grace*. He is currently working on a history of religion in Polynesia.

E .   A L I S O N   K A Y is professor of zoology at the University of Hawaiʻi. Her research interests center on the systematics of Pacific marine mollusks, the biogeography of the Pacific islands, and the history of natural history in the Pacific. She has recently published *Shells of Hawaiʻi.*

H E N R I K A   K U K L I C K is associate professor in the Department of History and Sociology of Science at the University of Pennsylvania, where she specializes in the sociology of knowledge and the history of the human sciences. Her most recent book is *The Savage Within: The Social History of British Anthropology, 1885–1945.*

J O H N   L A U R E N T is a lecturer in the Divison of Science and Technology at Griffith University, Brisbane, Queensland. His interests include the history of life sciences, evolutionary theory, and social and economic aspects of industrialization. With Margaret Campbell he is coauthor of *The Eye of Reason: Charles Darwin in Australasia* and editor of *Tom Mann's Social and Economic Writings.*

R O Y   M A C L E O D is professor of history at the University of Sydney, where he teaches the history of science and technology, the history of European expansion, Australian and British history, and the history of museums in Western society. He has published extensively in the history of nineteenth-century science and technology and has coedited with Philip Rehbock *Nature in Its Greatest Extent: Western Science in the Pacific.*

P A U L I N E   P A Y N E teaches at the University of South Australia and is a visiting fellow in the Department of History of the University of Adelaide. She has a special interest in the history of plant acclimatization in Australia and the network of contacts among nineteenth-century naturalists. She has recently published "Picturesque Scientific Gardening: Developing Adelaide Botanic Garden, 1865–1891," in *William Shakespeare's Adelaide, 1860–1930.*

P H I L I P   F .   R E H B O C K is professor of history and general science at the University of Hawaiʻi. He is the author of *The Philosophical Naturalists: Themes in Early Nineteenth-Century British Biology* (1983) and editor of *At Sea with the Scientifics: The "Challenger" Letters of Joseph Matkin* (1993). He also edits the *Pacific Circle Newsletter.*

S A R A   S O H M E R teaches at Texas Christian University. Her principal research interests lie in the intellectual and social influence of the British Empire. She has written about Sir Arthur Gordon and colonial Fiji and is at present working on the theological background of the Melanesian Mission.

J O H N   S T E N H O U S E is lecturer in history at the University of Otago. He is a specialist in nineteenth-century science and religion. He is currently working on a book about the reception of Darwinism in New Zealand.

D A V I D   R .   S T O D D A R T is professor of geography at the University of California, Berkeley, and is well known for his work in the history of geography (*On Geography and Its History,* 1986) and for his studies of coral reefs in the Seychelles and the Pacific.

Index

Page numbers of illustrations are in brackets.

aborigines (Australian): and advancement, 386; and civilization, 374–375; and economics, 387; and evolutionary anthropology, 381; and genocide, 476; inferior views of, 375–376; justification of taking over lands, 374; legal status of, 382–383; and natural law, 377; and phrenology, 375–376; as scientific data, 389; and Social Darwinism, 381; stage of development of, 388

aborigines (Tasmanian), 476–477

Aborigines Protection Society, 399

Academy of Natural Sciences, Philadelphia, 59, 225

acclimatization, 247, 251

adaptationism, 9; central factual belief of, 112; and conservatism, 113–114, 115; creationist, 114–115; and Darwin, 119, 124; debates over, 113, 134; environmentalist, 112; and evolutionary theory, 113; explanations of phenomena by, 114; functional approach to, 111–112, 114; and Gulick (John), 110–111, 120–121, 122, 125; and Lewontin, 133; and natural theology, 112; and neo-Darwinians, 112, 133; and politics, 113–114, 115–116, 134; and Paley, 113; strategy for research and evaluation, 112, 114

Adelaide, 239, 242, 251

Adelaide Botanic Gardens, 10, 239–240; and commercial network, 249–250; exchanges with, 248, 249; Palm House, 244, 254n25; Palm House as plant introduction center, 248; and practical application of natural history, 247; and Schomburgk, 242; and scientific culture, 245; Victoria House, 244; as visual interest, 246

Adventure (ship), 174

Agassiz, Alexander, 57, 194, 219, 222

age of science, 76

Alison, Robert, 173, 193

Allan, J., 173, 194

amateurs, 10; contributions to natural history, 232; and professionals 229–230, 333, 341, 455

American Association of Geologists and Naturalists, 30

American Journal of Conchology, 223

American Journal of Science, 28, 30, 31, 36

American Philosophical Society, 24

anatomy: comparative, 49; and evolutionary theory, 49, 146, 149–150; and morphology, 146; and politics, 150

Andes mountains, 173